379

7.50

D0474863

Education and the S
Volume II

Politics, Patriarchy and Practice

THE COLLEGE OF RI
AND YORK ST

EDS.

CA!

WITHDRAWN
1 7 MAY 2021

22446

Coll. of Ripon & York St John

3 8025 00118717 1

Education and the State
Volume II ← h. rec.

Politics, Patriarchy and Practice

Edited by
Roger Dale,
Geoff Esland,
Ross Fergusson
and
Madeleine MacDonald

The Falmer Press
*A member of the Taylor & Francis Group
in association with*
The Open University Press

COLLEGE OF RIPON
AND YORK ST. JOHN
YORK CAMPUS
LIBRARY

Selection and editorial material
copyright © The Open University 1981

All rights reserved. No part of this publication may be reproduced, stored in a retrieval system, or transmitted in any form or by any means, electronic, mechanical, photocopying recording, or otherwise, without the written permission of the Publisher.

First published 1981

ISBN   0 905273 17 6 Limp
        0 905273 18 4 Cased

Cover design by Pedro Pra Lopez
Printed and bound in Great Britain by
Taylor & Francis (Printers) Ltd.,
Basingstoke, Hampshire for
The Falmer Press
(*A member of the Taylor & Francis Group*)
Falmer House,
Barcombe, Lewes,
Sussex   BN8 5DL
England

COLLEGE OF RIPON AND
YORK ST. JOHN, YORK CAMPUS

CLASS NO.	ACCESSION NO.
370.19 DAL	77543.B
CHECKED	DATE
HK.	12-4-83

This reader is one part of an Open University integrated teaching system and the selection is therefore related to other material available to students. It is designed to evoke the critical understanding of students. Opinions expressed in it are not necessarily those of the course team or of the University.

ACKNOWLEDGEMENTS

We are grateful to the following for permission to reproduce copyright material:

The Hutchinson Publishing Company for JOHNSON, R. 'Really useful knowledge: radical education and working class culture, 1790–1848' and CLARKE, J. 'Capital and culture: the post war working class revisited' in J. CLARKE, C. CRITCHER and R. JOHNSON (Eds) *Working Class Culture*, 1979, London, Hutchinson.

President and Fellows of Harvard College for ANYON, J. 'Ideology and United States history textbooks', *Harvard Educational Review*, 1979, 44:3, abridged. Copyright © 1979 by President and Fellows of Harvard College.

HARGREAVES, J. 'The Political Economy of Mass Sport'. Copyright © 1981 J. Hargreaves.

The Open University Press for FERGUSSON, R. and MARDLE, G. *Education and the Political Economy of Leisure*; FITZ, J. *The Child as Legal Subject*; PURVIS, J. *Women and Teaching in the Nineteenth Century*. Copyright © 1981 The Open University Press.

The Editor *Time Out* for HEBDIGE, D. 'Subculture: image and noise' August 1979.

The Editor *Screen Education* for FRITH, S. and McROBBIE, A. 'Rock and sexuality' winter 1978–79 No. 29.

Routledge and Kegan Paul for BEECHEY, V. 'Women and production: a critical analysis of some sociological theories of women's work' in A. KUHN and A. M. WOLPE (Eds) *Feminism and Materialism*, 1978.

Croom Helm Ltd. for WOLPE, A. M. 'The official ideology of education for girls' and PARRY, N. and PARRY, J. 'The teachers and professionalism: failure of an occupational strategy' in M. FLUDE and J. AHIER (Eds) *Educability, Schools and Ideology*, 1976.

Gower Publishing Company for WILLIS, P. 'Patriarchy, racialism and Labour power' in P. WILLIS *Learning to Labour*, 1977, Chap. 6.

Pluto Press for HARTMANN, H. 'The unhappy marriage of marxism and feminism: towards a more progressive union' in SARGENT, L. (Ed) *The Unhappy Marriage of Marxism and Feminism: A Debate on Class and Patriarchy*, 1981, Pluto Press (Published in the USA by South End Press as *Women and Revolution*). Copyright © 1981 Pluto Press, South End Press and Heidi Hartmann.

The Editor *Feminist Review* for MURRAY, N. 'Socialism and feminism: women and the Cuban revolution' 1979 No. 2 (pp. 17–71) and No. 3 (pp. 99–108).

The Editor *Journal of Sociology and Social Welfare* for ADAMS, P. 'Social control or social wage: on the political economy of the "Welfare State"', 1978 Vol. 5, pp. 46–54.

Cambridge University Press for LAND, H. 'Who cares for the family?' *Journal of Social Policy* 1978, 7:3, pp. 257–84.

NFER for SHAW, J. 'In loco parentis' in *Journal of Moral Education*, 1977 Vol. 6 No. 3, pp. 181–90; and PATEMAN, T. 'Accountability, values and schooling' in A. BECHER and S. MACLURE (Eds) *Accountability in Education*, 1978.

The Editor *Victorian Studies* for MAY, M. 'Innocence and experience: the evolution of the concept of juvenile delinquency in the mid-nineteenth century' 1973, (XVII) pp. 7–29.

Dr I. Reid for DALE, R. 'Control, accountability and William Tyndale'. Copyright© 1981 I. Reid.

Woburn Press Limited for BOYSON, R. 'Collapse of confidence' in R. BOYSON *The Crisis in Education*, 1975, pp. 27–32.

University of California Press for LARSON, M. 'Monopolies of competence and bourgeois ideology' in M. LARSON *The Rise of Professionalism*, 1977, Chap. 12.

Harper and Row Limited for BACON, W. 'Professional control and the engineering of client consent' in W. BACON *Public Accountability and the Schooling System*, 1978, London, Harper and Row Ltd.

Contents

Introduction

This collection of readings is the *second* of two volumes compiled as a component of the Open University course *Society, Education and the State*. It is our hope that these two volumes will be of interest not only to Open University students, but also to a much larger group of readers who are interested in the sociology of education.

In terms of their overall structure and content the course and the Readers have been conceived as being in two parts. The first – as represented by the first volume – examines elements of the large-scale political and economic structures which affect educational provision, and the second – represented in this volume – is concerned with more specific areas of social policy and political practice. In Part One of the course, there is some consideration of the relationship between the economy and education, the nature of the nation-state, and the role played by education in national development; and, in Part Two, the topics include the politics of school culture, sexual divisions and patriarchy, the social construction of childhood and the family, and the politics of teaching.

The readings in the first section of this collection are concerned with schooling and the politics of culture. This is an area of the sociology of education which has elicited a good deal of interest during the past decade. Originating from the resurgence of interest in the sociology of knowledge which took place during the late sixties, the analysis of educational culture has tended to remain at the level of competing interest groups – professional organizations and subject associations, for example; and the approach usually adopted has been the analysis of the content of school syllabuses and text books to the neglect of wider political and economic concerns. In compiling this selection of articles, we have, therefore, sought to move beyond this conception of the politics of culture by extending it where possible to the analysis of class politics and theories of the state.

This section opens with Richard Johnson's paper 'Really Useful Knowledge' which examines the radical tradition in popular education during the period 1790 to 1848. Johnson suggests that what characterised this tradition was opposition to all forms of 'provided' education, on the grounds that it 'threatened subjection'. So developed was its critique of 'provided education' that 'radicalism developed its own curricula and pedagogies, its own definition of "really useful knowledge"'.

Jean Anyon contributes a study of history textbooks in the United States. In her examination of the content of seventeen, widely-used, secondary school texts dealing with economic and labour history, she argues that the prevailing patterns of interpretation given to events described in these books are much more favourable to the interests of capital than to those of unions or socialists.

While Anyon's paper examines school culture as a manifestation of ruling ideology, John Clarke in 'Capital and Culture: the Post-War Working Class Revisited', details a number of trends in capitalist development in Britain since the last war which have led to the transformation of several central elements of working-class culture. An important part of his analysis is his attempt to relate this process to state policy.

A form of culture which is being increasingly recognised by sociologists as having been absorbed into the state apparatus is sport. John Hargreaves's article 'The Political Economy of Mass Sport' criticises the liberal notions of sport as 'enjoyment' and 'fulfilment through leisure' and argues instead that many of the features of sport are directly attributable to developments in the capitalist state.

A similar argument is made by Ross Fergusson and George Mardle in their paper 'Education and the Political Economy of Leisure'. They challenge the value of 'education for leisure' in its current popular conception, as well as the belief that technology (and particularly the micro processor revolution) will lead to more leisure. They argue that the industrialization of leisure has led to the expansion of a huge consumer market which materially conditions the ways in which 'leisure' can be experienced.

The two articles by Hebdige and Frith and McRobbie examine areas of popular culture as forms of subcultural resistance. While Hebdige traces the sources of the style and the social construction of meanings in skinhead and punk subcultures as 'lived experience', Frith and McRobbie are concerned with the social construction of gender within popular music. They look at the contradictions between the definitions of masculinity and femininity as they are differently constructed within rock music and pop music, and examine how this relates to their audiences and to the form and packaging of the music.

What the analysis of cultural forms in this first section reveals is the importance of recognising the impact on youth life styles and culture of institutions and ideological agencies other than schools. Many early social and sexual identities are formed in the family and this critical area of social life and its relationship to education requires investigation.

In the case of women, in particular, the family has a special significance as a future work place. Sociology has often failed to analyse the impact of the critical division between the worlds of the family and social production, tending to neglect the impact of the historical delegation of domestic roles to women and 'economic' roles to men.

By treating 'work' as that activity found only in the wage labour process, there is a danger of ignoring the work performed by women in the home. The explicit focus of studies of the vocational aspect of schooling has been the preparation for paid employment to the neglect of unpaid domestic labour. Further, it should be recognised that the sexual division of labour between and within both domestic and wage labour is a critical factor, along with the class structure, affecting the shape of education.

In Section Two, Veronica Beechey identifies and critiques various theories of women's position, both in the family and in waged work. She develops an analysis of the advantages to capital of female labour and relates this to women's domestic role.

The relations between family and work for women, as transmitted by education, are examined by Anne Marie Wolpe. In her article she identifies a 'common code' of government policy based on the assumption that a 'woman's place is in the home'. The pattern of education particularly in the area of curricular provision, is shown to reinforce the two structures of inequality: those of social class and gender. The integration of and contradictions between these sets of power relations are taken up again in the article by Madeleine MacDonald who claims that the reproduction of gender relations is part of bourgeois hegemony. She argues that it is important to recognise that the definition of masculinity and femininity are both historically specific and class specific. The ideology of gender is transmitted implicitly and explicitly through schooling, 'recontextualizing' the class based, familial forms of gender relations. This argument is closely related to Paul Willis's analysis of the forms of class and gender resistance of working class 'lads' to school culture. In the extract from his book *Learning to Labour*, class and gender are brought together in their relations of complementarity and contradiction.

The last two articles in this section present the debate over the position and significance of 'women's work'. Heidi Hartmann considers the arguments concerning patriarchy and capitalism as sources of sexual inequality and puts forward the possibilities for a synthesis. Nicola Murray, in her study of Cuba, shows that in a socialist country, where men and women are treated ideologically as equals and where women play a considerable role in the economy, gender divisions and inequalities still persist, especially in the domestic sphere.

In all these analyses of the sexual division of labour, it is recognised that the state either in its educational policy or in its welfare policy has intervened in specific ways in the relations between the family and the economy. In Section Three this topic is investigated in more depth. In Paul Adams's article, a central contradiction in the work of the welfare state (and we might add, of state apparatuses in general) is isolated and discussed. The foci of his paper are, first, the debates about whether the welfare state is primarily a form of social control, and, hence, intrinsically oppressive, whatever form it takes; and second, debates about the existence, size and value of the social wage. Educational provision is clearly central to both of these debates.

Hilary Land in 'Who Cares for the Family?' investigates the assumptions behind a particular set of welfare policies which can be categorised broadly as 'family policy'. Within these policies, one finds the assumption of a bourgeois family form – the male breadwinner, the dependent housekeeping wife and dependent children. This affects not only women's economic position, but also results, for example, in the uneven development of child care provision affecting the patterns of women's employment. Further, as Jenny Shaw shows, state policies delineate specific concepts of parenthood and childhood which are most clearly seen in the development of mass schooling. In the area of the education and care of children, the state acts in *loco parentis*, assuming responsibility over and above parental rights. Margaret May's article, which is concerned with juvenile crime in the nineteenth century, shows that an important element of the state's responsibility lay in the growing tendency to designate child crime as 'juvenile delinquency' thereby relinquishing the child of total responsibility for his/her actions and investing it in parents.

The legal construction of childhood is a part of a complex process in which childhood is differentially constituted through a whole range of different discourses. John Fitz describes this complexity in his analysis of political, legal, economic and cultural discourses which specifically make children dependent on their parents and the state.

One distinctive feature of the course, *Society, Education and the State*, is that it identifies schools as 'sites of struggle' in which class and interest groups strive for favourable positions and conditions. The last section of this volume is concerned with some contemporary manifestations of this. During the 1970s, 'political' activity by teachers and parents became more public than at any time since the 1944 Education Act. Part of Roger Dale's paper is devoted to an outline analysis of the specific causes of the emerging contestation over the control of education. He focuses on the state's reassertion of its role, stimulated and justified by the case of the William Tyndale School. Major questions of control and accountability were generated by this 'politicization' of education, whose chief theme was a populist attack from the Right on what had become social democratic orthodoxy. Some central components of this attack are set out in the piece by Rhodes Boyson, perhaps its chief political orchestrator.

In these politicized contexts, teachers are primarily identified as *employees* who negotiate terms and conditions of employment and the degree of control they exert over the work they do; parents are primarily *consumers* of a service which they may criticize or seek to alter, while pupils are primarily *actors* in schools, not just 'acted on' by teachers and the institution.

Perhaps the most fundamental single issue here is the claim by teachers that as professionals they have 'monopolies of competence' which justify their right to make and execute educational decisions. On the other hand, the engagement of teachers in struggles over pay and conditions is for many incompatible with the notion of professionalism. Further, parental claims for accounts to be given of the progress of their children's education, and the right to participate in the organization of schooling may be seen as eroding professional claims to monopoly. Larson's paper is therefore an apt contribution to the section. She problematizes the concept of professionalism and locates monopolies of competence among professional groups generally in the class and commodity character of the social relations of production in capitalism. The role of ideology in the development of professionalism is emphasized, especially that of educationally-based ideologies which legitimate restrictive access to professional cadres. Parry and Parry in their article look at the teaching profession, and specifically the historical failure of teachers to attain professional status comparable with that of the traditional professions. The authors identify the state as playing a significant role in this curtailment, to prevent the dissipation of its own control over education. Purvis's contribution situates the position of teachers still more precisely, drawing on the generally neglected but crucial factor of gender in the history of the occupation. Her historical study shows how factors of both class and gender affected induction into this expanding and predominantly female new 'profession'.

Within popular conceptions of education 'accountability' has become a blanket term, often used with little consciousness of its varying meanings and complex ramifications. A frequent application is in the context of schools' accountability to parents, but as Pateman's paper shows, account may equally be rendered with social need, use of public resources or professional colleagues as the reference points.

This is followed by two studies which show that control as well as accountability is a major aspect of teachers' work. In its analysis of the ways in which the Tyndale case reinforced existing anti-progressive moves, Dale's paper shows the enactment of conflicts which were both produced by and a stimulus to demands for 'accountability'.

Finally, in an empirical study of the effects of greater parent participation in school government in Sheffield, Bacon, in the chapter from his book, demonstrates the tendency towards incorporation and domestication of legitimate parental concerns within the existing machinery of educational administration.

Acknowledgements

In compiling this Reader we would like to acknowledge the help of the other members of the *Society, Education and the State* course team, particularly David Davies, Rosemary Deem, John Fitz, Jenny Ozga, Jenny Shaw and Geoff Whitty. We are grateful to Olive Banks for her comments on the development of the Reader. The editors would also like to thank Denise Hamilton and Tracey Lenton for their secretarial assistance.

I
Schooling and the Politics of Culture

1 'Really Useful Knowledge': Radical Education and Working-Class Culture, 1790–1848

Richard Johnson

Introduction

One of the most interesting developments in working-class history has been the rediscovery of popular educational traditions, the springs of action of which owed little to philanthropic, ecclesiastical or state provision. [...] In 1960 Brian Simon's *Studies in the History of Education* drew attention to the continuity and the liveliness of independent popular education from Jacobinism to Chartism. In 1961, J.F.C. Harrison's *Learning and Living* examined traditions of adult self-education in one locality. Harold Silver's important book, *The Concept of Popular Education* (1965), looked at 'developments in attitudes to the education of the people' more generally, but focused especially on Owen and Owenism. Thompson's *The Making of the English Working Class* (1963) permitted a fuller contextualization of others' findings, but also stressed the intellectual character of early-nineteenth-century radicalism and the role of 'the articulate consciousness of the self-taught'.[1] These themes have become more explicit in later studies of Owenism and Chartism and of the radical press, the main 'educational' medium.[2] Related to radical traditions, but not yet connected in the historiography, were other educational resources which have been receiving increasing attention from historians – especially the extent and uses of private schools.[3] Some recent studies of Sunday schools have shown the co-existence of schools under popular control with more clearly philanthropic institutions.[4] There is, however, no adequate study of the other important popular educational resource: the working-class family itself.

The radical press remains the obvious route of entry into popular educational practices and dilemmas. It was extremely articulate, indeed talkative, providing a weekly set of commentaries on everyday life and politics. Although it is the main source for what follows, this use is in itself problematic, posing additional questions which must be answered *en route*. For we cannot assume that the attitudes of radical leaders and writers were those of 'the workers' (any more than we can assume that radicalism was 'unrepresentative' or the downwards extension of middle-class

Source: CLARKE, J., CRITCHER, C., JOHNSON, R. (Eds.) (1979) *Working Class Culture*, London, Hutchinson.

3

'ideas').[5] For one thing, radicals differed a lot on some essential matters. For another, popular opinion itself was not homogeneous. Moreover, radical leaders were clearly involved in a process that was part mediation or expression of some popular feelings, and part a forming or 'education' of them, an attempt to achieve, from very diverse materials, some unity of will and direction. This necessarily involved fostering some tendencies and opposing others. The image of the educator or 'schoolmaster' is itself interesting here. It was one of the commonest guises adopted by radical journalists.[6] Though it was an identity often adopted jokingly and as a conscious play upon Henry Brougham's populist 'schoolmaster abroad' speeches of the 1820s, it was an image that constructed some distance between 'teachers' and 'pupils', despite the involvement in a common enterprise. It is important, then, to understand the particular position of leaders and journalists within radical movements and, more generally, within the popular classes as a whole. It is necessary, in other words, to face squarely the problem of the 'popularity' of radicalism. This is an especially important question for the concerns of this essay, which puzzles around the relation between various kinds of radicalism, understood as 'educative' or transformative ideologies, and the conditions of existence and lived culture of some of the groups which radicalism addressed. But first it is necessary to describe some salient features of radical education over this period, concentrating, at first, on some common elements. Later we shall look, more discriminatingly, at some internal differences and changes over time.

The Radical Dilemma

There were four main aspects to 'radical education'. First, radicals conducted a running critique of all forms of 'provided' education. This covered the whole gamut of schooling enterprises from clerically dominated Anglican Sunday schools, through Cobbett's 'Bell and Lancaster work', to the state-aided (and usually Anglican) public day schools of the mid century. It also embraced all the institutes, clubs and media designed to influence the older pupil – everything from tracts to mechanics institutes. Plans for a more centralized state system of schooling were also opposed, a feature to which we will return. This tradition, then, was sharply oppositional: it revolved around a contestation of orthodoxies (and some un-orthodoxies too) both in theory and practice. Nor was this critique limited to formally 'educational' institutions. In its later phases radicalism developed a practical grasp and a theoretical understanding of cultural and ideological struggle in a more general sense.

The second main feature was the development of alternative educational goals. At one level these embraced a vision of a whole alternative future – a future in which educational utopias, among other needs, could actually be achieved. At another, radicalism developed its own curricula and pedagogies, its own definition of 'really useful knowledge', a characteristically radical *content*, a sense of what it was really important to know.

Thirdly, radicalism conducted an important internal debate about education as a political strategy or as a means of changing the world. Like most aspects of counter-education, this debate was also directed at dominant middle-class conceptions of the relation between education and politics, especially the argument that 'national education' was a necessary condition for the granting of universal suffrage. But it expressed real radical dilemmas too.

Finally, radical movements developed a vigorous and varied educational practice. The distinctive feature was, at first sight, an emphasis upon informing mature understandings and upon the education of men and women as adult citizens of a more just social order. But radicals were also concerned with men and women as educators of their own children and they improvised forms for this task too. It might, however, be truer to say that the child-adult distinction was itself less stressed in this tradition, or in parts of it, than in the contemporary middle-class culture of childhood. This is one reason why, in what follows, no large distinction is made between the education of 'children' and 'adults'. Such a distinction is not found in nature by educators, but has actually, in large part, been constructed.

We can move beyond a rather descriptive listing like this by seeing these elements as aspects of a particular, lived, dilemma. This dilemma was not unique to early nineteenth-century radicals. It is arguable that it represents the *typical* popular educational dilemma under capitalist social conditions. Nineteenth-century radicals, however, certainly experienced it with a particular sharpness. On the one hand, they valued the acquisition of knowledge very highly indeed, often with a quite abstract passion. Knowledge or 'enlightenment' was *generally* sought: it was a good in itself, a use value. This passion can be traced in many working-class autobiographies in which the fervent 'pursuit of knowledge' always looms large, in the language and educational stance of the unstamped press, in the popular reception of quite abstract texts, and in an educational rhetoric as exalted and sometimes as high-flown as the more familiar Broughamite language of middle-class liberals.

[...]

At the same time, however, radicals were aware of the poverty of educational resources to hand – a recognition often enforced by personal experience. This was partly a quantitative scarcity – lack of schools, lack of books, lack of energy, lack of time. But there was also a qualitative question involved. In the course of the period some of the quantitative deficiencies were supplied: certainly from the 1830s there was a growth, in real terms, of educational facilities of the provided kind, if not of opportunities for their use. Yet as 'facilities' grew, the dilemma actually deepened. The quality of what was on offer never matched the aspirations. Far indeed from promising liberation, provided education threatened subjection. It seemed at best a laughable and irrelevant divergence (*useless* knowledge in fact); or at worst, a species of tyranny, an outward extension of the power of factory master, or priest, or corrupt state apparatus. There is a continuity of comment of this kind from Paine's initial warnings on the educational tendencies of hereditary monarchies and established religions to the caveats of the *Northern Star* on government education schemes. Paine taught radicals that monarchy, being based on so irrational a device as inheritance, tended to 'buy reason up' and that priests were employed to keep the people ignorant.[7] Cobbett, the original de-schooler, extended this to cover schools and schoolmasters. Note the industrial and political analogies:

> He is their over-looker; he is a spy upon them; his authority is maintained
> by his absolute power of punishment; the parent commits them to that
> power; to be taught is to be held in restraint; and, as the sparks fly upwards,
> the teaching and restraint will not be divided in the estimation of the boy.[8]

Early radical journalists put each new educational innovation into a place already
prepared for it in Painite theory. Schooling was not about 'political education' at
all, not about 'rights' and 'liberties'; it was about 'servility', 'slavery' and 'surveillance', about government spies in every parish, about the tyranny of the schoolroom.
This theme was elaborated in a hundred ingenious ways: reporting injustice in
individual schools, parodying hymns, catechisms and teaching methods, exposing
Dr. Bell's sinecure, stressing the ideological rationale of schooling by which all
evils were ascribed to 'popular ignorance'.[9] By the 1830s new forms of provided
education had appeared, especially mechanics institutes, infant schools and the
Society for the Diffusion of Useful Knowledge (SDUK), some of which were less
obviously 'knowledge-denying' than tracts or monitorial schools. Yet radicals
maintained a critical opposition. The SDUK was universally ridiculed: infant
schools were attacked by Owenites (as a corruption of Owen's ideals) and parodied
in the Chartist press;[10] and mechanics institutes, the most popular of the innovations,
were very cautiously evaluated and, on the ground, openly opposed or instrumen-
tally used.[11] *The English Chartist Circular*'s comment on the SDUK was typical:

> Their determination is to stifle inquiry respecting the great principles which
> question their right to larger shares of the national produce than those
> which the physical producers of the wealth themselves enjoy.[12]

There was also a host of jokes on all possible variants of the epithet 'useful knowledge'.

> In conformity with the advice of Lord Brougham and the Useful Know-
> ledge Society, the Milton fisherman, finding their occupation gone, have
> resolved to become capitalists forthwith.[13]

'Why', it was asked, 'did not the lass Victoria learn *really* useful knowledge by
being apprenticed to a milliner?'[14] 'What' asked the *Poor Man's Guardian*, 'is useful
ignorance? – ignorance useful to constitutional tyrants'.[15] One editor of the Unstamped even produced a one-off issue of a little thing called 'The Penny Comic
Magazine of an Amorous, Clamorous, Uproarious and Glorious Society for the
Diffusion of Broad Grins'.[16]

It was '*really* useful knowledge', then, that was important. But 'education-
mongers' offered the opposite. They didn't offer 'education' at all; only, in Cobbett's
coinage, 'Heddekashun', a very different thing.[17] So how was really useful knowledge to be got? How were radicals to educate themselves, their children and their
class within cramping limits of time, and income? The main answer for the whole
of this period was by their own collective enterprise. The preferred strategy was
substitutional. They were to do it themselves. A series of solutions of this kind were

improvised, all resourceful, though none wholly adequate. Radical education may be understood as the history of these attempts.

Forms

The key feature was *in*formality. Certainly, Owenites and Chartists did found their own educational institutions and even planned a whole alternative system. Secular Sunday schools and Owenite Halls of Science, for instance, represent the most visible, formalized (and best documented) aspects of activity. They remain extremely interesting. Yet to concentrate on counter-institutions would be seriously to misread the character of the radical response and the nature of the transition in the practices of cultural reproduction through which working people were living. There is a danger, too, of separating out 'the educational' and constructing a story parallel to but different from the usual tales of schools and colleges.[18] Radical education was not just different in content from orthodox schooling: its formal principles were different. It was constructed in a wholly different way. There is also a temptation to exaggerate the extent and, especially, the permanence of such institutions in collusion with the invariably euphoric reporting of their activities.

Typically, then, educational pursuits were not separated out and labelled 'school' or 'institute' or even 'rational recreation' They did not typically occur in purpose-built premises or places appropriated for one purpose. The typical forms were improvised, haphazard and therefore ephemeral, having little permanent existence beyond the more immediate needs of individuals and groups. Educational forms were closely related to other activities or inserted within them, temporally and spatially. Men and women learned as they acted and were encouraged to teach their children, too, out of an accumulated experience. The distinction between 'education' (i.e. school) and not-education-at-all (everything outside school) was certainly in the process of construction in this period, but radicals breached it all the time. As George Jacob Holyoake put it, 'knowledge lies everywhere to hand for those who observe and think'.[19] It lay in nature, in a few much-prized books, but above all in the social circumstances of everyday life.

Radical education cannot be understood aside from inherited educational resources. It rested on this basis but also developed and enriched it. We mean the whole range of indigenous educational resources, indigenous in the sense that they were under popular control or within the reach of some popular contestation. Struggle of some kind was possible, of course, in every type of school or institute but there were also whole areas that were relatively immune from direct intervention or compulsion by capital or capital's agencies. We include, then, the educational resources of family, neighbourhood and even place of work, whether within the household or outside it, the acquisition of literacy from mothers or fathers, the use of the knowledgeable friend or neighbour, or the 'scholar' in neighbouring town or village, the work-place discussion and formal and informal apprenticeships, the extensive networks of private schools and, in many cases, the local Sunday schools, most un-school-like of the new devices, excellently adapted to working-class needs.

On top of this legacy, which in nineteenth-century conditions was very fragile, radicals made their own cultural inventions. These included the various kinds of communal reading and discussion groups, the facilities for newspapers in pub, coffee house or reading room, the broader cultural politics of Chartist or Owenite branch-life, the institution of the travelling lecturer who, often indistinguishable from 'missionary' or demagogue, toured the radical centres, and, above all, the radical press, the most successful radical invention and an extremely flexible (and therefore ubiquitous) educational form.

The product of these two levels of activity may best be thought of as a series of educational networks. 'Network' is a better word than 'system', suggesting a limited availability, fragile existence and a highly contingent use. The ability to use them, even at high points of radical activity, was always heavily dependent on chance individual combinations of more structural features. Accordingly, the working-class intellectual was (and is) a rare creation. The fully educated working man and, still more, working woman was, in Thomas Wright's phrase, 'an accidental being'.[20]
[...]

Press

It was, perhaps, the press, in each distinctive phase, that epitomized the forms of radical education. Its general historical importance is now well established. In the first phase it was the main source of unity: '1816–20 were, above all, years in which popular Radicalism took its style from the hand-press and the weekly periodical'.[21] The unstamped press from 1830 to 1836 was both an educative force, developing much later Chartist theory, and a practical example of the struggle against unjust laws and oppressive government.[22] More recently, it has been established that the press was important within the dynamics of Chartism itself and that 'the establishment of a national newspaper [the *Northern Star*] was a vital prerequisite to the emergence of the Chartist party'.[23]

The political importance of the press was closely linked to its versatility as an educational form. It was a resource that could be used with great flexibility. It could be carefully studied and pondered over, as the more expository parts of, say, the *Poor Man's Guardian* must have been. It could be read aloud in declamatory style in pub or public place as Cobbett's or O'Connor's addresses were.[24] It reached its 'pupils' at different levels of literacy and preparedness for study. The conjunction, it is true, sounds somewhat paradoxical: because of our experience of the modern popular press, we are not used to thinking of a newspaper as an educative medium. An example may convince. We can take the *Northern Star* as the hardest case, the most newspaperly of the radical media and that with the strongest reputation for sheer demagoguery.

The *Star* was certainly a newspaper. It 'could compete with any adversary for coverage', using paid journalists and local correspondents.[25] It remains, as a result, the best source for the study of Chartism everywhere. Yet the *Star* was also saturated with an educational content, even if we interpret 'education' in the most conventional sense. It contained regular advertisements and reviews of radical literature, drew attention to travelling lecturers likely to appeal to popular audiences, noted prosecutions of flogging schoolmasters (presumably to warn readers off such offenders) and published Charles Dickens's exposé of boarding schools from *Nicholas Nickleby*[26] It gave special attention to Sunday schools, noting the opening of new ones, reporting on meetings of Sunday school teachers and covering the doings of Sunday school unions in Chartist localities. [. . .] In all these ways, quite aside from its 'teaching', we can certainly see the *Star* as an educational medium. The distinction between 'physical' and 'moral' force Chartism and the tendency to identify O'Connor with the latter has distorted understandings of the *Star* as a newspaper and of O'Connor as a leader.[27] A study of the newspaper itself does not support the contention of R.C. Gammage, Chartism's first historian, that O'Connor 'never sought to raise the Chartist body by enlightening its members'.[28]

Content

Perhaps the phrase 'really useful knowledge' is the best starting point. It was more than just a parody of the Society for the Diffusion of Useful Knowledge. It was a way of distancing working-class aims from some immediate (capitalist) conception of utility and from recreational or diversionary notions. It expressed the conviction that real knowledge served practical ends, ends, that is, for the knower. The insistence on this was unanimous:

> This knowledge will be of the best kind because it will be practical. [The *Co-operator*, an early Owenite journal]
> All useful knowledge consists in the acquirement of ideas concerning our conditions in life. [*The Pioneer*, an Owenite/trade union journal]
> It is a wrong use of words to call a man an ignorant man, who well understands the business he has to carry on . . . . [Cobbett]
> What we want to be informed about is – *how to get out of our present troubles*. [*Poor Man's Guardian*]
> A man may be amused and instructed by scientific literature but the language which describes his wrongs clings to his mind with an unparalleled pertinacity. [*Poor Man's Guardian*][29]

A concern that knowledge should be relevant to the experienced problems of life was reflected in the criticisms of the SDUK and of the fare of mechanics institutes as trivial and childish.[30] A slightly different criticism was sometimes addressed to lecturers and to the more 'philosophical' of fellow radicals: a criticism of wilful abstractness or abstruseness, of the failure to speak plainly. When a reviewer in the *Pioneer* exhorted his readers 'to call on men of talent to instruct you in the highest branches of science', a fine Cobbett-like editorial, probably by James Morrison, put him in his place:

> No proud, conceited scholar knows the way – the rugged path that we

are forced to travel; they sit them down and sigh, and make a puny wail
of human nature; they fill their writings full of quaint allusions, which we
can fix no meaning to; they are by far too classical for our poor knowledge-
box; they preach up temperance, and build no places for our sober meetings
... but we will make them bend to suit our circumstances.[31]

There is a lot going on in these few pungent sentences. There is a hostility to the
scholar and a recognition that his skills may dominate or mystify. There is a moment
of self-deprecation ('Poor knowledge-box'). But there is also a sense of the idealism
or triviality of much 'preaching' and of the absence of that really materialist grasp
of conditions which 'we' ourselves (for all our lack of learning) actually possess.
There is also a determination to work through the problems politically, to make
the 'intellectuals' work *for* us. Very similar themes appear in a running debate
within radicalism between those who argued that we remain ignorant and need
to get knowledge and those who inverted the intellectual pyramid and argued that
'we' were really wiser than 'they'.

Radicals, however, also argued that their conception of knowledge was wide,
much more liberal than philanthropic offerings. Education should be comprehensive
in *every* meaning of the word: widely available and extensive in content. The
language of universal enlightenment occurs again and again in radical propaganda,
the contrast being with the confining of knowledge by monopoly or control. In
one of its earthier analogies, the *Poor Man's Guardian* compared knowledge with
capital and with manure:

If manure be suffered to lie in idle heaps, it breeds stink and vermin. If
properly diffused, it vivifies and fertilizes. The same is true of capital and
knowledge. A monopoly of either breeds filth and abomination. A proper
diffusion of them fills a country with joy and abundance.[32]

[...]

The 'practical' and the 'liberal' were not seen as incompatible as they tend to be
in modern education debates. For the practical embraced 'all known facts' and 'the
attainment of truth'. Despite the stress on a relation to the knower's experience,
there is no narrowly *pragmatic* conception of knowledge here. Knowledge is not
just a political instrument; the search for 'truth' matters.

Radicals did distinguish, however, between different kinds of knowledge and the
practical priorities between them. While a really full or human education, embracing
a knowledge of man and nature, would certainly be achieved once the Charter had
been won or the New Moral World ushered in, some substantive understandings
had a special priority, here and now. Certain truths had a pressing immediacy.
They were indispensable means to emancipation. These truths were several simple
insights. Once grasped they provided explanations for whole areas of experience
and fact. Once these truths were understood, the old world could indeed be shaken.

[...] There were three main components in what we might term the 'spearhead
knowledge' of early-nineteenth-century radicalism. For the radical mainstream,
running from Jacobinism through Cobbett and the unstamped and into the Chartist

movement, 'political knowledge' maintained its pre-eminence. As a number of studies have now shown, Paine's popular radical liberalism was the most powerful continuing influence on radical political theory.[33] Yet it is important to stress the historical distance that separates Paine's world of the French and American Revolutions from the Britain of the 1830s. The changes had been very great, not least within the British state. This was not just a question of the Reform Act of 1832, the bringing of industrial interests within 'the constitution' and the exclusion of the propertyless. Under Whig auspices after 1832 the state was increasingly employed in a dynamic and transformative manner both to discipline individual capitals and to secure the conditions of capital accumulation as a whole. This involved attacking the customary defences of the poor and handling the hostility which this itself produced, both by coercive means and by modifying the most aggressively forward policies. Radicals schooled in natural right theory and the 'aristocratic' character of state and church had to come to some understanding of Poor Law, Factory Acts, the professionalization of civilian police, the reform of secondary punishments and important changes in the criminal law. [. . .]

Something of these changes was grasped in later radical theory, especially in the *Poor Man's Guardian* and the *Northern Star*. While retaining the theory of natural rights as a kind of moral underpinning of the demand for universal suffrage and, certainly, on occasion, speaking of the evils of taxation, the *Guardian* changed Paine's political sociology and developed a more active, interventionist view of 'government'. From the Reform Act, the *Guardian* learnt to draw relations of power (and exploitation) between property as a whole and the working class, not, as in Paine, between 'aristocracy' and 'people'.[34] The *Guardian* was much more interested too in the law and in the actual operations of government: government was an instrument of great power – hence the absolute priority of changing it and the centrality of political solutions. [. . .] The primary strategic problem was how to secure a 'government of the whole people to protect the whole people'. This once achieved 'the majority' would be in a position to introduce 'Owenism, St. Simonism or any other -ism' that would ensure the well-being of the whole.[35] This was the core of what the *Guardian* called 'knowledge calculated to make you free'.[36]

Like 'political knowledge', the Owenite's 'social science' or 'science of society' incorporated a central ethical notion and a simple principle of social explanation. In advanced versions of 'political knowledge' these were the rights of man and an extreme (political) democracy and the principle of the class nature of the state. Owenism centred on 'community' and a rational altruism and the principle of the educative force of competitive social relationships and institutions. Social co-operation among equals-in-circumstances was the only enduring source of progress and happiness. (It was also 'true Christianity', unlike the priestly kinds.) But why was Society so unlike what Reason prescribed? The explanation hinged on the socializing force of institutions and, in the end, on a fairly mechanical environmentalism. To live in this old immoral world was to become irrational, to have one's character misshapen as competitive, disharmonious and violent, and to learn the great untruth that the fault lay with oneself. The competitiveness of the economic system was reinforced by a whole range of social institutions. There was little indeed which did not, in the Owenite analysis, count as an ideological resource. But it was in relation to three key institutions – the family, the church and the school – that Owenite ideas were most forcibly expressed: in Owenite feminism, in Owenite secularism and in Owenite educational theory.[37] Owenism, then, added whole dimensions to the analysis of privations and a much more rounded view of liberation. It also tended to counter the overwhelmingly conspiratorial view of ruling-class actions promulgated by most of the radical press. [...]

The third main element of spearhead knowledge concerned questions of poverty and exploitation. How was it, in the midst of the production of wealth, that the labourers remained so poor? Economic justice prescribed that the labourer should have the full fruits of his toil; 'labour economics' or 'moral' or 'co-operative political economy' showed how capitalists stole a proportion in the shape of a 'tax' called profit. Though such theories gave a central place to capital, unlike the older notions of poverty through taxation or land theft, the capitalist still tended to be understood in his role as factor, merchant or external organizer of production, and exploitation was still understood as something that happened in exchange. The characteristic solution was to attempt to cut out the middle man from the process altogether and subject production and distribution to communal control.[38]

When radicals spoke of 'really useful knowledge' they usually meant one or other or all of these understandings of existing circumstances. As Patricia Hollis has argued the radical repertoire was built accumulatively not in some simple developmental sequence towards the more 'socialist' elements. Newer insights tended to be expressed in the older rhetoric.[39] Yet these understandings were very powerful. They embraced, after all, a theory of economic exploitation, a theory of the class character of the state and a theory of social or cultural domination, understood as the formation of social character.

'How to Do as Many Useful Things as Possible'

It is not possible to do justice here to all the elements in radical conceptions of knowledge. Chartism, for instance, was possessed of a rich literary culture. There was a widespread popular interest in the natural sciences, important in some forms of radicalism for its iconoclastic relation to 'Superstition' and 'Church Christianity'. A more complete treatment should also consider the startling modernity of Owenite experiments in the education of children, especially the stress on the child's own activity, the width of the curriculum and the insistence on reasonable adult behaviour towards the young.[40] One more theme must suffice: the relation of knowledge to production, or what is now often summed up (misleadingly) as the question of 'skills'.

Cobbett's approach to this question is particularly interesting.[41] Like all radicals he was concerned with political education. 'I was', he wrote, with typical immodesty and a grain of truth, 'the teacher of the nation: the great source of political knowledge'. [42] But he added a stock of notions about the education of children, attempting to distinguish a real 'education' (a word worth rescuing) from mere 'Heddekashun'.

Education meant 'bringing up', 'breeding up' or 'rearing up'. It included the cultivation of 'everything with regard to the *mind* as well as the *body* of the child'.[43] It embraced book-learning where this was useful, but much more besides. One central concern was to teach the child to earn a living, to acquire an economic independence – a 'competence' in both sets of meanings of the word. Such an education should occur almost imperceptibly in the course of play or labour. 'Heddekashun' by contrast was artificial, coercive and divorced from real needs. It involved learning irrelevancies from books. It was a thing quite outside the control of parents and children, resting on alien purposes. It meant 'taking boys and girls from their father's and mother's houses, and sending them to what is called a school ...'.[44]

The two most important constituents of 'rearing up' were an emphasis on practical skills and on the educative context of the home. Since Cobbett almost always had in mind the village labourer or small farmer, his prescriptions often have an old-fashioned or 'Tory' ring. He sometimes used the language of a traditionalist squire or farmer, especially when blaming 'Heddekashun' for encouraging artificial social ambitions.[45] Yet the appropriate education of the labourer or small farmer was not particularly limiting. The first priority was to teach the practical skills of husbandry and of 'cottage economy': gardening, rearing animals, making bread, beer, bacon, butter and cheese, tending trees, and, for boys, ploughing, hedging and ditching. Farmers must know how to ride, hunt, shoot and manage accounts. A healthy body and sober habits were also important. Yet more literary skills, as tools, should also be accessible to all. 'Book-learning is by no means to be despised; and it is a thing that may be laudably sought after by persons in all states of life'.[46] So when Cobbett praised the native wisdom of the untutored person, it was not to justify the withholding of literacy, a common argument among 'Tories'.[47] Cobbett was concerned, rather, to stress the value and rootedness of common sense and customary knowledge and to show the inadequacy of purely literary or abstract study. This was most startlingly expressed in a defence of the illiterate.

> Men are not to be called *ignorant* merely because they cannot make upon
> paper certain marks with a pen, or because they do not know the meaning
> of such marks when made by others.[48]

By the same rule, those whom the world called wise were often very stupid. Of the editor of the *Morning Chronicle* and of others with a facility for words, he wrote, 'they were extremely enlightened, but they had no knowledge'.[49]

Cobbett's positive evaluation of more literary skills was expressed more fully in his *Advice to Young Men*, and his *Grammar of the English Language*, works which ought to establish his reputation as a conscious educator. These texts were certainly intended for a popular audience, though one that was almost wholly male. *Advice to Young Men* was sub-titled 'and incidentally to Young Women' and addressed to 'every father'; the *Grammar* was intended for 'soldiers, sailors, apprentices and ploughboys'. (Cobbett was indeed the original patriarch, a theme to which we will return.) In the *Grammar* Cobbett sought to democratize the subject and to rescue it from its association with dead languages. He understood the connection between forms of language and social domination and saw the teaching of grammar as a way of protecting the ordinary man 'from being the willing slave of the rich and titled part of the community'.[50] Arithmetic too was a 'thing of everyday utility'.[51] History also was valuable, as a study of 'how these things came'. Cobbett actually wrote his own history book, but he was teaching how these things (tithes, taxes, the National Debt and his whole demonology) came, all the time.[52]

His curriculum, then, had the same feature as other radical versions. Working back from the living situation of adults, he ended with a range of 'competences' that combined the practical and the liberal.

His stress on the educative role of the family was linked to his political suspicion of schools. But we cannot understand this part of his writing without remembering two points made about Cobbett in *The Making of the English Working Class*: his 'personalisation of political issues' and the fact that 'his outlook approximated most closely to the ideology of the small producers'.[53] The central experience in his educational writing is Cobbett the father. Moreover, he actually lived (or envisaged) a situation in which production, domestic labour and the reproduction of skills all remained within the control of the father in the family of the direct producer. In such a situation the natural way for boys or girls to learn was alongside father or mother in the ordinary tasks of the day. All Cobbett's descriptions emphasize such learning situations; learning to make hurdles by helping father at work in a Hampshire copse; learning to manage a farm and read and write letters through the medium of a hamper that passed from family to prison cell; the daring image of the Sandhill, a description of a childhood game to set beside the philanthropic ban on play.[54] His own children were taught 'indirectly'. Things were made available – ink, pens and paper – 'and everyone scrabbled about as he or she pleased'. So 'the book-learning crept in of its own accord, by imperceptible degrees'. Cobbett's conclusions, then, appear equally inevitable:

> What need had we of *schools*? What need of *teachers*? What need of scolding or force, to induce children to read and write and love books?[55]

Cobbett's personalisms were based on rather special circumstances, 'a marvellous concatenation of circumstances such as can hardly befall one man out of a thousand', according to the *Poor Man's Guardian's* critique.[56] As writer and farmer, engaged (between politics, prison and exile) in two unalienated forms of labour, Cobbett spent much time at home in conditions of economic independence. (One is also curious about the relative roles of Mr. and Mrs. Cobbett in the 'rearing up' of their children.) If he expressed, in ideal form educational practices appropriate to the small producer household, he expressed them at a time when they were becoming less easy to realize.

Cobbett's ideal united mental and manual labour through the father's control of production. Owenites argued that monopoly or distortion of knowledge was a feature of capitalist industry. Capital seized hold of the secrets of the trades (once reproduced within the labourer's culture) and made of their workers 'unthinking slaves'.[57] Although these themes are everywhere present in the theory and practice of co-operation, they were most elaborately expressed by the 'early Socialist', William Thompson.[58]

Thompson argued that capitalist production tended to divorce labour from a knowledge of productive processes, to divide, in Marx's terms, mental and manual labour, conception and execution. He also argued that 'commercial society' had a more general effect on the production of knowledge itself. There was a direct interest in the development and application of the physical sciences which, by multiplying machinery, would enrich the wealthy. Political and moral sciences, however, were neglected or shaped according to the interests of the rich. In the absence of a knowledge of 'the natural laws of distribution', machinery became a means of oppression. In co-operative activity and ultimately in a new world, mental and manual labour would be reunited and knowledge of man and nature develop in harmony. Co-operative activity was often a conscious living out of these themes. It aimed at re-appropriating the capitalist's control of production and exchange. As the *Birmingham Co-operative Herald* put it:

> Labourers must become capitalists, and must acquire knowledge to regulate their labour on a large and united scale before they will be able to enjoy the whole product of their labour.[59]

The knowledge part of this was important: the Co-operative equivalent of Cobbett's 'how to do as many useful things as possible' was how to repossess the knowledge and skills appropriated by capital. The activity of the collective organization of 'affairs', including affairs of business, was itself an important education. [...]

Popularity

It is difficult, perhaps foolish, to try to weigh the impact of the solutions we have discussed – their 'popularity' – in some simple quantitative sense. [...] It may be more useful to approach the broader problem somewhat differently.

As our knowledge of popular movements, especially of Chartism and its antecedents, deepens, much of an older anonymity has been dispersed. It is possible now to identify and name levels of leadership well beyond the kind of national figures discussed in Cole's *Chartist Portraits* and subsequent biographies. For some localities a local leadership has been described quite closely. These were the people whom we have termed, with deliberate looseness, 'radicals' throughout this study. They were the journalists, the demagogues, the lecturers, the national and provincial leaders, the organizers, directors and 'educators' of radical movements. We may refer to many of these people as 'intellectuals'. The value of this term is to mark both the coherence of understanding that was developed and the 'educative' functions that were performed. We might even speak of radicals, and especially Chartists and Owenites, as constituting political parties or proto-parties. In some analyses of party, indeed, the terms party and intellectual are closely connected. For Gramsci, for example, parties were organizations that enabled the production of intellectuals whose experiences and allegiances were, organically, those of the class which they served. Certainly some such distinction – between party and class – between radical 'intellectual' and those whom they addressed – is in this context a useful one. We may then speak of a more or a less 'internal' or 'organic' relation between the two.[60] The question of the 'popularity of radicalism' becomes, then, more qualitative and relational.

There are, of course, great difficulties in answering this question too: it needs to be explored for each movement, each locality and perhaps for each major leader. Edward Thompson's comparison of Owen and Cobbett underlines the importance of individuality:

> If Cobbett's writings can be seen as a relationship with his readers Owen's can be seen as ideological raw material diffused among working-people, and worked up by them into different products.[61]

We might none the less risk the generalization that from 1816 to the early 1840s the relationship between radical leadership and working-class people was extraordinarily close.

One common, but not decisive, test of the organicism of a leadership is its social class origins. It is a common test because it is 'obvious' that people of working-class origin will have a more intimate knowledge of the problems of their class and a stronger sense of loyalty than others. It is not 'decisive' because there seem to have been very many exceptions to this rule: renegades, 'gentleman agitators', 'intellectuals'. The relationship between some of the radicals who were not working class and their working-class 'constituents' seems often to have been peculiarly close – John Fielden, Feargus O'Connor and Bronterre O'Brien are exemplary cases.[62] It would be wrong, however, to regard Chartism or its predecessors as typically led by middle-class people. Perhaps the most important feature of nineteenth-century radicalism was its capacity to produce an indigenous leadership. It is not difficult to understand why this was so, for working people with an inclination towards mental labour *had* to stay within their own class, or occupy positions of great social ambiguity like elementary or private schoolmastering or journalism or lecturing. There were few open roads to co-option. At the same time an education and a sort of career were available within radical movements themselves.

The more decisive tests of organicism are those discussed by Gramsci in a 'note' on Italian idealism, though, as usual, the problems of popular communist organization were not far from his mind:

> One could only have had … an organic quality of thought if there had existed the same unity between the intellectuals and the simple as there should be between theory and practice. That is, if the intellectuals had been organically the intellectuals of those masses, and if they had worked out and made coherent the principles and the problems raised by the masses in their practical activity … . Is a philosophical movement properly so called when it is devoted to creating a specialised culture among restricted intellectual groups, or rather when, or only when, in the process of elaborat-

ing a form of thought superior to 'common sense' and coherent on a scientific plane, it never forgets to remain in contact with the 'simple' and indeed finds in this contact the source of the problem it sets out to study and to resolve? Only by this contact does a philosophy become 'historical', purify itself of intellectualistic elements of an individual character and become life.[63]

Early nineteenth-century radicalism did indeed find in the everyday life of the masses 'the source of the problems it set out to study and resolve'. 'Spearhead knowledge' centred, as we have seen, on the experiences of poverty, political oppression and social and cultural apartheid. It gave a wider, more 'historical', more coherent view of everyday life than customary or individual understandings. This was possible, in part, because the commonest inhibitions to such an internal relation were weakly developed. There was nowhere else but contemporary ex- perience from which an appropriate theory could derive: no pre-existing socialist doctrine to be learnt and therefore no danger of the rigidity or autonomy of dogmas. Perhaps there was a tendency of Painite theory to crystallize thus, but, in general, there were simply no historical parallels for the situation of working people in England from which relevant theory might have been derived. A similar argument relates to forms of organization. Though radical groups can be considered parties in a looser Gramscian sense, they were hardly parties on a stricter Leninist model. But organizational looseness had compensations. There were few organizational orthodoxies either, little growth of bureaucracies, little of the more extreme kinds of internal division between 'officials' and 'rank and file' which were to dominate trade union, social democratic and communist politics. The main inhibition to a notably democratic practice was the *amour propre* and charismatic character of some leaders, who, however, could be jettisoned or ignored. In this sense, radicalism had little except its 'popularity' on which to depend. Many of the formal characteristics of its education project stem from this: informality for instance, and the 'practical', 'unintellectualistic' (had we better say unacademic?) character of its 'theory'.

[. . .]

Notes and References

1 SIMON, B. (1960) *Studies in the History of Education, 1780–1870*, Lawrence and Wishart; HARRISON, J.F.C. (1961) *Learning and Living 1790–1960*, Routledge and Kegan Paul; SILVER, H. (1965) *The Concept of Popular Education*, MacGibbon and Kee; THOMPSON, E.P. (1963) *The Making of the English Working Class*, Gollancz, especially pp. 711–45. Also important for first opening up many questions was WEBB, R.K. (1955) *The British Working Class Reader 1790–1848*, Allen and Unwin.

2 Especially HOLLIS, P. (1970) *The Pauper Press*, Oxford University Press; WIENER, J.H. (1969) *The War of the Unstamped*, Cornell University Press; THOMPSON, D. (1971) *The Early Chartists*, Macmillan; EPSTEIN, J.A. (1976) 'Feargus O'Connor and the *Northern Star*', *International Review of Social History* Vol. 21, Part 1, pp. 51–97; YEO, E. (1971) 'Robert Owen and radical culture', in POLLARD, S. and SALT, T. (Eds.) (1971) *Robert Owen: Prophet of the Poor*, Macmillan; HARRISON, J.F.C. (1969) *Robert Owen and Owenites in England and America*, Routledge and Kegan Paul.

3 The importance of private schooling before 1870 has been stressed by those who now favour a return to market principles in education. See especially WEST, E.G. (1970) 'Resource allocation and growth in early nineteenth-century British education', *Economic History Review*, Vol. 13, No. 1, April. For an

example of the kind of careful local study that we badly need see FIELD, J. (1978) 'Private Schools in Portsmouth and Southampton 1850–1870', *Journal of Educational History and Administration*, Vol. X, No. 2, pp. 8–14.

4 The major study of Sunday Schools – LAQUEUR, T.W. (1976) *Religion and Respectability: Sunday Schools and English Working Class Culture*, Yale University Press – argues that Sunday Schools as such were working-class institutions, democratically controlled. For an interesting example of a local study which shows the variety of practices under the term 'Sunday School' see FROST, M. (1978) 'Working-class education in Birmingham 1780–1850', University of Birmingham, unpublished M. Litt. thesis.

5 For the first of these faults see SIMON, B. (1960) *op. cit.*, p. 275; the latter simplifications are commoner in conservative historiography.

6 For Cobbett see page 12 of this chapter but Wooller, Carlile, O'Brien and O'Connor, among others, used this description of themselves or others.

7 PAINE, T. (1791) *The Rights of Man*, London, J. Johnson, reprinted (Ed.) COLLINS, H. (1969) Penguin, Harmondsworth, especially p. 163.

8 COBBETT, W. (1829) *Advice to Young Men*, reprinted (1906) London, Henry Frowde, p. 261.

9 E.g. *Black Dwarf*, 4 March 1818; Cobbett's or Hone's version of the catechism or Cobbett's 'Sunday School Hymn'; *Black Dwarf*, 6 October 1819; *Political Register*, 7 December 1833, p. 603.

10 For infants schools see *New Moral World*, 8 July 1837; and *Northern Star*, 7 January 1843. But for a more favourable view see the *Midlands Counties Illuminator* (Thomas Cooper's paper), 20 March 1841.

11 Even the most favourable assessments of the popularity of the mechanics' institutes are open to the interpretation that the institutes were used for their 'really useful' content, e.g. the late acquisition of skills of literacy. See for example ROYLE, E. (1971) 'Mechanics institutes and the working classes 1840–1860', *Historical Journal*, Vol. 14, where it is shown that elementary classes teaching the three Rs were the most popular aspect.

12 *English Chartist Circular*, No. 37, p. 145.

13 *Poor Man's Guardian*, 18 May 1833.

14 *Ibid.*, 22 June 1833.

15 *Ibid.*, 24 September 1831.

16 Listed in WIENER, J.H. (1970) *A Descriptive Finding List of Unstamped British Periodicals 1830–1836*, London, Bibliographical Society.

17 'Heddekashun' was defined in COBBETT (1822) *Cottage Economy*, London, C. Clements, reprinted (1850) London, Ann Cobbett, p. 4.

18 For a similar argument see YEO, E. (1971) *op. cit.*, p. 108, Note 2.

19 HOLYOAKE, G.J. (1892) *Sixty years of an Agitator's Life*, London, T.F. Unwin, Vol. 1, p. 4.

20 [Thomas Wright] *The Great Unwashed by a Journeyman Engineer* (1868), reprinted (1970) Cass, p. 7.

21 THOMPSON, E.P. (1963) *op. cit.* p. 674.

22 For the best account of the unstamped as, itself, a political force see WIENER, J.H. (1969) *op. cit.*; for the best account of radical ideology in this phase see HOLLIS, P. (1970) *op. cit.*

23 EPSTEIN, J.A. (1976) *op. cit.*, p. 95.

24 For Cobbett see THOMPSON, E.P. (1963) *op. cit.*, p. 749; for O'Connor see EPSTEIN, J.A. (1976) *op. cit.*, p. 84.

25 *Ibid.*, p. 79.

26 For lectures see *Northern Star*, (1838) 5 May, (1838) 2 June, (1839) 28 July; for schoolmasters see (1838) 25 August; for Dickens see (1838), *passim*.

27 For this argument in full see EPSTEIN, J.A. (1976) *op. cit. passim*.

28 GAMMAGE, R.C. (1969) *History of the Chartist Movement 1837–1854*, London, Merlin Press, p. 197.

29 *Co-operator*, (1830) 1 January; *Pioneer*, (1834) 31 May; *Political Register*, (1833) 21 September, p. 731; *Poor Man's Guardian*, (1834) 25 October and 14 April ('Letter from a "labourer" in Poplar').

30 For a typical attack on this score see *Le Bonnett Rouge* (journal of the neo-Jacobin, Lorymer), (1833) 16 February.

31 *Pioneer*, (1834) 25 January.

32 *Poor Man's Guardian*, (1834) 14 June.

33 E.g. HOLLIS, P. (1970) *op. cit.*, p. 219.

34 E.g. *Poor Man's Guardian*, (1831) 26 March, Leader on the reform bill, and, for a more developed version, the leader (1834) 14 June.

35 *Ibid.*, (1833) 30 November.

36 *Ibid.*, (1832) 14 April.

37 The most 'authoritative' source for Owenite theory was the *New Moral World*, the 'official' journal of the movement. But see HARRISON, J.F.C. (1969) *op. cit.* and THOMPSON, E.P. (1963) *op. cit.*, pp. 779–807, for the two most interesting contemporary interpretations.

38 For a fuller acount see HALÉVY, E. (1903) *Thomas Hodgskin 1787–1869*, London; PANKHURST, R. (1954) *William Thompson (1775–1833): Britain's Pioneer Socialist, Feminist and Co-operator*, London, Watts and Co. For their influence on working-class theory see HOLLIS, P. (1970) *op. cit.* and THOMPSON, E.P. (1963) *op. cit.*

39 HOLLIS, P. (1970) *op. cit.*, p. 225.

40 On Owenite educational ideas see especially SILVER, H. (1965) *op. cit.*, and HARRISON, J.F.C. (1969) *op. cit.*

41 He was not at all the Tory obscurantist that his vote against the education measures of 1833 has some-times suggested to educational historians.

42 *Political Register*, (1830) 10 April.

43 COBBETT, W. (1850) *Cottage Economy, op. cit.*, pp. 9–10.

44 *Political Register*, (1833) 7 December, p. 581.

45 E.g. COBBETT, W. (1850) *op. cit.*, pp. 10–14. In this way, and with a typical inconsistency, he managed to blame philanthropy both for destroying an old order and trying to maintain it!

46 COBBETT, W. (1829) *Advice to Young Men, op. cit.*, p. 40.

47 For a typical but intelligent argument of the Tory kind see (John Weyland) (1808) *Letter to a Country Gentleman on the Education of the Lower Orders*, London.

48 COBBETT, W. (1829) *op. cit.*, p. 40.

49 Quoted in REITZEL, W. (Ed.) (1967) *The Autobiography of William Cobbett*, Faber, p. 194.

50 COBBETT, W. (1829) *op. cit.*, p. 48.

51 *Ibid.*, p. 41.

52 His own history book was *History of the Protestant Reformation*, of which Cobbett boasted: 'unquestion-ably the book of greatest circulation in the whole world, the Bible only excepted'.

53 THOMPSON, E.P. (1963) *op. cit.*, pp. 755 and 759.

54 *Political Register*, (1833) 21 September, p. 735; REITZEL, W. (1967) *op. cit.*, pp. 123–5; COBBETT, W. (1830) Rural Rides, London, William Cobbett, reprinted by Penguin (1967),p. 41.

55 COBBETT, W. (1829) *op. cit.*, pp. 247–55.

56 *Poor Man's Guardian*, (1833) 14 September.

57 E.g. Shepherd Smith's lecture on Education, *Crisis*, 31 August 1833.

58 What follows is drawn mainly from *An Inquiry into the Principles and Distribution of Wealth*, but see the similar argument in *Crisis*, (1832) 21 April.

59 *Birmingham Co-operative Herald*, (1829) 1 June. This is a part-quote from THOMPSON, W. *Labour Defended*.

60 For Gramsci's discussion of parties based on the inter-war Italian experience see HOARE, Q. and NOWELL-SMITH, G. (1971) *Selections from the Prison Notebooks of Antonio Gramsci*, Lawrence and Wishart, *passim*. The distinction between 'organic' and 'traditional' intellectuals is central to Gramsci's discussion of party and working-class culture.

61 THOMPSON, E.P. (1963) *op. cit.*, p. 789.

62 On Fielden see RICHARDS, P. (1975) 'The state and the working class 1833–1841', University of Bir-mingham unpublished Ph.D. thesis; on O'Connor see EPSTEIN, J.A. (1976) *op. cit.*, and (1977) 'Feargus O'Connor and the English working-class movement', University of Birmingham unpublished Ph.D. thesis.

63 HOARE, Q. and NOWELL-SMITH, G. (1971) *op. cit.*, p. 330.

2 Ideology and United States History Textbooks

Jean Anyon

Textbooks are social products that can be examined in the context of their time, place, and function. Those produced in this country are designed and marketed by a publishing industry that is big business – with annual sales of several billion dollars – and that increasingly is owned by corporate conglomerates.[1] CBS owns Holt, Rinehart and Winston, Fawcett Publications, Praeger Publications, and W.B. Saunders, a science textbook house. RCA, which owns NBC, in a merger arrangement with Harcourt Brace Jovanovitch owns Random House, which owns Vintage. IBM recently acquired Science Research Associates. Xerox owns Ginn, American Educational Publications ('My Weekly Reader'), Learning Materials, Inc., and R.R. Bowker, publisher of the leading trade magazines, *Publisher's Weekly* and *Library Journal*. Gulf and Western, one of the largest of the multinational conglomerates, owns Simon and Schuster.[2]

Exactly how influential are contemporary publishing companies? While publishing is definitely a large industry, the sale of its product is nevertheless dependent upon decisions by consumers. Textbook content is influenced by the educational expectations of parents, school personnel, school boards, and state selection committees. If, however, one looks at the larger publishing companies with their multinational 'parents', one sees that they constitute the only source of nationally distributed books and textbooks. According to industry analysts, only forty hardcover houses in the country have the resources to produce a book profitably on a nationwide basis.[3] The larger publishing companies are thus able to make certain views and curriculum materials widely available and to withhold others from national distribution.
[. . .]

Methodology

This study used seventeen well-known, secondary school United States history

Source: Harvard Educational Review (44.3) (1979), pp. 361–86.

textbooks that appear on board of education lists of 'Books Approved for Use' in both of two large, urban school systems in the Northeast (see Notes). The two school systems were chosen because they have substantial numbers of both minority and white students from poor and working-class families. For many of these students the history textbooks they read are likely to be their major source of information concerning United States history.

The seventeen textbooks vary little from publisher to publisher and from year to year. Although some have more information on Blacks and women than others and some include reproductions of primary source documents while others do not, all books cover a considerable number of the same persons, places, and events in United States history. All use a common descriptive vocabulary when they discuss political and economic leaders, institutions, and social events. Finally, the judgments they make as to what constitute social problems and solutions are also remarkably similar.

The content areas of the history textbooks to be analyzed are economic and labor union developments during the period of rapid industrialization and social change from the Civil War to World War I. These developments involved substantial conflict of interest and struggle for social power. In reports of historical developments that involve group conflict it is possible to ascertain 'whose' knowledge is provided, and to assess if that knowledge legitimates the prerogatives of any group at the expense of any other.

Although it would have been equally appropriate to have analyzed the treatment of black history, women's history, or any other topic involving conflict between groups in society. economic and labor history was chosen partly because it has been largely ignored by those who have recently examined curriculum content, and partly because the relationships and social conflicts between employers and employees reveal basic configurations of resource and power in our society.

All the chapters in the seventeen textbooks that pertained to the period between 1865 and 1917 were examined to determine whether the information they contained was in any way biased. Those years constituted a crucial period in the growth of the United States economy. Mechanization and expansion of the productive forces and the consolidation of industries into large corporations (for example, Standard Oil, Western Electric, and US Steel) transformed an agricultural, entrepreneurial economy into a powerful corporate one. By the beginning of World War I, industrialization and incorporation had produced considerable wealth for some, an affluent middle class, and economic and social problems that have endured: urban poor, persistent unemployment and marginally employed workers; labor-management conflict; low wages and poor working conditions for many of the non-unionized;[4] and the control of a major portion of the United States economic resources by a relatively small number of corporations.[5]

Economic Developments

In all the textbooks studied, discussion of this period of expansion includes the extension of the railroads, communications, and industry, new inventions, and the contributions of the industrialists to the cheap and efficient production of consumer goods. The aspects of these developments considered salutary are emphasized in the textbooks, and their discussion consumes substantial portions of the chapters.[6] Other developments, such as economic concentration and workers' problems, are only briefly discussed and the solutions proposed for them support the activities of some social groups and not others. The textbook discussions of the development of business concentration provide a case in point.

All the books consider business monopolies and trusts to be a problem.[7] The way they treat social responses to this problem, however, actually disguises and rationalizes the continuation of economic concentration. Several books grossly overestimate the effectiveness of antitrust and similar legislation. The following passage, for example, does not mention that many of the legal steps alluded to failed:

> During the seven years he served as President [Theodore] Roosevelt brought 44 lawsuits against the trusts. The two Presidents who followed him rolled up even better records. William Howard Taft took 90 monopolies to court. Woodrow Wilson busted even more trusts. . . . But it was Teddy Roosevelt who blazed the trail. . . . Trusts and monopolies were broken up. Then the great good that industry had done for our country carried us forward to better times for everybody.[8]

While this and two additional textbooks make exaggerated claims,[9] most of the textbooks are more accurate in their report of 'trust-busting'.

The fourteen remaining books are more circumspect when they discuss this aspect of politics of the Progressive Era.[10] Each book provides several pages of description (very often in favorable terms, as in the quotation above) of the activities and intentions of 'trust-buster' Teddy Roosevelt and the legislation passed under Woodrow Wilson.[11] These descriptions are usually part of, or accompanied by, passages in which the Progressive Era itself is lauded as a period of social progress and reform. Only a few lines mentioning that the trust-busting laws were either narrowly construed by the courts or largely unenforced can be found interspersed with descriptions of implied good intentions.[12]

These brief statements concerning the limited results of government antitrust legislation are offered in the textbooks without any comment as to their implications or consequences. By attaching value to only partially successful legislation and by omitting discussion of the actual results, the textbooks encourage belief in the notion that industrial concentration – monopolies, holding companies, and trusts – will be prevented or controlled through legislation. Since, on the contrary, legislative efforts have been only partially successful, the textbooks indirectly facilitate economic concentration.

All but one of the textbooks describe the laws and the period itself in terms of reform and progress.[13] This vocabulary is common in descriptions of the politics of the time, but it does not represent the only interpretation, nor is it politically neutral. The words 'progress' and 'reform' evoke symbolic meanings that have ideological import. With respect to trust-busting, for example, the labels suggest responsive political institutions and good intentions on the part of political and economic leaders, and so serve to rationalize the failure of the legislation to control powerful economic groups. These consequences of the textbook vocabulary become clear when other, contrasting labels that might have been used are considered.

Some historians have suggested that the antitrust legislation was not intended to radically alter the activities of big business, but was a politically conservative response by political and economic leaders to popular pressure for more fundamental change.[14] They argue that the new laws were not imposed on business, but were designed with the explicit co-operation and advice of various national business groups.[15] Further, since the laws did not remove power from big business, and since other laws of the period did not change unpopular economic income inequities, the primary purpose of these laws can be seen not as reform, but as the maintenance of social and economic inequality. The legislation was designed to ensure the legitimacy, and thus the stability and survival, of industrial capitalism and the power of the large corporation.

One may not agree with this argument. However, the use of the words 'conservative' and 'maintenance' to describe trust-busting activities and their consequences highlights the ameliorative connotations of the labels 'reform' and 'progress'. By selective use of vocabulary, then, ideological support is given to activities of powerful economic and political groups that justifies popular support for them.

Economic developments detrimental to the industrial worker of the period, including low wages and poor working conditions, are only briefly discussed.[16] While most books express or imply sympathy for the plight of the worker during the period of industrialization, the explanations they offer actually legitimate the workers' position of suffering. The most commonly used explanations are along the following lines:

> After the Civil War several developments influenced the position of workers. First ... millions of immigrants settled in large cities. These immigrants formed a ready supply of unskilled labor and were willing to work for low wages under poor working conditions. Second, the relation between employer and employee was changing. ... [A]s Theodore Roosevelt observed: 'A few generations before, the boss had known every man in his shop. ... In the small establishment there had been a friendly human relationship between employer and employee. ... There was no such relation between the great railway magnates ... and the one hundred and fifty thousand men who worked in the mines. ... In addition, work became increasingly mechanized, with the worker tending to function like a machine'.[17]

While these explanations are not inaccurate, they tell only one side of the story. For example, attributing low wages to the willingness of unskilled immigrants blames the victims of low wages for their own plight. Some scholars have argued, to the contrary, that immigrant workers were used by employers to keep wages as low as possible, just as Blacks, women, and other underemployed groups of workers are today. They argue that industrialists at the turn of the century were aware of the benefits of an abundant supply of immigrant workers and took steps to increase the number available.[18]

By alleging a causal relationship between the attitudes of immigrants and the position of workers, however, the reader's attention is deflected from the owner's activities and intentions and from the otherwise obvious economic relationship between low wages and increased profits. While four textbooks do include the profit motive as one of the causes of low wages during the period,[19] two suggest that it no longer causes problems – it was an evil of industrialization[20] – and two others argue that it was used in excess by only a few businessmen, 'certain hard-driving manufacturers . . . [who] thought that wages . . . must be cut to the bone in order to raise profits'.[21] More commonly, however, the relation between the activities of immigrants and the disadvantaged position of workers as presented in these textbooks disguises and rationalizes the relationship between increased owners' profits and decreased workers' wages.

The second point made by most textbooks (and also represented in the quotation above) is that poor working conditions stemmed from the inability of owners to care for workers because of the increased size of the firm.[22] The source of this argument can be traced to a popular belief expressed by businessmen at the turn of the century. Industrialists often lamented the loss of personal contact between worker and owner and argued that it would benefit worker, society, and industry.[23] This argument motivated companies to sponsor educational activities for employees – lectures and classes in industrial efficiency, civil and moral responsibility, and family life. These activities, although allegedly for the benefit of the workers, have been described by some scholars as providing a mechanism by which employers could instill self-control in vast numbers of employees with whom they, as 'bosses', no longer had intimate personal contact. The following example is taken from an English lesson taught to immigrant employees at International Harvester in the early 1900s:

> I hear the whistle. I must hurry. I hear the five minutes whistle. It is time
> to go into the shop. . . . I change my clothes and get ready to work. . . . I
> work until the whistle blows to quit. I leave my place nice and clean.[24]

Critics have also argued that the machine-like quality of work that the textbooks attribute to mechanization was caused to a considerable degree by business practices designed to make industrial production more efficient. Many measures (for example, scientific management of work) increased worker alienation by delegating to managers all responsibility for planning and for decisions formerly made by the workers themselves, including decisions regarding the production processes to be utilized and the type and pace of the daily work to be done.[25]

These alternative arguments could have been used by the textbook authors to help explain the problems of workers. None is impartial, but together with those offered in the texts, they might have provided a more balanced discussion with a full range of views on the problem.

[. . .]

Labor Unions

The period of rapid industrialization between the Civil War and World War I was one of intense and often violent conflict between business interests and the new industrial work force. There are various ways in which this conflict might be presented. It might be described as a rebellion by workers against industrial exploitation and economic inequality. From this perspective, one would emphasize strikes and lockouts, focusing perhaps on those confrontations that were successful from labor's point of view. One might also describe problems common to all workers and provide details on the union activities that attempted to unite workers to the challenge of industrialists.

A second approach might present labor unions as illegitimate organizations that interfere with an owner's right to hire and fire and workers' rights to work where and for whom they please. Adherents of this view might describe the strikes and labor-organizing efforts of the period as the result of 'foreign' or anti-American influence, government regulation of industry as violating individual rights and principles of free enterprise, and unions as making unreasonable and inflationary demands.

Still another view might describe labor unions as necessary for the protection of the rights of workers in a democracy. The interests of all parties are supposedly served by the peaceful resolution of conflict. Such a narrative might criticize confrontation, such as strikes, and sanction the use of political and social avenues for reaching consensus, emphasizing the activities of unions that respected the prevailing arrangements of power and recourse and that were willing to operate within those constraints.

Despite the variety of possible descriptions, textbook characterizations of labor history are strikingly narrow and unsympathetic to the more radical segments of the union movement. The average length of the section in the texts on labor history is six pages. Most strikes are not even mentioned, and although there were more than 30,000 during the period,[26] the texts only describe a few of them. Fourteen of the seventeen books choose from among the same three strikes, ones that were especially violent and were failures from labor's point of view: the railroad strike of 1877, the Homestead strike of 1892, the Pullman strike of 1894.[27] Each of these strikes represented a severe setback for the labor movement, leading either to the demise of a particular union or to the withdrawal of support by the middle class.[28]

The authors of the textbooks may have chosen these particular strikes to demonstrate the difficulties faced by early unions; several imply that these strikes show what labor was up against. Whatever their intentions, however, the effect is to cast doubt on striking as a valid course of action. The historically inaccurate impression is given that strikes fail as a method of recourse. Nine books go further, stating that strikes only hurt labor's cause, are costly, and result in violence.[29]

One successful strike is discussed in fifteen of the books, although usually in accounts of Progressive reform rather than in the section on labor history.[30] This is the anthracite-coal strike of 1902, which was resolved in favor of the workers by the intervention of President Theodore Roosevelt. Thirteen of the textbooks state that this strike showed that 'President Roosevelt [and the federal government] treated workers fairly',[31] suggesting that strikes are only successful if government intervenes, and that government mediation is a fruitful and more appropriate recourse in labor disputes.

This suggestion is strengthened by the textbooks discussion of labor laws, also most often found in the sections on Progressive reform. State or federal laws passed to improve conditions for working men, women, and children are described in these terms: 'State laws ... prohibited the employment of children. ... More than half of the states limited the work week ... to 60 hours. .... The [third] type of ... law established a minimum wage'.[32] Some historians have argued that this legislation did not substantially alter the lives of most workers. They cite the fact that much of this legislation was declared unconstitutional by the Supreme Court. For example, the Supreme Court declared the laws against child labor unconstitutional in 1918 and again in 1919.[33]

Fourteen of the textbooks, however, present the labor laws either without noting that they were overturned, or as examples of social progress even though they were overturned.[34] None mentions that many businesses simply disregarded the laws, nor asks what the implications are when the Supreme Court decides that laws allegedly passed to constrain business powers are unconstitutional. The omission of successful strikes and the implied success of political avenues for resolution of conflict suggest a desire to avoid conflict and to facilitate consensus.[35]

The labor organization at the turn of the century that is emphasized in textbook discussions is the American Federation of Labor (AFL). Not coincidentally, it was also the only major labor group at that time that accepted the new corporate order and whose leaders advocated bargaining and union contracts rather than confrontation and changes in the social structure. As president of the AFL, Samuel Gompers, argued against confrontation with business and in support of labor-management co-operation. The use of strikes by AFL locals was not sanctioned by union leadership. Gompers argued throughout his career that labor unions and business trusts were similar organizations and were necessary forms of social co-operation. They were 'voluntary associations for production and distribution'.[36]

While the AFL is almost always described in favorable terms by the textbooks, radical unions are usually either disparaged or simply ignored. A count of all paragraphs in the seventeen books in which labor unions active between 1865 and 1917 are discussed reveals ninety-two paragraphs in which the AFL is mentioned and ninety paragraphs in which all other labor unions are referred to, including the Knights of Labor, the National Labor Union, the American Railway Union, the Western Federation of Miners, the United Mine Workers, and the Industrial Workers of the World. In other words, the AFL receives as much discussion as all other unions combined.[37]

Most AFL local affiliates admitted only skilled workers. This generally eliminated Blacks, recent immigrants, and women, most of whom were unskilled. Only two textbooks criticize these exclusionary practices.[38] Eleven argue that reliance by the AFL on the skilled worker was a major reason for its growth and success.[39] No textbook mentions Samuel Gompers's co-operation with industrialists in suppressing strikes by other unions or his frequent attempts to undermine radical labor groups.[40] The books praise Gompers's pragmatism and character, which they contrast to what they call weak, belligerent, and intolerant leaders of the radical unions.[41] A successful and legitimate labor union is thus implicitly defined by the textbooks as an organization of skilled workers who accept and co-operate with the prevailing corporate and political orderings.

Several historical circumstances that contributed to the AFL's success are not discussed in the textbooks. While reliance on the skilled and therefore better paid and more continuously employed worker certainly provided stability, the AFL was also not decimated by political trials, as was, for example, the major socialist union of the time, the Industrial Workers of the World (IWW).[42] AFL leaders were not harassed or hanged between 1865 and 1917, as were a number of radical union members and leaders.[43] It can be argued, then, that the strength and legitimacy of the AFL was a result at least in part of its relative immunity from business violence and legal harassment. As one historian has argued, 'Much of the business support that was given Gompers and the AFL was the result of a widespread agreement in business circles to uphold conservative unionism as against the socialists, and, after 1905, as against the IWW. Gompers played on this constantly'.[44] There is also evidence that, within the AFL, Gompers's view of the role and function of unions was often challenged by union members, many of whom argued that the union should 'declare in favor of socialism'.[45]

The IWW, whose leaders favored strikes and were opposed to contracts with employers and to the business values and power structure of capitalism, is ignored by all but five of the textbooks, despite the fact that it organized such well-known and successful strikes as Lawrence, Massachusetts, Western Mining, and Northwest lumber camp strikes, and the well-known but unsuccessful Paterson, N.J., strike.[46] One of the books misnames the IWW the International Workers of the World;[47] one says it and other radical groups took advantage of workers.[48] While all books outline portions of the AFL platform – only two of the four books do the same for the IWW.[49] One describes the IWW in some detail and seems respectful of it but, in contrast to some reports of the period, blames the IWW for the violence that occurred.[50]

No textbook indicates that the leaders of the IWW or other radical unions were supported by any other groups in American society. *The Rise of the American Nation* states that of all the radicals, Emma Goldman was 'the most feared and hated'[51] implying that she and other radicals were feared and hated by all Americans. In fact, Emma Goldman was well liked by some groups of working people, as were other radicals, two of whom, Bill Haywood and Eugene Debs, were often idolized as folk heroes.[52] The claim that radical organizations were feared and hated in the United States may, of course, be used to rationalize government and business attempts to limit the activities of these groups.

The books in this study praise co-operation between labor unions and business owners; they do not, however, seem to value co-operation between the various groups within the labor movement. The antagonisms between skilled and unskilled, between various immigrant groups, and between black and white are presented by thirteen of the books as natural and inevitable, a result of their belonging to separate interest groups with different problems. Textbooks suggest that skilled and unskilled workers had nothing in common and that unskilled workers and immigrants were a threat to the labor movement:

> Laborers in different crafts and industries had little interest in working for common goals. Unskilled laborers were too often undisciplined and too willing to use violence.[53]
>
> Skilled workers especially disliked the [Knights of Labor's] policy of taking in unskilled workers, with whom they felt they had little or nothing in common. ... Many immigrants had left Europe partly to be as free as possible from all sorts of restrictions. Thus they did not like labor unions, with their dues, their rules, and their insistence that no one work for less than a certain wage.[54]

While divisions in the workforce did result from competition for jobs, cultural and language differences, and other factors, business owners no doubt benefited from these divisions and often promoted them.[55] Historians point out that it was not uncommon for owners to import immigrants or Southern Blacks to take the jobs of striking workers.[56] Owners also hired workers who could not communicate because of language differences in order to impede the unionization of a shop. Ethnic segregation was the rule in factories after 1880, where the various immigrant groups were placed in different areas of a shop to ensure no more than minimal contact.[57] Thirteen of the textbooks either do not mention this, or do not relate it to divisions in the work force.[58] There is relatively little textbook discussion of the substantial contributions of immigrants to the labor movement during this period. No textbooks, for example, discuss any of the strikes well known for the involvement of immigrants of many nationalities, including those in Lawrence in 1912, Paterson in 1913, and the New York City garment-worker strikes between 1865 and 1917.

Not only are workers portrayed as naturally divided, but their numbers are underestimated: the emphasis on the AFL and skilled workers, to the exclusion of unskilled workers, immigrants, Blacks, and women, contributes to this impression. Only one book discusses the several black unions of the time,[59] and only one describes the contribution of women as strikers, speakers, organizers, and union leaders.[60]

Industrialists and Labor Conflict

Historians are well aware that individual industrialists of the time actively attempted to prevent the formation of labor unions. As the United States Commission on Industrial Relations, in a report issued in 1916, stated: 'Freedom does not exist either politically, industrially or socially for workers trying to organize'. The Commission found that the use of thugs, spies and hired gunmen was general throughout the country in the employers' efforts to keep the open shop. ... Almost without exception the employees of large corporations are unorganized as a result of the active and aggressive 'non-union' policy of the corporation managements. ... Our Rockefellers, Morgans, Fricks, Astors, Vanderbilts [and Carnegies] can do no industrial wrong because all effective action and direct responsibility is shifted from them to executive officials.[61]

One industrialist exclaimed of his power to put down a strike with armed guards, 'I can hire one half of the working class to kill the other half'.[62]

[...]

Fourteen of the textbooks provide a very different picture of the industrialists. Here is one example: 'Carnegie, more than anyone else, made the US a great steel-producing country. ... After Carnegie sold his company, he spent all his time helping other people with his money and writing. He helped build libraries, improve schools, and keep peace between the countries of the world. He gave away a lot of money'.[63] Carnegie, of course, did give away a great deal of money, as did other industrialists, but to present this information while ignoring his vigorous and well-known antiunion activities is to omit evidence about the way Carnegie accumulated his fortune by exploiting labor.

The emphasis on 'bread and butter unionism' with its focus on wages and conditions now dominates organized labor. Unions in the United States have until recently concentrated their attention on industrial workers. Although this has brought considerable power to these unions and economic well-being to their workers, it has also resulted in the exclusion of approximately 80 per cent of the American work force from union representation. Large numbers of workers who are unskilled, who are of minority or immigrant status, or who are women, are still unrepresented by unions, though they constitute the majority of workers in low-wage sectors of the economy such as clerical, service, and sales, where the conditions of employment are often marginal.

The social philosophy regarding workers and unions transmitted by the textbooks benefits primarily those unions that have accepted the legitimacy of, and have been empowered by, the United States business establishment. Thus, the accounts not only benefit those powerful unions but also those who own and manage business, while failing to legitimize the needs, perspectives, and histories of those groups who benefit only marginally from the activities of organized labor and those groups who would alter the distribution of economic and labor power.

Curriculum and Social Interest

This analysis of the way seventeen textbooks describe a critical period in United States economic and labor history demonstrates that the story told is not neutral *vis-à-vis* the perspectives of the various groups involved. A whole range of curriculum selections favors the interests of the wealthy and powerful. Although presented as unbiased, the historical interpretations provide ideological justification for the activities and prerogatives of these groups and do not legitimize points of view and priorities of groups that compete with these established interests for social acceptance and support.

Ideological support for powerful social groups can be found in schoolbooks throughout our history. The religious catechisms in eighteenth-century readers, for example, supported the social power of the colonial church.[64] Both Southern and Northern textbooks of the nineteenth century contained degrading descriptions of the Negro race that could be used to justify the power of whites over Blacks. Ruth Elson reports, for example, that her analysis of one thousand nineteenth-century schoolbooks revealed that the following descriptions of Blacks are typical: 'They [Negroes] are a brutish people, having little more of humanity but the form. ... Their mental powers, in general, participate in the imbecility of their bodies. ... Africa has justly been called the country of monsters. ... Even man in this quarter of the world exists in a state of lowest barbarism'.[65] American textbooks of that period also provided support for the rising industrial classes. Elson argues that, in histories and readers of the late nineteenth century, businessmen are 'heroes of the American tradition'.[66] She presents the following schoolbook quotation as typical: 'The man who has the original ability to bring a thousand workers together, and keep them steadily employed, cheaply and skillfully to produce the materials for their labor is entitled to a large reward for this difficult service'.[67] Here one sees a rationale for the social privileges of business owners. One also sees in these textbooks a potential source of unsympathetic attitudes toward labor unions. Elson states that in nineteenth-century textbooks, labor organizers were depicted as 'destroyers of American institutions and traditions'.[68] In all but one of the books she analyzed, labor organizations are

> equated with violence. ... Very often the words 'strike' and 'riot' are used interchangeably. ... Property destruction is always carefully detailed while grievances of the workmen are not. ... Among the strikers are 'the idle and vicious', and the 'dangerous classes'. ... Violence is the only context in which the organization of labor appears.[69]

Thus, even in earlier United States schoolbooks than our own, the activities of powerful groups were justified while those of contending groups were not.

There is ample evidence that not only textbooks, but other aspects of education as well, have served the interests of powerful groups. It was not unusual during the nineteenth and in the early twentieth century for individual corporations to provide educational activities for their employees. Westinghouse, Heinz, National Cash Register, Wanamaker's and Filene's department stores, Illinois Steel, International Harvester, Curtis Publishing Company, and the Pullman Company, among others, offered training in industrial skills and in the moral and social benefits of the new industrial order.[70] Through company-sponsored lectures, classes in family life and citizenship, and sometimes in company schools, the working classes and their children were educated to industrial, social, and civic responsibility.[71]

Business groups such as the National Civic Federation, the National Association of Corporation Schools, and the National Association of Manufacturers argued that the public schools should take responsibility for this kind of education. Business groups and many individual businessmen argued for a public school curriculum broad enough to ensure both vocational efficiency and social responsibility.[72] Samuel Gompers, as a member of the prestigious National Civic Federation, joined this call for public education of workers, arguing that in public institutions workers would not be exposed to the antilabor sentiments expressed in the corporation schools.[73]

Between the Civil War and World War I national business groups successfully promoted specific changes in the public school curriculum that supported their needs. Public schools began to take on the responsibility and the expense for industrial training. Vocational education in the public school curriculum was a service to the corporations, insofar as it provided them with competently trained workers.[74]

[...]

The analysis of history textbooks here suggests that the priorities of specific groups now powerful in the United States industrial hierarchy are expressed as well by a hidden structure of interests in the social studies curriculum. Although obscured by the claims of objectivity, a set of ideological judgments and beliefs can be identified that provide support for the activities of powerful groups.

Conclusion

If school knowledge is examined as a social product, it suggests a great deal about the society that produces and uses it. It reveals which groups have power and demonstrates that the views of these groups are expressed and legitimized in the school curriculum. It can also identify social groups that are not empowered by the economic and social patterns in our society and do not have their views, activities, and priorities represented in the school curriculum. The present analysis suggests that the United States working class is one such group;[75] the poor may be another. Omissions, stereotypes, and distortions that remain in 'updated' social studies textbook accounts of Native Americans, Blacks, and women reflect the relative powerlessness of these groups.[76]

Despite periodic changes in curriculum content, an underlying concern for the perspectives of dominant groups has remained. Recent references in textbooks to successful minority group members, deletions of Cold War aggressiveness, and revisions of Native American history are examples of changes that have not altered the basic ideology. Even in the most 'radical' curriculum ever to penetrate the schools in the United States, that of Professor Harold Rugg in the 1930s, ideological support was offered for the fundamental arrangements of political and economic power.[77] By identifying the ideology of power in curriculum content, then, we make apparent an underlying perspective that has provided continuity over generations of students.

The school curriculum has contributed to the formation of attitudes that make it easier for powerful groups, those whose knowledge is legitimized by school studies, to manage and control society. Textbooks not only express the dominant groups' ideologies, but also help to form attitudes in support of their social position. Indeed the importance of ideology to the power of dominant groups increases as the use of overt social coercion declines. In the twentieth century, the authority of tradition and the legitimacy of visible methods of control, such as force, have diminished. Government and other powerful groups increasingly justify their activities by appeals to 'reason', to the logic of evidence, and to the consent of populations,[78] the public is ostensibly called upon to make intelligent social choices.

Inasmuch as social choices are likely to be made on the basis of the social knowledge and symbolic meanings that are available, what one knows about social groups and processes is central to one's decisions. The perceived legitimacy of certain ideas increases their acceptance and utilization. Social agencies, such as the schools, the media, and government, whose functions include the dissemination of information, are major sources of knowledge that is both available and socially approved. If the views embedded in the information disseminated by these agencies predispose people to accept some values and not others, support some groups' activities and not others, and exclude some choices as unacceptable, then they provide invisible intellectual, internalized, and perhaps unconscious boundaries to social choice. These boundaries are a basis for social management and control.[79]

Textbook history illustrates one way of imposing beliefs and constraining choice. Textbooks offer concrete examples and thus substantive instruction in past 'success' and 'failure' in social, economic, and political matters. Governmental reform and labor-management co-operation are characterized as successful methods of social recourse, whereas confrontation and strikes are depicted as failures. Evidence of what constitutes success or failure, whether or not it coincides with actual fact, provides a compelling guide for making choices today.[80]

Alvin Gouldner has recently argued that ideological accounts of how society works, of what succeeds and what fails, have associated with them specific actions that should be taken.[81] These 'command implications', if internalized, direct social action. The command implications of the business and labor history in the textbooks analyzed in this study, for example, are actions that support or restrain – but do not seek to redistribute – social and economic power. The command implications of the textbook version of the methods appropriate for solving economic and labor problems and the view of consensual and orderly social change inherent in them are actions that maintain the balance of power in society; confrontation between contending groups which could increase the likelihood of changes in the power structure are not implied.[82]

The textbook reports of work, wealth, and the problems of industrial workers imply that we should regard the poor as responsible for their own poverty: poverty is a consequence of the failure of individuals, rather than of the failure of society to distribute economic resources universally. This ideology encourages education and other actions that attempt to change the individual, while leaving the unequal economic structures intact.

Finally, textbooks promote the idea that there is no working class in the United

States, and contribute to the myth that workers are middle class. The schoolbooks provide no label with which to unify as one group with a set of distinct concerns all those wage and salaried persons who are industrial laborers, craftspersons, clerical workers, or service, sales, and technical workers.[83] Without such a label, workers are not easily called to mind as a group, and the objective fact of the working class has no subjective reality. In this way the textbooks predispose workers and others against actions on behalf of the interests working people have in common. Predictably, then, we will not find school textbooks that are written from the point of view of the working class. Textbook economics that discusses or promotes management techniques or ways of increasing profit and worker efficiency is socially legitimate; textbook economics that identifies or promotes working-class resistance to these activities is likely to be regarded as politicized or ideological.

Social meanings in school history can contribute to management and control by the imposition of ideological boundaries, by predisposing some choices and not others, by legitimating some ideas, activities, and groups, and not others. The conceptual legitimacy conferred by school knowledge on powerful social groups is metabolized into power that is real when members of society in their everyday decisions support – or fail to challenge – prevailing hierarchies. The idea that certain groups have legitimate social power leads to the expectation that these groups deserve our support and contending ones do not.

The textbooks' failure to promote a working-class identity may be advantageous to powerful business groups. A recent article in *Fortune*, a journal of corporate executive opinion, reminds its readers that capitalist groups in this country enjoy a legitimacy and political stability that their counterparts in Europe, threatened by 'class-conscious labor unions' and Eurocommunism, do not. This article suggests why capitalism is less secure in Europe than it is in America: 'Capitalism has never had the secure hold in European culture and in the popular imagination that it has had in the US. This may be partly true because the US has never had a proletariat . . . that so regarded itself, while the European working class has never fully shared the American belief that the little man can make it big'.[84] This article attributes the political stability of capitalism in part to a lack of working-class consciousness. Indeed, the working class in the United States is unique among all of the industrialized capitalist nations of the world in that it did not produce a labor movement that successfully promoted class consciousness. A history curriculum that inhibits the formation of a 'proletariat that so regards itself' increases the power of business owners.

[. . .]

This article has utilized a mode of inquiry that is suggested by the interest theory of ideology and has attempted to assess the social meaning of commonalities in United States history textbook content. This approach highlights the ideological characteristics of what schools teach, suggests that social groups with power have had their perspectives legitimized and indicates that school curricula can lay a subjective basis for social control. It does not, however, imply resignation in the face of persistent and unpalatable curriculum distortions. Perhaps the most important conclusion to be drawn from the point of view expressed here is that the school curriculum as a major contributor to social attitudes can be used to change those attitudes. To argue that ideologies influence behavior is to accord real power to symbols and symbolic forms in education. Just as the public school curriculum has hitherto supported patterns of power and domination, so can it be used to foster autonomy and social change.

Social change is intimately connected with changes in available cultural symbols and meanings. Although it is probably true that ideological shifts in curriculum are ultimately a reflection of shifts in social power, it is also true that the availability of ideological alternatives increases the likelihood of power shifts and changes.
[...]

Notes and References

The US history textbooks used in this study are those that appeared on the most recent board of education lists of 'Books Approved for Use' as of July, 1878, in New York City (1975 with a supplement in 1976) and Newark, New Jersey (1977). The author analyzed the latest editions of these books that were available as of 1 January, 1979.

1 *New York Times*, (1977) 23 October, pp. 3–4. See also *New York Times*, (1978) 1 August, p. 1, and SCHILLER, H. (1973) *The Mind Managers*, Boston, Beacon Press.
2 See the following: *New York Times*, (1976) 24 October, pp. 3–5; (1977) 23 October; SCHILLER, H. (1973) *op. cit.*, pp. 68–9; and *New York Times*, (1976) 1 August, p. F5.
3 *New York Times*, (1977) 23 October, pp. 3–1.
4 In 1967, only 22.7 per cent of the total labor force was unionized; in 1974, only 21.7 per cent. *Handbook of Labor Statistics*, (1966–77) Washington DC, US Government Printing Office.
5 By 1904, the top 4 per cent of American concerns produced 57 per cent of the total industrial output by value. See WEINSTEIN, J. (1968) *The Corporate Ideal in the Liberal State: 1900–1918*, Boston, Beacon Press, p. 63. By 1929, 100 large companies had legal control of approximately 40 per cent of the total assets of all manufacturing corporations, and 44 per cent of their net capital assets (land, machines, etc.); the largest 200 corporations legally controlled 48 per cent of the assets and 58 per cent of the net capital assets reported by all corporations other than banks; see Gardner Means (1964) *Economic Concentration*, from Hearings before the Subcommittee on Antitrust and Monopoly of the Committee on the Judiciary, 88th Cong., Senate, 2nd Sess., pursuant to Senate Resolution 262, Part 1: Overall and Conglomerate Aspects, Washington DC, US Government Printing Office. In EDWARDS, R.C., REICH, M. and WEISSKOPF, T.E. (Eds.) (1972) *The Capitalistic System*, Englewood Cliffs, NJ, Prentice Hall, pp. 147, 150. In recent years several new waves of industrial merger and acquisition have taken place; see 'The Great Takeover Binge: It Could Rival the Craze of the 1960s, but Now the Giants are Dealing in Cash', *Business Week*, (1977) 14 November, pp. 176–84.
   In agriculture, similar concentration exists: less than 0.2 per cent of all food manufacturers in the United States control approximately 50 per cent of the assets of the food industry. ([June 1966] *The Structure of Food Manufacturing*, a report by the staff of the Federal Trade Commission [Technical Study, No. 8], National Commission on Food Marketing, p. 19); PARKER, R.C. (21 May 1974) testimony before US Congress, Senate, Consumer Economics Subcommittee of the Joint Economic Committee, p. 4. Cited by LAPPE, F.M. and COLLINS, J. (1977) *World Hunger: Ten Myths*, San Francisco, California, Institute for Food and Development Policy, p. 26.
6 See BRAGDON H., McCUTCHEN, S. and COLE, C. (1973) *History of a Free People*, New York, Macmillan, in which 47 of 60 pages are devoted to aspects of industrialization considered salutary; or WEISBERGER, B. (1972) The *Impact of our Past*, Boston, Houghton Miflin, in which 38 of 51 pages are so used; or WOOD, L., GABRIEL, R. and BILLER, E. (1975) *America: Its Peoples and Values*, New York, Harcourt, Brace, Jovanovitch, in which 51 of 63 pages are so used.
7 See REICH, J., STRICKLAND, A. and BILLER, E. (1971) *Building the United States*, New York, Harcourt, p. 436; GRAFF, H. (1977) *The Free and the Brave*, Chicago, Rand McNally, p. 556; also WEISBERGER, B. (1976) *op. cit.*, p. 488.
8 BRANSON, M. (1977) *American History for Today*, Lexington, Mass., Ginn, pp. 295, 360.

9 See WOOD, L., GABRIEL, R. and BILLER, E. (1975) *op. cit.*, p. 847; also WADE, R., WILDER, H. and WADE, L. (1972) *A History of the United States*, Boston, Houghton Miflin. This book states that 'effective antitrust laws were adopted' [p. 568].

10 See GRAFF, H. (1977) *op. cit.*, pp. 556–77; also WEISBERGER, B. (1976) *op. cit.*, pp. 488–93; and REICH, J., STRICKLAND, A. and BILLER, E. (1971) *op. cit.*, pp. 436–40.

11 See OKUN, M. and BRONZ, S. (1973) *Challenge of America*, New York, Holt, Rinehart and Winston, pp. 549–52, 556–68. Also TODD, L. and CURTI, M. (1973) *Rise of the American Nation*, New York, Holt, Rinehart and Winston, pp. 469–74 and 478–85; also SCHWARTZ, S. and O'CONNOR, J. (1975) *Exploring our Nation's History*, New York, Globe, pp. 413–26.

12 See OKUN, M. and BRONZ, S. (1973) *op. cit.*, pp. 557–8; also TODD, L. and CURTI, M. (1973) *op. cit.*, pp. 472 and 483; also SCHWARTZ, S. and O'CONNOR, J. (1975) *op. cit.*, p. 420.

13 See the chapter entitled 'A New Day of Reform', in GRAFF, H. (1977) *op. cit.*, pp. 556–77; or Unit Eight, 'The Arrival of Reform' and Chaps. 5 and 6, in TODD, L. and CURTI, M. (1973) *op. cit.*, pp. 464–86. Only one textbook (MADGIC, R., SEABERG, S., STOPSKY, F. and WINKS, R. [1975] *The American Experience*, Reading, Mass., Addison-Wesley) does *not* characterize the laws as examples of progress or reform. Rather, this textbook calls the federal legislation a 'conservative bulwark against more radical state laws' (p. 286).

14 There are several varieties of this argument. See WILLIAMS, W.A. (1961) *Contours of American History*, Cleveland, World Publishing; KOLKO, G. (1963) *Triumph of Conservatism*, New York, Free Press of Glencoe; WEINSTEIN, J. (1968) *op. cit.*; and SPRING, J. (1972) *Education and the Rise of the Corporate State*, Boston, Beacon.

15 See WEINSTEIN, J. (1968) *op. cit.*, Introd., p. ix, and Chaps. 1, 2, 3 and 6.

16 See OKUN, M. and BRONZ, S. (1973) *op. cit.*, p. 463 (two paragraphs), and p. 473 (one paragraph); WEISBERGER, B. *op. cit.*, p. 495 (two paragraphs) and p. 494 (one paragraph); BRAGDON, H., McCUTCHEN, S. and COLE, C. (1973) *op. cit.*, p. 537 (one paragraph).

17 MADGIC, R., SEABERG, S., STOPSKY, F. and WINKS, R. (1975) *op. cit.*, p. 275. All of the textbooks surveyed included at least one of the explanations offered in the passage cited. A typical comment on the role of immigrant workers is in TODD, L. and CURTI, M. (1973) *op. cit.*, 'The immigrants had an enormous influence on American life. Although some settled on farms, the great majority moved to the densely crowded slum areas of the cities. Here they competed with the native-born Americans for housing, thereby driving up housing costs. Most immediate of all, however, was their effect upon established workers. Immigrants competed with established American wage earners for jobs, thereby lowering wages' (p. 442). See also OKUN, M. and BRONZ, S. (1973) *op. cit.*, p. 462; and LEINWAND, G. (1975) *The Pageant of American History*, Boston, Allyn and Bacon, p. 323.

18 See KORMAN, G. (1967) *Industrialization, Immigrants and Americanizers: a view from Milwaukee*, Madison, Wis., State Historical Society of Wisconson. Also LURIA, D.B. (1974) 'Trends in the Determinants Underlying the Process of Social Stratification: Boston, 1880–1920' *Review of Radical Political Economics*, 6, No. 2, pp. 98–109; and BRODY, D. (1960) *Steelworkers in America*, New York, Harper and Row, esp. Chap. 5.

19 OKUN, M. and BRONZ, S. (1973) *op. cit.*, p. 463; WEISBERGER, B. (1976) *op. cit.*, p. 495; GRAFF, H. (1977) *op. cit.*, p. 518; and LEINWAND, G. (1975) *op. cit.*, p. 325.

20 LEINWAND, G., (1975) *op. cit.*, and OKUN, M. and BRONZ, S., (1973) *op. cit.*

21 WEISBERGER, B. (1976) *op. cit.*, p. 495; see also GRAFF, H. (1977) *op. cit.*

22 In contrast to this argument are less flattering view of the intentions of business owners. See MARGLIN, S.A. (1974) 'What Do Bosses Do? The Origins and Functions of Hierarchy in Capitalist Production', *The Review of Radical Political Economics*, 6, No. 2, pp. 38–60. See also PAGE, J. and O'BRIEN, M. (1973) *Bitter Wages*, New York, Grossman.

23 SPRING, J. (1972) *op. cit.*, p. 24. See also TOLMAN, W.H. (1909) *Social Engineering*, New York, McGraw, p. 24; COOK, E.W. (1906) *Betterment: Individual, Social and Industrial*, New York, F.A. Stokes; FILENE, E.A. (1907) 'The Social Improvement of Grammar School Graduates in Business Life', *Social Education Quarterly*, 1, pp. 146–55.

24 THE NEWT DAVIDSON COLLECTIVE (1974) *Crisis at CUNY*, New York, author, p. 34.

25 BRAVERMAN, H. (1974) *Labor and Monopoly Capital: The Degradation of Work in the Twentieth Century*, New York, Monthly Review Press. See also MARGLIN, S.A. (1974) *op. cit.* and STONE, K. (1974) 'The Origins of Job Structures in the Steel Industry', *The Review of Radical Political Economics*, 6, No. 2, pp. 61–97.

26 Estimates by labor historians place the figure higher than 30,000. RICHTER, I. (1976) Fellow, Woodrow Wilson Center for Scholars, Personal Communication.

27 All books except WOOD, L., GABRIEL, R. and BILLER, E. (1975) *op. cit.*, TODD, L. and CURTI, M. (1973) *op. cit.*; and REICH, J., STRICKLAND, A. and BILLER, E. (1971) *op. cit.*, discuss one or more of these three strikes. Two books mention – in passing – the Lawrence, Massachusetts, strike of 1912,

and what is known as the Coeur d'Alene 'Massacre'. The Railroad Strike of 1885 was successful from a labor point of view, and while no book discusses it in any detail, five books mention it as having taken place. For representative reports of strikes, see LEINWAND, G. (1975) *op. cit.*, pp. 324–5; WILDER, H., LADLUM, R. and BROWN, H. (1975) *This is America's Story*, Boston, Houghton Miflin, pp. 486–91; and BRAGDON, H., MCCUTCHEN, S. and COLE, C. (1973) *op. cit.*, pp. 435–8.

28 See, among others, BOYER, R. and MORAIS, H. (1970) *Labor's Untold Story*, 3rd Edition, New York, United Electrical Radio and Machine Workers of America.

29 See SCHAFER, B., AUGSPERGER, E. and MCLEMORE, R. (1973) *United States History for High School*, River Forest, Illinois, Laidlaw, p. 405; BRANSON, M. (1977) *op. cit.*, p. 347; BRAGDON, H., MCCUTCHEN, S. and COLE, C. *op. cit.*, p. 435.

30 See LEINWAND, G. (1975) *op. cit.*, pp. 341–2; OKUN, M. and BRONZ, S., *op. cit.*, p. 554; and REICH, J., STRICKLAND, A. and BILLER, E. (1971) pp. 438–9.

31 REICH, J., STRICKLAND, A. and BILLER, E. (1971) *op. cit.*, p. 438.

32 WADE, R., WILDER, H. and WADE, L. (1972) *op. cit.*, p. 555. See also TODD, L. and CURTI, M. (1973) *op. cit.*, p. 493; and SCHAFER, B., AUGSPERGER, E. and MCLEMORE, R. (1973) *op. cit.*, pp. 445–6.

33 See MELTZER, M. (1967) *Bread and Roses: The Struggles of American Labor, 1865–1915*, New York, Alfred A. Knopf; see also BOYER, R. and MORAIS, H. (1970) *op. cit.*

34 See GRAFF, H. (1977) *op. cit.*, p. 575; WILDER, H., LUDLUM, R. and BROWN, H. (1975) *op. cit.*, pp. 492–3; SCHAFER, B., AUGSPERGER, E. and MCLEMORE, R. (1973) *op. cit.*, pp. 445–6; and the section entitled, 'Improving Conditions for American Industrial Workers', in TODD, L. and CURTI, M. (1973) *op. cit.*, pp. 493–4.

35 Other studies of social science materials have reported that the subject of social conflict is either absent from educational curriculum materials or, if present, is discussed within the framework of a search for resolution and social consensus. See TURNER, M. (1971) *Materials for Civics, Government and Problems and Democracy*, Boulder, Colorado, Social Science and Educational Consortium; APPLE, M. (1971) 'The Hidden Curriculum and the Nature of Conflict', *Interchange*, 2, No. 4, pp. 27–40; FOX, T. and HESS, R.D. (1972) 'An Analysis of Social Conflict in Social Studies Textbooks', Final Report, Project No. 1-1-116, Washington DC, US Department of Health, Education and Welfare. See also ANYON, J. (1978) 'Elementary Social Studies Textbooks and Legitimating Knowledge', *Theory and Research in Social Education*, 6, No. 3, pp. 40–5.

36 GOMPERS, S. (1948) *Seventy Years of Life and Labor*, 11, New York, E.P. Dutton, p. 110. Indeed Gompers held, as did many businessmen, that 'trusts should not be suppressed, but regulated and helped to develop constructive control . . . ', pp. 20–2.

37 The following are representative of the contrast in description of the AFL and radical labor unions. WEISBERGER, B. (1976) *op. cit.*, cites the Knights of Labor's goal of 'co-operating in ownership and sharing the profits' as 'ignoring economic realities', p. 496; this is contrasted with 'the AFL's careful planning', p. 497. OKUN, M. and BRONZ, S. (1973) *op. cit.*, characterizes a radical union (The American Railway Union of Eugene Debs) as having 'leaders who were weak', p. 463, and states that Gompers was a 'shrewd and able man', p. 465. The authors describe the 'bloody and unsuccessful' Homestead and Pullman strikes, and say that 'In both cases the AFL was careful not to get deeply involved', p. 469. WADE, R., WILDER, H. and WADE, L. (1972) *op. cit.*, state that the AFL 'set realistic goals for itself', p. 478, while a 'belligerent union called the IWW called for the overthrow of the government . . . ', p. 551. This text also remarks, 'Nor would Gompers have anything to do with radicals, anarchists or anyone advocating changes in the capitalist system', p. 478. This textbook did not mention – nor did any other – that during the early part of Gompers' career he was a socialist. *History of a Free People* argues that Gompers is a responsible labor leader, p. 435, as opposed to a 'lunatic fringe' of anarchists [who] preached that violence was necessary to destroy capitalism', p. 435.

38 TODD, L. and CURTI, M. (1973) *op. cit.*, p. 448; DAVIS, B., ARANOFF, D. and DAVIS, C. (1969) *Background for Tomorrow: An American History*, New York, Macmillan, p. 574.

39 The following excerpts are representative: ' . . . through its policy of organizing only skilled workers and through Gompers' leadership, the AFL steadily gained members' see OKUN and BRONZ, (1973) *op. cit.* p. 649; 'The idea of bringing all workers together in one big union [such as the Knights of Labor] did not work well. The workmen did not have enough interests in common' see WOOD, L., GABRIEL, R. and BILLER, E. (1975), *op. cit.*, p. 460. In contrast, the AFL's success is attributed to its being ' . . . a craft union, in which the members have interests in common', p. 649.

40 See BOYER, R. and MORAIS, H. (1970) *op. cit.*, pp. 181–2, 204. See also BRODY, D. (1960) *op. cit.*, esp. Chap. 5.

41 See the quotes in Note 39 as examples. The descriptive term 'intolerant' is used in *History of a Free People* to describe a leader of the IWW, p. 536.

42 See BOYER, R. and MORAIS, H. (1970) *op. cit.*, p. 198

43 See KORNBLUH, J. (1972) *Rebel voices: an IWW Anthology*, Ann Arbor, Michigan, University of Michigan Press, p. 162; BOYER, R. and MORAIS, H. (1970) *op. cit.*; FONER, P. (1965) *The Industrial Workers of the World*, New York, International Publishers; and DUBOFSKY, M. (1969) *We Shall Be All*, New York, Quadrangle, *New York Times* publication. See also the following autobiographies and biographies: HAYWOOD, W.D. (1969) *The Autobiography of Big Bill Haywood*, New York, International Publishers; GINGER, R. (1970) *Eugene V. Debs: The Making of an American Radical*, New York, Macmillan; GOLD-MAN, E. (1970) *Living My Life*, New York, Dover Publications; and FLYNN, E.G. (1974) *The Rebel Girl: An Autobiography*, New York, New World Paperbacks.

44 WEINSTEIN, J. (1968) *op. cit.*, p. 21.

45 *Ibid.*

46 MADGIC *et al.*, (1975) *op. cit.*, pp. 280–2; WEISBERGER, B. (1976) *op. cit.*, p. 501; OKUN and BRONZ (1973) *op. cit.*, p. 563; DAVIS *et al.*, (1969) *op. cit.*, p. 418; WADE *et al.*, (1972) *op. cit.*, p. 551.

47 OKUN and BRONZ (1973) *op. cit.*, p. 563.

48 WADE *et al.*, (1972) *op. cit.*, p. 551.

49 MADGIC *et al.*, (1975) *op. cit.*, pp. 280–1; WEISBERGER *op. cit.*, p. 501.

50 MADGIC *et al.*, (1975) *op. cit.*, p. 281.

51 TODD and CURTI, (1973) *op. cit.*, p. 449. This statement is representative of a textbook pattern in which it is sometimes stated that 'Americans' or 'the Public' as a unified group, hold various beliefs. For example, BRANSON (1977) *op. cit.*, p. 348.

52 CONLIN, J. (1968) *Big Bill Haywood and the Radical Union Movement* Syracuse, NY, Syracuse University Press, p. viii.

53 BRAGDON *et al.*, (1973) *op. cit.*, p. 437.

54 TODD and CURTI (1973) *op. cit.*, pp. 445–6. See also, OKUN and BRONZ, (1973) *op. cit.*, p. 469; GRAFF, (1977) *op. cit.*, pp. 505 and 509.

55 MELTZER, (1967) *op. cit.*, pp. 95–7; see also KOLKO, G. (1976) *Main Currents in Modern American History*, New York, Harper and Row, pp. 92–3. Also BRODY, (1960) *op. cit.*; BOYER and MORAIS (1970) *op. cit.*

56 See LURIA, (1974) *op. cit.*; BRODY, (1960) *op. cit.*, for the use of immigrants. For the use of Blacks, see FONER, P. (1974) *Organized Labor and the Black Worker, 1619–1973*, New York, International Publishers.

57 MELTZER, (1967) *op. cit.*, pp. 95–7; see also BRODY (1960) *op. cit.*, esp. Chap. 5, and KOLKO (1976) *op. cit.*, p. 75.

58 While seven books mention the use by industry of strike breakers, lockouts etc., and cite them as examples of owners' power, no book considers the divisive effects of these activities on the labor force. See WEISBERGER, (1976) *op. cit.*, p. 497; LEINWAND (1975) *op. cit.*, pp. 325, 326; CURRENT, R., DE CONDE, A. and DANTE, H. (1974) *US History: A Developing Nation; US History: A World Power*, 2 volumes, Glenview, Illinois, Scott Foreman, p. 319. One book does argue, however, that the exclusion of the Blacks from the labor movement weakened it. See TODD and CURTI (1973) *op. cit.*, pp. 447–8.

59 See TODD and CURTI, (1973) *op. cit.*, pp. 447–8.

60 ABRAMOWITZ J. (1979) *American History*, Chicago, Follett, p. 436. There are also two sentences in TODD and CURTI (1973) *op. cit.*, about an upper-class women's group (p. 447); the following sentence appears in GRAFF (1977) *op. cit.*, 'Many women were among the strikers', pp. 506–7.

61 Final Report of the Commission on Industrial Relations (Washington, D.C. 1915), in BOYER and MORAIS, *op. cit.*, pp. 184, 186.

62 BOYER and MORAIS (1970) *op. cit.*, p. 72.

63 GRAFF (1977) *op. cit.*, p. 476. See also WILDER *et al.*, pp. 474, 560; WEISBERGER (1976) *op. cit.*, p. 439 and WADE *et al.*, (1972) *op. cit.*, pp. 315. 370.

64 For examples of these textbooks see SMITH, N.B. (1965) *American Reading Instruction*, Newark, Delaware, the International Reading Association.

65 ELSON, R. (1964) *Guardians of Tradition: American Schoolbooks of the Nineteenth Century*, Lincoln, University of Nebraska Press, p. 87.

66 *Ibid.*, p. 256.

67 *Ibid.*

68 *Ibid.*

69 *Ibid.*, pp. 249, 250.

70 SPRING, J. (1972) *op. cit.*, pp. 22–43. See also WEINSTEIN, J. (1968) *op. cit.*, pp. 19–20.

71 SPRING (1972) *op. cit.*, p. 22; pp. 23–43.

72 SPRING (1972) *op. cit.*, p. 43. See also CALLAHAN, R. (1962) *Education and the Cult of Efficiency*, Chicago, University of Chicago Press, Chap. 1. Also, FISHER, B. (1967) *Industrial Education*, Madison, Wisconsin, University of Wiscosin Press, pp. 113–4, cited by SPRING, (1972) *op. cit.*, p. 43. See also GORELICK, S. (1975) *Social Control, Social Mobility, and the Eastern European Jews: An Analysis of Public Education in New York City, 1880–1924*. Dissertation, Columbia University.

73 SPRING (1972) *op. cit.*, p. 42.
74 For a discussion of early vocational education, see SPRING, (1972) *op. cit.*, pp. 91–108; also, CALLAHAN R. (1962) *op. cit.* In an unusual attack by a member of the educational community on the agitation for vocational education, the superintendent of schools in New York City wrote in 1914 that ' ... the educational world is now seething [with agitation] for the introduction of industrial or trade teaching in the public schools. That agitation, as everyone knows, originated with the manufacturers ... demanding that the state, after taxing consumers for fifty years, through a protective tariff, in order to fill the pockets of manufacturers, should then proceed to pay the bills for training their workmen', MAXWELL, W. (1914) 'On a certain arrogance in Educational Theorists', *Educational Review*, 47, pp. 195–276. Cited by CALLAHAN (1962) *op. cit.*, pp. 13–4.
75 A recent study of basal readers suggests a bias against working-class jobs in these textbooks as well. See LUKER, W., JENKINS, F. and ABERNATHY, L. (1974) 'Elementary School Basal Readers and Work Mode Bias', *Journal of Economic Education*, 4, Spring, pp. 92–6.
76 See COUNCIL ON INTERRACIAL BOOKS FOR CHILDREN, (1977) *Stereotypes, Distortions and Omissions in US History Textbooks*, New York, Racism and Sexism Resource Center for Educators. Also, BALTIMORE FEMINIST PROJECT (1976) *Sexism and Racism in Popular Basal Readers: 1964–1976*, New York, Racism and Sexism Resource Center for Educators.
77 See CARBONE, P.F. Jr., (1977) *The Social and Educational Thought of Harold Rugg*, Durham, North Carolina, Duke University Press; and FITZGERALD, F. (1979) 'History Textbooks (Parts I–III)', *The New Yorker*, 26 February 1979, 5 March 1979, and 12 March 1979.
78 See GOULDNER, A. (1970) *The Coming Crisis of Western Sociology*, New York, Basic Books for this argument. See also BERNSTEIN, B. (1971) *Class, Codes and Control*, London, Routledge and Kegan Paul, for discussion of visible and invisible controls, and social agencies through which invisible control can be exercised.
79 See DAWE, A. (1970) 'The Two Sociologies', *British Journal of Sociology*, 21, No. 2, pp. 207–18; and YOUNG, M.F.D. (Ed.) (1971) *Knowledge and Control*, London, Collier-Macmillan, for insightful discussions of control as the imposition of meaning.
80 BLUM, A. (1971) 'The Corpus of Knowledge as a Normative Order', in YOUNG, M.F.D. (Ed.) *Knowledge and Control*, London, Collier-Macmillan, pp. 117–32.
81 GOULDNER, A. (1976) *The Dialectic of Ideology and Technology*, New York, Seabury Press, p. 206.
82 In an analysis of elementary school social studies textbooks, Fox and HESS in 'An Analysis of Social Conflict in Social Studies Textbooks', found that 'it would seem from the social studies textbooks we analyzed that American youth are expected to believe that virtually every existing social problem is resolvable with established knowledge and practices' p. 83.
83 Wage and salaried workers in the groups cited comprised, in 1970, 69 per cent of the non-agricultural labor force, or 55.3 million persons. See BRAVERMAN, H. (1974) *Labor and Monopoly Capital: The Degradation of Work in the Twentieth Century*, New York, Monthly Review Press, p. 379.
84 BALL R. (1978) 'The Surprising New Optimism of Europe's COE's (Chief Executive Officers)', *Fortune*, 14 August, p. 112.

3 Capital and Culture: The Post War Working Class Revisited

John Clarke

[...]

We may begin by detailing some trends in capitalist development in Britain since the war, those with most pertinence for working-class life. None of these tendencies were new in the period; they are often long-term trends in capital accumulation that have been intensified, proceeding at a greater pace or with a deeper impact on social relations. Among these trends we would want to point to the growing tendency to the concentration and centralization of capitals; the expansion of labour processes that are based on production-line technologies and forms of control; the continuing decline of 'heavy industry' and the movement of capital into modern 'lighter' forms of production, most notably the production of consumer durables; and major shifts in the composition of labour power – the secular tendency to 'de-skilling', the separation of 'conception' and 'execution' and the creation of new technical or control skills, the shift of labour out of direct production and into circulation and distribution, and the expansion of labour within the state.[1]

Concentration and centralization as well as the policies of large-scale companies often involve shifts in the geographical distribution of capital – shifts which must be understood in an international as well as a regional and national framework. Localities that suffer the sudden withdrawal of capital also suffer major disruptions in their patterns of social and cultural life.[2] Cultural forms that have developed, for instance, in a close connection with the original division of labour, may lose their very rationale. From the point of view of capital, its mobility requires the mobility of labour. It therefore also requires the continual fractioning of the local and more fixed patterns of reproduction: it specifically requires the destruction of locality as a major form through which working people experience their social life. The resistance of locally bound labour to capital's migration has, in turn, produced state policies that seek a greater conformity – here in the form of industrial grants to tempt capital to move to pools of labour, there in the form of mobility and redundancy payments to encourage labourers to pursue capital.[3]

Source: CLARKE, J., CRITCHER, C., JOHNSON, R. (Eds.) (1979) *Working Class Culture*, London, Hutchinson, Chap. 10, pp. 238–53.

The stripping of capital from an area and less dramatic forms of 'industrial reorganization' always have effects upon local forms of culture, the forms in which labour is actually reproduced. Thus Cohen shows how, in the East End, the rationalization of the docks has had profound consequences for forms of family life based upon neighbourhood patterns and upon inter-generational recruitment to the dominant male occupations.[4] Similarly, the mobility of capital, has in many instances, deepened the division between home and work-place, between the social relationships of the world of production and those of family. This division has also been increased by forms of local state planning in which the industrial and residential zones of urban areas are sharply separated.

One way of understanding these changes has been in terms of the undermining of 'working-class community'. Some reservations have to be stated against this view. We must not take 'the working-class community' as the archetypal 'traditional' moment of the English working class as a whole, as a de-historicized sociology sometimes does. The working class has not produced such cultural forms everywhere, nor has it produced them continuously in the period up to the 1950s. Gareth Stedman Jones points, for example, to the growing physical distance between the man's place of labour and the domestic sphere as one of the changes underlying the cultural adaptations of skilled workers in late-nineteenth-century London.[5] We would argue that the particular cultural form – 'working-class community' – rests especially on a close, dovetailed relationship between work and non-work and a geographical concentration of intra-class social relationships of all kinds. Hoggart's Hunslet or Hessle Road did seem to rest on the continuity of work and home. Yet if the patterns in Hunslet (or Ashton) were particular, localism in a looser sense has been a pervasive mode of working-class culture. A class culture has often been identified with specifically local experiences, relationships and practices; it has been articulated around specifically local points of reference, contact and conflict. To some extent, then, in the 1950s and 1960s, the structures of localism and even, for some sections, of 'community' have been undercut by the combined effects of changes in production and the effects of political and social policies. This has affected the primary forms of identification and antagonism – Hoggart's 'us' and 'them'. It may involve a greater sense of dislocation from 'them' in the form of local agencies of control and regulation: contacts and conflicts with police or schools or local councils may indeed be systematically deparochialized.[6]

Though, at one level, these tendencies are functional for capital accumulation, they also produce new problems in the cultural and political domains which themselves require new forms of state intervention. For example, both Cockburn and Corrigan have shown the decline of working-class involvement in local forms of political representation and a reduction in the legitimacy attributed to them.[7] Schools have complained of the decline of parental involvement in the education of children; the police have spoken of a loss of public confidence and a decline of community commitment to the control and reporting of crime. Housing authorities have complained about the reluctance of tenants to identify with their area and 'take pride' in its maintenance.[8] A common response to these forms of disengagement has been to attempt to reconstitute local identification and commitment –

hence community work, community schools, community liaison, community development and so on.

This partial and uneven reconstruction of British capital also involved other changes, especially those associated with the demand for an extended application of scientific knowledge to the labour process and more sophisticated methods of control of labour. We may doubt if the expansion of the education system since 1944 can wholly or even mainly be explained in terms of capital's requirements: the tendency to a more egalitarian provision owed as much to the need to win the consent of different classes of parents and to retain an alliance with the teachers.[9] But the reorganization of education, which included the coming of universal state secondary education and some expansion of the tertiary sector, undoubtedly had effects upon established patterns of working-class culture. For example, it restructured the age relations which shape both the internal social relationships of the family and the family economy itself. Most obviously, these changes defer, for different lengths of time, the entry of children of the family to full-time waged labour, thus necessitating new economic adjustments within the family patterns of reproduction. In addition, this reorganization of the educational apparatus produced a new range of possible 'career' patterns for working-class youth, affecting in different ways their relations to their located cultural patterns of street, neighbourhood and friendship groupings, and to the passage through the educational apparatus to waged labour. It also provided some of the symbolic indices of differentiation which mark out these different trajectories (e.g. the secondary modern boy, technical college boy or grammar school girl).

This reoganization of education also raises other central questions for our concerns here, for it is not simply a case of an administrative recording of an agency which is in some sense external to the working class. It involves the political and ideological interpellation of the class into the processes of politics and education. Crucial here are the symbolic figures of 'equality' and 'achievement' as expressions of working-class demands articulated through the complex mechanisms of social-democratic politics.[10] This political representation of a working class presence is no simple ideological mystification through which the working classes are bemused, but a representation that must be taken seriously as exerting definite force, what Poulantzas calls 'pertinent effects', on both lived experience *and* the material forms of reconstructed institutions. Even where institutions meet a logic required by capital, their form and direction are never the outcome of a simple unidirectional imposition by capital. They involve a complex political work of concession and compromise, if only to secure the legitimacy of the state in popular opinion. Thus, for example, while parts of the welfare state may be attributed to capital's need for a healthy and stable work force, these needs in no sense prescribe a solution which takes the form of a universal and free National Health Service (as we are now learning by example).

The area of youth is one in which the changed conditions of existence of the working class and the destruction of existing cultural forms have had their most visible consequences in the construction of new cultural forms and practices. As Cohen and Hall *et al.* have shown, the emergence of particular youth sub-cultures in post-war Britain is made possible by the changing material conditions of the working class (the reorganization of education, changes in the composition of labour power, and the reconstruction of local economies).[11] These processes had specific effects on the local forms of class reproduction and cultural representations – the material and cultural elements of communities. But they also had specific consequences for the structure of age relations within the working class and for the ideological representation of 'youth'. The expansion of youth employment laid the basis for the greater financial autonomy of working-class youth within the family economy, and underpinned the creation of the 'youth market'. But this greater financial autonomy (especially in the form of rising disposable incomes) also allowed the construction of new forms of youthful *cultural* autonomy – a separation from existing milieux and modes of informal regulation of adolescence.

But, as Hall *et al.* have argued, this autonomy of working-class youth cannot in any sense be taken as a severing of youth from class; rather, youth sub-cultural formations are elaborated on the terrain of class cultures but through the mechanisms of 'generational specificity'. The stylistic and symbolic repertoires of sub-cultures such as the Teds, Mods and Skinheads are cultural representations of the class's conditions of existence, and the changes taking place in them, but these representations are articulated through the position of youth within the class. For example, the style of the Mods involves the symbolic representation of affluence (and especially of affluent youth) through styles of conspicuous and highly developed consumption. From this standpoint the Mods appear to be the ideal representation of the affluence thesis, but the sub-cultural relations and practices which support this consumption also produce it in a form which is alien to that of the supposedly privatized and passive consumer of commodities. In the Mods, the commodities are transformed collectively into new uses and new cultural representations of the conditions of that particular fraction of working-class youth. These collective sub-cultural practices subvert the supposed role of the consumer, and transform the cultural meanings attached to the commodity – for example in the transformation of the motor scooter from a cheap and highly functional means of transport into an object of collective display.

The points raised here about youth have wider ramifications in relation to the affluence debate. There the dominant tendency was to assume that possession of similar objects or commodities by different groups necessarily indicated similar life-styles and outlooks. The possession of a car, fridge or television necessarily indicated a convergence of life-style with those who had previously been the privileged possessors of these commodities. As the example of the Mods shows, this conception suppresses the possibility of the same object or practice being located within different sets of relations and being endowed with different sets of cultural valuations. In this sense, the object or commodity is not unidimensional, but involves some (however limited) possibilities of being appropriated as a different sort of use value in a different class-cultural context. This is not to argue that the changes in commodities possessed by the working class (or sections of it) during the post-war period has had no consequences. These cannot, however, be reduced to an equalizing or convergence of cultural practices.

We have pointed to some of the tendencies undercutting locality, but it is equally important to note how other tendencies have registered on the family – another site of reproduction. Central among these has been a tension between capital and the state hinging around women's double position as the source of domestic labour and as a section of the reserve labour.[12] In the expansion and restructuring of post-war English capitalism, capital stood to benefit from women's roles as waged labourers in two main ways: first, in the expanding unskilled labour sector of the new light production industries, and secondly, in the rapid expansion of the service and distributive sectors. In both, of course, the key to the desirability of women's labour is its relative cheapness.[13] However, this requirement for cheap labour to intensify the profitability of such development conflicts with other demands bearing on the sexual division of labour. In part, it conflicts with wartime guarantees won by the trade unions about the priority to be given to employing men in the post-war period. More significantly, it conflicts with the state's concern to regulate and control the privatized reproduction of labor power. From the standpoint of the state, then, women's other function, as domestic labour, is of paramount importance, and a series of wartime investigations and studies raised the spectre of a maladjusted badly nourished and potentially incompetent future generation of bearers of labour power.[14] The central theme of these studies, and of subsequent state initiatives, was the centrality of the family and of the woman's position as wife and mother. From the state's standpoint, then, the employment of married women, at least, threatened to interrupt the necessary mechanism of generational reproduction, and thus required action by the state to secure those processes.[15]

Thus, for example, the establishment of the Children's Departments in local authorities at the end of the war must in part be seen as an attempt to construct a mechanism through which the state could monitor, and intervene in the 'private' processes of reproduction, and, where necessary, supplant the family (the incompetent, negligent or dangerous family, that is) with institutional alternatives.[16] In a different way, the state's control over the provision of alternative child care facilities such as nurseries provided a mechanism through which the state could intervene to change the balance between women's two functions.[17] In the post-war period the state's removal and reduction of institutional child care indicates its predominant commitment to returning women to the tasks of reproduction. This stress on reproduction in the activities of the state is also visible in Beveridge's conception of the 1946 National Insurance Act:

> The attitude of the housewife to gainful employment outside the home is not and should not be the same as that of the single woman. . . . In the next thirty years housewives as Mothers have vital work to do in ensuring the adequate continuance of the British race and British ideals in the world.[18]

These tensions act upon attempts to establish viable family economies among the working class, often dependent upon the need for two wages to maintain standards of living, in many cases producing the adaptation of part-time work by married

women.[19] In addition, in this period women were increasingly ideologically inter-
pellated into yet another role, that of the consumer of the new durables and domestic
goods by a capitalism striving to accomplish a mass domestic market for its products,
producing new images and conceptions of motherhood, housewifery and femininity.[20] We are in no position to be able to assess the consequences of these changes
in any systematic way, but in broad terms these conditions, together with the hidden
substratum of changes in contraceptive availability and practice, have substantially
unhinged the established practices and conceptions of the sexual division of labour
and its ideological, political and emotional concomitants in all classes (though
differently and unevenly, it is true).

The disruption of family and friendship patterns surrounding and supporting
domestic labour and especially child care through the processes of rehousing and
social reconstruction in the post-war period have, of course, been the focus of much
conventional sociological inquiry, but there are elements and aspects of these
processes which have been less remarked upon. For example, Cohen has pointed
out how the processes of rehousing not only involved the disruption of established
patterns of family relationships through enforced geographical mobility, but
involved their curtailment in the very material forms which such relocation took.[21]
He suggests that the patterns and models of house-building in the post-war period
were shaped by an invisible ideological norm of the nuclear family which excluded
other variants of family relationships by determining the physical and spatial
arrangement of housing. Thus, the 'ideal form' of reproduction is enshrined in
the very bricks and mortar within which reproduction takes place.

We would also want to indicate something of the way in which these reconstruc-
tions of housing in the hands of the local state have acted, together with larger
economic forces, to undercut other established practices of reproduction within
the working class. We have in mind here the activity of shopping as one vital (though
extremely hidden) element of domestic labour. The old estates and housing areas
with their variety of very local shopping facilities (the corner shop) produced
certain rhythms and relationships which organized shopping as a social activity.
New council and private housing estates have involved the replacement of local
shops with more centralized shopping areas. This process has gone on alongside the
tendency to concentration among distributive capital, with its steady supplanting of
the traditional petit-bourgeoisie. This centralization of shopping changes the rhythms
of shopping, creating pressures for adaptations and adjustments within working-
class culture. Thus the apparent supplanting of Saturday afternoon spectator sports
by Saturday afternoon family shopping in the 1950s is in no sense the 'free choice'
of a rational and free-floating consumer, but is in part determined by the changing
social conditions of shopping which require more systematic, large-scale expeditions
(and thus more 'rational' reproduction . . .). From this standpoint the 'disappearing
corner shop' is not a folk-tale derived from excessive viewing of 'Coronation Street',
but a direct consequence of the long-term tendencies of capital accumulation and
concentration, and a critical reorganization of the conditions of existence of
working-class culture. To grasp working-class culture as an empirical problem it is
necessary to hold on to both ends of this chain – on the one hand, the broad move-

ments of capital and, on the other, its specific, local consequences for the patterns of class reproduction.

Another related example of the consequences of the broad movements of capital for specific and local forms of class reproduction can be found in the position of the pub.[22] The pub has held a central position in the local articulation of working-class culture as a sort of 'colonized' institution which, though not formally owned by the class, has been internally moulded by the class's custom. Here certain customary rights and expectations could be enforced through what Foster in another context has called 'exclusive dealing',[23] and users of the pub stood in a relationship to publicans which might be described as 'membership'. In working-class culture, then, the pub has historically been a 'local' – a term signifying its patronage by an established local clientele who shaped the internal dynamics, relationships and patterns of drinking. In the post-war period the development of an oligopolistic brewing industry has led to critical economic and social changes in the public houses. First, it has led to a tendency for owners or tenants to be replaced by brewery-controlled managers, thus interrupting the relations of patronage between the clientele and the publican, and producing industrial rather than local domination of the internal dynamics and patterns of the pub. Second, the breweries have tended to rationalize (i.e. close) or 'improve' their pubs, with design changes having important consequences for the patterns and experience of drinking (e.g. the substitution of large lounges for a series of snugs, public bars and tap rooms). Much of this has been done in accordance with an image of a changing clientele identified by the breweries. The new consumer differs from the old in terms of age (s/he is young), class (s/he is classless) and taste (Campari not beer). The effect of this attempt to address the new consumer is to fundamentally change the social and economic conditions under which drinking takes place, that is, to change the determinants of a particular historically developed form of reproduction. We may borrow from Althusser to suggest that these changes in material conditions and signifying practices (and the commercial ideologies which guide them) function to interpellate a new identity for the drinker – that of the 'consumer' rather than the 'member'. This newly forged interpellation dissolves previous patterns and habits of 'how to drink' and substitutes for them new 'preferred' styles of drinking:

> It is high time that Andy Capp was given a new suit and a car and took his wife out to one of the many popular North East pubs where he can still enjoy his pint of beer and Florrie can have a glass of sauterne with her scampi and chips.[24]

(In the light of our earlier comment about how women were addressed as the new consumers, it is interesting that here it is Florrie who is to change her consumption patterns.)

This quotation serves to illustrate something of the complexity of the forms which the reorganization of capital takes at the point of consumption. It is not a matter of a neutral technical or financial process. It is a process born and conducted in ideological conceptions about 'the market' and the 'consumer' which are the professionalized variants of contemporary ideological and political discourses. Marketing ideologies about the consumer echo political ideologies about the disappearance of traditional class differences and the rise of an affluent, middle-class Britain. In a sense, these marketing ideologies and practices attempt to 'complete the circle' by producing precisely that affluent middle-class consumer they claim to have already recognized. Subsequently, of course, political ideologies register these changes as the changed conditions of political practice and debate.

Working-class cultural forms have also been disrupted by processes of class recomposition stemming in large part from the economic/productive formation of the class. The changing occupational structure, together with the deskilling and reskilling of labour, play a part in this, changing both the relations supporting occupational and trade union solidarities, and also the symbolic indices of internal differentiation within the class (craft skills, differentials, etc.). The most significant disruption of established class solidarities and differentiations, however, has been the importation of immigrant labour to meet both capital and the state's need for low waged labour.[25] Ethnic, national and racial divisions are not new to the structure and culture of the British working class, of course; for example, nationalist divisions between the indigenous working class and Irish immigrant labour, and the effects of imperial competition between the national and colonial work-forces have played an important role in the making and remaking of the English working class economically, politically and ideologically.[26]

What is new, however, is the internalization of racial differences within the national working class in visible and distinctive forms. For the sociologists, working-class culture has seemed always to refer nostalgically to some all-white golden age. It does not register the presence of the temples, Asian films and corner shops, reggae and rastafarianism; these are relegated to a different part of the sociological empire, the sociology of ethnic minorities or race relations. Yet these, too, are the forms in and through which labour is reproduced; they are also the cultural experiences, the material, from which new ideological and political forces address the class, or, more precisely, aim to divide it.

However, we must also not make the error of assuming that such divisions and the material for them is a recent consequence of the racial structuring of labour – the image of a working-class culture has always hidden a complexly stratified and divided class in which particular cultural forms have provided the symbols and signals of division. Regionalism and localism carried and reproduced in accent, vocabulary, dress and the varieties of local and civic pride have been a persistent source of suspicion, mistrust and hostility, while one of the most fertile grounds of intra-class differentiation has been the whole repertoire of 'respectability'.[27] Though drawing on work experience (and especially the distinction between employed and unemployed), the forms and practices of reproduction have acted as central symbolic formations in this repertoire. The rough-respectable division has been firmly lodged in the visible signs of the home, street, neighbourhood and patterns of consumption. As Robert Roberts has shown, it was the scrubbed and painted or polished front steps, the front room, the types of food, sobriety, orientation to schools, children's clothes, the best suit or coat – the very stuff of reproduction – which provided the material of intra-class division.[28] These repetoires have also been drawn on, added to and solidified by particular forms of ideological and political addresses to the class – the respectable trade unionists or labour politicians, the conservative appeal to freedom and the family life of Britain, the stigma of the visit from the welfare, school board man or social worker, the rough neighbourhood's reputation, the 'scroungers' and so on.[29] All of these have at different times provided mechanisms for the division of the class and the insertion of its 'respectable' elements into bourgeois political discourse and action.

In the processes of social reconstruction in post-war Britain some of these conditions and forms of the reproduction of the working class as a complexly stratified, divided and contradictory unity have been dissolved or put to one side. Blocks of flats and relative anonymity undermine the significance (or possibility) of the polished step; the mobility of labour tends against localism and the establishment of 'reputation'. But in their dissolution, new forms of division, new repertoires of signifying differentiation have been constructed and developed. The interruption and dissolution of established class practices of reproduction produced in their wake new tensions, divisions and contradictions requiring new cultural solutions, new forms of living the relation to the relation of production, new habits, forms of common sense and so on.

What we have said so far has been an attempt to point to the variety of processes of class struggle (in economic, political and ideological forms) which have transformed the conditions of existence of the working class in post-war Britain – processes which have acted to reorganize the sphere of production and the sphere of reproduction. In the transformation of those conditions of existence (and the dominant political and ideological representation of them), the basis of the cultural forms within which the working class represent those conditions, or live their experience of them, has been undermined. The change in those material conditions require the elaboration of new cultural practices and repertoires which are capable of producing (however partial and contradictory) new cultural frameworks in which to live the experiences of being working class.

We cannot detail the whole process of the transformation and reconstitution of working-class culture between 1945 and 1978, but we can offer some elements that seem to us to be involved in that process. Central to this is an awareness that what we are discussing is in no simple sense the overthrow of one working-class culture and its replacement by a new one. What we can be certain of is that the period with which we are dealing involves a process of cultural transition – a transition which begins not from some homogenous entity called working-class culture, but from a complex, uneven and contradictory ensemble, made up of internal contradictions, a range or repertoire of different 'cultural solutions' – trade unionism, religion, respectability, crime, domesticity, socialist politics, etc.[30] The process of transition involves both continuities and breaks; some elements continue unmodified, others are sustained in new forms and other disappear and are replaced by new cultural forms.

We may begin here with the central continuity – the persistence of the cultural forms and practices of solidarity based within production [...] the collective definitions of work, the cultural forms expressing resistance to work, and the transformation of those resistances into valued social identities (identities based in 'skills', 'masculinity' and 'being the bread-winner').[31] Here, in the process of socialized labour, workers have continued to forge positive, though partial, cultural responses based on collective solidarity, which transfers the necessities and degradations of waged labour into some form of valued cultural identification. That this is a culture of subordination which, in the process of resistance (of sabotage, of doing the bosses down, of absenteeism), continues to reproduce its own subordination (and the oppression of others – for example, women through the particular cultural valuations of masculinity) is beyond doubt. But it does form a persistent, though often hidden, element which provides core elements of working-class culture: work and the cultural strategies developed around it persist *underneath* the more apparent and visible changes in the patterns of working-class consumption which dominated the conceptions of affluence. The discipline of the wage relation persists throughout this supposed abolition of the working class.

But even here, some of the cultural forms are changed. Some of the conditions which are culturally represented within shop-floor cultures are modified. Skills are eroded and removed by managerial initiatives, dissolving established cultural patterns of location, hierarchy and identity, and removing resources for working-class resistance and struggle within production.[32] New, and often equally jealously guarded, hierarchies and forms of distinction are constructed within the process of production, but also new broader solidarities and identities are constructed out of the process of deskilling, involving cultural recognition of the forms in which labour becomes generalized and more interdependent.[33] New cultural foci and points of resistance become articulated around the changes which capital produces within the labour process. No longer the foreman as the personalized bearer of control, but the domination exercised by the pace of the production line itself.[34] No longer the patronizing self-assurances of the bosses, but an attack on the abstract intellectuals – the management scientists with their university training, who erode skills and pour scorn on the world of 'experience'.[35] In addition, the tendencies to both economic and political concentration in the period have produced new informal cultural resistances and responses. The greater distance from capital itself in this period, and the greater involvement of trade union organizations in national forms of economic planning and bargaining with industry and the state, creates the ground for the creation of new informal responses (or, more correctly, the elaboration of subterranean traditions of shop-floor resistance to a greater position of significance). The period of centralization of bargaining and planning from the 1950s is also the period of the growth of informal shop-floor action – unofficial disputes, the growth of shop steward power in representing shop-floor interests, the tendency of 'wage drift' through local control of output and bonus schemes, as well as the more 'individual' strategies of sabotage, absenteeism and high labour turnover.[36] All these developments had come to haunt political and managerial planning by the mid 1960s: they produced, among other things, the Donovan Commission, the Labour Party's 'In Place of Strife' and the Industrial Relations Act, as well as the neo-human-relations strategies of management (such as Volvo's semi-autonomous work groups, job rotation and job enrichment schemes), profit-sharing schemes and plans for worker directors.[37]

What we are faced with here is not the simple unfolding of some unidirectional historical logic, guided by the unerring hand of capital, but of new initiatives by capital changing the conditions and forms of resistance from within labour, requiring new 'solutions' from capital and the state and so on. It is a permanently contradictory process of class struggle, which may not always take the traditionally recognized correct or 'modern' forms but involves a variety of hidden and informal dimensions which may more closely resemble, in fact, the protests of Hobsbawm's 'primitive rebels'.

[...]

In all of this it is important not to proceed as if working-class cultural forms were made and remade within a vacuum, to take them as solely expressing, in some transparent way, the material conditions of the class. In the production of these 'imaginary relations', other representations and ideological ensembles make themselves felt and are drawn on. We have tried to indicate some of the ways in which new ideological initiatives have had specific consequences for the forms of working-class culture (in the production of new needs, in the creation of new sexual identities, etc.), but these are only some of the processes in which dominant ideological repertoires have penetrated and reshaped aspects of working-class culture.

The working class and its changing conditions of existence have been 'spoken to' in a variety of voices from within dominant ideologies, in attempts to provide favourable or harmonizing representations of these changing conditions.[38] These have included, for example, addressing the working class as the national interest in a variety of guises – from Macmillan's national interest of self-interests, to Wilson's 'progressive nation' forged in the 'white heat of the technological revolution' (not to mention the subsequent return to the Dunkirk spirit). More recently the Thatcherite strategy has called for the reconstitution of 'old' England, interpellating the working class as an aggregation of free and independent men and women. welded together through the values of the family but enmeshed and frustrated by the bureaucracies of creeping socialism. They have been addressed both by the state and by capital as 'consumers', a common identity aimed at overriding the 'sectional interests' of production. They have also been addressed as the 'English' whose way of life has been destroyed by the influx of black criminals and scroungers, whose streets are no longer safe to walk in, and who have been betrayed by 'liberal' politicians and intellectuals.

These attempts to organize or orchestrate cultural definitions work by addressing some aspect of changed conditions and offering relatively coherent ideological structures within which they can be 'realistically' represented (and also be removed from the deeper organizing structures of class relations and class struggle). These forms of address are not uni-vocal. They involve different fragments, or what Poulantzas terms 'sub-ensembles', of the dominant ideological repertoire.[39] Nor must we be led to assume any simple outcome from these ideological practices. They may, indeed, come to provide organizing themes for 'common sense', but they may also be rejected for their inability to render experience coherent and meaningful, or they may be subsumed as sub-themes within other cultural formations.

[. . .]

Notes and References

1 See, *inter alia*, BRAVERMAN, H. (1974) *Labor and Monopoly Capital*, New York, Monthly Review Press.
2 COMMUNITY DEVELOPMENT PROJECTS (1976) *The Costs of Industrial Growth*, HMSO; and COCKBURN, C. (1977) *The Local State*, London, Pluto Press.
3 CORRIGAN, P. and CORRIGAN, P. (1977) 'The Reconstruction of the State', Seminar Paper at CCCS, University of Birmingham, June.
4 COHEN, P. (1972) 'Subcultural conflict and working-class community', *Working Papers in Cultural Studies*, No. 2.
5 STEDMAN JONES, G. (1975) 'Notes on the remaking of the English working class', *Journal of Social History*.
6 See, for example, CAIN, M. (1973) *Society and the Policeman's Role*, Routledge and Kegan Paul; and HALL, S. (1974) 'Education and the crisis of the urban school', in Open University, *Issues in Urban Education*, Milton Keynes, Open University Press.
7 COCKBURN, C. (1977) *op. cit.*; and CORRIGAN. P. (1976) 'The community strategy, the state and class struggle, 1966–1976', Vienna, Paper presented to European Conference on Deviancy and Social Control, September.
8 COCKBURN, C. (1977) *op. cit.*, Chap. 4.
9 See FINN, D., GRANT, N. and JOHNSON, R. (1977) 'Social democracy, education and the Crisis', *Working Papers in Cultural Studies*, No. 10, University of Birmingham, Centre for Contemporary Cultural Studies.
10 *Ibid.*
11 COHEN, P. (1972) *op. cit.*; and HALL, S. and JEFFERSON, T. (Eds.) (1976) *Resistance Through Rituals*, Hutchinson.
12 See, *inter alia*, CONFERENCE OF SOCIALIST ECONOMICS (1976) *On the Political Economy of Women*, London, Stage One; SMITH, J. 'Women, work and the family', *International Socialism*, Nos. 100–1.
13 See SMITH, J. *op. cit.*
14 For example, the WOMEN'S STUDY GROUP ON WELFARE (1947) *The Neglected Child and His Family*, Oxford University Press.
15 See, for example, BLAND, L. *et al.*, (1978) 'Women and the reproduction of labour power', CCCS stencilled paper, University of Birmingham.
16 PACKMAN, J. (1976) *The Child's Generation*, Blackwell and Robertson.
17 CONFERENCE OF SOCIALIST ECONOMISTS (1976) *op. cit.*; SMITH, J. *op. cit.*
18 WILSON, L. (1977) *Women and the Welfare State*, Tavistock, pp. 151–2.
19 CONFERENCE OF SOCIALIST ECONOMISTS (1976) *op. cit.*
20 HALL, S. (forthcoming) 'Reformism and the legislation of consent', in *Permissiveness and Control*, National Deviancy Conference.
21 COHEN, P. (1972) *op. cit.*
22 HUTT, C. (1976) *The Decline of the English Pub*, Arrow; NEWMAN, B. and YOUNG, D. (unpublished manuscript) 'The pub as a leisure context', Dept. of Sociology, North-East London Polytechnic; and WHITEHEAD, A. (1977) 'Sexual antagonisms in Hertfordshire', in BARKER and ALLEN (Eds.) *Dependence and Exploitation in Work and Marriage*, Longman.
23 FOSTER, J. (1974) *Class Struggle in the Industrial Revolution*, Weidenfeld and Nicolson, p. 53.
24 HUTT, C. (1976) *op. cit.*, p. 128.
25 See CASTLES, S. and KOSACK, G. (1973) *The Immigrant Worker and the Class Structure*, Oxford University Press; and SIVANANDAN, A. (1976) *Race, Class and the State*, London, Institute of Race Relations.
26 See, for example, LENIN, V.I. (1969) *British Labour and British Imperialism*, Lawrence and Wishart; HARTMAN, P. and HUSBAND, C. (1974) *Racism and the Mass Media*, Davis-Poynter, Chaps. 1 and 2; and PEARSON, G. (1976) 'Paki-bashing in Lancashire', in MUNGHAM, G. and PEARSON, G. (Eds.) *Working Class Youth Culture*, Routledge and Kegan Paul.
27 See STEDMAN JONES, G. (1975) *op. cit.*; HALL, S. (1978) *Policing the Crisis*, Macmillan, Chap. 6; and DAMER, S. (1977) 'Wine Alley: the sociology of a dreadful enclosure', in WILES, P. (Ed.) *The Sociology*

of Crime and Delinquency in Britain, Martin Robertson.

28 ROBERTS, R. (1971) *The Classic Slum*, Harmondsworth, Penguin.

29 HALL, S. (1978) *op. cit.*, Chap. 6; and DUFF, E. and MARSDEN, D. (1977) *Workless*, Harmondsworth, Penguin.

30 See HALL, S. 'Subcultures, cultures and class', in HALL, S. and JEFFERSON, T. (1976) (Eds.) *op. cit.*

31 See also WILLIS, P. (1977) *Learning to Labour*, Farnborough, Saxon House.

32 See BEYNON, H. and NICHOLS, T. (1977) *Living With Capitalism*, Routledge and Kegan Paul; and NICHOLS, T. and ARMSTRONG, P. (1976) *Workers Divided*, Fontana.

33 See WILLIS, P. (1977) *op. cit.*

34 See BEYNON, H. (1975) *Working for Ford*, Harmondsworth, Penguin.

35 See HALL, S. *et al.*, (1978) *op. cit.*, Chap. 6.

36 See BEYNON, H. (1975) *op. cit.*

37 For a discussion of one example of neo-human-relations management, see NICHOLS, T. (May 1975) 'The "Socialism" of management', *Sociological Review*, Vol. 23, No. 2.

38 See HALL, S. *et al.*, (1978) *op. cit.*, Chap. 6, for an analysis of some elements of an 'English Ideology'.

39 POULANTZAS, N. (1973) *Political Power and Social Classes*, New Left Books, p. 210.

4   The Political Economy of Mass Sport

John Hargreaves

Until recently, sociologists have tended to ignore mass sport as a social phenomenon and, even when they have paid attention to it, the increasing importance of sport as a mechanism of social domination has largely escaped notice.[1] This paper sketches an approach to the problem and attempts to bring to bear on it insights from sociology, and economic and political theory, which hopefully at the same time illustrates the artificial nature of the barriers between these disciplines.

First, we need a theoretically adequate conception of politics that is not simply concerned with the activities of government and the state but with the whole range of social practices in which power and domination occur. An adequate conception of mass sport must relate to this conception of politics within the context of an overall social theory. There is no intention here to deal at length with the vexed question of what is sport, which in some ways can be a rather sterile exercise. Mass organized sport is a readily identifiable phenomenon and it is with this alone that we are here specifically concerned. However, there are problems arising from the manner in which concepts like play and leisure are related to sport which require clarification.

Among the numerous attempts to conceptualize sport, Huizinga's theory of play provides an interesting, convenient start for a discussion.[2] Huizinga regarded play as the most important element in the progress of civilization. The essence of play is its freedom and spontaneity, its quality as an end to be pursued for its own sake, having no other objective in view. The development of modern society has so eroded the opportunity for genuine play, in this sense, that Huizinga concludes modern civilization is in decline and that modern sport reflects this decline, having lost its constitutive quality of play. Unfortunately, rich as it is in insights about play, Huizinga's major work is a philosophy of history couched almost exclusively in aesthetic and moral categories. He possesses few concepts adequate for a social analysis of sport in modern capitalist society and his conclusions concerning the overall direction of history are unjustifiably pessimistic.[3]

In contrast to Huizinga's abstract, idealist theory of play, it is possible to find in Marx's work the basis for a concrete social analysis of play and sport. Alienated

Source: A revised version of a paper published in Parker, S. *et al.* (Eds.) (1975) *Sport and Leisure in Contemporary Society*, London, Leisure Studies Association, Conference Papers, I.

labour and leisure under capitalism is analysed in the light of men's distinguishing quality as 'species beings' and the potentialities for a qualitatively different society contained within capitalism itself. Men as 'species beings' distinguish themselves from animals by their creative power and purposive nature. Their powers and purposes are expressed, developed and realized through labour, and it is in the labour process that men change their nature and fashion their world. Capitalism, while increasing the productive powers of men, simultaneously reduces their labour to the status of a mere commodity, subject to the law of commodity production and therefore unfree, a denial of human nature.

In this analysis the possibility of conceptually confusing play and leisure with work does not arise, as it often does, for example, in the formalistic definitional disputes over these terms in the sociology of leisure. For example, it is said that 'work' may sometimes be simultaneously 'play', as in the case of the businessmen who enjoy their work for its own sake, or 'play' can be simultaneously 'work', as in the case of the professional sportsman. But for Marx alienation is not merely a psychological condition, nor is it a metaphysical notion connoting men's universal fate; nor is men's free, creative activity, their play, merely a state of mind. Play is a state of social being in which men's activities are freely chosen, in which those activities both reflect and enhance men's control over their existence. Within the context of capitalist society, therefore, the 'play' which is the product of the sports industry, or the 'play' which is associated with work, or the 'play' which is a form of character training in schools has a tendency to become alienated activity, not the freely chosen activity of the autonomous subject but, rather, activity in the service of repressive labour.[4]

It is interesting to see how Huizinga's critics in the sociology of sport have reacted to his ideas in their own attempt to provide a specifically sociological theory and also to contrast this predominant approach with that of Marx. Almost to a man, they have followed Caillois' rather restrictive assessment of Huizinga: his concept of play is alleged to be too diffuse, play is said to be only one among other dimensions of sport (in other words, it is demoted as a constitutive element of sport) and he is said to exaggerate the absence of play in contemporary sport.[5] The critics have instead preferred to examine what they consider to be the 'facts' of modern sport, as opposed to the 'value-judgments' of Huizinga and of others, presumably like Marx, who use a broader notion of play.

It is obvious that, far from avoiding value-judgments, they simply substitute for Huizinga's idealist notion of play their own preference for play as it exists today. Dunning, for example, argues that the play element in modern sport could not be completely eradicated, since large numbers of people are attracted to it (the case he cites is soccer attendances), and that the increasing organization of modern sport is a technical prerequisite for its 'democratization', that is, for spreading sport to a more socially heterogeneous public. A balance is therefore thought to be possible between organization and playful spontaneity.[6]

The argument is not very convincing: after all there are cases, such as Imperial Rome and Nazi Germany, where the mass following attracted to sport did, no doubt, find it enjoyable; yet it seems reasonably clear that the enjoyment derived from sport in these cases also provided power holders with the opportunity of using sport to counteract divisive tendencies.[7] The fact that large numbers of people are attracted to sport is very important, but it is something requiring very careful interpretation. The difficulty comes out very clearly in Dunning's assertion that it is possible to strike a balance between the need for organization in sport and the need for spontaneity. However, he gives no concrete indication of how this is to be accomplished. If categories like 'enjoyment' are simply taken over from the conventional wisdom concerning sport, there is no way of assessing the nature and the particular function of that phenomenon, that is, whether the enjoyment expresses autonomy and spontaneity, or whether it is in some way associated with attempts to exert power and influence. A critical theory raises these questions; a positivist approach ignores them. Despite its faults, at least Huizinga's theory of play is in some sense critical, in that it draws attention to questions about the quality of life in modern societies and to their capacity to serve people's needs – and these are also, of course, ultimately political and social questions, as Marx well realized.

Most sports sociologists, both functionalists and others, relate the emergence of the modern pattern of sport on a large scale to the emergence of industrial capitalism, which took place first in early nineteenth-century Britain and later spread to the rest of the developed world, and which introduced a new structure of society and new patterns of 'work' and 'leisure'. In functionalist theory sport tends to be viewed as a type of leisure activity which performs positive functions for the maintenance of social systems. One of the most explicit of the various versions of this view comes out in Dumazedier's analysis of leisure.[8] Leisure as such, and sport as a type of leisure, has three functions: recreation, recuperation and free development of the individual. There are several other accounts of the social function of sport, some of which do not explicitly employ a functionalist theory but say substantially the same thing.[9]

A number of related points can be made against this predominant approach. First, it makes the historically specific social roles of contemporary society universal. In particular, work roles are viewed as inevitably unrewarding, boring and frustrating for the majority of people. This goes deeper than a mere description of the typical work condition experienced by large numbers of individuals in industrial society: it is an assertion of an inescapable condition demanded by any conceivable modern society. Linked to this assumption is another: there must be some social mechanism to ensure adjustment of individuals to this situation, otherwise social stability is threatened. From this point of view the problem of adjustment to the social system is eased so long as the expansion of leisure time is administered correctly. This, then, is the sociological rationale for the so-called 'problem of leisure', a topic which crops up also in less esoteric areas than sociology, like modern liberal educational theory for example.[10]

The individual in industrial society is to fulfill himself in leisure activities, in compensation for the deprivations and inevitable frustrations experienced in work and social life in general. Leisure pursuits send him back refreshed, recovered and reconciled to further deprivation and frustration, to the nature of work and life in industrial society. From this terrain, typical practical policy problems are how to get government to provide more money for sporting leisure facilities, or how the 'educator', especially the physical educator, can teach individuals to use their leisure wisely by selecting their appropriate leisure pursuits, including sports, from an ever-widening list of leisure activities.

This whole approach to leisure and sport is riddled with value-judgment and ideology of a particular kind. It accepts and perpetuates the destructive dichotomy between work and leisure which, as both Marx and Weber noted, is a categorization peculiar to capitalist society. The revised, contemporary notion of the relation between work and leisure differs from Weber's 'Protestant Ethic', however, only in so far as consumption of leisure becomes a kind of duty as well as work. The guilt induced in individuals by puritanism for an unproductive existence has been supplemented by the guilt for not consuming one's leisure 'productively'. The approach is implicitly political in so far as sport and leisure is conceptualized purely as a mode of adjustment to social systems. Thus society is reified: the existence of an impersonal force is postulated which is presented as 'the needs of society' or 'functional prerequisites' of society, to which individuals must adjust in their leisure. Such reification conceals the extent to which real individuals and groups have the power and wherewithal to see that others 'adjust' to their own specific requirements, passed off as the 'needs of society'.

The alternative view, which does not conceal itself as the neutral, a-political 'view of the social scientist' (Dumazedier), is that there is no theoretical or practical reason why leisure should be considered merely from the point of view of how to adjust people to the social system; but there is every reason to question the demand for adaptation. The assumption underpinning the 'necessity of adjustment' view could be none other than that we already have the best of all possible worlds and all reasonable men recognize the necessity of adjustment. In effect, this particular conceptualization of sport, and the theory of its functions for the individual and for society, purges the discussion of mass sport of any critical content. Instead we are presented with the point of view of the benevolent administrator, whose social engineering task is to see that people are properly adjusted. Sport and leisure come to be seen through the rose-tinted spectacles of consensus politics.

Modern capitalism faced qualitatively new kinds of problems in the post-war era, problems which up to recently it managed remarkably well, with a great deal of sophistication. After the experience of the depression, it was learnt that full employment was a prerequisite of social stability. The successful application of neo-Keynesian economic policies after the war resulted in an unprecedented period of economic growth and a rise in the general standard of living. However, the 'affluent' society produces new problems from the point of view of dominant groups. Paradoxically, with more leisure time, higher levels of education, full employment and rising expectations, people became potentially more critical and more dissatisfied. The capital punishment of industry and commerce – dismissal – no longer contained the same terrors for employees as in the old days of unemployment, and besides the worker was more likely to be supported by a stronger trade union organization. The problem of motivating individuals to produce took on a new dimension.

Here the sphere of non-work, including sports, becomes increasingly important. A modern economy typically experiences a relatively greater growth of the tertiary or services sector compared with the primary and manufacturing sectors. Disposable income is spent increasingly on consumption of goods and services provided by what one could call the 'leisure industrial complex'. This sector expands to meet this increased demand, and itself attempts to expand demand further through advertising and other methods.

So, the first point to note about this expansion in leisure activities, and mass sport in particular, is that it is highly commercialized. As far as the private sector is concerned, there would be no point in producing the vast range of goods and services involved if there was not already a demand for them and consequently a profit to be made in fulfilling that demand.[11] It is not that Machiavellian capitalists deliberately get together to compensate people for their dissatisfactions by expanding the leisure industries so that, for example, the workforce will be better motivated to produce, having been compensated by a more satisfying leisure. It is that the particular nature of work in capitalist society itself produced in the worker a reaction to it, which takes the form of a demand for a fuller life in the form of leisure. This demand is formulated within the terms of a pre-existing autonomous cultural tradition, of which sporting pastimes are an important part. But the demand for compensation in leisure can also be exploited profitably by the private sector, if necessary in conjunction with the state, through the provision of a vast range of goods and services.

The demand for leisure goods and services may be seen as one particular form of the search of autonomy, which may itself, within the context of capitalist society, provide opportunities for dominant groups to exert control. Society in general, and work in particular, can be more bearable if non-work is in some sense relatively different and more satisfying.[12] It should be stressed that social integration is nevertheless always problematic for power holders and by no means automatic – as the case of 'soccer hooliganism' demonstrates.[13] Also it must be remembered that the expansion and continued existence of the 'leisure industrial complex' is premised on the possibilities of continued economic expansion. If the economy proves unstable and incapable of raising the standard of living in accord with expectations, or even of maintaining present levels, the frustrated expectations generated in the consumption of leisure may prove to be an explosive political force.

The private sector, however, by no means wholly satisfies demand for leisure, particularly sporting leisure. This is why it is necessary to examine in some detail the contribution of government and the state in this sphere. The role of the state in modern Western economies tends to be confined to those spheres which the private sector cannot or will not manage, but which nevertheless are necessary as an infrastructure for its activities to continue. In Britain the state has, for example, only taken over economic control of those industries which were unprofitable, or which needed very large injections of capital, and which might only be profitable in the very long term.[14] Also, the state functions as the overall co-ordinating mechanism of the economy. State intervention in the provision of sporting leisure fills the gap left by the failure of the market and represents an attempt to co-ordinate the overall provision of sporting leisure activities. The Mexican case provides an interesting illustration of the possibilities open to the state in this respect.

The 'Unidades', or State Social Security organizations, are government and industry – financed social centres, sports camps and hospitals, all in one campus. These were the brainchild of the ruling party's intellectuals and were introduced in the late 1950s in order to help cope with the problem of a declining economy and a work-force which badly lacked incentives to produce. It was realized that the Mexican masses were far more interested in using their initiative and energies in leisure pursuits like football, so the Unidades were made attractive as work training centres by providing them with good facilities and training courses for soccer. Football training was made available only to those willing to take special courses in a trade. In 1971 there were 96 Unidades and in the capital alone there were 36 Unidades soccer training centres.

There is some reason to think that the social security scheme helped guarantee production for Mexican industrialists and that it was associated with the regeneration of the Mexican economy. To a significant extent, the success of the scheme can be attributed to the centrality of soccer in the popular consciousness.[15] The more the state acts to co-ordinate the economic activity of society as a whole, the more it tends to manage the provision of leisure and sporting leisure. This places the relation of the state to sport in societies like Russia in perspective.[16]

Important as examples like the USSR are of the political use of sport, they stand out for commentators precisely because the party-state is so unashamedly involved on a grand scale, which is not yet true of the liberal democracies of the West. The dominant assumption which makes such examples of state control so impressive and indeed 'horrifying' to Western commentators is that politics is synonymous with the activity of the formally constituted, 'legitimate' political apparatus. Therefore it follows from this assumption, and it is axiomatic for commentators, that where the state's or government's activity is, relatively absent from sport it has no connection with politics. Where the state and government are only marginally involved and sport is organized by formally autonomous institutions, as in the West by and large, the direct intervention by government in sport is either seen as an unfortunate lapse due to the example of other, corrupt governments, or as a legitimate interest in the provision of leisure for the population. A sports administrator like McIntosh, for example, views instances of Western governments cashing in on international sport as a regrettable capitulation to the temptations put in their way, rather than as a sociologically significant occurrence.[17]

This kind of invidious comparison – between those societies in which government unambiguously uses sport as a political tool, by organizing sport directly on a massive scale, and societies like our own where government plays an increasing, but still marginal, role in the organization of sport for the masses – is misleading in two ways. First, it diverts attention away from the political importance of sport not organized by the state; it therefore tends to underemphasize the total resources of Western societies devoted to sporting activity, whether from 'public' or 'private' sources. Second, it considerably underestimates the political significance of the role already played by the state in sport in these societies. There is no good reason for thinking that sport is of less political significance in the West than it is in 'totalitarian' regimes.

In Britain it has been the state, rather than the private sector, which has provided sports facilities like swimming pools, sports fields, gymnasia, etc. requiring heavy capital investment. On the whole, entrepreneurs have not shown very much interest in providing these facilities on their own initiative. State provision out of taxation, which comes from the general public, has saved entrepreneurs the risks involved in the heavy capital investment required. At the same time they have profited from the government contracts for these facilities. State encouragement of sports creates a demand from participants for sports equipment and services, and this more immediately profitable aspect is provided by the private sector. In Britain the state has played a considerable part in promoting 'sports consciousness' through the schools and this again feeds back into the private sector as a demand for its products. Leisure, especially sporting leisure, has the great advantage, from the point of view of providing business with opportunities, that it is capable of generating an almost infinitely elastic demand for goods and services. There are always new ways of using leisure in sport.

There is no doubt that in Britain state promotion of sport is increasingly seen as an admirable agency of social control. A few years ago, the idea that in Britain, the home of the gentleman amateur, there should be a Minister of Sport, a state sponsored Sports Council, and a Parliamentary Sports Committee, would have been greeted with incredulity. Yet since 1962 in effect there has been a Minister of Sport. Central and local government aid to sport, though still on a relatively small scale, has steadily increased in real terms since the early 1960s.

The Sports Council as part of this effort is clearly concerned with Britain's success in international competition and its obvious political kudos. Its concern for international success even extends to school-children, for it sees a need for wide encouragement of special talent in children throughout Britain, and even school sports associations are grant aided by the Sports Council for local, national and international competition.[18] Just as in Russia and other countries, the awarding of honours by the state for sporting achievement is now standard practice in Britain.

Since at least the publication of the Wolfenden Report on Sport and Leisure, which recommended government financial support of sport and recreation, the justification for increased government aid to and interest in sport has been the so-called problem of leisure, particularly as it affects youth. There would be a reluctance to admit that the concern is with social control, but that in fact is what is involved. Bannister, former Chairman of the Sports Council, makes the point explicitly:

> Is there yet a real conviction that an economically sensible investment now, will help to avert *social* [my emphasis] and medical ills of the future, and will add greatly to people's happiness?[19]

The Sports Council and the Ministry of Sport are in the business of producing happiness, so when the leisure industry's production goes wrong, as it were, as in the case of 'soccer hooliganism', it is the duty of the Minister to step in and to correct the malfunction in the apparatus. In this case the phrase used by the Sports Council's Chairman about 'helping to avert social ills' takes on a less euphemistic, more sinister tone. It means, concretely, military-style defences of football grounds, heavier sentences for 'hooligans', and support for the profit-seeking football entrepreneurs who want to switch the spectator off and on at will.

If the total resources devoted to sport by both public and private sectors are taken into account (that is, capital stock in tracks, fields, pools, gymnasia, golf courses, etc.) and if the amount of time and money spent on sport via the sports industrial complex is added (that is, spectatorism, active participation, buying equipment, reading journals, etc.) it is likely that, in an economically advanced society like Britain, the resources in time, money and effort *per capita* devoted to sport are greater than in societies like Russia. The significant difference is not in the degree of sports fanaticism, but rather in the degree of overall co-ordination of all this activity by the state. Although the scale of its activities is small at the moment, the state in Britain has made some definite moves in that direction.

The close connection between business and sport can be seen in other ways: first, the place businessmen occupy on the controlling bodies of clubs and nationally organized 'autonomous' sports bodies. It is doubtful whether there is much money to be made, directly anyway, by businessmen who sit on controlling bodies, although that does not mean that the running of an organized sport like soccer in Britain is not big business – it is and very much so.[20] They do it out of genuine interest, for prestige, and they are useful in raising funds. But since there is in general very little financial reward for being an official on the governing body of a sport or of a sports club (most of which are voluntary positions), businessmen, who more than any other group in society have the resources and time to serve on voluntary bodies, tend to be very well represented on sports bodies of various kinds. Businessmen are not generally renowned for their radical politics or values. Controlling bodies have the ultimate say over policy, and they can get rid of even powerful professionals like soccer managers if the need arises. It is likely, then, that the influence of business-men in sport will be in a broadly conservative direction: that is, the values of business in particular, and bourgeois culture in general, will tend to be those most influential in the running of organized sport.

Second, sport is increasingly promoted and financed by business as a form of advertising for itself. The Sports Council attempts to tap this source of revenue for sport by putting sports bodies in contact with potential business advertisers – another example of the tie-up between the state, sports bodies and business.

A further point needs to be made about the political role of autonomous sports bodies in Britain. Under dictatorial, authoritarian regimes nationalism and other dominant values are more or less blatantly promoted by the government itself; in the West much the same function is performed by the independent sports bodies themselves and by the media. The major voluntary autonomous bodies like the MCC, FA, AAA, take international competition extremely seriously – to the extent that, in practice, it is the pinnacle of their activities, absorbing a great deal of time, money and effort. It could be argued that the heavy involvement of these bodies in international competition, in which the prestige of the nation is at stake, is not to enhance Britain's prestige but to stimulate interest in the sport itself, and to promote international goodwill. The actual conduct of these bodies does not bear this out. Even if it were true that the intentions were not nationalistic, it would still be the case that nationalism tends to be promoted by international sport, and there is little evidence at all that it promotes goodwill. For example, the typical conception of the role of the sportsman in international competition held by sports officials universally, British included, is as a 'good ambassador' for his country. What this tends to mean is that the sports representative is expected to embody the supposed national virtues, one of which is curiously universal: the sportsman is not to embarrass his country in the eyes of its rivals in any way. Woe betide anyone who does. There are many examples of competitors being penalized for transgressing the sacred standards and thus embarrassing their country. Independent sports bodies show no inclination to give up the panoply of national and militaristic symbols and sentiment which usually surround international contests. It seems they are just as enthusiastic to promote their country's image and to enhance its political prestige as any government is.

It has often been noted that sport has both a ritualistic and a dramatic aspect and that ritual and drama can be regarded as forms of communication and thus of learning.[21] Ritual can aptly be viewed as 'meaning in action' and anthropologists, particularly, have examined ritual as a mode of asserting values and beliefs in different cultures and as one of the many ways in which the culture of a society or its subcultures are transferred from generation to generation. The dramatic aspect of sport is probably most important of all for this analysis. Drama suspends and transforms immediate reality in order to convey meaning. Fantasy is therefore inseparable from drama. Drama is play with its own conventions and rules which in varying ways simplify or abstract from the world in order to convey meaning. Sport as ritual and as drama, then, possesses qualities and provides a setting which appeals to everyone: it is a play involving enjoyment, imagination and fantasy; there is an outcome which is indeterminate and therefore exciting. Sport is thus a simplified form of drama, and a ritual in which individuals can in some way recognize and play out the typical problems they face and have to resolve in their real lives.

The media play an important part in the promotion of sports consciousness through their dramatization of sports. It is no exaggeration to say that the media tend to treat success in international competition as a drama of national survival. Sports are accorded the same if not greater prominence than politics and war. This should not surprise us, absurd as it is from one point of view. Media coverage of international competition is invariably focused on the fortunes of the national team or individual representatives of the nation rather than an even coverage of the competition as a whole. The most obvious example is the Olympic Games when attention is increasingly focused on the medal table and how the nation stands in relation to others. From an analytic point of view, it matters not whether in fact the nation wins or loses: the point to note is that in the media's focus on the nation's fortunes, sport becomes a means by which the audience can identify with the nation and associate their own fortunes with it.

The sports drama, as it is presented in the media, just as it helps to promote nationalism in the way indicated, also tends to do the same for other values, ideas and sentiments already present in the culture which have political significance. One way certain values may be reinforced and celebrated is in the way sportsmen are treated as heroes and, more rarely, as villains. An example from America illustrates the point, where the presentation of race issues in the media is obviously politically significant. Joe Louis was judged by the American press of his time as a 'worthy' champion, whereas the only previous black holder of the world heavyweight boxing title, Jack Johnson, was not. Worthiness in this context was being a 'good nigger' and knowing his place, a value other blacks were supposed to hold at the time, and one which plainly Johnson did not exemplify.

In this country the 'official' heroes, as it were, are the Bobby Charltons, Bobby Moores, etc., – but not the Georgie Bests. These heroes represent the conventional virtues: respectability, modesty, stoicism, non-controversiality, law-abidingness. Politicians when performing for the media often cash in on the prevailing 'sports consciousness': former Prime Minister Harold Wilson likened his cabinet to a soccer team; Nixon's first remark to the returning lunar astronauts for all the world to hear on TV was about the latest ballgame score. The message contained in this folksy idiom for the audience is that the politician is a 'normal chap' or 'regular guy', for that, in terms of the consensus, is what sport is supposed to be about: sensible, ordinary, wholesome enjoyment with an element of excitement thrown in.[22] The politician associates himself with, and at the same time uses for his own and his group's benefit, the centrality of sport in the culture; the media facilitate and convey the performance to a wide audience. This is why on the great sporting occasions status figures and figures of authority are invariably present.

Proportionally the total amount of time and space devoted to sport in the media can only be described as enormous, and this effort can nowadays literally reach a worldwide audience. One estimate of the size of audience for the final of the 1974 World Cup was 1,000,000,000. It would be simplistic, however, to argue, merely on the basis of the sheer amount of sports coverage in the media and the sheer size of the audience reached, that the media are the point of origin and the determining factor in audience reactions to sport. Rather, the influence of the media is to provide a channel of communication for, and therefore to reinforce in the long run, the dominant values, ideas and sentiments present in the culture. If sports consciousness, whether it be in the form of passive consumption of spectacles or active participation, does have political significance as a form of social control, then exposure to sport via the media reinforces, strengthens and encourages the habit of watching or participating in sport and therefore, in this way, it can be said to contribute significantly to the political role of sport.

It has been suggested that the media help to promote nationalism and certain other conventional values in the way they present sporting activity. However, these are only the most obvious manifestations of hegemonic values in sport, and by no means necessarily the most important ones. It is necessary to further characterize the core elements of the hegemonic culture, which clearly have a political content, in order to see further sport's role in the culture.[23]

The British Conservative Party, for example, is one clear institutional and ideological expression of hegemonic culture in Britain, but it is only one expression. The kind of values and ideas which it presents in, as it were, 'ideal-typical' form are present in and cut across British culture as a whole. Therefore it should not be thought that the following sketch of hegemonic political values in Britain is synonymous with Tory values and ideas, but rather that this party more closely embodies them than other institutions. In this broad sense, 'conservativism' then, coheres about the following key ideas and values: the nation takes precedence over all other interests and has a special value; there is a necessity and a positive value in a hierarchical ordering of society; individuals are inherently unequal; social position is a result of individuals taking advantage of their talents; the competitive instinct is fundamental to human behaviour in society; individuals are inherently aggressive and anti-social, and consequently there is a strong need for social controls; change only comes gradually and therefore the very existence of social institutions is a justification for their necessity; and it is generally unwise to question the established rules of behaviour.

These values and ideas can be summarized in terms of three themes and their polar opposites:

1   Individualism and competition versus co-operation and solidarity.

2   Leadership and hierarchy versus democratic control.

3   Discipline and conformity versus critical rationalism.

Let us see how this might work with sport in British schools. It is fairly clear that the organization and cultural ethos of the 'public schools' was the embodiment of conservatism as it has been discussed so far. These schools strongly put into practice the idea that sports have a value in 'character training', and in a weakened, but still significant form, this concern with sport as having 'educational' value passed into the real 'public schools' run by the state, not surprisingly, since in many ways the private schools served as the model for the latter. Sport in British schools is highly organized with an important place in the curriculum.

The fact that sport is inherently competitive, in the sense that there has to be an outcome to the contest, with oneself or with others, makes it an admirable mode of socialization into culturally specific competitive mores of this society. Individual success requires a certain kind of discipline, self-reliance, toughness and individual initiative. Participation in organized competitive sport may be seen as a ritual re-hearsal for the rigours of real competitive life in society. To the victor in the sporting struggle goes the glory, status and satisfaction of defeating the opponent on track, field, etc. To the victor in the social struggle for individual success go material spoils and social status. Participation in sports is a way of imparting and acquiring both the ethic of individualism and the psychological motivation to perform as an individual in the broader social context. The sports coach attempts to teach aggression, determination, the will to win, and to impart the confidence that overcomes anxiety and fear, without completely dispelling them. Above all, perhaps, school sports teach that competitive individualism is a normal, unavoidable feature of social life. Just as there are winners and losers in sport, there must be winners and losers in society.

There is most probably no empirical connection between individual success in school sport and social success, and it is not necessary that this be so. The way socialization into the competitive individualism of bourgeois society probably 'works' is as a contribution to a pervasive cultural ethos. What is important is that individuals attempt to abide by the ethics, that is, actually attempt to put them into practice. Such ideas, acquired at an early age, can become part of a framework of thought and a means of judging the justice of one's fate.

This leads to the second theme, sport as socialization into conformity with the dominant rules and values. Though at first sight it may seem that conformity is contradicted by the theme of individualism, on reflection they are complementary rather than contradictory. Any form of competition requires rules, and in modern team games they have reached a high stage of formalization. Now, in bourgeois ideology, competition also has its limits, sometimes referred to as 'fair' and 'unfair' competition. Market competition has its rules for, like any competition it must be ordered: 'players' must know which rules are permitted and which not. Above all, if society is to maintain itself, there cannot be a continual questioning of the rules and everyone must accept them. It is a cardinal principle of bourgeois democracy that everyone is equal before the law or, in other words, the rules of this form of society are neutral. To challenge this is to subvert society.

The part played by rules of sport in political socialization is absolutely crucial. A whole series of analogues exists between what is taught in sport and what one is required to believe in bourgeois society: first, attitude to rules as such. One is taught that the rules of a particular sport are given; one plays by the rules. The very definition of 'playing fair' or 'being a good sportsman' is playing according to the rules – even when one thinks the decision is unjust. One is supposed to accept the decision of the umpire or referee without question, the logic being that the rules are neutral, and that the referees neutrally interpret them. The fact that the terminology and imagery of sport is often vividly present in political rhetoric and debate is not merely figurative or accidental or merely 'a way of speaking'. It is an appeal to a previously established way of understanding.

The same elementary conceptions of justice and equality in the rules of sport are the rationale and ideology of social practice in the society. Just as abiding by the rules makes one a true sportsman, so abiding by and not questioning the rules and ideas of consensual politics makes one a 'good' normal citizen, as opposed to a crank, extremist or fanatic. Just as in the heat of sporting competition we learn to accept the judgement of a neutral referee, so in the heat of social competition and social conflict, say, an industrial relations dispute, we learn it is reasonable to appoint 'neutral' arbitrators or judges to sort it out according to the established rules of political fair play. The ramifications and connections between sport and politics are almost endless in the context of their rules.

The third theme common to organized sport and consensual politics is their stress on hierarchy and leadership, and loyalty to it. Like conformity, this theme may seem to conflict with competitive individualism, but again they are complementary. In team games and sports, as opposed to individual pursuits, there is both competition against an opposition and co-operation with one's own team members. In the British public schools, fitting in with the team and supporting it has a special value. Pulling behind the leader, supporting the whole team, at the expense of one's own inclinations, makes for success of the team. A team needs more than skill; it needs morale, and a good leader's job is to hold his team together, to provide an example to the men. A leader both shapes and expresses the common determination of the team to win. Here both the values of comradeship and the individual's need for identity and security are exploited simultaneously. The team provides a way of finding personal worth for the individual by merging and identifying with a greater whole.

Again, the parallels with the political imagery, rhetoric and ideology of the right are obvious. The right has always stressed the desirability of strong leadership, which overrides national differences (particularly in an emergency) in 'the national interest'. The whole tendency of organized sport is to convey an intense respect, admiration, even adulation for heroic leader figures. Outstanding figures in sport are held up as heroes to emulate, and so the cult of leadership is prominent in sport. In right-wing political theory the leader-hero is a man of strength, action and decision – a lion, hence the political right tend to be suspicious and intolerant of intellectuals. In schools those who are good at sports may in some cases enjoy an equal if not higher prestige than their more intellectually-inclined peers.

There are a number of other scattered indications that the values of the right are fairly strongly represented in sport. In the upsurge of student militancy in the sixties, for example, radical students often found themselves opposed by the more sporty ones. In Britain the rugby authorities have consistently opposed moves to bring pressure to bear on South Africa to desegregate its sport. It would be interesting to examine in this connection the social character of the physical education world, for there are some indications that it is one of the more conservatively-oriented elements in education. For example, physical education colleges and departments are well known for being run in a relatively authoritarian manner, and there is a greater stress among physical education personnel on symbols and behaviour that those on the right of the political spectrum tend to worry about: conformity to particular modes of dress, appearance and 'bearing', a hyper-concern with discipline, order and established 'standards', especially with hygiene, cleanliness, attention to minute detail and technical efficiency.

Since the association between sport and the wielding of power has, to a large extent, been neglected in the literature on sport, this paper has concentrated on the opportunities organized sport provides for dominant groups to exert power and influence in sport. However, it is very important to also bear in mind that to note this aspect does not entail the proposition that sport as such necessarily functions to maintain the *status quo*. There are, after all, significant differences between sports, and these need to be thoroughly investigated: between say, cricket and football in Britain; between cricket here in Britain and the West Indies; between professional and 'shamateur', *versus* genuinely amateur sports; and between nationally *versus* locally organized sport. As in other areas of life where attempts are made to exert power and influence, sport can also become the focus of conflict and the means of expressing differences between groups and classes, and so it frequently becomes a locus of resistance to attempts from above to control those below.

Notes and References

1 Loy, J.W. and Kenyon, G.S. (1969) (Eds.) *Sport, Culture and Society*, Macmillan; Dunning, E. (1971) (Ed.) *The Sociology of Sport*, London, Cass; Talamini, J.T. and Page, C.H. (1973) (Eds.) *Sport and Society: an anthology*; Sage, G.H. (1973) (Ed.) *Sport and American Society*, London, Addison Wesley; Albonico, R. and Pfister-Binz, K. (1971) (Eds.) *Sociology of Sport*, Basel; Mangan, J.A. (1973) *Physical Education and Sport: sociological and cultural perspectives*, Oxford, Blackwell.

2 Huizinga, J. (1970) *Homo Ludens*, Paladin.

3 Like many cultural and social conservatives, his critique of modern society is based on an idyllic view of an irretrievable past, and the assumption that modern society is in deep decline, for which the masses tend to be blamed.

4 For Marx's earlier theory of alienation see Easton, L.D. and Guddat, K.H. (1967) (Eds.) *Writings of the Young Marx on Philosophy and Society*, New York, Anchor. For Marx's more mature views on alienated labour see Marx, K. *Capital*, Vol. 1, Moscow, Foreign Languages Publishing House, (1961).

5 Loy, J.W. (1969) 'The nature of sport' in Loy, J.W. and Kenyon, G.S. *op. cit.*

6 Dunning, E. (1971) *op. cit.*, p. 5. See also Page, C.H. (1973) 'Pervasive themes in the study of sport', in Talamini, J.T. and Page. C.H. *op. cit.*

7 McIntosh, P. (1957) *Landmarks in the History of Physical Education*, London, Routledge and Kegan Paul; Mandell, R. (1972) *The Nazi Olympics*, London, Souvenir Press.

8 Dumazadier, J. (1964) 'The point of view of the social scientist', in Jokl, E. and Simon, E. (Eds.) *International Research in Sport and Physical Education*, Springfield, Mass., Thomas. On the historical development of leisure, recreation and sport in Britain see Malcolmson, R.W. (1973) *Popular Recreations in English Society 1700–1850*, Cambridge, Cambridge University Press; Bailey, P. (1978) *Leisure and Class in Victorian England*, London, Hutchinson.

9 For work that is explicitly functionalist see Kenyon, G.S. and Loy, J.W. (1969) 'Towards a sociology of sport', in Loy, J.W. and Kenyon, G.S. *op. cit.*; Luschen, G. (1967) 'The sociology of sport', *Current Sociology;* Edwards, H. (1973) *The Sociology of Sport Dorsey;* Guttman, A. (1978) *From Ritual to Record*, New York, Columbia University Press. Most other work in the sociology of sport is implicitly functionalist in the sense that it takes the existing social structure for granted.

10 Roberts, K. (1970) *Leisure*, London, Longmans, contains a particularly blatant statement of this view.

11 The fact that a lot of sports are not actually profitable for those who directly run and participate in them (for example, many of the English Football League clubs) and rely on patronage or sponsorship, should not be allowed to obscure the equally hard fact that organized sport these days is very big business indeed, and that it does make money for some people. One example is the profit derived from ownership of TV rights to sports spectacles.

12 Mallet, S. (1964) *The New Working Class*, Paris; Goldthorpe, J.H., Lockwood, D., Bechhofer, F. and Platt, J. (1969) *The Affluent Worker in the Class Structure*, Cambridge University Press; Burns, T. (1973) 'Leisure in industrial society', in Smith, M.A. *et al.* (Eds.) *Leisure and Society in Britain*, London, Allen Lane. All these studies conclude that non-work is more satisfying for workers than work itself.

13 Taylor, I. (1971) 'Soccer consciousness and soccer hooliganism', in Cohen, S. (Ed.) *Images of Deviance*, Harmondsworth, Penguin.

14 Miliband, R. (1968) *The State in Capitalist Society*, London, Wiedenfeld and Nicholson; Gamble, A. and Walton, P. (1977) *Capitalism in Crisis*, London, Macmillan.

15 Taylor, I. (unpublished paper) 'Social control through sport'. The plausibility of Taylor's claim is somewhat weakened by the fact that it is not supported by evidence on the subsequent performance of the Mexican economy.

16 Riordan, J. (1978) *Sport in Soviet Society*, London, Blackwell. Since at least 1925, sport has been used by the party-state as a political tool.

17 McIntosh, P. (1963) *Sport and Society*, London, Watts. It should be noted that the attempt to bring pressure to bear on Russia, by threatening to withdraw from the Moscow Olympics, shows that Western governments are openly prepared to use sport as a political weapon.

18 Capital investment in the public sector on sports facilities increased from £28 m. in 1965–66 to £48 m. in the year 1971–72 and in 1972–73 it reached £80 m. The figure does not take into account what is likely to be a much larger overall figure for capital investment in commercially-run private facilities like race tracks, bowling alleys, business-provided facilities for employees, facilities in private schools etc.

19 Sports Council Annual Report, 1972–73, p. 3.

20 For some details of the links between business personnel and sports see Brohm, J.-M. (1978) *Sport:*

A Prisoner of Measured Time, Inklinks; HOCH, P. (1972) *Rip Off the Big Game*. Doubleday; DAVIES, H. (1972) *The Glory Game*, London, Sphere; TAYLOR, I. (n.d.) *op. cit.*

21 HARGREAVES, J. (forthcoming) *Sport and Hegemony* Macmillan. See also LUKES, S. (1975) 'Political ritual and social integration' *Sociology*, Vol. 9, No. 2; PATTERSON, O. (1969) 'The cricket ritual in the West Indies', *New Society*, No. 352, 26 June.

22 HALL, S. (1978) 'The treatment of football hooliganism in the press', in INGHAM, R. *Football Hooliganism*, Interaction Imprints.

23 For the concept of hegemony see *Gramsci, A.* (1971) *The Prison Notebooks*, London, Lawrence and Wishart (edited and introduced by HOARE, Q. and NOWELL SMITH, P.).

5 Education and the Political Economy of Leisure

Ross Fergusson and George Mardle

How education relates to the mode and social relations of capitalist production has been one of the major preoccupations of the sociology of education during the 1970s. Two important factors have supported this development: first, an increased conceptual awareness of the role of political economy in educational processes, second, the dominant political consensus which has demanded a far greater articulation of the link between industrial needs and educational provision. Whilst we do not intend to ignore these developments we want to argue that such a concentration on the economic and industrial infrastructure has blinded us to a problem of potentially equal importance, namely leisure. For as the interest in our productive performance may only have started as a minor skirmish in the mid 70s, so also could the minimal noises currently made about leisure achieve such a meteoric rise. It is our contention that we ignore this area at our peril, not only in relation to its importance as a concomitant to any fully developed analysis of capitalist production but also in its complex relation to the nature and form of educational provision in our society. It is the concern of this paper to explore these dimensions of the arguments which we feel will make a contribution at this early stage to such an analysis.

'Age of leisure' and 'education for leisure' slogans made their early debuts in anticipation of the 80s. The 1978 Trades Union Congress was almost preoccupied with the theme. The Presidential address from David Basnett was the keynote:

> There is a need for our society to consider fundamental changes to accommodate ourselves to the fact that there will not be the demand for as many working hours as there has been in the past. We need to contemplate the reorganization of society so that we can give precedence to positive leisure rather than destructive idleness.
>
> We must see education and training not as occupying a period at the beginning of our lives, but as being a constant requirement throughout our lives. We must ensure that education is concerned with the promotion

Source: First published in this volume.

of effective social needs and cultural values as much as being a preparation for the discipline of work.

In sharing work we also need to structure our society and our time so that leisure and education, health and recreation compliment, but are no longer subservient to, the need to create wealth.[1]

It was of course the predicted microelectronics revolution which stimulated the preoccupation. The TUC resolved to press the government to:

give consideration to the opportunities which may be offered as a result of the new technology for greater leisure time

declare publicly their concern at the prospect of the resulting unemployment and support the move towards a shorter working week, month, year or lifetime with no deterioration in living standards[2]

Congress continued the theme in 1979, and it promises to become increasingly significant in union-management negotiations.[3]

We hardly need to list the gloomy unemployment predictions for the 1980s from pundits, economists and forecasting agencies: five million out of work by the 1990s is a frequently quoted figure.[4] Certainly predictions of two million unemployed during the 1980s are hardly even regarded as controversial.[5] Of course, all these figures would be considerably inflated were they to take account of large numbers of people who are effectively unemployed but never register as such – typically housewives and pensioners who would like to work.[6]

To most commentators the general reason for this trend is as self evident as the precise mechanics of it are complex: technological development means that machines increasingly take over production and require less and less human supervision. Deskilling and unemployment are the hallmarks of the highly mechanized industrial society, and the coming revolution in microelectronics will give the whole trend an unprecedented boost. This view is now commonplace, and typified in expositions like Clive Jenkins' *The Collapse of Work*[7] and Tom Forester's early *New Society* article on the silicon chip.[8] He argues:

... higher economic growth, far from mopping up unemployment, may lead to more unemployment. Growth leads to greater investment in new technology like microprocessors, which in time have a dramatic effect on productivity and therefore growth spells disaster for jobs.[9]

But the arguments are not all pessimistic. Some make the leap of faith conceptually by converting mass unemployment into the sci-fi society of leisure: a utopia of minimum working hours and maximum leisure. Furthermore, as with our society of increased production, it is education which will be able to welcome in this wonderful world. The process will, it seems, operate at two levels – first, by widening the definition of education such that it becomes another of the expanding service industries;[10] second, and perhaps more important in this context, by preparing pupils for their life of leisure in a variety of ways, from 'cultural enrichment' to consumer education.

The theme of education for leisure is clearly not a new one.[11] However, what we wish to argue in the remainder of this paper is that such concerns as have been voiced about it have tended to be reactions to a fairly well developed set of social conditions. Furthermore since they have come through in the rhetoric of educational policy the arguments have mystified and over-simplified the more complex social conditions within which they are embedded. In essence the rhetoric has implicitly taken for granted three problematic dichotomies which are characteristics of social and economic existence in the capitalist mode of production – namely work and leisure, production and consumption, the public and the private person. The dichotomies are congruent and complementary: work (wage labour) is the site of productive activity in which the public person relates in the public work role in a public setting; leisure (time away from work) is centrally devoted to consumption performed in the private context of the home in the private social grouping, the family.[12] In what follows we want to problematize the three dichotomies by situating them historically and pointing out some of the assumptions and interests underlying them. Schematically, we can construct a periodization of attitudes to the three dichotomies both in the educational system and in the wider society. This will be a broad-brush picture, representing trends and emphases, not dramatic swings or hard and fast changes.

Post War Recovery

Our first period, the end of World War II to the early 1960s, is identifiable as a period of post war recovery and consolidation. Both in education and work there was a clear production orientation. Optimistic visions of the meritocratic future achieved through scientific progress 'white-hot technology' and the growing economic cake matched up with relatively full employment and the assertion of the right to work. State education was clearly seen as being in the service of production – most notably in the unprecedented expansion of post-compulsory education in this period. The Petry and Barlow Committees of the 1940s resulted in the National Advisory Council on Education for Industry and Commerce which initiated, in the 1950s, that major symbol of education-industry links, the sandwich course. Technical college status was raised and 'education for technology' became a slogan of the Eden administration. The 1962 *Anderson Report* gave technical students grant parity and in 1964 the industrial training boards were set up to decide course administration and content. The commitment to the tripartite system and secondary schooling was re-affirmed, largely on the grounds of the differential maximization of manpower potential. Primary schooling epitomized 'traditional methods'[13] and above all the very climate of activity inspired the development of human capital theory as the major legitimation of the system. Leisure provision was not a significant issue in education or society. It was not seen as the business of school, employer or state to intervene. It was more a space between work, a secondary reward for the primary activity of production. It did not constitute a rationale for a healthy society, but was in essence a private matter for the individual.

Early 1960s – Mid 1970s

The 1960s are noted for their rejection of the values of the post war era. The emphasis shifted. The individual, the private person, was seen as neglected in the mass social enterprize. Simultaneously the fruits of post war recovery were enjoyed in increasingly conspicuous and affluent consumption and were rejected, typically by young people, as hollow materialism. The classic researches of the period showed that work had ceased to be a 'central life interest', particularly in the blue collar sector.[14] Leisure potential expanded greatly: the histories of the period point to the increasing availability of cheap cars as the most significant single factor – perhaps only the most obvious tip of an ice-berg of consumption.[15]

Much of this change in emphasis was very clearly reflected in education. The individual child was moved to the centre of the curriculum, subject barriers dissolved, discussions opened; desirable skills and knowledge were approached as they related to the child's interests and propensities. In secondary schooling much of the then current advocacy of comprehensivization gave social values parity with economic values. The modern curricular methods pioneered in this period were later to be decried as failing to provide the skills required by the economic system. Tertiary education became more 'open' after Robbins, with unprecedented expansions in the 'liberal' arts and social sciences as well as in science. The writing of the deschoolers at the end of this period articulated some of the more radical philosophical links between the critique of materialistic industrial activities and the failures of schooling which the 1960s educational progressives had tried to address.[16]

The Late Seventies

By the mid 1970s the balance was tipping. Conciliatory explanations for economic decline were sought, and an education system which had reduced its emphasis on skills in favour of personal development became a prime target.[17] This was a central theme of Callaghan's 1976 Ruskin College speech at the beginning of the 'Great Debate' whose refrain was the re-establishment of education-industry links:

> The goals of our education from nursery school through to adult education are clear enough. They are to equip children to the best of their ability for a lively constructive place in society and also fit them to do a job of work. Not one or the other, but both. For many years the accent was simply on fitting a so-called inferior group of children with just enough learning to earn their living in the factory ... The balance was wrong in the past. We have a responsibility now to see that we do not get it wrong in the other direction. There is no virtue in producing socially well adjusted members of society who are unemployed because they do not have the skills ...

Despite its emphasis on balance, the interpretation of this keynote speech for the late 1970s saw it as placing emphasis on the production orientation. The speeches, the papers and the educational press of the late 1970s were preoccupied with skills, training and the service of declining industry.

Yet, for all its similarity in orientation to the first period we considered, this era does not merely represent a cyclical return to a production focus, but rather a definite progression, a qualitatively different orientation from the earlier period. It is not a reaction to prevailing economic conditions, but is a more complex ideological intervention. The point is that, whereas the prevailing objective conditions of the productive forces could be seen to link closely with the ideological rhetoric of the 1950s – mid 1970s,[18] it is much more difficult to substantiate such a link in the current arguments. Central to this is the difficulty in reconciling the net de-skilling of work (mechanization, plus atomization of tasks) and the net upskilling of work entrants (qualification inflation) with protestations of insufficient skilled manpower. In consequence the rhetoric of balance provides a neat ideological fulcrum upon which to balance the role of education. It is merely a matter of adjustment, not a matter of fundamental change.

Within this historical consideration of the relationship between work, leisure and education, we have sought to identify those key elements of policy which have influenced our understanding of the relationship. For, in so much as such rhetoric seeks to locate production as public activity and leisure as a private activity, then policy can only mystify the more complex and subtle logic of capitalist production. In order to suggest an alternative hypothesis we now want to consider the analysis of work and leisure in relation to the particular social formation and conditions in which they are embedded.

Following Marx, we begin from the premise that productive activity is the essential and distinguishing characteristic of human beings: through that activity they realize themselves. Now, insofar as work (i.e. wage labour) in modern society can be equated with production and leisure with consumption, to dichotomize the two conceptually in time, in place, and in social organization is to distort an essential human process. There is nothing natural or given about the dichotomy, and most industrial/anthropological studies of leisure point to the indistinguishability of work and leisure in many societies.[19] We want to argue that the dichotomy is historically specific and integral to the very logic of capitalist society. In such society leisure is predominantly ameliorative and is the logical counterpart of alienated production: 'free' leisure supposedly offers the opportunity for self-determination denied in production, providing consumption – oriented 'activity contexts'[20] which seem to justify the tedium of production. But in fact the commodities consumed in leisure remain as separate and alien to their consumer as the commodities he produces in work; the dialectic between subject and object is stunted. Leisure, then, comes to serve a social control function, ameliorating the deleterious effects of the mode of production. In so much as work and leisure may themselves be considered as a dichotomy inherent in industrial society, the particular social formation fosters another dichotomy, that between production and consumption. Alienated consumption – in which a product becomes an anonymous appropriated commodity, divorced of its social life and witless of its dialectical relationship with the process of which it is a consequence – increasingly becomes the sequel to alienated production, under which the overriding aim to arrive at an appropriable and tangible commodity to which an exchange value can be tacked denies the social process of production and perverts it from end-in-itself to means-to-the-end of producing commodity. As man is compelled to alienated production under capitalism, he is restricted to the role of energy-expending catalyst, both unchanged by and not objectified in the act of production. The alienated consumer does not metabolize but merely digests the commodities he acquires. The rationale lies not in being sustained and developed by the product (the counterpart of true social production) but in consuming for its own sake, a distraction from the failure to develop imposed by economy-centred rather than person-centred production.

Within the totality of productive activity this dichotomy is equally applicable to the institutionalization of leisure activities. The Sunday-driving syndrome in which the passenger consumes but does not touch or know the countryside; the package holiday on which the tourist takes 'a programmed gawk at strangers'[21]; the reduction of the sportsman to armchair spectator; the elevation of vital life functions like eating to saleable leisure forms like gastronomy; all epitomize the conversion of leisure into institutionalized alienated consumption.

Adorno and Horkheimer elaborate a similar argument describing the rendition of culture as a consumable leisure commodity in which consumer and consumed never dialectically transform each other:

> The man with leisure has to accept what the culture manufacturers offer him. Kant's formalism still expected a contribution from the individual, who was thought to relate the varied experiences of the senses to fundamental concepts; but industry robs the individual of his function. Its prime service to the customer is to do his schematizing for him.[22]

Thus the alienated consumer of the mass culture commodity does not bring himself to a painting, a book, a film to complete it and give it the life which it must lack until it is perceived; rather it is presented to him complete, divorced from its social context and oblivious to his perception. He leaves it having seen an objective thing, and this reification means that the only subsequent satisfactory action must be more of the same.

The ameliorative quality of leisure, to which we have referred, is nothing new: it has frequently been argued in the past that the personal spending power conferred by wage-labour, and the availability of extensive variations within a minor range of consumer commodities on which it can be exercised, is the major practical condition which ensures the continuation of the capitalist project. There are, however, limitations to the ameliorative efficacy of purchasing goods as compensation for alienating work. Apart from the limitations inherent in the poor pay of workers and the finite nature of physical resources, the Saturday spending spree or the occasional splash out on an expensive consumer durable do not extend their 'satisfaction' to all non-work time. In contrast, the leisure commodity offers more: the television emits constantly consumable images, the car offers infinite weekend cruising. Traditional research points strongly to the ameliorative effects of leisure – primarily by correlating work and leisure styles which demonstrate the most passive, consumption-oriented leisure forms to be most popular among that sector of the population which experiences the most (psychologically) alienating work.[23] Others view the link as quite simply the popular utilization of whatever is available by way of an improvement on work: the utilization of prescribed activity contexts. However one approaches or explains the link, the importance of ameliorative leisure seems clear if one imagines the complete withdrawal of such provision in the contemporary context. The problems of disaffected youth excluded from or uncatered for by existing institutional leisure (the usual account of vandalism) would arguably extend through the population. Few police constabulary bosses would be slow to anticipate the threat to civil order if electric power was cut and the pubs and clubs closed on a warm Saturday night.

Leisure does not only have an ameliorative effect. In diverse ways it confirms the 'naturalness' of the particular social world. This is particularly true of the culture of mass media – the epitome of industrialized leisure. The constant subjection of leisure consumers to identifiable images of society – and the confinement of discussion, questioning, choice and experiment within the familiar parameters – can only serve to ensure the deep legitimation of those parameters as natural. This correspondence is neither an insignificant coincidence, nor the result of a conspiracy, but what Adorno and Horkheimer describe as 'a circle of manipulation and retroactive need'.[24] The careful selector mechanisms which control access to the mass media of the culture industry are geared to the satisfaction of a level of popular demand which they themselves have helped to create and define. Thus, for Adorno and Horkheimer, the indistinguishability of the world portrayed by the culture industry and the world of work is so great that 'as soon as the very existence of these institutions no longer made it obligatory to use them, there would be no great urge to do so'.[25]

The phenomenal worlds of the soap opera, the sitcom, the news bulletin, the strip cartoon, the film romance; the omnipresence of the pop-station in factory, shop and restaurant serve to bind leisure and work along certain lines, which become increasingly taken for granted:

> Amusement under late capitalism is the prolongation of work. It is sought after as an escape from the mechanized work process, and to recruit strength in order to be able to cope with it again. But at the same time mechanization has such power over a man's leisure and happiness, and so profoundly determines the manufacture of amusement goods, that his experiences are inevitably after-images of the work process itself. The ostensible content is merely a faded foreground, what sinks in is the automatic succession of standardized operations. What happens at work, in the factory or in the office can only be escaped from by approximation to it in one's leisure time. All amusement suffers from this incurable malady. Pleasure hardens into boredom because, if it is to remain pleasure, it must not demand any effort and therefore moves rigorously into the worn grooves of association.[26]

We are therefore suggesting that the dichotomy of work/production with leisure/consumption can be located within the specific development of conditions of capitalist production. Furthermore, changes in emphasis on either side of such polarities by educational policies represent no more than idological reactions to those conditions. But the new, and somewhat more complex, conditions now evident give rise to a more subtle and interventionist role by the state and, therefore, a wider role for education in such a process. The current overt concern with the production emphasis merely mystifies this more insiduous development, ignoring both the aspects of production already with us, and the structural involvement of the state in a form of mass leisure which offers to make unemployment invisible while ensuring capital accumulation.

The Coming Age of Leisure?

As we noted earlier it is technological advancement, most recently in the form of microprocessors, which has occasioned alarm about unemployment – which has, itself, become converted into an emphasis on the coming leisure age. Historically there is little evidence to support this connection. Indeed, the correlation may be the inverse: as Wilensky observes, man in modern industrial society may just have regained the position of his thirteenth century counterpart in terms of real leisure time.[27]

An increasing number of commentators are now agreed that, in effect, industrial societies generally are not leisured societies.[28] In so far as it is possible to dichotomize work and leisure in them, historical and contemporary 'less developed' economies are characterized by greater leisure time. Among the explanations for this are: seasonal and diurnal time limits to production (especially primary production) in non-industrial societies and the absorption of increased productive capacity in increased ranges of consumption in industrial societies.[29] Even by comparison with other periods since industrialization, technologically-based promises of increased leisure in the second half of the twentieth century have been almost completely unfounded. Marglin argues that the centralization of production which was the hallmark of industrialization was previously inspired by the desire to extract increased productive effort from every worker i.e. to diminish his leisure time.[30] If this thesis is correct, then the early nineteenth century probably represents the most dramatic single reduction in available leisure time; and the reforms of later that century into the Victorian era – typically the Ten Hours Bill – the most dramatic increases. De Grazia shows that in the USA the most significant reductions in working hours since 1850 occured during the first three decades of the twentieth century, when the average working week shrank from 60.1 to 45.7 hours.[31] In England the working week became a slender 40 minutes shorter between 1948 and 1968.[32]

We would argue that this pattern, that hours worked remain constant while supposedly labour saving technology proliferates, represents a precedent in the capitalist mode of production, and one which will no more be broken by the inception of microprocessors than it was by the industrial application of centrally generated electricity. So long as the analysis of applications of new technologies assumes that the range of future economic and productive activity remains static, projections inevitably predict job-loss/reduced working hours. But by vastly extending production the steam engine, for example, created work, rather than eliminated it. At the very least new technologies require trainers and servicers; in some cases they merely transform work, in others they extend services.[33] It is instructive to consider why the unemployment predicted at the beginning of the computer revolution never materialized. At one level, clerks merely 'became' card punchers or tape operators; at another, the frenetic updating of hardware called for constant retraining in software; at yet another, the potential of information retrieval was dramatically improved.

A further explanation is precisely that leisure is a consumption activity. De Grazia has documented the way in which options for increased leisure are effectively whittled away by the desire to own more leisure-specific goods.[34] Another explanation which has been little explored is that the time/labour saving capacity of many goods – particularly domestic devices – is exaggerated if not illusory. The rationale for production of such goods is that they attract high profits and for purchase that, while for members of higher socio-economic echelons they *are* time saving, they merely confer status by emulation on those lower echelons for whom they save no time.[35]

The significance of proclamations of the leisure age then, cannot be explained primarily in technological terms. They *may* be the beginning of a period of accommodation to new conditions of production which are probably several decades away, but the first tremors of which are being felt in the economy now. Rather, microprocessors offer a technocratic legitimation of an adjustment which is necessary for rather different reasons.

The Structural Significance of Leisure

Paradoxically we agree with the pundits that unemployment will occasion the society of leisure. It will however be some years hence and will result from the saturation of commodity markets and not from technological unemployment in itself. The market for tangible commodities as vehicles for capital accumulation is probably capable of coping with the redeployment of surplus labour *post* the micro-electronic revolution into other industries. But that capacity is not infinite. Saturation point comes when the population cannot be sold any more goods (without themselves developing an increased potential for capital accumulation). Added to this, the increasing cost of raw materials from dwindling reserves inhibits the continued accumulation of capital through the high turnover of low-cost, short-life, fast-obsolescent goods. This poses a serious threat, though not in essence a new one: with mass production and limitations on resource use, modern capitalism has turned increasingly to the service sector as a location for selling something 'useful' at a profit. The amount of social productive power devoted to the manufacture of tangible commodities in this country is relatively tiny already. Half the population works for a wage and, of them, only one third actually contribute to the production of anything tangible, while only one third of *their* working life is spent at work (and still less, presumably, actually working).[36] This represents $3\frac{1}{2}$ per cent of the total social time available. So, even adding a liberal 25 per cent for that proportion of the population excluded from useful production by youth, old age or infirmity, one hour's work per (fit) person per day could maintain current levels of output of material goods. Hitherto this minimal requirement has been disguised by the existence of a mass of tertiary sector jobs – office workers, bureaucrats, distributive trades etc. Now even this burgeoning sector may be unable, as we know it, to contain surplus productive power; the finite nature of consumption of tangible commodities within the current distribution of wealth becomes increasingly apparent. Increased diversification into service/leisure-based industries may merely be presenting a new enslavement to divided wage labour. More people become obliged to work longer to earn the exchange which buys more leisure commodities where production itself ties more people to the very same division of labour. In consequence both work and leisure can be seen as part of the same set of social conditions. Thus the leisure industry, in common with other forms of commodity activity, facilitates the appropriation of social productive power. More importantly it also embodies an unprecedented capacity for the accumulation of capital. Its inessential nature makes it a potent means for acquiring profit. Pricing is minimally tied to commonplace raw materials, so that everyday points of comparison for judging 'fairness' of price are almost impossible. The market forces of supply and demand have an almost free hand. For the economic system which has long struggled to balance credibility in production with built-in obsolecence, minimal durability, increasingly frequent fashion phases etc., the possibility of selling a seat at a film, a nightclub or on a holiday tour is an undreamt of gift, for they can be repeatedly resold and the market can almost infinitely absorb more. There is no precedent for the elasticity of the leisure market.[37]

The industrialization of leisure which we describe got under way in the 1960s. The qualitative difference in the 1980s anticipation of the leisure age lies in the significance of state intervention in leisure provision. Two facets of the intervention are indicative of the transmogrification of leisure from family concern through industrial enterprise and now to mask for unemployment: the particular emergent form of state intervention makes leisure an act both of compulsory consumption and social control. The extent and nature of this intervention is beginning to be documented elsewhere. Briefly, the major areas of provision are emerging as sport, the arts, adult education and youth organizations. John Hargreaves indicates that the state acts in 'those spheres which the private sector cannot or will not manage but which, nevertheless, are necessary as an infrastructure for its activities to continue'.[38] But what is of greater significance is that state provision differs from private sector provision in effectively constituting *compulsory* consumption of services – not merely in the sense that payment through taxation is compulsory but because the use of facilities provided becomes institutionalized within a world of limited 'activity contexts'. Leisure, thereby, is brought into the mainstream of economic activity and effectively ensures further capital accumulation – both through the servicing provided by private enterprise, which is always an adjunct of state provision, and through the differential redistribution of resources effected by any state intervention in their collection and rechannelling.

The element of social control effected by state intervention typically has some parallels with the enterprises of the more paternalistic early industrialists who made 'the firm' provide in all spheres for their workers. The compulsory consumption of facilities ensures that free time is devoted to 'approved' activities – a low key act of containment – but also offers the opportunity for sponsoring socially valued attitudes, from competitiveness in sport to the accumulation of received knowledge which characterizes the curricula of adult education.

Particularly telling in this context as a form of state intervention are the job creation programmes which proliferated in the late 1970s. They indicate precisely how, as we have argued, leisure and unemployment increasingly promise to become different facets of the same thing. The professed intention of the programmes was to reduce unemployment (albeit it with an element of training/rehabilitation) but the brief of programme organizers, to avoid competing with existing local pro-ductive enterprise, effectively meant that activity was confined to economically peripheral projects which often resembled leisure activities – renovating old locomotives, rural conservation work, etc. As with leisure, apparently economically insignificant activity is tied in to the economic structure.

Increasingly, therefore, as the involvement of the state in leisure and its projection as a public rather than private concern becomes evident, we might expect a congruent role for education. Whilst its precise form and content may only be projected we nevertheless have some historical evidence from which to extrapolate. It is to a consideration of that which we now turn.

Education and Leisure

The earliest calls for education for leisure since the war, to which we alluded at the beginning of this paper, typically confirmed the conception of leisure as an ameliorative adjunct to alienated production. Almost all came within the con-sumption orientated period we defined as early 1960s to early 1970s and almost all tended to be premised on the same anticipation of deskilled mechanized alienating production which reappears in the modern 1980s versions as technological un-employment.

The emergence of interest in education for leisure can be traced to the report of a government commission in 1959, the *Crowther Report*, in which there was a relatively novel suggestion that the proposed County Colleges (which never materialized) should devote some of their part-time continuing education of the young post-school workforce to stimulating 'hobby-type' interests which had been formed in school but were readily dropped by most individuals on starting work. In the following years there were some classic statements which took this up. In 1961, E.B. Castle wrote:

On leaving school many [pupils] will enter the world of the conveyor belt. In this world, young persons are living two lives at the same time – a nut-tapping life and a dream life. The problem for teachers is: How shall we enrich the young worker's dream life? And the solution ... possibly lies in richly educated emotions, so that while he is turning his screws and she is filling her cigarette packet, daydreams arise from a healthier sub-conscious.[39]

In essence, education was not, therefore, to be designed for production in its narrowest sense but also for making the accepted alienation of productive activity bearable. Ironically the *Newsom Report* (1963) takes this quote to task, using it as the leading quotation of an important section, but countering it with an approach which is in essence the corollary not the antithesis of the values implicit in Castle's statement. In Newsom the idea developed that education should direct itself towards leisure as an alternative to providing skills which would never be used by what have become known as 'Newsom children', condemned to tedious and nauseous jobs. The emphasis therefore switches from ignoring work to a more positive idea of living for leisure. Choosing judiciously between leisure time experiences becomes identified as an important educational objective. Personal development for a fulfilling leisure life ousts development of marketable job skills as the major pre-occupation of schools. The unsatisfactory nature of production, and a mode of production which consigns increasing numbers of children to the employment scrap heap are never questioned; the contradiction between this acceptance and the recognition that the same children have talents worth cultivating for leisure is never realized.

By 1965 this attitude was beginning to be incorporated into the staple diet of most intending teachers – Musgrave's multi-editioned text *The Sociology of Education*:

Can the schools help the future workers both to use their increasing leisure and to find satisfaction in a life marked by an uninteresting job ... [They] can teach children how to make the best use of their spare time. Life away from work will be full enough to compensate for the *dullness* of time spent at work. Secondly schools can teach in such a way that children want to continue to learn. Then men and women will have the desire and the intellectual equipment with which to seek a worthwhile life away from their jobs.[40]

'Continuing education' became a theme of the 1970s with education identified as an expanding leisure form. In some countries it is a major facet of state intervention in the provision of leisure – in Sweden for example, part-time adult education has a larger population than the schools.[41] The interest is encouraged by the international bureaucracies – the OECD, for instance, has made strong recommendations for its development.[42] In this country the Open University – and particularly its Continuing Education unit – offers this new leisure form.

By extending these arguments it might be assumed that the prescriptions of the past will, in essence, be re-interpreted in the light of present circumstances. We base this assumption not on particular requirements specified by advocates but precisely on the fact that demands for education for leisure have always tended to be vague in the area of content, presumably on the assumption that it is self-evident or would be self-directing. If this is so, we would anticipate the following elements in a 'curriculum for leisure':

Consumer education, geared to facilitating judicious selection between leisure and commodity choices to the end of 'maximizing possibilities for self development and minimizing exploitation'.

Cultural education geared primarily to the consumption but also the production of music, painting, film, theatre, literature etc.

Sport education

The cultivation of 'hobby' interests.

The significance of such a curriculum within the political economic context we have described should be evident, at least in so far as it represents a set of social relations of consumption congruent to the current prevailing social relations to production.[43]

The leisure curriculum threatens to trivialize, domesticate and contain social productive power in the mass of the population in the same way as the society of leisure is the recasting of the society of unemployment. A consumption orientation in education presents no attractive alternative to even the most slavish of production orientations. Yet unless we develop more rigorous attempts to understand the complexity of the work/leisure dichotomy in capitalist society it is one we shall end up with, not simply as yet another re-orientation but one which, like current preoccupations, is more subtle and diffuse.

As yet alternatives which recognise this analysis and its implications are few and remain underdeveloped.[44] But, in general terms at least, we would argue that educationalists should not be tempted by the utopian visions of the leisure society in constructing curricula in the last two decades of the century. The social productive individual must remain at the centre. The challenge is to arrive at a production orientation in education which sits between a slavish induction into the capitalist division of labour and the domestication of social productive power in peripheral activities which currently characterize so-called 'productive' leisure.

Acknowledgement

The authors would like to thank Madeleine MacDonald for her helpful comments on an earlier draft.

Notes and References

1 Report of the 110th Annual Trades Union Congress, 1978, London, Trades Union Congress.

2 *Ibid.*, from composite motions 9.12, pp. 477–8.

3 See, for example, JENKINS, C. and SHERMAN, B. (1977) *Computers and the Unions*, London, Longman, especially Chap. 13.

4 Discussed by FORESTER, T. (1978) 'Society with chips and without jobs', *New Society*, 16 November, pp. 387–8. Indeed this figure is arguably conservative if one takes account of the projected growth in the Labour force by $2\frac{1}{4}$ million (9 per cent) between 1976 and 1991. (Department of Employment Gazette, June 1979, London HMSO).

5 The first editions of the weekly press for the 80s, for example, bristled with such statistics (e.g. *Now*, (1980) 1 January).

6 COUNTER INFORMATION SERVICES (1979) *Who's next for the chop*, Anti Report number 14, London, CIS, estimates that official statistics cover only 77 per cent of those wanting work.

7 JENKINS, C. (1979) *The Collapse of Work*.

8 FORESTER, T. (1978) *op. cit.*

9 Most of the predominantly journalistic (and pessimistic) writing on this subject leaves out of account why it is that these technologies get developed while other crucial technologies (e.g. the exploitation of 'natural' energy) remain on the drawing board. The argument that it is the desire to guarantee increasing profit which impels selective technological development remains in the blind spot of most commentators' vision.

10 It is assumed that machines and microprocessors will not take over such areas, an assumption already under threat.

11 Most of the traditional arguments are rehearsed in Stanley Parker's books on the sociology of leisure, which appeared during the 1970s.

12 Of course, this conceptualization has several limitations. It ignores the whole element of *production* in leisure – and we take this up later. It also ignores that large proportion of the population engaged in labour – typically domestic labour – but not for a wage, for whom the split is far less clear cut; this requires separate treatment which space does not permit. It may also seem to trivialize the ameliorative effects of leisure: but the whole point is that leisure 'really does' make up for work for many people who prefer the goods at a price to no goods at no price. TAYLOR, L. and COHEN, S. (1976) *Escape attempts*, London, Allen Lane, document this graphically. We do not wish to suggest that all activity in capitalist society is inevitably an epiphenomenon of the mode of production; but we do wish to show its significant influence in the sphere of leisure.

13 A theme returned to in the 1970s when it was inferred that in previous time such methods had usefully served a 'healthy economy'.

14 Most notably DUBIN, R. (1963) 'Industrial workers' worlds', in SMIGEL, E. (Ed.) *Work and Leisure*, New Haven, College and University Press; GOLDTHORPE, J., LOCKWOOD, D., BECHHOFER, F. and PLATT, J. (1968) *The Affluent Worker*, Cambridge, Cambridge University Press.

15 In the same period there were enormous increases in such areas as package holidays, eating out, the hardware and software of hi-fi and television. There was also a heavy increase in secondary consumption – e.g. roads.

16 This is not to deny the argument that such liberal ideology functions as a more covert but equally effective form of control. But whatever the *effect*, it is difficult to deny the sincerity and articulated motivations of individual progressives without positing a conspiracy theory.

17 For two excellent articulations of this complex process see HALL, S. (1979) 'The great moving right show', *Marxism Today*, January, and the UNIVERSITY OF BIRMINGHAM CENTRE FOR CONTEMPORARY CULTURAL STUDIES EDUCATION GROUP (forthcoming 1981) *Unpopular Education*, London, Hutchinson.

18 It is possible for instance to argue that, given the economic situation and the 'laws' of capitalist production the post war production orientation in educational rhetoric and practice, particularly at tertiary level, was rational and effective. Similarly the rhetoric and practice of the 60s period 'made sense' in exploiting its comparative affluence in response to shifting intellectual values and a bulge in the age cohort reaching tertiary level.

19 See for example PARKER, S. (1971) *The Future of Work and Leisure*, London, MacGibbon and Kee, Chap. 3.

20 'Activity contexts' (typically work, community and the natural environment) are a central theme in GINTIS, H. (1972) 'Towards a Political Economy of Education', reproduced in DALE, R., ESLAND, G. and MACDONALD, M. (Eds.) (1976) *Schooling and Capitalism*, London, Routledge and Kegan Paul. Gintis writes:

These activity contexts as I shall show are structured in turn by the way people structure their *productive relations*. The study of activity contexts in capitalist society must begin with an understanding of the basic economic institutions which regulate their historical development (p. 11 Emphasis in original).

21 – to use Ivan Illich's phrase from *Disabling Professions*, (1977) London, Calder and Boyars.

22 ADORNO, T. and HORKHEIMER, M. (1973) 'The Culture Industry: enlightenment as mass deception', in CURRAN, J. *et al.*, (Eds.) (1977) *Mass Communication and Society*, London. Edward Arnold, p. 124.

23 Typically FRIEDMANN, G. (1956) *The Anatomy of Work*, London, Heinemann.

24 *Op. cit.*, p. 121.

25 *Op. cit.*, p. 139. We take up this point of the obligatory use of institutions later in relation to state provision of leisure.

26 *Op. cit.*, p. 137.

27 Quoted in JOSEPHSON, E. and JOSEPHSON, M. (1962) *Man Alone*, p. 29.

28 E.g. PARKER, S. (1975) 'Work and leisure: theory and fact', and BASINI, A. (1975) 'Education for leisure: a sociological critique', in HOWARTH, J. and SMITH, M.A. (Eds.) (1975) *Work and Leisure*, London, Lepus Books. This theme is also the burden of LINDER, S. (1970) *The Harried Leisure Class*, New York, Columbia University Press.

29 This is central theme of DE GRAZIA, S. (1962) *Of Time, Work and Leisure*, New York, 20th Century Fund Inc. see p. 223.

30 MARGLIN, S. (1976) 'What do bosses do?', in Gorz, A. (Ed.) *Division of Labour*, Brighton, Harvester Press.

31 *Ibid.*, p. 441.

32 United Nations Statistical Yearbooks for 1962 and 1970.

33 The 1979 TUC Annual Economic Review, for example, elaborates on this counter-argument to 'technological unemployment'.

34 *Ibid.*

35 A commodity is only time saving for any given individual in so far as it takes that individual less time to earn the money to buy it than the commodity takes to do the job in question as compared to another method of doing that job. Hence the time-saving capacity of a commodity cannot be generalized but is a function of the rate per unit time at which the potential user earns money. In practice, though, individuals tend to work on the assumption that time saving capacity is inherent in the commodity and never calculate its time saving value for their particular circumstances. The status conferred by possessing such a commodity is in real terms a greater attraction and the individual may actually 'lose' time in buying the commodity (i.e. spend longer earning to buy it than he realizes in using it). It is in this sense that technology may errode leisure. See FERGUSSON, R. (1978) *Education and the ecological crisis: a sociological perspective*, unpublished MA thesis, University of Keele.

36 Based on statistics presented by SCHUMACHER, E. (1973) *Small is Beautiful*, London, Sphere Books, p. 125.

37 Parker's statistics for 1973 show that leisure accounted for on average of 23.4 per cent of consumer expenditure. See PARKER, S. (1975) *op. cit.*, p. 118.

38 HARGREAVES, J. (1975) 'The political economy of mass sport', reproduced in this volume, p. 59.

39 CASTLE, E. (1961) *Ancient Education and Today*, Hammondsworth, Penguin Books, p. 82.

40 MUSGRAVE, P. (1965) *The Sociology of Education*, London, Methuen, p. 110.

41 Figures are cited by ILLICH, I. and VERNE, E. (1976) *Imprisoned in the Global Classroom*, London, Writers' and Readers' Publishing Co-operative, p. 20.

42 See for example ORGANIZATION FOR ECONOMIC COOPERATION AND DEVELOPMENT (1976) *Beyond Compulsory Schooling*, OECD.

43 BASINI, A. (1975) *op. cit.*, provides a good culturalist critique of the typically envisaged forms of education for leisure.

44 One example may be the 'black economy', i.e. production for money and barter outside the capitalist wage labour system. Gershuny and Pahl identify this as a form of resistance to unemployment and exploitation and predict the growth of the 'self service' economy where only commodities not services are bought in the formal economy. See GERSHUNY, J. and PAHL, R. (1980) 'Britain in the decade of the three economies', *New Society*, 3 January.

6   Subculture : Image and Noise

Dick Hebdige

The emergence of spectacular youth groups in the post-War period has frequently been interpreted in the mass media as symptomatic of a more general cultural decline. Since the invention of the term 'teen-ager' in the early 1950s, youth has been habitually invoked as a metaphor for change, as a sign of the troubled and troubling times. This process of symbolisation, amplification and 'moral panic' has been most adequately treated by those sociologists who operate a transactional model of deviant behaviour. For instance, Stan Cohen has described in detail how one particular moral panic (surrounding the mod-rocker conflict of the mid-1960s) was launched and sustained.[1] However, the imagery in which subcultures are presented in the media is frequently ambiguous. The members of a subculture are made to appear both more *and less* exotic than they actually are. They are seen both as dangerous aliens and boisterous kids, wild animals and wayward pets. Roland Barthes furnishes a key to this paradox in his description of 'identification' – one of the seven rhetorical figures which, according to Barthes (1972), distinguishes the meta-language of bourgeois mythology. He characterises the petit-bourgeois as a person ' . . . unable to imagine the Other . . . the Other is a scandal which threatens his existence'.[2]

Two basic strategies have been evolved for dealing with this threat. First, the Other can be trivialized, naturalized, domesticated. Here the difference is simply denied, 'Otherness is reduced to sameness'.[3] Alternatively, the Other can be transformed into meaningless exotica, a 'pure object, a spectacle, a clown'.[4] In this case, the difference is consigned to a place beyond analysis. Spectacular subcultures are continually being defined in precisely these terms. Soccer hooligans, for example, are typically placed beyond the 'bounds of common decency' and are classified as 'animals'.[5] On the other hand, the punks tended to be resituated by the press in the family, perhaps because members of the subculture seemed to deliberately obscure their origins and eagerly embraced their role as social outcasts. Certainly, like every other youth culture, punk was perceived as a threat to the family. Occa-

Source: Earlier versions of this article appeared as *Subculture: the meaning of style* and 'Putting on the style', in *Time Out*, August 1979, pp. 17–23. This version appears for the first time in this volume.

sionally, this threat was represented in literal terms. For example, the *Daily Mirror* (1 August, 1977) carried a photograph of a child lying in the road after a punk-ted confrontation under the headline 'Victim of the Punk Rock Punch Up: The Boy Who Fell Foul of the Mob'. In this case, punk's threat to the family was made 'real' (that could be my child!) through the ideological framing of photographic evidence which is popularly regarded as unproblematic.

None the less, on other occasions, the opposite line was taken. For whatever reason, the inevitable glut of articles gleefully denouncing the latest punk outrage was counterbalanced by an equal number of items devoted to the small details of punk family life. For instance, the 15 October, 1977 issue of *Woman's Own* carried an article entitled 'Punks and Mothers' which stressed the classless, fancy-dress aspects of punk. Photographs depicting punks with smiling mothers, reclining next to the family pool, playing with the family dog were placed above a text which dwelt on the ordinariness of individual punks: 'It's not as rocky horror as it appears' ... 'punk can be a family affair'; ... 'punks as it happens are non-political' and, most insidiously, albeit accurately: 'Johnny Rotten is as big a household name as Hughie Green'. Throughout the summer of 1977, the *People* and the *News of the World* ran items on punk babies and punk-ted weddings. All these articles served to minimize the Otherness so stridently proclaimed in punk style, and defined the subculture in precisely those terms which it sought most vehemently to resist and deny.

But how does a phenomenon like the punk subculture emerge, what functions does it fulfil for its members, and what subversive value, if any, can we attach to its distinctive forms? To answer these questions we must first examine in more detail the relationship between subculture and style.

Paul Willis (1978) first applied the term 'homology' to subculture (the term was originally used in an anthropological context by Levi-Strauss) in his study of hippies and motor-bike boys, using it to describe the symbolic fit between the values and life styles of a group, its subjective experience and the musical forms it uses to express or reinforce its focal concerns. In *Profane Culture*[6] Willis shows how, contrary to the popular myth which presents subcultures as lawless forms, the internal structure of any particular subculture is characterised by an extreme orderliness: each part is organically related to other parts and it is through the fit between them that the members of a subculture makes sense of the world. For instance, it was the homology between an alternative value system ('Tune in, turn on, drop out'), hallucinogenic drugs and acid rock which made the hippy culture cohere as a 'whole way of life' for individual hippies. This approach was extended and refined in *Resistance through Rituals*.[7] The authors explored the ways in which selected objects – items of dress, language, types of music etc. – were symbolically 'appropriated' by the members of a subculture and 'made to reflect, express and resonate ... aspects of group life'. In these 'objects the members of a subculture could see their central values held and reflected'.

The skinheads were cited to exemplify this principle. The boots, braces and cropped hair were only considered appropriate and, hence, meaningful because they communicated the desired qualities: 'hardness, masculinity, and working-classness'. In this way 'The symbolic objects – dress, appearance, language, ritual occasions, styles of interaction, music – were made to form a unity with the group's relations, situation, experience'. Clearly it was through a process of this kind that the punks were able to use objects to construct and communicate a distinctive group identity. By focussing on punk style, we can explore in greater detail the implications of the homology model for a study of subculture.

Punk made its sensational debut on the British streets during the long hot summer of 1976. In London, especially in the south west in the vicinity of the Kings Road, a new style was being generated combining elements drawn from a whole range of heterogeneous youth styles. Strands from David Bowie and glitter rock were woven together with elements from American proto punk (the Ramones, the Heartbreakers, Iggy Pop) from that faction within London pub rock (the 101-ers, the Gorillas etc.) inspired by the mod subculture of the 1960s, from the Canvey Island 40s revival and the Southend R & B bands (Dr. Feelgood, Lew Lewis etc.), from northern soul and from reggae.

This alliance of superficially incompatible musical traditions found ratification in an equally eclectic clothing style which reproduced the same kind of cacophony on the visual level. Early punk consisted of a chaos of quiffs and leather jackets, bum freezers and bovver boots, moddy crops and skinhead strides – all kept in place and out of time by safetypins and plastic clothes pegs, bondage straps and bits of string.

In fact, punk's irreverence and iconoclasm were cited in the press as factors behind the hostilities between teds and punks which were widely reported throughout the summer of 1977. Quite apart from the broad differences in the racial affiliations of the two groups (the teds were frequently identified with a tacit kind of racism, the punks with the newly formed Anti-Nazi League), teddy boys often objected in interviews to the punks' symbolic 'plundering' of the precious 1950s wardrobe (the drains, winklepickers etc.) and to the ironic and impious uses to which these 'sacred' artefacts were put when 'cut up' and reworked into punk style where they were contaminated by association. Behind punk's favoured 'cut ups' lay hints of disorder, of breakdown and category confusion: a desire not only to erode racial and gender boundaries but also to confuse chronological sequence by mixing up details from different periods.

The punk style signified chaos at every level. There was a homological relation between the trashy clothes and spikey hair, the pogo and amphetamine, the spitting, the vomiting, the format of the fanzines, the insurrectionary poses and the 'soulless', frantically driven music. In fact, we could say that punk style fitted together homologically precisely through its *lack of fit* (i.e. hole is to t-shirt as spitting is to applause as bin-liner is to garment as anarchy is to order) – by its refusal to cohere around a readily identifiable set of central values. It was instead characterised by its 'blankness' and in this it can be contrasted with the skinhead style.

Whereas the skinheads fetishised their class position in order to effect a 'magical' return to an imagined past (the 'classic slum'), the punks dislocated themselves from the parent culture and were positioned instead on the outside in a science fiction future. They played up their Otherness, 'happening' on the world as aliens' foundlings with no obvious ancestry (they even desecrated the family name inventing their own outrageous aliases). Though punk rituals, accents and objects were deliberately used to signify working-classness, it was difficult to pin this down exactly. Punk seemed to issue out of nameless housing estates, anonymous dole queues, slums-in-the-abstract. Though it claimed to speak for the neglected constituency of white lumpen youth, it did so in a language which was stilted – 'rendering' working-classness metaphorically in chains and hollow cheeks, 'dirty' clothing (stained jackets, tarty 'see through' blouses) and rough and ready diction. Moreover this working-classness stood in violent contradiction to that other great punk signified – sexual 'kinkiness'. The two forms of deviance – social and sexual – were juxtaposed to give an impression of multiple warping guaranteed to faze the most liberal and sympathetic of observers. Resorting to parody, the 'blank genera-tion' described itself in bondage through an assortment of darkly comic signifiers – straps and chains, strait jackets and rigid postures. For despite its proletarian accents, punk's voice was steeped in irony. In this way, although the punks referred con-tinually to the realities of school, work, family and class, these references only made sense at one remove: they were passed through the fractured circuitry of punk style and re-presented as noise disturbance, entropy.

How then do we trace the sources of the style and its meanings? How does a complex, self-reflexive unity like punk evolve? It would be misleading to read punk as a straightforward reflection of the fundamental conflict between dominant and subordinate classes and interests – between relatively powerful and powerless groups. The significations seem too specific, too strangely constructed, too arch and self conscious for such an interpretation to really satisfy. However, we can begin to account for punk's complexity – for the notion of style 'at one remove' – by focussing on the *generative role of the mass media* – on the ways in which the media indirectly shape and define the experience of the members of a subculture. In post war Britain, as Stuart Hall has argued (1977),[8] the media have 'progressively colonised the cultural and ideological spheres'. They provide us with the most available categories for classifying out the social world offering a symbolic frame-work within which the separate and fragmented pieces of the social totality appear to fit together and make sense. Not only do the media supply groups with sub-stantive images of other groups, they also relay back to people a 'picture' of their own lives which is 'contained', or 'framed' by the ideological discourses which surround and situate it.

Thus, much of the experience which finds itself encoded in subcultural style has already been subjected to a certain amount of prior handling by the media. And subcultures are, at least in part, responses to these more generalised media representa-tions. Elements taken from the received 'picture' of working class life (and of the social whole in general) are bound to find some echo in the various styles. For instance, there is no reason to suppose that subcultures spontaneously affirm only those *blocked* readings excluded from the airwaves and the newspapers (consciousness of subordinate status, a conflict model of society etc.). They also articulate some of the *preferred* meanings and interpretations, those favoured by and transmitted through the authorised channels of mass communication. The typical members of a working class youth culture in part contest and in part agree with the dominant definitions of who and what they are and there is a substantial amount of shared ideological ground between these forms and the larger, mainstream cultural formations.

For instance, the mod and skinhead styles of the 1960s have been interpreted as alternative manipulations of a complex iconography of class. According to this reading, the original mods – tellingly described in a newspaper of the time as 'pin neat, lively and clean' – explored the upwardly mobile option whereas the skinheads who followed in the late 1960s embraced an aggressively proletarian even lumpen identity. However, this elaboration of upward and downward options does not necessarily indicate any significant difference in the relative status of the jobs available to the average mod of 1964 and the skinhead of 1968 (though a census might indeed reveal such a difference). Still less does it reflect directly the fact that job opportunities open to working class youth in general actually diminished during the intervening period. Rather, the different styles represent negotiated responses to a contradictory mythology of class. In this mythology, the 'withering away of class' is paradoxically countered by an undiluted 'classfulness', a romantic conception of the traditional working class 'way of life' revived twice weekly on television programmes like *Coronation Street*. The mods and skinheads, then, in their different ways were 'handling' this mythology as much as the exigencies of their material condition. They were learning to live within or without that amorphous body of images and typifications made available in the mass media in which class is alternately overlooked and understated, denied and reduced to caricature.

In the same way, to return to our earlier example, the punks were not only responding *directly* to the 'realities of life in the late 70s' – increasing joblessness, changing moral standards, the rediscovery of poverty, the Depression etc. – they were *dramatising* what had come to be called 'Britain's decline' by constructing a language which was, in contrast to the prevailing rhetoric of the rock establishment, unmistakably relevant and 'down to earth' (hence the swearing, the references to 'fat hippies', the rags, the lumpen poses). The punks appropriated the rhetoric of crisis which constantly filled the airwaves and editorials and translated it back into tangible terms. In the gloomy apocalyptic ambience of the period – with widespread unemployment, with the ominous violence of the Notting Hill Carnival, Grunwick, Lewisham and Ladywood – it was 'fitting' that the punks should present themselves as 'degenerates'; as signs of the highly publicised decay which perfectly represented the atrophied condition of Great Britain.

Thus, while the various ensembles adopted by the punks undoubtedly expressed genuine aggression, frustration and anxiety, they were cast in a language which was generally available. They used a *topical* vocabulary. This accounts first, for the appropriateness of the punk metaphor both for the members of the subculture and for its opponents and, second, for the success of the punk subculture as spectacle: its ability to symptomatize a whole cluster of contemporary problems. It also helps to explain why a particular subculture catches on at a particular time, how it attracts new members and produces the requisite outraged responses from the relevant authorities (parents, employers, head teachers, councillors, pundits, police and MPs). In order to communicate disorder, the appropriate language must first be selected even if it is to be subverted. For punk to be dismissed as chaos, it had first to 'make sense' as noise.

If we follow this approach through we can read each spectacular subculture as an oblique set of responses to *particular* ideological configurations. Each style is written out of, produced across, the discursive formations which are in dominance at any one time. Each style plays back in a distorted form *contemporary* headlines, contemporary themes and issues. For instance, the glam rockers – the self consciously camp followers of Bowie, Roxy Music etc. – played with the available gender stereotypes in the early 1970s at the moment when feminist ideas and images were just beginning to filter through the media as commodities (e.g. *Cosmopolitan*). In the same way the mods ten years earlier had provided an ironic commentary on the rhetoric of affluence which was prevalent at the time. They dressed up to play down class differences or perhaps more subtly to accentuate them: the office boy in his handmade suit and Italian shoes could put the boss to shame neatly inverting the hierarchical equation of status and dress. The mods took the prevailing mid 1960s myths (limitless upward mobility, classlessness etc.) and gave them back as noise. Or as Dave Laing put it 'they looked alright but there was something in the way they moved that adults couldn't make out'.[9]

The current spate of revivals – the mods, skinheads, teds etc. – involves a more subtle inflection of dominant values and meaning. Subcultural style now constitutes a system-in-itself – a set of options which can be reworked again and again in a variety of combinations. In subculture, the generation of new styles has always been determined partly by a purely internal dialectic – by the destruction of existing codes and the formulation of new ones.

In each case the members of a subculture attempt to find in style their own 'immaculate' identity – one untouched by the cultures, both marginal and mainstream, which surround it. Each style thus defines itself *against* what has gone before and what is already there: skinhead v hippy; ted v punk; punk v hippy and now, inevitably, mod v punk. (A mod interviewed recently in the *Evening Standard* defined punks as 'hippies with zips'). But these internal conflicts and differences still signal deeper cultural tensions – conflicts which are *generally* divisive. For instance, the antagonism between punks and latter-day teds and skinheads appears to revolve at some level around the issues of race, 'ethnicity' and racism. The treatment of these issues in the dominant culture by the official agencies and institutions (the media, police, Parliament etc.) is of course profoundly confused and contradictory and, in their different ways, the punks and the ted and skinhead revivalists are handling those contradictions – seeking to resolve them through style.

For instance, it wasn't only *directly* through their support for the Rock Against Racism campaign that the early punks set out to combat racism. Despite their emphatic whiteness (their bleached roots) they also expressed in their music and their style an affinity with the exile status of young blacks ('Punks are niggers' – Richard Hell). The skinheads and teds, on the other hand, seem to represent a conservative, proletarian backlash to the radical 'working class' posturings of the new wave and part of that backlash, at least for some young revivalists, involves the espousal of some kind of racist ideology (though this in itself can be contradictory

– skinheads wearing Anti-Paki T-shirts can still dance to Jamaican rocksteady and call themselves rude boys).

The mod revival of 1979–80 can be read as a compromise solution. It seems to have emerged partly in reaction to punk (to punk's 'commercialisation' – its incorporation within the rock and fashion mainstreams; to punk polemics and the obviousness of the style). By contrast, the revived mod look was relatively muted and obscure and the lyrics of the new mod songs refrained from any overt 'political' or social commentary retreating back into the closed world of the Young Generation where the classic mod concerns: ('Think sharp, dress sharp, be sharp' in the words of the mod fanzine *Maximum Speed*) could be endlessly elaborated. None the less, punk's 'lime' on race was extended and refined by some of the mod revivalists in the movement back to ska – back to a less separatist form of Jamaican music than 'ethnic' roots reggae – where a fusion of rock and West Indian traditions seemed possible (e.g. The Specials, the Selecter etc.).

The revival of the mod subculture, thus, cannot be interpreted as an arbitrary reworking of purely aesthetic codes. In its revived form, the style was being used to express, reflect and 'magically' resolve a *specific* set of problems and contradictions. At the same time, the latter day mods could benefit from the subtlety of the style. They could pledge their allegiance to a sinister collective and still negotiate the contradictory demands of school, home and street.[10] And like their predecessors of the 1960s, they could enjoy that secret sense of superiority which dandyism makes possible – what Angela Carter calls the 'ambivalent triumph of the oppressed'.[11]

But in the end, of course, the victory is lost on all but the mods themselves. And ultimately the limits of symbolic resistance – of subversion through style – are glaringly apparent. Each subculture moves through a cycle of resistance and defusion and this cycle is situated within the larger cultural and commercial matrices. This occurs irrespective of the subculture's political orientation: the macrobiotic restaurants, craft shops and 'antique markets' of the hippies era were easily converted into punk boutiques and record shops. It also happens irrespective of the startling content of the style: punk clothing and insignia could be bought mail-order by the summer of 1977, and in September of that year *Cosmopolitan* ran a review of Zandra Rhodes' latest collection of couture follies which consisted entirely of variations on the punk theme. At the same time, the media perform their vital function of labelling subcultural deviance and situating it within the dominant framework of meanings. Throughout 1977 punk provided the tabloids with a fund of predictably sensational copy and the quality press with a catalogue of beautifully broken codes. Shock and horror headlines dominated the front pages (for example, 'Rotten Razored' *Daily Mirror*, 28 June, 1977) while inside, the editorials bristled with 'serious' commentary and the centre spreads and supplements contained delirious accounts of the latest fads and rituals (e.g. *Observer* supplements 30 January, 10 July, 1977). As the subculture begins to strike its own eminently marketable pose, as its vocabulary (both visual and verbal) becomes more and more familiar, so the referential context to which it can be most conveniently assigned is made increasingly apparent. Eventually each subculture is brought back into line: its members *returned*, as they are represented on TV and in the newspapers to the place where common sense would have them fit (as 'animals' certainly but also, as we have seen, 'in the family', 'out of work', 'up to date' etc.).

Subcultural deviance is thus simultaneously rendered 'explicable' and meaningless in the classrooms, courts and media at the same time as the 'secret' objects of subcultural style are put on display in every high street record shop and chain-store boutique. After all, this process is perhaps inevitable. For as we have seen subcultures are constructed, however obliquely, out of the headlines – out of the ideologies which prevail at any given time – and, though they parody those ideologies and puncture them and play them back as 'noise', eventually they themselves become part of the symphony. Punks and mods alike appear on the front pages as convenient metaphors for the period, as folk devils and villainous clowns. They become fodder for the Sunday supplements – spectacular 'signs of the times'.

Meanwhile the value of each subculture as a form of resistance seems to lie in its potential for scrambling the available categories, for subverting the familiar language in which the world is habitually described, experienced and reproduced, for *exceeding* current definitions of what is and is not possible in everyday life. From this perspective, subcultural styles can be read as subversive transformations of existing social and aesthetic codes and, above all, they should be seen as meaningful mutations. Sometimes these forms will be disfigured and disfiguring. At such time, no doubt, this will be their 'point'. They are counterposed against the symbolic order of structured appearances – the syntax which positions the producer over and against that which he or she produces. In the face of such an order, they are bound on occasion to assume monstrous and unnatural features.

In the last instance, then, subcultures express the tension between dominant and subordinate groups and classes. But they do this indirectly. The tension is *figuratively* expressed in the form of subcultural style and it is appropriate that we should turn here to a metaphor for our final definition of subculture. In one of his most influential essays, 'Ideology and Ideological State Apparatuses', Althusser describes how the different parts of the social formation – the family, education, the mass media, cultural and political institutions – together serve to perpetuate submission to the ruling ideology. However, these institutions do not perform this function through the direct transmission of 'ruling ideas'. Instead it is the way in which they work together in what Althusser calls a 'teeth-gritting harmony' that the ruling ideology is reproduced 'precisely in its contradictions'.[12] Throughout, I have interpreted subculture as a form of resistance in which experienced contradiction and objections to prevailing ideologies are obliquely represented in style. Specifically, I have used the term 'noise' to describe the challenge to symbolic order that such styles are seen to constitute. Perhaps it would be more accurate and more telling to think of this noise as the flip-side to Althusser's 'teeth-gritting harmony'.

Notes and References

1 COHEN, S. (1972) *Folk Devils and Moral Panics*, Paladin.
2 BARTHES, R. (1972) *Mythologies*, Paladin.
3 *Ibid.*
4 *Ibid.*
5 A football club manager was quoted on the *News at Ten* (Sunday, 12 March 1977) as saying 'These people aren't human beings'.
6 WILLIS, P. (1978) *Profane Culture*, Routledge and Kegan Paul.
7 HALL. S., JEFFERSON, T. and CLARKE, J. (Eds.) (1976) *Resistance Through Rituals*, Hutchinson.
8 HALL, S. (1977) 'Culture, the Media and the "ideological effect"', in CURRAN, J. *et al.*, (Eds.) *Mass Communications and Society*, Arnold.
9 LAING, D. (1969) *The Sound of our Time*, Sheen and Ward.
10 'I can wear the clothes to work' confided the mod in the *Evening Standard*, interview.
11 CARTER, A. (1976) 'The message in the spiked heel', *Spare Rib*, September.
12 ALTHUSSER, L. (1971) 'Ideology and ideological state apparatuses', in *Lenin and Philosophy and Other Essays*, New Left Books.

7 Rock and Sexuality

Simon Frith and Angela McRobbie

[. . .]

Of all the mass media rock is the most explicitly concerned with sexual expression. This reflects its function as a youth cultural form: rock treats the problems of puberty, it draws on and articulates the psychological and physical tensions of adolescence, it accompanies the moment when boys and girls learn their repertoire of public sexual behaviour. If rock's lyrics mostly follow the rules of romance, its musical elements, its sounds and rhythms draw on other conventions of sexual representation, and rock is highly charged emotionally even when its direct concern is non-sexual. It is the ever present background of dancing, dating, courting. 'Rock'n'roll' was originally a synonym for sex and the music has been a cause of moral panic since Elvis Presley first swivelled his hips in public. It has equally been a cause for the advocates of sexual permissiveness – the Sixties counter-culturalists claimed rock as 'liberating', the means by which the young would free themselves from adult hang-ups and repression. For a large section of post-war youth, rock music has been the aesthetic form most closely bound up with their first sexual experiences and difficulties, and to understand rock's relationship to sexuality isn't just an academic exercise – it is a necessary part of understanding how sexual feelings and attitudes are learnt.

Unfortunately, knowing that rock is important is not the same thing as knowing how it is important. The best writers on the subject state the contradictions without resolving them. On the one hand, there is something about rock that is experienced as liberating – in Sheila Rowbotham's words, sixties youth music was 'like a great release after all those super-consolation ballads'. On the other hand, rock has become synonymous with a male-defined sexuality: 'Under my thumb', sang the Stones, the archetypical rock group, 'stupid girl'. Some feminists have argued that rock is now essentially a male form of expression, that for women to make non-sexist music it is necessary to use sounds, structures and styles that cannot be heard as rock. This raises important questions about form and content, about the effect of male domination on rock's formal qualities as a mode of sexual expression. These

Source: Screen Education, (Winter 1978–79), No. 29.

are more difficult questions than is sometimes implied. Lyrics are not a sufficient clue to rock's meanings, nor can we deduce rock's sexual message directly from the male control of its conditions of production. Popular music is a complex mode of expression. It involves a combination of sound, rhythm, lyric, performance and image, and the apparently straightforward contrast that can be drawn, for example, between Tammy Wynette's *Stand By Your Man* (reactionary) and Helen Reddy's *I Am Woman* (progressive) works only at the lyrical level. It doesn't do justice to the overall meanings of these records: Tammy Wynette's country strength and confidence seem, musically, more valuable qualities than Helen Reddy's cute, show-biz self-consciousness. [. . .]

There are few clues, then, in the existing literature as to *how* rock works sexually. Left accounts of popular music focus either on its political economy or on its use in youth sub-cultures. In the former approach, rock's ideological content is derived from its commodity form, rock is explained as just another product of the mass entertainment industry. But if we confine ourselves to this approach alone, we cannot distinguish between the sexual messages of, say, the Stranglers and Siouxsie and the Banshees. The contrast between the former's offensive attempts to reassert stereotypes of male domination and the latter's challenge to those stereotypes is lost if we treat them simply as equivalent best-selling products of multi-national record companies. The problem of analysing the particular ideological work of a particular piece of music is avoided with the assumption that all commodities have the same effect. In the sub-cultural approach rock's ideological meaning is derived, by contrast, from the culture of its consumers. The immediate difficulty here is that existing accounts of youth sub-cultures describe them as, on the one hand, exclusively male, and, on the other hand, apparently asexual. But even a good culturalist account of rock would be inadequate for our purposes. Rock is not simply a cultural space that its young users can win for their own purposes. Rock, as an ideological and cultural form, has a crucial role to play in the process by which its users constitute their sexuality. It is that process we need to understand.

Our difficulty lies in the ease with which the analysis of rock as an aesthetic form can slip past the comparatively straightforward sociologies of record production and consumption. An obvious indication of this problem is the complex reference to the term 'rock' itself. As rock fans we know what we mean by rock empirically but the descriptive criteria we use are, in fact, diverse and inconsistent. 'Rock' is not just a matter of musical definition. It refers also to an audience (young, white), to a form of production (commercial), to an artistic ideology (rock has a creative integrity that 'pop' lacks). The result of this confusion is constant argument about whether an act or record is really rock and this is not just a matter of subjective disagreement. Records and artists have contradictory implications in themselves. The meaning of rock is not simply given by its musical form, but is struggled for. As a cultural product, a rock record has many layers of representation. The message of its lyrics may be undercut by its rhythmic or melodic conventions and, anyway, music's meanings don't reach their consumers directly. Rock is mediated by the way its performers are packaged, by the way it is situated as radio and dance music. Rock reaches its public via the 'gatekeepers' of the entertainment industry, who try to determine how people listen to it. The ideology of rock is not just a matter of notes and words.

One of the themes of this paper is that rock operates as both a form of sexual expression and as a form of sexual control. Expression and control are simultaneous aspects of the way rock works; the problem is to explain how rock gives ideological shape to its sexual representations. We reject the notion, central to the ideology of rock as counter-culture, that there is some sort of 'natural' sexuality which rock expresses and the blue meanies repress. Our starting point is that the most important ideological work done by rock is the *construction* of sexuality. We will describe rock's representations of masculinity and feminity and consider the contradictions involved in these representations. Our concern is to relate the effects of rock to its form – as music, as commodity, as culture, as entertainment.

Masculinity and Rock

Any analysis of the sexuality of rock must begin with the brute social fact that in terms of control and production, rock is a male form. The music business is male run; popular musicians, writers, creators, technicians, engineers and producers are mostly men. Female creative roles are limited and mediated through male notions of female ability. Women musicians who make it are almost always singers; the women in the business who make it are usually in publicity; in both roles success goes with a male-made female image. In general, popular music's images, values and sentiments are male products. Not only do we find men occupying every important role in the rock industry and in effect being responsible for the creation and construction of suitable female images, we also witness in rock the presentation and marketing of masculine styles. And we are offered not one definitive image of masculine sexuality, but a variety of male sexual poses which are most often expressed in terms of stereotypes. One useful way of exploring these is to consider 'cock rock', on the one hand, and 'teenybop', on the other.

By cock rock we mean music making in which performance is an explicit, crude and often aggressive expression of male sexuality – it's the style of rock presentation that links a rock and roller like Elvis Presley to rock stars like Mick Jagger, Roger Daltrey and Robert Plant. The most popular exponents of this form currently are Thin Lizzy – their album *Live and Dangerous* articulates cock rock's values very clearly. Cock rock performers are aggressive, dominating, boastful and constantly seek to remind the audience of their prowess, their control. Their stance is obvious in live shows; male bodies on display, plunging shirts and tight trousers, a visual emphasis on chest hair and genitals – their record sales depend on years of such appearances. In America, the mid-west concert belt has become the necessary starting point for cock rock success; in Britain the national popularity of acts like Thin Lizzy is the result of numberless tours of provincial dance halls. Cock rock shows are explicitly about male sexual performance (which may explain why so few girls go to them – the musicians are acting out a sexual iconography which in many ways is unfamiliar, frightening and distasteful to girls who are educated into understanding sex as something nice, soft, loving and private). In these performances mikes and guitars are phallic symbols; the music is loud, rhythmically insistent, built round techniques of arousal and climax; the lyrics are assertive and arrogant, though the exact words are less significant than the vocal styles involved, the shouting and screaming. The cock rock image is the rampant destructive male traveller, smashing hotels and groupies alike. Musically, such rock takes off from the sexual frankness of rhythm and blues but adds a cruder male physicality (hardness, control, virtuosity). Cock rockers' musical skills become synonymous with their sexual skills (hence Jimi Hendrix's simultaneous status as stud and guitar hero). Cock rockers are not bound by the conventions of the song form, but use their instruments to show 'what they've got', to give vent to their macho imagination. These are the men who take to the streets, take risks, live dangerously and, most of all, swagger untrammelled by responsibility, sexual and otherwise. And, what's more, they want to make this clear. Women, in their eyes, are either sexually aggressive and therefore doomed and unhappy, or else sexually repressed and therefore in need of male servicing. It's the woman, whether romanticised or not, who is seen as possessive, after a husband, anti-freedom, the ultimate restriction.

Teenybop, in contrast, is consumed almost exclusively by girls. What they're buying is also a representation of male sexuality (usually in the form of teen idols) but the nature of the image and the version of sexuality on display is quite distinct from that of the cock rocker. The teenybop idol's image is based on self-pity, vulnerability, and need. The image is of the young boy next door: sad, thoughtful, pretty and puppy-like. Lyrically his songs are about being let down and stood up, about loneliness and frustration; musically his form is a pop ballad/soft rock blend; less physical music than cock rock, drawing on older romantic conventions. In teenybop, male sexuality is transformed into a spiritual yearning carrying only hints of sexual interaction (see Les McKeown's soft swaying hips). [...] If cock rock plays on conventional concepts of male sexuality as rampant, animalistic, superficial, just-for-the-moment, teenybop plays on notions of female sexuality as being serious, diffuse and implying total emotional commitment. In teenybop cults live performance is less significant than pin-ups, posters and television appearances; in teenybop music, women emerge as unreliable, fickle, more selfish than men. It is men who are soft, romantic, easily hurt, loyal and anxious to find a true love who fulfils their definitions of what female sexuality should be about.

The resulting contrast between, say, Thin Lizzy fans and David Soul fans is obvious enough, but our argument is not intended to give a precise account of the rock market. There are overlaps and contradictions, girls put cock rock pin-ups on their bedroom walls and boys buy teenybop records. Likewise there are a whole range of stars who seek to occupy both categories at once – Rod Stewart can come across just as pathetic, puppy-like and maudlin as Donny Osmond, and John Travolta can be mean and nasty, one of the gang. But our cock rock/teenybop comparison does make clear the general point·we want to make: masculinity in rock is not determined by one all-embracing definition. Rather, rock offers a framework within which male sexuality can find a range of acceptable, heterosexual expressions. These images of masculinity are predicated on sexual divisions in the appropriation of rock. Thus we have the identity of the male consumer with the rock performer. Rock shows become a collective experience which are, in this respect, reminiscent of football matches and other occasions of male camaraderie – the general atmosphere is sexually exclusive, its euphoria depends on the absence of women. The teenybop performer, by contrast, addresses his female consumer as his object, potentially satisfying his sexual needs and his romantic and emotional demands. The teenybop fan should feel that her idol is addressing himself solely to her, her experience should be as his partner. [. . .]

From this perspective, the cock rock/teenybop contrast is clearly something general in rock, applicable to other genres. Male identity with the performer is expressed not only in sexual terms but also as a looser appropriation of rock musicians' dominance and power, confidence and control. It is boys who become interested in rock as music, who become hi-fi experts, who hope to become musicians, technicians or music businessmen. It is boys who form the core of the rock audience, who are intellectually interested in rock, who become rock critics and collectors. (The readership of *Sounds*, *New Musical Express* and *Melody Maker* and the audience for the *Old Grey Whistle Test* are two thirds male; John Peel's radio show listeners are ninety per cent male.) It is boys who experience rock as a collective culture, a shared male world of fellow fans and fellow musicians. The problems facing a woman seeking to enter the rock world as a participant are clear. A girl is supposed to be an individual listener, she is not encouraged to develop the skills and knowledge to become a performer. In sixth form and student culture, just as much as in teenybop music, girls are expected to be passive, as they listen quietly to rock poets, and brood in their bed-sits to Leonard Cohen, Cat Stevens or Jackson Browne. Women, whatever their musical tastes, have little opportunity and get little encouragement to be performers themselves. This is another aspect of rock's sexual ideology of collective male activity and individual female passivity.

Music, Femininity and Domestic Ideology

Male dominance in the rock business is evident in both the packaging and the musical careers of female rock stars. [. . .] Indeed, one of the most startling features of the history of British popular music has been the speed with which talented women singers, of all types, from Lulu through Dusty Springfield to Kate Bush, have been turned into family entertainers, become regulars on television variety shows, fallen into slapstick routines and taken their show-biz places as smiling, charming hostesses. Female musicians have rarely been able to make their own musical versions of the oppositional, rebellious hard edges that male rock can embody. Our argument is not that male stars don't experience the same pressures to be bland entertainers, but that female stars have little possibility of resisting such pressures. It may have been necessary for Cliff Richard and Tommy Steele to become all-round entertainers in the 1950s, but one of the consequences of the rise of rock in the 1960s was that mass success was no longer necessarily based on the respectable conventions of show-biz; sexual outrage became an aspect of rock's mass appeal. But for men only. The rise of rock did not extend the opportunities for women; notions of a woman's musical place have hardly changed. The one new success route opened to women was to become the singer/songwriter/folkie lady – long haired, pure voiced, self-accompanied on acoustic guitar. But whatever the ability, integrity and toughness of Joan Baez, Judy Collins, Sandy Denny and the others, their musical appeal, the way they were sold, reinforced in rock the qualities traditionally linked with female singers – sensitivity, passivity and sweetness. For women rockers to become hard aggressive performers it was necessary for them, as Jerry Garcia commented on Janis Joplin, to become 'one of the boys'. Some women did make it this way – Grace Slick, Maggie Bell, Christine McVie – but none of them did it without considerable pain, frustration and, in the case of Janis Joplin herself, tragedy.

Perhaps the only way of resisting the pressures pushing women musicians into conventional stereotypes (and stereotyping is an inevitable result of commercialisation) was to do as Joni Mitchell did and avoid prolonged contact with the mass media. [. . .] She, like Joan Armatrading, is rewarded with an 'awkward' reputation and despite their artistic achievements, theirs is not the popular image of the woman musician. For that we have to look at a group like Abba. The boy/girl group is a common entertainment device in both pop and disco music (Coco, the Dooleys, on the one hand, Boney M and Rose Royce on the other), and Abba provide the clearest example of the sexual divisions of labour such groups involve: the men make the music (they write and arrange, play the guitars and keyboards), the women are glamorous (they dress up and sing what they're told, their instruments are their 'natural' voices and bodies).

[. . .] In rock, women have little control of their music, their images, their performances; to succeed they have to fit into male grooves. The subordination of women in rock is little different from their subordination in other occupations. As unskilled rock workers, women are a source of cheap labour, a pool of talent from which the successes are chosen more for their appropriate appearance than for their musical talents.

But the problems of women in rock reach much further than those of surviving the business. Oppressive images of women are built into the very foundations of the pop/rock edifice, into its production, its consumption and even into its musical structures. Pop music reaches its public via a variety of gatekeepers – the radio producers of BBC and commercial broadcasting, the television producers of *Top of the Pops* and the *Old Grey Whistle Test*, the film producers of *Saturday Night Fever* and *Grease*. Disc jockeys at discos and dances, writers in music papers and girls' magazines, compete to interpret musical meanings. [. . .]

Teenage magazines have used pop star images, male and female, to illustrate their romantic fantasies and practical hints since their origin in the 1950s. *Jackie*, for example, the highest selling girls' weekly magazine, interprets music for its readers exclusively in terms of romance. The magazine is dependent for its appeal on pop, carrying two or three large pop pin-ups each week, but never actually deals with music.[1] It doesn't review records, never hints that girls could learn an instrument of form a band, should take music seriously as either a hobby or a career. Music is reduced to its stars, to idols' looks and likes. Head and shoulders shots loom out of the centre and back pages, symbols of dreamily smiling male mastery. Nothing else in *Jackie* is allowed such uncluttered space – even the cover girl has to compete for readers' attention with the week's list of features and offers. Pop stars in *Jackie's* account of them, are not just pretty faces. Romance rests on more than good looks; the stars also have 'personality'. Each pin-up uses facial expression and background location to tell readers something about the stars's character – David Essex's pert cheekiness, David Cassidy's crumpled sweetness, Les Mc-Keown's reassuring homeliness. There is an obvious continuity in the visual appeal of teenybop idols, from Elvis Presley to John Travolta – an unformed sensuality, something sulky and unfinished in the mouth and jaw, eyes that are intense but detached. Sexiness, but sexiness that isn't physically rooted, that suggests a dreamy, fantasy fulfilment. These images tell us more about the ideology of female than male sexuality: the plot is revealed in the home settings of *Jackie's* photographs. Teenage music is not, after all, a matter of sex and drugs and careless-ness. These stars are just like us, they're rich and successful and love their families, they come from ordinary pasts and have ordinary ambitions – marriage, settling down.

Girls are encouraged from all directions to interpret their sexuality in terms of romance, to give priority to notions of love, feeling, commitment, the moment of bliss. In endorsing these values girls prepare themselves for their lives as wives and mothers, where the same notions take on different labels – sacrifice, service and fidelity. In Sue Sharpe's words:

> Women mean love and the home while men stand for work and the external world ... women provide the intimate personal relationships which are not sanctioned in the work organisation ... women are syn-onymous with softness and tenderness, love and care, something you are glad to come home from work to.[2]

Music is an important medium for the communication of this ideological message and its influence extends much further than our analysis of teenybop has so far made clear. The BBC's day-time music shows on Radio 1 and 2, for example, are aimed primarily at housewives and their emphasis is consequently on mainstream pop, on romantic ballads, and a lightweight bouncy beat. On these shows there is little new wave music, few of the progressive, heavy, punk or reggae sounds which creep into the playlists once the kids, the students, the male workers, are thought to be back from school and class and job. The BBC's musically interesting pro-grammes are broadcast at night and the weekend, when men can listen, and this programming policy is shared by commercial stations. The recurrent phrase in radio producers' meetings remains: 'we can't really play *that* to housewives!'

Music has a function for women at work too, as Lindsay Cooper has pointed out.[3] Many employees provide piped music or Radio 1 for their female employees – indeed, piped music in a factory is a good indicator of a female workforce – and the service industries in which women work – offices, shops – also tend to have pop as a permanent backdrop. Music, like clean and pretty industrial design, is thought to soften the workplace, making it homely and personal, increasing female productivity and lessening female job dissatisfaction. Pop's romantic connotations are not only important for socialising teenagers, they also function to bring the sphere of the personal, the home, into the sphere of the impersonal, the factory. Music feminises the workplace, it provides women workers with aesthetic symbols of their domestic identity, it helps them discount the significance of the boring and futile tasks on which they're actually engaged. If talk, gossip, passing round photos and displaying engagement rings indirectly help women overcome the tedium of their work, then the pop music supplied by management is a direct attempt to foster a feminine culture, in order to deflect women from more threatening collective activities as workers. Women's music at work, as much as girls' music at home, symbolises the world that is 'naturally' theirs, the world of the emotions, of caring, feeling, loving and sacrificing.

There's a feature on Simon Bates's morning Radio 1 show in which listeners send in the stories they attach to particular records. [. . .] This request spot illustrates with remarkable clarity how closely music is linked with women's emotional lives and how important music is in giving sexual emotions their romantic gloss. The teenybop mode of musical appropriation has a general resonance for the ideology of femininity and domesticity. A similar argument could be made with reference to cock rock and male sexuality, showing how the values and emotions that are taken to be 'naturally' male are articulated in all male-aimed pop music. But music is, in significant respects, less important for male than for female sexual ideology. 'Maleness' gets much of its essential expression in work, manual and intellectual; it isn't, as 'femaleness' is for women, confined to the aesthetic, emotional sphere. Boys can express their sexuality more directly than girls. They are allowed to display physical as well as spiritual desire, to get carried away. The excitement of cock rock is suggestive not of the home and privacy but rather of the boozy togetherness of the boys who are, in Thin Lizzy's classic song, 'back in town'.

Of course male sex is no more 'naturally' wild and uncontrollable than feminine sexuality is passive, meek and sensitive. Both are ideological constructs, but there is a crucial difference in the way the ideologies and the musics work. Cock rock allows for direct physical and psychological expressions of sexuality: pop in contrast is about romance, about female crushes and emotional affairs. Pop songs aimed at the female audience deny or repress sexuality. Their accounts of relationships echo the picture strips in girls' comics, the short stories in women's magazines. The standard plots in all these forms are the same: the 'ordinary' boy who turns out to be the special man, the wolf who must be physically resisted to be spiritually tamed, and so on. Ideologies of love are multi-media products and teenage girls have little choice but to interpret their sexual feelings in terms of romance – few alternative readings are available.[4] This remains true even though we recognise that pop music is not experienced as an ideological imposition. Music is used by young people for their own expressive purposes and girls, for example, use pop as a weapon against parents, schools and other authorities. At school they cover their books with pop pin-ups, carve their idols' names on their desks, slip out to listen to cassettes or trannies in the toilets. In the youth club, music is a means of distancing girls from official club activities. They use it to detach themselves from their clubs leaders' attempts to make them participate in 'constructive' pursuits. The girls sit round their record players and radios, at home and school and youth clubs, and become unapproachable in their involvement with their music. Music also gives girls the chance to express a collective identity, to go out *en masse*, to take part in activities unacceptable in other spheres. Unlike their brothers, girls have little chance to travel about together. As groups of girls they don't go to football matches, relax in pubs, get publicly drunk. Teenage girls' lives are usually confined to the locality of their homes; they have less money than boys, less free time, less independence of parental control. A live pop concert is, then, a landmark among their leisure activities. [...]

These moments of teenybop solidarity are a sharp and necessary contrast to the usual use of pop records in bedroom culture, as the music to which girls wash their hair, practice make-up and day-dream, as the background music of domestic tasks – babysitting, housework – which girls unlike boys are already expected to do. But the ritual 'resistance' involved in these uses of music is not ideological. Rather, girls' use of teenybop music for their own puposes confirms the musical ideology of femininity. The vision of freedom on which these girls are drawing is a vision of the freedom to be individual wives, mothers, lovers, of the freedom to be glamorous, desirable sex objects for men.[5] For the contradictions involved in popular music's sexuality we have to look elsewhere, to the cock rock side of our ideal type distinction, to rock's ideological break with pop, to its qualities as beat music, its functions for dance.

Rock Contradictions

The audience for rock isn't only boys. If the music tends to treat women as objects, it does, unlike teenybop romance, also acknowledge in its direct physicality that women have sexual urges of their own. In attacking or ignoring conventions of sexual decency, obligation and security, cock rockers do, in some respects, challenge the ways in which those conventions are limiting – on women as well as on men. Women can contrast rock expression to the respectable images they are offered elsewhere – hence the feminist importance of the few female rock stars like Janis Joplin, hence the moral panics about rock's corrupting effects. The rock ideology of freedom from domesticity has an obvious importance for girls, even if it embodies an alternative mode of sexual expression.

There are ambiguities in rock's insistent presentation of men as sex objects. These presentations are unusually direct – no other entertainers flaunt their sexuality at an audience as obviously as rock performers. 'Is there anybody here with any Irish in them?' Phil Lynott of Thin Lizzy asks in passing on the *Live and Dangerous* LP, 'Is there any of the girls who would like a little more Irish in them?' Sexual groupies are a more common feature of stars' lives in rock than in other forms of entertainment and cock rock often implies female sexual aggression, intimates that women can be ruthless in the pursuit of *their* sex objects. Numerous cock rock songs – the Stones' for example – express a deep fear of women, and in some cases, like that of the Stranglers, this fear seems pathological, which reflects the fact that the macho stance of cock rockers is as much a fantasy for men as teenybop romance is for women. [. . .]

Cock rock presents an ideal world of sex without physical or emotional difficulties, in which all men are attractive and potent and have endless opportunities to prove it. However powerfully expressed, this remains an ideal, ideological world, and the alternative, teenybop mode of masculine vulnerability is, consequently, a complementary source of clues as to how sexuality should be articulated. The imagery of the cheated, unhappy man is central to sophisticated adult-oriented rock and if the immediate object of such performers is female sympathy, girls aren't their only listeners. Even the most macho rockers have in their repertoire some suitably soppy songs with which to celebrate true (lustless) love – listen to the Stones' *Angie* for an example. Rock, in other words, carries messages of male self-doubt and self-pity to accompany its hints of female confidence and aggression. Some of the most interesting rock performers have deliberately used the resulting sexual ambiguities and ironies. We can find in rock the image of the pathetic stud or the salacious boy next door, or, as in Lesley Gore's *You Don't Own Me*, the feminist teenybopper. We can point too at the ambivalent sexuality of David Bowie, Lou Reed and Bryan Ferry, at the camp teenybop styles of Gary Glitter and Suzi Quatro, at the disconcertingly 'macho' performances of a female group like the Runaways. These references to the uses made of rock conventions by individual performers lead us to the question of form: how are the conventions of sexuality we've been discussing embodied in rock?

This is a complex question and all we can do here is point to some of the work that needs to be done before we can answer it adequately. Firstly, then, we need to look at the *history* of rock. We need to investigate how rock'n'roll originally affected youthful presentations of sexuality and how these presentations have changed in rock's subsequent development. Most rock analysts look at the emergence of rock'n'roll as the only event needing explanation. Rock'n'roll's subsequent corruption and 'emasculation' (note the word) are understood as a straightforward effect of the rock business's attempt to control its market or as an aspect of American institutional racism. [. . .] But, from our perspective, the process of 'decline' – the successful creation of teenybop idols like Fabian, the sales shift from crude dance music to well-crafted romantic ballads, the late-50s popularity of sweet black music and girl groups like the Shirelles – must be analysed in equal detail. The decline of rock'n'roll rested on a process of 'feminisation'.

The most interesting sexual aspect of the emergence of British beat in the mid-sixties was its blurring of the by then conventional teenage distinction between girls' music – soft ballads – and boys' music – hard line rock'n'roll. There was still a contrast between, say, the Beatles and the Stones – the one a girls' band, the other a boys' band – but it was a contrast not easily maintained. The British sound in general, the Beatles in particular, fused a rough r&b beat with yearning vocal harmonies derived from black and white romantic pop. The resulting music articulated simultaneously the conventions of feminine and masculine sexuality, and the Beatles' own image was ambiguous, neither boys-together aggression nor boy-next-door pathos. This ambiguity was symbolised in Lennon and McCartney's unusual lyrical use of the third person – 'I saw *her* standing there'. '*She* loves *you*'. In performance, the Beatles did not make an issue of their own sexual status, did not, despite the screaming girls, treat the audience as their sexual object. The mods from this period turned out to be the most interesting of Britain's post-war youth groups – offering girls a more visible, active and collective role (particularly on the dance floor) than in previous or subsequent groups and allowing boys the vanity, the petulance, the soft sharpness that are usually regarded as sissy. Given this, the most important thing about late sixties rock was not its well discussed, counter-cultural origins, but the way in which it was consolidated as the central form of mass youth music in its cock rock form, as a male form of expression. The 'progressive' music of which everyone expected so much in 1967–68 became, in its popular form, the heavy metal macho style of Led Zeppelin, on the one hand, and the technically facile hi-fi formula of Yes, on the other. If the commercialisation of rock'n'roll in the 1950s was a process of 'feminisation', the commercialisation of rock in the 1960s was a process of 'masculinisation'.

In the seventies, rock's sexual moments have been more particular in their effects but no less difficult to account for. Where did glam and glitter rock come from? Why did youth music suddenly become a means for the expression of sexual ambiguity? Rock was used this way not only by obviously arty performers like Lou Reed and David Bowie, but also by mainstream teenybop packages like the Sweet and by mainstream rockers like Rod Stewart. The most recent issue for debate has been punk's sexual meaning. Punk involved an attack on both romantic and permissive conventions and in their refusal to let their sexuality be constructed as a commodity some punks went as far as to deny their sexuality any significance at all. 'My love lies limp', boasted Mark Perry of Alternative TV. 'What is sex anyway?' asked Johnny Rotten, 'Just thirty seconds of squelching noises'. Punk was the first form of rock not to rest on love songs, and one of its effects has been to allow female voices to be heard that are not often allowed expression on record, stage or radio – shrill, assertive, impure individual voices, the sounds of singers like Poly Styrene, Siouxsie, Fay Fife of the Rezillos, Pauline of Penetration. Punk's female musicians have a strident insistency that is far removed from the appeal of most post-war glamour girls. The historical problem is to explain their commercial success, to account for the punks' interruption of the long-standing rock equation of sex and pleasure.[6]

These questions can only be answered by placing rock in its cultural and ideological context as a form of entertainment, but a second major task for rock analysts is to study the sexual language of its musical roots – rhythm and blues, soul, country, folk and the rest. The difficulty is to work out the relationship of form and content. Compare, for example, Bob Dylan's and Bob Marley's current use of their supporting women singers. Dylan is a sophisticated rock star, the most significant voice of the music's cultural claims, including its claim to be sexually liberating. His most recent lyrics, at least, reflect a critical self-understanding that isn't obviously sexist. But musically and visually his back-up trio are used only as a source of glamour, their traditional pop use. Marley is an orthodox Rastafarian, subscribes to a belief, an institution, a way of life in which women have as sub-ordinate a place as in any other sexually repressive religion. And yet Marley's I-Threes sing and present themselves with grace and dignity, with independence and power. In general, it seems that soul and country musics, blatantly sexist in their organisation and presentation, in their lyrical themes and concerns, allow their female performers an autonomous musical power that is rarely achieved by women in rock. [. . .]

This comparison raises the difficult issue of musical realism. It has long been commonplace to contrast folk and pop music by reference to their treatments of 'reality'. Pop music is, in Hayakawa's famous formula, a matter of 'idealisation/frustration/demoralisation'; a folk form like the blues, in contrast, deals with 'the facts of life'.[7] Hayakawa's argument rested on lyrical analysis but the same point is often made in musical terms – it is a rock critical cliché, for example, to compare the 'earthy' instrumentation of rhythm and blues with the 'bland' string arrange-ments of Tin Pan Alley pop. A. L. Lloyd rests his assessment of the importance of folk music (contrasted with the 'insubstantial world of the modern commercial hit') on its truth to the experience of its creators. If folk songs contain 'the longing for a better life', their essence is still consolation not escapism:

> Generally the folk song makers chose to express their longing by trans-posing the world on to an imaginative plane, not trying to escape from it, but colouring it with fantasy, turning bitter, even brutal facts of life into something beautiful, tragic, honourable, so that when singer and listeners return to reality at the end of the song, the environment is not changed but they are better fitted to grapple with it.[8]

Such consolation was derived not just from folk songs' lyrical and aesthetic effects, but also from the collective basis of their creation and performance – women's songs, for example, became a means of sharing the common experience of sexual dependence and betrayal. This argument can be applied to the realistic elements of a commercial country performance like Tammy Wynette's. But the problem remains: is musical realism simply a matter of accurate description and consequent acceptance of 'the way things are', or can it involve the analysis of appearances, a challenge to 'given' social forms?

In analysing the sexual effects of rock, a further distinction needs to be made between rock realism – the use of music to express the experience of 'real' sexual situations – and rock naturalism – the use of music to express 'natural' sexuality. An important aspect of rock ideology is the argument that sexuality is asocial, that is a means of spontaneous physical expression which is beset on all sides by the social forces of sexual repression. Rhythm, for example, the defining element of rock as a musical genre, is taken to be naturally sexual. What this means is unclear. What would be the sexual message of a cock rock dancing class like *Honky Tonk Woman* if its lyrics were removed? Rock's hard beat may not, itself, speak in terms of male domination, power or aggression, but the question is whether it says anything, in itself. Rock critics describe beat as 'earthy' or 'bouncy' or 'sensual' or 'crude', and so reach for the sorts of distinctions we need to make, but such descriptive terms reflect the fact that rhythmic meaning comes from a musical and ideological context. [...]

Sexual Expression /Sexual Control

The recurrent theme of this article has been that music is a means of sexual expression and as such is important as a mode of sexual control. Both in its presentation and in its use, rock has confirmed traditional definitions of what constitutes masculinity and femininity, and reinforces their expression in leisure pursuits. The dominant mode of control in popular music (the mode which is clearly embodied in teenybop culture) is the ideology of romance, which is itself the icing on the harsh ideology of domesticity. Romance is the central value of show biz and light entertainment and in as far as pop musicians reach their public through radio, television and the press, they express traditional show biz notions of glamour, femininity and so forth.[9] These media are crucial for establishing the appeal of certain types of pop star (like Tom Jones, Gilbert O'Sullivan, Elton John) and – as we have already argued – they are particularly significant in determining the career possibilities of female musicians.

It was against this bland show business background that rock was, and is, experienced as sexually startling. Rock, since its origins in rock'n'roll, has given youth a more blatant means of sexual expression than is available elsewhere in the mass media and has therefore posed much more difficult problems of sexual control. Rock's rhythmic insistence can be heard as a sexual insistence and girls have always been thought by mass moralists to be especially at risk; the music so obviously denies the concept of feminine respectability. In short, the ideology of youth developed in the 1960s by rock (among other media) had as its sexual component the assumption that a satisfying sexual relationship meant 'spontaneity', 'free expression' and the 'equality of pleasure'. Sex in many ways came to be thought of as *best* experienced outside the restrictive sphere of marriage, with all its notions of true love and eternal monogamy. The point is, however, that this was a male defined principle and at worst simply meant a greater emphasis on male sexual freedom. Rock never was about unrestricted, unconfined sexuality. Its expression may not have been controlled through the domestic ideology basic to pop as entertainment, but it has had its own mode of control, a mode which is clearly embodied in cock rock and which can be related to the general ideology of permissiveness that emerged in the 1960s, to the 'liberated' emphasis on everyone's right to sexual choice, opportunity and gratification.

One of the most important activities to analyse if we're going to understand how sexual ideology works is dancing. The dance floor is the most public setting for music as sexual expression, and it is the place where pop and rock conventions overlap. For teenybop girls music is for dancing, and rock, too, for all its delusions of male grandeur, is still essentially a dance form. Girls have always flocked to dance halls and their reasons haven't just been to find a husband: dance is the one leisure activity in which girls and young women play a dominant role. Dancing for them is creative and physically satisfying. But more than this dancing is also a socially sanctioned sexual activity – at least it becomes so when the boys, confident with booze, leave the bar and the corners to look for a partner from the mass of dancing girls. One function of dance as entertainment, from Salome to Pan's People, has been to arouse men with female display. That is not a function of most contemporary youth dancing, though. This remains an aspect of girls' own pleasure, even in the cattle market context of a provincial dance hall. The girls are still concerned to attract the lurking boys, but through their clothes, make-up and appearance – not through their dancing. This is equally true of boys' dances – their energy and agility is not being displayed to draw girls' attention and the most dedicated young dancers in Britain, the Northern soul fans, are completely self absorbed. Indeed Legs and Co's weekly attempts on *Top of the Pops* to impose 'dance-as-sexual-come-on' on current dance music is embarrassing in its misunderstanding.

[In conclusion we need to make one remark:] rock's sexual effect is not just on the construction of femininity and masculinity. Rock also contributes to the more diffuse process of the sexualisation of leisure. The capitalist mode of production rests on a double distinction between work and pleasure, between work and home. The alienation of the worker from the means of production means that the satisfaction of his or her needs becomes focused on *leisure* and on the *family*. Under capitalism, sexual expression is constituted as an individual leisure need – compare this with pre-capitalist modes of production, in which sexual expression is an aspect of a collective relationship with nature. This has numerous consequences – the exchange of sex as a commodity, the exchange of commodities as sex – and means that we have to refer mass entertainment (films as well as music) to a theory of leisure as well as to a theory of ideology.

In writing this article we have been conscious of our lack of an adequate theory of leisure. Underlying our analysis of rock and sexuality have been some nagging questions. What would non-sexist music sound like? Can rock be non-sexist? How can we counter rock's dominant sexual messages? These issues aren't purely ideological, matters of rock criticism. The sexual meaning of rock can't be read off independently of the sexual meaning of rock consumption, and the sexual meaning of rock consumption derives from the capitalist organisation of production. So far we have described the ways in which rock constitutes sexuality for its listeners. Our last point is that sexuality is constituted in the very act of consumption.

Notes and References

1 A 1967 issue of *Petticoat* magazine went so far as to urge girls to stop buying records and spend the money they saved on clothes, holiday and make-up. 'Borrow records from your boyfriend instead', the magazine suggested.

2 SHARPE, S. (1976) *Just Like A Girl*, Harmondsworth, Penguin.

3 COOPER, L. (1977) 'Women, Music and Feminism', in *Musics*, October.

4 Although it would support this argument, we don't analyze lyrics. This has often been a crude way of assessing musical meaning and, anyway, an excellent study of lyrical messages already exists – GODDARD, T. 'Popular music', in KING, J. and STOTT, M. (1977) *Is This Your Life?*, Virago.

5 This argument is taken from the detailed analysis of girl culture in McROBBIE, A. (1978) 'Working class girls and the culture of femininity', in WOMEN'S STUDIES GROUP *Women Take Issue*, Hutchinson.

6 It is ironic that Tom Robinson's rock expression of gay pleasures and pressures, while made commercially possible by punk's sexual ambiguity, uses an orthodox musical form, many of the conventions of which are drawn from cock rock.

7 HAYAKAWA, S.I. (1957) 'Popular songs vs. the facts of life', in ROSENBERG, B. and WHITE, D.M. (Eds.) *Mass Culture*, Free Press.

8 LLOYD, A.L. (1975) *Folk Song in England*, Paladin, p. 170.

9 For analysis of these values see DYER, R. (1973) *Light Entertainment*, British Film Institute.

2
Schooling and Patriarchy

8 Women and Production: A Critical Analysis of Some Sociological Theories of Women's Work

Veronica Beechey

Despite the emergence of important new areas of theoretical discussion within the women's liberation movement, such as analyses of domestic labour and the concept of patriarchy, and despite the substantial growth of research by feminist historians into the history of women, relatively little attention has been paid to the problems involved in analyzing the position of female wage labour in the capitalist mode of production. In attempting to understand the material basis of women's position in the family at the same time as countering the view – certainly common within sociology – that women's position in the family is definable in cultural terms, marxist feminists have tended to concentrate their work on the question of domestic labour and its productivity. One result of this concentration has been that the analysis of domestic labour has become isolated from the analysis of female wage labour, which has itself not been the subject of very much theoretical discussion either within the women's movement or within marxist theory.[1]

My purpose here is to discuss some of the problems involved in analysing female wage labour, through developing a critique of a number of approaches to the question; and the paper is divided into four sections. The first is a discussion of the conceptual framework for analysing the family which has been developed by Talcott Parsons.[2] This constitutes the classic sociological analysis of the family, and provides the foundation for most subsequent sociological work on the family and the position of women. This is followed in the second section by a discussion of empirical studies of 'women's two roles' which have been developed within British sociology, and which combine a modified structural functionalist framework with empirical research on working women and the family structure. The third section considers the conception of a dual labour market which has been developed within economics as a radical critique of neoclassical economics and which Barron and Norris[3] have utilized to analyse the occupational position of women. The last section of the paper discusses, albeit schematically, some of the problems which are raised for a marxist feminist analysis of female wage labour by Marx's analysis in *Capital*.[4] [. . .]

Source: An abridged version of a paper in KUHN, A. and WOLPE, A.M. (Eds.) (1978) *Feminism and Materialism*, London, Routledge and Kegan Paul.

I

In considering those aspects of Talcott Parsons's theory which have been important in providing a framework for empirical sociological studies of the family and the differentiation of sex roles, I do not attempt to provide a comprehensive overview or critique of Parsons' work, but rather will refer to relevant and representative sections of that work. In *Essays in Sociological Theory* Parsons examines the relationship between the kinship system and the wider society, locating his analysis within a discussion of the problems involved in determining class status, which he defines as 'the status of any given individual in the system of stratification in a society may be regarded as a resultant of the common valuations underlying the attribution of status to him in each of . . . six respects'[5] – membership in a kinship unit, personal qualities, achievements, possessions, authority and power. Parsons focuses on the ascription of status through membership in a kinship unit, and the achievement of status through position in the occupational structure. Although he is inconsistent in that at times he regards kinship as the primary determinant of social status while at others occupational position is presented as determinant, the overall thrust of Parsons's argument suggests that the dominant patterning of the occupational system in an industrial society requires a high degree of social mobility and equality of opportunity in order that individuals can attain their 'natural levels' within the occupational structure:

> We determine status very largely on the basis of achievement within an occupational system which is in turn organized primarily in terms of universalistic criteria of performance and status within functionally specialized fields. This dominant pattern of the occupational sphere requires at least a relatively high degree of 'equality of opportunity' which in turn means that status cannot be determined primarily by birth or membership in kinship units.[6]

However, Parsons continues, such an occupational system coexists with a strong institutional emphasis on the ties of kinship since 'the values associated with the family, notably the marriage bond and the parent-child relationship, are among the most strongly emphasized in our society'.[7] This suggests a contradictory relationship between the occupational system and the kinship system which is a potential source of disharmony. However, Parsons argues that this contradictory relationship has been largely resolved within the industrial societies, since the family has developed in such a way as to minimize the strain between the kinship system and the occupational system:

> The conjugal family with dependent children, which is the dominant unit in our society, is, of all types of kinship unit, the one which is probably the least exposed to strain and possible breaking-up by the dispersion of its members both geographically and with respect to stratification in the modern type of occupational hierarchy.[8]

This is because it has developed an internal structure which is adapted to the functional requirements of the occupational system.

The key to this internal structure lies in the segregation of sex roles. For, Parsons argues, if all members of the family were equally involved in competition within the occupational structure, there might be a very serious strain on the solidarity of the family unit. Thus a segregation of sex roles has emerged to ensure that their respective incumbents do not come into competition with each other. Parsons defines this sex role differentiation, which corresponds to the differentiation of family and economy in industrial societies in *Family: Socialization and Interaction Process*,[9] in terms of a structural differentiation between instrumental and expressive roles. The instrumental role involves goal attainment and adaptation and is basically concerned with the relationship between the family and the wider society, while the expressive role involves integration and is defined in terms of the internal structure and functions of the family. Parsons' analysis of the structural differentiation of sex roles is underpinned by the evidence from Bales' analysis of small groups, from which it is argued that there exists a tendency for all small groups to be structurally differentiated so that some persons take on leadership roles while others take on subordinate roles. For Parsons the conjugal family is no exception. While it is in principle possible for either men or women to hold expressive or instrumental roles, Parsons argues that men fulfil instrumental ones while women fulfil expressive ones. The reason he gives is that women are involved in the bearing and early nursing of children, and are therefore best adapted to performing internal expressive roles, while the absence of men from these activities makes them best adapted to instrumental ones. Since the tension between the kinship system and the occupational system requires a clear segregation of sex roles, the man is ascribed the instrumental role while the woman is removed from competition within the occupational system by her confinement within the family.

Since Parsons' definition of class status is defined in terms of social evaluations and since sex roles are defined in normative terms, it follows that his analysis precludes consideration of economic factors. Thus the woman's role in the family is portrayed in cultural terms, and the question of the economic role of the woman's domestic labour which has been emphasized by many feminist writers is ruled out by a theoretical sleight of hand. This has led Middleton to state that 'in academic sociology the view that female activity in the home is essentially cultural has often been associated with a denial of the proposition that women do in fact constitute a subordinate group at all'.[10] Although the fact that women work outside the home is acknowledged by Parsons, the economic implication of women's wage labour is ignored, since the role of women continues to be defined in expressive terms. This is because, according to Parsons, the number of women in the labour force with young children is small and is not increasing, and the kind of job which the woman does 'tends to be of a qualitatively different type and not a status which seriously competes with that of her husband as the primary status-giver or income-earner'.[11] He can therefore conclude that:

It seems quite safe in general to say that the adult feminine role has not ceased to be anchored primarily in the internal affairs of the family, as wife, mother and manager of the household, while the role of the adult male is primarily anchored in the occupational world, in his job and through it by his status-giving and income-earning functions for the family. Even if, as seems possible, it should come about that the average married women had some kind of job, it seems most unlikely that this relative balance would be upset; that either the roles would be reversed, or their qualitative differentiation in these respects completely erased.[12] [. . .]

Parsons is aware in *Essays in Sociological Theory* that such sex role segregation presents problems for the egalitarian system of values within American society. Even though women's status is evaluated on a different basis from men's, however, Parsons insists that the status of women is equal to that of men. He states, somewhat ambivalently, in his essay 'An analytical approach to the theory of stratification' that members of kinship groups are

> in certain respects treated as 'equals' regardless of the fact that by definition they must differ in sex and age, and very generally do in other qualities, and in achievements, authority and possessions. Even though for these latter reasons they are differently valued to a high degree, that is still an element of status which they share equally and in respect of which the only differentiation tolerated is that involved in the socially approved differences of the sex and age status.[13]

He furthermore argues that the marriage pattern is a relationship of equals, and does not involve structural superordination and subordination, because the wife's status is ascribed on the basis of her husband's, which in turn derives from his occupational position: 'in a system not resembling the caste type, husband and wife need not be rigidly equal by birth, although they *become* so by marriage' (p. 78, my emphasis). Thus inequalities between men and women disappear, for Parsons, because the woman's social status is ascribed on the basis of her husband's. The married woman, by definition, has an equal social status to her husband. In his 'A revised analytical approach to the theory of social stratification', Parsons does in fact recognize more explicitly the contradiction between the dominant egalitarian values and sex role segregation, and ultimately accepts some degree of inequality as being functionally necessary:

> it follows that the preservation of a functioning family system even of our type is incompatible with complete equality of opportunity. It is a basic limitation on the full implementation of our paramount value system, which is attributable to its conflict with the functional exigencies of personality and cultural stabilization and socialization.[14]

Parsons recognises that such a situation is unstable, since the wife is denied any occupational definition of her role, and suggests that the housewife may try to modify the domestic role by adopting what he describes as the 'glamour pattern' (which attempts to emphasize feminine values), or the 'common humanistic element' (emphasizing 'civilized' values), instead of adhering to domestic values in defining her status. Parsons's version of the feminine dilemma is described as follows:

> In our society, . . . occupational status has tremendous weight in the scale of prestige values. The fact that the normal married woman is debarred from testing or demonstrating her fundamental equality with her husband in competitive occupational achievement creates a demand for a functional equivalent. At least in the middle classes, however, this cannot be found in the utilitarian functions of the role of housewife since these are treated as relatively menial functions . . . it may be concluded that the feminine role is a conspicuous focus of the strains inherent in our social structure, and not the least of the sources of these strains is to be found in the functional difficulties in the integration of our kinship system with the rest of the social structure.[15]

In *Family: Socialization and Interaction Process*[16] this analysis had undergone a number of modifications, several of which are of relevance to the present discussion. First, in his essay on 'The American family: its relations to personality and to the social structure', Parsons[17] adds an evolutionary component, arguing that the family has become more specialized as a result of industrialization, having lost some of the functions which it used to exercise on behalf of society, such as its role as a unit of economic production, its significance in the political power system, and its functions as a direct agency of integration within the wider society, while gaining new functions on behalf of personality (namely as an agency for the primary socialization of children, and for the stabilization of adult personalities). A second modification is discernible in his more clearly developed theory of socialization, which draws heavily from psycho-analytic insights: in contrast with the earlier *Essays* in which the social differentiation of sex roles is located in an analysis of the contradictory tensions between the occupational system and the kinship system, Parsons argues in *Family: Socialization and Interaction Process* that it is primarily on account of the socialization functions of the family that there is a social, as distinct from a purely reproductive, differentiation of sex roles. One consequence of this increased emphasis on socialization is that the tensions between the occupational system and the kinship system and the resulting strains on the woman's role which Parsons discusses in the *Essays* assume a lesser importance. He is no longer concerned primarily with the structural sources of tension which would be dysfunctional for the social system, but with equilibrating processes, the most important of which, so far as the family is concerned, is socialization. Parsons appears not only to regard socialization as the principal function of the nuclear family, but also to regard the isolated nuclear family as the social institution which is best adapted to the socialization process. [. . .]

The explanation Parsons offers for the apparent universality of the nuclear family is threefold. First, it is an adaptive response to the functional prerequisites of tension management and pattern maintenance. Second, it is best adapted to fulfil the psychoanalytically defined needs of the individual in the process of socialization.

And third, it results from the biological fact that women bear and nurse children. Thus both the structure of the nuclear family and the sex role divisions within it, within Parsons' analysis, are overdetermined by a combination of social, psychological and biological elements.

What I am suggesting, then, is that in *Essays in Sociological Theory* Parsons places the position of women within an analysis of the contradictory demands of the occupational system and the kinship system in industrial societies; and I have criticized this mode of conceptualization for its concentration upon evaluative and normative factors, a preoccupation which has led Parsons to ignore the economic role of women within the home as domestic labourers and also to ignore the significance of women's wage labour. Parsons' conceptual framework necessarily excludes the possibility of any analysis of the sources of sexual inequality which locate it in terms of the organization of the capitalist mode of production. [...]

II

There has emerged in postwar Britain a fairly coherent body of sociological studies which have been concerned with married women working, and with the implications of this for relationships within the family. The pioneer study, Myrdal and Klein's *Women's Two Roles*, first appeared in 1956.[18] This has been followed by other similar studies such as Klein's *Britain's Married Women Workers* and Yudkin and Holme's *Working Mothers and Their Children*,[19] some of which – for example Fogarty, Rapoport and Rapoport's *Sex, Career and Family*[20] – have restricted themselves to women engaged in professional occupations. Other studies have considered the impact of women working on the structure of the family: Rapoport and Rapoport's *Dual Career Families*[21] and Young and Willmott's *The Symmetrical Family*.[22] Most of these investigations have been policy oriented – written with the objectives of investigating barriers against women working, of influencing social policies which would make it easier for women to work (policies concerning nursery provision, maternity leave and so on) and advocating the reorganization of working in order that women's labour can increasingly be drawn upon, (for example, by developing more flexible hours of work, part-time work). Recognizing the shortage of labour which existed during the postwar period in Britain, the studies have shared the assumption that married women are an important source of labour at all levels of the occupational structure, and have investigated the social characteristics of women who work, when in their life cycles they work, what problems they face when they work and so on, amassing a considerable amount of evidence on these questions. I am not concerned with their particular empirical findings here, but rather with an examination of the theoretical framework within which these studies have been undertaken, and I shall attempt to show how their focus upon what economists call the 'supply' of labour has led them to ignore some important questions concerned with the structuring of women's employment.

These studies have accepted elements of Parsons's functionalist framework, but in an *ad hoc* way, and since they are formulated as empirical studies their functionalist assumptions are not always explicit. Such assumptions become evident, however, in the central place occupied in these analyses by the concept of sex roles: the position of both men and women within the social structure is defined in terms of the social expectations of a person holding a particular role, social positions being defined in normative terms. While these studies share with Parsons a notion of sex roles understood in terms of normative expectations, they lack the macrosociological analysis which Parsons provides, in his early *Essays*, of the tensions between the demands of the occupational system and the kinship system in industrial societies. Thus, instead of providing an analysis of tensions whose roots are located at a societal level, the empirical studies locate tensions for the individual women as resulting from the existence of different sets of normative expectations. The basis of women's social position is therefore defined, as in the title of Myrdal and Klein's book, precisely as a tension between two roles, housewife and worker, a tension which does lead the authors to speak of a 'feminine dilemma' determined by the 'typical' conflicts which women subjectively experience between their career and familial roles. No analysis of the social/historical foundations of these conflicts is provided.

Where these studies do depart from Parsons, however, is in their recognition that many women go out to work, and they furthermore advocate changes in social policies which would make it easier for women to work outside the home, especially when they do not have young children. Women's position is therefore not defined in terms of the Parsonian expressive-instrumental dichotomy, since the studies recognize that many women fulfil aspects of both roles. Klein argues that 'the number of . . . social roles has . . . been increased and the forum on which they are enacted been widened'.[23] However, the studies do accept the fundamental Parsonian functionalist thesis that industrialization has modified the functions of the family by removing production to factories, which employ individuals and not families, and which supply goods and services outside the home. And they agree with Parsons that the family, shorn of many of its economic and educational functions, has been left with two major functions: socialization, and providing a focal point for lasting affections. However, they then develop what might be described as a reformulated functionalist thesis, by which I mean a thesis that there has emerged in postwar Britain, as a response to a demand for labour, a further development involving the re-entry of women into the world of work, and the subsequent combination of family and work life. The effects of women performing 'two roles', it is argued, may lead to the emergence of new forms of family: the dual career family described by Rapoport and Rapoport,[24] and the symmetrical family described by Young and Willmott.[25] Thus Klein,[26] for example, argues that there has been a tendency for the traditional patriarchal family to be replaced by a new, more democratic family form characterized by a relationship of partnership between husband and wife, which among other things encourages the relative independence of children. [. . .]

The change which these empirical studies document are ascribed in twin sources: the impact of industrialization and the normative march towards democracy. These factors, either alone or taken together, do not provide a satisfactory explanation, however. The studies first of all posit industrialization as a kind of *deus ex machina*, without specifying which elements of industrialization bring about particular changes. Capitalist industrialization involves a process of uneven development, and the labour process is transformed in different ways in different branches of production. Thus some industries (for example, the sweated or domestic industries which arose as a consequence of the development of modern industry, forming an underbelly of the industrial revolution, and providing an extremely important locus of female labour) remain relatively labour intensive (Alexander),[27] while others undergo rapid mechanization (for example, first spinning and then weaving in textiles, the latter remaining an important area of women's employment in nineteenth-century Britain). An adequate explanation of the impact of industrialization would require an analysis of the development of modern industry and the relationship between changes in the labour process and the employment of women in different branches of production. Likewise, any analysis couched in terms of the demand for labour would have to explain why in some conditions and not in others there is a demand of female labour (for example, in weaving, but in large numbers of mills not in spinning as industrialization proceeded), and how this demand is related to the organization of the labour process in particular industries as well as to the availability of other sources of labour. It is inadequate to postulate industrialization *per se* as an explanatory factor without specifying which elements of the development of industrial capitalism bring about particular changes, and without showing how these changes affect the demand for female labour.

A second problem with these studies is that their analysis is founded on various taken-for-granted assumptions the bases of which themselves require explanation. Thus the increased employment of married women is ascribed by Klein to the expansion of administrative, education, welfare and other services, which she describes as 'the very types of work which women are thought to be particularly well fitted to perform'. Myrdal and Klein[28] likewise provide no explanation of the re-establishment of pre-war conditions after the Second World War, but merely describe the closure of day nurseries and the cutting down of part-time jobs as part of the urge to go 'back to normal'. An adequate explanation of these phenomena, however, would have to consider why women are brought into employment in some conditions of labour scarcity – for example, during both world wars – to analyse the extent to which the sexual division of labour was modified under the impact of women working, and to examine its subsequent restructuring as after both wars women were excluded from employment in many industries and occupations. This would involve an analysis of a number of different levels: changes in the labour process, state policies, trade union agreements, values and beliefs around the family and women working. The authors of the empirical sociological studies are evidently aware of the importance of ideological factors in influencing the employment of women, but any such awareness tends to take the form of the kind of broad generalizations about the advance of progress, affluence and so on common in the postwar period in which they were writing. [. . .]

A similar tone of optimism pervades Young and Willmott's book, *The Symmetrical Family*,[29] in which the consequences of the increasing numbers of married women working for the family structure are analyzed. The authors argue that there have been three stages in the development of the family, from the pre-industrial family through the family of individual wage earners to the symmetrical family. In the symmetrical family, the former unity of husband and wife is restored around the functions of consumption, the couple is privatized and home centred, the nuclear family is more important than the extended family and sex roles are less segregated. The concept of the symmetrical family preserves the notion of differentiated sex roles, on a 'separate but equal' basis. Young and Willmott argue, on extremely flimsy evidence, that the symmetrical family enjoys more equality since there is increased financial partnership, more work sharing (their criterion for this being that men help with one task once a week!), and men work less while women work more – hence the symmetry. Thus 'a partnership in leisure has . . . succeeded a partnership in work'. Like the Rapoports, Young and Willmott assume that this new form of family, the harbinger of the future, will be diffused from the middle to the lower classes. A major problem with *The Symmetrical Family*, as with the optimistic beliefs of Myrdal and Klein, is that it is based upon an article of faith, upon a general optimistic belief in the long march towards democracy which is presumed to emerge as a natural outgrowth of a broad evolutionary process. Instead of taking such optimistic beliefs as given, however, it is necessary to explain why women were for so long excluded from the extension of democratic rights, and to show how their gradual inclusion within the body politic so far as legal and political rights are concerned has resulted not from an evolutionary process but from feminist struggle. Furthermore, it is important to explain why, even when some political and juridical rights have been achieved, the economic position of women has remained subordinated to that of men.

I have, in the preceding pages, suggested a number of criticisms of empirical sociological studies of 'women's two roles'. First, I have argued that they share the functionalist preoccupation with normative expectations. One result of this has been the obliteration of the economic role of female wage labour and domestic labour; a further consequence has been the pervasive optimistic belief in the long march of progress, which the studies accept as an article of faith. Second, I have suggested that the tensions which Parsons locates *structurally* within the organization of society have become reduced to individual role conflicts, and no explanation is provided of the foundations of these role conflicts within the organization of society. Third, no analysis is provided of the conditions which gave rise to the sexual division of labour, the existence of which, in fact, the studies take for granted. Finally, no analysis is provided of the labour process. One result of the fact that these empirical studies offer no analysis of the ways in which the capitalist labour process structures the organization of work and the demand for labour on the one hand, nor the basis of the sexual division of labour and its relationship to the labour process on the other, is that no explanation can be provided for the concentration of women in unskilled occupations in certain branches of manufacturing industry and in service occupations, nor for the fact that much 'women's work' is part time and low paid. In the next part of this paper I turn to the dual labour market approach which claims to constitute such an explanation.

III

Unlike the empirical sociological studies which I have discussed above, dual labour market theories locate the subordination of woman within an analysis of the labour market. Barron and Norris describe their departure from conventional sociological accounts in these terms:

> To borrow the terminology of economics, the sociologists have concentrated upon the supply side of the situation and have paid less attention to the demand side. Although they have pointed out that demand factors are important (for example, by showing that female labour force participation rates have shown sharp upsurges in times of high demand for labour) they have been less observant about the structure of the labour market into which women have been drawn and have had little to say about the forces which maintain that structure.[30]

Their objective is therefore to suggest a framework by means of which the nature and causes of occupational differences between the sexes can be approached, drawing on the concept of the dual labour market. [...]

Essential to the notion of the dual labour market is the assumption that the labour market is segmented into a number of structures. The most common approach differentiates two sectors, primary and secondary labour markets, and Barron and Norris describe the differences between these sectors:

> Primary sector jobs have relatively high earnings, good fringe benefits, good working conditions, a high degree of job security and good opportunities for advancement, while secondary jobs have relatively low earnings levels, poor working conditions, and negligible opportunities for advancement, and a low degree of job security. ... The difference between the opportunities for advancement offered by jobs in the primary sector and those in the secondary sector is usually related to the existence of structured internal labour markets to which primary jobs are attached. A highly structured internal labour market contains a set of jobs organized hierarchically in terms of skill level and rewards, where recruitment to higher positions in the hierarchy is predominantly from lower positions in the same hierarchy and not from the external labour market. Only the lowest positions in the firm's job hierarchy are not filled from within the organisation by promotion. Secondary jobs, on the other hand, are not part of a structured internal market; recruits to these jobs tend to come from outside the organization and will go back outside the organization onto the open labour market when they leave the job. Furthermore, because of the low skill level requirement for most secondary jobs, training is non-existent or minimal, so that secondary workers rarely acquire skills which they can use to advance their status on the open market.[31]

Not only, therefore, is there a segmentation of labour markets: there is also a segmentation of workers into primary and secondary sectors. As Gordon points out,[32] one problem with the dual labour market approach arises in differentiating between characteristics of occupations in different sectors and their holders, which frequently become conflated. This problem becomes apparent in the last section of Barron and Norris's paper, where they describe the characteristics of secondary occupations and then examine the 'fit' between common 'female' characteristics and these occupations, yet never actually demonstrate that in concrete situations women are employed in particular secondary occupations for these reasons.

The dual labour market approach claims that there is a restricted movement of workers between the two sectors of the labour market and that mobility in the hierarchically organized primary labour market tends to be upward, while in the secondary labour market it is horizontal. Thus primary employees are more likely to be mobile within hierarchically organized career structures in the firm, while secondary employees tend to move between industries and occupations (for example, in and out of unskilled and semi-skilled jobs). It postulates the existence of a division also among employers into primary and secondary groups. Some theorists,[33] assume that employers in the monopoly sector of the economy act as primary employers, utilizing an internal labour market in monopolistic enterprises; while employers in the competitive sector adopt a secondary strategy. Edwards attempts to tie the distinction between primary and secondary employers into distinction (as used by O'Connor, for example[34]) between monopolistic, competitive and state sectors of the economy. Barron and Norris do not tie primary employers into the monopoly sector in this way, however, but rather assume that primary employers can exist in different sectors of the economy. Various explanations have been advanced as to why employers adopt different recruitment strategies. Gordon[35] argues that the division between primary and secondary labour markets stems from employers' reactions to two problems: first, the need to promote employee stability in certain jobs; and second, the need to prevent the growth of class consciousness among certain sectors of the working class. However, Barron and Norris modify these arguments, suggesting that the attempt to create a primary labour market arises from the need to tie skilled workers into the firm and thus to reduce labour turnover among groups of workers with scarce skills, and from the need to buy off groups of workers in the face of demands for improved pay and working conditions. The strategies adopted by employers in the primary sector to reduce turnover and buy off sectors of workers have important implications for the structure of jobs in the secondary sector, particularly as far as levels of security and earnings are concerned. It therefore follows that 'in so far as it is in the interests of employers to maintain and expand the primary sector, it is also in their interest to ensure that instability and low earnings are retained in the secondary sector'.[36] This becomes easier, Barron and Norris point out, if there exists a readily available supply of labour which is prepared to accept the inferior pay, job security, job status and working conditions which are offered by the majority of employers in the secondary sector: a reserve army of labour.

Having characterized the primary and secondary labour markets as emerging from strategies adopted by employers to cope with labour market and consumer market fluctuations, Barron and Norris attempt to demonstrate that the female labour force can be characterized in terms of the concept of the secondary labour market. They argue that women's pay is significantly lower than men's, and that there is a high degree of occupational segmentation between male and female workers; that there is some evidence that women are more likely to be made redundant than men and thus to have a higher degree of job insecurity; that men are more likely to be upwardly mobile than women; and finally that women have limited opportunities for advancement, tending instead to be horizontally mobile. In this way it can be argued that women workers conform to all the criteria of secondary labour market employees. The concluding part of Barron and Norris's paper is concerned with the question of *why* women are confined to the secondary labour market. They argue that there are five major attributes which make a particular group likely to be a source of secondary workers, and that women possess each of them. These attributes are:

1   workers are easily dispensable, whether voluntarily or involuntarily;

2   they can be sharply differentiated from workers in the primary labour market by some conventional social difference;

3   they have a relatively low inclination to acquire valuable training and experience;

4   they are low on 'economism' – that is, they do not rate economic rewards highly;

5   they are relatively unlikely to develop solidaristic relations with fellow workers.

This part of the analysis is problematic, partly because little evidence is offered that these attributes actually are significant in concrete situations: the suggestion that women possess them relies heavily upon inference from stereotypical assumptions, and such a suggestion also casts doubt on their general claim that women's position can be explained in terms which are internal to the labour market. However, before discussing this particular problem, which is concerned with the application of the dual labour market approach to women, I first want to make some general comments about the dual labour market approach's characterization of the labour process.

The principal advantage of this approach is its emphasis that where women are employed it is in unskilled and semi-skilled jobs in particular occupations and industries, many of which provide little job security and are poorly paid. Thus Barron and Norris provide evidence to demonstrate that the employment situation of women is not equal to that of men (especially of white men), although it may share characteristics with those of certain other groups of workers, for example immigrant, Asian or black workers. In locating the reasons for this inequality within different employer strategies which are *de facto* discriminatory, the approach counters the view derived from neoclassical economics that individuals are allocated to occupational positions purely by the play of market forces. It also counters technological determinism by analyzing the role that management plays in structuring the labour process. Nevertheless dual labour market theories do encounter a number of problems, especially at the level of explanation. Some of these are general difficulties which exist independently of whether the approach is being used to analyze the position of women workers, while others apply specifically to the attempt to extend dual labour market analysis to women's employment. The first problem is suggested by Edwards when he argues that 'while the dual labour market theory may allow us to classify market behaviour, it does not necessarily explain it. . . . We must return to the sphere of production for an adequate explanation'.[37] As it stands the dual labour market approach is generally descriptive and taxonomic: it does not adequately explain the growth of the segmented labour market. This is because it abstracts the question of employers' behaviour in the labour market from an analysis of the labour process, specifically from an analysis of the productive forces as they are manifested in technological developments, and of the relations of production as they are embodied in class struggle.

Gordon suggests that the dual labour market approach is not inconsistent with a class analysis:

> The dual labour market theory offers a specific analysis of the labour market which can be interpreted in class terms, but the dual labour market theory itself does not rely on the concept, does not link the distinction between primary and secondary markets to other potential class divisions, and does not consistently base its hypotheses on evaluations of the group interests of employers or employees in either market.[38]

But Barron and Norris's explanation is only a partial one, for two reasons. First, it only makes sense to talk about employer strategies in the context of a concrete analysis of the organization of the labour process. Braverman[39] attempts to do this by tying the question of the different strategies adopted by capital and its representatives for organizing the labour process into an analysis of capital accumulation. The question of capitalist control over the labour market and the labour process is extremely important, but an adequate analysis needs to be far more specific than Barron and Norris's discussion. The second reason why their explanation is partial is that Barron and Norris, like Braverman, ignore the fact that the organization of trade unions and other forms of shop floor organization can be an important constraint upon capital's capacity to pursue a rational labour market strategy in terms of its interests. Apprenticeship regulations, for example, or trade union practices may impose constraints upon employers' decisions. A clear example of this is to be found in arguments concerning the recent British equal-pay legislation. The Confederation of British Industries had for some time been in favour of such legislation so long as it was linked with a package which would abolish protective legislation for women, presumably because this would enable employers to develop a more rational labour market strategy without restrictions upon the mobility and use of labour. The Trade Union Congress successfully resisted this demand, however, and an Equal Pay Act was passed in 1970 which retained protective legislation for women (although the Equal Opportunities Commission has a statutory duty to review the protective laws and to advise the government as to whether they should be repealed, amended or left as they are, so the future of these laws is by no means guaranteed). Any analysis of capital's labour market strategies, whether on a national or a local level, must consider the ways in which organized labour, both formally and informally (through custom and practice and shop floor organization), may in certain circumstances impose constraints upon capital's ability to pursue its interests. Such an analysis must also consider the ways in which organized labour fails to represent the interests of its membership – or certain sectors of it – by adopting policies which do not challenge capital's domination of the labour process. The forms of struggle between capital and labour over the organization of the labour process, and the implications of different forms of struggle for the position of female wage labourers within the labour process, are important questions to be investigated.

Having pointed to some of the problems involved in the dual labour market approach in general, I shall now consider further problems which arise from its application to female employment. My first point is that the major concentrations of female employment exist in different sectors of the economy, women being distributed horizontally – employed in particular industries and occupations – and vertically – employed mainly as unskilled and semi-skilled workers. In the conflation of the multifarious forms of employment into a heterogeneous category of secondary sector workers, the important differences between these predominantly female occupations become submerged. My second point is that much of the postwar expansion of women's employment has taken place in the state sector (nursing, teaching, cleaning and catering, clerical work and social work, for example). It is not clear from Barron and Norris's paper, however, how the dual labour market analysis might apply to the state sector in terms of changes in consumer demand, and employers' strategies in response to these changes. If state sector workers are categorized merely as secondary workers in the economy and the dynamics of their employment are seen to follow from employers' attempts to create a stable primary labour market, the important questions of the determinants of the demand for female labour in the state sector and the specificity of the position of employees in that sector are ignored.

A third, and crucial, problem concerns the fact that the dual labour market approach relegates the sexual division of labour to the status of an exogeneous variable, while the dynamics of the labour market are assumed to be the determinant factor in explaining the position of female labour. Barron and Norris's conceptual framework is essentially Weberian in this respect:

> The question of women's place in the family – the household sexual division of labour – will be relegated to the status of an explanatory factor which contributes to, but does not of itself determine, the differentiation between the sexes in their work roles. ... The approach adopted in this paper ... emphasizes the importance of considering the structure of the labour market and women's place within it as one cause among several of women's overall social position. Indeed a degree of causal circularity is assumed in the discussion which follows; ideological factors are seen as contributing to the preservation of the existing job structure for women, while the job structure is seen as a principal determinant of the inferior status of women as a social group and of the sexist ideology which helps to maintain their position.[40]

The list of attributes which Barron and Norris provide in the final part of their paper exactly indicates the importance of the family and of assumptions which justify the sexual division of labour in determining the attributes with which women enter the labour market. In fact, only one of the five attributes which Barron and Norris list arises intrinsically from the labour market situation of women (this is the lack of solidarism, which is ascribed to the fact that many women work in small establishments, work part time and so on). Given the salience of extrinsic criteria which derive from women's role in the family and from ideological representations of this role, it is difficult to understand why Barron and Norris attempt to locate their explanation solely within the internal dynamics of the labour market. They describe a 'vicious cycle' between ascriptive characteristics, such as sex, and the labour market:

> When ascriptive characteristics like sex are used as selection criteria this will have the effect of confining the groups so delineated to the secondary sector over the whole of their working lives. . . . The actual confinement of particular groups to the secondary sector will result in their having higher rates of labour turnover and job mobility. Thus a 'vicious cycle' is created which reinforces the discriminating power of the trait which was made the basis of the selection criterion, and the labelling process becomes self-fulfilling.[41]

But the failure to analyse a situation in which criteria like sex or gender become socially significant results in the 'vicious cycle' approaching a tautological explanation. What is in fact required is a theory which links the organization of the labour process to the sexual division of labour; it is of fundamental importance to analyze the relationship between the family and the organization of production in the process of capital accumulation. In the next section I discuss relevant sections of Marx's analysis in *Capital*,[42] the main project of which is a critical analysis of capitalist production.

IV

In this part of the paper I shall discuss two aspects of Marx's analysis in volume one of *Capital* which are in my view essential for understanding the position of female wage labour in the capitalist mode of production.[43] The first is Marx's analysis of the labour process, and specifically his discussion of the transition from manufacture to modern industry. The second is his concept of the industrial reserve army.

For Marx, manufacture and modern industry are two forms of organization of the labour process, which is defined in *Capital* as a relationship between the labourer (who has nothing to sell but his/her labour power), the object of labour and the instruments of labour (such as tools and machinery). The labour process in any period is a product of the development of the forces of production, and embraces both the forces and relations of production. Manufacture, according to Marx, is the characteristic form of labour process throughout the manufacturing period of the capitalist mode of production, before this mode of production has taken hold of all branches of production and drawn them into the system of commodity production. Its basis lies in handicrafts, and production takes place in the workshop. As far as the actual organization of the labour process is concerned, the important characteristics of manufacture are twofold. First, traditional handicrafts are broken down into a succession of manual operations in the workshop, such that 'each workman becomes exclusively assigned to a partial function, and that for the rest of his life, his labour-power is turned into the organ of this detail function'.[44] That is, there is a specialization of functions, or a developed division or labour based upon co-operation among those working in a particular workshop, among the detail labourers who together comprize the collective labourer. Second, these different functions are arranged according to a hierarchy of concrete labours with a corresponding scale of wages. At the bottom of this hierarchy emerges a class of unskilled labourers. Marx argues that since manufacture adapts detail operations to varying degrees of maturity, strength and development of labour power, this is in theory conducive to the employment of women and children, but that 'this tendency as a whole is wrecked on the habits and the resistance of the male labourers',[45] who jealously insist on maintaining apprenticeships even when these become unnecessary.

This system of production, with its hierarchy of concrete labours and subjective division of labour, gives way to modern industry, to 'real' capitalist control, Marx argues, when machines are created which can make machinery. In modern industry the instruments of labour, the workman's tools, are converted into machines, and there emerges a new form of division of labour in which the worker becomes a mere appendage of the machine. The most important characteristics of modern industry as far as the present discussion is concerned are first of all that, since the worker's skill has been handed over to the machine, the use of machinery provides the precondition for the abolition of the division of labour which was based on manufacture:

> Along with the tool, the skill of the workman in handling it passes over to the machine. The capabilities of the tool are emancipated from the restraints that are inseparable from human labour-power. Thereby the technical foundation on which is based the division of labour in manufacture, is swept away. Hence, in the place of the hierarchy of specialized workmen that characterizes manufacture, there steps, in the automatic factory, a tendency to equalize and reduce to one and the same level every kind of work that has to be done by the minders of the machines; in the place of the artificially produced differentiations of the detail workmen, step natural differences of age and sex.[46]

That is, the manufacturing division of labour with its hierarchy of concrete labours is no longer inherent in the labour process as it was in manufacture. However, Marx argues that the division of labour hangs on through what he calls traditional habit, and becomes in modern industry a way of intensifying exploitation through fostering competition. Thus there exists a contradiction between the technical necessities of modern industry and the social character inherent in its capitalist form, such that 'the life-long speciality of handling one and the same tool, now becomes the life-long speciality of serving one and the same machine'.[47]

Second, Marx argues that there exists a tendency in modern industry towards the substitution of unskilled labour for skilled, female labour for male, young labour for mature. He ascribes this tendency to the fact that machinery dispenses with the need for muscular strength, an argument founded upon naturalistic assumptions that women's physical strength is less than men's:

> In so far as machinery dispenses with muscular power, it becomes a means of employing labourers of slight muscular strength, and those whose bodily development is incomplete, but whose limbs are all the more supple. The labour of women and children was, therefore, the first thing sought for by capitalists who used machinery. That mighty substitute for labour and labourers was forthwith changed into a means for increasing the number of wage-labourers by enrolling, under the direct sway of capital, every member of the workman's family, without distinction of age or sex.[48]

Third, Marx argues that the excessive employment of women and children serves to break down the resistance which male operatives had to the development of machinery in the manufacturing period; that is, the existence of female labour is used by capital to foster competition.

Fourth, Marx argues that modern industry gives rise to intensified production outside factories, in the form of outwork, sweating, and so on, a new form of domestic industry in which women and children are extensively employed.

Finally, Marx argues that the more extensive employment of women and children gives rise to a new form of family and relations between the sexes:

> However terrible and disgusting the dissolution, under the capitalist system, of the old family ties may appear, nevertheless, modern industry, by assigning as it does an important part in the process of production, outside the domestic sphere, to women, to young persons, and to children of both sexes, creates a new economic foundation for a higher form of the family and of the relations between the sexes.[49]

This becomes a central tenet of Engels who argues in *The Origin of the Family, Private Property and the State* that:

> since large-scale industry has transferred the woman from the house to the labour market and the factory and makes her, often enough, the bread-winner of the family, the last remnants of male domination in the proletarian home have lost all foundation.[50]

and thereby concludes that 'the first premise for the emancipation of women is the reintroduction of the entire female sex into public industry' (p. 510). It is important to emphasize that both Marx and Engels constitute the form of the labour process and also the form of the family as matters for historical investigation.

Although Marx does not discuss in any detail the advantages to capital of employing female labour, it is possible to cull a number of arguments from his discussion at different points in *Capital*. These hinge, in one way or another, on the theory of value. Jean Gardiner[51] and others, [...] have pointed to the ways in which women's domestic labour can lower the value of labour power by producing use values which contribute to the reproduction of labour power in the home. It is also important to consider the relationship between female wage labour and the value of labour power, and to show how capital utilizes female wage labour in ways which are economically advantageous to it. The first advantage to capital of the tendency for modern industry to employ all the members of the workman's family is that the value of labour power tends to be lowered since the costs of reproduction are spread over all the members of the population. Thus the portion of the working day in which the labourer works for himself is lowered, and more surplus value is thereby extracted.

> The value of labour-power was determined, not only by the labour-time necessary to maintain the individual adult labourer, but also by that necessary to maintain his family. Machinery, by throwing every member of that family on to the labour-market, spreads the value of the man's labour-power over his whole family. It thus depreciate his labour-power. To purchase the labour-power of a family of four workers may, perhaps, cost more than it formerly did to purchase the labour-power of the head of the family, but, in return, four days' labour takes the place of one, and their price falls in proportion to the excess of the surplus labour of four over the surplus labour of one. In order that the family may live, four people must now, not only labour, but expend surplus-labour for the capitalist. Thus we see, that machinery, while augmenting the human material that forms that principal object of capital's exploiting power, at the same time raises the degree of exploitation.[52]

This tendency is generalized from Marx's analysis of the textiles industry in which men, women and children were extensively employed in the early stages of modern industry.

Marx also suggests at various points in his argument that while the value of labour power is theoretically assumed to be averaged for a given society, in practice labour power will have different values. As determinants of these concrete differences in the value of labour power he cites a number of factors, including the expenses involved in training, natural diversity and the part played by the labour of women and children. This raises the question of whether female labour power has a lower value, and if so, why. One reason might be that women have less training, and therefore the costs of reproducing their labour power are lower; a second that, by virtue of the existence of the family, women are not expected themselves to bear the costs of reproduction. Since male wages are paid on the assumption that men are responsible for the costs of reproduction, and since it is generally assumed that women have husbands to provide for them and their children, the value of labour power can be lowered since it is assumed that women in the family do not have to bear the costs of reproduction.

The advantage to capital of female labour power having a lower value parallels the tendency, noted by Marx, to pay wages below the value of labour power. This is commonly the case with female wage rates, which can be lower because of the assumption that women are subsidiary workers and their husbands' wages are responsible for the costs of reproduction. Marx states that the

> Forcible reduction of wages below ... [the] value [for labour power] plays ... in practice too important a part. ... It, in fact, transforms within certain limits, the labourer's necessary consumption-fund into a fund for the accumulation of capital.[53]

As far as women are concerned, it is only possible to pay wage rates below the value of labour power because of the existence of the family, and because of the assumption that a woman is partly dependent upon her husband's wages within the family. It is this tendency to pay women wages below the value of labour power which is responsible for the plight of single, working-class women, widows and female-headed, single-parent families – the impoverished needlewomen and shop-workers of the nineteenth century, many of whom were forced into prostitution, and the single-parent family of today. The point is that even where women do not have husbands – or fathers – to support them, in patriarchal ideology their social position is defined in terms of the family as a patriarchal structure. A fourth advantage to capital of female labour concerns the circulation of commodities. Marx suggests in a footnote that the employment of women leads to an increased demand for ready made articles, and hence speeds up the circulation process. He states that when

> certain family functions, such as nursing and suckling children, cannot be entirely suppressed, the mothers confiscated by capital, must try substitutes of some sort. Domestic work, such as sewing and mending, must be replaced by the purchase of ready-made articles. Hence, the diminished expenditure of labour in the house is accompanied by an increased expenditure of money. The cost of keeping the family increases, and balances the greater income.[54]

This theme is taken up by Braverman[55] in his chapter on the 'The universal market' in which he discusses how capital took over tasks such as food production and processing, clothes production, and so on, which were formerly undertaken within the domestic economy at the same time as employing women as wage labourers to perform these tasks. That is, women's work leads to an increased demand for consumer goods, while the demand for female wage labour historically has been linked to the development of consumer goods manufacturing industries, according to Braverman. (It should perhaps be noted, however, that Braverman does not sufficiently link his discussion of the universal market with his analysis of the labour process; and thereby loses sight of the fact that it is because of the family that capital is able to draw on female labour in particular ways as a form of industrial reserve army.)

A final advantage to capital of employing female wage labourers which is discussed by Marx in his chapters on the labour process is that it breaks down male workers' resistance to capitalist development which had existed in the manufacturing period.

He states that 'by the excessive addition of women and children to the ranks of the workers, machinery at last breaks down the resistance which the male operatives in the manufacturing period continued to oppose to the despotism of capital'.[56] One implication of this is that the introduction of women and children, while being advantageous to capital, is at the same time resisted by the male workers who struggle to maintain their position of privilege. That is, it suggests that the introduction of women and children into modern industry is a source of class struggle. This can itself be an important source of divisions within the working class.

Before returning to discuss some of the problems which this analysis raises, I shall now turn to the second aspect of Marx's analysis which is relevant to an analysis of female wage labour, the concept of the industrial reserve army. For Marx an industrial reserve army[57] or relative surplus population is both a necessary product and a lever of capital accumulation, a condition of the existence of the capitalist mode of production:

> It forms a disposable industrial reserve army, that belongs to capital quite as absolutely as if the latter had bred it at its own cost. Independently of the limits of the actual increase of population, it creates, for the changing needs of the sell-expansion of capital, a mass of human material always ready for exploitation.[58]

This is not the case in the early stages of capitalism where capital composition changes slowly, but rather emerges in the transition of modern industry where capitalist control of the labour process is generalized. At this point an industrial reserve army becomes a permanent feature of capital accumulation. Thus:

> The course characteristic of modern industry . . . depends on the constant formation, the greater or less absorption, and the re-formation, of the industrial reserve army of surplus-population. In their turn, the varying phases of the industrial cycle recruit the surplus population, and become one of the most energetic agents of its reproduction.[59]

When accumulation develops in old branches of production, or penetrates new branches of production, 'there must be the possibility of throwing great masses of men suddenly on the decisive points without injury to the scale of production in other spheres'.[60] This requires a relative surplus population which is independent of the natural limits of the population. In the discussion below I shall concentrate upon three questions which are raised by Marx's analysis. First, how is the concept defined? Second, what are the functions of the industrial reserve army? And third, can female labour be described in terms of the concept of the industrial reserve army?

The concept of the industrial reserve army, or relative surplus population, is not very precisely defined by Marx, and this imprecision has given rise to various interpretations in subsequent marxist writings. At some points Marx distinguishes between the active labour army and the industrial reserve army, implying that these are mutually exclusive categories, while at others he describes the major forms of the industrial reserve army as all being part of the active labour army. Marx further distinguishes between three forms of industrial reserve army:

1 the floating form, whereby labourers are sometimes repelled and sometimes attracted into the centres of modern industry. This is linked to the argument that the demand for labour in the centres of modern industry tends to substitute unskilled for skilled labour, women for men, and youths for adults;

2 the latent form, which exists among the agricultural population which is displaced by the capitalist penetration of agriculture;

3 the stagnant form, comprising labourers who are irregularly employed, for example, in domestic industry, whose members are recruited from the supernumerary forces of modern industry and agriculture.

Below these are the categories of pauperism and the 'lazarus layers'.

Marx's analysis contains two elements. There is first of all a theory of the tendency for capital accumulation both to attract and to repel labour which suggests that the structuring of the working class by the labour process is a dynamic process, and that the process of capital accumulation generates considerable amounts of underemployment. The tendency towards attraction of labour resulting from capital accumulation in particular branches of production then raises the question of the sources of labour which become part of the working class, while the tendency towards repulsion raises the question of the destiny of the labourers, whether employed or unemployed (for example, the tendency towards marginalization of certain groups of workers in Latin America suggested by Obregon[61] and the tendency discussed by Jean Gardiner[62] for women rendered unemployed in manufacturing industry in Britain to be absorbed into the service sector). The second element of Marx's analysis is a theory of the functions of the industrial reserve army. He argues that it provides a disposable and flexible population. That is, it provides labour power which can be absorbed in expanding branches of production when capital accumulation creates a demand for it, and repelled when the conditions of production no longer require it. It is therefore a crucial component of capital accumulation, as Obregon[63] points out, essential to the analysis of economic cycles (the industrial reserve army being disposable in the recession) and to the analysis of the penetration of the capitalist mode of production into new branches of production. It is also seen as a condition of competition among workers, the degree of intensity of which depends on the pressure of the relative surplus population. This competitive pressure has two consequences. It depresses wage levels: Marx argues that the general movements of wages are regulated by the expansion and contraction of the industrial reserve army, which in turn corresponds to periodic changes in the industrial cycle. It also forces workers to submit to increases in the rate of exploitation through the pressure of unemployment. Finally, it counteracts the tendency for the rate of profit to fall. The sources of reserve labour which Marx mentions are modern industry itself, which tends to repel labourers as machinery is introduced, and agriculture, which repels labourers as capitalism develops. Clearly women can be repelled, alongside men, in either of these ways – whether they are is, of course, a matter for concrete investigation. The question which I want to raise here, however, is whether the family is *per se* a source like any other of the industrial reserve army or whether married women drawn into production from the family constitute a specific form of industrial reserve army which is different from the forms described by Marx. I have already suggested certain advantages to capital in employing female labour, and will now consider whether further advantages accrue if married women constitute an industrial reserve army.

I would argue that married women function as a disposable and flexible labour force in particular ways, and that the specificity of the position of women arises from their domestic role in the family and the prevalent assumption that this is their primary role. There are several ways in which married women can more easily be made redundant – disposed of – than men. They are less likely to be strongly unionized than men; if made redundant, they are less likely to be in jobs covered by the Redundancy Payments Act; in Britain at the moment married women paying a married woman's national insurance contribution receive less state benefits; and unless they register as unemployed, women do not appear in the unemployment statistics, which accounts for a massive under-numeration of female unemployment. Thus women who are made redundant are able to disappear virtually without trace back into the family. I would also argue that women are more likely to be a flexible working population, being horizontally mobile and willing to take on part-time work. This relates to the assumption that their primary place is in the home, an assumption actually embodied in state policies which, [...] virtually compel women to accept movement into and out of jobs at different periods of their life cycle. Female employment also poses particular pressure on wages since women's wage rates are substantially lower than men's. The fact that women's wages can be paid below the value of labour power means that women, as part of the industrial reserve army, constitute a particularly intense pressure on wage levels. It appears, therefore, that women form a specific element of the industrial reserve army by virtue of the sexual division of labour which consigns them to the family and inscribes a set of assumptions about women's roles. While they can occupy Marx's floating, latent and stagnant categories, married women also have a position which derives specifically from their role in the family.

It is, of course, a matter for concrete historical analysis to establish which sources of industrial reserve army are at various conjunctures drawn upon by capital, this being determined by the availability of various sources of reserve labour and by political expediency, as well as by the relative economic advantages offered by different groups of labour, such as married women and migrant workers, who are partially dependent upon sources other than their own wages for the costs of reproducing their labour power. In the last instance, the question of who actually comprises the industrial reserve army of labour turns on class relations, as two examples from Britain indicate. First, during the First World War, because trade unions objected to the employment of coloured labour, women, drawn mainly from the family and from domestic service, as well as from sweated trades, became a significant reserve for the war effort. After initial objections to dilution and to the employment of women, especially on non-munitions work, a number of agreements were reached between the Amalgamated Society for Engineers and the government, and the Trades Union Congress and the government, which while granting women equal piece rates refused them equal time rates, and moreover ensured that jobs would be vacated for men at the end of the war. The employment of women as a reserve thus offered advantages both to capital, since lower wages could be paid (both by not paying equal time rates and by *de facto* not paying equal piece rates), and also to skilled workers, who could secure the return to the *status quo ante* after the war, at least as far as the exclusion of women from skilled jobs was concerned. A second example emerged during the 1960s when it became politically expedient to restrict immigration to Britain from the Commonwealth to particular occupational groups, thereby rendering women an important source of the industrial reserve army. [...]

It is important to assess the limitations of the marxist analysis discussed here, and to put forward some questions which require further consideration. My basic argument at this point is that a marxist explanation which considers the family-production relationship to be central is able to explain the vertical division of labour: that is, it can explain the tendency for women to be employed in unskilled and semi-skilled jobs in the centres of modern industry and for women to be employed in the sweated trades which flourished as an outgrowth of capitalist industrialization. It cannot, however, explain the horizontal division of labour: that is, it cannot adequately explain why there has emerged a demand for female labour in some centres of modern industry – such as textiles, clothing and footwear, leather goods, food, drink and tobacco production, as well as certain sectors of engineering (electrical engineering and instrument engineering, for example) – but not in others, such as shipbuilding and machine engineering, mining and quarrying, construction and metal manufacture. The tendency has been for analyses of female wage labour to focus upon the appropriation of women's domestic labour into factories with the development of capitalist commodity production, and to show that women perform similar tasks in the factories to those which they perform in the home. Thus Braverman, for example describes how women were drawn into employment in food processing, clothes manufacture and so on, as these activities became appropriated from the family by capitalist commodity production. And the apparent symmetry between women's wage work and domestic labour has led the Power of Women Collective to conclude in *All Work and No Pay*[64] that all forms of women's work are really housework. A glance at the principal occupations of women in nineteenth century Britain does indicate some symmetry between women's domestic labour and other forms of female wage labour, the major occupations for women in 1851 being domestic servant, milliner, worker in cotton manufacture, washerwoman, mangler and laundrykeeper. It is important to emphasize, however, that the view that women's work is a kind of extension of domestic labour is too simplistic (Taylor).[65] While women's wage labour may seem to mirror domestic labour in particular periods, it is essential to penetrate beneath surface appearances and to recognize that wage labour has a different relationship to the organization of production than does domestic labour. As well as analysing the organization of the labour process along the lines already suggested, the analysis of the horizontal division of labour, in order to try to explain why at certain moments some industries and trades have generated a demand for female labour, would also have to consider alternative sources of labour (were women the only available reserve army?), trade union policies relating to the recruitment of women, state policies towards both the employment of women and the family, and attitudes towards women working in particular kinds of occupation. Since the thrust of my argument here has been to emphasize the necessity of integrating an analysis of the sexual division of labour which consigns women to the family into an analysis of the capitalist labour process, I shall conclude by outlining, very briefly, how I see the relationship between the two spheres of production and family in the capitalist mode of production. Prior to the development of industrial capitalism, production took place in the household alongside reproduction and consumption. One of the consequences of the development of modern industry has been that production was largely removed from the family to the factory (although in practice many women continued to work in the home and in small workshops attached to the home). The sphere of production thus became separated from the family, which retained 'functions' which can be discussed by reference to two sets of concepts, reproduction and consumption.

As production moved to the factories with the development of modern industry, a new form of family emerged to fulfil the function of reproducing the commodity labour power, on both a generational and a day-to-day basis. Generational reproduction involves biological reproduction, the regulation of sexuality, and the socialization of children, while day-to-day reproduction involves numerous tasks of domestic labour such as shopping, cooking meals, washing, cleaning and caring. The two forms of reproduction of labour power inscribe biological, economic and ideological components, which are the tasks of domestic labour. The family is furthermore involved in the reproduction of the social relations of production which are in capitalist society both class relations and gender relations. The specific role of the family here involves, on one hand, the transmission of property/propertylessness (the major functions of the family in class societies according to Engels)[66] and, on the other, the reproduction of patriarchal ideology. [...] Like the reproduction of labour power these take place on both a generational and a day-to-day basis. The family also operates as a primary locus of consumption, which is essential to the circulation of commodities in the capitalist mode of production. The relationship between the three elements – production, reproduction and consumption – changes historically, the forms of reproduction and consumption, and therefore the forms of the family and of the sexual division of labour within it, being determined in the last instance by changes in the mode of production. According to this mode of analysis, therefore, the sexual division of labour in the family, which Parsons explains in purely normative terms, is ascribed a material basis. An adequate analysis of the family and of the position of women both as domestic labourers and as wage labourers must provide a theory of the relationship between these elements, which functionalist sociology fails to do. Furthermore, an analysis of female wage labour must integrate an analysis of the labour process with an analysis of the family which defines the specificity of the position of female wage labour, which Braverman and Marx fail to do. It has been the object of this paper to point to some of the problems involved in this task through discussion of a number of approaches to the analysis of women's wage labour. Clearly much more work needs to be done on the subject. My purpose here has been simply to attempt to clarify some of the questions involved in providing a marxist feminist analysis of female wage labour.

Acknowledgements

This paper was written in June 1976 and slightly revised in September, 1977 for publication. I am grateful to many feminists, friends and colleagues, especially in the Coventry–Birmingham area and at the University of Warwick for helpful discussions of the issues raised in the paper, and in particular to Colleen Chesterman, Annette Kuhn and AnnMarie Wolpe for detailed comments on the original version of this paper.

Notes and References

1 Since this paper was first written, the paper by ADAMSON, O., BROWN, C., HARRISON, J. and PRICE, J. (1976), 'Women's oppression under capitalism', *Revolutionary Communist*, No. 5, pp. 2–48, has been published. This emphasizes the interrelationship between women's wage labour and domestic labour.

2 PARSONS, T. (1954) *Essays in Sociological Theory*, New York, Free Press.

3 All references are to an unpublished version of Barron and Norris's paper 'Sexual divisions and dual labour market' presented at the annual conference of the British Sociological Association in 1974. A slightly revised version is published in BARKER, D.L. and ALLEN, S. (Eds.) (1976) *Dependence and Exploitation in Work and Marriage*, London, Longman.

4 My own ideas on the relevance of Marx's analysis in *Capital* for an understanding of female wage labour have developed since I first wrote this paper. See BEECHEY, V. (1977) 'Some notes on female wage labour in capitalist production', in *Capital and Class*, (3), pp. 45–66.

5 PARSONS, T. (1954) *op. cit.*, p. 76.

6 *Ibid.*, pp. 78–9.

7 *Ibid.*, p. 79.

8 *Ibid.*, p. 79.

9 PARSONS, T. and BALES, R.F. (1956) *Family: Socialization and Interaction Process*, London, Routledge and Kegan Paul.

10 MIDDLETON, C. (1974) 'Sexual inequality and stratification theory' in PARKIN, F. *The Social Analysis of Class Structure*, London, Tavistock, p. 180.

11 PARSONS, T. and BALES, R.F. (1956) *op. cit.*, p. 14.

12 *Ibid.*, pp. 14–5.

13 PARSONS, T. (1954) *op. cit.*, p. 77.

14 *Ibid.*, p. 422.

15 PARSONS, T. (1954) *op. cit.*, pp. 193–4.

16 PARSONS, T. and BALES, R.F. (1956) *op. cit.*

17 *Ibid.*

18 MYRDAL, A. and KLEIN, V. (1970) *Women's Two Roles*, London, Routledge and Kegan Paul.

19 KLEIN, V. (1965) *Britain's Married Women Workers*, London, Routledge and Kegan Paul; YUDKIN, S. and HOLME, A. (1969) *Working Mothers and their Children*, London, Sphere.

20 FOGARTY, M.P., RAPOPORT, R. and RAPOPORT, R.N. (1971) *Sex, Career and Family*, London, Allen and Unwin.

21 RAPOPORT, R. and RAPOPORT, R.N. (1971) *Dual Career Families*, Harmondsworth, Penguin.

22 YOUNG, M. and WILLMOTT, P. (1975) *The Symmetrical Family*, Harmondsworth, Penguin.

23 KLEIN, V. (1965) *op. cit.*, p. 18.

24 RAPOPORT, R. and RAPOPORT, R.N. (1971) *op. cit.*

25 YOUNG, M. and WILLMOTT, P. (1975) *op. cit.*

26 KLEIN, V. (1965) *op. cit.*

27 ALEXANDER, S. (1976) 'Women's work in nineteenth-century London: a study of the years 1820–50', in MITCHELL, J. and OAKLEY, A. *The Rights and Wrongs of Women*, Harmondsworth, Penguin.

28 MYRDAL, A. and KLEIN, V. (1970) *op. cit.*

29 YOUNG, M. and WILLMOTT, P. (1975) *op. cit.*

30 BARRON, R.D. and NORRIS, G.M. (1974) 'Sexual divisions and the dual labour market', paper presented at the BSA Annual Conference, p. 2.

31 BARRON, R.D. and NORRIS, G.M. (1974) *op. cit.*, pp. 12–3.

32 GORDON, D.M. (1972) *Theories of Poverty and Underemployment*, Boston, D.C. Heath, p. 88.

33 BLUESTONE, B. (1970) 'The tripartite economy: labor markets and the working poor', *Poverty and Human Resources Abstracts*, July–August, pp. 15–35; EDWARDS, R.C. (1975) 'The social relations of production in the firm and labor market structure', *Politics and Society*, Vol. 5, pp. 83–108.

34 O'CONNOR, J. (1973) *The Fiscal Crisis of the State*, New York, St. Martin's Press.

35 GORDON, D.M. (1972) *op. cit.*

36 BARRON, R.D. and NORRIS, G.M. (1974) *op. cit.*, pp. 23–4.

37 EDWARDS, R.C. (1975) *op. cit.*, p. 88.

38 GORDON, D.M. (1972) *op. cit.*, p. 88.

39 BRAVERMAN, H. (1974) *Labor and Monopoly Capital*, New York, Monthly Review Press.

40 BARRON, R.D. and NORRIS, G.M. (1974) *op. cit.*, p. 1.

41 *Ibid.*, p. 39.

42 MARX, K. (1867) *Capital*, Vol. 1. This edition 1967, New York, International Publishers.

43 This section relies heavily upon collective discussions within the Women and Labour Process Group, of which I am a member.

44 MARX, K. (1867) *op. cit.*, (1967) p. 339.

45 *Ibid.*, p. 367.

46 *Ibid.*, p. 420.

47 *Ibid.*, p. 422.

48 *Ibid.*, p. 394.

49 *Ibid.*, pp. 489–90.

50 ENGELS, F. (1884) *The origin of the family, private property and the state*, in MARK, K. and ENGELS, F., *Selected Works*, (1968) London, Lawrence and Wishart, p. 508.

51 GARDINER, J. (1975) 'Women's Domestic Labour', *New Left Review*, No. 89, pp. 47–58.

52 MARX, K. (1867) *op. cit.*, (1967) p. 395.

53 *Ibid.*, p. 599.

54 *Ibid.*, p. 395, footnote.

55 BRAVERMAN, H. (1974) *op. cit.*

56 MARX, K. (1867) *op. cit.*, (1967) p. 402.

57 I develop the analysis of women as an industrial reserve army and the question of the similarities between married women and other groups in the industrial reserve army (e.g. immigrants, and migrant workers), in BEECHEY, V. (1977) *op. cit.*

58 MARX, K. (1867) *op. cit.*, (1967) p. 632.

59 *Ibid.*, p. 633.

60 *Ibid.*, p. 632.

61 OBREGON, A.Q. (1974) 'The marginal pole of the economy and the marginalized labour force', *Economy and Society*, Vol. 3, pp. 393–428.

62 GARDINER, J. (1975) *op. cit.*

63 OBREGON, A.Q. (1974) *op. cit.*

64 POWER OF WOMEN COLLECTIVE (1975) *All Work and No Pay*, Bristol, Falling Wall Press.

65 TAYLOR, B. (1975–76) 'Our Labour and Our Power', *Red Rag*, No. 10, pp. 18–20.

66 ENGELS, F. (1884) *The origin of the family, private property and the state*, in MARX, K. and ENGELS, F. *Selected Works*, London, Lawrence and Wishart, (1968).

9   The Official Ideology of Education for Girls

Ann Marie Wolpe

Introduction

It is well known that the nature, form and content of education for children is inextricably linked with their future roles in adult society. The education process is a highly complex one. In equipping children for these adult roles a whole range of different forms of knowledge are transmitted. They include the basic fundamental skills of numeracy and literacy essential in an industrial society; they also include the learning of certain types of skills which are necessary for many vocational type jobs; the development of abstract reasoning is encouraged among particular sets of children. In addition to all this, education ensures the transmission of the dominant cultural values specific to the society in that point in time. Bourdieu has emphasized this latter point in the following statement:

> If it be accepted that culture ... is a common code enabling all those possessing that code to attach the same meaning to the same words, and conversely, to express the same meaningful intention through the same words, it is clear that the school which is responsible for handing on that culture, is the fundamental factor in the cultural consensus in as far as it represents the sharing of a common sense which is the prerequisite for communications. Individuals owe to their schooling, first and foremost a whole collection of commonplaces, conveying not only common speech and language but also areas of encounter and agreement, common problems and common methods of approaching those common problems.[1]

One aspect of the 'common code' with all the relevant 'collection of commonplaces' is that which relates to the different expected forms of behaviour of men and women, boys and girls. The code which relates to gender differentiation embraces an ideology regarding the nature and form of appropriate gender behaviour. From childhood on through to adulthood there is a complex set of beliefs not only concerning the basic major roles of the two genders in adult society but also the way in which

Source: FLUDE, M. and AHIER, J. (1976) *Educability, Schools and Ideology*, Croom Helm.

children as well as adults should behave and manifest these basic differences. The dominant ideology legitimates in a complex and multivaried manner the way in which children are reared and taught to act appropriately.

It is true to say that at a very early age children (in fact by the time they have reached their third year) are clearly able to identify masculine and feminine roles particularly in relation to broad categories of behaviour characteristic of the division of labour of their parents both in the home and in the occupational structure of society. In addition to this, young children themselves very soon learn to identify with the appropriate gender roles. This is expressed in different forms of overt behaviour which are manifest in their everyday lives at home, in play, and subsequently when they begin their schooling.[2] In other words, children at an early age, have already internalised important elements of the ideology about the different roles that men and women play in our society.

The processes which contribute to this are complex and closely interrelated. In the early formative years, the family institution is the main medium for the transmission of this ideology. But very soon the influence of peer group, mass media and schooling come into the picture and contribute to the reinforcement of these beliefs.

However, recognising that young school-going children have internalized to some extent the notions about their own gender identities, and developed gender-appropriate forms of behaviour, it is suggested that the period of latent or early adolescence is a crucial phase of development.[3] It is at this period of transition from childhood to adulthood that these notions relating to masculine and feminine roles become clarified and reinforced, and perhaps even redefined in adult terms. This period of the life cycle which represents an apprenticeship for adult status is of critical importance in this regard and the role of the secondary school in terms of defining the situation, as Bourdieu has said, 'the fundamental factor in the cultural consensus' cannot be underestimated.

While there is a consistency in the common code relating to the position of men and women as stated throughout the educational process, nevertheless the secondary school does, for most children, introduce a new element. For the majority of children the secondary school stage represents a new experience. It is at this point that they first are introduced to a totally new situation in which new school subjects are taught by specialists in those subjects and attend class within the framework of a set period.

At this stage of their lives it would appear that irrespective of their differences both boys and girls react to this new situation with shared enthusiasm. Their interests converge and there does not yet appear to be the polarisation which characterises the genders in the upper levels of the school. Overall, girls and boys appear equally receptive to new areas of study that go to make up the curriculum, although there are individual variations in the degree of their enthusiasm which do not seem to be related to gender difference. Yet within a relatively short space of time this situation has undergone a marked change. Girls, as is well known, tend to follow a curriculum which excludes a whole range of subjects, particularly mathematics, physical sciences, and, as could be expected, vocationally oriented subjects related to the trades. They pursue in the main those subjects which are regarded as more suitable for females, such as subjects by definition being 'feminine', home economics, the arts, business studies, (which is shorthand and typing) etc.

Notwithstanding the prevailing ideology that egalitarianism of opportunity exists for both boys and girls alike, their educational experience results in marked differences in their respective levels of attainment and range of subjects passed in qualifying examinations. In any event, by this time, girls have come to limit their own occupational and educational horizons. Their aspirations about their future employment and the realization of these aspirations for the vast majority of girls does not go beyond the scope of what are regarded as 'suitable' feminine jobs. And to this extent the curriculum that girls pursue is appropriate both to their occupational roles in the labour market as well as their roles as wives and mothers.

It could, therefore, be said that the secondary school institutionalises the dominant female gender role. This institutionalization is the result of a number of different processes and structures which characterise the average secondary school. One important aspect covers the ideology of gender differentiation. It is this ideology that provides the legitimation of the various actions, processes and form of teaching that go to making up the school in its entirety. Not only is the ideology expressed in a number of official state documents which provide the guide line for the overall form and nature that secondary schooling should take but it also filters down and becomes part of the 'common code' of the practitioners themselves. The teachers not only share parts of the 'common code' of cultural values but also through the structure imposed by the school organisation itself must transmit much of this ideology.

However, in order to make an initial attempt to understand part of this whole process it is proposed to examine the stated official ideology of the form education should take for girls. In order to do so three educational reports which have appeared in England over the past thirty years (known by their more popular titles as the Norwood, Crowther and Newsom reports)[4] will be examined. Although these three reports were concerned with reformist notions about the nature of education for large numbers of the children in the country and were compiled over a thirty year period, it is interesting to note that they all have several features in common. In the first instance authors of these reports are unaware of the fact that they have taken for granted their own implicit ideological assumptions. The type of question they are likely to ask and the way in which they interpret the answers, and the data they are given, indicates quite clearly their own beliefs. The form of the final report can be seen to display their own system of beliefs. Furthermore, in spite of the different social conditions prevailing at the time of the compilation and presentation of their data, all three reports have consistently shown that they view the school-going population as predominantly homogeneous, boys and girls together. Where they have considered educational problems for girls as distinct from those of boys they have revealed that they have presupposed what will and should be the lives of girls as adults. In other words, they have shown that they accept implicitly the dominant cultural values of the society and have disregarded in the main the stark substantive data of the situation – they have been guided by their ideological assumptions rather than by a disciplined analysis.

These three reports will be examined in some detail in order to illustrate this point substantively. The contradiction between their ideological assumptions and the basic structural features will be drawn, although no attempt will be made to explain this.

Official Ideological Statements

The first document to be examined is the Norwood Report. This was published one year prior to the 1944 Education Act which successfully extended the availability of secondary education to all children in this country.[5] The terms of reference of the Norwood Report were:

> to consider suggested changes in the secondary school curriculum and the question of school examination in relation thereto.

When it began its work the Committee felt that although their terms of reference were highly specific they could not do justice to these problems at all until they had considered what they regarded as a fundamental problem, *viz* the whole purpose of secondary education. Their conceptualization of this problem, and the policies which they formulated, provide a key to the form which secondary and further education has taken since World War II. As will be demonstrated below, their basic ideological position about girls and the nature of their education should take has not been questioned in any significant way by subsequent reports.

The Norwood Report began from a standpoint which was innovative in that they were concerned with the individual child. This was reflected in their statement that education was 'to help each individual realize the full powers of his personality, body, mind and spirit – in a thorough active membership of the Society'.[6] The way was blazoned for the notion of secondary education moving from a teacher-centred orientation to a child-centred one, a philosophical approach which is still dominant today. Essentially they promulgated a change in the relationship between teacher and pupil. The pupil was no longer seen as a passively receptive object within a teaching situation. Rather, the child's own interest was seen as playing a crucial part in the educational process. The child's education was largely to be determined through a uniformity in the pace and rate and process of learning.[7]

In pursuance of this they considered that the needs of children differed according to their 'special interests and aptitudes'. The school population was not seen as being comprised of an undiversified whole. Rather, owing to differences in abilities and their related development, some means would have to be found whereby an 'education most suited to them'[8] could be provided.

The emphasis on 'special interests' becomes crucial. The Norwood Report, as indeed do subsequent reports, demarcates areas of 'natural interests' which cut across the genders; put in the crudest terms, boys' interests are seen as being dominated by their future occupational roles, whereas girls' interests are, in the main, confined to their future roles as wives and mothers.

Because boys are to become the supporters of their future families, their interests are defined almost exclusively in these terms; their secondary schooling is consequently directly related to the types of jobs they will pursue in their adult lives. Likewise because girls are likely to marry and become wives and mothers their secondary education is directly linked to what is seen as their major role in life. This simple dichotomy is seen as immutable and little attention is paid to the fact that women in fact play a dual role – both as wives/mothers and as workers, as is the case with men. In other words the family institution is related only to women without any reference to the part that men play within the family structure.

Curiously, the report failed to recognise the contradiction between their notion of education catering for *individual* interests and aptitudes of all children and the conclusion they reach whereby they classify all boys as having a primary concern with their future work and all girls as being wrapped up in their forthcoming familial roles. In other words they classify the school population into two major groups, i.e. boys and girls, and each of these two groups is seen as comprising a homogeneous whole. They were then able to conclude that the nature of educational facilities for girls must differ from that of boys if their notion of catering for the 'special interests and aptitudes' was to be taken to its logical conclusion.

The curriculum becomes the medium for catering for these differences. The Norwood Report said that it 'must be varied and flexible if it is to offer the nurture of most benefit to the individual'.[9] The flexibility of the curriculum could then cater for these differences thereby equipping children for what the report sees as the ultimate goal of education. Further, the differences in the educational system must apply within each group.

Their ultimate goal of education is defined in terms of the children fitting into the adult world in which they will function as 'citizens and workers with hand and brain in a society of fellow citizens and fellow workers'.[10]

A further difficulty is encountered when they nevertheless define children as falling into three main categories which are determined by their 'level of ability'. According to Norwood the high ability children are interested in learning for its own sake. The next level are those who can apply their knowledge – 'He often has an uncanny insight into the intricacies of mechanism whereas the subtleties of language construction are too delicate for him'.[11] The third group is the one which takes in the children of average and below average ability – the child who characteristically deals 'more easily with concrete things rather than with ideas ... he often fails to relate his knowledge or skill to other branches of activity ... he may be incapable of a long series of connected steps'.[12]

Through this classification system, the report effectively overlooked class differences. The basis for their stratification of pupils was according to differential levels of ability. The effect of this distinction was of extreme importance as it resulted in a proposal for a tripartite system of education which would cater for these groups. They said 'within a framework of secondary education the needs for the three broad groups of pupils ... should be met within three broad types of secondary education, each type containing the possibility of variation and each school offering alternative courses which would yet keep the school true to type'.[13] In this way they maintained that they would follow through their notions that schools must not impose or inflict on children a curriculum that failed to take into account the specific, individual wishes and personal involvements or commitments. This would assure the child-centred orientation of the school of the future.

The educational form for the grammar school would cater for the élite who would pursue knowledge for its own sake, for the vocational school the form is self-evident, and for the modern school provision would be made for an overall education which aimed at awakening interest in many aspects of life. It is clear that this formulation is linked primarily with their ultimate aim of education equipping children to fit into the two distinct worlds – work and citizenship. Equally concise, from the way in which they described the attributes of each school, is their notion of the world of work. The grammar school products are the élite in so far as they are the ones who will enter 'the learned professions or who have taken up higher administrative or business posts',[14] whereas the second group clearly comprise the future technicians needed by industry. And the third group caters for the *majority* of the working population – those who work with their hands, who will receive a 'practical and concrete' orientation which will enable them to supply the demands of the labour market for unskilled or semi-skilled operations. It can therefore be seen that their ideological position justifies the role of education in so far as it is directly related to a reproduction of the labour requirements of the society based on the *status quo*.

It appears obvious that the report does not view women, in general as being an integral part of the world of work. Only when they consider in detail the ideal constituent content of specific subjects in the curriculum do they link women with some forms of work. This occurs specifically in regard to their discussion on domestic subjects. Although the report was written during World War II when women had moved into skilled jobs which previously had been the terrain of men who were now on active service, this was regarded as a purely temporary intrusion as the following statement reveals:

> The view has been expressed that as a result of the experience of war, women have undertaken work which hitherto has been regarded as men's work, and men have found themselves increasingly concerned with domestic matters. It is therefore suggested that girls should have an opportunity of learning handicraft and boys domestic subjects. We do not ourselves contemplate a state of affairs in which every boys' school should have a kitchen for the teaching of cooking and every girls' school a workshop. Normally, we believe, such opportunity must be offered to those who desire it through 'scouting' or 'guiding' or similar interests. In coeducational schools, however, facilities are already available and in some schools a few boys show themselves interested in cooking and a few girls in carpentry. This is a development which we would bring to the notice of coeducational schools in general.[15]

At that point in time the inroads women were making into the hitherto jealously preserved jobs of men was not overlooked by the trade unions. They were well

trained recruits; the nature of the technological education itself; the brain drain of qualified technologists; the need to recruit the 'best' graduates into industry away from academic careers – all these areas were examined separately in an attempt to meet the projected manpower targets set by the various reports of the manpower planning sections.

It had been quite clear for some time that the secondary schools were failing to produce the 'able' young man who could pursue a technological course at university level. Not only did this refer to the grammar schools but also to some extent to the secondary modern schools. Whilst the manpower plans were geared entirely to this question of the *skilled* technologist, there were additional problems occurring at the lower levels of the occupational structure. Not only was there a shortage of skilled personnel but an ever increasing demand for a technician group, nonetheless skilled but not required to play a managerial or decision-making role expected of the technologist group. The technological changes were also reflected in an overall decrease of purely unskilled jobs and a general increase of semiskilled jobs.

The whole issue of whether the education system was meeting its stated aims of 'producing citizens who are fitted by character, knowledge and skill to play their full part in an increasingly educated and responsible society' was raised by a Ministry of Education document in 1958.[20] This document ruefully stated that a large number of children did not appear to receive the type of education to which they were suited. Well-known sociological studies subsequently pointed to the fact that the extension of educational facilities has been of benefit almost exclusively to the middle classes[21] and that amongst the working classes there was an estimated wastage of 30,000 children each year who could easily have benefited from specialist training.[22]

In 1959 the Crowther Report was published. This committee had been established to consider:

> in relation to the changing social and industrial needs of our society and the needs of the individual citizens, the education of boys and girls between 15 and 18 in particular; to consider the balance at various levels of general and specialised studies between these ages and to examine the inter-relationship of the various stages of education.[23]

The changes they spoke of referred to the decrease in absolute numbers of unskilled jobs and an increase in the level of skills demanded by the occupations which had emerged as a direct consequence of technological developments. They formulated the resultant problems in terms of 'the need to reassess what must be attempted by people of only average intelligence',[24] i.e. the pupils of the then secondary modern schools.

The implication of what they were saying reflects both on the schools and on the level of attainment of their pupils. In the past the nature of the occupations was such that employers did not demand much from the new labour recruits in the form of intellectual skills. Because the children of secondary modern schools were defined as those with 'average' or 'below average' ability, they were regarded as incapable of performing jobs which might require any initiative at all. In concentrating precisely on those pupils who would in the future become the unskilled and semi-skilled workers, they accepted that there was an inevitable limit on the level of achievement of such pupils. And it is interesting to note that their concern was with boys and girls alike.

There is no doubt that the Crowther Report conceptualised the difficulties in terms of the innate abilities of the children who themselves represented the main problem area. They did not pose the question in terms of whether the schools, the whole educational system and indeed the socioeconomic conditions could be the major source of all the problems.

Unlike the Norwood Report, the Crowther Report, not only through its terms of reference, but by virtue of the educational system, was concerned with what happened to children who left school at the age of fifteen and then began their vocational training for specific jobs.

Here they did display some insight into the relationship between the labour market and the educational system which laid the foundation for the type of training the new labour recruits would receive after leaving school. They said:

> ... further education has grown up as a hand maiden of employment. For the overwhelming majority of boys and girls in future education, the choice of job (or at least the type of employment) comes first, and the entry into further education courses follows as a consequence, either as a condition of employment (as with part-time day release) or as a means of obtaining the qualifications for a specific employment (as with girls' full-time commercial courses) or as a means of obtaining promotion. English further education cannot be understood without realizing that virtually everything that exists in it has come into existence as a conscious answer to a demand arising from industry or from individual workers.[25]

But when they came to speak of the proportion of boys to girls in education they pointed out the discrepancies that existed:

> In full-time education there is virtually no difference in numbers between boys and girls – a quarter of each (25.5 and 24.9 respectively) are either at school or full-time students in colleges of further education. But when we turn to part-time education, the picture is entirely different for boys and girls. There are very nearly as many boys in part-time day classes as in full-time education during these years, but only 5 to 6 per cent of the girls get part-time day release.[26]

Although the figures for full-time education are almost identical between boys and girls they pointed out that most girls pursued full-time courses in shorthand and typing, of which, they scathingly commented 'the educational value, though by no means non-existent, is distinctly limited'.[27]

They attributed the very small number of women in part-time courses to two main reasons. The first they laid at the doorstep of employers themselves as they 'cannot look forward to a sufficiently long period of assistance to justify him in providing day release'.[28] But the more important reason they attributed to the type of jobs women were employed in, particularly as 'the bulk of women's employment is not in fields where considerable technical knowledge is required'.[29] Teaching, social work, the health services, the clothing trades and commerce are the occupations usually thought of when the school curriculum is planned, although they did recognize that there are other occupations which women might follow after marriage. But these they did not specify or consider in any way.[30] In this way the report neatly side-stepped the main issues concerning girls and their employment. On this basis the report could conveniently ignore that section of economic life where thousands of women work but where the skills they require are provided by in-service training programmes.

In accepting their own assumptions, not based on evidence concerning the areas in which women work, credence was given to their statements made in regard to what they considered to be the special interest of girls *qua* girls. This in turn affected their schooling and subsequent jobs. Crowther saw these processes as being a function of the girls' interests themselves. They emphasised that owing to the demographic aspects of the increasing numbers of women marrying before their twenties, there were apparent dysjunctions in an education system which treated young women on the threshold of marriage as though they were still children. Although they differentiated between ability strata of all girls there was still a common theme running through their discussions on girls. That was their 'special interests as women'.

In regard to the higher ability groups, Crowther felt that provision was being made for those girls to enter into higher institutions where they might follow careers, but here their own specific interests as women were being neglected. But for the lower ability groups, because it had been demonstrated that these girls would soon embark on their marriage careers, it was felt that the educational system was neglecting them, particularly as the curriculum was not making sufficient provision for their developing interests in matrimony and all that involved; whereas with boys of the same age group their interests lay in what work they would be doing on completion of their schooling.

Following the notion of child-centred education whose ultimate aims should result in the 'creation of intelligent and responsible citizens', they said, in a revealing passage that 'the prospect of courtship and marriage should rightly influence the education of the adolescent girl ... her direct interest in dress, personal experience and in problems of human relations should be given a central place in her education'.[31]

Thus it can be seen that the Crowther Report still adhered to the dichotomy established by Norwood whereby a sharp division was drawn between what was seen as the overriding interests that divided boys and girls. However, there is a transformation evidenced in the Crowther Report which dissolved the dichotomy between the worlds of work and citizenship. They accepted the fact that women's roles did cross the boundaries and that they did not exist only in the world of citizenship, but nevertheless they introduced a new dichotomy into the world of work in which they relegated women to those jobs which did not require 'considerable technical knowledge'.

The Newsom Committee continued the work of Crowther. They were set up to

consider the education between the ages of 13 and 16 of pupils of average
or less than average ability who are or will be following full-time courses
either at schools or in establishments of further education. The term
education shall be understood to include extra-curricular activities.[32]

Their report was published in 1963 at a time when the country was still in the throes
of the economic problems which were related to the manpower shortages mentioned
above. Whilst the select committees on manpower problems were concentrating
on the shortfall of technologists and its possible solution, there was an equally
serious problem in regard to the dearth of technicians with specialist knowledge.
It was not surprising, therefore, that the Newsom Committee was set up to consider
that latter sector of the school population from which such people could be recruited.

They formulated the problem in almost identical terms to the Crowther Report.
They stressed the changes that had occurred in the occupational structure, *viz* the
diminution of unskilled jobs, and related the needs for greater numbers of skilled
workers to the educational system. They recognized that the 'average and below
average pupils are sufficiently educable to supply the additional talent', and thereby
meet the demands of the labour market.

Unlike Crowther they did recognize that women might be specifically affected
by these technological changes both in occupational and personal terms:

> This is a century which has seen, and is still seeing, marked changes in the
> status and economic role of women. Girls themselves need to be made aware
> of the new opportunities which may be open to them, and boys and girls
> will be faced with evolving a new concept of partnership in personal
> relations at work and in marriage.[33]

Unfortunately they did not qualify what they meant by the changes in 'status and
economic terms'. But whatever they did have in mind, they obviously did not
attribute any real significance to this so-called change because a few pages later they
seemed to have forgotten all this when they discussed in concrete terms the type of
occupations available to the majority of girls.

> The main groups of occupations most widely taken up by girls – jobs in
> offices, in shops, in catering, work in the clothing industry and other
> manufacturing trades – can all provide material for courses at more than
> one level of ability.[34]

Presumably they were thinking in terms of management, either at shop floor level,
or at the middle management level which could suit girls of higher ability.

Notwithstanding this they return, as could be expected, to what they consider
to be the overriding single element, and that is girls' interest in marriage. In accordance with the now well-established ideological notion that education should
primarily be concerned with satisfying the individual's needs and interests, and
because girls are believed to have a consensual interest in marriage, this should be
the major concern of education. Their statement in this regard echoed the sentiment
expressed in the Crowther Report.

Common to all these reports are the patent contradictions between their educational ideologies on the one hand and the way in which they define what happens to women in the occupational structure. Whereas the Norwood Report quite categorically ignores the role of women as workers, the other two reports accede only partially to the reality of the situation. These latter two prescribe the working roles of women to 'traditional' female occupations.

Conclusion

None of the Reports makes any attempt whatsoever to consider or analyse the concrete facts relating to the employment of girls and women. They accepted, without question, the popularly held beliefs of the time that women's main role was the domestic one and work in the world outside the home was peripheral and of little consequence.

Historically women's roles have been inextricably entwined in the productive processes of the communities in which they have lived. This was so in 1944 and the position has not altered since then, but as mentioned above, the Norwood Report failed totally to recognize that women did constitute an essential section of the working population. The report regarded women's work as of a purely temporary character and overlooked the fact that women provide a constant source of labour power. They were expressing the dominant ideology of the period. In addition to this their ideology reflected their elitist approach to education in general. Their overriding concern was with those pupils who would comprise the top sectors in the occupational hierarchy. As women were not deemed to comprise any signficant element in this group they were not considered at all. Conversely because the bulk of the working population comprised products of what they regarded as the less significant sector of the school population their disregard for both girls and boys in this sector was on a par. Hence they could totally overlook girls in the school population.

Their oversight, if it can be called that, was not due to lack of information. Presumably they could have obtained any amount of substantive data concerning the position of women in employment had they consulted the relevant government department or social scientists. Indeed shortly after the Norwood Report was published the Ministry of Labour and National Service published a document which was aimed at assisting enquiries from women who had been on active service and who might wish to resume employment in industry. They said that women, who comprised roughly one third of the working population were employed in the following groups of employment, although large numbers had been employed as domestics. The groups were:

(i)   Service industries such as shops, laundries, domestic service, transport, catering and entertainments.

(ii)   Manufacturing industries, such as textiles, clothing and food.

(iii) Professional occupations, such as nursing and teaching.

(iv)   Clerical occupations.

(v)   Extractive industries, such as agriculture, horticulture, mining.[35]

The book then went on to examine in detail general information including the location, description of the manufacturing process, wages, working conditions, recruitment, training and post-war prospects in a wide range of industries, which included engineering, glass and plastics. It was quite clear that none of the jobs were newly created ones but that women had worked in all these different industries *prior* to the war.

By the time the Crowther Report was published the post-war years' employment situation had become stabilized and certain definite trends were evident. Analysis of Ministry of Labour figures clearly showed that there was a general, overall diminution in occupations at the lower end of the scale. Despite this, women's position had not changed markedly. They still clustered at the lower end, working predominantly in unskilled and semiskilled occupations. In 1951 women represented 28.4 per cent of *all* manual workers. So while the Crowther Report emphasised the need for an overall increase in levels of skills, a need which had emanated from the productive processes, women's position had not qualitatively altered.

Crowther's approach to the question of future education begged the whole issue. All they could say was that when girls did follow further education courses it was in courses for shorthand and typing, and not in industrial spheres. Consequently for the 2,406,000 women who had been employed in manufacturing and industrial processes, most were unlikely to have had any training except on the job, nor was the situation likely to alter in the forseeable future. Women represented (as they still do) cheap labour power. It is possible to see why the Crowther Report ignored this not insignificant number of women in industry for they reported that 'women work in teaching, social work, health services, clothing industry and commerce'. But what were the actual numbers involved and did these categories comprise the majority of women workers? The first three occupations fall under *one* broad heading, according to the standard Industrial Classification, *viz* Professional and Scientific Services which in 1959 comprised 16.72 per cent of the total number of women workers. Clothing industry accounted for 5.25 per cent, while in commerce (and here it is difficult to know exactly which group of workers were meant but taking it as women employed in insurance, banking and finance) only 2.95 per cent of the total number of women were working. This left the remaining 75 per cent of women employees totally unaccounted for.[36]

The Crowther Report did not question the popular myth that these listed occupations were predominantly 'feminine' ones. If they had done so they would not have been able to link these occupational categories with the so-called interests of girls. By definition only those occupations which were singled out were regarded as occupations which most suited girls and thereby there could be no conflict with their dominant interests. The principle of child-centred education could be demonstrated to be operating smoothly. This is a completely tautological 'explanation'. In addition, they failed to explain how men were found in these 'feminine' occupations, although men who work in the health services, or teaching, or even the clothing industry are not defined as following feminine pursuits.

An additional explanation which can account for Crowther's lack of concern for so-called 'lower ability' girls, the ones who would go into all those occupations not specified, would be their assumption that as these girls were likely to marry at an early age their source as labour power was not of any consequence. They failed to take into account the phenomenon of married women workers.

The Newsom Report continued in the myth-upholding roles of its predecessors. They said that 'this century has seen marked changes in the status and economic role of women'. If they were referring to the fact that women no longer worked as domestic servants then no fault can be found. But presumably this was not what they meant. Rather they must have been referring to the general changes brought about by technology with resultant totally *new* occupations. The switchboard operator no longer plugs in and plugs out – most systems are automatic; typewriters are electric; electronic systems have altered so much of routine work; records are computerised or punched out; central heating has replaced the grate which had to be blacked daily. Certainly occupations have altered considerably, but the role women play in the occupational system has not qualitatively altered. While work may not be as physically demanding as previously was the case, women's jobs are still those which require minimal skill, or skill quickly acquired through marginal training schemes.

Viewing the situation at the time, a Ministry of Labour report in 1967 summed up the situation:

> These analyses of changes in the female employment suggest that the growth of nearly 850,000 between 1951 and 1961 (virtually identical to the growth in male employment) did not result in any significant extension of female employment into 'new' occupation groups. However, two industries which have traditionally employed a large number of women – textiles and miscellaneous services both experienced a substantial decline in female employment. Other industries, notably in the Services Sector, recorded significant increases in both numbers and proportions. Viewed from the occupational aspect, the two growth points for female employment, measured in terms of both numbers and proportions, have been the clerical and unskilled occupations.[37]

So much for the changes referred to in the Newsom report. When they actually listed the types of occupations which girls follow they specifically mentioned offices, shops, catering, clothing industry and other manufacturing industry. This again gives a biased view. For example while the clothing industry employed 448,500 women in 1961, engineering and electrical sectors employed just under 100,000 *more* women. In all over two million women were employed in manufacturing, extractive and primary industries, whereas only 965,700 were employed in textiles, leather, clothing and footwear.

Where the improvement in status of women's employment comes from, Newsom fails to say. If they were equating pay with status then they were hopelessly out of touch. As early as 1948 a PEP book on women in employment commented on the lower level of pay women received and the obvious reasons advanced for this by a Royal Commission on equal pay. They accepted these but went on to say that the

> reasons given by the Commission as secondary, but none the less of considerable importance, were that *women tended to offer their services on easier terms than men, and that they were less well organized.*[38]

So far the discussion has been based on the actual distribution of women workers. This information is given in order to illustrate the misconceptions and the biased view with which these reports view the occupational roles of girls and women.

However, there is an additional dimension to the occupational roles of women. This is the low status that women occupy throughout the whole work spectrum in the country. Here status is taken to refer to both the low level of skill and the relatively low level of pay they receive for their labour. In regard to the low level of skill, women, other than those in professional services, are employed mainly as unskilled or semiskilled operators.[39]

Furthermore the whole question of pay has been well documented by economists and sociologists; women's pay is relatively lower than that of men.[40] This applies not only to women who perform work similar to that of men, but also has an effect on the whole industries. For example, in the clothing industry which has always been defined as a 'traditional' female type of work, the overall wages are lower than that of other industries. This has consequences for the men as well because although their wages are nevertheless higher than those paid to women, in comparison with other industries their average wage is lower.[41]

Even professional workers do not escape this differential. Routh has said in regard to professional occupations that 'though professional fees for those working on their own account are generally the same, and though equal pay has been applied in the public service for some time to the professionally qualified, age distribution, time worked and prejudice continue to lower women's earnings, so that we may guess that for all women professionals, the average would be about 75 per cent of that for men'.[42]

Women can be said to represent 'supplementary labour power'. They have been consistently employed in all aspects of the economic life of the country both in significant numbers and at low statuses. It is not within the scope of this paper to do more than set out these propositions, and no attempt can be made here to explain this phenomenon. However, the value in raising these aspects and providing some empirical evidence to support the statement is to highlight the total lack of meaningful remarks made by official documents in regard to girls' education with future reference to their adult lives. Although they believe, and women in the main no doubt also hold similar views, that their main function in life is as wives and mothers, nevertheless for over a third of the female population their adult lives are likely to be spent in employment *outside* the home. There is a failure to equip girls through the education system for this other important part of their lives – their contribution to the economic life of the country. It could be concluded that the consequence of this situation is to produce an adaptable, pliable and docile female labour source with only marginal skills.

In conclusion it can be said that none of the three reports considered the reality of the situation which applies to such a large proportion of women, *viz* as workers *outside* the home. Their focus on women and marriage provides them with a means of extricating themselves from this situation. The stated overriding concern of girls with their future marriages provides them with the means of legitimation for this omission. Having established this dichotomy between the world of work and marriage all three reports are able to provide an ideological basis for the perpetuation of an education system which does not open up new vistas or possibilities to the majority of girls.

Notes and References

1 BOURDIEU, P. (1971) 'Systems of Education and Systems of Thought', in YOUNG, M. (Ed.) *Knowledge and Control*, Collier-Macmillan, pp. 190–1;
2 For a review article in which these findings are adequately set out see MUSSEN, P.H. (1969) 'Early Sex-Role Development', in GOSLIN, D.A. (Ed.) *Handbook of Socialization Theory and Research*, Russell Sage Foundation; MACCOBY, E.E. (1966) (Ed.) *The Development of Sex Differences*, Stamford University Press. For an interesting analysis of the enforcement of sex-roles in preschool children through picture books see WEITZMANN, L.J. (1972) 'Sex Role Socialization in Picture Books for Pre-School Children', *American Journal of Sociology*, Vol. 77, (6) May, pp. 1125–50.
3 There is a large body of work on the adolescent and aspects of their socialization. A particularly useful work in this regard is by DOUVAN, E. and ADELSON, J. (1966) *The Adolescent Experience*, John Wiley.
4 Report of the Committee of the Secondary School Examinations Council, (1943, reprinted 1946) *Curriculum and Examinations in Secondary Schools*, HMSO, (*The Norwood Report*); Report of the Central Advisory Council for Education (1959) *15–18* Ministry of Education, Vol. 1, HMSO, (*The Crowther Report*); Report of the Central Advisory Council for Education (England) (1963, sixth impression 1969) *Half Our Future*, DES, (*The Newsom Report*).
5 This Act was said to 'have completely revolutionized educational facilities for all children in requiring local authorities to provide for all senior pupils a unified system of secondary education and offering such variety of instruction and training as may be desirable in view of their [pupils'] different ages, abilities and aptitudes, and of different period for which they may be expected to remain at school'. TAYLOR, G. and SAUDERS, J.B. (1971) *The New Laws of Education*, Butterworths, 7th Edition.
6 Norwood Report, *op. cit.*, p. vii.
7 This approach was founded in Jacques Rousseau's work and has had a very direct influence on subsequent philosophers in education, particularly in Britain and America. Its influence is most noticeable in primary schools. For an account of the philosophical foundations see ENTWHISTLE, N.J. (1970) *Child-centred Education*, Methuen and Co.; for the effect of this notion see BERNSTEIN, B. and DAVIS, B. (1969) 'Some sociological comment on Plowden', in PETERS, R.S. (Ed.) *Perspectives on Plowden*, Routledge and Kegan Paul.
8 Norwood Report, *op. cit.*, p. i.
9 *Ibid.*, p. i.
10 *Ibid.*, p. viii.
11 *Ibid.*, p. 3.
12 *Ibid.*, p. 3.
13 *Ibid.*, p. 14.
14 *Ibid.*, p. 7.
15 *Ibid.*, p. 20.
16 'When the National Government was formed, however, under Mr. Churchill, in May 1940, production was, at last, placed on a wartime footing, and Trade Unions were, at length, fully associated with the national effort. The Emergency Powers (Defence) Bill gave the Government powers over the entire resources of the country. At the same time, Mr. Attlee, in introducing the Bill as Deputy Leader of the House of Commons, assured the workers that their rights would remain alive, and would be secured by an addition to the fair wages clause whereby any employers who did not restore customs or conditions set aside for the duration would be ineligible to go on the list of Government Contractors.' HAMILTON,

M.A. (1941) *Woman at Work*, London, Labour Book Service. Agreements were reached with Trade Unions concerned on these issues, for example the AEU who regarded women as temporary workers did not admit them to membership of the Union at this point in time.

17 RANDEL, M. *et al.*, (1968) *Equality for Women*, Fabian Research Series, 268, p. 7.

18 *Scientific Man Power 1946*, Cmd. 6824, HMSO, 1947 (The Barlow Commission).

19 Technical Education, Cmd. 9703, 1957, HMSO, 1956.

20 MINISTRY OF EDUCATION (December 1958) *Secondary Education for all, A New Drive*, Cmd. 604, HMSO, p. 10.

21 See, for example, JACKSON, B. and MARSDEN, D. (1968) *Education and the Working Class*, Pelican; HALSEY, A.J., FLOUD, J. and ANDERSON, C.A. (1961) *Education, Economy and Society*, Collier-Macmillan.

22 DOUGLAS, J.W.B., ROSS, J.M. and SIMPSON, H.R. (1968) *All Our Future*, Peter Davies.

23 Crowther Report, *op. cit.* p. xxvii.

24 *Ibid.*, p. 333.

25 *Ibid.*, p. 333.

26 *Ibid.*, p. 124.

27 *Ibid.*, p. 124.

28 *Ibid.*, p. 124.

29 *Ibid.*, p. 124.

30 *Ibid.*, p. 33.

31 *Ibid.*, p. 34.

32 Newsom Report, *op. cit.*, p. 5.

33 *Ibid.*, p. 28.

34 *Ibid.*, p. 37.

35 MINISTRY OF LABOUR AND NATIONAL SERVICE (1945) *Women in Industry*, p. 6. The attitude expressed in this work on unskilled labour should be cited. They said 'the change in the emphasis from skill may have led to some increase in the monotony of work; it is generally accepted, however, that great numbers of men and women find such work to be congenial', p. 8.

36 These figures are dreived from DEPARTMENT OF EMPLOYMENT AND PRODUCTIVITY (1971) *British Labour Statistics: Historical Abstract*, 1886–1968, DEP, p. 253.

37 MINISTRY OF LABOUR (1967) *Manpower Studies No. 6: Occupational Changes 1951–1961*, HMSO, p. 14.

38 PEP (1948) *Employment of Women*, p. 44.

39 An example of this can be illustrated by the following figures. As at April 1970, of the 2,701,000 women employed in manufacturing industries: 1,943,000 or 71.93 per cent were employed as operative, 758,000 or 28.06 per cent were employed in administrative, technical or clerical posts. Source: DEP (1972) *British Labour Statistics Yearbook 1970*. Furthermore Routh showed that 'the number of skilled men increased by 11 per cent between 1911 and 1951, but the number of women in skilled jobs fell by 34 per cent; ROUTH, G. (1965) *Occupations and Pay in Great Britain 1906–1960*, Cambridge University Press.

40 See, for example, ROUTH, G. (1965) *op. cit.*; HUNT, A. (March 1968) *A Social Survey of Women's Employment*, Government Social Survey, (SS. 379).

41 The following table illustrates their position:
Average weekly earnings of manual men and women.

	Clothing Industry		All Manufacturing Industry
	Women s. d.	Men s. d.	Men s. d.
1944	54.10	106.7	130.9
1959	132.0	233.8	271.9
1963	148.4	286.6	332.4

Source: *British Labour Statistics: Historical Abstract 1886–1968*, DEP, 1971.

42 ROUTH, G. (1965) *op. cit.*, p. 67.

10 Schooling and the Reproduction of Class and Gender Relations

Madeleine MacDonald

In 1967, Quintin Hoare wrote,

> British education is from a rational point of view grotesque, from a moral one, intolerable and from a human one tragic. . . . Predictably, the Labour Party has at no time offered a global challenge to the present system. It has at most stood for its expansion and the elimination of some of its most flagrantly undemocratic features. It has never seriously threatened the most important of these: the continued existence of the public schools, and sexual discrimination against girls in every type of school. Above all, it has never attacked the vital centre of the system, the curriculum, the *content* of what is taught.[1]

These remarks are still valid not just for the Labour Party, but also for sociologists of education. This may seem a curious statement to make, particularly given the development of sociology of the curriculum over the last decade and the more recent flowering of feminist analysis of schooling within the discipline. However, whilst the diversity and range of material is considerable and its critical stance not disputed, I shall argue in this paper first that what is still lacking in the studies of the curriculum is that 'vital centre' – the *content* of school subjects. [. . .] Second, although there is now more research on patterns of sexual discrimination in schools, this research still retains a marginal status. By and large, it has not been integrated into the 'radical' critiques of schooling which tend to weight theories of education towards class analysis. There has been a noticeable neglect of race and sexual structures in schooling, as integral and not subsidiary elements of capitalism. [. . .]

My concern in this paper with these two 'forgotten' subjects of school analysis is part of an attempt to answer the same central theoretical question. I am interested in the ways schooling may be involved in the processes of legitimation and hence of reproduction of class and gender relations under capitalism. (The complications which an analysis of racial hierarchies brings, requires another article). Here, I

Source: First published in BARTON, L., MEIGHAN, R. and WALKER, S. (Eds.) (1981) *Schooling, Ideology and Curriculum*, Barcombe, Falmer Press.

shall focus specifically on the structure and content of school culture as represented in the curriculum. The position I shall take is, first, that one cannot isolate out one sex or one social class. One has to remember that these categories exist within a set of social relations. In particular, the category of gender, which is socially constructed, only has meaning when the concepts of masculinity and femininity are recognized as a pair which exist in a relationship of complementarity and antithesis.

Simone de Beauvoir[2] describes the relation by using a Hegelian distinction between Subject and Other. Man is the Subject, the absolute and woman is the Other. Within this duality, the definition of woman is constructed *relative* to man:

> The terms *masculine* and *feminine* are used symmetrically only as a matter of form, as on legal papers. In actuality the relation of the two sexes is not quite like that of two electrical poles, for man represents both the positive and the neutral, as is indicated by the common use of *man* to designate human beings in general, whereas woman represents only the negative, defined by limiting criteria, without reciprocity.[3]

The assumption I hold is that both class relations and gender relations, while they exist within their own histories, can nevertheless be so closely interwoven that it is theoretically very difficult to draw them apart within specific historic conjunctures. The development of capitalism is one such conjuncture where one finds patriarchal relations of male dominance and control over women buttressing the structure of class domination. In a wide variety of 'sites' such as the work place, the family, the law and the educational system, there are the hierarchies of class and also of sex. Further, in so far as class relations (in other words the division between capital and labour) constitute the primary element of the capitalist social formation, they limit and structure the form of gender relations, the division between male and female properties and identities. I do not believe that one can disassociate the ideological forms of masculinity and femininity, in their historical specificity, from either the material basis of patriarchy nor from the class structure. If one definition of femininity or masculinity is dominant, it is the product of patriarchal relations and also the product of class dominance, even though these two structures may exist in contradiction.

Within capitalism, the relations of class and gender take a unique form. They are brought together, for example, in the maintenance of capitalist social relations of production – where male dominance reinforces the authority of supervisors, managers and experts.[4] At a more fundamental level, the coincidence of these two structures, facilitates the reproduction of the work force, required by that mode of production. Biological reproduction of workers occurs within a particular family mode, which is characterised in capitalism by a patriarchal household, monogamy, and a domestic sexual division of labour which delegates to woman the prime responsibility for child care and early education. Social reproduction of the work force occurs through the extension of this domestic division of labour (supposedly derived from the biological role of woman in childbearing) to the division, within capitalism, of social production and the domestic sphere. A correspondence is maintained between the public (male) worlds and the private (female) realms. This coincidence, I would argue, is one of the major factors in the reproduction of the male and female work force which, in the capitalist mode of production, is organized largely along the lines of sex segregation. The division between work and the family represents a 'split' or separation between production of commodities for exchange and the production of use values such as food, garments etc. for consumption in the family. However, this becomes 'misrecognized' or falsely perceived when it appears that the division is based upon the 'natural instincts and interests' of men in work and women in the family. Thus, the usefulness for capital of this division, and the additional superior status attributed to productive work because of its 'masculine' association, is hidden in the ideology of sex differences.

What it is important to recognise is that the congruence of these two structures is not natural but socially imposed and, as a result, has to be continually reinforced through the legal, political and educational agencies of the state, if it is to be maintained.[5] The context of this imposition is that of bourgeois hegemony, of the attempt by the bourgeoisie to gain the consent of women to a definition of femininity which locates their primary role as keepers of the home with only secondary involvement in waged work. Also the consent of men has to be won to a definition of masculinity which involves their leaving their homes to go out to work and to be responsible for the family income. If such consent can be won, the ideological conditions are more likely to be ensured for the daily and generational reproduction of the wage labour force through the unpaid work of the wife and mother.[6] Also, the recruitment of working class women is facilitated, because of their domestic commitments, into those occupations which require little skill, are badly paid, are often part-time and normally lack any prospects. Other advantages for capital also arise from this sexual division of labour across the divide of work and family life. Zaretsky,[7] for instance, suggests the psychiatric advantages of the family to capital by the alleviation of class aggression and alienation, through the 'hiving off' of the world of personal relations from the materialistic and harsh world of work. Women in the family become either a stabilizing emotional force or alternatively the victims of male violence. Further, the state can be relieved of the responsibility of catering for such functions as early childhood care and education, sick nursing, care of the aged etc. These can be delegated to the family and especially to women.

It is therefore within the context of bourgeois hegemony that we can understand the dominant pattern of state education where women have been implicitly oriented, if not overtly prepared, for domesticity and men for the world of work.[8] Whilst for men schooling has been directed largely towards the discipline of the work place, the development of mass schooling for women has taken a different direction. As Davin[9] argues, if state education developed solely as a result of a need for a skilled work force or alternatively to educate politically a newly enfranchised working class, this could only explain the development of schools for men, as women did not fall into either category. Extending Johnson's[10] argument, that the school was meant to compensate for a morally deficient family (held responsible for the decay in society), Davin presents the view that,

a further aim of schooling was to impose on working-class children the bourgeois view of family functions and responsibilities. Education was to form a new generation of parents (especially mothers) whose children would not be wild, but dependent and amenable ... [11]

The bourgeois form of family which schools were to establish as a 'stabilizing force' was composed of the male breadwinner, the dependent housekeeping wife and dependent children. In her analysis of Board School readers of the turn of the century, Davin concludes that,

> ... it is worth noticing that their tendency, both through the behaviour they advocated – unselfishness, compassion, devotion to housewifely industry and family duty – and through the situations which they presented as natural to women, was to direct girls towards an exclusively domestic role, even at the expense of school.[12]

We can understand the social relations of schooling not just as attempts to prepare for class obedience but also to prepare women for their role, subordinate to men. In both the reproduction of the social relations of production and the work force, we must therefore recognise the *dual* locations of family and work, not just for women but for men as well. Education for one sphere has implications for men and women's roles within the other. For working class men the contradictions between these two worlds are clear: at school they learn to expect forms of control and discipline when they become workers but they also learn about the expected dominance of men over women in the home and at work. In some way they have to balance and contextualize these two different behavioural repertoires. Working class women on the other hand experience dual forms of control, both as workers and as women, and also the contradictions of trying physically and emotionally to cope with both domestic and wage work. The role of schooling in the reproduction of the capitalist mode of production, I believe, is not therefore just to do with the reproduction of a work force through basic skill training, nor is it just to do with reproduction of the social relations of production through the hidden curriculum of discipline and authority. The work of the school facilitates the maintenance *in the long run* of the work force and the social relations of production through the transmission of a set of gender relations, its association with the division between domestic and waged labour, and all the contradictions this entails.

Care must be taken however, when generalizing this to all stages of capitalist development. With the growth of corporate capitalism and the emergence of the welfare state we can see an increased intervention of the state and the economy into the privatized world of the family. [...] Patriarchy, as a set of power relations, may well conflict with the structure of advanced capitalism. This can be seen in the case of Sweden where the state has attempted, and yet failed, to combat sexual discrimination in families, the communities and the schools. The advantages to be gained by capital in the breakdown of patriarchical families would lie in the 'releasing' of married women from the home and domestic chores for waged work in the commodity production system.[13] Patriarchal structures in the families of different social classes also may have different relations to the labour process and capital. Dorothy

Smith,[14] for example, argues that the family of the managerial classes has been incorporated into the bureaucracies of corporate capitalism. The family of the business executive (and in particular his wife) now stands in what she called a 'subcontractual' relationship to the corporate enterprise, transmitting its culture and values and reflecting its authority structures. Humphries,[15] on the other hand, argues that historically the working class family stood in opposition to capital because in the protected world of home life the working class could maintain and transmit its own culture and values. The weakening not only of the boundaries between the family and the economy but also of the domestic division of labour amongst the middle classes has to some extent heralded in attempts to break down sex segregation in the schools and to construct and transmit a new set of gender relations, more appropriate for corporate capitalism.

The impression we have to keep is of the dynamics of class and gender relations through the development of capitalism but, more than that, it is also important to remember the existence of class and sexual struggle. The dualities of capital and labour and male and female, constitute not only social dichotomies but also hierarchies upon which both material and symbolic power is based. Inside these hierarchies the dialectics of class and sexual struggles are waged. If we wish to understand the role of schooling as one site of the reproduction of the socio-sexual division of labour, we must also be aware of the stakes of these *two* forms of struggle and their interrelations. Certainly there is now an interest in the forms of popular struggle over and in education, in forms of class resistance and the nature of the final compromises. However, this perspective has not really affected feminist analyses. There seems to be little recognition of sexual struggle particularly in the educational arena. [. . .] Yet there is a history of women's fight for education not merely as a means of social mobility but also of sexual liberation. More than that, there must be a 'hidden' history of women's class struggle in and outside the classroom to resist and reject bourgeois definitions of femininity transmitted with such persistence through every cultural agency.

The analysis of class and gender relations requires I believe a theory of 'identity formation' – the patterns and processes which define, limit and transmit the range of models available to individuals to identify with. I make no assumption however that these structures will necessarily describe individual or group identities but I do assume that they will represent social priorities and the cultural framework within which individuals acquire a sense of themselves. The mistake, I believe, that many theories of education make, is to assume that social identities are formed through the experience of cultural forms without ever testing this. The experience can be as little as 'contact', as active as 'consumption' such as the buying of a book or a record, or as deep as the process of 'unconscious internalization' or 'acquizition' of structural principles. It is at this point that our theories of education are at their most deterministic and make their greatest theoretical leaps. The learner is either assumed to be passive or 'naked' in the sense of being unaffected or unformed by any previous experience, and therefore incapable of resisting social pressures. Further what is noticeable is how often these theories assume that individuals are what they are supposed to become. The working class is often talked of as passive, quiescent, docile or uncritical because educationalists since the nineteenth century have wanted it to be, or because the school is seen to be a place of discipline and control. Yet as Willis[16] so succinctly puts it, 'merely because capital would like to treat workers as robots does not mean they are robots'.[17] Similarly women in feminist accounts whether they are sociological or historical, tend to take on the mantle of femininity and passivity without any stuggle. In attempting to move away from biological determinism in the explanation of sex differences, such theories often fall into the trap of *social* determinism. There is a sense in which, in feminist writings, that women are 'oversocialized'. Take, for example, this statement by Simone de Beauvoir:

> The passivity that is the essential characteristic of the 'feminine' women is a trait that develops in her from the earliest years. But it is wrong to assert a biological datum is concerned; it is in fact a destiny imposed upon her by her teachers and by society.[18]

The formation of identity is a highly complex process which cannot be *assumed* to be successful at either the conscious or unconscious levels of learning. Ideally what we need is an analysis not just of the production and transmission of cultural messages but also the reception of cultural messages before we can judge the impact of these forms. Further, it is important to understand the part played by school culture in a wider context. In an age of mass media and a wide variety of cultural agencies, we can no longer justify concentrating upon schools, in isolation, as the sole or even dominant creator of meanings, class and sexual identities and consciousness. We need to investigate the relationship between 'external' cultural resources and internal school culture in both its complementary and antagonistic aspects. As Bernstein[19] has already pointed out, the consciousness of the ruling class and the consciousness of the working class are less likely to be dominated by the mode of education than by the mode of production. In contrast, it is the consciousness of the new middle classes (called by Bernstein the agents of symbolic control) which is constituted by the mode of education and only indirectly by the mode of production. This view is supported by Willis who argues that the distinction between work and culture must be broken down particularly in the analysis of male working class identities. He claims:

> ... not only can work be analysed from a cultural point of view, but it must occupy a *central* place in any full sense of culture. Most people spend their prime waking hours at work, base their identity on work activities and are defined by others essentially through their relation to work.[20]

[...]

In the next section of this paper, I shall go back to the sociology of the curriculum to try and draw out elements of a theory of class and gender relations. The analysis will be of necessity exploratory. I shall concentrate on the structure of school culture first, and then move onto school texts.

The first body of theory I shall look at is that of cultural reproduction, to see what a structuralist account of class and gender relations in schooling could look like.

Within this category one can place Basil Bernstein's theory of educational codes and Pierre Bourdieu's work on cultural codes.[21] The theme here, is that culture has, through education, been divided into two categories – the legitimate and the illegitimate. This dichotomy also reflects the division between public and private knowledge, between culture and common sense, between school knowledge and family and community experience. Further, the transmission through educational institutions of specific forms of culture not merely ensures the reproduction of that culture but also of the class structure it supports and is supported by. Culture, according to Bourdieu, symbolically

> reproduces in transfigured and therefore unrecognisable form, the structure of prevalent socio-economic relationships – it produces a representation of the social world immediately adjusted to the structure of socio-economic relationships which are consequently perceived as natural, so contributing to the symbolic buttressing of the existing balance of forces.[22]

The structural division and relations between forms of knowledge, according to Bourdieu and indeed Bernstein as well, is a far more significant aspect of the formation of social identities than the *actual* selection of knowledge and *its* hidden message. What is important is the acquisition of the rules and principles which govern the structural hierarchies of culture. Indeed for Bernstein[23] the word 'contents' signifies merely how a period of time is filled in the school timetable. Thus a curriculum is defined 'in terms of the principles by which certain periods of time and their contents are brought in to a special relationship with each other'.[24] What is central to Bernstein's analysis is whether a school subject has high or low status, whether it is compulsory or optional and what relation it bears to other subjects in terms of the strength or weakness of its boundaries.

In both Bernstein's and Bourdieu's structuralist accounts of schooling, social identities are formed through a process of internalization of three core classifications – those of age, sex and social class. The structures of age relations, sex relations and class relations are to be found, for example, in the family, the school and the work place. While their analyses of these classifications and their interrelations remain underdeveloped, one can still see what direction that analysis might take if we look at Bourdieu's *Outline of a Theory of Practice*.[25] In this study of the Kayble society, in Algeria, Bourdieu identified structural correspondences between the sexual division of labour and symbolic oppositions.[26] The categories of masculine and feminine were found *objectified* in the dichotomies of the right and left hands or the division between religion and magic, between external space such as the market and the fields, and internal space – the home. When the child learns to use these structural divisions of gender and their objectified form in the divisions of time, space and objects, according to Bourdieu, he or she also constructs his or her social identity. This social identity is composed first of a sexual identity which is learnt through simultaneously experiencing the mother's and father's body as well as the sexual division of labour within the home. It is also made up by a whole system of social meanings and values, a body language of gestures, postures, and a physical bearing (what Bourdieu calls body hexis), a form of speech and a language. The child experiencing the structural organization of the economic, the social and the cultural, will learn to relate to his or her own body, to other individuals and to nature according to the same principles. For the female child among the Kayble, for example, the experience is one of learning 'inner-directedness' or what Bourdieu called a *centripetal* orientation. The male child, by contrast, will be outer-directed – he will have a *centrifugal* orientation which will be expressed in the outward displays of virility and by his involvement in work, politics and war. The process is what Bourdieu called *embodiment*, which determines not merely the child's social identity but also his or her physical and sexual presence.

In terms of the relevance of this account for an analysis of institutionalised education, we need to ask the following questions. Is it possible to identify similar *dialectics of embodiment and objectification* in the culture of a class society? Is there any reality in talking of correspondences between the structure of gender relations, of masculinity and femininity and the divisions of school knowledge? In the world of formal education, it is certainly not difficult to identify numerous sets of oppositions which divide and distance forms of knowledge and their associated activities. For example, we can find the dichotomies of public and private knowledge, politics and psychology, reason and emotion, science and art, technology and nature, reality and fantasy. Further, as Spender[27] has noticed, there are also the methodological distinctions between hard and soft data, objectivity and subjectivity. The difficulty is of judging, at more than a common sense level, the relationship of these classifications to the social definitions of masculinity and femininity. As Roberts put it:

> How polarization and dichotomization affect thought systems is still open
> to much consideration. The 'we and they', the 'foe and friend', the 'reward
> and punishment' – the ubiquitous and fallacious paired opposites are
> obvious. What is unclear is the extent to which social sex polarization
> provides the basis of such dualistic thinking.[28]

Certainly much of the literature on school subjects and sex segregation within the school, places great emphasis on the fact that some subjects are perceived as either masculine or feminine. The 'masculinity' of science or the 'femininity' of domestic science can be seen as contributing to the unwillingness of girls to choose the former and of boys to study the latter.[29] The question is, how does such characterization occur which limits the range of choice of school subjects for the different sexes? Is it purely through the unconscious manipulations of teachers using restricted gender definitions or is it the effect of the different patterns of men's and women's employment? Certainly both might enter the hidden curriculum of the school and affect the students' choice of subject. Bourdieu[30] suggests that the process of gender attribution to both students and academic disciplines is dialectical. The transference of femininity, for example, from the student to the school subject and back again to the student exemplifies the dialectic of objectification and embodiment:

> ... the objective mechanisms which channel girls preferentially towards
> the Arts faculties and within them, towards certain specialities (such as

modern languages, art history or French) owe part of their effectivity to a social definition of the 'feminine' qualities which they help to form; in other words, to the internalization of the external necessity imposed by this definition of feminine studies. In order for a destiny, which is the objective product of the social relations defining the female condition at a given moment in time, to be transmuted into a vocation, it is necessary and sufficient that girls (and all those around them, not least their families) should be unconsciously guided by the prejudice ... that there is an elective affinity between so-called 'feminine' qualities and 'literary' qualities such as sensitivity to the imponderable nuances of sentiment or a taste for the imprecise preciosities of style.[31]

In this description of the process, women's educational route becomes a self fulfilling prophecy once one has imposed a specific definition of femininity. The question which one has to ask is, 'how do academic disciplines or school subjects change their gender?'. Why do some subjects change from appearing as masculine to being viewed as essentially feminine (such as the social sciences) or alternatively change in the other direction (e.g. education)? The answer must lie, to a great extent, in the pressures exerted on the school and universities by the changing pattern of employment of men and women in the labour force. However, the attribution of gender to specific subjects is also part of class culture and its operation in the school is, I shall argue, one of the means for legitimating the structure of class domination.

In the family, the child learns the class-based definitions of masculinity and femininity, as well as a certain sexual division of labour. When the child enters the school this experience is challenged by a very specific set of gender relations – what I shall call, following Bernstein, a *gender code*.[32] The school's gender code sets up the categories of masculine and feminine as well as the boundaries and relations of power between them. While variations of the dominant gender code are possible in different types of school,[33] what is transmitted is essentially the form of gender relations which is specific to the ruling class. It represents the morality of the bourgeoisie, it legitimates in its ideal family form, as Davin[34] argued, the bourgeois family. In this sense, we can see the work of the school as involving the process of what Bernstein called *recontextualizing*, where the familial form of gender relations is converted into that of the dominant class. Because of this process the concepts of masculinity and femininity can be found to vary in different historic periods within schooling, affecting both the provision and the 'image' of school subjects. According to Bernstein, the informal everyday experience and everyday communication within the family and peer groups which shape social identities feed into and 'create procedures and performances fundamental to formal education. However, formal education also selects, and re-focusses and abstracts from such experiences and in so doing de-contextualizes it'.[35] The process begins with this de-contextualizing of the behaviours and competences invoked in the contexts of the home and community. They are thus freed from their dependence on these evoking contexts and, through a process of recontextualizing, become generalizable and abstract.

Thus the 'practical mastery',[36] acquired through imitation of actions in the home, is converted (if the process is successful) into 'symbolic mastery' of the school discourses. One of the aspects of this process in the context of class society, is the recontextualization of definitions of masculinity and femininity into the class based, and hence arbitrary, classification of school knowledge. The notions of appropriate behaviours for each sex is converted into the appropriate academic disciplines. Despite the actual availability of all subjects, girls and boys of different classes learn the new ideology of sex differences which mixes a theory of biological sex differences with expected gender differences of intelligence, ability, interests and ambitions, making it appear 'natural' that boys and girls should study different school subjects.

The process of recontextualizing, even of decontextualizing, may, however, not always be effective, especially where the family structure and culture differs considerably from the school. Let us look for a moment at the distinction between mental and manual labour which is integral to the capitalist labour process. In bourgeois culture it is transposed with the hierarchy of male over female – in other words mental labour is equated with the masculine and manual work or practical skills with the female. The dominant gender code within school is likely to transmit this pairing of two hierarchies. However, as Willis[37] has shown in *Learning to Labour*, working class boys confronted with this dual structure have two choices – either they conform, with the result that they lose credibility with their own class and deny their masculine sexuality. Alternatively they can reject the message of the school. Significantly, the conformist or 'ear'ole' is labelled as effeminate or cissy. The 'lads' on the other hand, in their resistance to bourgeois culture, invert the school hierarchy of mental over manual, celebrating the manual and physical working class masculinity. This inversion is in line with the 'lads' family culture and in particular with that of their fathers. Thus, in resistance, 'manual labour is associated with the social superiority of masculinity, and mental labour with the social inferiority of femininity'.[38] On the shop floor, as well, this convergence of manual labour with masculinity has political repercussions:

> ... where the principle of general abstract labour has emptied work of significance from the inside, a transformed patriarchy has filled it with significance from the outside. Discontent with work is turned away from a political discontent and confused in its logic by a huge detour into the symbolic sexual realm.[39]

The failure of the school to 'recontextualize' the masculinity of these 'lads' into academic rather than physical displays, has reinforced the probability of their occupational destiny and the diffusion of their class discontent. On the other hand, those 'ear'oles' who conformed have been swept into acceptance of bourgeois culture. In both cases, the resolution of the conflict between sexual and class identities and school culture helps contain opposition to school order and, later, to the class divisions of the mode of production.

In the case of working class girls, the classification of mental work as male and manual work as female, is less problematic as it is often reinforced rather than resisted by the family culture. We must however, be careful to distinguish between the application of the 'manual' category to working class and middle class women. In the case of the working class, manual labour either refers to the form of waged labour practised by this group of women or alternatively to their unpaid domestic labour. In this case of school will legitimate the equating of domesticity, of marriage and of motherhood with femininity. For the middle class girl, manual labour can either mean skilled work in secretarial or administrative occupations or alternatively the more 'practical' professions such as social work or nursing. The forms of class resistance to the imposition of bourgeois definitions of femininity by working class women takes the form of exaggerated celebration of domestic life and the over-emphasis of 'female' interests. Paradoxically the work of Willis, McRobbie and Sharpe[40] has shown that both these forms of class resistance to the school, which involve the celebration of working class definitions of masculinity and femininity, have confirmed rather than broken down the cycle of class reproduction. *They undermine neither the sexual nor the social division of labour.* In both cases, mental labour and the high status/high income professions, are delegated and legitimated as the preserve of the male bourgeoisie and to a lesser extent the female bourgeoisie. The formation of sexual identities in the home and the school are therefore critical elements of the reproduction of the class structure.

[. . .]

Let us now turn to the analysis of school texts. These texts represent a system of choices from the 'external' culture – whether we are talking about a body of litera-ture, a range of photographs, a set of experiments drawn from the science depart-ments of universities, or history textbooks produced by educational publishers. Despite the diversity of resources available to teachers, the research on school texts reveals a pervasive ideology – that of legitimacy of the *status quo*. This message, according to Gerard MacDonald[41] has become hidden in school textbooks which once were the vehicle for an overt ideology of conservatism based on religion.

> Textbooks present a particular ideological position which can best be described as the politics of stasis. The existing order, whether natural or social, is presented as what Marx calls an 'exterior fatality'. Textbook knowledge glosses or ignores the extent to which our world is a human project. It does not help towards either real understanding or real alterna-tives. Resigned quiescence is no longer an overt message in textbooks. Instead it has become their hidden agenda.[42]

School texts are characterized by their 'untouchable' and apolitical nature. They are received as the truths of a 'declassed' cultural heritage. Whether we are talking about science (Young)[43] or social science (Whitty)[44] or literature (Hand)[45] or music (Vuilliamy),[46] the analyses show the uncritical orientation of texts towards both the selection of 'facts' and their presentation within an ideology which leaves unchallenged the *status quo*. Children, if working class, are faced with a presentation of the real world which does not correspond to their 'lived' experience, or alter-natively with a view of the world as far too stable to be amenable to active reform.

[. . .]

Yet while the force of these analyses makes disbelief difficult, what, one must ask, is the nature of the ideology which is transmitted through these texts? Is there no attempt to form social identities? Is it really the case that the working class child is unlikely to acquire any sense of identity – only alienation – from school? There is little analysis of the actual representations of social class, in texts which makes it extremely difficult to answer this question. [...] Most of the research on the content of school texts (rather than the form) has been with a view to identifying potential sources of sexism and racism.

In terms of sexism, there are a number of studies of school and university texts which use several different methodologies – some quantitative and some qualitative. What they have in common is their interest in identifying the ways in which gender, and in particular women are represented. If anything, most of the studies, especially the quantitative research, tend to assume the existence of a sexual division of labour and look for its representation in the subject matter. Also, they search for consistency, rather than diversity, of images of women with the result that they identify the existence of sex role stereotypes and gender stereotypes. In addition, there is little concern with class analysis so that the overall impression is that cultural forms exist purely within a patriarchal society without any impact from capital's involvement and control over agencies of cultural production. Whereas the sociology of school knowledge, described above, has neglected, by and large, this source of cultural domination and sexual oppression, feminist analysis of school culture and the mass media has, to a considerable extent, neglected the forms of class control in the production and transmission of knowledge.

The picture which emerges from these exploratory and rather descriptive studies is, nevertheless, not only interesting but also very depressing. While we might have thought that the gains won by women in political, economic and sexual spheres would be reflected in the cultural media, if anything this research shows just how deeply embedded are sexual ideologies and how 'conservative'. The impression gained is one of women's inferiority, her domesticity, her lack of intelligence, ability, sense of adventure or creativity. In the studies undertaken in the United States (where the majority of content analysis is found) and Britain, the analyses of school texts in, for example, domestic science,[47] history,[48] and literature[49] are complemented by those at university level in such disciplines as sociology,[50] anthroplogy,[51] psychology,[52] political science,[53] and community studies.[54] The message is still the same – there is a consistent distorted model of woman which not merely misrepresents her activities in social life but does nothing to correct the social patterns of discrimination. From the fantasy world of children's books[55] to the male bias of academic disciplines which purport to be 'value-free', one finds a persistent pattern of representations of women which can only be construed as the ideological wing of patriarchy. This pattern has three basis elements:

1   Women suffer from invisibility – which one author called her 'symbolic annihilation'. Women are absent actors in the histories of Western civilization. They do not appear as active participants in such diverse fields as history, politics, literature drama or art. Except for the heroine who portrays the

individualized rather than the collective struggles of women, most women are present in passive roles.

2   When women do appear, they are generally in low status or 'second-rate' jobs. The occupations they fill are most likely to be traditional, limited in prospect and narrow in range. Even in children's reading schemes, in the world of fantasy, women's prospects are not much better. Lobban,[56] for example, found in her study of children's readers that, in contrast to the thirty-three occupations shown for adult men, only eight were available for adult women – mum, granny, princess, queen, witch, handywomen about the house, teacher and shop assistant. However, what is more important is that women do not appear in employment nor in typically female jobs in the ratio in which they are actually found in the economy. If anything there is an under-representation of women in paid work with an over-representation of their financial dependence on men. Spence[57] noticed this in the case of British magazine photographs:

> The visual representation of women as not having to work, as the glamour-ous property of men, harks back to the tradition of bourgeois painting. It effectively displaces the idea that women *do* work, and so inhibits their sense of themselves as workers. In fact according to the Equal Oppor-tunities Commission, women make up 37 per cent of the paid work force.[58]

The image of the female is no less arbitrary and distorted. What is interesting is that the differences between the sexes appears to increase as they move from child-hood to adulthood. Take for example Dohrmann's conclusions[59] from a study of children's educational television programmes:

> The male child is accorded the most laudable pattern: ingenuity, achieve-ment, bravery-rescue. The female child, while rewarded and achieving, is also a follower, an object of insult, and helpless. The adult female is even more uniformly passive, adding routine service, incompetence, and admiration of others to her behavioural repertory. The adult male excels in rewarding, performing occupationally-related tasks, putting others down and picking them up in the rescue role.[60]

3   There is an over-riding emphasis on women's domesticity. The message comes across not as any subtle or hidden code but rather with a degree of repetition that can only be described as ideological bombardment. The assumption first of all appears to be that women have never left the home and, if they had, it must have been unwillingly. This is then limited even further by the portrayal, for example, of women in advertisements selling the products of those two 'feminine' locations in the home – the kitchen and the bathroom.[61]

This pattern can be traced from television drama to commercials, from newspapers to magazines to comics.[62] Against this background of cultural invasion into the home and the community, the school takes its place as just one competitor for the right to present the legitimate gender model which the child is encouraged to follow. In the United States, it is already the case that young children spend more time watching television than in school. Thus we cannot say that the message of the school is the only source of class and sexual identity formation nor indeed necessarily the dominant one. Yet the amount of time and effort spent on school texts is considerably greater than that spent on a short television programme, a once read magazine, a galanced at advertisement in the street. What we can suggest is that the message of school texts is most likely to represent in its purest form the ideological statement of the ruling class or, at least, those values which it considers essential to transmit. Because of this, I believe, it is extremely important that we analyse school texts in all their variety.

The tools for such analysis are being developed to a large extent outside the sociology of education. It is impossible to delve too deeply here into the vast body of literature which covers content analysis, semiotics, cultural histories etc. However, what I would like to do is to make some observations and draw some conclusions from this research. First, what is interesting about this research on culture is that it reveals a considerable split between the world of the family and that of work. Certainly, the equation between women and the home and men and public life appears to be carried in most media. If any message exists, it is the ideology of this division. Cultural texts are, therefore, a further 'site' for the reproduction of the 'dual spheres', reinforced not just by the ascription of gender to each sphere but also by the recontextualizing of masculinity and femininity in each setting. [. . .]

In television commercials in the States, for example, a difference was noticed in the portrayal of masculinity. In this vivid description, one finds the distinction between the image of the man at home and the man in the world outside:

> The image of the American man in TV commercials as muscular, knowledgeable, dominating, independent, sexy, cosmopolitan, athletic, authoritative and aggressive exists only when he is seen away from his family. In embarrassing contrast the American father and husband is portrayed as passive and stupid, infantile and emasculated. . . . But outside the house, trouble is what he is looking for. Swift as a panther, stealthy as a cougar, free as a mustang he speeds to his rendevous with status, independence and violence.[63]

The definitions of femininity and masculinity which we find in cultural texts are not then simple, homogenous stereotypes but rather ideological products which if they are pulled together with all their contradictions into a coherent pattern represent one aspect of bourgeois hegemony. The existence of a dominant gender code does not however rule out the possibility of dominated or subordinated codes which reshape the dominant message of patriarchy into the requirements of specific audiences. This process of recontextualizing *within* one cultural form can be seen most clearly in Frith and McRobbie's research[64] into popular forms of music. Here, without all the statistical manipulations of content analysis, they identify two 'ideological' models of gender relations. The first exists in rock music primarily for a male audience. Masculinity is portrayed by the 'rampant destructive male traveller, smashing hotels and groupies alike ... ' Women, in the eyes of these men, are

> either sexually aggressive and therefore doomed and unhappy or else sexually repressed and therefore in need of male servicing. It's the woman, whether romanticized or not, who is seen as possessive, after a husband, anti-freedom, the ultimate restriction.[65]

Teenybop music in contrast, played to a largely female audience of housewives and factory workers, presents a different model of sexuality. As the authors argue,

> If cock rock plays on conventional concepts of male sexuality as rampant, animalistic, superficial, just-for-the-moment, teenybop plays on notions of female sexuality as being serious, diffuse and implying total emotional commitment. ... It is men who are soft, romantic, easily hurt, loyal and anxious to find a true love who fulfills their definition of what female sexuality should be about?[66]

Frith and McRobbie argue that within each musical form one can find a range of models or definitions of sexuality, mediated by the words of the song, the rhythms and beat of the music, the packaging and image of the singer or group. What their analysis reveals is the complexity of the ideological struggle to define and contain sexual identities within the framework of class culture.

This complexity can also be found in McRobbie's[67] analysis of the school girl magazine *Jackie*. Here she uses semiology to provide a method for such research, a form of analysis which has become increasingly popular in cultural studies. The advantages of this form of analysis are that it has

> more to offer than traditional content analysis if only because it is not solely concerned with the numerative *appearance* of content, but with the messages which such 'contents' signify. ... Quantification is therefore rejected and replaced with understanding media messages as *structured wholes* and combinations of structures, polarities and oppositions are endowed with greater significance than their mere numerative existence.[68]

As a result, she is able to draw out five different subcodes of femininity which relate to beauty, fashion, pop-music, personal/domestic life and romance. What is important here is that the magazine is examined not just as a social product but also as an active agent in the *production* of new meanings. The problem, therefore, is not one of trying to fit these representations of women to the realities of their lives but rather to recognize the ideological 'work' carried out by these texts in the *reconstruction* rather than the reproduction of gender definitions and relations.

By analysing the combinations of various representations of femininity or masculinity within one set of texts, one is also more likely to be made aware of the contradictions which can arise between different gender definitions. Take for example, the contradictory sets of female ideals; the capable consumer housewife versus the dependent incapable wife; the insatiable temptress and the passive sex object; the all embracing earth mother versus the childlike doll. Another example can be found in the excellent analysis of 1950s texts in three domains of motherhood, education and sexuality by the Birmingham Feminist History Group.[69] Here they located the ideological conflict between the liberal concept of equal opportunity and the bourgeois ideal of separate spheres for each sex, which was resolved in the 1950s in the ideology of the two sexes being 'equal but different'. Further they identified the contradictory pressures upon married women both to return to work and to act as efficient and dedicated wives and mothers. Thus the apparent 'unity' of the 1950s under their scrutiny, collapsed into 'contradictions, tensions and divisions'. They found that

> There was no one representation of women; but the struggle for primacy
> of one set of representations concerned with marriage, home and family,
> is systematically victorious throughout our period'.[70]

What I have argued is that not only must we be aware of the complexity of definitions of gender relations in culture. [. . .] The question I believe we should be asking is not just what relation do the representations found within texts bear to 'lived' relations but also what is the relevance of that message for capital. The struggle to define and contain sexuality, is no less a problem for capital than containing the force of class opposition and preparing the working class for the rigours of the work place. [. . .]

The history of hegemonic control over relations between the sexes has been fraught with crises which have affected mainly the middle classes and sectors of the ruling class. After each period of puritanism, Gramsci argues, there is a crisis of libertinism which only marginally affects the working class – through the depravement of their women. However, what is important in Gramsci's argument is that gender relations, or more specifically sexual relations, are linked to the methods of production and patterns of work within a mode of production. For example, he links the relative stability of sexual unions among the peasants to the system of agricultural work in the countryside. With the introduction of Fordism, the rationalization of work, Gramsci argued, made it important that the working class hold a new sexual ethic – that of monogamy:

> The truth is that a new type of man demanded by the rationalization of
> production and work cannot be developed until the sexual instinct has been
> suitably regulated and until it too has been rationalized.[71]

Rigorous discipline at work demands discipline of the sexual instincts and with it, according to Gramsci, comes the strengthening of the ideology of the family and the stability of sexual relations. The reason for the 'puritanical' initiatives of the industrialists such as Ford, into working class families (controlling the consumption of alcohol and 'womanizing') could be found in the necessity of reproducing the work force in fit state for the discipline of the new work methods. Capital needed to preserve 'outside of work, a certain psycho-physical equilibrium which prevents a physiological collapse of the worker, exhausted by the new methods of production'.[72]

In these brief notes Gramsci argues that not only are the relations between the sexes historical products, related to the development of capitalism, but also that these relations are areas in which consent has to be won. To create and make new moralities 'second nature', to win consent for the arbitrary division of social life into male and female worlds of public and private activities is no easy task and perhaps that is why there is such ideological pressure from educational and cultural agencies of the state. It is not that capital has *succeeded* in creating classed and sexed subjects, suitably adjusted to the rigours of work in the home and the work place, but rather that no day can go by without it *trying*.

Notes and References

1 HOARE, Q. (1967) 'Education: Programmes and Men', *New Left Review*, Vol. 32, pp. 40–52. *Ibid.*, p. 40.
2 DE BEAUVOIR, S. (1972) *The Second Sex*, London, Penguin edition.
3 *Ibid.*, p. 15.
4 See HARTMANN, H. (1976) 'Capitalism, Patriarchy and Job Segregation by Sex', *Signs: Journal of Women in Culture and Society*, Vol. 1, No. 3, Part 2, Spring, pp. 137–69 and GEE, M. (1978) 'The Capitalist Labour Process and Women Workers'. Paper given at the Conference of Socialist Economists Annual Conference, Bradford.
5 See LAND, H. (1978) 'Who cares for the Family?', *Journal of Social Policy*, Vol. 7, No. 3, pp. 257–84 (reproduced in this volume).
6 For a brief summary of the 'domestic labour debate' which analyses the economic implications and advantages to capital of women's household work see FEE, T. 'Domestic Labour: an analysis of housework and its relation to the production process', *Review of Radical Political Economics*, Vol. 8, No. 1, Spring, pp. 1–8.
7 ZARETSKY, E. (1973) *Capitalism, the Family and Personal Life*, New York, Harper Colophon Books.
8 DYEHOUSE, C. (1977) 'Good Wives and Little Mothers; Social Anxieties and School Girls' Curriculum 1890–1920', *Oxford Review of Education*, Vol. 3, No. 1, pp. 21–36; SHARPE, S. (1976) *Just Like a Girl*, Harmondsworth, Pelican; DEEM, R. (1978) *Women and Schooling*, London, Routledge and Kegan Paul; WOLPE, A.M. (1977) *Some Processes of Sexist Education*, London, WRRC pamphlet, and (1976) 'The Official Ideology of Education for Girls', in FLUDE, M. and AHIER, J. (Eds.) *Educability, Schools and Ideology*, London, Croom Helm (produced in this volume); articles by DELAMONT, S. in DELAMONT, S. and DUFFIN, L. (Ed.) (1978) *The Nineteenth Century Woman*, London, Croom Helm.
9 The 1869 Franchise Act created approximately a million new voters none of which were women: see DAVIN, A. (1979) 'Mind you do as you are told, reading books for Board School Girls', *Feminist Review*, No. 3, pp. 89–98.
10 JOHNSON, R. (1970) 'Educational Policy and Social Control in Early Victorian England', *Past and Present*, No. 49.
11 DAVIN, A. *op. cit.*, (Note 9), p. 90.
12 *Ibid.*, p. 98.
13 The state also acted against patriarchal family structures during the two world wars, by encouraging the employment of women in wage labour. The child care facilities established during this period were later to be closed down when women were directed back to the home.
14 SMITH, D. (1975) 'Women, the Family and Corporate Capitalism', *Berkeley Journal of Sociology*, Vol. XX, pp. 55–90.
15 HUMPHRIES, J. (1977) 'Class Struggle and the Persistence of the Working Class Family', *Cambridge Journal of Economics*, No. 3, Vol. 1, pp. 241–58.
16 WILLIS, P. (1979) 'Shop Floor Culture, Masculinity and the Wage Form', in CLARKE, J., CRITCHER, C. and JOHNSON, R. (Eds.) *Working Class Culture*, London, Hutchison.
17 *Ibid.*, p. 187.
18 DE BEAUVOIR, S. quoted in FREEMAN, J. (1970) 'Growing up Girlish', *Trans-Action*, Vol. 8, November–December, pp. 36–43.
19 BERNSTEIN, B. (1977) 'Aspects of the Relation between Education and Production', in *Class, Codes and Control*, Vol. III, Routledge and Kegan Paul, 2nd edition.
20 WILLIS, P. *op. cit.*, (Note 16), p. 186.
21 For a critical analysis of the work of Bernstein and Bourdieu, see MACDONALD, M. (1977) *Curriculum and Cultural Reproduction*, E202, Block 3, Milton Keynes, Open University Press.
22 BOURDIEU, P. (1971) 'The Thinkable and the Unthinkable', *Times Literary Supplement*, 15 October, p. 1255.

23 BERNSTEIN, B. (1977) 'On the Curriculum', in *Class Codes and Control*, Vol. III, London, Routledge and Kegan Paul, 2nd edition.

24 *Ibid.*, p. 79.

25 BOURDIEU, P. (1977) *Outline of a Theory of Practive*, London, Cambridge University Press.

26 For an outline of this theory see MACDONALD, M. 'Cultural Reproduction: The Pedagogy of Sexuality', *Screen Education*, Autumn/Winter, No. 32/33, 1979, pp. 143–53.

27 SPENDER, D. (1978) 'Educational Research and the Feminist Perspective', Paper presented at the

28 ROBERTS, J. quoted in SPENDER, D. *ibid.*

29 See, for example, KELLY, A. (1975) 'A Discouraging Process: How Girls are eased out of Science'. Paper presented at the Conference on Girls and Science Education, Chelsea College, 19–20 March; WYNN, B. (1977) 'Domestic Subjects and the Sexual Division of Labour', in WHITTY, G. *School Knowledge and Social Control*, E202, Block 3, Milton Keynes, Open University Press.

30 BOURDIEU, P. (1977) *Reproduction in Education, Society and Culture*, London, Sage.

31 *Ibid.*, p. 78.

32 For a description of gender codes see MACDONALD, M. (1980) 'Socio-cultural Reproduction and Women's Education', in DEEM, R. (Ed.) *Schooling for Women's Work*, London, Routledge and Kegan Paul.

33 CLARRICOATES, K. (1980) 'The importance of being earnest ... Emma ... Tom ... Jane ...: The Perception and Categorisation of Gender Conformity and Gender Deviation in Primary Schools', in DEEM, R. *op. cit.*, (Note 32).

34 DAVIN. A. *op. cit.*, (Note 9).

35 BERNSTEIN, B. (1977) *op. cit.*, (Note 19), p. 30.

36 For the distinction between practical and symbolic mastery see BOURDIEU, P. *op. cit.*, (Notes 25 and 30).

37 WILLIS, P. (1978) *Learning to Labour*, Farnborough, Saxon House.

38 *Ibid.*, p. 148.

39 WILLIS, P. *op. cit.*, (Note 16), p. 198.

40 WILLIS, P. *op. cit.*, (Note 37); MCROBBIE, A. (1978) 'Working Class Girls and the Culture of Femininity', in *Women Take Issue*, Women's Studies Group, Centre for Contemporary Culture Studies, London, Hutchinson; SHARPE, S. *op. cit.*, (Note 8).

41 MADCONALD, G. (1976) 'The Politics of Educational Publishing' in WHITTY, G. and YOUNG, M. (Eds.) *Explorations in the Politics of School Knowledge*, Driffield, Nafferton Books.

42 *Ibid.*, p. 223.

43 YOUNG, M. (1976) 'The Schooling of Science', in WHITTY, G. and YOUNG, M. (Note 41), *op. cit.*

44 WHITTY, G. (1976) 'Studying Society: for social change and social control', in WHITTY, G. and YOUNG, M. (Note 41), *op. cit.*

45 HAND, N. (1976) 'What is English', in WHITTY, G. and YOUNG, M. (Note 41), *op. cit.*

46 VUILLIAMY, G. (1976) 'What Counts as School Music', in WHITTY, G. and YOUNG, M. (Note 41), *op. cit.*

47 See WYNN, B. *op. cit.*, (Note 29).

48 TRECKER, J.L. (1971) 'Women in US History High School Textbooks', *Social Education*, March, pp. 249–60, 338. ANYON, J. (1979) 'Ideology and United States History Textbooks', *Harvard Educational Review*, Vol. 49, No. 3, August, pp. 361–86 (reproduced in this volume).

49 WOLFF, C.G. (1972) 'A Mirror for Men: Stereotypes of Women in Literature', *Massachusetts Review*, Vol. 13, pp. 205–18, see also articles in STACEY, S., BEREAUD, S. and DANIELS, J. (Eds.) (1974) *And Jill came tumbling after*, New York, Dell.

50 EHRLICH, C. (1971) 'The Male Sociologist's Burden: The Place of Women in Marriage and Family Texts', *Journal of Marriage and the Family*, Vol. 33, August, pp. 421–30.

51 SLOCUM, S. (1975) 'Woman the Gatherer: Male Bias in Anthropology', in REITER, R. (Ed.) *Towards an Anthropology of Women*, New York, Monthly Review Press.

52 WEISSTEIN, N. (1971) 'Psychology Constructs the Female , in GORNICK, V. and MORAN, B.K. (Eds.) *Women in Sexist Society*, New York, Basic Books.

53 BOURQUE, S. and GROSSHOLTZ, J. (1974) 'Politics and Unnatural Politics, Political Science Looks at Female Participation', *Politics and Society*, Winter, pp. 225–66.

54 FRANKENBERG, R. (1976) 'In the Production of their Lives, Men (?) Sex and Gender in British Community Studies', in BARKER, D.L. and ALLEN, S. (Eds.) *Sexual Divisions and Society*, London, Tavistock.

55 See, for example, LOBBAN, G. (1975) 'Sex Roles in Reading Schemes', *Educational Review*, Vol. 27, No. 3, June, pp. 202–10; WEITZMAN, L.J. *et al.*, (1976) 'Sex Role Socialization Picture Books for Pre-School Children', in *Sexism in Children's Books*, Children's Rights Workshop, No. 2, London, Writers' and Readers' Publishing Co-operative; DIXON, B. (1977) *Catching Them Young (No. 1) Sex, Race*

and Class in Children's Fiction, London, Pluto Press; WOMEN ON WORDS AND IMAGES (1975) *Dick and Jane as Victims*, P.O. Box 2163, Princeton NJ 08540.

56 LOBBAN, G. (1978) 'The Influence of the School on Sex Role Stereotyping', in CHETWYND, J. and HARTNETT, O. (Eds.) *The Sex Role System*, London, Routledge and Kegan Paul.

57 SPENCE, J. (1978) 'What do People do, all Day; Class and Gender in Images of Women', *Screen Education*, Winter, No. 29, pp. 29–45.

58 *Ibid.*, p. 31.

59 DOHRMANN, R. (1975) 'A Gender Profile of Children's Educational T.V.', *Journal of Communication*, Vol. 25, No. 4, pp. 56–65.

60 *Ibid.*, pp. 62–3.

61 See, for example, COURTNEY, A.E. and WHIPPLE. T.W. (1974) 'Women in T.V. Commercials', *Journal of Communication*, Vol. 24, No. 2, pp. 110–18.

62 For good summaries of research see BUSBY, L.J. (1975) 'Sex Role Research on The Mass Media', *Journal of Communication*, Vol. 25, No. 4, pp. 107–31 and UNESCO (1979) 'Mass Media: The Image, Role and Social Conditions of Women', *Reports and Papers on Mass Communication*, No. 84.

63 BARDWICK, J.M. and SCHUMANN, S.I. (1975) 'Portrait of American Men and Women in T.V. Commercials', *Psychology*, IV, (4), pp. 18–23, quoted to BUSBY, L.J. *op. cit.*, (Note 62), p. 116.

64 FRITH, S. and McROBBIE, A. (1978) 'Rock and Sexuality', in *Screen Education*, No. 29, Winter, pp. 3–20 (reproduced in this volume).

65 *Ibid.*, p. 7.

66 *Ibid.*, p. 7.

67 McROBBIE, A. (1978) 'Jackie: an Ideology of Adolescent Femininity', CCCS, Stencilled Occasional Paper, No. 53.

68 *Ibid.*, p. 11. For other example of semiotics see CCCS Women's Studies Group, 'Images of Women in the Media', CCCS, Occasional Paper, No. 3.

69 BIRMINGHAM FEMINIST HISTORY GROUP (1979) 'Feminism as Femininity in the Nineteen Fifties', *Feminist Review*, No. 3, pp. 48–65.

70 *Ibid.*, p. 64.

71 GRAMSCI, A. (1971) *Selections from the Prison Notebooks*, translated by HOARE, Q. and NOWELL-SMITH, G., London, Lawrence and Wishart, p. 296.

72 *Ibid.*, p. 303.

Paul Willis

[...]

The ethnographic account reminds us again and again that there is only one social outcome. Gigantic forces in conflict resolve into one reality – not serial realities allowing us to read back their pure determinants and forwards their proper outcomes. The pure logic of cultural penetration runs straight only on the page. In reality simultaneous forces of distortion, limitation and mystification resolve this pure logic into a partial logic. In the way in which it is actually effective in the world the half-rejection and cultural penetration of the present social organisation by the counter-school culture becomes an always provisional, bare, sceptical, yet finally accepting accommodation within the *status quo*. It nevertheless, however, contradictorily maintains a degree of conviction of movement, insight and subjective validation in individuals even as they accept this subordination. In the present tangled knot of ideological entrapments in contemporary capitalism the most remarkable demonstration of this contradiction is that of a nascent cultural understanding of abstract labour and class solidarity amongst disaffected working class kids being delivered into a particular subjective affirmation and 'free' giving of manual labour power.

Divisions

Cultural penetrations are repressed, disorganised and prevented from reaching their full potential or a political articulation by deep, basic and disorientating divisions. The two most important are those between mental and manual labour and those of gender. (Racism which is also significant here is dealt with in a later section.)

The rejection of the school, and the cultural penetration of the unfairness of the 'equivalent' it offers can be seen as the rejection of individualism. It is also, however, simultaneously the rejection of mental activity in general. In the moment of the defeat of individualism its mark of separation passes. Individualism is defeated

Source: An abridged version of WILLIS, P. (1977) *Learning to Labour*, Gower (Saxon House), Chap. 6.

not for itself but for its part in the school masque where mental work is associated with unjustified authority, with qualifications whose promise is illusory. Individualism is penetrated therefore at the cost of a practical division of human capacity and a yielding of the power to properly exercise one half of it. As one kind of solidarity is won, deeper structural unity is lost. Although 'the lads' stand together, they do so on this side of the line with individualism and mental activity on the other. The human world is divided into those who are 'good with their hands' or 'good with their heads'. The burden of the cultural penetration that all work is the same is thrown mainly on to a notion that all *manual* work is the same. Manual labouring comes to take on, somehow, a significance and critical expression for its owner's social position and identity which is no part of its own proper nature.

We can see here the profound, unintended and contradictory importance of the institution of the school. Aspects of the dominant ideology are informally defeated there, but that defeat passes a larger structure more unconsciously and more naturalised for its very furnacing in (pyrrhic) victory. Capitalism can afford to yield individualism amongst the working class but not division. Individualism is penetrated by the counter-school culture but it actually produces division.

The other great division which disorientates cultural penetration is that between male and female. It is, at least in part, an internally produced division. The male counter-school culture promotes its own sexism – even celebrates it as part of its overall confidence.

The characteristic style of speech and movement, even in the absence of females, always holds something of the masculine spectacle. The ability to take the initiative, to make others laugh, to do unexpected or amusing things, to naturally take the active complement to the appreciative passive, these are all profoundly masculine attributes of the culture, and permanent goals for individuals in it. Not only this but a more concrete hallmark of being a member of the culture is to have either sexual experience or at least aspirations which are exploitative and hypocritical. Girls are pursued, sometimes roughly, for their sexual favours, often dropped and labelled 'loose' when they are given. Girls are asked to be sexy and inviting as well as pure and monogamous: to be consumed and not be consumed. The counter-school culture emphasises sexual division at the same moment that it penetrates the artificiality of individualistic division.

In its sexism the counter-school culture reflects the wider working class culture. This is partly, of course, because it turns to some of the wider class models for guidance during *differentiation* of the school educational paradigm. As he becomes disillusioned with the school, for instance, one of 'the lads' finds one of the most deep-seated and abiding models of sexual division and domination in the working home. Members of the counter-school culture are also much more likely to find a job – out of necessity – than are the conformists, and to experience a particular kind of sexism, both directed at them personally and as an aspect of the working environment in general. It becomes for them part of the worldliness and superior style of that whole working class culture of the workplace which they admire and are busily reconstructing in relation to the particular oppositions and determinants of the school.

Although there may be an institutionalised sexism in our schools, it is not as strong as the reproduced sexism of the informal level of its working class male oppositional culture. Schools must be given some credit for holding out a degree of liberalism and formalistic equality. It is no product of the school's manifest intentions that sexism and profoundly naturalized divisions arise in more virulent forms at the moment when its own authority is broken. All the same it plays out a vital and systematic, if unintended, role in the reproduction of a class society.

Labour Power and Patriarchy

The cultural penetrations examined may even have survived the disorientation and schism caused by the divisions outlined above if they had remained divisions in the abstract or separate from each other. As it is, there is further complex fusion of these divisions absolutely characteristic, in micro form, of a knot of meanings central to the stability of the capitalist system itself and appearing in all of its manifestations. Let us now consider this knot.

The mental/manual distinction alone presents a fertile field for the construction of naturalised divisions in human capacities. What is surprising is that a portion, including such as 'the lads', of those who make up the social whole are content to voluntarily take upon themselves the definition and consequent material outcomes of being manual labourers. This is surprising since in the capitalist mobilization of the mental/manual distinction it is conventionally, and according to the dominant ideology, the mental labourers who have the legitimised right to superior material and cultural conditions. Mental work is held to be more exacting and therefore to justify higher rewards. It is not difficult to explain why that which is ideologically seen as desirable and which is really rewarding materially should be pursued. The fact that all do not aspire to the rewards and satisfactions of mental labour is what is in need of explanation. Just because capitalism needs a split such as this does not explain why its need its satisfied. It is only in a perfectly reflective empirical world that the shape of a need determines the inevitability of its satisfaction. Moreover, the real mechanisms at play in the satisfaction of this need are covered over and mystified, and hidden from view by the way in which the dominant ideology, and the meritocratic view of what happens in schools for instance, really do seem to assume that all are trying to achieve broadly the same aims in life.

The way in which we are all expected to pursue the same aims suggests that those at the bottom of a class society are there apparently, and they believe it for themselves, because of their own smaller capacity to achieve these aims. All accept, so to speak, the same rules, meanings and goals of the game – and also what counts as winning and losing. In fact, of course, as the humanistic developments in education and careers counselling partly recognize but wrongly interpret, this model could never actually work under modern conditions. It assumes that the lower factions of the working class are really a sub-species: It is more feudalism than capitalism. Though it is usually misrecognized, one of the things which keeps the capitalist system stable, and is one of its complex wonders, is that an important section of the subordinate class do not accept the proffered reality of the steady diminution of their own capacities. Instead they reverse the valuation of the mental/manual gradient by which they are measured. 'The lads' under study here prefer (for the moment), and affirm themselves through, manual labour. This, of course, provides the missing link for a social chain of class distinctions. All other classes above this can celebrate, justify, and see a comparative base for their own superiority in the mental mode in the currency of the dominant ideology. The 'ear'oles' conformism, for instance, takes on a more rational appearance when judged against the self-disqualification of 'the lads'. Whether or not there is that much difference in the actual work they do, they can gain some advantage and social approval from defining it, their relationship to it, and their own identity in a relatively more mental mode.

A reverse polarization of a too well-learned distinction neatly complements the dominant ideology and gives it a sounding board for the subjective creation of identities in labour for all those factions above the lowest. Without this clinching inversion of the ideological order at its lowest reach in relation to the giving of labour power the system could not be stable. No amount of conditioning in state agencies could provide a fully human identity for those at the bottom of the class structure: coercion or permanent struggle, not free consent in submission, would be the basis of the social order.

This important inversion, however, is not achieved within the proper logic of capitalist production. Nor is it produced in the division of labour spontaneously. It is produced in the concrete articulation on the site of social classes of two structures which in capitalism can only be separated in abstraction and whose forms have now become part of it. These are patriarchy and the distinction between mental and manual labour. *The form of the articulation is of the cross-valorization and association of the two key terms in the two sets of structures.* The polarization of the two structures become crossed. Manual labour is associated with the social superiority of masculinity, and mental labour with the social inferiority of femininity. In particular manual labour is imbued with a masculine tone and nature which renders it positively expressive of more than its intrinsic focus in work.

Gender and mental/manual difference provide the atavistic divisions to be worked up into contemporary concrete cultural forms and relationships, but it is only the learning that division is not always and automatically to its own disadvantage which prevents sectors of the working class from seeing division as oppression. For 'the lads', a division in which they take themselves to be favoured (the sexual) overlies, becomes part of, and finally partially changes the valency of a division in which they are disadvantaged (mental/manual labour power).[1]

It is often overlooked that where two sets of divisions are lived out in the same concrete space they cannot remain separate. The pressure of consciousness and culture which work upon their own materials in their own location and seek a kind of unity will not live separately in two systems of ideas which both occur in the compression of their own life space. Such systems can only be separated in abstraction. As ethnography reminds us it is not a theoretical capacity but an empirical imperative that there must be a conjunction of systems. The secret of the continuation of both sets of divisions in labour and gender lies, at least partly, in their lived profane conjunction under the class system of capitalism, and not in their own pure logics. In this crossover conjunction the masculine – in its own proper field a state or formalistic law of superior status – becomes movement, action, assertion. An essence, which, it can be argued, is trans-historical, is given a style and a concrete worldly form of expression under capitalism. Manual labour power – in its own proper field neutral or even dissociated physical work on nature – becomes dominance and a form of election. It is given an expressive purpose.

If a form of patriarchy buttresses the mental/manual division of labour, this division, in its turn, strengthens and helps to reproduce modern forms of sexual division and oppression. It is precisely because there are divisions at school and work which operate objectively to their disfavour but which can be understood and inverted in patriarchal terms that those gender terms must themselves be continuously reproduced and legitimated. If the currency of femininity were revalued then that of mental work would have to be too. A member of the counter-school culture can only believe in the effeminacy of white collar and office work so long as wives, girlfriends and mothers are regarded as restricted, inferior and incapable of certain things. As we have seen, there is ample evidence of this belief amongst 'the lads'. The ideology of domesticity they impose on girlfriends, the patterns of homely and subcultural capacity and incapacity, all underwrite the restricted role of women. It is from the ideological division of labour, not simply from the domesticity of the house or patriarchal ideology that some of the real determinants and rationales of these practices spring.[2] For our immediate purposes the result of this cross-valorization is that the flow of cultural penetration, and particularly its nascent appreciation of general abstract labour, is diverted into a surprizing affirmation of labour power. There are two important process. In the first place the association of different kinds of work with different sexual genders confirms the nature of division in the world of work. Mental activity for 'the lads' is not only barred because of their particular experience of the institution of the school, but also because it is regarded as effeminate. Many of their own mental activities and feelings are expressed and acted through the cultural, the stylish and the concrete. In the crucial, critical and classic shift, what they take as mental work becomes for 'the lads' mere 'pen-pushing', 'not really doing things' and, most importantly, 'cissy': it is not basically man's work or within the manly scope of action. We see at least why the 'ear'oles' are likely to be regarded as effeminate and passive 'cissies' by 'the lads', and why other names for conformists include 'pouf' or 'poufter', or 'wanker'. Despite their greater achievement and conventional hopes for the future, 'ear'oles' and their strategies can be ignored because the *mode* of their success can be discredited as passive, mental and lacking a robust masculinity.

In the second place the whole meaning of what masculinity stands for reinforces the sense in which the weight of the cultural penetration concerning labour power and the nature of modern work is thrown contradictorily on to an affirmation of manual labour power. There is a further infusion of meaning into manual labour power which is no part of its intrinsic nature.

Manual labour is suffused with masculine qualities and given certain sensual overtones for 'the lads'.[3] The toughness and awkwardness of physical work and effort – for itself and in the division of labour and for its strictly capitalist logic quite without intrinsic heroism or grandeur – takes on masculine lights and depths and assumes a significance beyond itself. Whatever the specific problems, so to speak, of the difficult task they are always essentially masculine problems. It takes masculine capacities to deal with them. We may say that where the principle of general abstract labour has emptied work of significance from the inside, a transformed patriarchy has filled it with significance from the outside. Discontent with work is hinged away from a political discontent and confused in its proper logic by a huge detour into the symbolic sexual realm.

The brutality of the working situation is partially re-interpreted into a heroic exercise of manly confrontation with *the task*. Difficult, uncomfortable or dangerous conditions are seen, not for themselves, but for their appropriateness to a masculine readiness and hardness. They are understood more through the toughness required to survive them, than in the nature of the imposition which asks them to be faced in the first place.

Though it is difficult to obtain stature in work itself, both what work provides and the very sacrifice and strength required to do it provides the materials for an elemental self-esteem. This self-esteem derives from the achievement of a purpose which not all – particularly women – are held capable of achieving. The wage packet is the provider of freedom, and independence: the particular prize of masculinity in work. This is the complement of, and is what makes possible, the fetishism of the wage packet. A trade is judged not for itself, nor even for its general financial return, but for its ability to provide the central, domestic, masculine role for its incumbent. Clearly money is part of this – but as a measure, not the essence. As Spanksy's father says, 'You can raise a family off polishing'. The male wage packet is held to be central, not simply because of its size, but because it is won in a masculine mode in confrontation with the 'real' world which is too tough for the woman. Thus the man in the domestic household is held to be the breadwinner, the worker, whilst the wife works for 'the extras'. Very often of course, the material importance of her wage may be much greater than this suggests, and certainly her domestic labour is the lynchpin of the whole household economy. The wage packet as a kind of symbol of machismo dictates the domestic culture and economy and tyrannizes both men and women.

In a more general sense in the machismo of manual work the will to finish a job, the will to really work, is posited as a masculine logic and not as the logic of exploitation. 'It's a man's want to be finished when he starts a job', says Joey's father about his heavy drop forging work. The very teleology of the process of work upon nature and the material power involved in that becomes through the conflation of masculinity and manual work a property of masculinity and not of production. Masculinity is power in its own right, and if its immediate expression is in the completion of work for another, then what of it? It has to be expressed somewhere because it is a quality of being. That is the destiny which a certain kind of self-esteem and dignity seem naturally to bring. Where the intransigence and hardness of a task might bring weakness, or collective opposition or questioning, an over-ride of masculinity – transferred teleology of production – can cut in to push back fatigue and rational assessment of purpose.[4]

And if the nature of masculinity in work becomes a style of teleology, completion, femininity is associated with a fixed state. Its labour power is considered as an onto-logical state of being, not a teleological process of becoming. Housework is not completion, it is maintenance of status. Cooking, washing and cleaning reproduce what was there before. Certainly in a sense housework is never completed – but neither is it as difficult or productive as masculine work is held to be. Female domestic work is simply subsumed under *being* 'mum' or 'housewife'. 'Mum' will always do it, and should always be expected to do it. It is part of the definition of what she *is*, as the wage packet and the productive world of work is of what 'dad' is.

Far from patriarchy and its associated values being an unexplained relic of previous societies, it is one of the very pivots of capitalism in its complex, unintended preparation of labour power and reproduction of the social order. It helps to provide the real human and cultural conditions which in their continuously deconstructed, reconstructed, fragile, uncertain, unintended and contradictory ways actually allow subordinate roles to be taken on 'freely' within liberal democracy. We have the elemental, though finally illusory, reversal of real conditions in experience which is necessary for the 'free' functioning of consciousness and will in finally determinate conditions. What begins as, or has the potential to be, an insight about the com-monality of the giving of labour, and of the identity of the working class, amongst 'the lads' and in the counter-school culture becomes broken down into an assertion about manual labour only, and then distorted into strange affirmation of it. Labour comes to express aspects of an essence or quality not intrinsically part of its nature or relation to capital. More concretely, in an important sense it is because 'the lads' known division and superiority in courtship, in the home, on the street, in the pub, and in the family that they understand and accept division at school and work and find short term celebration and long term accommodation within its least favourable term.

Masculinity must not, however, be too simply posed. It has many dimensions and edges. In one way it is a half-blind, regressive machismo which brings self-destructive violence, aggression and division to relationships within the working class. In another way, imparting something of what lies behind it, masculinity expresses impulses which can be progressive. Behind the expression of masculinity lies an affirmation of manual labour power and behind that (though mediated and distorted) a sense of the uniqueness of the commodity of labour power and of the way in which general abstract labour unites and connects all kinds of concrete labour. The masculine disdain for qualifications, for all its prejudice, carries still a kind of 'insight' into the divisive nature of certification, and into the way in which mental work and technicism are mobilised ideologically primarily to maintain class relations rather than to select the most efficient or to increase productive efficiency.

It is in the understanding of this contradictory complex of masculinity and the strange articulation of sexual and labour divisions that we have the beginnings of an answer to the problem outlined earlier: why that which is conventionally registered, artificially defined and ideologically imbued as the least desirable and satisfying work (manual work) should be taken on voluntarily, and even with some enthusiasm by an important group in society – at least for long enough in their youth to be trapped forever.

Manual work is *seen* significantly differently by this group. Its stigma becomes *positively* expressive. Such work is undertaken in part to express things other than its objectives or dominant ideologically ascribed identity within the capitalist system. These things are not themselves without an aetiological 'rationality' which though displaced and transposed is potentially more adequate than some of those accounts which directly define manual work as inferior.

It is the unlikely hard stone at the bottom of the social system of self-selection into manual work which allows, in the currents of ideology against it, 'new classes' to effervesce upwards in experiential relations of ascendence.[5] For instance both the conformists and the non-conformists of this study are, in fact, working class and objectively doing similar work in a similar position *vis-á-vis* the productive proceeds. Yet the conformists can believe themselves, especially equipped with qualifications, to be in 'better' jobs than, and to be a 'different kind of person' from, 'the lads'. And once such a division is founded in the working class, of course, it massively legitimates the position of the middle class: not capitalism but their own mental capacities keep them where they are.

Racialism and Labour Power

Racial division helps, as with labour and gender divisions, to found the whole epistemological category and possibility of division. It also provides an evident underclass which is more heavily exploited than the white working class, and is therefore indirectly and partially exploited by the working class itself (at least lessening their own exploitation); it also provides an ideological object for feelings about the degeneracy of others and the superiority of the self (thus reinforcing the dominant ideological terms which make the comparison possible). Racism therefore divides the working class both materially and ideologically.

There is also a sense, however, in which racism tones the sensual giving of labour power for sections of the white working class such as 'the lads' in a way which leads to further nuanced affirmation of a particular kind of labouring. It marks the bottom limit of the scope of masculinity and delivers it not as a vulgar assertion of everything physical and menial, but as a more carefully judged cultural category. Since immigrant racial groups are likely to take the worst and roughest jobs, they are also potentially likely to be harder and more masculine. It is untenable that another social group should take the mantle of masculine assertiveness, so such jobs are further reclassified to fall off the cultural scale of masculinity into the 'dirty', 'messy' and 'unsocial' category.

A complex map of occupations therefore develops which does not have a single principle of organisation. Very light or mental work is marked down as 'cissy' but the heaviest and most uncompromising work is not necessarily masculine. It can be marked down as dirty and unacceptable through association with immigrant labour.

Racism must be understood with respect more to the complex social definition of labour power under capitalism than to any pure and inevitable ethnic hostility.

There are variations, of course, in relations and social definitions between the races. West Indian males seem to have preserved a degree of machismo from the real and imputed degradation of their conditions (it would be interesting to see how far this is related to their sense of their own labour power). Certainly some white working class hostility towards young West Indians seems to be based on kind of sexual jealousy. Of course just as his work situation is downgraded from the masculine to the dirty, so the West Indian's supposed sexual prowess can be downgraded from the natural to the disgusting.

In the case of Asians there seems to be evidence of an opposite move on the basic cultural scale of work so that successful shopkeepers, businessmen and students are defined by many working class whites such as 'the lads' as 'cissy', passive and lacking aggression alongside conformist, effeminate whites (c.f. 'queer-bashing' and 'Paki-bashing'). Some of the virulence of this response may be accounted for by the perception of this move upwards (and into its set of characteristic prejudices) in relation to the feeling that the Asians should really belong with the rough and dirty workers anyway. There is a confusion about which category of prejudice to apply, and in a certain sense the Asians suffer from both.

If the basic general thesis of the contradictory cultural forms in which labour is prepared has any validity, however, it should also throw light upon such preparation amongst immigrant groups.[6]

Certainly in the case of some young second generation West Indians their cultural responses and processes can be likened to those of 'the lads'. They are in some respects more advanced in a way which shows up aspects of the present situation more clearly. Such lads have, for the most part, grown up and been educated in England and have had broadly the same experiences as their white fellow pupils at school and in and around the neighbourhood and district – from a structural point of view anyway. It may be suggested that this will have led their informal culture to certain kinds of mediated 'insights' about the nature of the school and the labour market similar to those amongst the white lads. They also, however, inherit from the West Indies a culture of wagelessness and poverty. It appears to them as if there is a viable possibility of surviving without wages – or in some cases without any kind of official and visible means of support at all. This opens up the possibility, therefore, of certain accurate insights about the nature of their future being carried forward not as an affirmation of a certain kind of work but as a *refusal* of all work.

This is not to say that their culture, and the actions springing from its logic, are without mystification or are not finally distorted and made partial in their own ways. However, if they close the circle too early by a refusal to work not properly based on an analysis of, and politically articulated with, the real conditions and possibilities of this society, they highlight the half-completed nature of the white response with its contradictory mixture of penetration, rationality, distortion and final incorporation.

As structural unemployment becomes a permanent feature of this society and some sections of white youth are forced into long term unemployment there may well develop a white ethnic culture of wagelessness (borrowing very likely from the West Indian one, though compare the currently emerging phenomenon of punk rock culture). A necessity might be turned into an invention and, through the cultural mediation, the option of not working become a more widespread 'freely' chosen response. The question of the cultural reproduction of an under class is as full of significance as that of the reproduction of the manual working class. We cannot, however, pursue it here.

Notes and References

1 The basic cross-valorization discussed here is relevant to groups other than the male working class. The association, for instance, of femininity with mental work implies a contradiction for working class women. Masculinity is an aspect of their *class* cultural identity no matter what their feminine gender on other grounds. This association also implies for middle class women a further restriction, passivity, and inherent absurdity of their social and cultural roles even than their gender definition implies. We have here elements towards an explanation of the women's movement, its class origin, and to forms of working class antagonism to it.

For middle class males there are also contradictions between a class and cultural (patriarchal) defini-tion of their masculinity. They are by no means immune from the inversion of the occupational gradient accomplished and underpinned by patriarchal values in an important area of working class culture. For the class base and origins of the developing 'Men's Movement' see TOLSON, A. (1976) *The Limits of Masculinity*, Tavistock.

The male working class case presented in the main text is not, of course, without contradictions. Racial complexities threaten it from one side, and the reduction of work experience which allows – even given the scope of ideological play – masculine experiences threaten it from the other.

2 Juliet Mitchell's important book attempts to demonstrate the strict redundancy of patriarchal forms in modern capitalism. Both as outlined by Engels in his materialist analysis (*The Origins of the Family, Private Property and the State*), and in Mitchell's account of the cultural analyses of Freud and Levi-Strauss, patriarchy now seems to be superfluous. For Mitchell, apparently, it lives on as an historical trace without any continuously and relevantly reproduced logic or justification. Not only this, but patriarchy and capitalism are preserved as two quite distinct entities by Mitchell (p. 379). This leads her to posit an untenable dualistic politics (pp. 406, 414 and 415). She asserts that the systems are in contradiction but there is no actual depiction of the process of struggle between, or dialectical trans-formation of, both. We are dealing here surely with a contradiction that lies ultimately within *one* complex and differentiated unit, an *internal* contradiction specific to the complex balance of modern capitalism. It is precisely the oblique conjunction of the capitalist mode of production and patriarchy which make them difficult to sort out at the level of consciousness. It is the inheritance of pre-capitalist forms and their profane and complex determinate relation with (and partly constituting it) a specific and determinant kind of capitalist mode of production which helps to divert the insights bred at the cultural level, and more properly focused on specifically capitalist relations, into reactionary, immobile or neutral forms. What does indeed confound the pure logic of the system also confounds working class culture.

More generally, this book highlights the potential danger of the women's movement being vitiated by a too-short-run notion of a patriarchal sexism which oppresses them directly in some way outside capitalism. The need is for a dialectical and connected notion of a determinate capitalist patriarchy which transforms and fixes the whole social totality. This clearly has important implications for men as well as women – though it is undoubtedly women who suffer the sharpest most obvious and visible oppression. MITCHELL, J. (1974) *Psychoanalysis and Feminism*, Penguin.

3 Masculinity is so deeply embedded in the giving of manual labour that we might actually question the 'objectivity' of those methods which aim to intensify and increase the efficiency of labour. The role of transformed patriarchal influences within the productive process as it has been intensified by capitalism has hardly been touched on. The intertwining of patriarchal forms in capitalism means, in fact, that there is no pure way in which we can picture abstract labour. The techniques of Ford, Taylor and Gilbreth might not be so pure as they suppose. Even the codifications and reductions of modern organisation and methods, especially as they are resisted in shopfloor culture in what are often essentially

masculine forms, cannot remove atavistic traces of swagger, unnecessary movement and the expression of an essence which is essentially foreign to production *qua* production. Indeed we may say that in an unintended way some of this swagger is institutionalised and given a kind of legitimation which escapes the notice of the rate setter. Certainly we may regard it as an unpredictable area which gives space and microstrategies for time wasting, systematic soldiering and resistance to intensification of the labour process.

It may even be argued much more speculatively that the particular physical style given to production in this way has more than provided the detail of concrete forms and experiential relations to production, but has altered the course of industrialization itself. The peculiarly obstinate and trenchant form of the *mechanical* industrial revolution we know and still largely have, and its inability to fully give way to a more cybernetic industrial process when the technical processes are at hand, suggest that there are profound cultural gearings as well as more important structural factors keeping us to a certain kind of physical, visible, and mechanical work upon nature.

It is possible that this masculine style of expression influences the form of struggle and conflict in work. Certainly the union official or shop steward uses particular shopfloor cultural forms to mobilise the men – the spectacle or bluff, or strong and combative language – which are suffused with masculine feelings. This establishes a real expression of anger and opposition which may be very effective in the short term, and is certainly a force to be reckoned with. But it may be that longer term objectives simply cannot be conceptualized in this way, and are to a certain extent made inoperative by default at the face to face grassroots level. The masculine style of confrontation demands an appropriate and honourable resolution: visible and immediate concessions. If this is its price, however, it can be bought off at it. But the visibility of the concessions won in this way, especially in the form of a larger, masculine wage packet, may actually conceal longer term defeats over the less visible issues of control and ownership. It is possible to satisfy violent and possibly even frightening demands by short term, visible and dramatic concessions without changing any of those basic arrangements which the violence might appear to threaten. There are many other important strands of course, long term and continuing historical factors which must be given precedence, and this is simply speculation, but the particular combination of an affirmation of manual labour in a masculine and immediate style may have an important, though as yet unexamined role, in the particular social democratic and short run economic perspective so characteristic of the British labour movement.

In this light the question of the emergence of new classes under capitalism is less interesting than the question of the reproduction of the old in new conditions. My general argument carries more theoretical implications for the status of the division mental/manual in relation to the development of 'new' classes than is relevant to outline in the main text.

In my view it is important to separate the following categories: distillation upwards of skill and control in the productive powers, the mental/manual ideological division; ideological class division; and real class divisions. The distillation upwards of skill is a real thing in capitalism. Quite apart from its meaning in the ideological realm it is an objective and necessary hallmark of capitalism that it sets further back the limits on production. It removes the constraints of immediate wants and direct appropriation and opens up the variable capacity of labour to produce up to the limits of social resistance or technical competence. Pushing back the limits of technical competence under capitalism means the progressive distillation upwards of control and planning and the intensification of labour.

This real tendency in productive capitalism provides a framework for a cultural and social interpretation of a division between mental and manual labour. The classic transference of collective properties of a system onto individual differences and qualities can be seen. It is here that the scope is essentially created for the rolling back of social constraints on production. It establishes the possibility of division.

For the wage earning working class, objective differences produced by the distillation upwards of control and planning produce little internal division for themselves. The actual experience of work for most blue collar people is very similar. With de-skilling, centralization and rationalization there is really only a marginal difference between working at one machine in the tool room, and working at the same machine on the production line. The commonality of experience persists even through the proliferation of differentiated conditions of work. Even obvious differences (e.g. between white and blue overalls) pall into insignificance beside the standard minute and standardized procedures. For the working class, the objective differences they face are much less important than the ideological resonances these bear. These resonances concern, at least in part, an articulation of sexism upon the mutual/manual division. The form of the mental/manual division as it returns to production is therefore profoundly different from the material base which supports its interpretation – especially in its patriarchal and sexist associations. Just because capitalism needs and can benefit from ideological distortions and visions of this kind does not mean that it will be supplied with them.

The mental/manual division is therefore artificial: it is a construction upon the real which is dislocated from its originating structure, transformed and re-applied. It is nevertheless made, however, to partly bear the weight of class divisions. These are of two sorts: first, internal divisions of consciousness within what is objectively the working class, so that those doing the same basic kinds of work believe themselves to be socially diverse; and second, real class divisions which it helps to present as differences only in competence. The middle class is legitimated in part with a currency arising ultimately from an objective tendency of the forces of production. The real tendency of the distillation upwards of skill and control is made to serve as the basis of ideological class divisions quite out of its context in the forces of production. Social divisions are presented and defended as productive divisions and in a society where production and the economy constitute the main ideological discourse this transference of legitimation proves near impenetrable.

The vital move in all this is the ideological transformation of real productive tendencies into sexually imbued mental/manual divisions. This is accomplished not by the inner laws of capital, nor by some obscure working of all time-structural factors, but with the help of contradictory, half-rational cultural and subjective processes.

Class divisions erected upon the mental/manual basis are, therefore, an illusion upon an illusion. Even insofar as the mental/manual division is legitimate it occurs strictly only within the working class. The mental aspects of labour – personalised as concrete mental labour in the illusion – engaged in expanding capitalist production through concentration and intensification are truly contributing to the expansion not the absorption of surplus [i.e. it is not middle class]. It is no logic of its own that such labour is taken over, simplified and re-interpreted – especially in the light of the frank adoption of what is taken to be manual labour elsewhere – and used for the purposes of maintaining and legitimizing class division. The objective distillation upwards of control and skill in the production process goes through some long loops into the cultural and the subjective and is also supplemented with new and specific inputs of meaning (sexism and school associations of 'mental' labour) before it appears socially as the mental/manual division.

It is wrong, however, to reserve the role of the maintenance of the social relations of production simply for the ideological. Similarly it is wrong to see the logic of capitalism as essentially that of the maintenance of the social relations of production. This occurs also, and in the same moment (and could not take place without), as the logic of expanded production works through the continuous reorganisation of the labour process, distillation upwards of skill and control, and intensification of labour. There is a dialectical relation between the two.

None of this is to deny that what we might loosely call 'mental labour' is not associated with the middle class. The work of managing capital, dividing surplus (even where some of it goes back to the working class), and maintaining the social relations of production certainly involves mental operations. It is difficult, however, to sort out activities which *look* similar but differ in having either a basically social or a productive function. The foregoing analysis does not relieve the problem of objective differentiation between classes and class factions.

However, since we have seen that the mental/manual division does not arise from production alone, but from external processes which overlay and make a certain sense of real productive tendencies but are different from them, we need not attempt to spirit away the real divisions of production as Poulantzas does in his concern to penetrate the ideological process. If the ideology at least partly arises elsewhere we can take the guilt out of seeing real demarcations in production. This should help in our identification of real class factions. See POULANTZAS, N. (1975) *Classes in Contemporary Capitalism*, New Left Books.

6 This is also true of the preparation of labour power amongst working class girls. It may be suggested that specific ideologies about sex roles – from familial models to mass media stereotypes – are taken up in the school context in specific kinds of practices which have implications for the diversion of cultural penetrations and for the subjective and collective development of a certain sense and definition of labour power. Wheedling around male teachers or challenging both them and female teachers with a direct sexuality, for instance, may help girls to think of their own vital powers as applicable, not to 'work' and 'industry', but to complex and contradictory sexual manipulation, comforting and familial construction of the 'home'.

Though I could not include girls in the focus of this research, the approach outlined here is equally applicable, at least at a formal level, to the study of girls in school.

12   The Unhappy Marriage of Marxism and Feminism: Towards a More Progressive Union

Heidi Hartmann

[...]

The 'marriage' of marxism and feminism has been like the marriage of husband and wife depicted in English common law: marxism and feminism are one, and that one is marxism.[1] [...]

The inequalities in this marriage, like most social phenomena, are no accident. Many marxists typically argue that feminism is at best less important than class conflict and at worst divisive of the working class. This political stance produces an analysis that absorbs feminism into the class struggle. Moreover, the analytic power of marxism with respect to capital has obscured its limitations with respect to sexism. We will argue here that while marxist analysis provides essential insight into the laws of historical development, and those of capital in particular, the categories of marxism are sex-blind. Only a specifically feminist analysis reveals the systemic character of relations between men and women. Yet feminist analysis by itself is inadequate because it has been blind to history and insufficiently materialist. Both marxist analysis, particularly its historical and materialist method, and feminist analysis, especially the identification of patriarchy as a social and historical structure, must be drawn upon if we are to understand the development of western capitalist societies and the predicament of women within them. In this essay we suggest a new direction for marxist feminist analysis.

I Marxism and the Woman Question

The 'woman question' has never been the 'feminist question'. The feminist question is directed at the causes of sexual inequality between women and men, of male dominance over women. Most marxist analyses of women's position take as their question the relationship of women to the economic system, rather than that of women to men, apparently assuming the latter will be explained in their discussion of the former. Marxist analysis of the woman question has taken three main forms.

Source: An abridged version of Heidi Hartmann's lead article in SARGENT, L (Ed) *The Unhappy Marriage of Marxism and Feminism: A Debate on Class and Patriarchy,* 1981 PLUTO PRESS.

All see women's oppression in our connection (or lack of it) to production. Defining women as part of the working class, these analyses consistently subsume women's relation to men under workers' relation to capital. First, early marxists, including Marx, Engels, Kautsky, and Lenin, saw capitalism drawing all women into the wage labor force, and saw this process destroying the sexual division of labor. Second, contemporary marxists have incorporated women into an analysis of 'everyday life' in capitalism. In this view, all aspects of our lives are seen to reproduce the capitalist system and we are all workers in that system. And third, marxist-feminists have focussed on housework and its relation to capital, some arguing that housework produces surplus value and that houseworkers work directly for capitalists. These three approaches are examined in turn.

Engels, in *Origins of the Family, Private Property and the State*, recognized the inferior position of women and attributed it to the institution of private property.[1] In bourgeois families, Engels argued, women had to serve their masters, be mono-gamous, and produce heirs to inherit property. Among proletarians, Engels argued, women were not oppressed, because there was no private property to be passed on. Engels argued further that as the extension of wage labor destroyed the small-holding peasantry, and women and children were incorporated into the wage labor force along with men, the authority of the male head of household was undermined, and patriarchal relations were destroyed.[2]

For Engels then, women's participation in the labor force was the key to their emancipation. Capitalism would abolish sex differences and treat all workers equally. Women would become economically independent of men and would participate on an equal footing with men in bringing about the proletarian revolu-tion. After the revolution, when all people would be workers and private property abolished, women would be emancipated from capital as well as from men. Marxists were aware of the hardships women's labor force participation meant for women and families, which resulted in women having two jobs, housework and wage work. Nevertheless, their emphasis was less on the continued subordination of women in the home than on the progressive character of capitalism's 'erosion' of patriarchal relations. Under socialism housework too would be collectivized and women relieved of their double burden. [...] Capital and private property, the early marxists argued, are the cause of women's particular oppression just as capital is the cause of the exploitation of workers in general.

Though aware of the deplorable situation of women in their time the early marxists failed to focus on the *differences* between men's and women's experiences under capitalism. They did not focus on the feminist questions – how and why women are oppressed as women. They did not, therefore, recognize the vested interest men had in women's continued subordination. As we argue in Part III below, men benefited from not having to do housework, from having their wives and daughters serve them and from having the better places in the labor market. Patriarchal relations, far from being atavistic leftovers, being rapidly outmoded by capitalism, as the early marxists suggested, have survived and thrived alongside it. And since capital and private property do not cause the oppression of women as *women*, their end alone will not result in the end of women's oppression.

Perhaps the most popular of the recent articles exemplifying the second marxist approach, the everyday life school, is the series by Eli Zaretsky in *Socialist Revolution*.[3] Zaretsky agrees with feminist analysis when he argues that sexism is not a new phenomenon produced by capitalism, but he stresses that the particular form sexism takes now has been shaped by capital. He focusses on the differential experiences of men and women under capitalism. Writing a century after Engels, once capitalism had matured, Zaretsky points out that capitalism has not incorporated all women into the labor force on equal terms with men. Rather capital has created a separation between the home, family, and personal life on the one hand and the workplace on the other.[4]

Sexism has become more virulent under capitalism, according to Zaretsky, because of this separation between wage work and home work. Women's increased oppression is caused by their exclusion from wage work. Zaretsky argues that while men are oppressed by having to do wage work, women are oppressed by not being allowed to do wage work. Women's exclusion from the wage labor force has been caused primarily by capitalism, because capitalism both creates wage work outside the home and requires women to work in the home in order to reproduce wage workers for the capitalist system. Women reproduce the labor force, provide psychological nurturance for workers, and provide an island of intimacy in a sea of alienation. In Zaretsky's view women are laboring for capital and not for men; it is only the separation of home from work place, and the privatization of housework brought about by capitalism that creates the *appearance* that women are working for men privately in the home. The difference between the *appearance*, that women work for men, and the *reality*, that women work for capital, has caused a misdirection of the energies of the women's movement. Women should recognize that women, too, are part of the working class, even though they work at home. In Zaretsky's view,

> the housewife emerged, alongside the proletarian [as] the two characteristic laborers of developed capitalist society,[5]

and the segmentation of their lives oppresses both the husband-proletarian and the wife-housekeeper. [...]

Zaretsky's analysis owes much to the feminist movement, but he ultimately argues for a redirection of that movement. Zaretsky has accepted the feminist argument that sexism predates capitalism; he has accepted much of the marxist feminist argument that housework is crucial to the reproduction of capital; he recognizes that housework is hard work and does not belittle it; and he uses the concepts of male supremacy and sexism. But his analysis ultimately rests on the notion of separation, on the concept of *division*, as the crux of the problem, a division attributable to capitalism. Like the 'complementary spheres' argument of the early twentieth century, which held that women's and men's spheres were complementary, separate but equally important, Zaretsky largely denies the existence and importance of *inequality* between men and women. His focus is on the relationship of women, the family, and the private sphere to capitalism. Moreover, even if capitalism created the private sphere, as Zaretsky argues, why did it happen that *women* work there, and *men* in the labor force? Surely this cannot be explained without reference to patriarchy, the systemic dominance of men over women. From our point of view, the problem in the family, the labor market, economy and society is not simply a division of labor between men and women, but a division that places men in a superior, and women in a subordinate, position.

Just as Engels sees private property as the capitalist contribution to women's oppression, so Zaretsky sees privacy. Because women are laboring privately at home they are oppressed. Zaretsky and Engels romanticize the preindustrial family and community – where men, women, adults, children worked together in family-centered enterprise and all participated in community life.

[...]

[Similarly] Mariarosa Dalla Costa's theoretical analysis of housework is essentially an argument about the relation of housework to capital and the place of housework in capitalist society and not about the relations of men and women as exemplified in housework.[6] Nevertheless, Dalla Costa's political position, that women should demand wages for housework, has vastly increased consciousness of the importance of housework among women in the women's movement. The demand was and still is debated in women's groups all over the United States. By making the claim that women at home not only provide essential services for capital by reproducing the labor force, but also create surplus value through that work,[7] Dalla Costa also vastly increased the left's consciousness of the importance of housework, and provoked a long debate on the relation of housework to capital.[8]

[...] But like the other marxist approaches reviewed here her approach focusses on capital – not on relations between men and women. The fact that men and women have differences of interest, *goals*, and strategies is obscured by her very powerful analysis of how the capitalist system keeps us all down, and the important and perhaps strategic role of women's work in this system. The rhetoric of feminism is present in Dalla Costa's writing (the oppression of women, struggle with men) but the focus of feminism is not. If it were, Dalla Costa might argue, for example, that the importance of housework as a social relation lies in its crucial role in perpetuating male supremacy. That women do housework, performing labor for men, is crucial to the maintenance of patriarchy.

Engels, Zaretsky, and Dalla Costa all fail to analyze the labor process within the family sufficiently. Who benefits from women's labor? Surely capitalists, but also surely men, who as husbands and fathers receive personalized services at home. The content and extent of the services may vary by class or ethnic or racial group, but the fact of their receipt does not. Men have a higher standard of living than women in terms of luxury consumption, leisure time, and personalized services. A materialist approach ought not to ignore this crucial point. It follows that men have a material interest in women's continued oppression. In the long run this may be 'false consciousness', since the majority of men could benefit from the abolition of hierarchy within the patriarchy. But in the short run this amounts to control over other people's labor, control which men are unwilling to relinquish voluntarily.

While the approach of the early marxists ignored housework and stressed women's labor force participation, the two more recent approaches emphasize housework to such an extent they ignore women's current role in the labor market. Nevertheless, all three attempt to include women in the category working class and to understand women's oppression as another aspect of class oppression. In doing so all give short shrift to the object of feminist analysis, the relations between women and men. [. . .]

Towards More Useful Marxist Feminism

Marxism is also a *method* of social analysis, historical dialectical materialism. By putting this method to the service of feminist questions, Juliet Mitchell and Shulamith Firestone suggest new directions for marxist feminism. [. . .]

> According to the materialistic conception, the determining factor in history is, in the final instance, the production and reproduction of immediate life. This, again, is of a twofold character: on the one side, the production of the means of existence, of food, clothing, and shelter and the tools necessary for that production; on the other side, the production of human beings themselves, the propagation of the species. The social organization under which the people of a particular historical epoch live is determined by both kinds of production. . . . [9]

This is the kind of analysis Mitchell has attempted. In her first essay, 'Women: The Longest Revolution', Mitchell examines both market work and the work of reproduction, sexuality, and child-rearing.[10]

Mitchell does not entirely succeed, perhaps because not all of women's work counts as production for her. Only market work is identified as production; the other spheres (loosely aggregated as the family) in which women work are identified as ideological. Patriarchy, which largely organizes reproduction, sexuality, and child-rearing, has no material base for Mitchell. *Women's Estate*, Mitchell's expansion of this essay, focusses much more on developing the analysis of women's market work than it does on developing the analysis of women's work within the family. The book is much more concerned with women's relation to, and work for, capital than with women's relation to, and work for, men; more influenced by marxism than by radical feminism. In a later work, *Psychoanalysis and Feminism*, Mitchell explores an important area for studying the relations between women and men, namely the formation of different, gender-based personalities by women and men.[11] Patriarchy operates, Mitchell seems to be saying, primarily in the psychological realm, where female and male children learn to be women and men. Here Mitchell focusses on the spheres she initially slighted, reproduction, sexuality, and child-rearing, but by placing them in the ideological realm, she continues the fundamental weakness of her earlier analysis. She clearly presents patriarchy as the fundamental ideological structure, just as capital is the fundamental economic structure:

> To put the matter schematically . . . we are . . . dealing with two autonomous areas: the economic mode of capitalism and the ideological mode of patriarchy.[12]

Although Mitchell discusses their interpenetration, her failure to give patriarchy a material base in the relation between women's and men's labor power, and her similar failure to note the material aspects of the process of personality formation and gender creation, limits the usefulness of her analysis.

Shulamith Firestone bridges marxism and feminism by bringing materialist analysis to bear on patriarchy.[13] Her use of materialist analysis is not as ambivalent as Mitchell's. The dialectic of sex, she says, is the fundamental historical dialectic, and the material base of patriarchy is the work women do reproducing the species. The importance of Firestone's work in using marxism to analyze women's position, in asserting the existence of a material base to patriarchy, cannot be overestimated. But it suffers from an overemphasis on biology and reproduction. What we need to understand is how sex (a biological fact) becomes gender (a social phenomenon). It is necessary to place all of women's work in its social and historical context, not to focus only on reproduction. Although Firestone's work offers a new and feminist use of marxist methodology, her insistence on the primacy of men's dominance over women as the cornerstone on which all other oppression (class, age, race) rests, suggests that her book is more properly grouped with the radical feminists than with the marxist feminists. Her work remains the most complete statement of the radical feminist position.

[...]

II Radical Feminism and Patriarchy

The great thrust of radical feminist writing has been directed to the documentation of the slogan 'the personal is political'. Women's discontent, they argued, is not the neurotic lament of the maladjusted, but a response to a social structure in which women are systematically dominated, exploited and oppressed. Women's inferior position in the labor market, the male-centered emotional structure of middle-class marriage, the use of women in advertising, the so-called understanding of women's psyche as neurotic – popularized by academic and clinical psychology – aspect after aspect of women's lives in advanced capitalist society was researched and analyzed. The radical feminist literature is enormous and defies easy summary. At the same time, its focus on psychology is consistent. The New York Radical Feminists' organizing document was 'The Politics of the Ego'. 'The personal is political' means, for radical feminists, that the original and basic class division is between the sexes, and that the motive force in history is the striving of men for power and domination over women, the dialectic of sex.[14]

Accordingly, Firestone rewrote Freud to understand the development of boys and girls into men and women in terms of power.[15] Her characterizations of what are 'male' and 'female' character traits are typical of radical feminist writing. The male seeks power and domination; he is ego-centric and individualistic, competitive and pragmatic; the 'technological mode', according to Firestone, is male. The female is nurturant, artistic, and philosophical; the 'aesthetic mode' is female.

No doubt the idea that the 'aesthetic mode' is female would have come as quite a shock to the ancient Greeks. Here lies the error of radical feminist analysis: the 'dialectic of sex' as radical feminists present it projects 'male' and 'female' characteristics as they appear in the present back into all of history. Radical feminist analysis has greatest strength in its insights into the present. Its greatest weakness is a focus on the psychological which blinds it to history.

The reason for this lies not only in radical feminist method, but also in the nature of patriarchy itself, for patriarchy is a strikingly resilient form of social organization. Radical feminists use 'patriarchy' to refer to a social system characterized by male domination over women. Kate Millet's definition is classic:

> our society . . . is a patriarchy. The fact is evident at once if one recalls that the military, industry, technology, universities, science, political offices, finances – in short, every avenue of power within the society, including the coercive force of the police, is entirely in male hands.[16]

This radical feminist definition of patriarchy applies to most societies we know of and cannot distinguish among them. The use of history by radical feminists is typically limited to providing examples of the existence of patriarchy in all times and places.[17]
[...]

Towards a Definition of Patriarchy

We can usefully define patriarchy as a set of social relations between men, which have a material base, and which, though hierarchical, establish or create inter-dependence and solidarity among men that enable them to dominate women. Though patriarchy is hierarchical and men of different classes, races, or ethnic groups have different places in the patriarchy, they also are united in their shared relationship of dominance over their women; they are dependent on each other to maintain that domination. Hierarchies 'work' at least in part because they create vested interests in the status quo. Those at the higher levels can 'buy off' those at the lower levels by offering them power over those still lower. In the hierarchy of patriarchy, all men, whatever their rank in the patriarchy, are bought off by being able to control at least some women. [...]

The material base upon which patriarchy rests lies most fundamentally in men's control over women's labor power. Men maintain this control by excluding women from access to some essential productive resources (in capitalist societies, for example, jobs that pay living wages) and by restricting women's sexuality.[18] Monogamous heterosexual marriage is one relatively recent and efficient form that seems to allow men to control both these areas. Controlling women's access to resources and their sexuality, in turn, allows men to control women's labor power, both for the purpose of serving men in many personal and sexual ways and for the purpose of rearing children. The services women render men, and which exonerate men from having to perform many unpleasant tasks (like cleaning toilets) occur outside as well as inside the family setting. Examples outside the family include the harassment of women workers and students by male bosses and professors as well as the common use of secretaries to run personal errands, make coffee, and provide 'sexy' surroundings. Rearing children (whether or not the children's labor power is of immediate benefit to their fathers) is nevertheless a crucial task in perpetuating patriarchy as a system. Just as class society must be reproduced by schools, work places, consumption norms, etc., so must patriarchal social relations. In our society children are generally reared by women at home, women socially defined and recognized as inferior to men, while men appear in the domestic picture only rarely. Children raised in this way generally learn their places in the gender hierarchy well. Central to this process, however, are the areas outside the home where patriarchal behaviours are taught and the inferior position of women enforced and reinforced: churches, schools, sports, clubs, unions, armies, factories, offices, health centers, the media, etc.

The material base of patriarchy, then, does not rest solely on child-rearing in the family, but on all the social structures that enable men to control women's labor. The aspects of social structures that perpetuate patriarchy are theoretically identifiable, hence separable from their other aspects. Gayle Rubin has increased our ability to identify the patriarchal element of these social structures enormously by identifying 'sex/gender systems':

> a 'sex/gender system' is the set of arrangements by which a society trans-
> forms biological sexuality into products of human activity, and in which
> these transformed sexual needs are satisfied.[19]

We are born female and male, biological sexes, but we are created women and man, socially recognized genders. *How* we are so created is that second aspect of the *mode* of production of which Engels spoke, 'the production of human beings themselves, the propagation of the species'.

How people propagate the species is socially determined. For example, if people are biologically sexually polymorphous, reproduction would be accidental. The strict division of labor by sex, a social invention common to all known societies, creates two very separate genders and a need for men and women to get together for economic reasons. It thus helps direct their sexual needs towards heterosexual fulfilment. Although it is theoretically possible that a sexual division of labor should not imply inequality between the sexes, in most known societies, the socially acceptable division of labor by sex is one which accords lower status to women's work. The sexual division of labor is also the underpinning of sexual subcultures in which men and women experience life differently; it is the material base of male power which is exercised (in our society) not just in not doing housework and in securing superior employment, but psychologically as well.

How people meet their sexual needs, how they reproduce, how they inculcate social norms in new generations, how they learn gender, how it feels to be a man or a woman – all occur in the realm Rubin labels the sex gender system. Rubin emphasizes the influence of kinship (which tells you with whom you can satisfy sexual needs) and the development of gender-specific personalities via child-rearing and the 'oedipal machine'. In addition, however, we can use the concept of the sex/gender system to examine all other social institutions for the roles they play in defining and reinforcing gender hierarchies. Rubin notes that theoretically a sex/gender system could be female dominant, male dominant, or egalitarian, but declines to label various known sex/gender systems or to periodize history accordingly. We choose to label our present sex/gender system patriarchy, because it appropriately captures the notions of hierarchy and male dominance which we see as central to the present system.

Economic production (what marxists are used to referring to as *the* mode of production) and the production of people in the sex/gender sphere both determine 'the social organization under which the people of a particular historical epoch and a particular country live', according to Engels. The whole of society, then, can only be understood by looking at both these types of production and reproduction, people and things.[20] There is no such thing as 'pure capitalism', nor does 'pure patriarchy' exist, for they must of necessity coexist. What exists is patriarchal capitalism, or patriarchal feudalism, or egalitarian hunting/gathering societies, or matriarchal horticultural societies, or patriarchal horticultural societies, and so on. There appears to be no *necessary* connection between *changes* in the one aspect of production and changes in the other. A society could undergo transition from capitalism to socialism, for example, and remain patriarchal.[21] Common sense, history, and our experience tell us, however, that these two aspects of production are so closely intertwined, that change in one ordinarily creates movement, tension, or contradiction in the other.

Racial hierarchies can also be understood in this context. Further elaboration may be possible along the lines of defining 'color/race systems', arenas of social life that take biological color and turn it into a social category, race. Racial hierarchies, like gender hierarchies, are aspects of our social organization, of how people are produced and reproduced. They are not fundamentally ideological; they constitute that second aspect of our mode of production, the production and reproduction of people. [. . .]

Capitalist development creates the places for a hierarchy of workers, but traditional marxist categories cannot tell us who will fill which places. Gender and racial hierarchies determine who fills the empty places. *Patriarchy is not simply hierarchical organization*, but hierarchy in which *particular* people fill *particular* places. It is in studying patriarchy that we learn why it is women who are dominated and how. While we believe that most known societies have been patriarchal, we do not view patriarchy as a universal, unchanging phenomenon. Rather patriarchy, the set of interrelations among men that allows men to dominate women, has changed in form and intensity over time. It is crucial that the relation of men's interdependence to their ability to dominate women be examined in historical societies. It is crucial that the hierarchy among men, and their differential access to patriarchal benefits, be examined. Surely, class, race, nationality, and even marital status and sexual orientation, as well as the obvious age, come into play here. And women of different class, race, national, marital status, or sexual orientation groups are subjected to different degrees of patriarchal power. Women may themselves exercise class, race, or national power, or even patriarchal power (through their family connections) over men lower in the patriarchal hierarchy than their own male kin.
[. . .]

III The Partnership of Patriarchy and Capital

How are we to recognize patriarchal social relations in capitalist societies? It appears as if each woman is oppressed by her own man alone; her oppression seems a private affair. Relationships among men and among families seem equally fragmented. It is hard to recognize relationships among men, and between men and women, as systematically patriarchal. We argue, however, that patriarchy as a system of relations between men and women exists in capitalism, and that in capitalist societies a healthy and strong partnership exists between patriarchy and capital. Yet if one begins with the concept of patriarchy and an understanding of the capitalist mode of production, one recognizes immediately that the partnership of patriarchy and capital was not inevitable; men and capitalists often have conflicting interests, particularly over the use of women's labor power. Here is one way in which this conflict might manifest itself: the vast majority of men might want their women at home to personally service them. A smaller number of men, who are capitalists, might want most women (not their own) to work in the wage labour market. In examining the tensions of this conflict over women's labour power historically, we will be able to identify the material base of patriarchal relations in capitalist societies, as well as the basis for the partnership between capital and patriarchy.

Industrialization and the Development of Family Wages

Marxists made quite logical inferences from a selection of the social phenomena they witnessed in the nineteenth century. But they ultimately underestimated the strength of the pre-existing patriarchal social forces with which fledgling capital had to contend and the need for capital to adjust to these forces. The industrial revolution was drawing all people into the labor force, including women and children; in fact the first factories used child and female labor almost exclusively.[22] That women and children could earn wages separately from men both undermined authority relations (as discussed in Part I above) and kept wages low for everyone. Kautsky, writing in 1892, described the process this way:

> [Then with] the wife and young children of the working-man . . . able to take care of themselves, the wages of the male worker can safely be reduced to the level of his own personal needs without the risk of stopping the fresh supply of labor power.
>
> The labor of women and children, moreover, affords the additional advantage that these are less capable of resistance than men [sic]; and their introduction into the ranks of the workers increases tremendously the quantity of labor that is offered for sale in the market.
>
> Accordingly, the labor of women and children . . . also diminishes [the] capacity [of the male worker] for resistance in that it overstocks the market; owing to both these circumstances it lowers the wages of the working-man.[23]

The terrible effects on working class family life of the low wages and of the forced participation of all family members in the labor force were recognized by marxists. Kautsky wrote:

> The capitalist system of production does not in most cases destroy the single household of the working-man, but robs it of all but its unpleasant features. The activity of woman today in industrial pursuits . . . means an increase of her former burden by a new one. *But one cannot serve two masters.* The household of the working-man suffers whenever his wife must help to earn the daily bread.[24]

Working men as well as Kautsky recognized the disadvantages of female wage-labor. Not only were women 'cheap competition' but working women were their very wives, who could not 'serve two masters' well.

Male workers resisted the wholesale entrance of women and children into the labor force, and sought to exclude them from union membership and the labor force as well. In 1846 the *Ten-Hours' Advocate* stated:

> It is needless for us to say, that all attempts to improve the morals and physical condition of female factory workers will be abortive, unless their hours are materially reduced. Indeed we may go so far as to say, that married females would be much better occupied in performing the domestic duties of the household, than following the nevertiring motion of machinery. We therefore hope the day is not distant, when the husband will be able to provide for his wife and family, without sending the former to endure the drudgery of a cotton mill.[25]

While the problem of cheap competition could have been solved by organizing the wage-earning women and youths, the problem of disrupted family life could not be. Men reserved union protection for men and argued for protective labor laws for women and children.[26] Protective labor laws, while they may have ameliorated some of the worst abuses of female and child labor, also limited the participation of adult women in many 'male' jobs. Men sought to keep high wage jobs for themselves and to raise male wages generally. They argued for wages sufficient for their wage labor alone to support their families. This 'family wage' system gradually came to be the norm for stable working class families at the end of the nineteenth century and the beginning of the twentieth.[27] Several observers have declared the non-wage working wife to be part of the standard of living of male workers.[28] Instead of fighting for equal wages for men and women, male workers sought the 'family wage', wanting to retain their wives' services at home. In the absence of patriarchy a unified working class might have confronted capitalism, but patriarchal social relations divided the working class, allowing one part (men) to be bought off at the expense of the other (women). Both the hierarchy between men and the solidarity among them were crucial in this process of resolution. 'Family wages' may be understood as a resolution of the conflict over women's labor power which was occurring between patriarchal and capitalist interests at that time.

Family wages for most adult men imply men's acceptance, and collusion in, lower wages for others, young people, women and socially defined inferior men as well

(Irish, blacks, etc., the lowest groups in the patriarchal hierarchy who are denied many of the patriarchal benefits). Lower wages for women and children and inferior men are enforced by job segregation in the labor market, in turn maintained by unions and management as well as by auxiliary institutions like schools, training programs, and even families. Job segregation by sex, by ensuring that women have the lower paid jobs, both assures women's economic dependence on men and reinforces notions of appropriate spheres for women and men. For most men, then, the development of family wages secured the material base of male domination in two ways. First women earn lower wages than men. The lower pay women receive in the labor market perpetuates men's material advantage over women and encourages women to choose wifery as a career. Second, then, women do housework, childcare, and perform other services at home which benefit men directly.[29] Women's home responsibilities in turn reinforce their inferior labor market position.[30]

The resolution that developed in the early twentieth century can be seen to benefit capitalist interests as well as patriarchal interests. Capitalists, it is often argued, recognized that in the extreme conditions which prevailed in the early nineteenth century industrialization, working class families could not adequately reproduce themselves. They realized that housewives produced and maintained healthier workers than wage-working wives and that educated children became better workers than non-educated ones. The bargain, paying family wages to men and keeping women home, suited the capitalists at the time as well as the male workers. Although the terms of the bargain have altered over time, it is still true that the family and women's work in the family serve capital by providing a labor force and serve men as the space in which they exercise their privilege. Women, working to serve men and their families, also serve capital as consumers.[31] The family is also the place where dominance and submission are learned, as Firestone, the Frankfurt School, and many others have explained.[32] Obedient children become obedient workers; girls and boys each learn their proper roles.

While the family wage shows that capitalism adjusts to patriarchy, the changing status of children shows that patriarchy adjusts to capital. Children, like women, came to be excluded from wage labor. As children's ability to earn money declined, their legal relationship to their parents changed. At the beginning of the industrial era in the United States, fulfilling children's need for their fathers was thought to be crucial, even primary, to their happy development; fathers had legal priority in cases of contested custody. Carol Brown has shown that as children's ability to contribute to the economic well-being of the family declined, mothers came increasingly to be viewed as crucial to the happy development of their children, and gained legal priority in cases of contested custody.[33] Here patriarchy adapted to the changing economic role of children: when children were productive, men claimed them; as children became unproductive, they were given to women.

The Partnership in the Twentieth Century

The prediction of nineteenth century marxists that patriarchy would wither away in the face of capitalism's need to proletarianize everyone has not come true. Not only did they underestimate the strength and flexibility of patriarchy, they also overestimated the strength of capital. They envisioned the new social force of capitalism, which had torn feudal relations apart, as virtually all powerful. Contemporary observers are in a better position to see the difference between the tendencies of 'pure' capitalism and those of 'actual' capitalism as it confronts historical forces in everyday practice. Discussions of the 'partnership' between capital and racial orders and of labor market segmentation provide additional examples of how 'pure' capitalist forces meet up with historical reality. Great flexibility has been displayed by capitalism in this process.

Marxists who have studied South Africa argue that although racial orders may not allow the equal proletarianization of everyone, this does not mean that racial barriers prevent capital accumulation.[34] In the abstract, analysts could argue about which arrangements would allow capitalists to extract 'the most' surplus value. Yet in a particular historical situation, capitalists must be concerned with social control, the resistance of groups of workers, and the intervention of the state. The state might intervene in order to reproduce the society as a whole; it might be necessary to police some capitalists, to overcome the worst tendencies of capital. Taking these factors into account, capital*ists* maximize greatest *practicable* profits. If for purposes of social control, capitalists organize work in a particular way, nothing about capital itself determines who (that is, which individuals with which ascriptive characteristics) shall occupy the higher, and who the lower rungs of the wage labor force. It helps, of course, that capitalists themselves are likely to be of the dominant social group and hence racist (and sexist). Capitalism inherits the ascribed characteristics of the dominant groups as well as of the subordinate ones.

Recent arguments about the tendency of monopoly capital to create labor market segmentation are consistent with this understanding.[35] Where capitalists purposely segment the labor force, using ascriptive characteristics to divide the working class, this clearly derives from the need for social control rather than accumulation imperatives in the narrow sense.[36] And over time, not all such divisive attempts are either successful (in dividing) nor profitable. The ability of capital to shape the workforce depends both on the particular imperatives of accumulation in a narrow sense and on social forces within a society which may encourage/force capital to adapt. [...]

If the first element of our argument about the course of capitalist development is that capital is not all-powerful, the second is that capital is tremendously flexible. Capital accumulation encounters pre-existing social forms, and both destroys them and adapts to them. The 'adaptation' of capital can be seen as a reflection of the *strength* of these pre-existing forms to persevere in new environments. Yet even as they persevere, they are not unchanged. The ideology with which race and sex are understood today, for example, is strongly shaped by the reinforcement of racial and sexual divisions in the accumulation process.

The Family and the Family Wage Today

We argued above, that, with respect to capitalism and patriarchy, the adaptation, or mutual accommodation, took the form of the development of the family wage in the early twentieth century. The family wage cemented the partnership between patriarchy and capital. Despite women's increased labor force participation, particularly rapid since World War II, the family wage is still, we argue, the cornerstone of the present sexual division of labor – in which women are primarily responsible for housework and men primarily for wage work. Women's lower wages in the labor market (combined with the need for children to be reared by someone) assure the continued existence of the family as a necessary income-pooling unit. The family, supported by the family wage, thus allows the control of women's labor by men both within and without the family.

Though women's increased wage work may cause stress for the family (similar to the stress Kautsky and Engels noted in the nineteenth century), it would be wrong to think that as a consequence, the concepts and the realities of the family and of the sexual division of labor will soon disappear. The sexual division of labor reappears in the labor market, where women work at women's jobs, often the very jobs they used to do only at home – food preparation and service, cleaning of all kinds, caring for people, and so on. As these jobs are low-status and low-paying patriarchal relations remain intact, though their material base shifts somewhat from the family to the wage differential. Carol Brown, for example, has argued that we are moving from 'family-based' to 'industrially-based' patriarchy within capitalism.[37]

Industrially-based patriarchal relations are enforced in a variety of ways. Union contracts which specify lower wages, lesser benefits, and fewer advancement opportunities for women are not just atavistic hangovers – a case of sexist attitudes or male supremacist ideology – they maintain the material base of the patriarchal system. While some would go so far as to argue that patriarchy is already absent from the family (see, for example, Stewart Ewen, *Captains of Consciousness*),[38] we would not. Although the terms of the compromise between capital and patriarchy are changing as additional tasks formerly located in the family are capitalized, and the location of the deployment of women's labor power shifts,[39] it is nevertheless true, as we have argued above, that the wage differential caused by the extreme job segregation in the labor market reinforces the family, and, with it, the domestic division of labor, by encouraging women to marry. The 'ideal' of the family wage – that a man can earn enough to support an entire family – may be given way to a new ideal that both men and women contribute through wage earning to the cash income of the family. The wage differential, then, will become increasingly necessary in perpetuating patriarchy, the male control of women's labor power. The wage differential will aid in *defining* women's work as secondary to men's at the same time as it necessitates women's actual continued economic dependence on men. The sexual division of labor in the labor market and elsewhere should be understood as a manifestation of patriarchy which serves to perpetuate it.

Many people have argued that though the partnership between capital and patriarchy exists now, it may *in the long run* prove intolerable to capitalism; capital may eventually destroy both familial relations and patriarchy. The logic of the argument is that capitalist social relations (of which the family is not an example) tend to become universalized, that as women are increasingly able to earn money they will increasingly refuse to submit to subordination in the family, and that since the family is oppressive particularly to women and children, it will collapse as soon as people can support themselves outside it.

We do not think that the patriarchal relations embodied in the family can be destroyed so easily by capital, and we see little evidence that the family system is presently disintegrating. Although the increasingl labor force participation of women has made divorce more feasible, the incentives to divorce are not overwhelming for women. Women's wages allow very few women to support themselves and their children independently and adequately. The evidence for the decay of the traditional family is weak, at best. The divorce rate has not so much increased, as· it has evened out among classes; moreover, the remarriage rate is also very high. Up until the 1970 census, the first-marriage rate was continuing its historic decline. Since 1970 people seem to have been delaying marriage and childbearing, but most recently, the birth rate has begun to increase again. It is true that larger proportions of the population are now living outside traditional families. Young people, especially, are leaving their parents' homes and establishing their own households before they marry and start traditional families. Older people, especially women, are finding themselves alone in their own households after their children are grown and they experience separation or death of a spouse. Nevertheless, trends indicate that the new generations of young people will form nuclear families at some time in their adult lives in higher proportions than ever before. The cohorts, or groups of people, born since 1930 have much higher rates of eventual marriage and child-rearing than previous cohorts. The duration of marriage and childrearing may be shortening, but its incidence is still spreading.[40]

The argument that capital 'destroys' the family also overlooks the social forces which make family life appealing. Despite critiques of nuclear families as psychologically destructive, in a competitive society the family still meets real needs for many people. This is true not only of long-term monogamy, but even more so for raising children. Single parents bear both financial and psychic burdens. For working class women, in particular, these burdens make the 'independence' of labor force participation illusory. Single parent families have recently been seen by policy analysts as transitional family formations which become two-parent families upon remarriage.[41]

It could be that the effects of women's increasing labor force participation are found in a declining sexual division of labor within the family, rather than in more frequent divorce, but evidence for this is also lacking. Statistics on who does housework, even in families with wage earning wives, show little change in recent years; women still do most of it.[42] The 'double day' is a reality for wage-working women. This is hardly surprising since the sexual division of labor outside the family, in the labor market, keeps women financially dependent on men – even when they earn a wage themselves. The future of patriarchy does not, however, rest solely on the future of familial relations. For patriarchy, like capital, can be surprisingly flexible and adaptable.

Whether or not the patriarchal division of labor, inside the family and elsewhere, is 'ultimately' intolerable to capital, it is shaping capitalism now. As we illustrate below, patriarchy both legitimates capitalist control and delegitimates certain forms of struggle against capital.

Ideology in the Twentieth Century

Patriarchy, by establishing and legitimating hierarchy among men (by allowing men of all groups to control at least some women), reinforces capitalist control, and capitalist values shape the definition of patriarchal good.

The psychological phenomena Firestone identifies are particular examples of what happens in relationships of dependence and domination. They follow from the realities of men's social power – which women are denied – but they are shaped by the fact that they happen in the context of a capitalist society. If we examine the characteristic of men as radical feminists describe them – competitive, rationalistic, dominating – they are much like our description of the dominant values of capitalist society.

This 'coincidence' may be explained in two ways. In the first instance, men, as wage-laborers, are absorbed in capitalist social relations at work, driven into the competition these relations prescribe, and absorb the corresponding values.[43] The radical feminist description of men was not altogether out of line for capitalist societies. Secondly, even when men and women do not actually behave in the way sexual norms prescribe, men *claim for themselves* those characteristics which are valued in the dominant ideology. So, for example, the authors of *Crestwood Heights* found that while the men, who were professionals, spent their days manipulating subordinates (often using techniques that appeal to fundamentally irrational motives to elicit the preferred behaviour), men and women characterized men as 'rational and pragmatic'. And while the women devoted great energies to studying scientific methods of child-rearing and child development, men and women in Crestwood Heights characterized women as 'irrational and emotional'.[44]

This helps to account not only for 'male' and 'female' characteristics in capitalist societies, but for the particular form sexist ideology takes in capitalist societies. Just as women's work serves the dual purpose of perpetuating male domination and capitalist production, so sexist ideology serves the dual purpose of glorifying male characteristics/capitalist values, and denigrating female characteristics/social need. [...]

A parallel argument demonstrating the partnership of patriarchy and capitalism may be made about the sexual division of labor in the work force. The sexual division of labor places women in low-paying jobs, and in tasks thought to be appropriate to women's role. Women are teachers, welfare workers, and the great majority of workers in the health fields. The nurturant roles that women play in these jobs are of low status in part because men denigrate women's work. They are also of low status because capitalism emphasizes personal independence and the ability of private enterprise to meet social needs, emphases contradicted by the need for collectively-provided social services. As long as the social importance of nurturant tasks can be denigrated because women perform them, the confrontation of capital's priority on exchange value by a demand for use value can be avoided. In this way, it is not feminism, but sexism that divides and debilitates the working class.

IV Towards a More Progressive Union

Many problems remain for us to explore. Patriarchy as we have used it here remains more a descriptive term than an analytical one. If we think marxism alone inadequate, and radical feminism itself insufficient, then we need to develop new categories. What makes our task a difficult one is that the same features, such as the division of labor, often reinforce both patriarchy and capitalism, and in a thoroughly patriarchal capitalist society, it is hard to isolate the mechanisms of patriarchy. Nevertheless, this is what we must do. We have pointed to some starting places: looking at who benefits from women's labor power, uncovering the material base of patriarchy, investigating the mechanisms of hierarchy and solidarity among men. The questions we must ask are endless.
[. . .]

Notes and References

1 ENGELS, F. *The Origin of the Family, Private Property and the State*, edited, with an introduction by Eleanor Burke Leacock, New York, International Publishers (1972).
2 ENGELS, F. *The Condition of the Working Class in England*, Stanford, California, Stanford University Press (1958). See esp. pp. 162–6 and 296.
3 ZARETSKY, E. (1973) 'Capitalism, the Family, and Personal Life', *Socialist Revolution*, Part 1 in Nos. 13–14, January–April, pp. 66–125, and Part 11 in No. 15, May–June, pp. 19–70. Also ZARETSKY, E. (1974) 'Socialist Politics and the Family', *Socialist Revolution* (now *Socialist Review*), No. 19, January–March, pp. 83–98, and (1976) *Capitalism, the Family and Personal Life*, New York, Harper and Row. Insofar as they claim their analyses are relevant to women, BROWN, B. (1973) *Marx, Freud and the Critique of Everyday Life*, New York, Monthly Review Press, and LEFEBVRE, H. (1971) *Everyday Life in the Modern World*, New York, Harper and Row, may be grouped with Zaretsky.
4 In this Zaretsky is following BENSTON, M. (1969) 'The Political Economy of Women's Liberation', *Monthly Review*, Vol. 21, No. 4, September, pp. 13–27, who made the cornerstone of her analysis that women have a different relation to capitalism than men. She argued that women at home produce use values, and that men in the labor market produce exchange values.
5 ZARETSKY, E. (1973) *op. cit.*, Part 1, p. 114.
6 DALLA COSTA, M. (1973) 'Women and the subversion of the community', in DALLA COSTA, M. and JAMES, S. *The Power of Women and the Subversion of the Community*, Bristol, England, Falling Wall Press, 2nd edn.
7 The text of the article reads: 'We have to make clear that, within the wage, domestic work produces not merely use values, but is essential to the production of surplus value', p. 31. Note 12 reads: 'What we mean precisely is that housework as work is *productive* in the Marxian sense, that is, producing surplus value', p. 52, original emphasis. To our knowledge this claim has never been made more rigorously by the wages for housework group. Nevertheless, marxists have responded to the claim copiously.
8 The literature of the debate includes VOGEL, L. (1973) 'The Earthly Family', *Radical America*, Vol. 7, Nos. 4–5, July–October, pp. 9–50; GERSTEIN, I. (1973) 'Domestic Work and Capitalism', *Radical America*, Vol. 7, No. 4–5, July–October, pp. 101–28; HARRISON, J. (1973) 'Political Economy of Housework', *Bulletin of the Conference of Socialist Economists*, Vol. 3, No. 1; SECCOMBE, W. (1974) 'The Housewife and her Labour under Capitalism', *New Left Review*, No. 83, February, pp. 3–24; COULSON, M., MAGAS, B. and WAINWRIGHT, H. (1975) '"The Housewife and her Labour under Capitalism", A Critique', *New Left Review*, No. 89, January–February, pp. 59–71; GARDINER, J. (1975) 'Women's Domestic Labour', *New Left Review*, No. 89, January–Febuary, pp. 47–58; GOUGH, I. and HARRISON, J.

(1975) 'Unproductive Labour and Housework Again', *Bulletin of the Conference of Socialist Economists*, Vol. 4, No. 1; GARDINER, J., HIMMELWEIT, S. and MACKINTOSH, M. (1975) 'Women's Domestic Labour', *Bulletin of the Conference of Socialist Economists*, Vol. 4, No. 2; SECCOMBE, W. (1975) 'Domestic Labour: Reply to Critics', *New Left Review*, No. 94, November–December, pp. 85–96; FEE, T. (Spring 1976) 'Domestic Labour: An analysis of Housework and its Relation to the Production Process', *Review of Radical Political Economics*, Vol. 8, No. 1, pp. 1–8; HIMMELWEIT, S. and MOHUN, S. (March 1977) 'Domestic Labour and Capital', *Cambridge Journal of Economics*, Vol. 1, No. 1, pp. 15–31.

9 ENGELS, F. (1972) *op. cit.*, 'Preface to the First Edition', pp. 71–2. The continuation of the quotation reads, ' . . . by the stage of development of labor on the one hand and of the family on the other'. It is interesting that, by implication, labor is excluded from occurring within the family; this is precisely the blind spot we want to overcome in this essay.

10 MITCHELL, J. (1966) 'Women: The Longest Revolution', *New Left Review*, No. 40, November–December, pp. 11–37, also reprinted by the New England Free Press.

11 MITCHELL, J. (1974) *Psychoanalysis and Feminism*, New York, Pantheon Books.

12 *Ibid.*, p. 412.

13 FIRESTON, E.S. (1971) *The Dialectic of Sex*, New York, Bantam Books.

14 NEW YORK RADICAL FEMINISTS (1971) 'Politics of Ego: A Manifesto for New York Radical Feminists'. in HOLE, J. and LEVINE, E. (Eds.) *Rebirth of Feminism*, New York, Quadrangle Press, pp. 440–3. 'Radical Feminists' are those feminists who argue that the most fundamental dynamic of history is men's striving to dominate women. 'Radical' in this context does *not* mean anti-capitalist, socialist, countercultural, etc., but has the specific meaning of this set of feminist beliefs or group of feminists. Additional writings of radical feminists, of whom the New York Radical Feminists were probably the most influential, can be found in KOEDT, A. (Ed.) (1972) *Radical Feminism*, New York, Quadrangle Press.

15 Focussing on power was an important step forward in the feminist critique of Freud. Firestone argues, for example, that if little girls 'envied' penises it was because they recognized that little boys grew up to be members of a powerful class and little girls grew up to be dominated by them. Powerlessness, not neurosis, was the heart of women's situation. More recently, feminists have criticized Firestone for rejecting the usefulness of the concept of the unconscious. In seeking to explain the strength and continuation of male dominance, recent feminist writing has emphasised the fundamental nature of gender-based personality differences, their origin in the unconscious, and the difficulty of their eradication. See DINNERSTEIN, D. (1977) *The Mermaid and the Minotaur*, New York, Harper Colophon Books; CHODOROW, N. (1978) *The Reproduction of Mothering*, Berkeley, University of California Press, and FLAX, J. (June 1978) 'The Conflict Between Nurturance and Autonomy in Mother-Daughter Relationships and Within Feminism', *Feminist Studies*, Vol. 4, No. 2, pp. 141–89.

16 MILLETT, K. (1971) *Sexual Politics*, New York, Avon Books, p. 25.

17 One example of this type of radical feminist history is BROWNMILLER, S. (1975) *Against Our Will, Men, Women and Rape*, New York, Simon and Schuster.

18 The particular ways in which men control women's access to important economic resources and restrict their sexuality vary enormously, both from society to society, from sub-group to sub-group, and across time. The examples we use to illustrate patriarchy in this section, however, are drawn primarily from the experience of whites in western capitalist countries. The diversity is shown in REITER, R.R. (Ed.) (1975) *Towards an Anthropology of Women*, New York, Monthly Review Press; ROSALDO, M. and LAMPHERE, L. (Eds.) (1974) *Woman, Culture and Society*, Stanford, California, Stanford University Press, and LEIBOWITZ, L. (1978) *Females, Males, Families: A Biosocial Approach*, North Scituate, Mass., Duxbury Press. The control of women's sexuality is tightly linked to the place of children. An understanding of the demand (by men and capitalists) for children is crucial to understanding changes in women's subordination.

   Where children are needed for their present or future labor power, women's sexuality will tend to be directed towards reproduction and childrearing. When children are seen as superfluous, women's sexuality for other than reproductive purposes is encouraged, but men will attempt to direct it towards satisfying male needs.

19 RUBIN, G. (1975) 'The Traffic in Women', in REITER (Ed.) *op. cit.*, p. 159.

20 Himmelweit and Mohun point out that both aspects of production (people and things) are logically necessary to describe a mode of production because by definition a mode of production must be capable of reproducing itself. Marx, though recognizing capitalism's need for people did not concern himself with how they were produced or what the connections between the two aspects of production were. See HIMMELWEIT and MOHUN, (1977) *op. cit.*, Note 8 above.

21 For an excellent discussion of one such transition to socialism, see WEINBAUM, B. (1976) 'Women in Transition to Socialism: Perspectives on the Chinese Case', *Review of Radical Political Economics*,

Vol. 8, No. 1, Spring, pp. 34–58.

22 It is important to remember that in the pre-industrial period, women contributed a large share to their families' subsistence – either by participating an a family craft or by agricultural activities. The new departure, then, was not that women earned income, but that they did so beyond their husbands' or fathers' control. CLARK, A. (1969) *The Working Life of Women in the Seventeenth Century*, New York, Kelly, and PINCHBECK, I. (1969) *Women Workers in the Industrial Revolution 1750–1850*, New York, Kelly, describe women's pre-industrial economic roles and the changes that occurred as capitalism progressed. It seems to be the case that Marx, Engels and Kautsly were not fully aware of women's economic role before capitalism.

23 KAUTSKY, K. (1971) *The Class Struggle*, New York, Norton, pp. 25–6.

24 We might add, 'outside the household', KAUTSKY, K. (1971) *op. cit.*, p. 26, our emphasis.

25 Cited in SMELSER, N. (1959) *Social Change and the Industrial Revolution*, Chicago, University of Chicago Press, p. 301.

26 Just as the factory laws were enacted for the benefit of all capitalists against the protest of some, so too, protective legislation for women and children may have been enacted by the state with a view toward the reproduction of the working class. Only a completely instrumentalist view of the state would deny that the factory laws and protective legislation legitimate the state by providing concessions and are responses to the demands of the working class itself.

27 A reading of CLARK, A. (1969) *op. cit.*, and PINCHBECK, I. (1969) *op. cit.*, suggests that the expropriation of production from the home was followed by a social adjustment process creating the social norm of the family wage. HARTMANN, H. (1974) in *Capitalism and Women's Work in the Home*, Yale University, unpublished Ph.D. dissertation, forthcoming, Temple University Press (1980) argues, based on qualitative data, that this process occurred in the US in the early twentieth century. The 'family wage' resolution has probably been undermined in the post World War II period. BELL, C.S. (1974) in 'Working Women's Contributions to Family Income', *Eastern Economic Journal*, Vol. 1, No. 3, July, pp. 185–201, presents current data and argues that it is now incorrect to assume that the man is the primary earner in the family. Yet whatever the *actual* situation today or earlier in the century, we would argue that the social norm *was* and *is* that men should earn enough to support their families. To say it has been the norm is not to say that it has been universally achieved. In fact, it is precisely the failure to achieve the norm that is noteworthy. Hence the observation that in the absence of sufficiently high wages, 'normative' family patterns disappear, as for example, amongst immigrants in the nineteenth century and third world Americans today.

28 HARTMANN, H. (1974) *op. cit.*, argues that the non-working wife was generally regarded as part of the male standard of living in the early twentieth century (see p. 136, Note 6) and GERSTEIN, I. (1973) *op. cit.*, Note 8, suggests that the norm of the working wife enters into the determination of the value of male labor power (see p. 121).

29 The importance of the fact that women perform labor services for men in the home cannot be over-emphasized. As Pat Mainardi said in 'The Politics of Housework', 'the measure of your oppression is his resistance' in MORGAN, R. (Ed.) (1970) *Sisterhood is Powerful*, New York, Vintage Books, p. 451. Her article, perhaps as important for us as Firestone on love, is an analysis of power relations between women and men as exemplified by housework.

30 Libby Zimmerman has explored the relation of membership in the primary and secondary labor markets to family patterns in New England. See ZIMMERMAN, L. (1977) 'Women in the economy: a case study Lynn, Massachusetts, 1760–1974, Heller School, Brandeis, Unpublished Ph.D. dissertation. Batya Weinbaum is currently exploring the relationship between family roles and places in the labor market. See WEINBAUM, B. (Fall, 1977) 'Redefining the question of revolution', *Review of Radical Political Economics*, Vol. 9, No. 3, pp. 54, 78, and (1978) '*The Curious Courtship of Women's Liberation and Socialism*, Boston, South End Press. Studies of the interaction of capitalism and patriarchy can be found in EISENSTEIN, Z. (Ed.) (1978) *Capitalist Patriarchy and the Case for Socialist Faminist Revolution*, New York, Monthly Review Press.

31 See WEINBAUM, B. and BRIDGES, A. (1976) 'The Other Side of the Paycheck: Monopoly Capital and the Structure of Consumption', *Monthly Review*, Vol. 28, No. 3, July–August, pp. 88–103, for a discussion of women's consumption work.

32 For the work of the Frankfurt School, see HORKHEIMER, M. (1972) 'Authority and the Family', in *Critical Theory*, New York, Herder and Herder; and FRANKFURT INSTITUTE OF SOCIAL RESEARCH (1972) 'The Family', in *Aspects of Sociology*, Boston, Beacon.

33 BROWN, C. (1975) 'Patriarchal Capitalism and the Female-Headed Family', *Social Scientist*, (India), Nos. 40–1, November–December, pp. 28–39.

34 For more on racial orders, see GREENBERG, S. (1976) 'Business enterprise in a racial order', *Politics and Society*, Vol. 6, No. 2, pp. 213–40, and BURRAWAY, M. (1972) *The Color of Class in the Coppermines: From*

African Advancement to Zambianization, Manchester, England, Manchester University Press, Zambia Papers No. 7.

35 See REICH, M., GORDON, D. and EDWARDS, R. (1973) 'A theory of labor market segmentation', *American Economic Review*, Vol. 63, No. 2, May, pp. 359–65, and the book they edited (1975) *Labor Market Segmentation*, Lexington, Mass., D.C. Heath.

36 See GORDON, D.M. (1976) 'Capitalist efficiency and socialist efficiency', *Monthly Review*, Vol. 28, No. 3, July–August, pp. 19–39, for a discussion of qualitative efficiency (social control needs) and quantitative efficiency (accumulation needs).

37 BROWN, C. (1975) *op. cit.*

38 EWEN, S. (1976) *Captains of Consciousness*, New York, Random House.

39 Jean Gardiner, in 'Women's Domestic Labour' (Note 8) clarifies the causes for the shift in location of women's labor, from capital's point of view. She examines what capital needs (in terms of the level of real wages, the supply of labor, and the size of markets) at various stages of growth and of the business cycle. She argues that in times of boom or rapid growth it is likely that socializing housework (or more accurately capitalizing it) would be the dominant tendency, and that in times of recession, housework will be maintained in its present form. In attempting to assess the likely direction of the British economy, however, Gardiner does not assess the economic needs of patriarchy. We argue in this eassy that unless one takes patriarchy as well as capital into account one cannot adequately assess the likely direction of the economic system.

40 For the proportion of people in nuclear families, see UHLENBERG, P. (1974) 'Cohort Variations in Family Life Cycle Experiences of US Females', *Journal of Marriage and the Family*, Vol. 36, No. 5, May, pp. 284–92. For remarriage rates see GLICK, P.C. and NORTON, A.J. (1974) 'Perspectives on the Recent Upturn in Divorce and Remarriage', *Demography*, Vol. 10, pp. 301–14. For divorce and income levels see NORTON, A.J. and GLICK, P.C. (1976) 'Marital Instability: Past, Present and Future', *Journal of Social Issues*, Vol. 32, No. 1, pp. 5–20. Also see BANE, M.J. (1976) *Here to Stay: American Families in the Twentieth Century*, New York, Basic Books.

41 ROSS, H.L. and SAWHILL, I.B. (1975) *Time of Transition: The Growth of Families Headed by Women*, Washington DC, The Urban Institute.

42 See WALKER, K.E. and WOODS, M.E. (1976) *Time Use: A Measure of Household Production of Family Goods and Services*, Washington DC, American Home Economics Association.

43 This should provide some clues to class differences in sexism, which we cannot explore here.

44 See SEELEY, J.R. *et al.*, (1956) *Crestwood Heights*, Toronto, University of Toronto Press, pp. 382–94. While men's place may be characterized as 'in production', this does not mean that women's place is simply 'not in production' – her tasks, too, are shaped by capital. Her non-wage work is a resolution, on a day-to-day basis, of production for exchange with socially determined need, the provision of use values in a capitalist society (this is the context of consumption). See WEINBAUM, B. and BRIDGES, A. (1976) *op. cit.*, for a more complete discussion of this argument. The fact that women provide 'merely' use values in a society dominated by exchange values can be used to denigrate women.

13   Socialism and Feminism: Women and the Cuban Revolution

Nicola Murray

[. . .]

Introduction

'The production of life, both of one's own in labour and of fresh life in procreation, now appears as a double relationship: on the one hand as a natural, on the other as a social relationship'.[1] Thus, in *The German Ideology*, Marx and Engels prepared the way for a 'concrete study of women's condition as an historically changing aspect of the material situation',[2] a study which must examine the relations of reproduction as well as those of production. *The Origin of the Family, Private Property and the State* was Engels's[3] attempt at such a study. In it he linked the subordination of women to the emergence of private property in the means of production, which, given monogamous marriage and women's tasks of child-rearing and domestic labour, led to their exclusion from social productive labour and thus to their dependence on their male partners. If, then, exclusion from extra-domestic tasks is the cause of women's inferior status, the assumption of such tasks will help to bring about emancipation:

> The emancipation of women becomes possible only when women are enabled to take part in production on a large, social scale, and when domestic duties require their attention only to a minor degree. And this has become possible only as a result of modern large-scale industry which not only permits of the participation of women in production in large numbers, but actually calls for it and, moreover, strives to convert private domestic work also into a public industry.[4]

And the emancipation of women will become actual with the abolition of the private property which was the cause of their subordination. [. . .]

[Yet] as Beverley Brown has argued,[5] Engels's analysis is itself premised on certain

Source: An abridged version of an article published in two parts in *Feminist Review*, (1979), Nos. 2 (pp. 57–71) and 3 (pp. 99–108).

assumptions about women which are such that the policies of states which ground their practice on his theoretical work are bound to be incapable of recognizing the full extent of women's oppression. Firstly, he assumes that it is women's 'natural' desire to restrict their sexual relationships to one man only, this being the origin of monogamy; and secondly, he assumes a 'natural' (i.e. preceding and external to social relations) division of labour in the primitive (and modern) family, whereby the woman performs household and child-rearing tasks while the man hunts, and then places this 'natural' division of labour at the 'origin' of women's oppression because it allows men to acquire private property in the form of herds of cattle. By identifying particular social relations as an unchanging part of human societies and attempting to locate in them the 'origin' of women's subordination, Engels fails to recognize that these social relations are historically specific – after all, the division of labour between men and women varies from tribe to tribe as well as from 'modern' state to state – and becomes enmeshed in the search for the 'original sin' rather than engaging in an historically specific analysis; he is also unable to explain why it is that the sexual division of labour *subordinates* women. Without suggesting that there is a one-to-one correlation between Engels's analysis and the current practice of socialist states, we can nevertheless note certain strands which can be traced to his two assumptions and their implications. The family is regarded as the basic unit of socialist society, and the morality of socialists is held to depend upon this. Sexual liberation is not articulated as an issue that has anything to do with socialism. [...]

And, whether socialized or private, certain tasks continue to be assigned to women on the basis of an imputed 'natural' ability to perform them (e.g. childcare, even in nurseries, is a job done by women only). It is these elements with which I am particularly concerned in this article.

Recent writings within the women's liberation movement have tried to analyze the specificity of women's oppression using a marxist framework, and have suggested that 'woman's condition must be seen as resulting from the unity of different elements [each of which] has its own autonomy although each is ultimately, but only ultimately, determined by economic factors'.[6] [...]

The four elements which may be identified as forming the specific structure of the position of women, are, following Mitchell: production, reproduction, sexuality and the socialization of children. In this article, I examine these four structures within Cuban society, and the ways in which they are changing; but I have avoided discussing them separately in order better to represent the way in which they are 'overdetermined' – that is, the fact that each element reacts upon and contradicts or reinforces the others. As Mitchell has stated 'The liberation of women can only be achieved if all four structures . . . are transformed'.[7]

In taking the data available to me and presenting them in the form of a narrative, I am aware that I have failed to a large extent to convey the full 'reality' of the position of Cuban women. In part, this stems from the fact that most of my material consists of written accounts, and very little of it is based on the time I actually spent in Cuba in 1978. Also, I have deliberately adopted a critical stance in an attempt to stress what I feel are the implications of the Cuban, and other socialist states' approach to the liberation of women, although perhaps a more 'balanced' critique would have done justice to the complexities and contradictions involved. [. . .]

I should state here that my admiration for the Cuban revolution and sympathy for the Cuban people is deeply felt, lest it should seem at times that I have fallen into the comfortable position of a western feminist whose privileged luxury it is to be critical; I am only too aware of the constant struggle in which all Cubans are engaged. But it is also the very fact that so many western socialists have turned to Cuba as a model, and to Ché Guevara and Castro as heroes, that encourages me to be so critical. [. . .]

The Position of Women in Cuba before 1959

It is crucial to point out that the divisions of class and race cut through and over-determine sexual divisions within Cuban society. The Cuban economy in the nineteenth century was based on sugar and, until its abolition in 1880, on slavery. As in other West Indian islands and in the southern states of the USA, the socio-economic conditions resulting from slavery were such as to undermine the traditional male role of husband and father, and produced 'matrifocal' families and more 'independent' women. The extreme physical exertion necessary in sugar-plantation work resulted in fewer women being imported from Africa than men; such women slaves as there were probably worked as domestic servants, and possibly at piling rather than cutting the sugar-cane. The latter is a division of labour which, with few exceptions, persists in Cuba today: 'Our experience in Cuba is that men cut cane. Women pile the cane. As a result of our practice in cane-cutting we find this to be a productive experience'.[8] As Martinez-Alier[9] stresses, the thesis of the matri-focality of Caribbean societies assumes a social homogeneity which certainly was not the case in Cuba; we may note here the strong contrast between 'matriarchal' black families and 'patriarchal' white (Spanish origin) families (cf Burkett[10]). In the latter, there was an especially strict division between women's and men's 'spheres' – *casa* (house) and *calle* (street) – reflected in beliefs about what constituted appropriate behaviour for the sexes; and yet class cut through that ideology: working-class and peasant women were 'liberated' by economic necessity from some of these restrictions, but this only 'freed' them for economic exploitation and did little to change the conditions of their sexual subordination. In general, the specific constellation of attitudes and ideas known as *machismo* (virility) entailed a double standard as regards sex-roles: 'manly honour . . . associated with penetration, womanly with its prevention' and 'elaborate game[s] played among men for social status, in which the woman [was] expected to play a passive role. The prize [being] not the woman, but the esteem of the other man'.[11] The corollaries of this (again, varying with social class) were chaperoning, extreme estimation of virginity in women, the isolation of women from each other and the centring of women's lives around their relationships with men and the family, and – the other side of the coin – prostitution. In a sense, then, 'a particular kind of female assertion was acceptable',[12] but generally only inasmuch as Cuban women's 'subservience in production [was] obscured by their *assumed* dominance in their own world – the family'.[13] Both within marriages and within the free consensual unions which were much more common among poor and black people, relations between men and women were based on jealousy, and 'paradoxically, the preoccupation with the idealized purity of women goes hand in hand with a wide suspicion of their easy surrender to temptation'.[14]

[...]

The structure of the Cuban economy was, then, not such as to afford wide employment opportunities for women outside the rural smallholding economy – the major area of employment for working-class women was domestic service, and for middle class women teaching or office and shop work. In 1903, 70 per cent of employed women were domestic servants, and the majority of the remainder worked in the tobacco industry. In 1919, 50 per cent were domestic servants, 33 per cent worked in the tobacco and other light industries, 5 per cent in agriculture, and the remainder in services, commerce and transport.[15] By the eve of the revolution, 70 per cent of all employed women were domestic servants,[16] while those who were in industry were still concentrated in textiles, foodstuffs and tobacco.[17] Women accounted for less than 3 per cent of the workforce in paid agricultural labour, fishing, mining, construction and transport, in 1957; 9 per cent in commerce; 19 per cent in industry; but they were 48 per cent of employees in the service sector, and 90 per cent of all domestic servants (Moreno, 1971;[18] Purcell, 1973).[19] Female unemployment was lower than male (11.8 per cent compared with 17.1 per cent in 1956–57), but this only records those seeking work. Most women did not in fact go out to work, as Table 1 shows

Table 1 Proportion of total female population in paid employment

Year	Percentage of total
1919	11.9
1931	6.2
1943	3.7
1953	14.7
1958	14.2

Sources: Mesa-Lago, 1972;[20] Camarano, 1970.[21]

although out of a sample of 69 women from the former slum district of Buena Ventura in Havana, 91 per cent had had paid jobs before the revolution. 64.9 per cent of all Cuban women were housewives in 1958, and another 19.3 per cent were 'seeking work'. Women accounted for a small (but slowly growing) proportion of the total labour-force: 10 per cent in 1943, 14 per cent in 1956–67.[22] This was not only the result of the industrial structure of the country and the belief that women should not go out to work, but also because 'it was logical that in a country where there were hundreds of thousands of men without work, there would be little or no work opportunities for women'.[23] With the belief that birth-control would promote women's infidelity and undermine men's authority (see above), women were rarely able to exert any control over their fertility; women and children were a man's property and proof of his virility, and thus family size tended to be large. Given extreme poverty added to this, domestic labour was both arduous and time-consuming. There were few nursery facilities: privately-run nurseries were for the children of the rich, and the thirty-seven creches which existed in 1958 gave health rather than educational care, and were for 'needy' cases only.[24] If women did go out to work, the eldest daughter was often kept back from school to look after her younger sisters and brothers, thus reinforcing her underprivileged position and undermining her future position in the labour market. Although in such a society most women were assigned, and had to accept, a passive role, there were nevertheless some women who protested. Many were in the 'equal constitutional rights' school: women who demanded the vote, perhaps even 'equal opportunities', and who had not contemplated the wider social changes necessary to enable women to take up equal opportunities. Women were involved in the Wars of Independence in 1868 and 1895 – mainly as nurses, although some also fought in battle (a pattern repeated in the nationalist struggle in the 1950s) – but they were not granted the vote under the Cuban constitution of 1901 in spite of the efforts of a sympathetic male lobby to secure this. This, and also the growth of various (predominantly middle-class white) suffrage organizations in the 1910s and 1920s parallelled the world-wide suffrage movements of the early twentieth century.

[. . .]

Changing Women's Roles: First Steps

It is important to stress that Castro and the others in the Rebel Army did not come to Havana [on the 1 January, 1959] and oust Batista as communists. Theirs had been a nationalist struggle, directed at their country's dictator, and although their hostility to the USA indicated their recognition that its support of Batista had served its own economic interests, their struggle was articulated through Cuban-nationalist not anti-imperialist rhetoric. [. . .] It was not until 1961 that Cuba was declared communist. [. . .] The threat of invasion by the USA was growing, and so too was local resistance in the form of industrial sabotage and other disruptions. Given this political climate, it was crucial that popular support for the revolution be mobilized, and it was around this time that the 'mass organizations' were founded: the Committees for the Defence of the Revolution (CDRs), which are small units organized street by street; the CTC and the ANAP, the organizations of workers and peasants respectively; and the *Federacion de Mujeres Cubanas* (FMC), the Cuban Women's Federation. The latter was founded on 23 August 1960, through the merging of several previously-existing women's organizations, and counted an initial membership of some 100,000.[25]

It was also becoming apparent that economic expansion was rapidly transforming the nature of the problem of labour supply in Cuba from that of serious unemploy-ment and under-employment to that of a growing shortage of labour. The stated purpose of the FMC was to 'prepare women educationally, politically and socially to participate in the revolution . . . Its main functions are the incorporation of women in work and raising the educational consciousness of women' (Vilma Espin, President of the FMC, quoted in Purcell, 1973).[26] The 1962 Ministry of Labour's manpower (sic) plans for the period 1961–65 allowed for an increase of only 9 per cent in 'other outside labour-force (housewives, pensioners, etc.)'.[27] but this must have been allowing for the re-training which the FMC was undertaking with women already in paid employment – former maids, for example, were the source of employees to fill many positions in the early years of the revolution.

Although it would be a misrepresentation to suggest that the FMC was founded solely in order to tackle the political and labour problems of these early years, it is fair to say that 'Cuba required that women join the revolutionary effort for pragmatic as well as egalitarian and moral reasons',[28] and it is nevertheless the case that its purpose was 'more that of representing government policy to women than of representing women to government'.[29] Membership is now vast – 2,051,906 women in 1975, that is 77 per cent of women aged 14 and over – but as Lewis points out,[30] its study-groups, while playing 'an important role in the ideological training of all Cubans, especially women', are led by a cadre around a specific topic or text, and do not promote the same mutual support and self-awareness as do 'conscious-ness-raising' groups in the feminist movements within contemporary capitalist societies. 'There is a tremendous distance between the subservient, dependent, apolitical, homebound model of the traditional Latin woman, and the militant, independent, politicized and community-minded model of the socialist women',[31] and to bridge this distance requires not only material but also emotional support – especially in view of male resistance to this kind of change. This 'model of the socialist woman' is, moreover, in contradiction – or at least coexists in tension with – the emphasis in Cuban state policy on the role of the family. Socialism was to entail the demise of the traditional marriage based on female subordination in which the husband 'is the bourgeois; the wife represents the proletariat',[32] but would herald in its place a new and stronger marriage, based on the equal partnership of man and woman, which would form the 'essential nucleus' of socialist society. Thus, although divorce was made easier – and increased from 8.5 per 100 marriages in 1959 to 30.2 per 100 in 1974[33] – marriage was encouraged, and there was a 'collective marriage' programme whereby those who had been living in free consensual unions could formalize their relationship: the number of marriages increased dramatically – from just over 30,000 in 1958 to 85,000 in 1969.[34] Marriage was important to many people because it was formerly a luxury which only the rich could afford – the same was true of make-up, and both retained a symbolic meaning which increased their popularity. For marriage itself to be an 'equal partnership' (in Engels's terms), it is necessary both that women be economically independent (involved in social productive labour); and also that many of the tasks normally carried out in the home (by the woman), such as child-care and domestic labour, be socialized (or if not socialized, then shared by man and woman equally). How far has this gone in Cuba?

Cuba 'has chosen to spend a larger percentage of her gross national product on day-care than almost any other country in the world'.[35] In 1962 the FMC was given the task of creating a national network of nurseries (*circulos infantiles*) and from 109 with capacity for 10,470 children by the end of 1962, their total had reached 658 with places for over 55,000 children by 1975.[36] They take children from six weeks to six years of age, and provide medical care, meals and clothes which are washed on the premises to save parents' labour. Most are open from 6 a.m. to 6 p.m., but some have more flexible hours, and some will take 'boarders' from Monday to Friday. Until 1971 there was a sliding scale of charges made for nursery places, excepting those taken by the children of women agricultural workers, which were free. In January 1967, all places became free of charge, and this remained the case until recently. Since 1971, the Children's Institute (also under the aegis of the FMC) has been responsible for the *circulos*, for research on children, and for attempting to improve the training of day-care workers. Given the lack of trained nursery workers in 1962, paraprofessional staffs of *asistentes* were employed, consisting of inexperienced teenagers and older women whose 'qualification' was the fact that they had brought up their own children, and these staffs worked in a ratio of approximately 20:1 with qualified nursery-teachers. Only in 1971 did the Children's Institute found the *Escuelas de Educadoras* which teach three-year courses for nursery-workers.

[...]

Moreover, 'Cuba reflects the traditional view that women are the only proper caretakers of very young children'.[37] Not only does this mean that children are brought up in a situation, whether privatized or socialized, which reproduces traditional sex roles – certainly there are few signs of 'non-sexist' use of toys and roles in children's games and stories. But it also means that – ironically enough – in freeing one group of women from privatized child-care so that they may participate in social production, another group of women (the nursery workers), although themselves in paid employment become concentrated in a particular type of work: 'women's work'.

There have been other attempts at socializing domestic labour. Communal eating facilities are provided at People's Farms in particular but also in factories and schools; laundry services are being extended, as are such devices as refrigerators, which remove the need to shop daily. But although these facilities have been introduced, the economic situation in Cuba has been such that progress here must inevitably be slower – inevitably, that is, given that the liberation of women has not been prioritized to the extent that it might have been, and that there have been so many other necessary investments (industrial capital, schools, hospitals). Again, where these facilities are provided, the tendency is, as in capitalist societies, for women to be concentrated in the jobs: it is 'domestic' work in a social context, and is assumed to suit women better than it does men. Even if it is so that 'in Cuba, no-one looks down upon people who do clean-up work. They understand that all jobs in Cuba are equally crucial for the country's survival',[38] there is nevertheless a significant division of labour.

[...]

Increasing women's educational level should, in theory, be one way in which to enable them to escape sex-typed jobs. We might expect especially encouraging progress on this front in Cuba, as education has been a priority from the start of the revolution. There are two sides to this: the provision of educational facilities for children enables their mothers to go out to work; and the provision of educational opportunities both equally for boys and girls, and also for adult women, can give women access to new areas of work.

'School cities' have been constructed, in which young people study, do agricultural work and live during term-time; also, many peasant children were educated in large schools in the towns, although Cuban policy now is to build smaller schools nearer the villages. By 1970 there were 277,505 *becados* (state scholarships) or places for children at boarding schools, compared with only 76,834 in 1962; but these cannot account for more than 10 per cent of all schoolchildren.[39]

As regards sex-stereotyping in subject-choice at school and university, women have been encouraged to enter some traditionally male areas (where they often remain in the minority), and yet there are still specific types of training which remain 'women's work'. Given Cuba's need for indigenous skilled labour – most of the technicians in Cuba before 1959 were American, and of those who were Cuban, many were among those who chose to emigrate after 1959 – the average age of her technical workers is very young, and this has favoured women: all young people have been encouraged to acquire such skills. Thus, where women represented only 26 per cent of medical students in 1962, by 1970 they were 50 per cent.[40] But, on the other hand, all those who undertake training as nursery workers are women; and whereas women accounted for 85 per cent of education students in 1962, by 1970 they were 90 per cent of the total.[41] This pattern has been repeated in adult education, and also in the types of jobs which women have taken. Women now do all the jobs which men have always done; but where is the effort on men's part to learn to do the things that women have traditionally done?

In the literacy campaign in 1961, which reduced illiteracy from 23.6 per cent to 3.9 per cent, 55 per cent of the *brigadistas* (the schoolchildren who went to live with peasant families and taught them to read and write) were girls.[42] For these girls the change was enormous – independent, free of many of the restrictions of their own family life – and this also had some impact on the Cuban public in general, as the campaign was known about and publicized everywhere. Women accounted for 56 per cent of those who became literate as a result of the campaign, and for them too, the effects must have been enormous: not only did their literacy enable them to be more involved and aware of events outside of their immediate environment, but they were also able to partake in follow-up courses through which they could reach sixth-Grade level (the end of primary schooling), and then perhaps beyond to secondary and higher education.

There were also educational and retraining programmes directed specifically at women. As we have seen, there were large numbers of domestic servants at the beginning of the revolution, whose former employers were going abroad and whose labour was needed elsewhere. By August 1962, sixty special schools had been set up in which a total of 19,000 former domestic servants were enrolled,[43] and a further 10,000 had already been found new jobs.[44] There were evening classes for those who were still employed as domestic servants, teaching literacy and perhaps another skill such as typing; and there were full-time courses for specific occupations – mainly commercial and administrative skills, but also, for example, taxi-driving.

By 1967, there were only 5,500 women still taking these courses. The FMC also established special schools and courses for peasant women. In 1961, 1,000 were taught to read and write, and also took courses in dressmaking, cooking and hygiene; they were then given a sewing-machine to take back to their villages to instruct the other women. In 1963, the Ana Betancourt School for Peasant Women was opened in Miramar, a former bourgeois suburb of Havana, and this continued to train peasant women until 1975, when smaller schools started to be built in the country-side. Prostitutes were invited to attend 'rehabilitation' schools and were found jobs in factories – this suggests harsh treatment of these women, but may be a result of the lack of information available to me as to how the campaign to eliminate prostitution (not entirely successful, from what I could see in Havana) was carried out.

The FMC also ran other educational projects aimed at giving women skills to enable them to enter the labour-force. But what all have in common and we shall see that this is reflected in the distribution of women within the labour-force, is that they were educated in what are traditionally regarded as 'female' skills – dressmaking, cooking, health-care. On the one hand, in a poor and badly-educated country, such education is vital, and given that women are the people who tend to perform the tasks associated with these skills, then these courses were inevitable. But on the other hand, such specialization by sex cannot help but reinforce the assumption that such tasks fall naturally to women. Is it possible to choose not to reinforce sex stereotypes in such a situation? This is the dilemma facing Angola at the moment, where women are being trained in just such skills which are vital to the health and welfare of her people, and yet which will confirm women in specific positions within social relations.

Health education for Cuban women was not restricted to childcare and hygiene, however. Contraception has become freely available to all who ask for it, but although contraceptive advice is given to pregnant women, there is no national policy to promote family limitation. There was no suggestion that having children in large numbers may be oppressive, and women's control of their own bodies was apparently never an issue. The pre-revolutionary law permitting abortion 'only when carrying the child to term would "endanger the health or life of the woman"'[45] seems to remain in the statutes (I have been hindered here by an almost complete lack of information on this subject), but in practice the availability of abortion 'depends to a great extent on the attitudes of the individual doctor, and to a certain degree on the persistence of the woman in her demands'[46] – a state of affairs not so very different from Britain! Babies remain, however, the proof of 'manhood'. Sterilization is available only to women who are over thirty-eight and have five or more children. Many of the traditional Cuban ideas about women and sexuality remain unchallenged – it is felt that the encouragement of sexual freedom could only be an excuse for men further to exploit women sexually, given the strength of *machismo* ideology – that is, instead of challenging *machismo*, sexuality as a terrain of political practice is ignored. [...]

We must now ask what effect all these changes have had on women's involvement in paid labour. This can be seen in Table 2, although the table is incomplete owing to lack of data.

Table 2 Participation of women in the paid labour-force

Year	Number (000s)	Proportion of total labour-force (%)
1958	194	14.0
1962	258	
1964	282	
1966	344	
1968		15.6
1969	393	17.7
1970	421.4	
1974	590	25.3
1975	647	

Sources: Castro, quoted in Bonachea and Valdes, 1972; Mesa-Lago, 1972; Leiner, 1974; Castro, 1966b; Lewis, Lewis Rigdon, 1977; *Granma Weekly Review*, 28 December 1975; Castro, 1974.[47]

In spite of intensive campaigning to persuade women to enter the paid labour-force, the proportion of women of working age who were in paid employment had risen only to 22 per cent by 1970;[48] by 1975, this had increased to 30 per cent. This was a very low participation rate in comparison with the Eastern European states, and even in comparison with such capitalist states as Italy and Spain.[49]

Those women who are in paid labour, moreover, are concentrated in particular sectors of the economy, and they are less likely than men to hold 'management' posts (see Table 3). Women perform particular types of work wherever they are employed (see Table 4), and, as we have already seen above, they are still concentrated in the traditional nurturing and service roles. In the absence of any information as

Table 3 Women as proportion of labour-force by sector

Employing agency	Women as proportion of total labour-force (%)	Women as proportion of management (%)
Ministry of Public Health	64	31.5
Ministry of Education	58	40
Cuba Tabaco	53	8.1
Ministry of Milk-processing Industries	41	20.4
National Tourism Institute	41	15.7
Ministry of National Trade	36	26.6
Ministry of Food Industries	18	5.8
National Institute of Agrarian Reform	9	1.9
Ministry of Sugar	7	3.3

Source: Federacion de Mujeres Cubanas, 1975.

Table 4 Occupational structure 1975

Occupational Category	Women as proportion of total (%)
Administration	67.5
Technician	49.1
Service Worker	48.7
Manager	15.3
Production Worker	11.6

Source: Partido Comunista de Cuba, 1976.

to the wage-scales and gradations upon which basis wage-differentials are calculated, we can only speculate as to whether 'women's work' is liable to be classified as less skilled and therefore paid less. [. . .]

In part, this distribution comes as no surprise, given the type of education which we have seen comprised the FMC courses for adult women; thus the large proportion of women technicians stems from the shortage of indigenous skilled labour as we noted. It has, however, also been deliberate government policy to assign women to certain types of jobs – to 'jobs that cannot be accomplished with machinery, jobs which are not hard physical labour, and not jobs unsuitable for women. They must be jobs which women are completely capable of carrying out'.[50] Which jobs can women be considered to be 'capable of carrying out'? Categorization is based on observation of the type of work which women have previously done, and premises itself on the assumption that this distribution reflects a 'natural' division of labour. Such categorizations are reinforced by the centrality of sugar cultivation in the Cuban economy – not only does it entail physical exertion for which women have rarely been socialized, but also the economy's precarious health has encouraged an emphasis on productivity (in an attempt to outgrow its dependence on exports of sugar, tobacco and nickel, and on imports of many capital and consumer goods) which, when combined with *a priori* assumptions that women's productivity will be less in certain occupations than men's, makes any challenge to such categorizations highly unlikely. There is no substantive evidence to support such assumptions with regard to most occupations, and even where sheer physical strength is at issue, the distribution curves of average strength for men and women will always show large numbers of women stronger than large numbers of men. It is possible that such assumptions were based on higher rates of turnover and absenteeism among women because of their family commitments (I do not have data on this), and certainly, as we shall see, measures have now been taken to alleviate such problems. But I would say that to a large extent it is ideology, not 'hard facts' (although what 'harder fact' is there than a belief which has such far-reaching effects?), which is responsible for this occupational segregation.

This division of labour was enshrined in Resolutions 47 and 48 of the CTC Congress (Cuban TUC) in 1966. Resolution 47 reserved certain jobs vacated by men to be taken on only by women; and Resolution 48 excluded women from certain jobs (unfortunately, I cannot say what jobs were included in which category). The aim of the resolutions was to provide more jobs for women, but – again entailing certain *a priori* assumptions – to ensure that these were the ones in which they would be 'most productive'; some of the exclusions, to be fair, were on grounds of health to protect women's reproductive capacities. Resolution 47 does appear to have improved women's position to some extent: many of the new state management jobs which were created as a result of the nationalization of small businesses in 1968 were taken by women; and during the concentrated campaign by the FMC to mobilize women to join the labour force in 1969 in preparation for the next year's sugar harvest, which it was intended should achieve the goal of 10 million tons, nearly a quarter of the women who started paid employment were in jobs previously held by men.[51] It may be, however, that many of those nationalized enterprises were run by voluntary female labour.[52] This is an aspect of the Cuban labour market which we have not yet considered, and one which particularly affects women. It has been estimated that in 1967, approximately 10 per cent of all labour performed was voluntary, and of this, up to 5 per cent was done by 'unemployed housewives'.[53] [...]

With regard specifically to women, voluntary labour is seen as a first step towards incorporating them into the paid labour force. It does not bear the same connotations as does the term 'voluntary work' in Britain – it is very definitely a political action, and has nothing to do with 'do-gooding' – but it is nearly all in typically 'feminine' areas of work: running 'children's interest circles' in the evenings; helping out in schools, hospitals and in hygiene and inoculation campaigns. Through doing such work, women are intended to become acquainted with work discipline, and also to realize the social need for them to enter paid employment. But, [...] women wishing to enter the paid labour-force may well face problems with child-care arrangements; moreover, they are becoming experienced in specific types of work which will restrict their choice of employment.

Women's Changing Roles: Further Considerations

[...] Although the increase in the number of women in the labour-force was greater between 1968 and 1969 than between the ten years 1958 to 1968,[54] of all those women who entered the labour-force in 1969, 76 per cent – three-quarters – dropped out of it within the year.[55] Table 5 shows that this pattern continued in subsequent years.

Table 5   Women joining the workforce

Year	Number incorporated during that year	Net increase or decrease
1969	106,258	25,477
1970	124,504	55,310
1971	86,188	−63,174
1972	130,843	37,263
1973	138,437	72,279
1974	127,694	69,748
Total	713,924	196,903

Source: Partido Comunista de Cuba, 1976.

During the campaign of the FMC (*Federacion de Mujeres Cubanas*) to mobilize women into the labour-force in 1969, although over 100,000 had joined, nearly 300,000 of those who were approached door-to-door had refused. Fifty-nine per cent were said to have done so because of family obligations, and 41 per cent because of 'ideological obstacles'.[56] Lewis observed that in Buena Ventura 91 per cent of his sample of women had been in paid employment before the revolution, but by 1969 only 17 per cent had jobs outside the home, and another 9 per cent within their homes. For many formerly poverty-stricken women who had had to work from sheer economic necessity, 'liberation' meant release from outside work, taking care of their own homes, and having time to spend with their children,[57] although it is difficult to estimate how many women felt this. The FMC commissioned a special survey to investigate women's reasons for leaving the paid labour-force, and this stated these to be: inability to cope with domestic and family chores; lack of effective services to lighten this domestic load; the scarcity of consumer goods, which lessened the economic incentive to work; poor work conditions; work-centre administrators' lack of understanding of the (unspecified) 'specific' problems of women; and their own misconception of the role of women in socialist society.[58]

Moreover, those women who were in paid employment or involved in the mass organizations were not being promoted in proportion to their numbers. Women were already under-represented within their membership, and even more seriously so in higher positions. [. . .]

The *Partido Comunista* commissioned a survey of 5,168 male and female workers in 211 workplaces, asking them what they thought were the factors which militated against the promotion of women. The answers were: domestic labour (85.7 per cent); child-care (83 per cent); the 'low cultural level of women' (lack of further education?) (51.5 per cent), the lack of policies of promoting women (38 per cent); resistance from women's husbands (26.2 per cent), and the fact that the administration assumes that women's domestic tasks will adversely affect their work (22.8 per cent). The following comment made by a Cuban man in 1970 draws together what were to become the preoccupations of policy in the 1970s: 'If you ask me if women have total equality now in Cuba, I would say no. There is now a framework that will allow the equality of men and women in all senses, but many of the problems still have to be solved on the level of the home. In each home, the solution to these problems will depend on the level of consciousness of the woman and the man'.[59]
[. . .]

In 1974, a nation-wide offensive to this effect took place when, as part of the preparation for the second congress of the FMC, discussions were held all over the island around the 'theses' (papers on which study and discussion can be focused) for the second congress and also around the draft 'Family Code', the latter being a piece of legislation which was put into effect on International Women's Day in 1975. Organized discussion took place in workplaces and in the mass organizations (as now happens with much proposed legislation), but the debate continued 'in grocery stores, on buses, in waiting-rooms'.[60] Articles 24 to 28 of the Family Code establish that men and women are to take equal responsibility for the upbringing of children and for domestic labour, and they are read out at all marriage ceremonies; thus it seems that a woman 'can now take her husband before a People's Court, and ultimately divorce him on the grounds that his behaviour and non-participation at home prevents her from being able to work or study'.[61]
[. . .]

The Cuban Constitution itself crystallizes both the contradictions which we have already noted in other legislation, and the particular political style which assumes that the state somehow takes care of its subjects. Article 35 enshrines the equality of rights and duties in marriage; Article 41 states that 'Discrimination because of race, colour, sex, or national origin is forbidden and will be pubished by law'. In Article 42, dealing with access to jobs, sex has suddenly disappeared – ' ... all citizens, regardless of race, colour, or national origin ... ' – but it reappears in Article 43:

> Women have the same rights as men in the economic, political, and social fields, and as far as the family goes. In order to assure the exercise of those rights, and especially the incorporation of women into socially organized work, the state sees to it that they are given jobs in keeping with their physical make-up.

Thus, although Resolutions 47 and 48 (see above) were in fact rescinded in 1973, the 1976 Constitution now risks the permanent categorization of the least physically demanding and most unskilled jobs as 'women's work'. The decision has apparently been taken to teach home economics to all schoolchildren, and both girls and boys have compulsory military training at school – but the Military Service Law is not used to draft women. Castro, while focusing on the many ways in which women remain unequal, has also said that there is a need for 'proletarian chivalry', for 'certain small privileges and certain small inequalities in favour of women'.[62] The question is, at what point does this stop being merely 'polite' and become rather a part of a sexual double standard which classifies women as more fragile and less capable than men, and which continues to oppress them? [...]

Conclusion

There are three principal features of contemporary Cuban society which may be regarded as hindering the liberation of Cuban women. Firstly, the fact that the aim of changing women's roles has been a government decision 'imposed' on them, rather than a goal which arose from a grass roots movement, together with the absence of 'consciousness-raising' groups, has impeded women's awareness of their own oppression. Secondly, the extraordinary strength and power of *machismo* within Cuban culture, the most deeply-rooted and least attacked (also least understood and investigated) area of women's subordination. And thirdly, an economic situation which, in spite of the facilitation of women's entry into production which resulted from the shortage of labour (a factor which may now be absent), yet nonetheless the need for maximum productivity, coupled with firmly-held beliefs about women's capabilities, has led to the confinement of the major part of women's employment to particular sectors of the economy, and to particular types of work within these.

Because of the material shortages which prevent the complete socialization of child-care and domestic labour, the Cubans have been forced to re-examine the 'natural' division of labour within the family unit, and have in consequence introduced some of the most advanced legislation in the world with regard to the sharing of household responsibilities. This legislation still fails to displace the primary burden of responsibility from the shoulders of the woman, and in some cases, indeed, is such that only she is able to undertake the dual roles of home and work. Even allowing for the limitations of this legislation, 'the *de facto* position of Cuban women is still in rather sharp contrast to their *de jure* status',[63] and the sustained ideological campaign amongst both women and men to bring these into line, and which was promised at the FMC Congress in 1974, has not yet begun.

If we return to the four elements which Mitchell identifies as constituting the structure of women's position – production, reproduction, sexuality, and the socialization of children – we see that despite the marked changes which have taken place since 1959 in all four elements, none has changed fundamentally. With regard specifically to production, as a result of deliberate discriminatory employment practices, the 'natural' division of labour, rather than being destroyed by recent legislation, is being displaced from the family into paid labour. While the concept of a labour 'market' may be inaccurate with regard to a socialist economy, and while the data available are insufficient to allow this hypothesis to be tested, I would suggest that the segregation and concentration by sex of Cuban employment statistics bears a marked resemblance to what is known as a 'dual labour market' – that is, a labour market which is divided into two sectors, the secondary one being characterized by lower pay and fewer opportunities for advancement, with women tending to be concentrated in the secondary sector. To gain full equality, women need not only the right to work or equal pay for equal work, but the right to do equal work, and this necessitates far-reaching changes in social behaviour. As we have seen, the framework has to some extent been provided which will allow women to do the same work as men; but until women believe themselves capable of this, and until there is a fundamental challenge to the ideology which assigns a 'natural' proclivity to the performance of certain tasks to individuals solely on the basis of their sex, that framework will remain useless.

But the failure to face the issue of ideological struggle head-on has not been the predominant cause of women's confinement to the secondary sector; ultimately, the determining factor has been the government's commitment to economic development over and above the liberation of women. It is not clear whether there would be a loss in terms of economic growth if the decision were taken to employ women in the same work as men (and men in the same work as women). But even were this the case, might not the application of a criterion of 'feminist efficiency'[64] to government policies such that all would maximize the ability of women to perform the same work as men (and of men to perform the same work as women) and minimize the possibility of sexist slippage back towards further male domination be the mark of a genuine commitment to the liberation of women? Otherwise, as Juliet Mitchell points out,[65] 'a mere permutation of the form of exploitation is achieved'. Is this what is happening in Cuba?

Acknowledgements

Thanks to Cynthia Cockburn, Jill Lewis, Maxine Molyneux and Emma Swan.

Notes and References

1 MARX, K. and ENGELS, F. (1846) *The German Ideology*, ARTHUR, C. (Ed.) (1970) London, Lawrence and Wishart, p. 50.
2 ROWBOTHAM, S. (1972) *Women, Resistance and Revolution*, Harmondsworth, Penguin, p. 67.
3 ENGELS, F. *The Origins of the Family, Private Property, and the State*, LEACOCK, N.B. (Ed.) (1972) New York, International Publishers, and Pathfinder Press.
4 ENGELS, F. *op. cit.*, p. 152.
5 BROWN, B. (1978) 'Natural and Social Division of Labour – Engels and the Domestic Labour Debate', *m/f* No. 1, pp. 25–47.
6 MITCHELL, J. (1971) *Women's Estate*, Harmondsworth, Penguin, p. 100.
7 *Ibid.*, p. 120.
8 LEVINSON, S. and BRIGHTMAN, C. (Eds.) (1971) *Venceremos Brigade*, New York, Simon and Schuster, p. 252.
9 MARTINEZ-ALIER, V. (1974) *Marriage, Class and Colour in Nineteenth Century Cuba*, Cambridge, Cambridge University Press.
10 BURKETT, E.C. (1977) 'In dubious Sisterhood – Race and Class in Spanish Colonial Latin America', *Latin American Perspectives*, Vol. IV, Nos. 1 and 2 (Issues 11 and 12).
11 FOX, G. (1973) 'Honour, Shame and Women's Liberation in Cuba – Views of Working-Class Emigré Men', in PESCATELLO, A. (Ed.) (1973) *Female and Male in Latin America*, Edinburgh, Edinburgh University Press.
12 ROWBOTHAM, S. (1972) *op. cit.*, p. 223.
13 MITCHELL, J. (1971) *op. cit.*, p. 99.
14 LEWIS, G.K. (1963) *Puerto Rico: Freedom and Power in the Caribbean*, London, Harper and Row.
15 RANDALL, M. (1975) *Cuban Women Now: Afterword 1974*, Toronto, The Women's Press.
16 CASTRO, F. (1974) 'The revolution has in Cuban women today an impressive political force', speech reprinted in FEDERATION DE MUIERES CUBANAS (1975) *Memories, Second Congress FMC*, La Habana, Cuba.
17 LEINER, M. (1974) *Children are the Revolution – Day-Care in Cuba*, New York, Viking Press, p. 8.
18 MORENO, (1971) 'From traditional to modern values', in MESA-LAGO, C. (Ed.) *Revolutionary Change in Cuba*, University of Pittsburgh Press.
19 PURCELL, S.K. (1973) 'Modernising Women for a modern society: The Cuban case', in PESCATELLO, A. (Ed.) *Female and Male in Latin America*, University of Pittsburgh Press.
20 MESA-LAGO, C. (1972) *Labor Force, Employment, Unemployment and Underemployment in Cuba: 1899–1970*, California, Sage.
21 CAMARANO, C. (1970) 'Cuban Women', *Leviathan*, May.
22 MORENO, (1971) *op. cit.*
23 CASTRO, F. (1966a) 'The New Role of Women in Cuban Society' – speech of 1 May 1966, reprinted in JENNESS, L. (1970) *Women and the Cuban Revolution*, New York, Pathfinder Press.
24 LEINER, M. (1974) *op. cit.*, p. 53.
25 PURCELL, S.K. (1973) *op. cit.*
26 *Ibid.*
27 SEERS, D. *et al.*, (1964) *Cuba: the Economic and Social Revolution*, University of North Carolina, p. 58.
28 LEINER, M. (1974) *op. cit.*, p. 11.
29 LEWIS, O., LEWIS, R.M. and RIGDON, S.M. (1977) *Four Women: Living the Revolution – An Oral History of Contemporary Cuba*, University of Illinois, p. xiii.
30 *Ibid.*, p. xvi.
31 *Ibid.*, p. xiii.
32 ENGELS, F. *op. cit.*, p. 81.
33 *Annuario Estadistico*, (1975).
34 *Boletin Estadistico*, (1971).
35 SOCIALIST CHILDCARE COLLECTIVE (undated) *Changing Childcare: Cuba, China and the Changing of our own Values*, London, Writers' and Readers' Publishing Co-operative.
36 *Annuario Estadistico*, (1975); SEDLEY, M. (1976) 'The Theory and Practice of Childcare in Cuba', *Britain-Cuba Scientific Liaison Committee Bulletin*, No. 6, February.
37 LEINER, M. (1974) *op. cit.*, p. 49.
38 LEVINSON, S. and BRIGHTMAN, C., (1971) *op. cit.*, p. 118.
39 BONACHEA, R.E. and VALDES, N.P. (Eds.) (1972) *Cuba in Revolution*, New York, Anchor Press.
40 SEERS, D. (1964) *op. cit.*; PURCELL, S.K. (1973) *op. cit.*

41 *Ibid.*
42 JOLLY, R. (1964) 'Education', in SEERS, D. (1964) *op. cit.*
43 PURCELL, S.K. (1973) *op. cit.*
44 JOLLY, R. *op. cit.*
45 STYCOS, J.M. (1971) *Ideology, Faith and Family Planning in Latin America*, New York, McGraw Hill.
46 LEWIS, LEWIS and RIGDON (1977) *op. cit.*, p. xxc.
47 BONACHEA and VALDES, (1972) *op. cit.*; MESA-LAGO, C. (1972) *op. cit.*; LEINER, M. (1974) *op. cit.*; CASTRO, F. (1966b) 'Revolution Within the Revolution' speech of 9 May 1966, reprinted in JENNESS, L. (1970) *op. cit.*; LEWIS, LEWIS and RIGDON, (1977) *op. cit.*; *Granma Weekly Review*, (English Edition) 5 January 1969 to 12 December 1976, La Habana, Cuba; CASTRO, F. (1974) 'The Revolution has in Cuban Women Today an Impressive Political Force' – speech of 1974, reprinted in *Federation de Mujeres Cubanas* (1975) *Memories, Second Congress* FMC, La Habana, Cuba.
48 BONACHEA, R.E. and VALDES, N.P. (1972) *op. cit.*
49 See the table in SAFFIOTI, H. (1977) 'Women, Mode of Production and Social Formation', *Latin American Perspectives*, Vol. IV, Nos. 1 and 2, p. 34.
50 Castro quoted in *Granma Weekly Review*, (1969) 16 March.
51 *Granma Weekly Review*, (1970) 25 January.
52 See HUBERMAN, L. and SWEEZY, P. (1969) *Socialism in Cuba*, New York, Monthly Review Press.
53 MESA-LAGO, C. (1972) *op. cit.*
54 MURRAY, N. (1969) *Feminist Review*, No. 2. See Table 2.
55 STUBBS, J. (1975) 'Cuba and the New Family Code', *Red Rag*, No. 9, June.
56 MORENO, (1971) *op. cit.*
57 LEWIS, LEWIS and RIGDON (1977) *op. cit.*, p. xv.
58 KING, M. (1977) 'Cuba's Attack on Women's Second Shift', *Latin American Perspectives*, Vol. IV, Nos. 1 and 2 (Issues 11 and 12).
59 Quoted in LEVINSON and BRIGHTMAN, (1971) *op. cit.*
60 RANDALL, M. (1975) *op. cit.*
61 SEDLEY, M. (1976) *op. cit.*
62 CASTRO, F. (1974) *op. cit.*
63 LEWIS, LEWIS and RIGDON (1977) *op. cit.*, p. xxi.
64 I have developed this concept from that of 'socialist efficiency' suggested by GORDON, D.M. (1976) 'Capitalist Efficiency and Socialist Efficiency', *Monthly Review*, 28, (3), July–August. He posed 'socialist efficiency' as a criterion by which to judge socialist policies in an effort to escape from the non-progressive organizational changes which tend to accompany concentration on measures judged according to their 'economic efficiency', and suggested that 'socialist efficiency [in the organization of production] maximizes the ability of the working-class to increase its domination of the means of production and minimizes the possibility of revisionist slippage back towards further ruling-class domination', whereas 'capitalist efficiency best reproduces capitalist control over the production process and minimizes proletarian resistance to that control'.
65 MITCHELL, J. (1971) *op. cit.*

3
Childhood, Schooling and the Welfare State

14 Social Control or Social Wage: On the Political Economy of the 'Welfare State'

Paul Adams

Discussion between liberal apologists for the 'welfare state' and their radical critics has tended in recent years to focus on the question of 'social control'. In this area the corporate liberals and social democrats (the 'welfare statists') are weak. They talk of the 'welfare state' as if, at least in principle, it represented the collective assumption by society of responsibility for the basic needs and dependencies of its members. Insofar as 'social control' is relevant for them, it has to do with society's exercise of restraint over the selfish pursuit of private profit.[1] Radical critics of the 'welfare state', on the other hand, point to its controlling and system-maintenance functions, but often neglect the real benefits it provides. They have exposed the police officer, the guard, or (to use the old Wobbly term) the head-fixer behind the caring smile of the social worker, the teacher, and the therapist. Even the provision of material benefits – social security, public welfare, health and housing subsidies – is seen as reinforcing or regulating market forces in the interests of order and efficiency, rather than modifying them to meet human need. Where conservatives have seen 'creeping socialism', radicals have seen the intervention of the capitalist state to stabilize and reinforce the system.

To remain on this terrain in a period of economic instability, fiscal crises, welfare cuts, and the general collapse of New Deal liberalism in the face of these developments, is an indulgence. It reflects a one-sided and therefore inadequate understanding of the 'welfare state'. Government social welfare programs do certainly have a social control function, but they in many cases also constitute part of what may be called the 'social wage'. My purpose here is to distinguish these elements, to draw attention to the concept of the social wage and some of its difficulties, and to draw some political conclusions.

I want to begin with certain conditions which are necessary for the accumulation of capital. Starting with the simplest possible model of capitalism as a mode of production (that is, a way in which people co-operate together to produce the means of life), we can see that the owners of capital must pay for the labor-power they buy at least a certain minimum. This must be enough to ensure the maintenance and

Source: Journal of Sociology and Social Welfare, (5), 1978, pp. 46–54.

reproduction of labor-power at an adequate level of health, education, and security. Adequacy is here a matter of what is required at a given level of technological and cultural development to produce an efficient work force. These capital costs of production include the maintenance not only of the presently active labor force but also of past and future workers. They must, that is, be sufficient to support the worker and his or her family.[2] If the worker is to be fit for the job, and the work force is not to be depleted, capital must pay at least a certain minimum for the labor-power it hires. We can imagine these costs being met entirely in the form of wages. Workers would then have to provide for their own immediate needs and those of their dependents (including their education), as well as insuring against the needs and dependencies of sickness, accidents, old age, unemployment and so on – all from their paychecks.

On the other hand, workers must produce for their employers not only the value of their own labor-power (that is, enough to cover the costs of its production), and not only enough to cover wear and tear on physical plant, etc., but also a surplus which, if the product can be sold and certain other conditions met, will enable the employers to reinvest, buying more machinery or hiring more workers. Out of this surplus, however, various expenses must also be met, including those of the capitalists' own living and the hire of their personal servants. More significantly for our purposes, these expenses include the costs of maintaining the social conditions in which production and accumulation can proceed on the basis of capitalist property relations.' We can imagine each capitalist meeting these expenses individually, hiring not only his/her own managers and security guards, but also ideologues and propagandists, private army, police, and human relations experts.

Historically, however, both the capital costs of production and the expenses of ensuring its taking place under capitalist relations have been met in part, an increasing part, through the state. This is so clearly the case with regard to the expenses of production that the state may be defined as that social institution with the primary function of maintaining order and harmony in the relations of production. The mechanisms for carrying out this function include army, police, courts, state bureaucracy, and school insofar as they serve an ideological or 'head-fixing' purpose. In whatever form these aspects of the state's activity are financed, they constitute in essence taxes on capital. That is, they are part of the price that capital has to pay for the maintenance of the system.

On the other hand, the state has also increasingly socialized the wage system, in the sense of taking over from individual capitals part of the task of providing for the production and reproduction of labor-power. Put differently, the worker's standard of living depends not only upon what he or she takes home in his or her paycheck, but also upon the goods and services provided by the state. Indeed, according to one minister in the British Labour government, Barbara Castle:

> The most important part of the standard of living of most of us depends on the great complex of services we call 'public expenditure'. They are not only the key to the quality of life; they are the key to equality. ... The great advances ... have come ... from better education, better health

services, better housing and better care of the old, the disabled and the handicapped in life.[3]

Castle gives special emphasis to that 6o per cent of 'public expenditure' which, in the government's calculations, goes to the 'social wage'. She goes so far as to claim that 'the taxman is the Robin Hood of our time, taking from those who can afford it the means whereby we can pay every worker the wage that really matters, the social wage'.[4]

The social wage, as I am using the term, does not include all public expenditure. It is defined as those costs of labor-power which take the form of benefits and services provided by the state, and is distinguished both from other forms of wage paid directly by the employer (take-home and fringe benefits) and from other types of state activity (policing or 'system-maintenance', as well as non-labor, or constant, social capital costs). The social wage is not, of course, co-extensive with government social welfare expenditures. These support a wide range of activities which may have either a 'social control' function (helping to police the existing social and economic order) or a social wage function (providing real benefits to workers and their families which improve their standard of living); or they may combine both functions.

When we move from the apparently clear distinction between social control (social expenses of production) and social wage (the labor element of social capital costs), to particular cases of social welfare expenditures, the problems multiply. Governments which employ the concept of the 'social wage' (these include Russia and New Zealand as well as Britain) tend to use it ideologically, to disguise the coercive or policing aspects of certain state activities. Thus, the British government calculates the social wage as the amount of current and capital public spending on a number of programs for each member of the working population. These programs include not only social security (both 'insurance' and assistance programs), health, education, and certain subsidies, including food, nationalized industries' price restraint, and transportation – but also, law and order.[5] The assumption is evidently that the primary function of the forces of law and order is the preservation of the lives and property of the working population.

James O'Connor, in *The Fiscal Crisis of the State*, distinguishes capital costs of production from expenses of production and describes how both have increasingly been socialized.[6] In dealing with specific programs, however, he assigns social security insurance programs to the former category but 'welfare' (assistance) programs to the latter. Here the assumption appears to be that welfare clients constitute a 'surplus population' who exist outside production but must, from a capitalist viewpoint, be kept alive in the interest of public order. This may, in part, be correct. But most welfare clients have worked before going on welfare, and will work again when they are off, while many continue to work while receiving benefits. [...]

Education and personal social services are areas where it is particularly difficult to separate social control from social wage elements. Real benefits may be provided which constitute an enhancement of the recipient's standard of living, while reduced provision may constitute a cut in real living standards. While teachers and social workers provide these benefits, however, they may at the same time act as policing agents through the exercise of more or less open coercion or as ideological agents for the transmission of dominant norms and values.[7]

Further difficulties arise when one attempts, as the British government is doing, to quantify the social wage and measure increases and decreases in it. Very large rates of increase may appears – a recent *Times* (London) article was headed 'Social Wage Trebled in Six Years'[8] – without there being any real improvement in the level of provision made to individual recipients. The increase may go entirely to cover the effects of general inflation, as well as disproportionate increases in land costs and interest rates, increased drug prices or payments to physicians, or increases in numbers of recipients due to such factors as higher unemployment, or a higher proportion of the old and young in the total population.[9] An adequate empirical measure of the social wage would need to include only those forms of provision which constitute (or to the extent that they constitute) real benefits rather than policing expenses – and this is a political question to which we cannot expect to find a satisfactory answer from any existing government. It would also need to record and aggregate real, physical improvement or declines in the quality and quantity of provision. I do not know whether these problems are soluble. The political importance of the social wage, however, does not depend on its calculability.

In specific social welfare programs, I have suggested, social control and social wage elements may be inextricably entangled. The distinction is important nonetheless. Those who see all social services simply and inherently as policing or social control activities and for whom that is a condemnation, have no obvious grounds for opposing cutbacks in social welfare expenditures. Radicals would presumably have no objection to cuts in funding for the army, police, or Central Intelligence Agency. How is social welfare different?

It is different, in my view, because cutbacks in social welfare expenditures can amount to a disguised wage cut and be part of a government strategy to hold down personal and social consumption in order to maintain profitability and encourage investment.[10] Such a strategy is difficult to resist, the more so if it is not perceived as an attack on workers' living standards. Cutbacks in education or health and welfare programs are not as direct or obvious (unless they involve transfer payments) as a reduction in one's take-home pay. They tend to affect most those least able to resist: the old, the young, the disabled, the sick. In the United States especially, it is possible to present such cuts as an increase in the proportion of one's earnings which are disposable by oneself rather than by the state, even though they may in fact constitute an overall reduction in living standards.

The concept of the social wage draws attention to the fact that social security, education, health programs, and welfare are as much part of the real income of working class families as the paycheck. The income is disposed of by the capitalist state on behalf of those families, who exercise neither individual nor collective control over it, but a cutback is a reduction in real income for all that.

Given the obvious advantages of the social wage as the locus for an attack on consumption, it is somewhat surprising that the British Labour government should, in the course of such an attack, seek to give the *concept* wide currency. In part, its doing so reflects the uneasy co-existence of a real, if misguided, concern with social justice on one hand and a commitment to maintaining the competitiveness and profitability of British industry in a hostile world on the other. The 'Joint Framework for Social Policies' developed by the Central Policy Review Staff for the government emphasizes the importance of developing an index of the social wage.[11] But it does so in the context of a need to rationalize and prioritize social expenditure in a period of economic difficulty. That is, cuts must be made, so let us ensure that what is left goes with maximum effectiveness where we consciously decide it should go. (In a similar vein, the last Labour government, of 1964–70, introduced its incomes policy with much discussion of how the better off workers should restrain themselves so that more could go to the lower-paid. In the event, wage controls proved effective *only* against the weaker and lower-paid sections of labor. In general, advances by lower paid workers occur in the wake of and depend on the gains won by stronger and better paid sections of workers.[12] In this case, too, we may be confident that business, not those in greatest need, will benefit from the prioritizing of cutbacks.)

Furthermore, the policy of relying on the co-operation of union bureaucrats to induce acceptance by their members of cuts in real wages, despite its current success, is uncertain and inadequate. The social wage provides another line of attack, and one which can be made to appear very reasonable. Government ministers and civil servants have pointed out the rapid rises in the social wage, while failing to mention some of the reasons for them discussed above. Thus Chancellor of the Exchequer Dennis Healey in his April 1975 Budget speech said that the social wage now amounted to £1000 for every adult member of the working population in Britain, and observed that the 'social wage has been increasing very much faster than ordinary wages – much faster than prices too'.[13] The Central Policy Review Staff's report notes that

> public expenditure has been growing faster than production as a whole, and expenditure on social programs has been growing faster than the rest of public expenditure.

'This', it affirms, 'cannot go on'.[14] In this context it is to the government's advantage to make the social wage visible, so that workers and others will feel personally responsible for the country's economic troubles and recognize the necessity of cuts in social spending so that inflation can be reduced and the economy restored to health.[15]

Cutting the social wage, then, is one way in which a government can try to switch resources from consumption to investment. It has many advantages, but is nevertheless a dangerous strategy because it translates the struggle over wages and profits from the economic to the political sphere. In doing so, it breaks down the reformist barriers between the economic and the political, between struggles over wages and conditions on one hand, and political power on the other. Many kinds of state intervention, from the use of police to break a picket line to the imposition of wage controls, involve workers in conflict with the state as well as the employer.

The social wage has assumed such importance in the last forty years[16] that the defense of living standards now leads beyond a conflict with employer over wages and conditions, and only incidentally with the state insofar as it actively intervenes. It also involves a struggle over social policy, over what proportion of the total social product should go to what purposes and who should decide. As both opponents of capitalism like O'Connor and supporters like Daniel Bell have pointed out, this increasing politicization of the economy holds dangers for the system in terms both of generating unmeetable demands and of undermining the legitimacy of the market.[17] What they usually have not pointed out is that while the economy has been politicized, the state has in turn been increasingly subordinated to the demands of the economy. The competitive drive to accumulate capital is no less compulsive, and no less the central dynamic of the system, for being increasingly international in form, or for involving the state. Competition has not become subordinate to political decision-making, but rather the reverse. Governments are more and more held responsible for the functioning of the economy, but subject as they are to the pressures of international competition, they have less and less room to maneuver.

As governments, especially in Europe, have attempted to solve the problems of their economies by cutting the social wage, so they have elicited a more generalized and political response from workers. In recent years, with the faltering of the twenty year post-war expansion and stability, workers have found that they cannot make gains, or defend what they have, by relying on union bureaucrats or fragmented and localized struggle. They can no longer rely on being able to make up for reduced public provision with increased fringe benefits or higher wages as they did in the 1950s and 1960s.[18] They are still far from a unified, class-wide political response, even in countries with a stronger socialist tradition and more socialist militants. But the experience that neither shop-floor militancy nor the negotiations of labour leaders have prevented the closure of schools and hospitals, or the decline of provision for the aging, has produced different kinds of action by industrial workers. In 1974, dockworkers, coalminers and others struck in support of nurses during their pay dispute in England. Construction workers went on strike in support of higher old age benefits in 1972, also in England. In Italy there have been major strikes over housing and social security, and other actions against rent, bus fare, and food price increases.[19] These struggles have sometimes involved elements of workers' control. That is, workers on the job and as consumers have demanded and in some instances taken some control of their 'social' wage – not only how much it should be but how it should be spent. The demand for workers' control of the social wage is, of course, a quite different demand from that of the conservative 'individualist' who wants it largely eliminated in favor of the individual paycheck, or higher corporate profits. This is true even though both demands express, from different perspectives, a suspicion of the state and its bureaucracy.[20]

A one-sided emphasis on the social control aspects of the welfare state, then, leaves one ill-equipped for the actual battles which have to be fought in defense of social welfare programs. Cutbacks in social expenditures have to be opposed as strongly as if they were reductions in wages (although successful opposition to such cuts requires that the reformist separation of the economic – trade-union – from the political – Labour Party, etc. – struggle be overcome, and that the economic power of working people be politically organized and directed). This does not imply uncritical acceptance of social welfare programs in their present form, including their coercive 'social control' aspects. Indeed, defending the social wage involves conflict with the state which is its guardian, but which at the same time subordinates it to other priorities. An effective defense is likely to bring that guardianship into question.

Notes and References

1 For example TITMUSS, R.M. (1974) *Social Policy: An Introduction*, London, George Allen and Unwin, as well as earlier essays.

2 Of course, one may ask of any actual social formation, to what extent is capital subsidized by (rather than paying for) women's labor in the home. cf. GARDINER, J. (1975) 'Women's Domestic Labour', *New Left Review*, 89, January–February, pp. 47–58. But this and related problems do not affect the very basic distinction I wish to make.

3 Cited by TRINDER, C. (1976) 'Inflation and the Social Wage', Chap. 4 of WILLMOTT, P. (Ed.) *Sharing Inflation? Poverty Report 1976*, London, Temple Smith, p. 58.

4 *Ibid.* The quote is from the *Financial Times*, 8 July 1975.

5 *Hansard*, 22 April 1975.

6 O'CONNOR, J. (1973) *The Fiscal Crisis of the State*, New York, St. Martin's Press.

7 LEONARD, P. (1965) 'Social Control, Class Values and Social Work Practice', *Social Work*, (UK), 22, 4 October, pp. 9–13.

8 *The Times*, (London), 21 July 1976.

9 TRINDER, C. (1976) *op. cit.*, pp. 59–60; KINCAID, J. (1971) 'The Decline of the Welfare State', in HARRIS, N. and PALMER, J. (Eds.), *World Crisis*, London, Hutchinson, KINCAID, J.C. (1973) *Poverty and Equality in Britain*, Harmondsworth, England, Penguin, p. 81ff.

10 Fine and Harris, in their critique of GOUGH I. (1975) ('State Expenditure in Advanced Capitalism', *New Left Review*, 92, pp. 53–92), reject the concept of the social wage and the notion that social services are an 'integral part of the real wage level of the working class'. Such a notion, they argue, rests upon a rejection of the law of value. The payment of wages by capital involves the exchange of commodities with equivalent values, whereas the state's social welfare provisions do not involve such an exchange of equivalents but *instead* is primarily determined by political struggle (FINE, B. and HARRIS, L. (1976) 'State Expenditure in Advanced Capitalism: A Critique', *New Left Review*, 98, pp. 96–112). But employers do not pay the full equivalent value of the labor-power they hire in the form of wages and fringe benefits. Part of the costs of the production of labor-power has been 'socialized' via the state. At present, American auto companies pay a substantial proportion of their wage bill in the form of voluntary health insurance premiums. If these premiums are eliminated in favor of a national health insurance program along the lines of the Health Security Act, would the value of an autoworker's labor-power suddenly drop? No, the employers would have to pay for their workers' health care via a tax instead of a premium, and they might thereby succeed in shifting part of their costs on to other sections of capital. It is not that the law of value is wrong, as Gough believes. The shift in labor costs from individual employer to capitalist state is simply part of the process of 'socialization' of capital, that is the process of the bureaucratic collectivization of capitalism, in which the law of value is partially negated, but on the basis of the law of value itself.

11 Central Policy Review Staff, (1975) *A Joint Framework for Social Policies*, London, HMSO.

12 CLIFF, T. and BARKER, C. (1966) *Incomes Policy, Legislation and Shop Stewards*, London, London Industrial Shop Stewards Defense Committee; KIDRON, M. (1970) *Western Capitalism Since the War*, revised ed., Harmondsworth, England, Penguin.

13 *Hansard*, 15 April 1976.

14 Central Policy Review Staff, (1975) *op. cit.*, Paras. 4, 5.

15 Counter Information Services and Community Development Project, *Cutting the Welfare State (Who Profits)*, London, CIS, CDP, n.d. This special report unfortunately includes various items (such as defense) in their calculation of the social wage which the government excluded in its claim that every adult worker receives £1,000 in social 'wages'.

16 The total social wage rose as a proportion of consumption from a third in the early 1950's (33 per cent in 1955) to two-fifths in the early 1960s (40 per cent in 1963) to a half in the late 1960's (53 per cent in 1969) to three-fifths in the early 1970s (59 per cent in 1973) (*Hansard*, 15 July 1975).

17 O'CONNOR, J. (1973) *op. cit.*; BELL, D. (Fall 1974) *The Public Interest*, 37, pp. 29–68; OFFE, C. (1973) 'The Abolition of Market Control and the Problem of Legitimacy', *Kapitalistate*, 1, pp. 109–16, and 2, pp. 73–83; HABERMAS, J. (1975) *Legitimation Crisis*, Boston, Beacon Press, pp. 62–3 et passim; BRITTAN, S. (1975) 'The Economic Contradictions of Democracy', *British Journal of Political Science*, 5, pp. 129–59.

18 KIDRON, M. (1970) *op. cit.*

19 CLIFF, T. (1975) *The Crisis: Social Contract or Socialism*, London, Pluto Press, pp. 89–90.

20 Owners of capital, especially smaller and more conservative ones, tend to see the state as a drain on their investable resources and as encroaching on their individual prerogatives. Insofar as the state functions to maintain the environment in which they can operate, however, it is for them a *necessary* evil. For workers, on the other hand, this necessity does not exist.

15 Who Cares for the Family?

Hilary Land

[. . .]

'The family must be regarded as the bulwark of a stable society', said the Archbishop of Canterbury in the opening speech in a major debate on the family which took place in the House of Lords in the summer of 1976.[1] There is no doubt that the family is a powerful force for maintaining the *status quo*. In particular it is an important mechanism for the transmission of existing inequalities. On the other hand the family manages, or is expected to manage, the tension between order and change and in this sense may facilitate rather than inhibit change. Paradoxically therefore the family both transmits culture *and* provides a counter-culture. Hence both the causes of and the solutions to various social ills are looked for within the family. It is not surprising that a government spokesman in the same debate declared 'The government believe implicitly in the family and recognise that the family needs all the support that society can give it . . . '. In other words governments do care about the family but the form which their concern takes is an important and delicate issue because the family is portrayed as a sanctuary – warm, welcoming and intimate, unlike the cold, ruthless, competitive society outside. Unless this haven, which is thought to be a frail institution, remains private and free from state intrusion then it will not be able to counteract the increasingly alienating effects of social and economic change.

[. . .]

This paper will first examine the assumptions underlying a variety of social policies which concern the division of unpaid labour within the family whereby women care for the young, the sick and the old and, most important, for able-bodied adult men (their husbands). While acknowledging that the time and work involved are not the only dimensions of caring and that particularly in the context of a loving relationship there are other aspects which are positive and rewarding, it is important for us to recognize that, if we ascribe to women the primary responsibility for providing domestic services for other members of the family, their daily lives are structured in a way which profoundly affects their opportunities in the wider

Source: Journal of Social Policy, (1978), (7.3), pp. 257–84.

society in general and the labour market in particular. Moreover, the fact that this work is unpaid means that women do not acquire any direct financial independence by doing it. The second part of the paper therefore will indicate how the division of unpaid labour within the family is an important determinant of women's opportunities in the labour market.

In order to appreciate the full extent of the work of caring within the family it is important not to restrict an examination of the family to the child-bearing stage of the life cycle. [. . .] [Further] it is essential to distinguish the needs and obligations which are presumed to arise from marriage from those which are presumed to arise from parenthood. When we are looking at families with young children it is too easy to equate marriage and parenthood. Marriage is after all a social contract regulated by church and state. With it goes a set of financial obligations for the man – in particular he must participate in the labour market in order to support his children and his wife. Women acquire a set of domestic duties which include caring for their children, their elderly or sick relatives and of course their husbands. One important consequence of the difference between the meaning of marriage for men and its meaning for women is that there is a conflict between a woman's responsibilites towards other members of her family and her activities in the labour market, whereas for most men there is not. As Alfred Marshall wrote at the turn of the century, when commenting on recent increases in women's wages, 'This is a great gain in so far as it tends to develop their faculties but an injury in so far as it tempts them to neglect their duty of building up a true home and of investing their effort in the Personal Capital of their children's character and abilities'.[2]

This paper will attempt to show that the priorities which women must accord to their paid work in the labour market, their unpaid work in the home and their leisure are as much a product of being wives as of being mothers.

Income Maintenance Systems and Responsibilities for Caring

The majority of married women have paid employment for most of their married lives. The economic activity rates for childless married women under forty years of age are the same as those for single women, and increasingly women with children have paid employment.[3] In half of all married couples under retirement age both husband and wife are earners. On average a wife's earnings represent 25 per cent of the family income.[4] For some families the wife's financial contribution is a very important means of keeping a family out of poverty. For example the Department of the Environment's second Inner Area study in Lambeth showed that among married couples with children under fifteen years of age in which the mother had full-time paid employment all had an income at least 20 per cent above supplementary benefit level. However, in those families in which the mother had part-time employment 6 per cent had an income below 20 per cent of supplementary benefit level, and where the mother did not have paid employment at all nearly one in four fell below this level.[5]

A wife's earnings then are an important means of maintaining a family's standard of living. It seems at first a little surprising therefore that among unemployed men the overall proportion with wives in paid employment is low. Among men dependent on supplementary benefit the proportion is even lower – one-third of the childless and only 1 per cent of those with children.[6] Part of the explanation lies in the fact that the social security system is based on the concept of one male bread-winner upon whom the rest of the family relies or *should* rely for financial support. The importance of the wife's financial contribution to the family is therefore ignored. Currently only £4 a week of a wife's earnings are disregarded. If she earns more than this then the extra dependency benefit is lost and in addition, for those on supple-mentary benefit, the benefit is reduced pound for pound. There is therefore a substantial incentive for a woman to give up paid work once her husband becomes unemployed, unless she has high enough earnings to maintain the whole family. Similarly there is evidence that the wives of men who become chronically sick are more likely to give up than to take up employment.[7] In other words the social security system ignores the fact that most families are dependent on *two* earners (and for many working-class families this has always been so);[8] it actively discourages role reversal and it encourages women to give priority to their responsibilities in the home. As a result the division of labour within the home remains unchanged even when the man is out of the labour market and dependent on state benefits. At the same time the experience of unemployment for the man is less intolerable than it might otherwise be. George Orwell, writing forty years ago about the lives of the unemployed, drew attention to the same phenomenon:

> ... so long as a man is married unemployment makes comparatively little alteration to his way of life. His home is impoverished but it is still a home, and it is noticeable everywhere that the anomalous position created by unemployment – the man being out of work while the woman's work continues as before – has not altered the relative status of the sexes. In working class homes it is the man who is the master and not, as in a middle class home, the woman or baby. Practically never, for instance, in a working class home, will you see the man doing a stroke of the housework. Un-employment has not changed this convention which on the face of it seems a little unfair. The man is idle from morning to night but the woman is as busy as ever – more so indeed, because she has to manage with less money. Yet so far as my experience goes the women do not protest. I believe that they, as well as the men, feel that a man would lose his manhood if, merely because he was out of work, he developed into a 'Mary Ann'.[9]

The interpretation of 'incapacity to work' in the national insurance scheme provides further examples of the assumptions made about a woman's primary responsibilities. The national insurance scheme created in 1911 was based on a large number of friendly societies and industrial associations which had developed during the previous century. Although some of them extended membership to women, the number of married women who joined was quite small because few could afford the premiums and in any case benefit was rarely paid during illness arising from pregnancy or childbirth. However, the new national insurance scheme had a much broader membership and included 700,000 married women, insured in their own right, many of whom had not been eligible for benefit before. Difficult questions about the circumstances in which sickness benefit should be paid were therefore raised on a much larger scale than hitherto. These issues could not be ignored because in the first years of the scheme many more women than had been expected to do so claimed sickness benefit, and in 1913 a committee was set up to find out why these 'excessive claims' had been made.[10]

The committee gave careful consideration to the meaning of 'incapacity to work'. Did it mean inability to follow one's usual occupation? For short periods of sickness when there was a good chance of returning to the same job, this was a reasonable interpretation, at least as far as men were concerned. For women it was different. As one witness explained, 'A man is working or he is ill. A woman is perhaps not working because some of the family are ill, or perhaps she is cleaning the house'.[11] Provided they were capable of doing the housework they were not deemed to be ill and therefore women found doing housework when the sick visitor called had their benefit withdrawn in spite of the fact that they were not fit enough to return to the mill or factory. What was recognized by only a few witnesses was how hard it was for a woman *not* to do any domestic work, however ill she felt. For example Marion Phillips, representing The Women's Labour League, told the committee:

> It is a very difficult problem to deal with mothers who are so used to waiting on the rest of the family that they do it unconsciously ... the working woman who has been so used to serving other people that even when she is ill she will go on doing it and it is recognized in her family as a natural thing.[12]

Men caught working on their allotment or garden were likewise disqualified, but, as Sidney Webb said to the committee, 'Gardens are not quite as common as teacups'.[13]

It was feared by many of the witnesses and indeed by the majority of the committee that the availability of sickness benefit had encouraged women to take time off from their paid employment. The secretary of an approved society with a membership of about 24,500, a third of whom were married, explained:

> With sickness benefit and husband's wages, she has sufficient to keep the family going, because she is saving the money she would have had to pay for having the children looked after ... and then there is washing and baking. She would have that to pay for. I consider that seven shillings and sixpence at home and being able to look after the children and to do the washing and baking herself would be equal to what she got by going out to work and having to pay for all these things.[14]

(This is evidence that, even when a woman does not actually do the household work herself, she is responsible for arranging *and* paying for it to be done.)

The committee (bar Mary Macarthur) found it easier to accept that the un-expectedly high number of claims for sickness benefits from women was due to an ignorance about insurance principles and a greater tendency to malinger than that it was because the health of many working women was very bad and because for the first time they could afford to take time off from work when they were ill. The committee therefore recommended that societies should convince women of the necessity to abstain from housework while they were receiving sickness benefit and should generally educate them about the principles of insurance.

Those who administer the national insurance sickness benefit scheme today still assume that if a woman is capable of housework then she is not in fact ill. The instructions issued by the Department of Health and Social Security (DHSS) to doctors concerning medical evidence for social security purposes ask them to consider the question of fitness for alternative work after a lengthy period of illness. As far as women are concerned this means assessing their capacity to perform household duties. The instructions state:

> If a woman has for some considerable time (perhaps 6 months or so) been advised to refrain from her normal paid employment but is nevertheless doing an amount of housework in her own home for which she could reasonably expect to be paid if it were done for an employer, there will generally be no grounds for continuing to issue statements of advice to refrain from work.[15]

Similarly DHSS visiting officers fill in a form which has a separate section for a woman ascertaining whether 'she is able to look after her family (if any) and do her own housework and laundry'. At the time of writing there were no such questions for men, either living alone or married. In other words in the last resort *all* women were expected to do housework in order to maintain themselves, or be maintained by a man. Men were not expected to do so until August 1977, when this assumption was challenged and a national insurance commissioner ruled that, where a man's capacity for work was at issue, 'If the evidence showed that he undertook household chores, as many men now do, or worked in the garden, that evidence would be admissible on the question whether he is capable of remunerative work'. As a result the instructions issue to doctors and DHSS visiting officers are going to be amended to apply to *all* claimants.[16]

[...]

The British income tax system recognizes a variety of family responsibilities by means of a series of allowances which the taxpayer is allowed to offset against his (or less often her) taxable income. Among these allowances is one for housekeepers, and the reason given for their introduction show similar assumptions about who does the work in the home. The housekeeper's allowance was first introduced in 1918. Initially it was only for widowers with dependent children but a year later it was extended to widowers without children. The Board of Inland Revenue in its evidence to the Royal Commission on the Taxation of Profits and Income of 1951–55 explained that 'The reason for this extension appears to have been the largely sentimental one that when a man's wife dies he cannot be expected to give up his home and therefore he must have someone to look after him . . . [the widow] . . . is already accustomed to look after the home herself'.[17]

Widows with children were, however, included in 1920; four years later the allowance was extended to childless widows. This seemed surprising in retrospect because, as the Inland Revenue Staff Federation told the same royal commission, 'It is not the death of the spouse but the lack of a *wife* who can keep house which may necessitate a housekeeper'.[18] Until the Second World War the tax system only recognized housekeepers who were female relatives and resident in the taxpayer's home. Evidence that they were being paid was not necessary. In other words women do the housework and look after a man and his children in return for their maintenance.

During the Second World War the definition of 'housekeeper' for tax purposes was broadened to include non-relatives, and any taxpayer with children employing a resident female housekeeper could claim it. However, a married man could only claim if his wife was permanently incapacitated, and a female taxpayer could only use the allowance if she was disabled or chronically sick, or supporting herself by full-time employment. In 1960 an additional allowance was introduced for taxpayers with children in the above categories. They did not have to have a resident housekeeper. However, married women with permanently incapacitated husbands were not eligible for either allowance because, a government spokesman explained, 'Though the work of looking after an invalid husband may be a serious tie to the wife, it does not prevent her from undertaking the normal responsibilities of looking after the children'.[19] It is clear that, even if married women are in full-time paid employment because their husbands cannot earn, they are still expected to carry out their 'normal responsibilites' in the home. Only women with children but without husbands to care for get additional tax relief. (In other words the key determinant is a woman's marital status rather than whether or not she is a mother.) In contrast men are not expected to combine paid employment with domestic work and are therefore helped with the cost of providing a substitute for a sick wife as well as an absent one. The substitute must be another woman.

[. . .]

The Interrelationship between Mothers' and Fathers' Employment and Day Care Provisions for Children

The provision of services which either share or replace the care which parents give their young children is based on similar assumptions. Although in the past hundred years the state has gradually taken from parents responsibilities for *educating* their children, it is not yet considered legitimate in Britain for the state to provide pre-school child *care* services either free or on anything approaching a universal basis. Since the Second World War local authority day nurseries have declined in number while nursery education places have doubled, and there are plans to provide sufficient places for all children from three to five years old whose parents wish them to attend. However, these nursery school places will only be provided for the majority on a part-time basis. The extension of nursery education is therefore not considered in the context of enabling mothers to take paid work outside the home but rather as a way of supplementing their skills and expertise. In other words education for the under-fives is increasingly seen as the province of professionals. The result is, as Bridget Plowden has pointed out, 'The confidence of parents in themselves as parents, in this rapidly changing society, where the urgent need is for confidence and security, has been lessened. It is "they" in nurseries and schools who know best, from the earliest months and years of a child's life . . . '.[20]

In contrast the work of caring is still firmly seen as the responsibility of the mother. Day care facilities do exist, but in 1975 two-thirds of legal day care (that is, day nurseries and registered child-minders) was provided by voluntary or private organizations. Even when numbers attending play groups are included, in 1974 only about a third of all children under five in England and Wales were known to be receiving some form of organized day care outside their families. This is half the number whose parents would like to use day care services. Access to a local authority day nursery is difficult, if not impossible, for the child from a 'normal' two-parent family. Even one-parent families may be refused a place, and some authorities will only accept children who are believed to be in danger of being battered and who are therefore on their 'at risk' register. Most mothers who do have paid work – and in 1974 it was estimated that one in three mothers of children under five were economically active (the majority part time) – have to rely on relatives (often grandmothers), neighbours or their own husbands. However, fathers of young children help mainly when the mother works part time: they rarely give sufficient help to enable the mother to take full-time employment.[21]

The justification for not providing more day care services, particularly nurseries, which are costly to run, is often based on a concern not to harm the emotional development of young children as well as on economic considerations. However, the evidence that the experience of day care outside the family is damaging to a child is not convincing. As Jack Tizard argued recently:

> Those such as Pringle (1974) who think that day care outside the home must be inevitably detrimental to the child's development (though it may be the lesser of the two evils) base their views essentially on two premises: first that the young children cannot accommodate to two environmental schemes rather than one (and this carries further implications that the home environment of a young child is in an undefined sense constant), secondly, that because of the child's attachment to his mother he can only function normally in her presence. Neither premise is true.
>
> The view that young children require constant mothering by the child's own mother or by a single mother substitute is of more than academic interest. It *provides the ideological (as opposed to the economic) basis both for the discouragement of day care services*, and for the current enthusiasm for the expansion of child-minding services rather than nursery services for those young children who simply cannot stay at home all day with their mother.[22]

Moreover, because the issue of day care for pre-school children is discussed predominantly in relation to mothers' employment, the use of such an ideological justification for restricting day care facilities serves to confirm the view that women's attachment to the labour market is, and should be, of secondary importance only.

As the Plowden committee, investigating the primary school system, stated in 1967, 'The extent to which mothers of young children should be encouraged by the provision of full-time nursery places to go out to work raises a question of principle'.[23] What is the principle? It is not that the needs of children must always take priority, although those who believe that day care outside the family is harmful to the child often present it as if this were so. For example the Plowden committee acknowledges that some mothers for 'exceptionally good reasons' might need full-time nursery places for their children although on the basis of its evidence the committee felt it generally undesirable, except to prevent a greater evil, to separate mother and child for a whole day.[24] These exceptionally good reasons included the necessity for the mother to make a financial contribution to the family income and the needs of the government's economic policy to employ women, as well as the importance of providing a child with an alternative to an inadequate home and poor parenting. However, the committee also stated that full-time day care was undesirable 'even for children who might tolerate separation *without* harm'. In other words it seems to be saying that a mother's place is in the home unless *economic* priorities require otherwise. However, this is not the full story.

During the Second World War, the economy required women, including women with young children, to participate fully in the labour market. The attitude towards day care services changed dramatically, and day nurseries were provided on a more extensive basis than ever before or since. Commenting on this change in government policy, Ferguson and Fitzgerald later wrote:

> Without this emphasis on child care would any government have embarked on a campaign – such a successful campaign – to encourage married women to work? Nurseries were partly an expression of the *right* of mothers willing to contribute to the war effort, to this sort of service ... The nursery ... was a contribution toward the feeling of *mutual responsibility* between government and the family.[25]

There were other policies too which helped women to combine paid work with their domestic responsibilities, for example the rapid development of the school meals service, factory canteen meals and civic restaurants. Government nutrition and food experts even went so far as to state publicly that the production of individual meals by individual housewives was wasteful both in economic and nutritional terms.[26]

As soon as the war was over, however, the propaganda switched to emphasizing the importance of 'the home' once again. The feeling of 'mutual responsibility' for child care dwindled rapidly and women were no longer considered to have the right to paid work. As a group of Oxford economists wrote in 1947, 'Custom also will fix a reasonably clear line of demarcation between those who may be regarded as employable and those (especially married women with children) who may be considered for practical purposes outside the field of paid employment'.[27]

This can partly be explained by the government's concern in the post-war period about its ability to maintain full employment, meaning a job for nearly every man – and so women were expected to make way for men returning from the armed forces.

In the event many married women did continue to participate in the labour market, but it should be remembered that the fifties were a time when the government made bigger efforts to recruit immigrant labour from the Commonwealth than to recruit married women, even those with qualifications. The other factor at work here may be men's concern not only that their wives are at home to look after their children but that they are available to provide domestic services for them.[28] Is it not more than a coincidence that the period in Britain when the state made the biggest deliberate attempts to relieve women of some of their responsibilities for caring for their children was a time when many men were absent from their homes? (It was estimated that by 1944 two-and-a-half million men in the armed forces were separated from their wives.) There is therefore a complex interaction between economic priorities and the wish of men to preserve the benefits which accrue to them from the traditional division of labour within the home.

Further evidence that it is easier to maintain this division of labour if women have the responsibility for looking after children *at home* can be seen from the Hungarian experience of the child care grant which was introduced in 1967. It is available for mothers who stay at home to care for their children until the age of three. The grants are generous and by 1973 78 per cent of mothers entitled to claim the grant were doing so.[29] However, there are some unfavourable consequences for women. There has been a growing reluctance of employers to take a young married woman for a qualified or responsible job (employers are obliged to keep the women's job open for her or to offer her a similar one). In addition Zsuza Ferge writes that research 'revealed that a significant proportion of mothers on grant claimed that their husbands did less housework than before the grant was consented ... though the amount of work obviously increased. *Thus the increased opportunity for the wife to fulfil the mother's function turns into an obligation to play the housewife role in full*'.

In Hungary therefore it is acknowledged that the grant cannot altogether replace the nurseries and the emphasis is shifting from discussion of a *mother's* wage to that of a *parent's* wage which would enable fathers to take a bigger share in the responsibility for children. (A father can already claim the grant if his wife is ill or absent.) This means that the responsibilities of child care are beginning to be discussed in relation to men's as well as women's employment patterns.

This has yet to happen in Britain. Much research has been done on the impact of the mother's employment on the development of children, but the effect of the nature of the father's occupation on family life has been largely neglected.[30] Those who are concerned about the effects of mothers' paid employment outside the home on the development of children would do well to examine the families of men whose jobs require them to work 'unsocial hours' or to be frequently absent from home or to be geographically mobile. An extreme example is the life of the families of men in the army.

In 1974 half of all men in the army were married and between them they had approximately 157,000 children. Roughly a third of the children were under five years, a third were of primary school age and the remainder were of secondary school age or over. The amount of mobility and separation experienced by these families was considerable. For example nearly a third of the families of soldiers and junior officers had moved at least four times in the previous five years. As a result two-thirds of secondary school children in the families of the senior ranks had been to at least six schools and nearly one in six had been to nine or more different schools. On average for all families except those of senior officers the husband had been absent for a total of three to four months out of the previous twelve. One in four soldiers and one in five junior officers had been separated from their wives for at least six out of the previous twelve months. This separation did not take place in a single block of time: there could be many distinct periods of separation of varying duration ranging from a four months' unaccompanied tour in Northern Ireland to two or three weeks' training. Altogether over a third had experienced six, seven or eight periods of separation in the previous two years and a further two-fifths had had nine or more periods of separation.

This combination of mobility and separation called 'turbulence' could occur at crucial times particularly for the young married soldier. In the first year of marriage a junior rank soldier had experienced an average of twenty weeks' separation from his wife and between one-quarter and a third had been absent during their wife's confinement.[31] Not surprisingly the wives, particularly of the young soldiers, experienced considerable loneliness and stress. Because the demands of army service gave them little opportunity to settle into a stable civilian community they were divorced from much of the resources and support to which civilians have access. Nevertheless their problems are only just beginning to be acknowledged by the army (not, however, to the extent of its agreeing to establish a family welfare service, as recommended by a recent committee of inquiry). It is assumed that, as long as the men are well provided for, the welfare of their families is assured.

It is to be hoped that this is an extreme example of the disruptive effects that a father's occupation can have on family life. Meanwhile most research studies measure a father's occupation in terms of the status or the economic resources which it brings to the family rather than in terms of how the nature of the job structures the daily lives of other members of the family and affects the emotional and intellectual development of the children. Conversely studies of mothers' employment tend to underplay the resulting financial contribution made to the family income and to emphasize the impact on children of their mothers' outside interests and absence from the home.

[...]

The Impact of Domestic Work on Men's and Women's Participation in the Labour Market

The above analysis of a few social policies shows that they are indeed based on consistent assumptions about the division of unpaid labour in the home and the respective priorities which men and women should accord to participating in the labour market. That these assumptions do not always have to be made explicit in the legislation or administrative rules suggests that we are looking at the outcome of a powerful set of ideologies concerning the family and that state social policies are one of the means by which these ideologies are sustained. The question now to be answered is who benefits from the maintenance of this pattern of dependencies and responsibilities within the family? In order to explore the economic benefits I shall examine the impact of women's domestic responsibilities on their opportunities and activities in the labour market. It would, however, be wrong to assume that the ideologies are solely a product of a capitalist economic system. The subordination of women is a phenomenon which predates the rise of capitalism in this country, and, although we need to know far more about how and why their subordination has been maintained although transformed as capitalism developed, we should also consider ways in which patriarchal values have interacted and even conflicted with economic priorities.

The amount of time taken up by women's domestic duties is one of the most important constraints on their daily lives. Hannah Mitchell, a working-class suffragette, described this graphically in her autobiography:

> The tyranny of meals is the worst snag in the housewife's lot. Her life is bounded in the north by breakfast, south by dinner, east by tea and in the west by supper, and the most sympathetic man can never understand that meals do not come up through the tablecloth but have to be planned, bought and cooked.[32]

But meals are only one of the many regular domestic tasks for which women are responsible. The physical care of young children requires attention at frequent intervals. Indeed the attendance allowance paid to those who are so ill that someone is needed to be present with them for a substantial part of the day or night (or both) is not available for children under the age of two years on the grounds that they all need constant attention. School-aged children do not require an adult's presence in the home to the same extent as a younger brother or sister but their mother's daily routine will have to become geared to the school day, which is shorter than a normal working day. In any case schools are not open for all fifty-two weeks of the year. The care of a sick or elderly person will demand differing amounts of attention spaced at varying intervals depending on the degree of their infirmity and their capacity for self-care. The domestic routine of all married women is likely to be affected to some extent by their husbands' working hours. In other words a woman's daily activities have to be timed to fit the needs of other members of the family. It is true that a man's paid employment fixes his hours too, but – with the reduction in the length of the working day which has taken place over the past hundred years – to a lesser extent, as William Beveridge noted thirty years ago · 'The housewife's job with a large family is frankly impossible and will remain so, unless some of what has now to be done separately in every home – washing all clothes, cooking every meal, being in charge of every child every moment when it is not in school – can be done communally outside the home'.[33] He therefore advocated amongst other services day and night nurseries and he went on to say, 'Nothing short of a revolution in housing would give to the working housewife the equivalent to the two hours of additional leisure a day on five days a week that has come to the wage earner in the past 70 years . . . '.[34] In these proposals Beveridge was trying to remedy what he called 'the defective appreciation of the housewife as an unpaid worker'. Unfortunately his assumptions about the economic dependency of married women led him to disregard the importance of their financial contribution to the family. He therefore helped to perpetuate a social security system which failed to meet the needs of many women.

It is often argued that the amount of time a woman need spend on her household tasks has been considerably reduced and that therefore she has more leisure or greater opportunities to take paid employment. There are two reasons put forward – technology has rendered domestic chores less labour intensive,[35] and husbands help in the home far more than used to be the case. On closer examination, however, this argument is not as soundly based as it first appears to be.

It is true that the development of a variety of household appliances has removed some of the drudgery from many domestic tasks, but this does not necessarily mean that women have to spend less time on their domestic responsibilities. First, not all households have labour-saving appliances. *The General Household Survey* shows that nearly three-quarters of households with economically active heads of households have a washing machine, although among the unskilled and semi-skilled the proportion is less than two-thirds.[36] Audrey Hunt found that among elderly recipients of a home help half had a vacuum cleaner, a fifth had a washing machine and nearly a quarter had no hot water supply.[37] Their housework could still be very hard work. The families most likely to have all the labour-saving devices are those which would have had domestic servants fifty years ago – instead of supervising people they now operate machines. Secondly, time-budget studies show that the total time women spend on their domestic tasks has declined very little in the last half-century. Full-time housewives living in urban areas still spend an average fifty-three hours a week.[38] What has changed is the way in which their time is distributed among the various tasks. The proportion of time spent on child care has increased and the time spent on cooking and cleaning has decreased. Data from the United States show that the more educated a mother is the more time she spends on child care.[39]

There is evidence that husbands help in the home more than they used to but the data need careful interpretation. Peter Willmott's and Michael Young's study, *The Symmetrical Family*, was based on couples aged between thirty and fifty, so their sample underrepresented those with very young children as well as those with sick or elderly dependants. We have already seen that the care of the sick, the young and the old falls disproportionately on women in the family. Willmott and Young also excluded some activities which require *regular* time and attention. For example they state that 'Such things not recorded as work might actually be so for housewives. A meal for example, is not counted as work although some mothers would think that feeding young children was'.[40] More comprehensive time-budget studies show, with remarkable consistency between countries, that women spend substantially more time on housework than men.[41]

Moreover a careful analysis of the tasks which men do in the home suggests that they do not substitute for their wife's time very much. Thus a study conducted in 1967 in the United States showed that in couples in which men helped with the physical care of the children the wife spent even *more* time herself on this task. If they helped with the preparation of meals the amount of the wife's time saved was only half that spent by the husband. In any case women spent ten times as much time as their husbands on meal preparation and the physical care of children.[42] Men helped more in activities relating to the children's social and educational development – activities which women also preferred but of which they did proportionately less. All these figures are averages, and, while some men do more, many do less. Audrey Hunt's study of women's employment in 1965 found that nearly a third of men gave their wives no help in the home. Altogether she found that a fifth of wives in paid employment had no help at all from other members of the household and had no paid help either.[43]

Women then are much more likely than men to be responsible for the routine domestic tasks in the home. It is therefore not surprising to find that 84 per cent of the four-and-a-quarter million part-time employees in 1975 were women, most of them married. In 1965 Audrey Hunt found that two-fifths of those working part time said that this was a consequence of having children to look after. One in six gave their responsibility for caring for their husbands as a reason.[44] The hours worked by those with children were often geared to the school day – a third of those working part time only did so during school hours and a further 7 per cent worked only evenings, early mornings or nights. 13 per cent gave up paid work during school holidays. Women with very young children were more likely to do paid work in their own homes – 16 per cent of working women with children under two years old did home work compared with 8 per cent of those with school-aged children.[45] Altogether a fifth of women working part time did so because they had the responsibility of an elderly or infirm person who was not necessarily living in the same household. Women responsible for an old person who was bedfast were the least likely to have paid employment at all.[46] So, although in some respects the national data on women's employment are incomplete and out of date, it is clear that a woman's availability for work is considerably constrained by her domestic circumstances.

From the employers' point of view this can be an advantage. Part-time employees have fewer rights than full-time employees (the *Employment Protection Act* has only recently been extended to those working sixteen or more hours a week). They therefore form a more flexible part of the labour force. Audrey Hunt's study of management attitudes towards women workers showed that one of the main advantages of part-time workers was that 'You can have them when you need them'.[47] They were also useful for jobs which did not require a full-time worker. In addition to greater flexibility they may also be cheaper. Married women with low earnings (less than £15 a week in 1977) will be counted as 'non-employable' and therefore no national insurance contribution need be paid. They are also less likely to have rights to sick pay or pensions from their employers. Promotion prospects are very limited – in only 17 per cent of the establishments included in Audrey Hunt's study did part-time workers have opportunities for promotion. Employers were sympathetic to women who needed time off to care for sick children and a fifth had a formal policy on the matter. However, less than 3 per cent granted *paid* leave for this reason.[48] In the face of this evidence it would be wrong to conclude that opportunities for part-time employment have grown out of a concern to enable women to combine paid employment with their domestic responsibilities.[49]

Conclusions

What needs to be understood is the complex interaction between the factors which structure the supply of particular sorts of jobs and those which determine the supply of certain types of labour. It is clear that many women and the minority of men with sole responsibility for the *care* of dependent children or adults[50] exchange some flexibility in working hours for considerably lower pay and prospects except when demand for their labour is *exceptionally* high, as it was during the Second World War.

There are other factors relating to a woman's primary commitment to her family which put her at a disadvantage in the labour market. First, she must find employment near home and, secondly, she is less likely than her husband to move in order to enhance her employment opportunities. Research in the United States has shown that, whereas a quarter of unemployed women mentioned their husband's job as a reason for not wanting to leave the area in which they were currently living, only 3 per cent of unemployed men gave their wife's job as a reason for wanting to stay. Looking at the employment prospects of those who had moved, the study concluded, 'For male workers inter-State mobility had the effect of decreasing the unemployment rate. However geographic mobility, especially long distance, decidedly worsens the unemployment situation for women, indicating that such migration was governed by factors other than personal economic opportunity'.[51]

In Britain *The General Household Survey* showed that in 1974 60 per cent of women who were out of the labour market gave domestic circumstances or pregnancy as a reason for leaving their last job.[52] When women do return after a break in employment they are often treated as new entrants and paid accordingly. Marriage and motherhood effectively 'deskill' women. Moreover in times of economic recession if one has left employment it becomes increasingly difficult to re-enter it. Unfortunately the official unemployment statistics in this country grossly underestimate the number of unemployed women because the figures are based on the number registering for work. Married women are less inclined to register because the majority are neither entitled to unemployment benefit, having 'opted out' of the national insurance scheme, nor able to claim supplementary benefit. As this 'option' is gradually withdrawn women's unemployment will become more visible. In the United States, where unemployment statistics are collected on an entirely different basis, the data show not only that women have higher rates of unemployment than men but that the unemployment situation of women has worsened over time.[53] It is not known whether this is the situation in Britain because the concept of the male bread-winner which is still deeply embedded in our social security system conveniently obscures the true dimensions of female unemployment, which in any case is regarded as a less important problem.

The perpetuation of an ideology which accords to women the primary responsibility for caring for other members of their family but at the same time takes for granted and therefore undervalues the time, work and skill which this involves ensures that there is always a supply of workers who are prepared to offer their labour on terms which are very favourable to employers. For this reason there have been periods when, in certain sectors of the economy at least, women have been used to undercut male wage rates or to drive some men out of the labour market altogether. Male trade unionists have understandably resisted such attempts on the part of employers, and one strategy they adopted was to restrict the sphere of women's employment. The Trades Union Congress told the Royal Commission on Equal Pay in 1944 that 'The trade unions have been compelled not only to uphold *but to promote*, a clear demarcation between men's and women's work – where such demarcation was possible – in order to protect the men's and thus indirectly women's rate of pay'.[54]

Thus the largely sex-segregated labour market observed in this country and many others is the result of the activities of organized labour as well as of changes in the technical means of production and the overall demand for labour. It should be noted that by behaving in this way men are acting in their own interests not only as workers but also as husbands and fathers who wish to retain as much as possible of the woman's labour in the home. Paradoxically the more men emphasize the importance of their own employment and their own wages, which must be higher than women's because unlike women they have families to support, the more they are bolstering up an ideology which says that men have a *duty* to take paid employment. However, there never has been a time in Britain when all, or even most, men have been able to earn wages high enough a support a family unaided. Consequently the reality for many women is that they have always had to combine paid employment with their domestic tasks. Most men do not have this obligation, and that is one of the advantages that marriage has for men. Moreover it is an advantage which is not exclusive to capitalist economies. Lenin, nearly fifty years ago, in a letter to Clara Zetkin, wrote that 'Very few husbands, not even the proletarians, think of how much they could lighten the burden and worries of their wives or relieve them entirely, if they lent a hand in their "women's work". But no, that would go against the "privilege and dignity" of the husband. He demands to have his rest and comfort'.[55]

The particular assumptions about the division of responsibilities between the sexes and the generations in the family which have been described in this paper therefore have an important impact both on the interests of the economically powerful and on those of individual men. These interests are not always entirely coincident. The state *does* intervene in the family, and it is not a question of whether or not to have family policies but of how explicit the values on which they are based are to be made. The fact that certain values favouring the interests of men rather than women have been embodied in a variety of social policies over a long period of time, both formally in the legislation and by the way in which they are allocated or used, indicates that social policies are a very important means by which these values, and hence major inequalities between the sexes, are maintained.

Notes and References

1 House of Lords Debates, Vol. 371, Col. 1, p. 260.
2 MARSHALL, A. (1901) *Elements of Economics of Industry*, third edition, London, Macmillan.
3 OPCS, 1971 *Census*, London, HMSO, 1971 – household composition tables: 10 per cent sample, Table 50.
4 HAMILL, L. (1977) *Wives as Sole and Joint Breadwinners*, Unpublished paper given to the Social Science Research Council Social Security Workshop.
5 Quoted from the Department of the Environment's second Inner Area study in WILLMOTT, P. 'The Role of the Family', in BUXTON, M. and CRAVEN, E. (1976) *The Uncertain Future*, London, Centre for Studies in Social Policy, p. 53.
6 SUPPLEMENTARY BENEFITS COMMISSION (SBC), (1977) *Annual Report 1976*, Cmnd. 6910, London, HMSO, p. 46.
7 See MARTIN, J. and MORGAN, D. (1975) *Prolonged Sickness and the Return to Work*, London, OPCS, HMSO.
8 See LAND, H. (1975) 'The Myth of the Male Breadwinner', *New Society*, 29:2, pp. 71–3.
9 ORWELL, G. (1937) *The Road to Wigan Pier*, Harmondsworth, Penguin Books, p. 72.
10 Departmental Committee on Sickness Benefit Claims under the Insurance Act, appointed in September 1913.
11 SICKNESS BENEFIT CLAIMS COMMITTEE, (1914) *Report and Minutes of Evidence*, Cd. 7688, Vol. 1, London, HMSO.
12 *Ibid.*, Vol. 3, p. 311.
13 *Ibid.*, Vol. 2, p. 435.
14 *Ibid.*, Vol. 1, p. 2.
15 *Medical Evidence for Social Security Purposes*, (1976) London, DHSS, p. 3.
16 Personal communication from Stanley Orme, Minister of Social Security, to Jo Tunnard, 26 October 1977.
17 Royal Commission on the Taxation of Profits and Incomes 1951–55, (1953) *Evidence*, Vol. 4, London, HMSO, p. 55.
18 *Ibid.*, Vol. 3, p. 18.
19 House of Commons Debates, Vol. 621, Col. 1, p. 558.
20 PLOWDEN, B. (1976) 'Low Cost Day Care Facilities and the Part Which is Being and Can be Played by Voluntary Organisations', in *Low Cost Day Provision for the Under-Fives*, London, DHSS, p. 17.
21 Moss, P. (1976) 'The Current Situation', in FONDA, N. and Moss, P. (Eds.) *Mothers in Employment*, London, Institute of Education, p. 24.
22 TIZARD, J. 'Effects of Day Care on Young Children', in FONDA, N. and Moss, P. *op. cit.*, p. 67 (my italics).
23 *Children and their Primary Schools*, (Plowden Report) (1965), Central Advisory Council for Education, Vol. 1, London, HMSO, p. 127.
24 *Ibid.*
25 FERGUSON, S. and FITZGERALD, K. (1954) *Studies in the Social Services*, London, HMSO, p. 211 (my italics).
26 ROYAL INSTITUTE OF GREAT BRITAIN, (1940) *The Nation's Larder*, London, George Bell and Sons, p. 95. This was a series of lectures given at the Royal Institute in the summer of 1940. Contributors included Lord Woolton, Minister of Food, John Boyd-Orr and Professor Mottram.
27 WORSWICK, P. (1947) 'The Stability and Flexibility of Full Employment', in BALOGH, T. (Ed.) *Economics of Full Employment*, Oxford, Basil Blackwell, p. 60.
28 I am indebted to Diana Barker for first pointing this out to me.
29 FERGE, Z. (April 1976) 'The Relation Between Paid and Unpaid Working Women', *Labor and Society*, p. 46.
30 There have been a few recent studies. See for example COHEN, G. (1975) *Absentee Husbands in Spiralist Families*, Civil Service College, London, mimeograph.
31 Army Welfare Inquiry Committee Report, (1976) Appendix C, London, HMSO.
32 MITCHELL, H. (1977) *The Hard Way Up*, London, Virago, p. 113.
33 BEVERIDGE, W. (1947) *Voluntary Action*, London, Allen and Unwin, p. 264.
34 *Ibid.*, p. 275.
35 See for example DEPARTMENT OF EMPLOYMENT, (1974) *Gazette*, January, p. 9.
36 OPCS, (1977) *The General Household Survey*, London, HMSO, p. 84.
37 HUNT, A. (1968) *The Home Help Service in England and Wales*, A Survey of women's employment,

Government Social Survey (S.S. 379), March, p. 191.

38 LEIBOWITZ, A. (1975) 'Women's Work in the Home', in LLOYD, C. (Ed.) *Sex Discrimination and the Division of Labour*, New York, Columbia University Press, p. 223.

39 *Ibid.*, p. 230.

40 WILLMOTT, P. and YOUNG, M. (1973) *The Symmetrical Family*, London, Routledge and Kegan Paul, p. 112.

41 BOULDING, E. (1976) 'Familial Constraints on Women's Work Roles', in BLAXALL, M. and REAGAN, B. *Women and the Workplace*, Chicago, University of Chicago Press, p. 112.

42 LEIBOWITZ, A. (1975) *op. cit.*, p. 239.

43 HUNT, A. (1968) *A Survey of Women's Employment*, Vol. 2, p. 205 (see note 37).

44 *Ibid.*, p. 52.

45 *Ibid.*, p. 164.

46 *Ibid.*, p. 180.

47 HUNT, A. (1975) *Management Attitudes and Practices Towards Women at Work*, OPCS, London, HMSO, p. 14.

48 *Ibid.*

49 DEPARTMENT OF EMPLOYMENT, *op. cit.*, p. 9.

50 See for example WILDING, P. and GEORGE, V. (1970) *Motherless Families*, London, Routledge and Kegan Paul.

51 NEIMI, B. (1975) 'Geographic Immobility and Labour Force Mobility: A Study of Female Labour Force Unemployment', in LLOYD, *op. cit.*, p. 76.

52 OPCS, (1973) *The General Household Survey*, p. 119.

53 NEIMI, B. (1975) *op. cit.*, p. 86.

54 *Report of the Royal Commission on Equal Pay*, 1944, Cmd. 6937, London, HMSO, p. 191 (my italics).

55 Quoted in SCOTT, H. (1976) *Women and Socialism: Experiences from Eastern Europe*, London, Allison and Busby, p. 199.

16 In Loco Parentis: *A Relationship Between Parent, State and Child*

Jenny Shaw

Abstract

For that the name of Parents being a most sweet and loving name men might thereby be allured the rather to the duties they owe; whether they should be duties that are to be performed to them, or which they should perform to their Inferioures.

For that at the first, in the beginning of the world, Parents were also Magistrates, Pastours and School masters.

Archbishop Ussher (1645)[1] in explaining why all superiors were called parents called upon the idea of patriarchal authority. This paper considers the social implications of the same philosophy as it is represented by the practice of education authorities standing *in loco parentis* to their pupils.

Introduction

A classical education is supposed to be particularly good for training scholars to think precisely, yet Latin terms are most usually inserted into English discourse just when the subject is getting dangerously ambiguous and confused. The case of the phrase *in loco parentis* is no exception and, despite its quasi-legal tone, the term is deceptive. It does not refer to a set of clearly-defined rights and duties which parents have and may, on occasion, transfer to some other responsible adult thereby empowering that person to take charge of their child. Rather it imparts a spurious air of legitimacy to some adult or agency in a struggle to establish and maintain power and authority, usually over the child but quite often over the natural parent or substitute.

Parents are not, and cannot be, ever present with their offspring, yet not everyone who ever looks after a child is defined as being *in loco parentis,* nor are the many adults and older children, who quite voluntarily take a caring, overseeing, stance

Source: Journal of Moral Education, (1977), Vol. 6, No. 3, pp. 181–90.

towards younger children, in general thought to be quasi-parents when they see a strange child safely across the road. Partly this is a question of specificity – children as a group appeal to an adult's general assumption of greater wisdom, confidence and experience – and many adults discharge what may be felt as a general obligation to look after children. Such an obligation is probably vested in the status of an adult and has little to do with the specific role and duties of a parent and even less to do with the particular child who receives the care. However, when the idea of *in loco parentis* is employed it is always in the context of a specific child or class of children and, moreover, it is likely that punishment as much as care will be received by the child.[2]

This last point is loosely related to another general feature of the term and its occasion. Affection is not an essential or even very significant part of the posited relationship, as it is in the case of many other instances of assumed or surrogate kinship. Anthropologists sometimes refer to 'fictive' kin when for social, and often personal, reasons someone acquires the honour and status of a kinsman. In such circumstances kindnesses, liking and, perhaps, mutual choice precede any public recognition of the relationship. However, emotions are not easily controlled and psychoanalytically oriented researchers are not alone in pointing out the difficulties that both individuals and organizations encounter if they fail to keep some check on the feelings that members have towards each other.[3] During the period when apprenticeship and domestic service (i.e. the practice of sending children to work as servants in other households than their own) was common for children over the age of 8–9, there was a conscious acknowledgement of the functional utility of such an arrangement. Much more labour could be extracted from a child servant if the relationship was not complicated by love, sympathy and identification.[4] The link between this and other examples of the custom *in loco parentis* is that the parental 'role' is both attenuated and only partially reassigned. Hence the question of which aspects are transferred, and whether they are handed over wholly or only in part, becomes central.

The range of social situations which occasion the use of the term *in loco parentis* is wide and has varied over time. Since the age of majority has been lowered, universities no longer vex themselves over the issue but local education authorities, social service departments, therapists, charities and insurance companies do. Probably the most important historical antecedent for this particular type of social relationship was the system of apprenticeship and, although it is not my concern to discuss contemporary variants, much of the ethical system informing that institution is critical for understanding its derivatives.[5] The process of transferring rights in and over children and the consequent sharing of responsibility is neither as clear nor as simple as it might seem. It is often quite hard to determine *who* actually is *in loco parentis*. Furthermore, a close study of the custom poses two essential questions. The first concerns what is done or transmitted through the practice and to whom. The second concerns how this is achieved.

Through examining some of the contexts in which the term *in loco parentis* is used I hope to illustrate procedures which are probably present on a much larger scale. These procedures are important because they facilitate transfers at a number of levels. Quite simply, there are transfers of a social and political kind in that parents lose real control over their children. They are deemed to delegate to the school the authority to act in their stead, which includes the right physically to assault the child if the circumstances are viewed as 'reasonable'. They lose the opportunity of controlling other aspects of their child's life such as what books he or she reads and maybe what clothes he or she is allowed to wear. At another level there is a transfer of quite a different kind, that is, a mass cognitive or ideological transformation. Intuitively, at least, it seems that schools are important in shaping how people come to see the world and their relationships within it and to share that view with others. Whilst I make no claim that this short essay can contribute much to the study of schools as agencies of ideological transmission, it might underline the point that ideologies are not just belief systems but also practices, and that schools underpin their intellectual and ideological activities with a set of very real non-ideational mechanisms.

The Organization of Responsibility

The immediate impulse behind this paper occurred whilst researching into the causes and correlates of children's absences from school. This research, which was exploratory, took the form of a case study of two schools within the same local education authority and is based on a series of interviews with pupils, staff and education welfare officers. Quite early on in the study I came to realize that, despite the apparent clarity of a situation where education up to the age of sixteen is compulsory, a striking feature was the considerable uncertainty which prevailed over whose responsibility it was to see that a child actually went to school.

The 1944 Education Act lays responsibility fairly and squarely on the shoulders of parents to see that their children receive efficient and full-time education suitable to their age and ability, but it qualifies this by permitting parents the right of exercising choice over the sort of education that their child receives. This choice is not unlimited, as it has to be 'compatible with the provision of efficient instruction and training and the avoidance of unreasonable public expenditure', but equally clearly the area of choice is not confined to issues of religious denomination nor just to the initial choice of a school. Besides the parent's duty the local authority has a corresponding obligation to provide suitable educational facilities which cater for the exercise of parents' rights; but, in practice, they assume that the majority of parents are content to accept whatever schools are offered to them. In return for the right of choosing their child's education, in principle, parents have a duty to ensure that child's attendance at the chosen school. This is part of the fiction that a 'contract to educate' a child is entered into between the state and its parents.

Unlike many other 'social contract' theories, the origins of such a contract are not obscured in mythological pre-history. Nevertheless, accounts of original contracts are not in themselves usually sufficient to justify current orderings and all such theories have to cope with the problem of explaining their capacity to exact continuing respect. An educational version would not avoid such problems. Indeed, although I am not primarily concerned to provide one, an historical account would note the high degree of unwillingness to enter into any such contract on the part of both the agents of the state and the parents.[6] Recognition of this reluctance is presumably evidenced by the setting up of specialized agencies and personnel to supervise attendance. Whatever current thinking lies behind the establishment of today's Educational Welfare Service, there can be no doubts that their predecessors, the 'special visitors' and 'attendance officers' of the old school boards, were seen as necessary adjuncts to the provision of compulsory state education. Experience swiftly showed that all parents did not eagerly take on that duty which was their part of the 'contract to educate'.

In the research mentioned above I found an amazing lack of agreement between all those who might be supposed to have some professional interest in the matter of attendance. Teachers tended to see the responsibility as belonging to the parents; parents, for their part, thought that teachers ought to be able to retain the interest of children if children were forced to attend school. Educational welfare officers whose paid job it is to see that children attend school might reasonably be expected to be, and be seen as, central to the issue, but in fact parents and schools generally seemed to treat them as peripheral; only the police had an axe to grind, in that they felt that they (the police) had to 'do more than their *share*' of taking children to court. The police considered that the education welfare officers waited until a child could be taken to court for some other offence, and then the matter of the child's attendance could be brought up virtually as any other business, thus making the police into the 'hard' men and letting the education welfare service off the 'nastier' part of their job. The educational welfare officers viewed the school and teachers as 'appalling'. The circle of blame is thus completed, with no one ever mentioning the child as having any responsibility.

One initial, but possibly instructive, mistake that I made in trying to trace these lines of responsibility was to confuse responsibility for the fact or 'cause' of the non-attendance with responsibility for the consequences of the absences once they had occurred. This was most visible over the issue of punishment, which I suggest is central to the process of transferring responsibility. Who, if anyone, is failing in their duties and who should be punished? In particular, do substitute parents such as local authorities ever get taken to court for failing to see that a child in their care goes to school in the same way that a natural parent does?

This raises a wider issue which is whether, when parental rights and duties are transferred (with varying degrees of state backing), a rather complex and *prescriptive* model of parent/child relationships is employed. In the case of natural parents the relationships are circumscribed by the state in the most minimal way by a set of *proscriptive* rules which only apply to extremes; i.e. parents can do most things short of physical harm. In fact probably two models of parenthood are operating, the good parent and the bad parent. One can be seen through the limits placed on natural parents and the other through the requirements placed on surrogate parents. This is not to imply that a higher standard of parental behaviour is demanded of surrogate parents than of natural parents; if local authorities are not treated as harshly as natural parents this cannot be so. However, it is often noted that a particular type and style of bringing up children is preferred, and this is especially visible through the processes of arranging adoption. The point is that multiple models of parental behaviour operate and that when trying to unravel what is meant by acting in the place of a parent we need to know which model is being invoked, reinforced and why. What are these models and from where do they come? In a paper comparing various forms of control and participation in education, Miriam David suggests and discusses a typology based on three ways of viewing the state's relationship with parents through the schooling of their children. She argues that the state can supplement, regulate or replace parental rights (or parents) and that in each case a particular family form is assumed.[7]

I am not so sure what that particular family form is. In looking for examples of the use of the term *in loco parentis* I found it hard to decide whether the notion of the parents being replaced (albeit temporarily) was grounded at all in any actual set of parents, middle or working class. In some ways the heavy paternalism of educational provision betrays the early assumption that state education was for those who would not otherwise provide an education for their children, i.e. the working classes. In other respects, namely the increasing consolidation of the system and its emphasis on selection, it bears the hallmark of generations of middle class parents who redirected the system according to their own needs and interests. Thus I came to favour the view that the implied parental model might in itself be almost classless, although use of such a model might well suit a particular class's interests. An ideal parent or ideal-type of parenthood is a powerful device and, as all sociologists know, exists to control more than just the imaginations of social scientists.

In the introduction to his second edition Barrell[8] notes that a new element was introduced to the doctrine of a *careful parent* by a then recent judgment. This placed a higher duty of care on the school than was expected in the home when the judge had ruled that 'the test of a reasonably prudent parent must be applied not in relation to the parent in the home but the parent applying his mind to school life'. The crux of the issue as seen by this author revolves around what can possibly be meant when a teacher is enjoined to act like a reasonable parent. His book is aimed at reassuring teachers, heads and local education authorities about the risks of litigation under various circumstances, and hence stresses the caution necessary when one's adversary is in effect an insurance company. Accordingly the duty of a schoolmaster appears to have been defined in 1893 by Mr. Justice Cave: 'The schoolmaster is bound to take such care of his boys as a careful father would take of his boys'. In most of the cases subsequently discussed the issue of carefulness or reasonableness depended on the age of the child and the activity taking place, a higher degree of supervision being required during instruction than during play. In several cases children who suffered quite severe injury were not awarded damages, on the ground 'that you would otherwise have to consider whether or not to expect a headmaster to show such an excessive degree of care that boys never get into mischief?' The distinction is not always easy to follow, and in particular I have a suspicion that what counts as instruction depends on gender. In 1911 a fourteen-year-old girl was asked to stoke the fire in the staffroom. Her pinafore caught light, and during the action brought against the teacher and the authority the judge awarded against the teacher initially but not the authority. After two appeals the teacher succeeded in getting the authority to share the 'blame', on the grounds that she had acted within the scope of her employment in asking the girl to perform the domestic task, for the 'Education Acts are designed to provide for education in its truest and widest sense. Such education includes the inculcation of habits of order, obedience and courtesy; such habits are taught by giving orders and if such orders are reasonable and proper under the circumstances . . . it would be extravagant to say that a teacher had no business to ask a child to perform small acts of courtesy for her or for others such as to fetch her pocket handkerchief from upstairs and the like'. More recently (1959) in Manchester another fourteen-year-old girl carried a pot of scalding hot tea to the staffroom along an awkward corridor and collided with another child coming out of a classroom. This time the court maintained that 'this was not a dangerous operation. Older girls had lessons in domestic science and carried out certain duties partly in furtherance of their duties and partly for staff convenience. This was part of their general training for life. If children of 14 were to be guarded against the least physical injury gymnastics would be abandoned and cookery classes would cease'.[9]

What emerges from these and other examples where the lines of school and state authority are carefully drawn and re-drawn is a gradual encroachment by the school. In cases where the school's right to discipline a child for misbehaviour outside the school gates has been challenged all have found in favour of the teacher for administering punishment. Further illustration of this process can be found by way of the regulation which requires that the local education authority make provision for regular medical and dental inspections and that anyone refusing to submit to the inspection (but not the recommended treatment) can be fined.[10] The crunch finally comes when distinction needs to be made between cases where the child is the offender and those where the parents had exercised control over the child to prevent him from acting in accordance with the school rules. In examples of the latter Barrell recommends that the child must not be punished although 'it is possible to consider suspending him with a view to expulsion if it appears that the parents' action is so subversive of school discipline as to break the contract to educate'.[11]

In the space of this paper it is not possible to provide comprehensive discussion of parental rights and duties, or indeed any general theory of rights. I assume that at birth a child has a right to be taken by its natural mother at least, and that the state recognizes this right.[12] Clearly, though, there are occasions when even that right is not secure. (In one extraordinary instance a child born to a mother, one of whose older children had been maltreated by her then husband, was taken into care by the social services department before the mother left hospital, even though neither the mother nor the father of this child [his first] had records of child assault.[13])

Teachers, Parents and Schools: A Three-Part Invention

School is probably the first really collective situation that anyone faces and the social relationships that are possible within it are vastly different from those of the home. In its turn the school faces organizational problems in managing both the transition into it and the range of possibilities that the situation offers. One strategy employed in coping with these is selectively to play up the presumed similarities or dissimilarities of the school with the home according to the task in hand. This is done only at a general level, for detailed knowledge of the pupils' home is not usually available, but the confidence with which assumptions are made about home background, e.g. in gauging what amounts of homework will be tolerated, in time becomes a reality of its own. The really detailed and unique features of childrens' homes become insignificant, and pupils pool what they bring to school of their homes to form the school-teachers' collective image. In ways not always so subtle, this image is fed back to children so that they measure themselves and their homes against it, for, in a context where the criteria of success are still not genuinely diverse or equally valued, all points of difference are treated normatively. If it were just a matter that the home was used as a foil for the school perhaps not much harm would be done or comment be worthwhile, but there is a deeper significance. In forcing the home into the background the school is reconstructing and elaborating the patterns and distribution of power in society.

The sources of power that schools might command are not easily identified. After all, schools are not directly involved in economic production, and the case for seeing them as powerful ideological forces has still to be made convincingly. Their structural importance seems to rest directly on a monopolistic control of certificates and indirectly on the labour market within which education levels can assume a critical position. But, as Bourdieu has shown, the scope of this argument is limited largely to the production of the educational system itself.[14] For most members of the labour force educational certificates are either non-existent or irrelevant. Much more significant are the consequences of a system which stresses differentiation and hierarchy, for it is along these dimensions that a school's claim to authority rests. The secret weapon of schooling is not a capacity to award or withhold occupational advantages to the next generation, but rather selectively to hand back some of the authority the state took from parents in the first place.

The concept of a 'reasonable parent' is used as a basis for discipline in schools and includes punishment 'rights'. It implies both that parents are fairly uniform and that they have no real grounds for objecting to the state acting in their stead. The state sets standards which parents have to meet, or be punished if they fail. It is in fact the vision of J.S. Mill.[15] Duties are created, but the supposed and associated parental rights are harder to determine. This can be very serious, as in the case of the Muslim parents in Bradford who wanted only to be able to exercise their right to choose single-sex schools for their daughters.[16] Many of the parental rights presumed to exist actually are hypothetical in that it is virtually impossible for parents to exercise them; for example, when local education authorities offer only coeducational schooling.

A more central point is that such 'rights' as do exist are not 'natural' but rather are invented by the state just at the point when they are, or are likely to be, removed. Recent interest in the rights of children can create an impression that parents have unlimited rights, such that the successful establishment by children of their rights can only diminish those of their parents. However, by no means is this calculation obvious. I do not wish to argue that parents are impotent, for they do indeed have powers, and schools are intensely interested in them; that is, both in how the parents use them and in the sense that they might be taken over. In the early days of the sociology of education a predominant theme was the fate of the upwardly mobile grammar school-boy who might become 'alienated' from his working class home and family; doubts about the value of a more 'open' or egalitarian education system were disguised as fears for the parents' loss of prestige and/or respect in the eyes of their sons. Selective concern for the feelings of parents remains and can be seen in any number of handbooks for teachers in managing the notoriously tricky relationship with parents,[17] but without exception the task is presented as one of how to coax the parents into co-operation with the aims of the school. Quite apart from the apparent impossibility of imagining that parental opposition could be a strength and resource, this attitude seems to indicate a half-conscious recognition that the basis of school authority is not only derived from the parental role, but is in some danger of being revoked.[18]

Sociology abounds with case studies and empirical illustrations of how roles and role-sets are institutionalized, so that to propose a study of the construction or consolidation of power that inheres in the various roles linked by the practice of *in loco parentis* would not add greatly to sociological knowledge.[19] Rather, what is of particular interest about this transformation, i.e. of the parental role *into* the legitimacy of school authority is the significance of the original idea of parental power. State education is often referred to as being paternalistic but, more to the point, is the underlying model of patriarchy. The debate in political philosophy over the source of patriarchal authority and its relation to the legitimacy of the state centred on the issue of whether the obedience of children to their parents was based on a notion of contract and social convention or on nature. Was a child's obligation to love, honour and obey its parents to be seen as based on the parents' original care of the child (a contract) or did the demand for obedience derive from the simple fact of generation and that children were *born* into their subordinate position? In a discussion of the nature of political obligation Schochet argues that in Stuart England the limits and duties of superiors flowed from the nature of fatherhood rather than from a prior and conditional agreement. 'Patriarchalism treats status as natural and supported authority and duty without reciprocity. The contract emphasized the conventional sources of status and ultimately led to limits on authority and the reciprocity of rights and duties'. Thus it was easy to conclude that a 'consciousness which already knew and understood the family and fatherhood was extended to include the political order and magistracy. Children who previously had no conception whatever of politics were introduced to the state and told that it was identical to the household. It made no difference that the king was not one's literal and biological father; neither was his master'.[20]

Such ideas as these may be discredited and arcane as legitimations of most aspects of modern government, but they persist in shaping the state's relationship to children and their parents.

The idea of parental authority is thought of as deriving historically and essentially from the rights of fatherhood. Two examples of this can be given and, though they are somewhat stretched, they illustrate the point. The first is taken from a historical context but one which is of considerable importance for understanding the allocation and re-allocation of the parental role, namely the institution of apprenticeship. The British custom of farming out children seemed most mysterious to some commentators of the time,[21] but, as mentioned earlier, it was primarily a system whereby economic rights in minors were transferred. The rights to services, once transferred, were held by the surrogate father (master) and not jointly with his wife. In an article on apprentices in London, Smith itemizes the sort of complaints that were successfully brought against masters for ill-treatment. In the case of one young apprentice this included being made to suffer 'because the maids were in a position of authority over him, as were the daughters of masters who he charged with being haughty in their dealings with him'. The author is obviously sympathetic, for he writes 'placing young gentlemen as apprentices led to a role confusion, as did subjugating apprentices to the wives, daughters and maids of the masters.[22] A more contemporary example is drawn from family case law, where the fundamental rights of a father were seen to be inalienable despite the fact that on the break-up of the marriage custody was granted to the mother. A mother had changed her child's name without informing the father, and he successfully brought a suit against her and got his name replaced on the child. Barrell, commenting on this case, says 'if there is any power to change an infant's name it resides with the natural guardian who is the father if he is still alive. An order for the custody is all that the name implies and does not abrogate all the rights of the father'.[23] Most recent analyses of the position of children in English society have stressed the abuses that they have long suffered and have regarded the intervention of the state as an almost wholly benign process, the good fairy in fact who looks after little children.[24] Essentially, the state is seen as a neutral third party which at least stands between children and their parents to set limits to the physical abuses and economic exploitation that might otherwise take place, and at best can positively further children's interests by providing a range of welfare services and the opportunities for self advancement through education. Clearly any singular analysis of the role and advance of state administration is liable to appear simplistic and, whilst I do not want to misrepresent those authors who have studied the recent history of children and child welfare, it is hard to reconcile such a consistently liberal progressive view with even the most cursory account of the introduction of compulsory state education in the nineteenth century. The history of that period bristles with the bitterness of the conflict over advantages and disadvantages, costs and benefits of constructing a system of state education. That those in favour of compulsory state education eventually 'won' is no indication of unanimity either of all those who argued for its introduction or, at a later date, of all those who worked within and through the system set up. It is hard to believe that the benefits of the system were so self-evident that opposition just disintegrated. Indeed, there are easily available records of the substantial protest that continued for some considerable time afterwards. A good question to ask would be what has happened to that protest?

Class and the Transformation of Protest

Currently, education is a little bit like sanitation, most people (save a few of the very wealthy) are only too glad to have the state take care of it and are in no hurry to demand its return to the people. Furthermore, most articulated opposition to compulsory state education is to the form rather than the fact of its existence. Coming, in the main, from middle class parents with a liberal individualistic perspective, their aim is reform from within rather than the unilateral opposition which characterized some sectors of the working class in the earlier period. Yet discerning the subtleties of class response to the facts of compulsory state education is not at all easy.

In a recent, much-publicized, confrontation between a group of teachers in a London school and the managers of that school, the working class parents of its pupils were represented (when represented at all) as being most out of sympathy with the methods that the teachers, reported as inspired by left wing views, were using.[25] Unfortunately, straightforward comparisons either in the present or over time between the responses of middle class and working class parents to the quality and extent of their children's education are not especially helpful. True, it is quite easy to show that those who get most out of the existing educational system, the middle class, are also the most vociferous and active in demanding delivery of the goods, and those who get least are the most acquiescent. It is also easy to conclude that these differential responses are the inevitable and uncomplicated product of objectively different class positions. Part of the difficulty lies in the observation, by no means novel, that children have a politically conservative effect. It is not just that people shift their hopes for a better world onto their children's lifetime and put up with their own deprivations as though that in itself would achieve better things for those children, but the case of one's own children, who are usually felt to be rather special, illustrates the possibility of conflict between individual and group interests in a very concrete way.

But, if the question of what has happened to that element of working class opposition to state education is a reasonable one to ask, then a number of other questions follow. It becomes inadequate to assume that just because the working class get so little out of an education system that is promoted for having the apparent qualities of being free and of offering equal opportunity for all to succeed, then a wholesale rejection of the system is a highly rational response. Teachers often believe that working class parents are not interested in the education of their children and take the discontinuities between the home and the school to be evidence of indifference or even opposition. Maybe the answer to my question is that the remains of working class parents' opposition to education is now situated in the minds of teachers. If so, this is an additional dimension to the double bind situation in which all parents, but working class parents in particular, find themselves. The principle of universal compulsory education is embodied in the Universal Declaration of Human Rights[26] which declares that everyone has the right to be educated, that education shall be free, but that it shall also be compulsory. The compulsion is binding on parents and children and on governments, but whereas the onerousness experienced by the state is of essentially a financial kind, parents find that their children are taken as a sort of hostage, and, furthermore, they find that they themselves are literally on a bail for their child's good behaviour (i.e. good attendance) at a school which they have theoretically chosen but in practice have not.

Conclusion

Paradoxes such as these may not be resolved by asking whether state education relies more or less explicitly on the ancient doctrine of patriarchal authority, but such an approach at least identifies the sources of some of the contradictions. An assumption common both to patriarchalism and the modern state is that children are a kind of property. In fact this is a very tangled issue, for if children are property to whom do they belong?

Parents seem to have no doubts that children belong to them, but the view that the State's investment in them (as human capital) also confers a measure of ownership is markedly persistent; and in our culture property rights are respected almost above all others.

It is all too easy to ignore the internal divisions within the adult world and assume that in the matter of the subordination or care of children that agreement as to what is best obtains. This obscures the stresses and strains of the process euphemistically known as 'socialization', and which include a conflict for the control of the young. In the course of such a conflict appeals to legitimating ideologies are made and agencies developed. The growth and extension of the practice of being *in loco parentis* is an example.

The main aim of this paper has been to suggest that as currently used the doctrine of *in loco parentis* is highly ideological. It appears to legitimate common but controversial practices within educational institutions by appealing to an apparent consensus of how good and reasonable parents should behave. That this model of parenthood is not grounded in any empirical or actual set of parental behaviours is a central reason for its success as a doctrine and for the procedures of which it is part.

These points are, in a sense, mainly historical. In particular, my claim that many of the apparent parental rights (e.g. to have their child educated) were invented by the state at the point when it began a new programme of social control (mass compulsory education) could only really be substantiated by a careful and competent historian. I would be encouraged in these arguments if historical research confirmed my impression that there has been a gradual shrinkage in the range of people thought, formally or informally, to have quasi-parental responsibilities over children. If from the middle of the nineteenth century onwards god-parents became ciphers and neighbours minded their own business, then the way was left open for the state to define and appropriate the model of responsibility for children.

Notes and References

1 ARCHBISHOP JAMES USSHER, (1945) 'Body of Divinitie', quoted in SCHOCHET, G.J. (1969) 'Man's attitudes in Stuart England', *Historical Journal*, 12.

2 NEWELL, P. (Ed.) (1972) *A Last Resort: Corporal Punishment in Schools*, Harmondsworth, Penguin.

3 MENZIES, I. (1960) 'A case study in the functioning of social systems as a defence against anxiety', *Human Relations*, 13, May.

4 MACFARLANE, A. (1970) *The Family Life of Ralph Josselin*, Cambridge, Cambridge University Press.

5 See p. 187.

6 RUBENSTEIN, D. (1969) *School Attendance in London 1870–1904, A Social History*, Hull, University of Hull.

7 DAVID, M. Lecturer in Social Administration, University of Bristol. 'Participation in education: a Comparative and Historical Perspective on Community and Family Roles', (unpublished).

8 BARRELL, G.R. (1958) *The Teacher and The Law*, London, Methuen.

9 *Ibid.*, p. 166.

10 In 1976 the responsibility for a school medical service was transferred from the DES to the DHSS.

11 BARRELL *op. cit.*, p. 184.

12 In referring to parental rights I follow the implicit assumption that parents are married. I would argue that a sexually differentiated model of parenthood is employed but I have not traced this differentiation to the institution of marriage, although I believe this to be the root. Once married parental rights dominate. NEWELL *op. cit.*, cites a case of a mother who was unable to prevent her child from being beaten at school, and, although she had custody, her separated husband and father colluded with the head of the school to support his exercise of corporal punishment. I have not searched for instances of how the fathers of illegitimate children would or could be treated.

13 *The Times*, 18 April 1974; 23 May 1974; 22 August 1974; 19 September 1974.

14 BOURDIEU, P. 'Cultural reproduction and social reproduction', in BROWN, R. (Ed.) (1973) *Knowledge, Education and Cultural Change*, London, Tavistock.

15 MILL J.S. in his essay 'Liberty' thought that the State should not itself provide education, unless the society was extremely backward, but that it should see that a child was educated at the charge of its parents. MILL, J.S. (1910) *Utilitarianism, Liberty and Representative Government*, London, Everyman.

16 *Times Educational Supplement*, 7 January 1974 and 25 January 1976.

17 CRAFT, M. (1972) *Linking Home and School*, (2nd edition), London, Longman.

18 The idea of there being a contract between parents and the state is notional indeed. It is quite hard to discern what principles of reciprocity might lie behind the disputes, some of which are mentioned above, as the bulk of legal judgments tend to reaffirm unequivocally that within the domain of state institutions a different set of ground rules apply to personal interaction. NEWELL, P., who provides many examples of legal judgments following law suits between parents and teachers, argues (*op. cit.*) that it is still an open question whether when a parent specifically expresses an opinion on the use of corporal punishment the local authority in question is under any obligation to comply.

19 COULSON, M. 'Role: a redundant concept in sociology', in JACKSON, J.A. (Ed.) (1972) *Role*, Cambridge, Cambridge University Press.

20 SCHOCHET, G.J. (1969) 'Patriarchalism, politics and mass attitudes in Stuart England', *Historical Journal*, 12, p. 421. See also SCHOCHET, G.J. (1967) 'Thomas Hobbes on the family and the state of nature', *Political Science Quarterly*, 82, and SCHOCHET, G.J. 'The family and the origins of the state in Locke's political philosophy', in YOLTON, J. (Ed.) (1969) *John Locke Problems and Perspectives*, Cambridge, Cambridge University Press.

21 MACFARLANE, A. *op. cit.*, p. 206.

22 SMITH, S. (1973) 'The London apprentices', *Past and Present*, 6, November.

23 BARRELL *op. cit.*, p. 136.

24 PINCHBECK, I. and HEWETT, M. (1969) *Children in English Society*, Vol. 1 and (1973) Vol. 2, London, Routledge and Kegan Paul.

25 AULD, R. (1976) *The William Tyndale Junior and Infants Schools*, Report of the Public Inquiry, London, ILEA.

26 *Universal Declaration of Human Rights*, adopted by the General Assembly of the United Nations, Article 26, 10 December 1948.

17   Innocence and Experience: The Evolution of the Concept of Juvenile Delinquency in the Mid-Nineteenth Century

Margaret May

> The latter [the delinquent] is a little stunted man already – he knows much and a great deal too much of what is called life – he can take care of his own immediate interests. He is self-reliant, he has so long directed or mis-directed his own actions and has so little trust in those about him, that he submits to no control and asks for no protection. He has consequently much to unlearn – he has to be turned again into a child. . . . [1]

Matthew Davenport Hill's portrayal of a juvenile delinquent epitomised the new attitude to the problem and treatment of delinquency in mid-nineteenth-century England. Hitherto the problem had received only limited attention and young offenders were punished in exactly the same way as adults. State recognition of Reformatory and Industrial Schools in 1854 and 1857 (17 and 18 Victoria, c. 86; 20 and 21 Victoria, c. 48) marked a radical change in penal policy. For the first time in a legislative enactment Parliament recognised juvenile delinquency as a distinct social phenomenon and accepted responsibility not only for young offenders, but also for children who, although not in conflict with the law, required 'care and protection'. Thus children coming before the courts were no longer regarded as 'little adults' but as beings in their own right entitled to special care because they lacked full responsibility for their actions. This change in status was accomplished by the introduction of reformatory rather than punitive treatment and also involved the assertion of new powers of state intervention in parent-child relationships. A reformatory system which clearly distinguished a child's offence from an adult's crime replaced a penal system which made little specialised provision for children. This departure culminated in Herbert Samuel's Children Act of 1908 (8 Edward VII, c. 17).

[. . .]

I

At the beginning of the nineteenth century few legal distinctions were drawn

Source: An abridged version of an article first published in *Victorian Studies*, (XVII), September (1973), pp. 7–29.

between the offence, mode of trial, or punishment of children and adults. But a limited concession was made for the capacities of infants. Centuries of judicial precedent had built up the principle of *doli capax* most clearly enunciated by Blackstone in 1796, 'the capacity of doing ill, or contracting guilt, is not so much measured by years and days, as by the strength of the delinquent's understanding and judgement'.[2] Up to the age of seven it was presumed that children were incapable of criminal intent and could not be held personally responsible for violations of the law; between the ages of seven and fourteen they were presumed innocent unless the prosecution proved their ability to 'discern between good and evil'; thereafter they were fully responsible.

These provisos were generally observed[3] but otherwise children were sentenced to the same retributive punishments as adults, graded by statute and judicial precedent according to the magnitude of the offence. Age by itself gave no right to special treatment and children were tried with the full publicity and formality of judge and jury or magistrate.[4] Young offenders were liable for all the main forms of punishment, capital conviction, transportation and imprisonment. They had no legal right to be treated differently, though individual magistrates might exercise a compassionate discretion. Thus although 103 children under fourteen received capital sentences at the Old Bailey between 1801 and 1836, all were commuted to transportation or imprisonment.[5] But such clemency was only a variant of a policy applied to all offenders in the early nineteenth century in the face of the stringent penal code (Radzinowicz, *Criminal Law*, I, 163). Children also shared the punishment of transportation; 780 males and 136 females under twenty-one were transported to Australia between 1812 and 1817 alone.

During the first half of the century, however, transportation and capital conviction gradually gave way to imprisonment as the chief form of punishment for all offenders. Again there was little differentiation between children and adults. Prisons at first were mere places of detention where offenders of all types and ages were huddled together indiscriminately. A Select Committee of 1818 found free association between prisoners common in most metropolitan and provincial gaols. Newgate, where 'children of the tenderest age were confined in the cells with prisoners of more mature age and more confirmed habits of crime', was but the most notorious of many. Similarly in Bristol, Fowell Buxton, the prison reformer, found that boys were allowed 'to intermingle with men' and all 'without distinction of age were in heavy irons'. At the better disciplined Gloucester and Salford prisons 'boys were treated as adults' and subject to the rigours of the treadmill.[6]

[...]

Prison reform passed through several phases, each employing different devices for eliminating contact between individual inmates. The first limited step was the introduction of classification in 1823, following various local experiments. But this categorisation of offenders by character and seriousness of offence, whilst entailing the separation of the inexperienced and the hardened, did not necessitate segregation by age. The sheer size of the prison population did, however, force several prisons to allocate separate 'wards' for juveniles and to establish prison schools. The obvious inadequacies of classification led to a more vigorous campaign in the 1830's and

1840's based on American successes.[7] The rival Separate and Silent Systems were enthusiastically advocated. Both aimed at eliminating corruption; the former by physical separation, the latter by enforced silence. Their protagonists had high expectations of both general deterrence and individual reformation. Following the appointment of William Crawford and Whitworth Russell as Prison Inspectors in 1836, the Separate System was widely adopted as the best cure for all offenders. It was applied with equal rigour to young and old. At Reading the child offender was placed in solitary confinement 'like a dog in a kennel', relieved only by the visits of officials, or, as at Wakefield, by extra schooling. Boys were even employed on the crank at Hampshire County Gaol. Meanwhile a parallel campaign to remove similar abuses from the transportation system brought some improvement but no change in status for the young offender. Efforts at classification included the introduction of a separate convict hulk in 1823 and a boys' penal colony at Point Puer in 1837; and as part of the general reorganisation of transportation, Parkhurst Prison was opened in 1838 to train boy transportees before embarkation. Despite all efforts at uniformity, however, the penal system was still characterised by great diversity.

But the strenuous attempts at improvement and the decline of association had an unexpected result. As mass contamination was reduced the special problem of the young offender was highlighted. New techniques of prison management and reform were allied with changing attitudes to the purpose of imprisonment itself. The reforms of the 1830's and 1840's with their emphasis on individual reformation shifted attention from the nature of the offence to the criminal himself. Significant changes in the character of penal administrators followed. Gradually the inefficient eighteenth-century gaoler was replaced by a new generation of prison governors and chaplains dedicated to proving the value of their reforms. They found the existence of ever-increasing numbers of children in the improved prisons an embarrassing impediment to reform. By 1850 Joshua Jebb, the Surveyor-General of Prisons, was admitting that he did 'not think that the present prisons are at all adapted to juveniles'.[8] It was this dissatisfaction, shared by prison officials, magistrates, and a small group of well-informed outsiders, which stimulated a search for new policies. Discontent was firmly based in their practical experience and drew its strength from clear evidence of failure. For the first time the crucial question of the suitability of imprisonment for children was raised.

The arguments familiar since Howard were given a new direction. Prisons were criticised not for mass corruption but corruption of the young. Recommittal statistics demonstrated that prison reform was producing the opposite effect to that intended. Juveniles were neither deterred nor converted, as the Reverend John Field, an assiduous supporter of the Separate System, was mortified to discover. John Clay was equally horrified to find a reconviction rate of 56 per cent in Preston in the 1840's. Juvenile recidivism was recognized by the Chaplain at Bath, the Reverend C.S. Osborne, who deduced 'once in gaol, always in gaol', was a truism for boys. 'They become trained to prison life' ('S.C. on Prison Discipline', p. 343).
[...]
These perceptions were firmly rooted in contemporary theory: associationist

psychology maintained that children developed in response to external stimuli. This was precluded by prison confinement, which starved them of the very spirit of childhood. The Governor of Cold Bath Fields, G.L. Chesterton, observed that 'the youthful mind is so elastic, the desire to play and the inclination for trifles are such that the bringing of boys like these under a strict system . . . which you assign to a grown-up person is a perfectly unnatural state for a boy' ('S.C. on Prison Discipline', p. 634). Prisons not only failed to meet a child's physical and mental needs, but he or she was positively harmed by the experience. Young offenders were contaminated directly by promiscuous association with adults in the unreformed gaols and indirectly tainted by the 'moral atmosphere' of the prison. This was but one facet of the major change in attitudes to childhood that characterized mid-Victorian social reform. Just as the Mixed General Workhouse, and indeed the early factory employment of children, were condemned for ruining childish innocence by the mere presence of adults, so prisons transmitted adult vices.

Disillusionment with imprisonment and fears that it only confirmed a criminal career extended beyond the prison walls. Uneven sentencing policy reflected the difficulties of many magistrates and judges in choosing the best procedure consistent with their knowledge of delinquency and the punishments permitted by law. The evidence of Graham Spiers, Sheriff of Edinburgh, to the 1847 Select Committee on Criminal Law exemplified long standing doubts: 'I have been puzzled, acting judicially, where a boy has been brought before me and found guilty of theft to know what to do'.[9] Some magistrates exercised their discretion through various devices for avoiding imprisonment. But the resultant inconsistencies in sentencing practice provoked further criticism on the one hand from those who felt juveniles were being treated too harshly and, on the other, from those who felt uncertainty was encouraging impunity.[10]

The pomp and ceremony of trial by jury for juveniles accused of more serious offences also perturbed court officials. The majesty of the law was undermined by the 'mockery' of formal and expensive trials of children too young to appreciate the solemnity of the occasion. Moreover the lengthy pre-trial detention of juveniles, often on very trivial offences, exposed them to all the depravity concentrated in the prison. In the 1820's a Warwickshire magistrate, J.E. Eardley-Wilmot, in an effort to salvage legal dignity, argued that minor offences by children should be classed as misdemeanors, not felonies, and children should be dealt with summarily. Magistrates in Petty Sessions should follow 'the domestic regulation of families', and provide punishments appropriate to children in order to avoid the stigma of public trial and imprisonment.[11] But his proposals were attacked because such differentiation between the child and the adult would deprive the child of the right of all free-born Englishmen to trial by jury – an unwarrantable interference with the liberty of the individual. This traditional equation of children and adults was challenged by an influential group of lawyers who argued that a child's freedom was largely illusory. He was not a free agent.[12] After prolonged wrangling the 1847 Summary Jurisdiction Act was passed giving power to try children under fourteen summarily for petty larceny. In 1850 this was extended to include children up to sixteen.[13] A combination of judicial self-interest, the need to reduce costs, and a growing awareness of the special rights of children thus produced the first statutory distinction between children and adults.

II

The growing discontent among prison administrators and magistrates was based not only on disenchantment with defective sentencing and imprisonment, but also on a new awareness of the nature and extent of juvenile delinquency. Whilst prison experiments isolated the problem of the young offender from that of the adult, other developments highlighted the existence of a large group of children who, though not technically law breakers, shared their characteristics. Segregation of the neglected and ill-behaved child was one result of the growth of a system of public education which provided only for the more tractable and fee-paying working-class, and a system of public assistance that made no direct provision for child neglect. Institutional differentiation was accompanied by the identification and delineation of delinquency as a special social problem, demanding distinctive action. Such categorisation was the direct result of the increasing availability of criminal statistics in the nineteenth century, and the corresponding growth in the scientific study of crime.

[...] The most notable early attempt at analysis was that of the London police magistrate, Patrick Colquhoun, whose belief that crime was spiralling led him to describe the types of crime flourishing in the metropolis and attack the penal system which 'vomitted' criminals back onto society. Large numbers of human predators, many commencing their careers in infancy, were at war with society.[14] A more precise insight into the extent and changing pattern of crime followed the introduction of the Home Office Returns in 1805. Though they did not distinguish adults and juveniles, they did reveal an apparently rapid rise in crime. Witnesses at Select Committees in the 1810's and 1820's repeatedly attributed this to an increase in juvenile offenders. So widespread was this impression that special local inquiries were held, notably in London in 1816 and in Surrey and Warwickshire in 1828. All confirmed a 'perfectly appalling' rise in crime committed at a much earlier age than formerly. It was ascribed primarily to parental neglect.[15]

These findings were reiterated with new authority in the 1830's and 1840's when more refined methods of inquiry and diagnosis were developed. Under Samuel Redgrave's supervision from 1834 the national returns were improved, and for the first time information on the age and education of offenders was provided.[16] Parallel prison reforms replaced the erratic and limited prison registers with compulsory uniform records, including details of age. This sudden flow of information and the absence of long-term statistics fostered a widespread belief in the escalation of crime. Some contemporaries realised that factors independent of the activities of criminals might be partly responsible. The more general impression, however, was that, despite growing industrial prosperity, crime was apparently increasing out of all proportion to the rise in population, and this increase was greatest among the young. Redgrave revealed a massive 600 per cent rise in crime between 1805 and 1842.[17] Prison convictions of under twenties increased from 6,803 in 1835 to 11,348 by 1844. By 1853 Sydney Turner, the future Inspector of Reformatory Schools and Chaplain of Red Hill School, estimated that 12,000 juveniles were being imprisoned annually. Anxious and frequently confused use of statistics generated the intense public alarm which was a major force behind the acceptance of new measures.

Such fears precipitated a flood of unofficial inquiries in the 1830's and 1840's, which both confirmed national trends and paved the way for social action. The emergence of juvenile delinquency as a distinct social problem can be traced through these investigations. The gradual accumulation of detailed information increasingly shifted from general studies of crime to specific consideration of delinquency. This was accompanied by various analytical processes which isolated juvenile delinquency from other social problems. The nature of the investigations was an important factor in this development. Most were empirical studies, the product of the daily experience and apprehensions of those whose occupations brought them into contact with young miscreants. Lawyers, magistrates, voluntary teachers and ministers of religion constructed a picture of delinquency which was widely accepted because of their professional status. Though the investigators claimed objectivity, their findings were inevitably coloured by their own prejudices and values. The concept of deviance implies behaviour which somehow differs from prevailing expectations.[18] The conditions discovered by these amateur social investigators violated their images of childhood. Throughout their writings comparison between the realities of slum childhood and their own sense of a protected childhood is implicit.

The most authoritative group of investigators was the self-styled 'moral statisticians' of the numerous statistical societies. Their work was of crucial importance in initiating the 'science' of criminology and in particular in drawing attention to the age of the offender. They developed the methods and tools of statistical inquiry, examining the 'moral topography' of different areas as well as the 'moral health' of the whole nation. In the words of R.W. Rawson, the first Secretary of the London Statistical Society, they believed that just as Newton had discovered universal laws governing the physical world, so 'moral phenomena may be found to be controlled and determined by peculiar laws. A simple accumulation of facts and figures would reveal the laws which regulate criminality' (*JSSL*, II [1839], 316–318).

In their search for verifiable facts and patterns of criminal behaviour they elaborated the first clear concept of juvenile delinquency. The key breakthrough was Rawson's demonstration in 1839 that the correlation between age and the type and number of offences was one fundamental 'law' of crime. Criminal activity began early in life and reached a peak between sixteen and twenty-five. Larceny and petty theft were the most characteristics offences. Joseph Fletcher, another prominent member, concluded that since over half of those sentenced were under twenty-five 'there is a population constantly being brought up to crime' (*JSSL*, VI [1843], 236).

His observation and the new consciousness of age were substantiated by a close scrutiny of criminal life and habits. Widespread concern with the early urban environment had produced a series of general studies of social conditions in the

1830's. J.P. Kay's influential survey of Manchester in 1832 revealed, among a mass of social problems, the prevalence of the 'moral leprosy', crime.[19] By the 1840's crime and delinquency were being treated as separate social questions, and not merely as illustrations of a general social disease. W.A. Miles' experience in London led him to distinguish criminals from the respectable working class, particularly 'a youthful population . . . devoted to crime, trained to it from infancy, adhering to it from education and circumstances . . . a race *sui generis*, differing from the rest of society not only in thoughts, habits and manners but even in appearance'.[20]

Another early study, William Beaver Neale's 'Juvenile Delinquency in Manchester', stressed 'the existence of a class of juvenile delinquents', concentrated in certain quarters of Manchester 'congenial to criminals'. Such areas were the source of both moral and physical 'contagion and pestilence'; children born and reared in them were 'predestined' to a life of crime. Neale traced the careers of such potential malefactors from 'the first step' juvenile vagrancy, through street selling which served as a guise for petty pilfering, to pickpocketing and organised crime. Parents often actively encouraged this process, forcing their offspring to beg and steal to satisfy their own whims. Lacking affection and supervision, the juvenile delinquent in consequence displayed his independence. He was 'in general a gambler and a drunkard' with an 'unnatural' interest in the opposite sex. But 'circumstances' and parental irresponsibility rather than 'innate depravity' produced such outrageous behaviour: of one hundred cases examined, sixty were the offspring of 'dishonest' and thirty of 'profligate' parents.[21]

[. . .]

Conceptualisation of this kind was sharpened by a concentration on those attributes which most distinguished this youthful group from other respectable and well-tutored children. The behaviour and familiarity with the adult world and its pleasures found among slum children contradicted middle-class standards of childhood morality and propriety. Horrified investigators could only describe such behaviour in terms of a savage animal-like existence. 'English Kaffirs', 'Street Arabs', 'ownerless dogs' were the epithets commonly applied, and strong contrasts were drawn with an idealised obedient middle-class child, sheltered by stringent but affectionate parental supervision from both the snares of the world and his own inability to decide for himself. This use of racial nomenclature was another method of designating a special group and reflected the apprehensions which the inquiries inspired. Lower-class standards of child-rearing were denounced, and the conduct of street children received universal condemnation. Their restless, uncontrolled and nomadic existence embraced all the symptoms of social disorganisation, and challenged the very foundations of an ordered society. Mere exposure to crime-infested areas seemed to generate anti-social conduct, whilst careful studies of the new prison records and inquiries among offenders themselves confirmed that the massive problem of adult crime was rooted in the progressive career of the delinquent child. The solution lay in catching the young recruit before he became too accustomed to his irregular mode of life.

A nation-wide accumulation of evidence rapidly convinced the public of this threat. Edward Rushton, Stipendiary Magistrate for Liverpool, encountered 'Hottentots' in his courts, reared 'without the constant care and judicious guidance of a vigilant mother'. The London magistrate, J. Buchanan, plotted the geography of delinquency in the capital, as did the more famous accounts of criminal areas, Mayhew's *London Labour and the London Poor*, and Beames' *Rookeries of London*. The latter described the London rookeries as 'beds of pestilence' and 'rendezvous of vice', nurseries of felons 'where children were trained as criminals under professional thieves and became addicted to drink and debauchery'. Even in Ipswich John Glyde's study of social conditions forced him to conclude that 'the mass of depravity among the rising generation is horrifying to witness'. Boys gambling openly on the streets on Sundays, and 'almost all, even from the boy of twelve, have acquired the habit of smoking; and obscene and disgusting language is continuously emanating from their lips'.[22]

'Can these be children?' was the inevitable question raised by the Reverend Micaiah Hill in his prize-winning essay of 1853, observing the amusements, the singing and dancing salons, and the extraordinary licentiousness shown by children at such gatherings. Young law-breakers and vagrants were 'never children in heart and mind', and concepts of childhood taken from the upper or middle class were 'utterly inapplicable'. Their unchildlike behaviour was the result of the pernicious environment in which they lived, and particularly of 'parents destitute of all sense of parental responsibility', who permitted 'license of an extent ruinous to childhood'. Delinquency rose from 'too early an exposure to the hardships and temptations of life' caused by large scale desertion, broken marriages or orphanage. Many children were driven to crime and vagrancy by sheer necessity.[23]

[. . .]

If the neglected and delinquent child was 'unlike other children', he or she was still not an adult. The process of isolating young malefactors was accompanied by the belief that unseemly habits were the product of a defective environment and abnormal conditioning. Multifarious causes were assigned, ranging from the unchecked curiosity and adventurousness of childhood to bad housing and the temptations presented by the new urban society. Most interpreters did not question the social system but were moralistic and policy-oriented. It was generally agreed that the absence of proper parental care was most to blame. Indeed the typology of delinquency was commonly expressed in terms of the parents' condition, from the orphaned to the abandoned or neglected child through to the child deliberately instructed in theft. Diagnosis in terms of parental neglect facilitated concrete action. It mirrored current preoccupations with the supreme importance of the home and the family in child socialisation. Children were 'copyists' who developed the habits of honesty, diligence and obedience through imitating those around them. Constant and vigilant parental surveillance was necessary to prevent the mistakes of inexperience. The child could not be held fully responsible for misconduct; he or she was 'more sinned against than sinning'.

This evaluation of childhood derived from the contemporary proliferation of child guidance manuals. Overlaid with New Testament and Romantic sentiments of childish innocence, it was most clearly and sensitively expressed by Mary Carpenter. Her clarion-call of 1851, *Reformatory Schools for the Perishing and Dangerous*

Classes and for Juvenile Offenders, defined the categories of children in a way which galvanized public opinion and led to the first positive state action. Her wide reading and personal experience of Ragged Schools led her to distinguish between the 'dangerous class' of young offenders, and the 'perishing class' of incipient criminals living a life of vagrancy or theft but not yet subject to the law and excluded from any schooling. The central characteristic of all wayward children was not physical destitution, nor lack of education, but moral destitution resulting from parental neglect. Her *Juvenile Delinquents – Their Condition and Treatment* in 1853 expanded this analysis. The young delinquent exhibited 'in almost every respect, qualities the very reverse of what we should desire to see in childhood; we have beheld them independent, self-reliant, advanced in the knowledge of evil. . . . ' Yet children were physically and mentally quite different beings from adults, less developed in both respects. By being placed in a position of 'dependence' within a properly organised family system they might be 'gradually restored to the true position of childhood' – the key to reformation.[24]

Her studies intersected the work of social investigators and the operation of the prison and education systems. As a teacher she had discovered the exclusivity of the British and National Schools which, for reasons of poverty, behaviour or appearance, did not admit the lowest social segments. Even the Sunday Schools, originally founded by Raikes for the very poorest, were by mid-century largely confined to the more industrious and respectable classes. Rudimentary literacy was, in her opinion, moreover, not the prime need of such children. Religious-based moral training was necessary to provide an understanding of the difference between right and wrong which parents had neglected. Even if moral instruction in schools were improved the lesson might be undermined in the home. Thus by restricting their curriculum and intake the existing schools had in fact helped to define the delinquent.

By aiding only those who sought assistance and dealing with children as appendages of their parents, Poor Law administration had a similar effect. The few suggestions for substituting the workhouse for prisons were sharply rebuked. Honesty and dishonesty were not to be confused; by breaking the law, the delinquent however destitute had cut himself off from the pauper. The future prison inspector, William Crawford, had as early as 1834 pointed to the folly of treating pauper and delinquent in the same way. In her evidence to the Select Committee of 1852, Mary Carpenter herself repeated the argument that 'the poorhouse is, in theory, a refuge for the physically destitute'. The victims of misfortune should not be tainted by association with the victims of vice however similar their situation might appear.[25] The 'moral orphan' required separate treatment.

III

Demands for remedial state action inevitably followed the discovery of these social and institutional outcasts. Spearheaded by Mary Carpenter and Matthew Davenport Hill, a prolonged and well-organised campaign for reform was launched. A powerful

cross-section of religious and political opinion adhered to it, harnessing the professional impetus to reform from magistrates and prison administrators to the
more emotional response of the humanitarians. The strength of their case lay with
an influential group of lawyers led by Charles Pearson, the City of London Solicitor.
New insights into the condition of delinquents prompted a revaluation of the
ancient principle of *doli capax*. They argued that the child's 'incapacity' to distinguish
between right and wrong should be more fully implemented, and 'that his age,
the neglect or vice of his parents, and the depraving circumstances of his childhood
should be taken into account'.[26] This was the basis of middle-class parental protection. The misbehaviour of their children brought parental chastisement, but
lower-class children were sent to prison for similar faults. Moreover the civil law
already made allowances for the young, and Mary Carpenter argued that the criminal
law should be assimilated to it: 'The law of England does not recognise the right of
a young person ... to contract matrimony, or enter into solemn engagements
without the consent of his parents. . . . The child is very rightly regarded in the eyes
of the law as incapable of acting wisely for himself and therefore under the control
of his parents' (M. Carpenter, *Reformatory Schools*, p. 286). Such comparisons were
reinforced by the example of the French Code Napoleon which stipulated that
children under sixteen acted *sans discernment* and acquitted them of the offence,
placing them under the care of the state for retraining. The English reformers
argued that all children lacked *discernment* and that the law should treat delinquents
'as a wise parent would in such circumstances'. Discipline commensurate with a
child's nature, not adult punishment, was necessary when a child proved 'by his
conduct that he is ignorant of his duty, deficient in principle and totally unfit to
guide himself' ('S.C. on Criminal and Destitute Juveniles', p. 118).
[...]

The 1852–53 Select Committee heard conflicting evidence on the delinquent's
capacity to distinguish between right and wrong and the age at which this capacity
was reached. Opinion on the age of discretion ranged from ten to sixteen. Clay,
while admitting that 'in many cases a child does not know he has committed a
crime', maintained that he knew it was wrongful as punishment would follow.
Sydney Turner believed that children 'are in fact aware of what they do' and knew
punishment would ensue, whilst Captain John Williams 'scarcely ever knew a
case in which a boy did not know he was doing wrong'.[27]

The vehemence of this controversy was seen at a special meeting of the Royal
Society of Arts in 1855. The main speaker, Jelinger Symons, attacked 'the belief
that juvenile offenders are little errant angels who require little else than fondling',
arguing that they could discern between right and wrong and should be punished
accordingly. Indeed reformation was impossible without such warning of the
consequences of misbehaviour. David Power, Recorder of Ipswich, disagreed
completely. Children should not be punished for their parents' neglect but rehabili-
tated. The traditionalists were represented by Mr. Elliott who attacked 'effeminate
and diseased sentimentality' and argued that 'juvenile offenders should be treated
as all other offenders', 'they must be hurt so that the idea of pain might be instantly
associated with crime in the minds of all evildoers'. Aversion therapy had been a

constant theme in utilitarian and traditional policy, and Elliott was supported by Lord Lyttleton who argued that *doli capax* had never meant 'that the crime of that child was not to be imputed to it because of a fault in the education of the child'.[28]

The sharp division of opinion led ultimately to legislative compromise. Mary Carpenter's proposals for Reformatory Schools for convicted offenders and Industrial Schools for the incipient criminal and neglected child were accepted.[29] The former were recognised in 1854, the latter in 1857 and similar measures were passed for Scotland and Ireland. Under the 1854 Act a system similar to that governing education in general was established, based on a partnership of state and voluntary bodies. Judges and magistrates were empowered to sentence children under sixteen on indictable or non-indictable offences to Reformatory Schools for a period of two to five years. Reformatory treatment was preceded by a prison sentence of at least fourteen days, later reduced to ten. Schools were to be managed by voluntary associations subject to state inspection and certification. Maintenance costs were met by the state and also by a parental contribution of up to 5s. a week. In 1857 local authorities were also given powers to finance the schools.

The legislation epitomised the attitudes to delinquency held up to the 1880's and embodied fundamental changes in the state's attitude to children. A more liberal intepretation of *doli capax* was sanctioned, acknowledging the essential differences between children and adults. For Adderley, the crux of his act was the recognition that 'children in the eyes of the law are not fully to blame', since they committed offences 'for want of knowing better'. Children for the first time were accepted as wards of state and new rights of enforcing parental responsibility were asserted. The legal age of delinquency was set at sixteen, following the French precedent, and corrective detention in the Reformatory ensured a 'child's punishment for a child's crime'.[30]

The discrimination between children and adults was not complete, however. Old traditions and fears were still strong. The act was only permissive and many magistrates continued to ignore it. Imprisonment of children, though at a dwindling rate, continued to the 1890's. Large sections of the public continued to regard delinquents as nuisances requiring a sharp lesson. Reformatory treatment itself was preceded by imprisonment, as a concession to those who maintained that without clear punishment the Reformatory would be an incentive to crime and parental neglect. Mary Carpenter and others continued to resent this, but the essential principle of a child's diminished responsibility was established.

This was particularly important in the context of a second dispute over state interference with parental rights. Reformatory Schools were intended to enforce parental responsibility, directly, by maintenance contributions and, indirectly, by warning that financial duties could not be avoided, as under the prisons, by child neglect. Parental maintenance was a new principle but its adoption was eased by the fact that convicted children were already in the state's custody. Industrial Schools raised the issue in a more acute form, embodying direct restrictions on parental control. Under the 1857 Act magistrates were empowered to sentence children aged between seven and fourteen to the Schools for any period up to their fifteenth birthday. The sentence was not preceded by imprisonment as the Act dealt only with children charged with vagrancy. Voluntary management was again combined with state aid.

The uncertain charge of vagrancy proved difficult to administer and was little used until an amendment in 1861 classified the children to be dealt with. This was broadened by a consolidating measure in 1866. A new category of children, those 'in need of care and protection' was thus introduced into English law. The 1866 act defined those requiring state care as 'any child under the age of fourteen found begging or receiving alms ... wandering, and not having a home or settled place or abode, or any visible means of subsistence, or [who] frequents the company of reputed thieves; any child apparently under the age of twelve years who, having committed an offence punishable by imprisonment or some less punishment, ought nevertheless, in the opinion of the justices, regard being had to his age, and to the circumstances of the case, to be sent to an Industrial school'. For the first time children 'beyond their parents' control' were also included.[31]

The experimental time limit placed on the Industrial Schools by the first two acts reveals their revolutionary implications. Again parents were to contribute to the maintenance of their children and be deprived of their right to bring them up as they wished. As early as 1834 William Crawford's monumental study of American institutions had declared, 'to separate children from their parents by committing them to a place of confinement ... for an act of vagrancy, or the mere accusation of such an act ... is a stretch of authority not reconcilable with the spirit of the English law'. Monckton Milnes, the presenter of a bill in 1849, found 'a strong objection to the enforcement of the responsibility of parents and guardians by legal means ... lay members of the House were unwilling to take upon themselves the establishment of so new a principle'.[32]

Yet the Reformatory and Industrial Schools permitted a substantial encroachment on parental freedom, by attempting to impose middle-class standards of child-rearing on lower-class parents. In declaring that 'we have proceeded on the principle that we must revere the parental duties as long as they are not abandoned', Matthew Davenport Hill voiced the reformers' awareness of the novelty of the legislation ('S.C. on Criminal and Destitute Juveniles', p. 41). Industrial Schools were founded on the belief that in some cases the welfare of the child and public safety necessitated the separation of parent and child. No parent should be allowed to bring up his child 'in such a way as to almost secure his becoming a criminal'.[33] Where a parent abrogated his duties the state had the right to act *in loco parentis*. Parents who failed to provide not only physical but mental and moral care had signed away their rights to their children. By upholding this fundamental principle, Industrial Schools provided the precedent for later legislation to protect the child, and paved the way for compulsory education.

Many of the promoters of Reformatory and Industrial Schools saw punishment of parents and enforcement of parental duties as the chief benefits of the acts. The decline in delinquency from the 1850's was frequently attributed to greater willingness among parents to keep their children off the streets. Legal sanctions for improved standards of parental training were one aspect of the legislation. Equally radical was the approach to the treatment of children in institutions. The schools aimed 'to train up the child in the way he should go', by providing all the elements for civilised development missing from the child's own home. Institutionalisation was based on the rehabilitative philosophy enunciated by Mary Carpenter, Hill, Turner, T.B. Ll. Baker and other contributors to the *Reformatory and Refuge Union Journal* and the *Transactions of the National Association for the Promotion of Social Science* from the 1850s.

There was general agreement on the main ingredients of reformation. Schools were to act as 'moral hospitals' and provide the corrective training to which children, as wards of state and victims of neglect rather than fully responsible law-breakers, were entitled. Treatment policies were based on a fixed concept of the needs of delinquents, who, reared to 'wild license' and 'self-action', needed in Turner's phrase to be 'remoulded and recast'. The Commander of the Reformatory Ship *Akbar* saw his task clearly, 'the first great change which has to be affected ... when they are received on board in their vagrant state is to make them "boys". They are too old, too knowing, too sharp when they come on board, too much up in the ways of the world'.[34] The re-creation of more acceptable patterns of behaviour was to be achieved by methods whose success had been demonstrated by a number of voluntary schools both in England and abroad before 1854.[35] Sentences should be sufficiently long to permit reformation and children should be removed from their 'haunts and associates' and placed in more amenable surroundings. The best situation was the countryside, the 'rural antidote to town poisoning'. Exemplary substitutes for defective parents and neighbourhood influences should be provided by a devoted staff who organised the school on the family system. The guidance of the upper classes missing in the slum areas was supplied by voluntary managers. A stringent retraining programme based on religion and work would prepare children for their restoration to society. Treatment of this nature, however, was not to elevate the child, but prepare him by the acquisition of industrious habits for a life of unremitting honesty and strenuous labour in his own social station. The 'object is not to make learned thieves but plain, honest men' (*Report of the Proceedings of a Conference* ... , p. 14).

Practical administration of these ideals proved another matter, and early optimism was often lost. Staffing and financial problems, the need to preserve less eligibility and safeguard the public, tended to outweigh child welfare. Hopes of providing a complete substitute for imprisonment were delayed to the 1890s. Defective enforcement of the acts, and the later charges that the discipline was over-severe, should not be allowed to disguise the revolutionary implications for the position of the child in society. The establishment of separate institutions gave the juvenile delinquent a new legal status. The operation of the English penal and educational systems and the perceptions of social investigators had resulted in new distinctions between the child and the adult. The acceptance of Mary Carpenter's belief that 'children should not be dealt with as men but as children', was a seminal point in the evolution of the modern child ('S.C. on Criminal and Destitute Juveniles', p. 119).

Notes and References

1 HILL, M.D. (1855) 'Practical Suggestions to the Founders of Reformatory Schools', in SYMONS, J.C. *On the Reformation of Young Offenders*, London, Routledge and Kegan Paul, p. 2.

2 BLACKSTONE, W. (1857) *Commentaries on the Laws of England*, London, John Murray, Vol. IV, p. 19.

3 'Answers of certain Judges, Select Committee of the House of Lords on the Execution of the Criminal Laws, especially respecting Juvenile Offenders and Transportation', *Parliamentary Papers*, 1847, Vol. VII, Appendix.

4 Like adults children were tried for lesser crimes before magistrates and for more serious crimes before the judges.

5 KNELL, B.E.F. (1965) 'Capital Punishment: Its Administration in Relation to Juvenile Offenders in the Nineteenth Century and Its Possible Administration in the Eighteenth', *British Journal of Criminology, Delinquency and Deviant Social Behaviour*, Vol. V, pp. 198–207.

6 'Select Committee within the City of London and Borough of Southwark and Newgate', P.P., 1818, Vol. VIII, p. 5; BUXTON, T.F. (1818) *An Inquiry Whether Crime and Misery are Produced or Prevented by our Present System of Prison Discipline*, 3rd edition, London, Arch., p. 133; 'Select Committee on Criminal Committals and Convictions'. P.P., 1828, Vol. VI, pp. 77, 93.

7 For a history of prison discipline see Fox, L.W., GRUENHUT, M., WEBB, S. and WEBB, B. (1922) *English Prisons under Local Government*, London, Longmans, Green; HENRIQUES, U.R.Q. (1972) 'The Rise and Decline of the Separate System of Prison Discipline', *Past and Present*, 54, pp. 61–93.

8 'Select Committee on Prison Discipline', P.P., 1850, Vol. XVII, p. 29.

9 'Select Committee on the Execution of the Criminal Law'. P.P., 1847, Vol. VII, p. 381.

10 HILL, M.D., for instance, introduced a system of probation in Birmingham.

11 EARDLEY-WILMOT, J.E. (1820) *A Second Letter to the Magistrates of Warwickshire on the Increase of Crime in General, but more particularly of Juvenile Delinquency*, London, Hodgson, p. 9.

12 See Evidence in 'Report of the Commissioners for Inquiring into the County Rates and Other Matters', P.P., 1836, Vol. XXVII and 'Third Report from the Commissioners on Criminal Law (Juvenile Offenders)'. P.P., 1837, Vol. XXXI.

13 10 and 11 Vic.c. 82; 13 and 14 Vic.c. 37; many of the legal protagonists were members of the Law Amendment Society and engaged in the reform and codification of the criminal law.

14 COLQUHOUN, P. (1796) *A Treatise on the Police of the Metropolis*, London, Fry.

15 *Report of the Committee for Investigating the Causes of the alarming increase of Juvenile Delinquency in the Metropolis*, London, Dove. 1816; EARDLEY-WILMOT, J.E. (1826) *A Letter to the Magistrates of England*, 2nd edition, London, Hatchard; JACKSON, R. (1828) *Considerations on the Increase of Crime*, London, Hatchard.

16 Age Statistics in 1834, education in 1835. In 1841, age statistics were changed to accord with the census. Age, sex and education statistics were discontinued in 1849 since reliable information was provided through the Prison Returns, first published in 1820, and reorganized as appendices to the Prison Inspectors' Reports in 1836. In 1854 age statistics were again changed to allow for Reformatory Schools.

17 *Journal of the Statistical Society of London*, Vol. IX, (1846), p. 177. Hereafter cited as JSSL.

18 COHEN, S. (1971) *Images of Deviance*, London, Penguin, pp. 9–24.

19 KAY, J.P. (1832) *The Moral and Physical Condition of the Working Classes Employed in the Cotton Manufacture of Manchester*, London, James Ridgway.

20 'Second Report of the Select Committee of the House of Lords on the Present State of the Several Gaols and Houses of Correction in England and Wales', P.P., 1835, Vol. XI, p. 395.

21 NEALE, W.B. (1840) *Juvenile Delinquency in Manchester, Its Causes and History, and Some Suggestions Concerning its Cure*, Manchester, Hamilton, pp. 8, 9, 13, 52ff.

22 RUSHTON, E. (1842) *Juvenile Delinquency*, London, Simpkin, Marshall, p. 13; BUCHANAN, W. (1846) *Remarks on the Causes and State of Juvenile Crime in the Metropolis*, London, Taylor; BEAMES, T. (1850) *The Rookeries of London: Past, Present and Prospective*, London, Bosworth, p. 119; GLYDE, J. (1857) *The Moral, Social and Religious Condition of Ipswich*, Ipswich, Burton, pp. 50–1.

23 HILL, M. and CORNWALLIS, C.F. (1853) *Two Prize Essays on Juvenile Delinquency*, London, Smith, Elder, pp. 49, 58, 59.

24 CARPENTER, M. (1851) *Reformatory Schools for the Children of the Perishing and Dangerous Classes, and for Juvenile Offenders*, London, Gilpin; CARPENTER, M. (1853) *Juvenile Delinquents – Their Condition and Treatment*, London, Cash, pp. 292, 298.

25 'Report of William Crawford on the Penitentiaries of the United States', P.P., 1834, Vol. XLV; 'Select Committee on Criminal and Destitute Juveniles', P.P., 1852, Vol. VII, p. 466.

26 *Report of the Proceedings of a Conference, . . .* p. 43.

27 'Select Committee on Criminal and Destitute Juveniles', P.P., 1852, Vol. VII, pp. 191–7; P.P., 1852–53, Vol. XXIII, p. 255.

28 SYMONS, J.C. (1855) *On the Reformation of Young Offenders*, London, Routledge, pp. 82–118.

29 Her recommendations and the legislation also owed much to the experiments, both at home and abroad, in voluntary Reformatory Schools.

30 *Irish Quarterly Review*, Vol. IX, (April 1859), p. 1.

31 29 and 30 Vic.c. 118; 25 and 26 Vic.c. 10. Under the 1857 Act Industrial Schools were placed under the Committee of Education and transferred to the Home Office in 1861.

32 'Report of William Crawford', P.P., 1834, Vol. XLV, p. 44; *Report of the Proceedings of a Conference,* . . . p. 38.

33 'Select Committee on Criminal and Destitute Juveniles', P.P., Vol. VII, p. 119.

34 TURNER, S. (1855) 'Reformatory Schools, A Letter to C.B. Adderley, MP', in SYMONS, J.C. *op. cit.*, p. 9; Irish Quarterly Review, Vol. VII, (1857), p. xlix.

35 Red Hill and Stretton in England, Mettray in France, and the Raube Haus in Germany.

18   The Child as Legal Subject

John Fitz

The English legal system is a very dispersed body of texts, institutions and professions. Unlike Continental systems, English law is uncodified; it has material
existence in the form of common law and equity, as public law and private law,
criminal law and civil law; courts exist in the form of Parliament, High Courts,
Crown Courts and Magistrates Courts (which are hierarchically arranged). Legal
texts exist as statutes, legal commentaries, parliamentary reports, law reports of
selected cases etc., each with different effects (commentaries may produce dicta,
but cannot be used as precedent). We can obtain a theoretical purchase in these
diverse practices, institutions and texts by seeing them as the very material which
constitutes legal subjects. By privileging the effectivity of these elements, we hope
to extend the currently available work on Marxist theory of the law.

Marxist theories of the law conceive the juridico-political as an element of the
superstructure; having material form as an apparatus of the State, and functioning
both repressively and ideologically[1] or coercively, and ideologically winning consent
of the governed. Major theorists in this tradition have privileged (from different
perspectives) the law as regulating and reproducing the property relations of
capitalism (e.g. laws concerning the right to hold and alienate private property,
including labour), and, the law as a mechanism for the reproduction of class relations.
We shall not challenge these conceptions as far as they go, but build on this work by
pointing out certain absences which will hopefully enable the legal system to be
opened up for analysis in areas, so far not fully developed.

If we do grant that the legal system is an expression of class relations, and the
legal system is a key means by which the ruling class retains its power, how then
do we theorise the legal form of social relations which are not primarily class relations. For example, how do we understand the legal constructs of rape, prostitution,
incest, the patriarchal nature of family law etc. Are these to be dismissed as bourgeois
constructs?

Some of these problems attend Pashukanis (1978)[2] in his attempt to derive the

Source: A considerably shortened version of a paper presented at the BSA Law and Society Conference,
University of Warwick, April 1979. First published in this volume.

legal form of bourgeois law from the commodity form. His work can only be very crudely glossed here. For Pashukanis, the legal subject 'is the very atom of juridic theory', and the law is a relationship between legal subjects. Pashukanis' legal subject is the analogue of the economic subject (as a possessor of a commodity equivalent, meeting other subjects at the level of exchange). The legal form comprises subjects as bearers of rights, meeting in dispute over the possession or pursuit of rights. His abstract derivation of the legal form from the commodity form realises two related problems (Hirst, P. 1979).[3] First, the legal subject is a simple 'read off' from the economic subject, thus allowing no real space for the processes of legal subjectification. Secondly, rights seem to be constituted outside the legal system, which therefore has no effect in constructing these rights; that is, rights take on some form of extra-legal quality. Rights are constructed in and through the legal system, and definite limits are placed on subjects by the law.

To recuperate the effectivity of the legal system, we can consider Hirst's proposition:

> Legal subjects are entities created through legal recognition which are capable (in forms of law) of initiating actions (suits, pleas, etc.,) and of supporting certain statuses (possession, responsibility, etc.). Such subjects exist only relative to legal recognition (they cannot exist in law otherwise, other entities are represented only as a possession of subjects or object of dispute between them). .... To be denied the status of a legal subject is not inconsequential, it is to be unable to initiate legal actions or to support the consequences ... [4]

The status, rights, privileges and disabilities afforded the legal subject are not given outside the legal system but in it and through it. Therefore it is necessary to recognise the specificity of the elements of the legal system in order to account for the differentiated subjectivity of individuals, corporate bodies, etc., for it is through the play between the various elements, that differentiation is constructed.

This paper then is refuting a theory based on the law in general, for as such, the law has no materiality. The law exists as a dispersed set of practices, institutions, texts and agents. Rather we shall treat the law as a discrete but related set of discourses; each discourse specified by the objects of which it purports to speak (marriage, property, contract, criminality, etc.), and each operating with a definite set of categories, concepts and notions and each discourse producing definite effects. There is little doubt that legal discourses, in English law, are hierarchially arranged; land law for instance provides a definite limit to space allowed for transformations within other areas of the legal system, as this paper will indicate.

We shall consider legal subjects as constituted by, and having a definite position in relationship to, separate and different discourses. This, we hope, will allow the multiple legal subjectivities possible for an individual to emerge, and to display some of the contradictions involved. Such a procedure will also display, in spite of an apparent diversity, the unity of the position of specific subject, in this instance, the child, over the totality of legal discourses, and make some tentative proposals about the regulating principles which seem to inform the unequal distribution of legal capacities.

This paper is concerned specifically with the constitution of children as legal subjects. It falls into three different sections. The first will consider the legal notion of infancy where some of the general conditions for the separation of the legal category child from the category adult emerge. The second will be concerned to understand the state/parent/child relationship. The last will briefly survey the position of the child in criminal law.

Infancy

Infancy in law is a 'technical' word; infancy describes that period prior to the age of majority and is given through a series of incapacities or exclusions. The denial of the right to hold property, either in the form of land, or written transfer; the incapacity to be a party to a contract (including marriage); the exclusion from public office; the incapacity to make testamentary depositions, collectively describes the legal infant. The possession of these capacities conversely describes the 'full' legal subject. Proscribing the use of alcohol, tobacco, street trading, sexual relations, etc., to persons deemed to be under age reinforces the separation of the infant and the adult. Presently, the age of majority is 18, though historically, it and the notion in infancy display remarkable transformations. Pollock and Maitland, for example, speak of the thirteenth century when

> There is more than one 'full age'. The young burgess is of full age when he can count money and measure cloth; the young sokeman when he is fifteen, the tenant by knight's service when he is twenty-one years old. In past times boys and girls had soon attained full age: life was rude and there was not much to learn ... In later days our law drew various lines at various stages in a child's life; Coke tells us of the seven ages of a woman; but the only line of general importance is drawn at one and twenty; and the *infant* – the one technical word that we have as a contrast for the person of full age – stands equally well for the new born babe and for the youth in his twenty-first year.[5]

Infancy is a *general* condition attaching to the young and has meaning only in its 'contrast' to the person of full age. But let us pursue the 'difference' in Coke's writing on infancy:

> Note that the full age of a man or woman to alien, demise let, contract, is one and twenty years. Before this age of twenty-one a man or woman is called an infant ... and certain privileges he hath in respect of his infancy.[6]

Macpherson writes of the different stages in the early part of the nineteenth century, but elaborates on the differentiated legal categories within infancy:

> A male at twelve years old may take the oath of allegiance; at fourteen is

at years of discretion, and therefore may consent or disagree to marriage, and may choose his guardian, and at twenty-one is at his own disposal and may alien his lands, goods and chattels. A female, also at seven years of age may be betrothed, or given in marriage; at nine is entitled to dower, at twelve is at the age of maturity, and therefore may consent or disagree to marriage; at fourteen, is at years of legal discretion, and may choose a guardian; and at twenty-one may dispose of herself and her lands.[7]

Finally, we may consider the Latey Report on the age of majority which had as its brief:

... to consider whether any changes are desirable in the law relating to contracts made by persons under twenty-one and to their power to hold and dispose of property, and in the law relating to marriage by such persons and to the power to make them wards of court.[8]

These dispersed texts display the subjectivity of the legal infant through their various incapacities, incapacities which separate them absolutely from the 'full' adult subject. Infancy is defined in the negative; a 'lack' of the capacities which are differentially distributed around the age of majority. For something like 600 years, in spite if its historical fluidity, the age of majority functions in a similar manner; it becomes the point of origin of a legal classification whereby subjects emerge as *either* infant or adult. We are not concerned here to trace systematically the changing age of majority (see James 1960, for a standard 'history'),[9] but to register its effectivity in English common law. By custom, through the courts and latterly by statute, majority has been fixed at 14, 21, and now 18 years old; the sites of struggle have focussed on *where* it should be drawn, not *whether* it should exist. Majority is a legal category with specific social, economic and juridical effects; determining and limiting, privileging and protecting, defining and distributing the possible social relationships of both infants and adults, thus contributing in a significant way to the fabric of 'the social'.

We now take the central differences between minority and majority to be the right to vote and to hold public office. Within the discourse of common law, however, these issues have never been of real concern. Rather the differences in common law of the infant *contra* the adult emerge through a reflection upon the relation of subject to property. The various capacities are formed, though by no means exclusively, in terms of possession, alienation and contract, as the extracts quoted above adequately demonstrate. Infancy is described in terms of the separation from the ownership of the means of production. Immediately, therefore, infants stand in a power relationship, with adults, but a power relationship which is *not* unambiguously repressive. The separation of infants from property is also constructed as a form of *protection* (from greedy lords, spendthrift parents, and the fraudulent schemes of money lenders and traders). Even in the thirteenth century when infants had some proprietory rights, and went before the courts as independent persons,[10] they rarely had free and unrestrained use or control over their land, goods and chattels. Where boys and girls inherited land:

in such cases, the father will usually be holding the land for his life as 'tenant by the law of England', but the fee will belong to the child'.[11]

In some cases, the wardship of the land (and therefore the use) belonged to a lord, not to the father, thereby retaining the infant/property separation.

We can now begin to understand that land law is central to the production of the legal infant. The protection and orderly transmission of land from one generation is perhaps the crucial determinant of the position of the *infant* in the law. We should not consider this concern for the sanctity of land as a simple 'reflection' of feudal or pre-capitalist legal discourse. For example, Latey's review of the evidence presented before the Select Committee displays exactly the same concern:

> It has been urged on us that in relation to land law which is such a basic feature of our legal system, there must be no room for uncertainty; that is the basis for the bald provision contained in S.1(6) of the Law of Property Act 1925, which creates an absolute prohibition against the holding by an infant of legal estate in land.[12]

The existence of the land law, its position as a 'basic feature' of the legal system, with its explicit 'exclusion' of infants, demonstrates the limits set to a debate, which to all intents and purposes, took as its object the extension of voting rights to eighteen year olds. Remember also Latey's brief was to examine the *laws* relating to property and contract; infancy enters as a side issue.

But the question must now be posed: where are the infants *without property*, where are the infants who will inherit nothing but the privilege or selling their labour? It is not too strong to insist that they are invisible in these texts. Is it simply the case, as Pollock and Maitland remark:

> But here again we have a good instance of the manner in which the law for the gentry becomes English common law.[13]

The absence of the property-less infant from the texts on infancy in fact speaks of the dispersed institution of common law and their hierarchial ordering. The separation of heirs to property from wage labourers is constituted through the court system. The courts of wards and liveries, equity courts and latterly the high courts constitute the child as a legal subject in cases of disputes about property. The property-less infant confronts the legal system, historically through the magistrates' courts. Infants thereby become subjects only in and through particular institutions; infancy as a general condition, thereby admits, through the subject/property relation, differentiated capacities, with infant subjects open to varying forms of protection. We will demonstrate this through a consideration of wardship and care orders, in the next section of the paper.

Cross-cutting the inequalities apparent through the subject/property relation, the texts also reveal the distribution of capacities by gender. There is little doubt that the male infant is the figure in dominance. The age of majority, in its universalised, statutory form, has its lineage in the *male* infants' passage to adulthood; the mantle was first assumed at the time that the male was able to bear arms in combat.[14] Equally the age of discretion is drawn at the time the male was recognised as a party whose contracts (specifically marriage) were binding and non-voidable. For the female infant, legal subjectivity articulates to a different set of values. Whereas the male infant/adult divide was *physical strength*, for the female, infant life is periodized through the stages of *marriage alliance*: dower, consent, contract. Customarily, the female moved out of wardship and guardianship earlier than the male infant, though never out of domination; the domain of the lord/ward/guardian merely precedes the domination of the husband. Marriage becomes an extended form of infancy (separation from property, inability to sue on her own behalf).

Infancy, then, is difference, dependence and subordination; materialized in the land law, the laws of wardship and guardianship, the laws of tort and contract (which for reasons of space we have not really considered here). Infancy is also a state of privilege and protection; the infant's restricted capacities to sue or be sued, their separation from property, is contradictorily the site of their dependence and the site of their privilege. And yet the legal discourses must ground the difference between the adult and the infant. The modality of the distribution of capacities must be rational and rationalized. Thus, in spite of the dispersed theoretical objects which together constitute the common law, there is a unity in the positioning of the child in relation to these (dispersed) theoretical objects.

The modality of the distribution of capacities is, in the last instance, through a political economy of 'reason'. Blackstone invokes it thus:

> [Children] are enfranchized at the years of discretion, or at that point which the law established (as some must be necessarily established) when the *empire of the father* or other guardian, gives place to the *empire of reason*[15] (My emphasis).

The age of majority operates as the age of full reason. The age of discretion, brought into play particularly in the discursive order of crime and punishment, marks the partial acquisition of reason. Criminal acts may be investigated punishment may follow, but, contradictorily the subject is as yet unready for the grave responsibilities of property ownership. The texts invoke infancy and madness, intrinsic qualities, which of themselves disqualify certain classes of subjects, Coke for instance:

> . . . a madman is only punished by his madness. And so it is of an infant, until he be the age of 14, which in law is accounted as the age of discretion.[16]

Reason is quantifiable and distributed by age. Those without reason, the infant and the mad, are punished by their lack of it. The courts can ascertain, through the application of certain techniques the quantity of reason. Macpherson, discussing the testimony of infants:

> the admissability of children depends not upon their possessing a competent degree of understanding, but also in part upon their having received a certain share of religious instruction.[17]

Reason is thus constructed within definite limits, which can be quantified by an examination of the child's knowledge of Christian doctrine. Macpherson displays the polymorphous nature of 'legal' reason when describing the offices an infant may hold:

> An infant seems capable of holding such offices as do not concern the administration of justice, *(but only require skill and diligence*; and these he may execute himself, or they may be exercised by deputy)[18] (My emphasis).

The infant may be therefore, park-keeper, gaoler, or forester, but not, steward of a manor, bailiff, factor, or receiver; not a juror, a private or officer in the army, priest nor deacon, a barrister, surgeon or apothecary.

A hundred and thirty years on we find in the Latey Report 'reason' invoked in a reconstruction job on young adults. Christian doctrine is not its measure (though the church was called on for its views) but the technology of medicine. Evidence from the British Medical Association established that the child of the late 1960s was more physically developed than the child of a century earlier, (earlier menarche, earlier physical maturation, etc.). Though the BMA were non-commital on the relationship between physical and psychological maturity, Latey concludes:

> there is good evidence however that children who are physically advanced for their age score higher in mental tests than their contempories.[19]

Ergo, young adults circa 1967 were capable of assuming responsibilities denied them a century ago. Thus the programming of legal capacities is dependant on the legal distribution of reason. We could take up a reprise in Coke and assert that in English common law, infants occupy a similar space to the mad.

The Doctrine of Parens Patriae: the State as the Wise and Supreme Parent

Simply stated, the medieval doctrine of *parens patriae* is:

> The sovereign, as parens patriae had a kind of guardianship over various classes of person, who from their legal disability stand in need of protection, such as idiots, infants and mental patients.[20]

We have already established the nature of the infants' 'legal disability' so we shall concern ourselves here with two related notions; parens patriae and guardianship, which will put into play a complex relationship between the state, parents and children. It is impossible here to write a full account of the complex 'history' of guardianship, and the related categories of custody and wardship; guardianship remains a notoriously difficult construct, even for legal historians and commentators to trace through all its various paths and by-ways. Medieval law recognised ten different types of guardianship,[21] while Coke lists four categories: his nineteenth century editor footnotes nine different types.[22] Legal commentaries on guardianship may be bracketed in two ways; those accounts which read its legal history as a series of successive blows against the absolute authority of a father over his children (see the various contributions to Graveson and Crane; 1957);[23] and those accounts which privilege the growing concern of the courts to enact judgements – in custody, wardship, divorce proceedings, etc. – which would be of benefit to the child (e.g. Stone, 1978).[24] The first seeks to establish the grounds of which married women emerge as legal subjects in their own right; the second brings together the parents and the state in constellation, through the doctrine of 'the welfare of the child'; this is the theme I shall develop here.

But first a return to the doctrine of *parens patriae*. Principally, the sovereign's concern with his subjects' legal disabilities, historically, was a concern not with their persons but their property, especially land. Heirs with property, and outside any specific wardship, came under the protection of the Monarch, who in turn had the use of the property during infancy. How this supreme parentage devolved upon the Equity Courts, specifically Chancery, is not clear.

Certainly, by the early nineteenth century, the question of Chancery Courts standing in *parens patriae* was not in dipute. But it was a limited jurisdiction. Lord Eldon (1825) maintained:

> ... the state must of necessity place somewhere a superintending power over those who cannot take care of themselves, and that the court represents the King as parens patriae.[25]

and he continues:

> that the court has not the means of acting except where it has property to act on; because it cannot take on itself the maintenance of all children in the Kingdom.[26]

Lord Cottenham speaking to the Custody of Infants Bill (1839), held that the Court of Chancery has a general jurisdiction over the *property* of infants, and where the infant has property, it exercises jurisdiction over the infant. Chancery Courts thus continued a customary separation between the guardianship of property and the guardianship over the person. The child had a case to plead only as a bearer of property; those without property were outside *parens patriae*. This is reaffirmed by Cotton L. J. in Re Agar-Ellis (1883) 24 Ch. D. 317).

> The Court does not exercise its jurisdiction except when either there is money paid into court under the Trustees Relief Act, and for this purpose £100 is held sufficient, or a suit instituted to administer trusts of money on the infant, not because the jurisdiction is not there but because the Court will not interfere as regards the Custody and tuition, where it has not the means of providing them.

But as the Chancery Court constituted *parens patriae* as applicable only to those with sufficient wherewithal to provide for their own subsistence, maintenance and tuition (i.e. child heirs), the discourse was simultaneously being decomposed. Cottenham (1847) in Re Spence 16 LJ (Ch. (NS) 309) recants his earlier position (see above) declaring:

The case in which the Court interferes on behalf of infants are not confined to those in which there is property. The Court interferes for the protection of infants qua infants by the virtue of the prerogative which belongs to the Crown as *parens patriae*.

Thus Cottenham in redefining the Court's responsibilities effectively reconstructs the doctrine of parens patriae, and the court's supreme parentage over *all* infants. Cottenham's statements though must be seen in a much broader transformation of the Chancery's court relation with the family. For the transformation of the doctrine of *parens patriae* was in tandem with the legal demolition of the absolute authority of the father as head of the household.

We can display this through a consideration of two cases. Re Agar-Ellis (*op. cit.*) in which a girl of 16 applied to the court, by writ of habeas corpus to remain in her mother's custody. The father was dead, but his 'presence' is given through his appointed testamentary guardians, who hold in law all the rights of the father. In common law a girl of 16 is at years of discretion and can therefore apply to the courts for a writ of habeas corpus. The court established however that the rules of equity prevail, therefore Brett M.R. summed up that the girl's writ:

> ... seems directly contrary to the laws of England which is that the father has control over the person, education and the conduct of his children until they are twenty-one years of age. That is the law.

The patriarchal discourse is further elaborated by Cotton, L.J.:

> ... this Court holds this principle – that when by birth a child is subject to the father, it is for the general interest of the families, and for the general interest of the children, and really for the interest of the particular infant, that the court should not, except in very extreme cases, interfere with the discretion of the father but leave to him that power which nature has given him by the birth of the child.

The material circumstances of the girl disappear in the celebration of the very principle of legal patriarchy; the 'natural' right of the father qua father to dominate his children. Her plea represents a threat to the social body, 'the general interests of children and the general interests of families' which the court entrusts to the good management of the patriarch. The girl's appeal was dismissed.

By contrast if Agar-Ellis celebrates legal patriarchy, the case of Reg v Gyngall (1892) 2QB 232 celebrates its decomposition. Gyngall is of some importance for its new reading of *parens patriae*, the elaboration of the notion 'the welfare of the child', and finally for the space created for the interventionist state. Lord Esher puts *parens patriae* in play in a revolutionary way:

> ... the Chancery Court was put to act on behalf of the Crown as being the guardian of all infants, in place of a parent, and as if it were the parent of the child, thus superseding the natural guardianship of the parent.

Chancery becomes the guardian of *all* children, it functions *as if* it were a parent, and importantly, its jurisdiction supersedes the natural guardianship of parents. Further, as 'the supreme parent of the child':

> The Court has to consider what is for the welfare of the child and for her happiness, what are her prospects. . . .

Thus the empire of the father and the natural rights of parents decompose in a judgement where Chancery 'acting as a wise and high minded parent' fabricates a direct relationship not only with child heirs but with all children. We can see the doctrine intact in the principles of the Guardianship of Minors Act 1971:

> In deciding the question of guardianship the court shall regard the welfare of the minor as the first and paramount consideration, and shall not take into consideration whether from any other point of view the claim of the father, or any right possessed at common law possessed by the father.[27]

The struggles and practices outside the legal system, the multiple components necessary for an analysis of the monumental shift registered in the Agar-Ellis case to Gyngall disposition, requires itself a minor thesis. It will have to be sufficient here to register the transformation, and the effects, which are basically two-fold.

Through the transformation of the doctrine of *parens patriae*, the Chancery Courts stand the child in relationship to a *custodial space*, a space formerly occupied only by the father, but a space which can now be 'filled' by a person (the father as natural guardian, or his appointed testamentary guardians), the courts (representing the Crown) or as Eldon suggests above, the state.

Secondly, the social relationships constituting the family, are no longer the private domain of the father. Where the child's welfare and happiness is at stake, Chancery provided the legal space for diverse agencies of the state to seek, through the courts, the power to intervene in the natural-parent/child relationship. Thus the web of common law and statute law, the judicial dispositions of the High Courts and magistrates benches, in cases related to marriage, divorce, custody and care, erected since the mid-nineteenth century, while invoking the principle of the 'welfare of the child', simultaneously opens up the family to judicial, social and medico-hygiene surveillance (confer Donzelot, 1979).[28] State agents and institutions do not, however, have *carte blanche*, but operate within definite limits.

It is useful here to consider the legal form of the state-parent-child relationship, which, tentatively, seems to involve the following principles:

a   Parental privileges and obligations are legal abstractions which can be distributed by the High Courts to certain classes of person (guardian ad litem, foster parents, etc.) or to certain institutions (local authorities can assume parental rights under the Children Act 1948.[29]

b   Guardians appointed by the courts (and this would include community homes, assessment centres etc.), assume the mantle of parents and have exclusive authority over the child (in terms of the denial/restriction of social practices, experiences, ideas, which are made available to the child).

c   The relationship between the natural parents and children is subordinate to the relationship between the courts and *its* children (the doctrine of *parens patriae*), thus providing the legal means by which state can remove children from the guardianship of natural parents.

d   The child cannot really consent, nor disagree to these arrangements (though the Children's Act 1975 does specify 'consultation'). What therefore comprises the child's happiness or welfare is the construct of parents (natural or surrogate), not the child.

e   Finally, far from being a legal subject in matters of custody, divorce, care orders, etc., the child becomes an *object* of dispute (between parents, and between parents and the state).

The legal constitution of a custodial space which can be 'filled' either by natural parents or 'institutions', by no means comprises an equivalence between natural and surrogate parents. Jenny Shaw (1977)[30] notes that while state apparatuses assume the rights, obligations and responsibilities of a parent, this does not include the other side of parental functions: to show love and affection. Further more, McEwan's (1976)[31] study of young offenders who commit offences while in care and control of the local authority, shows that the courts treat local authorities and natural parents quite differently. Local authorities bear no financial responsibility for fines and compensation imposed on juvenile offenders in its care; these are regarded as the responsibility of parents or guardians.

But so far we have only established the *general* terrain of the legal relationship between the parent and the child, and the hierarchy of authority over children, largely in terms of the law administered by the High Courts. We should not forget that the juvenile courts (formally created in 1908) are empowered to make dispositions in disputes between parents and state apparatuses. Further, the positioning of the child in the discourse of the magistrates court contrasts considerably with their discursive position, for instance, in the Family Division of the High Courts. Wardship proceedings and care order proceedings demonstrate this difference and provide an interesting comparison for two reasons. First, both are fundamentally ordered around the doctrine of the welfare of the child; secondly, wardship proceedings are more frequently being resorted to by natural parents to control wayward children, and, recently, Dunn, J. (141 JP 1977) encouraged local authorities to use wardship proceedings:

> because in many cases it is the only way in which orders can be made in the interests of the child, *untrammelled by the statutory provisions of the Children and Young Persons Act 1969 (147)* (My emphasis).

Section I of the Children and Young Persons Act 1969 empowers juvenile courts to hear and make dispositions on care proceedings brought by authorised persons (usually local authorities). Care proceedings can be initiated on the grounds of neglect, ill treatment, exposure to moral danger, a child being beyond parental control, or not receiving efficient full-time education. The proceedings are non-criminal, and, according to Lord Widgery, 'non-adversary, non-party' and should present the 'objective position of the child' (141 JP 472). Further, care cases should not 'provoke a contest between the local authority and the parent of the child' (Widgery, *ibid*).

The techniques for determining 'the objective position of the child' (Social Enquiry Reports, 'laying of information' by authorised persons, the questions raised by the bench, school reports), take place within the setting of the court, whose procedures are based on a tradition which is fundamentally adversarial and contestatory.

The constitution of the child in and through the family, is underscored by the system of legal representation in court, and the workings of the legal aid system. Legal aid is available to the child (though it seems inordinately difficult to get). However, it is the parents who instruct the defence, establishing the community interest between parent and child, sometimes with tragic results. The child is not represented independently of the family. The objective position of the child is established through the separate representation of the state and the family. What is at stake is the possession of the child, and under what conditions possession will take place. Through the processes and procedures of the juvenile court, the child's position to discourse is one of subject as object. That is, they have no *independent* legal personage in the system of legal representation; the child confronts the court through, and is constituted as the object of, a dispute, and is, therefore, invisible as a subject, visible as an object.

Wardship proceedings are somewhat homologous with care proceedings but provide a stark contrast to them. The effects of wardship proceedings, if an order is made, is to place the High Court as supreme parent of the child, rather than the local authority (though local authorities may act as the Courts agent).

The relationship of the child in the discourse in wardship cases however is radically different from the child in care proceedings. In the case of wardship, the child is represented by an Official Solicitor, appointed by the Court, whose sole consideration is to represent the child, independently of the other parties in the proceedings. Thus the child's position is that of an independent legal subject; the machinery exists through which the child's understanding of, and views about the proceedings, can be brought into play. Therefore the child confronts the Court, not as a subject only embedded within a family, but as a legal subject independent of it.

While one recent case is convincing evidence that wardship proceedings can work to the benefit of the child (Re D a minor 1976 Fam: Div: 185), the positive aspects of wardship proceedings should not mask the similarity of High Court procedures with those of the juvenile court. Both courts operated through secret written proofs, written by the technologists of medicine and social hygiene. Children cannot easily place themselves before any court, independently of the state or the family. Further, wardship and care proceedings are class-distributed; the very costs involved in high court hearings are sufficient to limit the number and nature of cases heard there. The contrast however, does underline a point made earlier, that different courts have different effects on the positioning of children in relationship to discourse, and, radically different effects on the social relations of children.

Children and Criminal Law

In 1831, a boy of thirteen was hanged at Maidstone, convicted of theft. After 1971, except in the case of homicide, children under the age of 14 could no longer by prosecuted for theft. The exclusion of children and young persons from adult criminal and penal processes will be only sketched here. It is an area well traversed by those interested in the nineteenth century conceptions of juvenile delinquency, those concerned with the formation, function and procedure of the juvenile court, and those whose concerns are the administration of justice and welfare in the juvenile courts.

The child's discursive positioning in criminal law, and criminal law itself can be conceived as sites of struggle (extra-legal, parliamentary struggle); the outcome of these struggles, briefly, were the demolition of an absolutist system of crime and punishment, and the insertion of the child into a system of discipline, reform and rehabilitation, existing as a concrete set of institutions (industrial schools, reform schools, borstals, juvenile courts, assessment centres, etc.). These institutions provide the formal boundaries between the adult legal subject and the child as a legal subject, in criminal law. The rituals and practices of these institutions in turn subjectify the child in a radically different manner from the adult.

The absolutist system of crime and punishment conceives crime as the physical manifestation of the morally evil mind. The criminal is held absolutely responsible for his/her criminal acts, and therefore after conviction, is to be punished according to the degree of transgression. Children over the age of criminal responsibility (which varied historically) were thus to be treated as a full legal subject, a position contradictory to previously discussed discourses. The dissolution of the absolutist system and specifically the removal of children and young persons from adult legal processes is an extremely complex transformation but the elements of such an account include:

1   Common law doctrines such as *mens rea* (guilty mind) and *doli incapax* (incapable of committing a crime) are the legal basis of the age of criminal responsibility, which always provided a measure of protection for the very young against the absolutist criminal and penal system. In the nineteenth century, below the age of seven, and presently, below the age of ten, a child is legally deemed not to be capable of committing a crime, because they do not have the necessary guilty mind. Criminal law demands evidence beyond all reasonable doubt that an offence has been committed by a defendant *and* that the prosecution must prove that the defendant has *mens rea*. In earlier times this meant that a child could be tried, convicted, but released because it did not have the necessary criminal capacity. The operation is now somewhat different; no trial is held because of the irrebuttable assumption (given through statute law) that no crime has been

committed, because the child does not have (in law) a criminal capacity. This fragile legal construct explodes when a child commits murder. The doctrine of *doli incapax* operates between the age of innocence and the age of discretion (age 14); a period during which the law recognises a *rebuttable* assumption that a child is incapable of committing a crime. The prosecution must demonstrate not only the committal of an offence, but show that a defendant knew the act to be wrong.

The exclusion of innocents from criminal law is something which seems never to be questioned in the texts. However, the existence age of responsibility provided one of the strategies for liberal reformers in their efforts to remove the young from the gaols and the hangman's noose. To extend the age of criminal responsibility was one strategy adopted.

2   In 1816 the Society for Investigating the Alarming Increase of Juvenile Delinquency in the Metropolis claimed that there were five significant causes of juvenile delinquency: i. the improper conduct of parents; ii. the want of education; iii. the want of suitable employment; iv. the violation of the Sabbath and habits of gambling in the streets; v. other auxiliary causes which aggravate and perpetuate evil (the severity of the criminal code, the state of the police, and, police discipline). More or less sophisticated versions of this account permeate the nineteenth century texts on juvenile crime (social investigations by individuals, or groups of child savers, parliamentary reports etc.). Schematically the 'field' on juvenile delinquency is constituted through the following:

a   'the alarming increase of juvenile crime' announces a 'new' problem, simultaneously delineating a 'new' social group ('child criminals' as opposed to criminals).

b   the child savers' pathological view of the working class family, environment and culture locates an object of study *and* the cause of crime.

c   the unchildlike behaviour of the working class young; their premature worldliness as a result of their familiarity with street life; their undisciplined upbringing manifest in lascivious behaviour, lack of thrift, industry and religious observance (May 1973: 21 Clarke *1975*: 6–7) contradicted (implicit) notions of childhood as a period of dependency and innocence.

d   the causal relationship between worldliness and crime is articulated through appeals to the new technologies of hygiene and medicine (crime as disease spreads contagiously, streets as 'moral sewers' to be cleansed by 'aeration', prisons as Houses of Contamination, 'mixing' the young with hardened criminals).

e   finally, and most importantly, the *decentring* of the child as the author of crime. Juvenile delinquency is embedded in the social environment and practices of the working class.

3   The social policies programmed by such an account of the causes of crime concretise through:

   a   the institutionalisation of the juvenile court, separating physically the child offender from the adult criminal. Different court procedures consecrating the separate existence of the child as a subject in criminal law.

   b   the insertion of the child offender into a set of practices designed not to punish, but to 'discipline' or 'treat' (reform schools, community homes etc.).

   c   a range of non-criminal offences (wandering, truancy, sexual promiscuity, loitering) detected by the police, the educational welfare officers etc. bring the activities of the 'street' into the purview of the juvenile court, and serve to indicate that the child to be in need of care and control.

In combination, these elements begin to provide the explanation for the specific form of the juvenile court on the one hand, and current conceptions of the young offender on the other. Principally, children have become 'decentred' subjects; they are no longer the authors of criminal acts. Nineteenth century child saving discourses and twentieth century penal and criminological theories, in their attempts to free the child from adult criminal proceedings, see offences as the product of the child's total social, cultural and economic conditions of existence. The conditions of existence are usually reduced in effect, to family background (see for example the official documents produced in the 10 years before the 1969 Act). The child thus confronts the juvenile court not because what it has done but for what it is. The judicial proceedings at the juvenile court take the form, not of an examination of the child but an investigation of the family. For what is at stake is not simply guilt or innocence but equally, whether the child is to remain within the family and under what conditions; in effect the modern juvenile court is equally a *de facto* family court.

The legal criminal child is further specified by age, class and gender, a specification which takes place through the work of the police (including the juvenile bureaux), the social workers' report, the magistrates court procedures, and through the discipline and treatment dispositions given in the courts. Thus specified as separate subjects, the very young, the female, the male, working class child is in receipt of highly specific attention from judicial-welfare agencies. Priestly, Fears *et al* (1977),[32] for example, indicate that West Country police have informally raised the age of criminal responsibility to twelve, rarely bringing to the notice of the courts, offences committed by children below that age. Children are thus inserted into periods of 'moral quarantine'. It would seem also that the police rarely bring to the notice of the court first-time offenders; they are dealt with by the juvenile bureau, if the offence is deemed to be not too serious. Margaret Casburn (1978)[33] in her excellent work on the Hackney juvenile court, indicates that girls are brought to the courts less often than boys, but receive stringent care and supervision orders for offences for which boys on similar charges are merely fined. The courts, it seems, constitute themselves as moral guardians when handing out dispositions to female offenders.

In terms of the criminal law, children are caught up in highly discretionary legal process; discretionary in that discipline and treatment are meted out in a legal process not safeguarded by some of the guarantees the 'fair trial' embedded in adult criminal legal process. Care orders for instance are open ended, unlike the system of determined lengths of punishment in the adult penal system. Section 53 children for example (those who have committed serious offences such as manslaughter or murder) are detained for an indeterminate period; the only comparison available seems to be with adults detained involuntarily under the Mental Health Acts. It is the discretionary nature of the criminal legal process as it confronts the young which is now under attack. Some commentators would like to see the welfare and criminal aspects of the juvenile court divided between two separate institutions, others would like to see the introduction of the Scottish Reporter system south of the border. Both positions fail to comprehend that neither of these 'solutions' take into account the always/already present processes of subjectification at work in the processes of juvenile justice and welfare; the individuation according to class, age and gender, which take place within the general separation of the adult from the child.

Conclusion

Through the historical analysis of discourses on infancy, *parens patriae* and criminal law we can begin to understand the complex and diffuse position of the child in law. This paper also indicates the importance of the High Courts in constituting children as legal subjects; studies which focus primarily on the processes of the juvenile court must be somewhat limited in their understanding of the complex relationship between law and class.

The problems which emerge from the tangled position of the child in law are two-fold; first, does the child emerge as a legal subject, and second, what is the nature of the legal subjectivity of that child.

In the first case, one leading commentator[34] has argued that:

> ... children tend to be objects of the law rather as animals are. And despite recent dicta to the contrary children do not have legal rights.

Now we may agree that the child has no legal rights (though this is problematic), but we must not equate legal subjectivity with the possession of rights. The non-possession of legal rights itself designates, albeit in the negative sense, a position, status or space (for example, the married woman in nineteenth century law, the guest-worker in European economies, the African and Coloured workers in South Africa), which speaks of the power relations of social formations through categories which the law excludes. The multiple discourses of English law do constitute a 'child', even if, as we have earlier indicated, that the child is conceived in a very negative sense by being forbidden to enter into or speak at certain judicial proceedings. The legal system, as in the case of the child, must work positively to position subjects who stand outside the law's domain. The legal system functions not only through positive recognition, but also by the process of exclusion.

In the context of the child in law, it is clear that in many judicial proceedings, the child is present as an object; disputed over in intra-familial cases of custody, homologous to the position of goods and chattels, whose ownership is to be settled in court. But is this not part of the process of the law's subjectification of the child – the transformation of human individuals of a certain age into the objects of dispute – between parents, and between parents and local authorities?

In other circumstances the recognition of the child as a legal subject is more positive. For example, except in the most exceptional circumstances the child as a legal subject is 'absent' from the process of 'adult' criminal procedures, but is 'present' in a system of juvenile justice. However the judiciary may want to argue that though the juvenile court is not a court in the proper sense (i.e. its proceedings are non-party, non-adversarial) *it is still a court*; cases are heard, dispositions are made on the basis of evidence which proves 'beyond reasonable doubt' or on 'the balance of probabilities' that an offence has been committed or that a child is not receiving reasonable care. Further, 'findings of guilt' or acquittal *are* operative concepts; discipline or treatment may result as a consequence. In these circumstances the child is on stage as a legal subject, however 'decentred' that subjectivity maybe.

To the second question, we must say that the law produces the child as a legal subject separate and different from adult subjects. The law's child is an incapacitated and negative subject; separated from the ownership of property, lacking reason, always positioned in relationship to a custodial space, the object of dispute, classified by age and gender – almost a non-person, incapable of acting on the world. It is rarely granted any autonomy from the set of social practices while the law constitutes around it. Thus in relationship to the social category adult, the child's position legally, is one of dependence and subordination.

We have indicated through historical analysis, the various struggles which have produced the current situation of the child in law. The child savers' struggles to remove children from adult criminal law and from gaols can be defended. But should we not look again at the whole problem of age, maturity, and responsibility? Is the discrepancy between the age of discretion for boys, set at 14 and girls set at 16, a necessary one? We know the age of consent was a tactic employed by Stead and others to prevent the exploitation of young girls in brothels, but does it have any relevance today? Rather, does it not now function in a purely repressive manner, legitimating the harsher care and supervision orders placed on female offenders (whose offences are often non-criminal)? The relations between parents and children, children and the courts is constituted in terms of possession (custody, guardianship, wardship); children are continually objectified as someone's property. The medieval origins of this construct are clear and stand in need of transformation.

Finally, the relationship between the law and the child is one of repressive protection. The repression-protection couple remains in constant tension and the question becomes whether the child's protection in law must always be at the price of a certain repression. How the protection-repression couple is to be dissolved, or indeed whether it needs to be, is not simply a problem inherent in legal relations, but confronts us in our theorising about the child and school, the child and work and, children and sexuality.

Notes and References

1 ALTHUSSER, L. (1971) *Lenin and Philosophy*, New Left Books; HUNT, A. (1976) 'Law, state and class struggle', *Marxism Today*, June.
2 PASHUKANIS, E.B. (1978) *Law and Marxism: A General Theory*, Ink Links.
3 HIRST, P. Q. (1976) 'Althusser and the theory of ideology', *Economy and Society*, 5, (4).
4 *Ibid.*, p. 401.
5 POLLOCK, F. and MAITLAND, F.W. (1968) *The History of English Law Before the time of Edward I*, (2nd edition), revised and reissued by SFC Milson, Cambridge University Press, pp. 438–9.
6 COKE, E. (1818) *A Systematic Arrangement of Lord Coke's 1st Institute of the Laws of England*, edition by THOMAS, J.H., 3 Vols., p. 170.
7 MACPHERSON, W. (1842) *A Treatise on the Law Relating to Infants*, A. Maxwell and Son, p. 337.
8 LATEY REPORT, (1967) *Report of the Committee on the Age of Majority*, Cmnd. 3342, HMSO, p. 13.
9 JAMES, J.E. (1960) The age of majority, *American Journal of Legal History*, Vol. 4.
10 POLLOCK, F. and MAITLAND, F.W. (1968) *op. cit.*, p. 439.
11 *Ibid.*
12 LATEY REPORT, (1967) *op. cit.*, p. 99.
13 POLLOCK, F. and MAITLAND, F.W. (1968) *op. cit.*, p. 439.
14 JAMES, T.E. (1960) *op. cit.*; RICHE, P. (1973) 'L'enfant dans le haut moyen age', *Annales de D.H.*
15 BLACKSTONE, W. (1775) *Commentaries on the Laws of England*, Vol. I, (7th edition), Clarendon, p. 453.
16 COKE, E. (1818) *op. cit.*, p. 47.
17 MACPHERSON, W. (1842) *op. cit.*, p. 453.
18 *Ibid.*, p. 448.
19 LATEY REPORT, (1967) *op. cit.*, p. 28.
20 *Jowitt's Dictionary of English Law*, (1977) (2nd edition), BOURKE, J. (Ed.), Sweet and Maxwell, p. 131.
21 POLLOCK and MAITLAND (1968) *op. cit.*, p. 444.
22 THOMAS, J.H. (Ed.) (1818) *op. cit.*, p. 151.
23 CRANE and GRAVESON, R.H. (1957) *A Century of Family Law*, Sweet and Maxwell.
24 STONE, O. (1978) 'The welfare of the child, in BAXTER and EBERTS (*op. cit.*).
25 Quoted in MACPHERSON, W. (1842) *op. cit.*, p. 100.
26 *Ibid.*, p. 101.
27 CLARKE HALL, W. and MORRISON, A.C.L. (1972) *Law Relating to Children and Young Persons*, (8th edition), Butterworths, p. 1198.
28 DONZELOT, J. (1979) 'La police des familles', review article by HODGES, J. and HUSSAIN, A. *Ideology and Consciousness*, No. 5, Spring.
29 CLARKE HALL, W. and MORRISON, A.C.L. (1972) *op. cit.*, p. 1199.
30 SHAW, J. (1977) 'In loco parentis', *Journal of Moral Education*, 6, (3).
31 McEWAN, J. (1976) 'The local authority as "guardian" of child offenders', CLR, p. 718.
32 PRIESTLEY, P., FEARS, D. and FULLER, R. (1977) *Justice for Juveniles: The 1969 Children and Young Persons Act: a case for reform*, Routledge and Kegan Paul.
33 CASBURN, M. (1978) 'Juvenile Justice for Girls', Unpublished MS; forthcoming WRRC pamphlet.
34 FREEMAN, M.D.A. (1974) 'Child law at the crossroads', *Current Legal Problems*, Stevens and Sons, p. 167.

4
Teacher Politics and Accountability

19 Control, Accountability and William Tyndale

Roger Dale

There can be few, if any, schools as well known as William Tyndale,[1] and even fewer whose names evoke such a varied range of (usually negative) reactions. It is the extent of this range which provides a major clue to the continuing importance and topicality of the Tyndale case. Other schools have, of course, achieved a similar notoriety, but this has typically been relatively short-lived, and confined to a single issue; the cases of Duane at Risinghill (see Berg[2]) and MacKenzie in Aberdeen (for a comparison of this case with Tyndale, see Little[3]), both centring on the attempts of charismatic headmasters to liberalise the regimes of working class secondary schools, provide evidence of this. While the efforts of the William Tyndale headmaster, Terry Ellis, and his staff to liberalise the school's regime were undoubtedly a major cause of the scandal which blew up around it, they would not, alone, have ensured its continuing perceived relevance. What made the Tyndale case unique was the number, variety and intensity of the reverberations it set up throughout the education world. The lessons that the Tyndale affair is seen to teach, or the most important issues it is thought to raise, reflect an impressive breadth of viewpoints.

The Tyndale affair is, for instance, often taken to be about progressive education and its failure. As Adam Hopkins[4] puts it, 'Here in a nutshell was all that anyone had ever dreaded about progressive practice'. This was the line most frequently pursued in the unanimously hostile press coverage of the affair. In these reports progressive education was linked to two further themes which were themselves developed independently by commentators after Tyndale, those of political indoctrination and falling standards – see Holland (1976)[5] for an account of the press reporting of the Tyndale affair: see also School Without Walls (1978).[6] The success of this press campaign can be seen in the use of 'William Tyndale type' as a handy adjective to damn teachers or schools as at once dangerously subversive and irresponsibly indifferent to standards.

The political indoctrination theme is picked out most clearly by Dolly Walker, the former Tyndale teacher, who played a major part in exposing what was going

Source: First published in this volume.

on at the school. Writing in the 1977 Black Paper, she refers to 'the heart of the matter, which the Auld Report assiduously evades, namely, the strong political motivation of the teachers whose educational thinking was entirely germane to their political thinking'[7] and she goes on to ask, 'Is it too fanciful to see that all that happened at the school reflects a highly successful policy *if the aim is to provide material for future revolution?*' (emphasis in original). Hopkins also sees this as a critical issue, arguing that 'anxiety about left wing teachers ... was given a powerful boost by the events at and surrounding William Tyndale school in 1975 and 1976', while 'in terms of public opinion ... it was undoubtedly the educational politics of William Tyndale which mattered most'[8].

Ironically, in view of this labelling of them, the Tyndale teachers' actions were not particularly well received amongst those left wing teacher groups they were taken to typify. They were criticized for 'not taking into account the larger forces outside the school',[9] presumably the very forces their right wing critics were blaming them for introducing. Similarly, Ken Jones' criticism in *Radical Education* that 'the response of the Tyndale teachers is unfortunately typical of the progressive legacy'[10] sets up improbable echoes of more conservative voices. (It should be noted that there is emphatically no intention here to suggest that because they were *apparently* attacked from both sides for opposite failings, that these attacks somehow cancel each other out and that the Tyndale teachers must, therefore, have 'got it about right'; the intention is rather to indicate how lessons from the particular set of events were articulated to very different political ends.)

Other important issues raised for the first time or revealed in a new light by the Tyndale case include the curriculum and the place of parents in schooling. For Becher and Maclure, for instance, writing on the politics of curriculum change:

> The William Tyndale episode offers a case study of innovative failure. It exemplifies, among other things, inept teacher-controlled curriculum development; an impotent local authority inspectorate; failure by the local authority to accept responsibility for the curriculum leading to the eventual collapse of the school when parents, teachers and managers pulled in different directions; the failure of the staff to carry the support of the parents, and the reluctance of the staff to compromise their own professional principles by seeking to persuade parents; and the conse-quences of internal staff division.[11]

'Parent power' was another major issue sparked off by Tyndale and taken up by the press; and the part played by parents in bringing about the downfall of the Tyndale teachers was seen as a highly significant and welcome manifestation of this power, signalling a victory for common sense, standards and values, over theory, experiment and subversion. However, a rather more searching analysis by David also gives the issue of parental rights a prominent place among the implications of the Tyndale affair. For her:

> The conflict centred on the control that both mothers and fathers could have over educational practice and their commensurate rights. ... The

dispute does indicate, albeit in stark and crude form, the boundaries of the relationship between parents, teachers, taught, government and administration which can be tolerated within the present system if social and sexual reproduction is to be maintained.[12]

In these two contributions, the common thread which ties together almost all the themes within the Tyndale affair has generated or rekindled becomes more apparent. It is the problem of the control of schooling and the accountability of schools and teachers to various sectors of 'the wider community'. The importance of this theme has been recognised by many of those who have written on the Tyndale affair – not least in the title of Gretton and Jackson's book – *William Tyndale: Collapse of a School – or a System?*. There has, though, been a tendency to simplify the problem, once it has been identified, and I want to spend the remainder of this paper indicating some of the complexities thrown up by a discussion of the issues of control and accountability as they are presented by the William Tyndale affair.

First, though, it is necessary to put that affair into rather clearer perspective. In demonstrating what a range of issues it raised, there is a danger of suggesting that what happened at William Tyndale *caused* these issues, that they were not matters of concern previously. Of course, this would be quite untrue. Already, for instance, there was considerable concern about standards, as the setting up of the Bullock committee on reading (in response to the 1972 NFER reading survey), and the creation of the Assessment of Performance Unit in 1974, demonstrate. Similarly the Taylor Committee on the government of schools was set up in April 1975, by the then Minister of Education, Reginald Prentice. At the same time, the Black Papers, with their strongly anti-progressive, pro-standards line had been enjoying increasing credibility, and increasingly strident support from most of the popular press. There was, then, undoubtedly an atmosphere of growing disenchantment with the achievements of the education system as a whole, and with some segments of the teaching profession in particular, well before Terry Ellis was even appointed to William Tyndale school. This feeling had not, though, yet reached a point where it could bring about the changes it specified as necessary for the rehabilitation of the education system. These desirable outcomes were unattainable owing to the lack of a fatal challenge to the dominant consensus on education and the pattern of effective control over it. At considerable risk of distortion, these may be briefly summarised as, respectively, a mildly progressive social democratic approach and a high level of teacher control over the day to day life of schools, and influence over educational policy.[13] What the William Tyndale affair did was to make these desirable ends attainable by simultaneously increasing the credibility of the right wing attack and undermining the dominant educational ideology and the legitimacy of the teachers' authority within the education system, both at classroom and national levels. William Tyndale acted as a catalyst, creating a climate which made possible what was being increasingly bruited as desirable. It was the wider context in which they occurred, then, rather than the actual happenings at Tyndale themselves, which made the affair 'the educational *cause celebre* of the decade'.

It certainly did produce a host of outcomes. Apart from the doubling of the ILEA primary inspectorate, the case appears to have been widely used 'to encourage the others'; all over the country, we may be sure, heads, inspectors, elected representatives and teachers were led to take a little extra care over what they wrote on blackboards, reports, memos and exercise books. The atmosphere created was one in which all concerned in the education system were perhaps somewhat more amenable to greater and more overt control and accountability in the education system. And in arguably the most important outcome of the Tyndale affair, the Prime Minister-initiated Great Debate and subsequent Green Paper,[14] control and accountability were certainly very prominent themes.

Control and Accountability, Post-Tyndale

Let us then examine what light can be shed on these issues, which I have already referred to as deceptively simple, by examining them in the light of discussions of what is taken to have happened at William Tyndale. I want to separate out for the purpose of this analysis three strands of the overall problem, those of the management of education, teachers' classroom autonomy, and teachers' wider professional autonomy.

The Management of Education

The Tyndale affair has been widely regarded as a management problem. It is seen as posing questions both about how conflict between individuals and groups can be settled, and about what institutional machinery is most likely to bring about this desirable end. Yet, as in so many other areas, what happened at William Tyndale served to bring concentrated attention to bear on a problem which was far from novel, through a dramatic demonstration of some of the more extreme difficulties the problem might entail.

It was already clear before 1975 that the basis of the management of the English education system, enshrined in the 1944 Education Act, was in a rapidly advancing state of decay. The social, economic and educational context of 1944 had been transformed by the late 1960's, placing an increasingly unabsorbable strain on the assumptions on which the system was based. The two most crucial assumptions were those of a balance of power, and a supra-political consensus. The 1944 Act sought to create a balance between central and local government and the teaching profession such that:

> power over the distribution of resources, over the organization and
> context of education was to be diffused among the different elements and
> no one of them was to be given a controlling voice ... the DES was not
> given strong formal powers to secure the implementation of its policies
> because it was assumed that both central government and local education
> authorities were managed by men of good will whose main concern was
> to improve the service and whose reflective judgements remained untainted
> by the intrusion of party ideology.[15]

The second part of that quotation is shot through with an ideology of supra party consensus on education; this was to be achieved through consultation with all interested parties. Thus, as Bogdanor further states:

> Were any element in the system to seek to use its formal powers to the full, the system could not work. Mutual constraint, as in the Hobbesian universe, is the precondition of success, and the war of all against all would make progress in education impossible. There must, therefore, be limits on the degree of politicization of the education service if it is to operate success-fully.[16]

There are at least five shortcomings to be noted with respect to this system of education management. First of all, it quite clearly does not reflect the situation in the system it was set up to control at all accurately. The comprehensive schools issue alone, culminating in the Tameside judgement, knocks the props out completely from under a system premissed on the exclusion of party politics from educational matters and some sort of permanently available central-local consensus. Second, as Bogdanor too points out, the system is ineffective in directing the education system into new pathways. Since 1944, the potential contribution of education to both individual and national economic prosperity has been widely acknowledged, but a system which rests on no one party taking an undue initiative in its direction has responded only slowly to the challenges contained in the role of education in the development of human capital. (This is not to suggest that the system of education management alone is responsible for this failure, very far from it.) Third, again as noted by Bogdanor, such a system is able to operate much better in periods of expansion than in periods of retrenchment, when squabbles between the parties to the consensus over the distribution of even scarcer resources may become inevitable. Fourth, there has been in recent years evidence of a change in the style of education management, at both national and local level, towards a 'managerialism' emphasising efficiency rather than broadening access (see David[17]), with the DES coming under the influence of a manpower planning ideology (see Tapper and Salter[18]). At a local level this has been accompanied by a growth in the size of local authorities following the 1974 reorganization of local government, and by the introduction in many of them of a system of 'corporate management' drawn from industrial and business use and intended primarily to increase efficiency (see Cockburn[19]). Finally, the assumptions have been challenged by an increasing desire for participation in the control of the education system by many of the groups affected by it but excluded from influence over it. As Bogdanor puts it,

> in particular the move towards greater participation in education has done much to undermine traditional arrangements. For the system of consultation worked best, when only a small number of interests were involved whose rank and file were content to defer to elites, and could, therefore, be relied upon to act 'sensibly'.[20]

(And what did William Tyndale do to that?!) As David has shown, pressure towards greater participation in the control of education was already building up in the late 1960s. At that time such pressure was associated with radical efforts at securing greater community control over schools; it is interesting that such moves were nowhere near as successful as the articulation of 'parent power' to a much more conservative political stance in the past three or four years, and it is difficult to avoid seeing an effect of William Tyndale here. What the Tyndale case was used to demonstrate was the importance of parents having some say in what was going on at their children's school, rather than an example, albeit rather flawed, of an attempt to set up a school more responsive to its local community than to perceived national priorities.

It is fairly clear that the Tyndale affair did have some effects in the area of the management of education. It served to deliver the final blow to the 1944 system by demonstrating that its several shortcomings could jointly lead to disaster. It had, perhaps, two particular effects in this area. First, it appeared to show that the pursuit of national economic goals could be not merely ignored but actually frustrated in a system where clear central leadership was absent; in this way it made the path to greater DES intervention in the education system much smoother. And second, it greatly enhanced the likelihood that the progress of parent participation in schooling would be articulated in a conservative rather than any kind of progressive or radical philosophy of schooling.

Teachers' Classroom Autonomy

The assumption that the education system was governed by a more or less implicit consensus about aims and objectives, strategies and tactics had considerable effects at the level of the management of individual schools, too. For, as Pateman (in this volume) argues, where the goals of schooling were expressed in terms of implicit understandings rather than explicit targets, this:

> increased the power of both teachers and inspectors. In the case of teachers it made it difficult for them to be held to account by either parents or managers with whom it was possible, if desired, to play a 'catch us if you can' game. In the case of inspectors, it required of them a hermeneutic understanding of the schools, the efficiency of which they were assessing ... Education, like medicine and the law, had its mysteries to which teachers and inspectors were privy, and parents and politicians were not.[21]

This approach is developed further in Dale and Trevitt-Smith. In a consensual situation teachers' classroom autonomy has plenty of space to develop – in such a situation:

> the extent to which a school board can hold teachers or a school to account for its performance is strictly limited, since by definition its members are not expert and can at best only claim to be able to identify cases of gross incompetence, gross inefficiency and plain corruption – and even here they may well feel constrained to rely on the advice of the head teacher or an inspector.[22]

Two common explanations of the Tyndale case, one from 'sympathetic liberals' and the other from more cynical radicals, become pertinent here. A common argument from people not unsympathetic to the Tyndale teachers is that what they were attempting was fine in theory (and some versions go on to indicate that similar things are being done with impunity in other schools) but they just were not very good at carrying through these admittedly very difficult practices and policies. Chaos inevitably ensued, to a degree that was interfering with any kind of effective education of the children. The more cynical view suggests that what happened to the Tyndale teachers merely confirms what we knew all along, namely that all the talk about professional autonomy was just a hoax – when it is put to the test, when someone actually treats it seriously, then its bogus nature is immediately revealed.

Both these arguments seem to be too simple and to ignore some of the complexities of the situation. The first argument assumes the persistence of a consensus about education; according to Pateman, a logical precondition for teacher autonomy ' . . . when the ends of education cease to be consensual . . . the claim to professional freedom logically collapses. For in such a situation there is no longer a neutral professional dealing in expertly-assessable means',[23] albeit one that has changed over the years and is now represented, in primary schools at any rate, by what might be called 'Plowdenism'. John White puts this very clearly: 'It is one of the ironies of this case that they were, after all, only putting into practice in a radical form the theories that had been pumped into them in their own training and which have, between Hadow and Plowden, become the official gospel of the primary world'.[24] Two points need to be made about this. First, the teachers at William Tyndale saw themselves as going well beyond Plowdenism – in April 1975 Brian Haddow had attacked 'the late 1960's style of informal progressive repression', advocated the abolition of 'pointless structure' and called for more egalitarian systems for staff and children. (The teachers' views on progressive education are set out in Ellis *et al*[25]). Thus, 'incompetent Plowdenism' seems an ineffective charge to lay at their door. Second, I have argued elsewhere[26] that the period of dominance of the Plowden consensus was already very much on the wane, and was yet another educational phenomenon whose end was hastened rather than directly brought about by its being dragged into the Tyndale affair. Effectively, then, teacher autonomy was being treated under a form assuming a consensus regime some time after a consensus could in fact be established. Hence the conditions for the kind of teacher autonomy premised on consensus were absent; it was only a matter of time before their absence was discovered.

The other pat response to the Tyndale affair – its exposure of the hoax of teacher autonomy – also rests on a number of rather fragile and vague assumptions about the nature of teacher autonomy. Essentially, they make the exercise of teacher autonomy far too voluntaristic, indeed far too easy. What they miss is the situated nature of teachers' classroom autonomy, and even, indeed, its political nature. Only its suppression is seen as a political act; its practice by teachers in situations like that at William Tyndale is seen rather as the expression of inalienable professional rights. Yet Pateman's argument shows that it is only in the relatively narrow – and in a sense self-defeating – context of working within a consensus framework that the assertion of teacher classroom autonomy – if that means doing something different from what is officially expected of them, which it usually implicitly does – is anything other than a political challenge which must be interpreted and acted on as such.

Oddly similar in some ways to this cynical interpretation of the Tyndale affair is the more popular and more right wing view which sees the teachers as abusing their power and deserving everything they got. This account, too, turns on a particular interpretation of teacher autonomy. There are very many, very widely recognised, constraints on teacher autonomy, some of which it is impossible for individual teachers to overcome – such as the teacher pupil ratio, the inability of schools to choose whom they will teach and so on – others of which it is possible, if very difficult, to overcome – such as the expectation that children will be taught the 3 R's or that they will not be tortured. Teachers have an implicit mandate to combat ignorance and indiscipline and they have to carry it out in particular circumstances (such as the teacher – pupil ratio, external examination demands) which themselves entail certain constraints.[27] Within these constraints, teachers are relatively free to carry out their duties as they will. They are only relatively free since, first, they remain at the bottom of a hierarchy of authority and subject to the immediate control of their head teacher and, second, the ways in which they exercise the freedom available to them are subject both to the constraints of the classroom situation, its 'hidden curriculum', and to the assumptions about what it is to be a teacher which they distil from their own pupil experience, their teacher training and their teacher experience.[28] One result of this, for instance, is to make a cognitive style of individualism very prominent among teachers.[29] It is for this reason, rather than any lack of imagination or initiative on the part of teachers, that what autonomy teachers have has both tended to be minimized in much writing about teaching, and to have had so confirmatory, rather than disruptive an effect on the education system. Consequent to this modifying of possible autonomy, it was possible for teachers to be granted a 'licensed autonomy' within the education system without danger of this leading to a revolutionary, or even radical, transformation of the system.

What the Tyndale teachers appear to have done, however, and what led to the charges of abuse of autonomy, was to step outside the implicit and internalized guidelines as to how what autonomy they had should be used, as much as to extend the area of autonomy itself. In exercising their autonomy, the Tyndale teachers both ignored their mandate (by reversing the priorities it contained) and ignored the prescriptions for practice contained within the sedimented common sense of the teaching profession. This dual negation in the exercise of their professional autonomy is the basis of the accusations of its abuse.

The effects on educational policy of this perceived abuse of their autonomy by the Tyndale teachers have derived from the two sides of that negation. Steps have been taken to ensure both that the mandate (to teach certain subjects like maths and reading) is actually made mandatory (through the specification of the remit of the APU) and to reinforce the already potent effect of experience and professional common sense (through more frequent and more detailed monitoring of teachers and school activities). It has led to an increasing emphasis on how educational knowledge is *consumed* at the expense of how it is *produced* – symbolized in the waxing of the Assessment of Performance Unit while the Schools Council wanes. It has led to a recognition of the political nature of teachers' classroom autonomy in a period when there is no clear consensus on educational goals, and a consequent attempt both to specify the aims and objectives of the education system more clearly and more explicitly, and to routinize teachers' accountability for the performance of their (newly specified) roles. What is involved is the replacement of teachers' professional judgement by bureaucratic accountability. No longer will teachers be able to use their professional expertise to play 'catch me if you can'; they will now have to play 'jumping through the hoops'.

The Influence of the Teaching Profession

The effect which the Tyndale case had on teacher autonomy was not, however, limited to the moves to limit teachers' classroom autonomy just outlined. The affair also had a notable effect on the whole standing of the teaching profession and on its power and influence in the corridors and conference rooms where education policy is made. This is particularly important, for it is possible to distinguish two rather different conceptions of teacher autonomy which frequently are combined with consequent confusion and lack of clarity. The first conception of teacher autonomy, which we might call the weak conception, would limit it to the free exercise of acknowledged expertise in executing in the school and classroom educational programmes designed elsewhere, over which teachers should have no greater say than anyone else. It is this conception which underlay the discussion in the previous section. The second, 'strong', conception would include the creation as well as the execution of educational programmes within the scope of teacher autonomy, on the basis that the teachers are the experts about education and that they alone, or they best, can decide what should be taught as well as how to teach it. Now these issues are the subject of a continuing philosophical and political debate which is not strictly relevant here. What is relevant is that the Tyndale affair had an important effect not only on the weak conception of teacher autonomy, an effect which as we saw in the previous section led to it being curtailed, but also on the strong conception. This is not because the Tyndale teachers were in any way closely associated with those levels of the teaching profession which exercise its influence over educational policy, or because they were in any way attempting directly to bring pressure to bear on national educational policy themselves. Far from it. They were, in fact, repudiated by their union, the National Union of Teachers, which represented not them, but the Deputy Head, Mrs. Chowles, at the Auld Inquiry and, though they received some initial support from their local association of the NUT in the form, for instance, of asking other local primary schools not to enrol children removed from William Tyndale, this appears not to have continued in the same way.

The two conceptions of teacher autonomy broadly divide the two major teacher unions, with the NUT holding very much more to the strong conception than the

NAS/UWT. Some idea of what this strong conception involves can be gained from the remarks of a former president of the NUT, and still a very influential figure in teacher politics, Max Morris, who is reported as saying at an NUT executive committee meeting that:

> the TUC [of whose General Council the NUT's secretary is a member] had ignored the views of the teacher unions over (the) Taylor (committee Report) [which may be summed up in the General Secretary's reference to it as 'a busy body's charter'], the views of the workers in the industry concerned. The TUC would never presume to ride roughshod over the wishes of one of the industrial unions – the miners, for instance – about developments in their industry [the TUC had asked the government for swift implementation of the Taylor Report].[30]

In a similar vein of 'what's good for teachers is good for education' are Morris' comments to the House of Commons Expenditure Committee:

> Every improvement in teachers' conditions is inevitably an improvement in the education of children in our schools. Equally every improvement in educational conditions within schools improves teachers' conditions. The two things go together like that[31].

It should be added that Bogdanor also quotes Terry Casey, General Secretary of the NAS/UWT, stating to the same committee that:

> one tends to look at educational problems from what seems to me a very rational point of view, that the interests of teachers in the end are completely consonant with the interests of the education service.

It had been and continues to be, however, increasingly difficult to sustain this approach, for a number of reasons, several of which appeared to be strengthened by what happened at William Tyndale. One basic cause was the generally declining economic state of the country. This inevitably led to ever more severe cuts in budgets for education, affecting both resources and manpower. The zenith of the NUT's influence had been reached, inevitably, in the decade of rapid educational expansion from the late 50's on, and such contraction not only closed off possible avenues of further expansion, but made it very difficult even to maintain the *status quo*. Again the Tyndale affair had no direct effect on this, but the atmosphere it created made it very much easier for such cuts to be implemented. That atmosphere had a similar effect on the teaching profession retaining its central role in educational decision making. As has been hinted above, the DES was very keen to give a more decisive lead to the education service, to bring it more into line with perceived national priorities, and 'clipping the teachers' wings' seems to have been regarded as an important part of this. Before Tyndale, though, this would have been politically very difficult to achieve, given the very entrenched and apparently well legitimated position the teaching profession held. Tyndale, together with other evidence (such as the alleged decline in literacy) of 'the failure of the schools to do what the nation required of them' made this 'wing clipping' much more feasible. It did this through creating a situation where the scapegoating of the education system for the nation's parlous economic condition could be converted into the scapegoating of the teachers, and thus absolve all other levels of the system from responsibility. Thus, the educational policy makers and implementers emerged from the attacks on the system they directed scot free, while the reputation of the teaching profession received a very damaging blow.

As well as being squeezed from the one side by the more aggressive stance being taken by central government, the NUT's influence was also being pressured from the other side by the development of 'parent power', and once more this development was far from being hindered by the Tyndale affair.

So, notwithstanding the NUT's explicit repudiation of the Tyndale teachers, what they are popularly interpreted as having done has made a significant contribution to the erosion of the teaching profession's influence on education policy. Its wings *have* been clipped by the DES – note, for instance, the Schools Council's new (1978) constitution which effectively removed it from teacher control. It has been forced onto the defensive both by cuts in educational budgets and by falling rolls, with the pressure they put on the maintenance of teachers' jobs. And the public reputation of the teaching profession has not been lower for a long time, something which has further weakened its ability to defend its influence and its interests; this is symbolically reflected in a public mention, however tentative – in the Green Paper – of the possibility of setting up machinery to sack incompetent teachers, a further erosion of teacher power which the effect of Tyndale made it much more difficult to resist.

Conclusion

It should by now be clear that the role attributed to the William Tyndale affair in respect of changes in the control of schools and the accountability of teachers is essentially a facilitative one. What happened at the school did not initiate or cause these shifts, whose consequences are not yet clear, but whose broad aim quite clearly is to restructure and redirect the education system. Both the successful completion and an intended outcome of this process involve cutting back the influence of the teachers at both classroom and policy levels. However, stating that the Tyndale affair enabled rather than caused these changes is not an entirely satisfactory way to conclude this analysis and I would like in this final section to examine, extremely briefly, what might be some of those causes.

I argued above that many of the trends and tendencies which Tyndale brought to fruition were present long before the school achieved its notoriety, and I want now to look at some of these trends and tendencies. Why, for instance, did the DES want to increase central control over education? Why did the dominant consensus break down? Why did parents want more say in their children's education? In sum, how had all these problems arisen and why was it necessary to solve them in these particular ways?

Very briefly, (the arguments in this paragraph are spelled out much more fully in Dale[32]), over the period since 1944, the economic, political, and ideological climates in which education operates had changed, and so had the contributions which it was assumed education could make at each of these levels. However, the changes at these levels are far from being mutually complementary but are in fact contradictory; it is from these contradictions that the education system gains its dynamic. Similarly, changes at one level do not always, or often, keep pace with changes at other levels, which results in considerable strain during the catching-up period. Concretely, over this period both the pressure to national economic success, and the contribution which it seemed education could make to it, increased. The manpowering function of education became dominant. Yet, because it was governed by a system set up with a different set of priorities in mind, and dominated ideologically by approaches which were often hostile to the manpowering function, the implementation of what the priority of that function entailed was substantially obstructed. Furthermore, the removal of these obstructions was no easy matter; what were seen as obstructions from the viewpoint of an increasingly frustrated central government were widely legitimated features of a well established education system. As I have suggested some of these features were beginning to lose their legitimacy well before the Tyndale affair blew up. There is, though, no doubt that it hastened the pace of educational change, even if the broad direction of that change was already clear.

However, that is perhaps slightly to underestimate the impact of Tyndale. As I have argued about that impact in another context[33] while the broad direction of change had nothing to do with the Tyndale affair, some details of the route taken might, without distortion, be regarded as attributable to it. So I might best conclude this piece by pointing out two fairly major features which are not entailed by the overall nature of the restructuring and redirection which the change of educational priorities is bringing about, but where the public representation of the William Tyndale case had a particularly potent impact. First, I think it made a major contribution to the articulation of 'parent power' to a conservative rather than a progressive or radical educational programme. There is little in the phenomenon of parent power itself which would necessarily predispose it in that direction, or that would necessarily lead to it being in opposition to, rather than in association with 'teacher power' (though on this latter point the approach of the teaching profession is clearly crucial); the example of what happened at Tyndale might be seen to have pushed it powerfully in that direction.

Second, the scapegoating of the education system for the nation's economic failures need not necessarily have led to the teacher sector of the system taking all the blame. If blame there was to allocate – which seems highly dubious, and to be itself a function of the uneven development of the various levels at which the education system operates – it seems at least plausible that it might be laid at the doors of at least some of the other parties to the education partnership. As it is, following William Tyndale (and also the Bullock report[34] which looked to the improvement of teachers for an improvement of reading standards), it is the performance of teachers which is being monitored and not that of any other part of the system.

In terms of the two concerns of this paper, then, it might be said that while the Tyndale affair did not bring about changes in control, or make accountability necessary, it did have a significant impact on how easily those changes could be made, on the details of the new form of control, and on who was to be held accountable to whom and for what.

Notes and References

1 I have not included any details of the Tyndale affair in the body of the article for two reasons. First, at least what are taken to be the main features of it seem by now to be part of 'what everyone knows' about education. In a sense it has become an educational catch phrase which requires no explanation, and it is at this level of comprehension and usage that it has had the effects which I attempt to analyse here. Second, in view of the catch phrase effect, what *actually* happened has become more and more remote from, and less and less relevant to, most issues. That this popular view of the affair is a distortion of what actually happened I am convinced, yet attempting to establish 'the truth of Tyndale' is not strictly germane to this present undertaking. I have, in fact carried out such an attempt in a television programme and two radio programmes (produced by Ken Little) on *The Case of William Tyndale* which I made for the Open University course E202, *Schooling and Society*. I would refer anyone wishing to know more of the detail of the case to those programmes (and to the notes accompanying them) and to the Auld Report, (AULD, R. (1976) *William Tyndale Junior and Infants Schools Public Inquiry: A Report to the Inner London Education Authority*, London, Inner London Education Authority), the teachers' book, (ELLIS, T., McWHIRTER, J., McCOLGAN, D. and HADDOW, B. (1976) *William Tyndale: the Teachers' Story*, London, Writers and Readers Publishing Co-operative), the Times Educational Supplement journalists' book, (GRETTON, J. and JACKSON, M. (1976) *William Tyndale: Collapse of a School – or a System?*, London, Allen and Unwin) and to Patricia Holland's article on the press treatment of the case, (HOLLAND, P. (1976) 'Scandal for Schools', *Times Educational Supplement*, 17 September). The teachers' view of developments since their dismissal is contained in a pamphlet entitled *Tyndale 1978* by Terry Ellis and Brian Haddow, available from them at 32 Clifton Court, Playford Road, London, N. 4.
2 BERG, L. (1968) *Risinghill: The Death of a Comprehensive School*, London, Penguin.
3 LITTLE, K. (1976) 'Town House to County Hall', *Times Educational Supplement*, 5 March.
4 HOPKINS, A. (1978) *The School Debate*, London, Penguin, p. 97.
5 HOLLAND, P. (1976) *op. cit.*
6 SCHOOL WITHOUT WALLS, (1978) *Lunatic Ideas: How the Press Reported Education in 1977*, London, Corner House Bookshops, pp. 10–2.
7 WALKER, D. (1977) 'William Tyndale', in COX, C.B. and BOYSON, R. (Eds.), *Black Paper 1977*, London, Temple Smith, pp. 38–41.
8 HOPKINS, A. (1978) *op. cit.*, pp. 95, 96.
9 *Teachers' Action*, No. 6, (1976).
10 JONES, K. (1976) 'Progressive Education and the Working Class', *Radical Education*, 6, pp. 6–9.
11 BECHER, A. and MACLURE, S. (1978) *The Politics of Curriculum Change*, London, Hutchinson, p. 175.
12 DAVID, M.E. (1978a) 'The Family-Education Couple: Towards an Analysis of the William Tyndale Dispute', in LITTLEJOHN, G. *et al.*, (Eds.) *Power and the State*, London, Croom Helm, p. 177).
13 These points are developed in DALE, R. (1979a) 'From Endorsement to Disintegration: Progressive Education from the Golden Age to the Green Paper', *British Journal of Educational Studies*, 28, 3 October; and DALE, R. (1979b) 'The Politicization of School Deviance: Reactions to William Tyndale', in BARTON, L. and MEIGHAN, R. (Eds.), *Schools, Pupils and Deviance*, Driffield, Nafferton.
14 DEPARTMENT OF EDUCATION AND SCIENCE, (1977) *Education in Schools: A Consultative Document*, London, HMSO, (Cmnd. 6869).
15 BOGDANOR, V. (1979) 'Power and Participation', *Oxford Review of Education*, 5, 2, pp. 157, 166.
16 *Ibid.*, p. 158.
17 DAVID, M.E. (1978b) 'Parents and Educational Politics in 1977', in BROWN, M. and BALDWIN, S. (Eds.) *The Year Book of Social Policy in Britain 1977*, London, Routledge and Kegan Paul, pp. 87–106.
18 TAPPER, E. and SALTER, B. (1978) *Education and the Political Order*, London, Macmillan, esp. Ch. 7.
19 COCKBURN, C. (1977) *The Local State*, London, Pluto Press.
20 BOGDANOR, V. (1979) *op. cit.*, p. 161.
21 PATEMAN, T. (1978) 'Accountability, Values and Schooling', in BECHER, A. and MACLURE, S. (Eds.)

Accountability in Education, Slough, NFER. (Reproduced in this volume.)

22 DALE, R. and TREVITT-SMITH, J. (1976) 'From Mystique to Technique: Completing the Bourgeois Revolution in Education', unpublished paper.

23 PATEMAN T. (1978) *op. cit.*

24 WHITE, J. (1977) 'Tyndale and the Left', *Forum*, 19, 2, p. 60.

25 ELLIS, T., McWHIRTER, J., McCOLGAN, D. and HADDOW, B. (1976) *William Tyndale: the Teachers' Story*, London, Writers and Readers Publishing Co-operative, esp. pp. 42–7.

26 DALE, R. (1979) *op. cit.*

27 See DALE, R. (1976) *The Structural Context of Teaching (Course E202 Unit 5)*, Milton Keynes, Open University; DALE, R. (1977) 'Implications of the Rediscovery of the Hidden Curriculum for the Sociology of Teaching', in GLEESON, D. (Ed.) *Identity and Structure: Issues in the Sociology of Education*, Driffield, Nafferton, pp. 44–54.

28 See DALE, R. (1977) *op. cit.*

29 DALE, R. (1976) *op. cit.*

30 *The Teacher*, (1978) 20 December, p. 7.

31 BOGDANOR, V. (1979) *op. cit.*, p. 162.

32 DALE, R. (forthcoming) *The State and Education Policy*, London, Routledge and Kegan Paul.

33 DALE, R. (1978) *op. cit.*

34 DEPARTMENT OF EDUCATION AND SCIENCE, (1975) *A Language for Life (Bullock Report)*, London, HMSO.

20 *Collapse of Confidence*

Rhodes Boyson

A healthy school system must win the allegiance of teachers, parents and the public. Among all three there is unmistakable evidence of a sharp fall in confidence.

The lack of confidence of teachers is shown by the numbers of qualified practitioners who leave the profession, the rapid turnover of staff in many parts of the country, the low qualifications of those entering the profession, and the increasing militancy of teachers who, like university students, adopt an 'us versus them' posture in dealing with senior colleagues or the authorities.

The wastage-rate of teachers in the early years of teaching is very high. After a three-year College of Education course costing the country some £3,000, four-fifths of the women and one-third of the men leave the profession within their first six years of teaching. Even among the number of women teachers who leave for childbirth, it is doubtful how many will return to education except under economic necessity.

There are two elements in the problem of teacher turnover. The first is the rapid turnover from school to school in the search for higher pay through special responsibility allowances, and the second is the flight of teachers from many urban authorities because of the pressure of living costs and the increasing difficulty in maintaining discipline. Both factors are ultimately influential in causing so many teachers to leave the profession. The flight of teachers from London and other cities is, however, a new phenomenon which is matched by the difficulty of staffing other public services in urban areas.

A survey by the Assistant Masters Association (AMA) in 1973, showed that between a quarter and a fifth of London teachers from both ILEA and the outer London boroughs, left each year. The highest figure was 29.8 per cent in Brent and the lowest was 17.3 per cent in Hillingdon. This disturbed and disturbing state of affairs cannot simply be blamed on low salaries which themselves reflect over a number of years the low esteem in which teachers are held by the rest of society.

There has always been a conflict in the minds of teachers as to whether they are a profession or a trade. Supporters of the view that teaching is a profession have

Source: BOYSON, R. (1975) *The Crisis in Education*, London, Woburn Press, Chap. 5, pp. 27–32.

aimed to create for themselves a highly responsible, highly respected image, believing that society would then be prepared to pay teachers high salaries. Those who saw teaching as a trade wished to ape the militant trade unionists, to negotiate vigorously and even belligerently with the employers and to strike if the terms offered were unsatisfactory.

The National Union of Schoolmasters, basically a union of career male teachers, has always been militant but well-controlled in the tradition of the old trade unions, taking action only with the approval or guidance of its national headquarters. It has organized courses for shop stewards in the schools and occasionally calls strikes in favour of higher wages or better conditions of service in some school or authority.

The National Union of Teachers, a large union whose strength lies in its primary school membership, has moved towards militancy, partially in defence of the living standards of its members and partially under the influence of Neo-Troskyist and rank-and-file groups which have taken over some branches that can only be kept as members if they are given their head. Like the militant university students, these branches look for confrontation with their employers not only to improve the conditions of service of their members but also to express political opposition to certain policies.

The end of teaching as a profession was signalled by the determination of the NUT in London from 1973–74 to cease to 'cover' for absent colleagues after three days, far more than by the NUT (or the NAS) joining in membership of the Trades Union Congress, a decision taken by the NUT Executive only after the proposal had been rejected by a ballot of members. The Joint Four teacher unions, the National Association of Head Teachers and the Professional Association of Teachers continue to make an attempt to keep the image of professionalism alive.

The growing disillusion of parents with the state educational system is shown in three ways: their refusal to send their children to certain schools to which the local education authorities have directed them, their objection to the teaching methods and values of certain schools which their children are attending, and the increased numbers sending their children to independent schools.

The ILEA has borne the brunt of parental protests against the way children are allocated to secondary schools. In 1972, of 33,000 primary pupils due for transfer to secondary schools, some 4,645 did not get the school of their first choice. Over 2,500 parents protested to the divisional officers but something like half of the parents accepted the schools they were then offered for their children.

Large groups of parents, however, continued to object to the schools they were offered. Their chief reasons were not that the schools were in old buildings or had a low teacher/pupil ratio, but that they objected to the low academic standards, the lax discipline and even the loose curriculum of these schools. Some 800 children were still out of school at the beginning of the September term, 1972, 560 remained out towards the end of September and 325 had not attended school by late October.

The protesting parents in Islington and Hackney, who were predominantly working-class, joined together to rent a hall and hire three teachers for their children. They continued to give the ILEA a worrying time: police had to clear demonstrators from at least one divisional office, parents chained themselves to the railings at

County Hall and held a school in the main foyer. Mr. Harvey Hinds, the chairman of the ILEA schools committee, was held hostage in a Stoke Newington school until police intervention secured his release.

It is significant that none of the parents who kept their children away from ILEA schools was prosecuted for the non-attendance of their sons and daughters and that almost all of them finished up obtaining either the school they wanted or an equally respected school for their children. It was February 1973 before the last of the 'rebellious' pupils entered a school of their choice.

Although the ILEA was more careful in its allocation of pupils in 1973, a smaller number of parents again kept their children from the schools offered and once more a school was opened in Islington and a teacher hired until the ILEA fed the pupils into the preferred schools as soon as the numbers were manageable.

Towards the end of 1973 there was also an increase in the number of Moslem immigrant parents who kept their girls out of school because they objected to mixed schools. Although this objection was based on social and religious rather than educational grounds, it illustrates discontent with the narrow choice provided by the local education authorities.

Leicestershire has seen at least two revolts against comprehensive secondary schools to whose methods and values many parents strongly objected. Parents of some 250 children at Countesthorpe College petitioned the Department of Education and Science for the right of parents to choose an education they considered best for their children. According to the local press, this petition was prepared because the parents considered the school was far too left-wing, progressive and permissive. The question of an inquiry into the organization of this school became an issue in the county elections in April 1973 and it was finally agreed that a Department of Education and Science (DES) inquiry into the school should be held.

Some hundred parents also objected to the lack of discipline, poor academic standards and lack of a competitive element at Wreake Valley Comprehensive College, Leicestershire, and a working party of governors, staff and parents was set up after the parents met the Board of Governors and the Principal in June 1973.

The objection of parents to particular schools is a sign of a breakdown of minimum standards in the state system during the past 20 years. Before that period there were 'identikit' grammar schools and secondary modern schools with dependable standards. Today there is no standard comprehensive school and parents often object to the school place their children are allocated in the bingo lottery of the state system. There is no longer a dependable general pattern of internal school organization or even in the general approach to the education of the young.

It is no doubt these growing discrepancies between state schools and the fear of parents that their children may be allocated to what are called 'sink' schools which help to account for the increased number of children entering independent education. Compared with 564 pupils in the ILEA who left the state sector at the time of transfer to secondary school at the age of 11 in 1971, the number had increased to 735 a year later.

Certainly the demand for independent education is increasing. The number of pupils in Headmasters' Conference schools increased from 84,700 in 1947 to 105,000 in 1967, while the number in direct grant schools rose from 62,000 to 78,000. The largest increase, however, has recently come in the preparatory schools taking pupils from 7–9 to 13 years. Despite the pressures of inflation on family expenditure, the total number of children attending these schools increased by 1,477 in 1972 and by a further 4,000 in 1973 to a total of 70,000. This is as much a vote of no confidence in the state educational system as it is a vote of confidence in the independent sector.

Recently, we have seen a marginal increase in Britain of interest in both 'free schools' and 'deschooling'. Free schools, with less discipline and an attempt at self-rule by pupils, are not new and support for them has risen and fallen over the last two hundred years. Despite the fame of A.S. Neill, however, 'free schools' are not a significant factor in the British educational system. Support for them outside certain middle-class intellectual families is small or non-existent and the total numbers attending such schools in Britain are less than the number enrolled in one average-sized secondary modern school.

It is the same segment of the intellectual middle-class, influenced by a romantic primitive view of life and Ivan Illich in America, which also toys with the idea of 'deschooling'. It is argued that structured education fulfils no useful purpose for pupils and lessens their own individuality and spontaneity whilst shaping them as tools for some authoritarian or conventional society. On this reckoning, schools should be closed and pupils should get their education from the real world. Its simplicity makes this an attractive if facile doctrine and its appeal to the social worker mentality should alert us to the danger of its influence spreading. That anyone takes 'deschooling' seriously in an urban industrialised society, however, shows how deep is the crisis of confidence in state education.

There is clearly enough evidence of widespread lack of confidence to prompt the question: Do these accumulating signs of breakdown in schools and universities spring from a common underlying cause?

Magali Larson

From Historical to Structural Analysis

Looking backward from the phenomenon of profession as it appears in contemporary social life, I have attempted to trace its underlying unity in terms of the double movement by which it is historically constituted. The visible characteristics of the professional phenomenon – professional association, cognitive base, institutionalized training, licensing, work autonomy, colleague 'control', code of ethics – have been considered from a double perspective: first, as structural elements of the *general* form of the professional project, and second, as specific resource elements, whose variable import is defined by different historical matrices.

As structural elements, these characteristics appear in various combinations in all the modern professions. As resources, however, they are qualitatively different in different historical contexts and therefore they vary in import or 'useableness'. In the nineteenth century, for instance, institutionalized training meant different things for the same professions in Britain and in the United States; the differences in meaning reflected larger differences in the whole structure of the social stratification system in each country, including the different ideological legitimations of inequality. A cognitive base, as the necessary premise of training, is necessary to every specific professional project, but in each project it had a different content; therefore, it occupied in each a different place among various strategic resources.

The history or 'genealogy' of the elements that appear combined in the complex structure of profession can be traced across historical time spans and contemporary functional boundaries.[1] This has been done, for instance, in histories of professional schools or professional associations, or in histories of the cognitive corpus of various present-day professions (such as histories of legal thought, of architectural styles, of engineering techniques, of medical arts). I have focused my account on the complex mobilization and organization of these elements by different types of professional projects. It is time now to turn once again from historical diversity to the underlying structural processes and structural effects, which give a unified and broader meaning to this diversity.

Source: This is an abridged version of LARSON, M. (1977) *The Rise of Professionalism*, University of California Press, Chap. 12.

As organizations of producers of relatively scarce and mostly intangible skills, modern professions first emerge from the personal ties of dependence characteristic of precapitalist social formations, and then organize, on the market model, various new or enlarged spheres of social activity. That is to say, ultimately, modern professions organize to exchange their services for *a price*. We have followed the diverse manifestations of this organizing project and underscored its inherent tendency toward monopoly.

From a broader analytical perspective, the professional project is part of a basic structural transformation – namely, the extension of exchange relations under capitalism to all areas of human activity. It is analytically useful to recall, very briefly, some of the well-known concepts by which Marx uncovers the essence of this process.

Marx's analysis of the *real* commodity form reveals, first, its dual nature: as *use-value*, a commodity's concrete utility is a function of the concrete needs that it can satisfy. Use-value only becomes a reality when the commodity 'has found a resting place . . . [when] it falls out of the sphere of exchange *into that of consumption*'.[2] That a commodity should be capable of satisfying the needs of some potential user is a necessary aspect of its twofold existence, and a *sine qua non* condition of *its exchange value*. As *exchange value*, or value, a commodity 'at first sight, presents itself as a quantiative relation, as the proportion in which values in use of one sort are exchanged for those of another sort, a relation constantly changing with time and place'.[3]

The institutionalization of exchange relations – which, obviously, presupposes some development of the social division of labor – establishes 'the distinction . . . between the utility of an object for the purposes of consumption and its utility for the purposes of exchange'.[4] The development and generalization of money, as the universal equivalent which expresses the quantitative relations between all circulating commodities, completes their 'metamorphosis': 'When they assume this money-shape, commodities strip off every trace of their natural use-value, and of the particular kind of labor to which they owe their creation, in order to transform themselves into the uniform, socially recognized incarnation of homogeneous human labor'.[5] Indeed, in the labor theory of value, 'the magnitude of the value of a commodity represents only the quantity of labor embodied in it'.[6] Labor, the 'value-creating substance', does not appear here as concrete labor, creating specific use-values, but under its abstract guise: it is *labor-time*, measured by its duration, which is itself a function of the average labor-power of society. 'The labor-time socially necessary is that required to produce an article under the normal conditions of production, and with the average degree of skill and intensity prevalent at the time'.[7]

Thus, the extension of market relations tends to generalize the double abstraction embodied in the commodity form: *value*, an abstract quantitative relation to the monetary equivalent, and *labor-time*, an abstract quantitative expression of the 'average labor-power of society', expended for purposes of exchange.

Labor-power, the 'value-creating substance', itself appears as a commodity on the market, inseparably from the appearance of capital: the appearance and the combination of these two structural elements signals 'a new epoch in the history of social production'. 'The capitalist epoch', Marx writes, 'is therefore characterized by this, that labor power takes in the eyes of the laborer himself the form of a commodity which is his property; his labor consequently becomes wage labor. On the other hand, it is only from this moment that the produce of labor universally becomes a commodity'.[8] Two central processes – relatively independent of each other and of variable historical form – constitute the 'prehistory' of capitalism: first, the constitution of money-capital and its concentration in the hands of potential entrepreneurs; and second, the separation of the worker from the means of production. The second process is reflected in the juridico-political evolution which allows the individual worker to *sell* his labor – which makes him, that is, 'the untrammelled owner of his capacity for labor, i.e. of his own person'.[9]

In sum, the penetration of market relations into all areas of life is immensely accelerated and completed by capitalism. This character inseparably links the extension of market relations to the rise of a modern class system and to a juridico-political ideology which *ideologically* makes the isolated individual into the essential unit of the social and political orders.

This is the historical matrix within which professions organize the markets for their services. The advance in the social division of labor and the breakdown of personal ties of dependence, which are crucial in the rise of capitalism, are also preconditions for the formation of modern professions. The problem is, now, to relate the structure of profession to the particular nature of the commodities which professions produce and sell.

The term 'fictitious commodity' is used by Karl Polanyi in reference to labor, land, and money – entities which are exchanged and organized into markets even though they do not correspond to the 'empirical definition of a commodity': 'The postulate that anything that is bought and sold must have been produced for sale', says Polanyi, 'is emphatically untrue in regard to them'.[10] A profound transformation in social structure and ideology is therefore necessary for such markets to arise. The change is deepest, and affects most directly the largest number of people, where labor is concerned. Since 'labor' stands for wage-earning human beings, the mobilization and organization of labor in function of market requirements changes, therefore, the very structure of social life. Society, Polanyi asserts, becomes determined by the economic system.

The general process by which the commodity fiction extended to practically all forms of human labor affected professionals as well. The growth and diversification of the professional sector of the middle class changed the character of profession: in their efforts to secure a clientele or an income, the providers of these services became increasingly exposed to the constraints of capitalist competition in expanded markets. Today, insofar as most professionals sell their labor power to an employer, they represent but a special case within the general pattern of labor organization in capitalist societies. What complicates this specific instance is the process by which entry into professional labor markets is organized. Professional aspirants must acquire specific skills with a view to their sale. They normally acquire them through a relatively long process of training in monopolistic centers for the 'production of producers'. This training – or this passage – connects the sale of professional labor power with the educational system – that is to say, with the principal legitimator of social inequality in advanced industrial capitalism. This intimate connection disguises the stark characteristics of wage labor by covering it with all the structural and ideological advantages derived from status stratification and from the specific ideology of professionalism.

This ideology derives from the model of profession that emerged in the first wave of professionalization: founded on the importance of training and tested competence, this model, however, did not correspond to the generalized sale of labor power. The first modern professions – essentially medicine and the law – typically provided intangible goods under the form of services sold directly to consumers. In my analysis, I have emphasized the requirements imposed upon this project by the market orientation: the necessary homogenization of these intangible goods according to relatively universalistic standards could only be achieved at the level of training. The necessity to standardize training introduces into the model of profession a principle of equivalence between quality and quantity: excellence, it is implied, can be measured by 'units of training' and by series of objective examinations. In our century, the generalization of bureaucratic patterns of recruitment reinforces the apparent equivalence between competence and length of training: while the use of IQ and other tests spreads at the lower and middle levels of the occupational hierarchy, expertise at the technical, professional and managerial levels tends to be equated with years of schooling and numbers of credentials.[11]

The differences that exist between the direct sale of professional services and the sale of professional labor power do not prevent the resort, in both situations, to a model of profession which corresponds only to the first. Before returning to the implications of this usage, I will attempt to state these differences with more structural precision, following the terms of Marx's analysis of the commodity form.

The labor which is standardized in the case of professional 'commodities' is, first and above all, that which goes into training. Training – considered as the co-operative activity of instructors and students – appears indeed as the production of a marketable commodity, namely, the special skills of the professional producer. These skills can therefore be considered as exchange value created, in fact, before professional services are actually transacted between the provider and the user. Homogenized years of schooling and standardized credentials provide a 'universal equivalent' into which these exchange values can be translated and by which they can be measured. The monopoly of instruction and credentialing appears, thus, as the structural condition for the creation of 'professional exchange value'.

The achievement of this monopoly of instruction depends on two related historical processes: the first is the process by which an organization of professional producers agrees upon a cognitive base and imposes a predominant definition of a professional commodity. The second is the rise and consolidation of national systems of education – the institutional infrastructure within which and by means of which such unified definitions of professional commodities can become predominant. In this sense, the creation of professional exchange value ultimately depends upon the state – or, more precisely, upon the state's monopolistic appropriation and organization of a social system of education and credentialing.

It is, however, inherently contradictory – as well as a departure from the strict commodity form – that the exchange value of professional skills should depend on cognitive and educational monopoly. This monopoly means that length of training can be arbitrarily determined. Taken together with the unquantifiable nature of intangible skills, the monopoly condition destroys the equivalence between length of professional training and a notion of the average labor time that is socially necessary for the production of a professional. Monopoly of training means, therefore, that the price of professional services is *not* the market expression of socially necessary length of training or average (educational) labor time.

Despite the distorting effects of monopoly, the production of special skills with a view to their sale creates exchange value. This value is vested in the individual. The social character of production is perhaps more visible in this case than in any other, for most education is subsidized by the state out of public funds; the products, however, are privately appropriated. Indeed, in the juridico-political framework of bourgeois society, the individual is the sole owner of his person and, therefore, of his socially produced special competences.[12] Professional training appears, therefore, as a lengthy process of production which, under special institutional conditions, creates exchange values and makes them the sole property of individuals. The *general* contradiction between the social nature of production and the private appropriation of its products is especially visible in the case of specialized training. We shall see later on how the ideology of profession addresses itself specifically to this contradiction.

In sum, the attempt to apply Marx's structural category of value to the 'professional commodity' indicates, in this first phase of analysis, three things.

First, professional training creates or preserves value (by transmitting the skills of the instructor to the student) in the person of the apprentice professional. The professional himself appears, therefore, as the product of congealed or materialized labor, as 'the use-value that has been produced for exchange'. From this point of view, professional training is, in Marxist terms, *productive* labor.

Second, when professional skills are viewed as commodities under the aspect of exchange value, their distinctiveness appears to be lodged in the professional monopoly over training. From this point of view, the monopoly over training contains an inherent contradiction: it appears to be a central condition for the effective creation of 'professional exchange value', and yet it tends to place the price of professional 'commodities' outside the realm of market determination.

Third, through standardized and monopolized education, professional skills acquire *an appearance* of measurability and comparability in terms of years of schooling. Length of training and tested competence clearly appear as means to 'objectify' professional skills, in the double sense that the skills acquire both a tangible, quantifiable expression *and* a 'universalistic' legitimation. While both years of schooling and credentialing are related to the market value of specific professional services, the relation appears to be ideological: indeed, it functions more as an implicit justification for the price of the professional commodity and for the privileges associated with professional work, than as the actual quantitative translation of 'average socially necessary labor time' into market value.

The first market-oriented phase of professionalization introduced a principle of objectification at the core of the professional commodity. Standards of value derived from this principle tended to displace (though never entirely to replace) precapitalist standards based on narrow monopolies of status, on the social position of the clientele, or on the personality and idiosyncratic biography of the professional. The particular aspects of use-value in the professional commodities limited the scope of this transformation.

Historically, the first professions to organize on a market basis were the classic 'personal' professions – most conspicuously, medicine and the law. The essential feature of these profession's product is that *it tends to be immediately used or consumed (as advice or ministration) by the client or consumer.* This means that the realization of use-value (its consumption) is immediate – that is, *independent of capitalist relations of production.*

In terms of Marx's theory of exploitation, this implies that professional labor sold on a market under the form of direct services – independently, that is, of capitalist relations of production – does not contribute to capitalist accumulation by producing surplus value. Since only labor which produces surplus value is *productive*, professional services sold directly on a market are, strictly speaking, unproductive.[13] 'It is labor which is *not exchanged with capital, but directly with revenue,* that is wages or profits (including, of course, the various categories of those who share as co-partners in capitalist profit, such as interest and rent)'.[14] Marx adds: 'The laborer himself can buy labor, that is commodities which are provided in the form of services. ... As buyer – that is a representative of money confronting commodity – the laborer is in absolutely the same category as the capitalist where the latter appears only as buyer'.[15] If we look at the 'classic' personal professions from the point of view of the use-value of their labor (historically organized into markets during the nineteenth century and later on), their typical ideology appears to be based on structural properties of the commodity or services they sell: any buyer can acquire their 'professional labor power' as a commodity for immediate consumption; and this kind of professional labor power does not enter *directly* into the process of capitalist reproduction and accumulation.

The ideal of universal service to 'all of mankind' appears, in fact, to reflect the equalizing and democratizing effects of the market (equalizing if compared, for instance, to aristocratic patronage which reserves professional labor power for the use of an élite): unproductive labor can potentially be purchased and consumed by all, whether they own capital or not. The claim of disinterestedness conceals, it is true, the potential venality of the transaction of services; it does nevertheless reflect the fact that this kind of professional labor remains outside (or removed from) the capitalist mode of production. As unproductive labor, it is therefore different in nature from the specific form that productive labor assumes under capitalism – that is, the form of wage-labor 'which, exchanged against the variable part of capital ... reproduces not only this part of capital (or the value of its own labor-power), but in addition produces surplus-value for the capitalist'.[16]

It can be noted, furthermore, that the unproductive character of the labor sold by the personal professions not only bestows upon them an appearance of 'class-lessness' (because their services can, in principle, be universally used), but also explains that close ties can be maintained with noncapitalist élites, at least in the transitional phase (i.e. 'the various categories of those who share as co-partners in the capitalist profit, such as interest and rent').

Let us consider now whether these structural connections between professional ideology and the sale of professional labor power can be extended beyond the personal professions. In the practice of the classic personal professions, the exchange of services typically tends to take place between the 'free' professional and his individual client. The immediate realization of use-value – accessible, in theory, to everyone – appears to be a predominant characteristic of this kind of market transaction. Because professional labor is not, here, exchanged with capital and does not participate directly in the production of surplus value, it is, in strict terms, unproductive. The free professional escapes, therefore, capitalist exploitation. This point immediately suggests a corollary: if a professional works in the service of a capitalist firm, '*the same* kind of labor may be *productive* (that was) unproductive' in a 'free' professional market. Marx writes: 'If we may take an example from outside the sphere of production of material objects, a schoolmaster is a productive laborer, when, in addition to belaboring the heads of his scholars, he works like a horse to enrich the school proprietor. That the latter has laid out his capital in a teaching factory, instead of a sausage factory, does not alter the relation'.[17] And he adds: 'An actor for example, or even a clown, according to this definition, is a productive laborer if he works in the service of a capitalist (an entrepreneur) to whom he returns more labor than he receives from him in the form of wages'.[18]

Professional labor which is performed for the benefit of a capitalist firm is therefore not structurally different from any other kind of labor which is subject to capitalist relations of production. From the point of view of exploitation, therefore, any kind of labor can become productive. From the point of view of capitalist accumulation – that is, the production and appropriation of surplus value – professional labor appears at first sight to have a relatively indirect connection with the actual production of commodities. Even the work of engineers consists typically of devising, planning, and supervising – tasks that are preliminary, parallel, or supraordinate in the physical process of production. This vague similarity among all the occupations generally regarded as professions merely indicates that the work in which these occupations engage is relatively removed from and 'superior' to the manual work typically performed by the industrial proletariat. This general trait cannot compensate for the crucial differences between these occupations.

Engineers and other 'technical devisers' emerged, typically, as salaried employees of either capitalist firms or public corporations in charge of building the infrastructure for economic growth. Accountants, as well as lawyers specialized in corporate affairs, typically reserve the use-value of their labor for capitalist clients, despite the appearances of professional 'freedom'. Furthermore, as changes in the organic composition of capital tend to bring about 'the massive reintroduction of intellectual labor into the process of production', expert labor becomes an integral part of production.[19] Expertise is either drawn from occupations already dependent on the capitalist firm or tends to be qualified as 'professional': the workers tend to seek professional status, or are granted 'professional' privileges, for reasons internal to the organization.[20] Finally, the kinds of professional services delivered within the bureaucratic framework of the welfare state seem to be in an altogether different category.[21] *Salaried* experts or professionals share one characteristic: the products of their activity do not normally reach an *open* market. What engineers, accountants, employed architects, business administrators, social workers, teachers at all levels, and salaried physicians and lawyers all exchange for income on specific labor markets is their labor power and the skills inherent in their persons. The products of their activity, however, remain within the purchasing organization, where they are used directly by employers or by clients of the organization.

Two relatively independent dimensions seem to be involved in the determination of these differences: the degree to which an expert occupation is subordinated to capitalist relations of production, and the degree to which its relation to the production of surplus value is direct or indirect.[22] A classification of professional situations on this basis is attempted in Table 1.

One important point must be made: the farther one moves from the classic market situation of the 'free' personal professions, the more purely ideological do the professional claims of disinterestedness and universality of service become. We have seen, indeed, that these claims, typical of the legitimizing ideology of profession, reflect the structural characteristics of unproductive labor and of a singular market situation. Such structural connections do not exist for professions which contribute to capitalist reproduction and accumulation more directly than do medicine or the law. Neither do the connections hold for salaried professionals – in particular, not for the organizational professions, either pure or technobureaucratic.

Insofar as the term 'profession' incorporates the connotations of universal service and of an exchange of labor power radically different from that typical of capitalism, the very extension of the term beyond the classic professional situation of 'free' and unproductive work is ideological. The sociological definitions which

Table 1 Relation of professional (or expert) services to capitalist production

Use-value of services	Services exchanged for capital	Services exchanged for revenue
Directly incorporated into production of surplus value	Expert services included within the corporation: professional and managerial (including freelance consulting)	Expert or professional services which contribute to the production of constant capital (in non-profit research and development)
Incorporated only indirectly (contribute to the reproduction of the labor force)	Contribute to the reproduction of the work force within the corporation or (rarely) in privately owned service firms (e.g. health professions, instruction of different kinds).	(a) Market situation: classic personal professions (b) Non-market situation: 'welfare' professions in the service of the state
Not incorporated	Supervisory or controlling services	Services related to 'law and order', containment, and ideological production (including 'free' professions)

include these elements are, therefore, contributing to the ideological assimilation of structurally different kinds of labor. This ideological extension of the term 'profession' applies to nonmarket and nonpersonal exchanges of skilled services the expectations and legitimations derived from the classic situation of unproductive professional labor. Historically, the force promoting both the ideological use and its ideological effects is *the status project* in which aspiring occupations are engaged.

Before turning to an analysis of the ideology of profession *per se*, I shall sum up the results of this attempt to apply Marx's structural categories to the 'professional commodity'. Table 2 presents the summary in diagrammatic form.

Table 2　Production of professional commodities and ideological production

| | Professional services considered under the aspect of | | |
| | Exchange value | Use-value | |
Principal characteristics		Market situation (personal professions)	Non-market situation (organizational professions)
Main locus of production	Training centers	Practice	Practice
Product characteristics	Skilled labor power, inherent to the person of the professional; socially produced, privately appropriated	Advice or ministration	Advice or ministration Research
Realization	Deferred to entry into labor market, after training	Immediate: product consumed as use-value (potentially accessible to all consumers)	Immediate: product consumed (or incorporated into other products) by specific clients or specific employers
Typical conditions of production	Monopoly of training and credentialing	Interpersonal exchange on a free market of services	Interpersonal services not purchased by client but provided by 'welfare-state' institutions; technical or scientific products consumed or incorporated within organization
Predominant appearance of product	Abstract, susceptible of being measured (quantitative expression: analogy between standardized education and homogenized labor-time)	Concrete, qualitative, related to client's needs, susceptible of differentiation in terms of status and style of life of clientele	Concrete, qualitative, either related to client or employer's needs or defined by bureaucratic regulations
Main ideological effect	False equivalence between credentials, length of training, and price of professional labor power	Universality of service, radical difference between professional mode of production and capitalist mode	Extension of the ideology of profession to structurally different kinds of work situation and conditions of production
General ideological premises	Individualism; skills as personal property	Individualism; equality among individual consumers or individual citizens	Ideology of expertise as the new foundation of inequality in the educational and occupational structure

This tentative analysis has located the points of departure of the professional commodity from *real* commodities: the services that professions historically organized to sell are, in fact, skilled labor-power, the price of which tends to be justified in terms of expertise and length of training. The conditions of monopoly in which these skills are produced, however, invalidate the apparent equivalence between market price and special training. Finally, in the *practice* of many professions, use-value predominates over exchange value: this appears to be the structural foundation of the ideology of profession as it is formulated, first, by the classic personal professions which initiate the movement toward organization of their markets in the competitive phase of capitalism. The particular structure of the 'commodity' exchanged on these markets indicates that the professional project of market organization is *not* a *direct* extension of capitalist relations of production: it represents, rather, an extension of exchange relations into new areas of life, as an effect of the generalized breakdown of the precapitalist *social* structure.

The origins of professions other than the classic ones (law, medicine, dentistry, and, with certain qualifications, architecture) are not typically found in 'free' markets of services. And the practice of the classic professions themselves is changed by the rise of organizations. In general, professions do not consolidate their privileges until the 'organizational revolution'. What this term stands for is, in fact, the end of liberal capitalism. In the transition toward the monopolistic phase, the occupations which attain or aspire to the status of the classic professions, and which contribute to spread the latter's self-justifying ideology, do not typically depend on the extension of exchange relations; their origins are located, rather, in the transformation of the forces and relations of production in the capitalist enterprise, in the new functions of the capitalist state, and in the elaboration of new forms of the dominant ideology.

The radical differences between work situations which are usually regarded as professions suggest one line of thought: the market project of the classic personal profession represented a necessary but nevertheless provisional and temporary stage in the status project that is generally called 'professionalization'. Despite the apparent independence of the professional providers, these special markets required institutional guarantees which tied them closely to the state – in particular, to a state-controlled system of education and credentialing. The consolidation of large organizations in the private sector and the expansion of state functions signal, in our century, a general retreat from the 'pure' market principle: in the large organizational units of the private or the public sector, greater predictability of operations tends to go hand in hand with the bureaucratization of functions and control.

In this phase, professionalization represents a collective attempt to protect and upgrade relatively specialized and differentiated activities: the privileges that are sought are justified by resorting to a model of profession which corresponds to the project and the practice of the market professions during the liberal phase of capitalism. In the first place, this ideological reference aims at legitimizing social inequality: it does so, on the one hand, by stressing the apparent fusion between educational and occupational hierarchies, and on the other, by tacitly assimilating the market professions' relative independence from the class structure and their ethical claims.

Secondly, one of the goals of professionalizing occupations – one of the privileges they pursue – is a measure of work autonomy. Autonomy in the organization of free markets of services went together with autonomy in determining the conditions of work in the first phase (or the first type) of professionalization. Such autonomy was obviously never conceded to the sellers of the typical labor-commodity, namely, the industrial proletariat. But it was not attained, either, by occupations which are often regarded as professions: the established clergy and the military, necessary though they were to the maintenance of the bourgeois state, *never* entered a market sphere. Nor did a 'free' profession like engineering, directly relevant to capitalist production, attain the control over its own work which characterizes the classic market professions; the project of the 'personal' professions was only a brief episode in the story of professionalization. This indicates that, today, the alleged conflict between bureaucracy and profession as modes of work organization is not so much a conflict between two different structures as it is a contrast between the structure of bureaucratic organizations and an ideology promoted by some of their members. The case of engineering suggests something else: that autonomy is more easily conceded when it concerns transactions between private persons than when it would impinge on the basic structure of decision-making in capitalist production.[23] For occupations which are encapsulated within (or dependent upon) large heteronomous organizations, the ideological appeal to the model of profession may represent an attempt to establish a last-ditch defense against subordination.

I have emphasized throughout this analysis that, today, the disparate occupational categories which we call 'professions' are essentially brought together *by ideology*. It is an ideology used by the leaders of professionalization projects and shared by the members of various occupations. It is also shared and sustained by the whole society, not excluding its social scientists. We must examine, now, the affinities between the ideology of profession and the dominant ideology of bourgeois societies. First, I shall look briefly at the ideological trunk from which the professional branch derives. Second, I will consider what functions the ideology of profession performs within the social division of labor, with regard to the specific groups of workers who claim professional status. Finally, we must ask, however tentatively, what the ideology of profession contributes, today, to the dominant ideology.

General Components of the Ideology of Profession

During the nineteenth-century phase of professionalization, the emergent ideology of profession incorporated several traditional or precapitalist components which can be viewed as *residues*. We have discussed these elements at an earlier stage as 'anti-market' principles.[24] Three of them are important here. The first is a work ethic derived from ideals of craftsmanship, which finds *intrinsic* value in work and is expressed in the notion of vocation or *calling*. This ethical notion is to be distinguished from the bourgeois entrepreneurial work ethic, in which work is a means toward capitalist accumulation, or in Weber's interpretation, a means toward salvation; in either case, the value of work is *extrinsic* to work itself. The second is the ideal of universal service; connected with the 'protection of the social fabric' against the subversive effects of the market, it tends to respect and define, in the transitional phase, pre-industrial ideals of community bonds and community responsibility. In this sense, it incorporates precapitalist legitimations of social inequality, which are reflected in the model of gentlemanly distinterestedness. Third, its ideological status model appears as a secularized version of the feudal notion of *noblesse oblige*, which embodied the nobility's ideological aversion to commercial pursuits and its belief, anchored in a religious view of the social world, that high rank imposes duties as well as conferring rights.

These elements can now be linked with more precision to the structure of the 'professional commodity'. The visibility or predominance of 'realized' use-value in the transaction of professional services emphasizes the concrete, qualitative aspects of the labor power expended; it appears, thus, as a direct support for the intrinsic value placed on work by the ideology of profession. The relative independence of the classic personal professions from capitalist production can be related, in turn, to the professions' particular affinity with status. Their detachment from the predominant relations of production gave the classic professions a measure of independence from the capitalist class structure and the possibility of maintaining social and ideological ties with precapitalist elites; the gentlemanly ideal, transferred by the nineteenth-century professions to their market project, is a manifestation of this apparent independence from class relations.

[...]

Despite the complexity and heterogeneity of its components, the ideology of profession cannot be considered independently of the dominant bourgeois ideology within which it is formed. At the center of the ideology of profession we find, necessarily, the general postulates of bourgeois ideology.

The notion that 'the individual is essentially the proprietor of his own person and capacities, for which he owes nothing to society' is a cornerstone of the bourgeois theory of democratic liberalism.[25] The model of society that emerges during the seventeenth-century crisis of the *ancien régime* is a market model, in which free individuals consent of their own will to the contrivances of political society in order to protect their own natural rights – and first and foremost, their right to property. In the foundations of liberal theory, the force that binds atomized individuals to each other is the market itself.[26]

A market society which is ideologically founded on the equal rights of free individuals but which equates freedom with possession involves an inescapable contradiction: it 'generates class differentials in effective rights and rationality, yet requires for its justification a postulate of equal natural rights and rationality'.[27] Thus, at the core of all liberal theories we find the impossibility of individual equality in a class society. Unable to achieve the impossible, ideology escapes the issue either by denying the centrality of class or by justifying it as part of the 'state of nature'. The possessive market model created by liberal theory is described by its contradictory foundations: individualism, property, egalitarianism, *and class.*

The possessions appropriated by the professional consist, typically, of practical and theoretical knowledge, under the form of a special *competence.* This form of property has two distinctive characteristics: on the one hand, it is inseparable from mind and self; on the other, it constitutes a resource that cannot be depleted. Because it cannot be depleted, the form of property characteristic of the professional escapes the dictates of scarcity. Insofar as high prices on a market are a function of supply and demand, they can be attained in a market of competent services by acting either upon demand (which is difficult, as we know) or upon supply. Relatively scarce supply can be obtained in two principal ways, both of which are predicated upon monopoly of training and a restrictive definition of what constitutes competence: the first is the implicit or explicit refusal to produce as many competent providers of services as demand calls for; the second is by conspiracy, among the competent providers of services, to withhold these services from the market.

A professional conspiracy to withhold services, although not impossible in theory, would be highly improbable, however. Like all forms of personal property, 'cognitive property' can be hoarded instead of being invested: only by its investment or application does cognitive property augment the available knowledge capital of a society or improve the lives of people who lack such knowledge. But historically, the class situation of the modernizing bourgeois professionals excluded the possiblity of such hoarding: they not only *had* to make a living, they had to make it through a market for their services. Unlike the traditional professionals, they could not depend on their élite patrons (or on their family fortunes) for subsistence. The disintegration of precapitalist ties of dependence, as well as the limitations inherent in the ownership of land and capital, forced the professional fraction of the bourgeoisie to seek and ensure alternative means of subsistence on the market. This was the essential structural factor in the mobilization of their cognitive property. It was complemented by a traditional ideological one: men who claim to have better than average competence – especially where the competence concerns vital collective needs – would be *immoral* if they did not apply it in the service of the community. Thus, the dictates of the capitalist division of labor combine with the dictates of traditional moral law to mobilize the competence appropriated by the individual professional.

This aspect largely accounts for the 'residual' persistence of a traditional ideal of service in the *contemporary* ideology of profession: the ideal of moral obligation to the collectivity is the main ideological response of profession to the contradiction between socially produced knowledge and its private appropriation. It appears, at the same time, as a justification and as a guarantee that such competence will, indeed, be 'returned to society'. Such an idealistic guarantee is not necessary, however, in a society where the large majority of people must sell their labor power in order to survive, and where special competences are sought with a view to their sale.

The ideal of service cannot solve the contradiction between the monopoly of training, which is the goal of professionalization projects, and the market situation, in which services are sold (in the classic personal professions) or skilled labor power is bought (in the case of salaried professionals). Monopoly of training can give a relatively high exchange value to the competence it produces, independently of the market; it allows, moreover, the creation of artificial scarcity, by means of which the theoretically inexhaustible knowledge resource becomes socially finite. The revelation that socially produced knowledge is privately monopolized (and artificially limited) challenges the egalitarian and democratic legitimations built into the dominant ideology. If, however, it can be convincingly established that the springs of knowledge flow for all who care to learn and are mentally capable of learning, the revelation is no longer as trenchant. The 'natural' laws of the market do not suffice to justify the high exchange value of the special competences produced by monopolistic training centers. But if those centers appear to be open to all who 'deserve' education, the individual appropriation of specially valued skills can be justified by another 'natural' law: namely, the unequal distribution of 'natural' intelligence and resolve, which maintains an inevitable selection process among individuals with equal rights and equal opportunities.

[...]

In short, the apparent equalization of educational opportunity transforms the impact of ideological egalitarianism: from being a source of contradiction and potential demystification, the principle of *equality among atomized individuals* becomes a central source of legitimacy for the class system. For, indeed, 'if all men start on some basis of equal potential ability, then the inequalities they experience in their lives are *not* arbitrary, they are the logical consequence of different personal drives to use those powers – in other words, social differences can now appear as questions of character, of moral resolve, will and competence'.[28]

The liberal and Utilitarian construction of the individual as a 'a natural unit of measurement in social science',[29] and as the basic unit of the social order, appears to be the cornerstone of the new system of inequality. Because the intervention of the state as universal educator appears to reestablish equality of opportunity at the outstart, special categories of individuals who *monopolize* competence appear to have *ipso facto* proved their ability. They may, thus, *legitimately* claim special prerogatives, both juridical and social.[30]

More generally, individualism appears to be a central ideological *process*, which runs across the whole social structure, its meaning and import differently articulated and modulated at each level of the structure.[31] Its essential effect is to produce the 'subjective illusion' by which the individual believes he acts as a free agent in identifying with the political and ideological structures of his society.

[...]

The particular relation that professionalism bears to individualism and to the subjective illusion deserves to be noted. Their special competence empowers professionals and experts to act in situations where laymen feel incompetent or baffled. In fact, the assumption by the public that the expert *is* competent creates a sort of pragmatic compulsion for the expert: to certify his worth in the eyes of the laity, he must act. Deferentially requested to intervene by his clients, the expert practitioner is compelled to do something; from this point of view, anything is better than nothing. As Freidson remarks: 'Indeed, so impressed is he by the perplexity of his clients and by his apparent capacity to deal with those perplexities, that the practitioner comes to consider himself an expert not only in the problems he is trained to deal with but in all human problems'.[32] Most particularly in the personal professions, the behavior of the expert asserts, ideologically, that a variety of ills – and, in particular, those that can most affect the person – have individual remedies. This reinforces the optimistic illusion of ideological individualism: personal problems of all kinds are purely private and admit, as such, individual and *ad hoc* solutions. In the predominant ideological way of addressing social issues and social relations experienced by individuals, therefore, structural causes, as well as collective action upon those causes, are relegated to a vaguely utopian realm. At the same time, the practitioner's 'compulsion to act' reiterates to the layman that education confers superior powers upon the individual and superior mastery over physical and social environments. The social worth of the educated individual, his greater social productivity, and the value of his time are asserted in relative and hierarchical terms: in a fusion of practical ability and moral superiority, the expert appears to be freer and more of a person than most others. Himself a choice victim of the subjective illusion, he is also, by his very existence and actions, an effective propagator of bourgeois individualism. It is along this crucial dimension that the ideology of profession and the 'possessive individualism' of expertise work to sustain the dominant ideology. We must attempt to discern the specific ways in which this is done.

[. . .]

A general starting point is the fact that a profession is by definition *organized*. As Stinchcombe remarks:

> Organizations are among the groups where the community of fate is shared *among unequals*. . . . In general, the fate of the organizational élite is more closely tied to the fate of the organization than is that of their 'inferiors'. . . . The more the subordinate's needs and wants are met by the organization, the more the superior controls the flow of these satisfactions, and the less the subordinate could meet these needs elsewhere, the less the upper classes have to court the subordinate's consent and compliance.[33]

The 'courting of consent and compliance' occurs, in the professions, through initial recruitment and during training. Professional socialization aims, in fact, at the internalization of special social controls: it takes, that is, standards defined by the profession's elites and makes them part of each individual's subjectivity. Insofar as this socialization is successful, the elites will be in control not only of material rewards but also of the kind of esteem that counts – the esteem granted by a reference group of major importance for the individual. While esteem is, ultimately, easier and cheaper to dispense than power or income, it holds for the recipient something more than the promise of influence; it is intimately bound up with a sense of self, precisely because professions are *ideologically* constructed as occupations that one enters *by calling*, or at least by choice. As such, they appear to express an essential dimension of the self.

The less this is so, the more purely instrumental the choice becomes, and the less important the moral reward of colleague esteem appears in comparison with material rewards, which may or may not be controlled by colleagues. *The erosion of the ideological notion of calling tends, therefore, to undermine a powerful element of social control within a profession.* Obviously, the existence of alternative professional élites also diminishes the control over the self-esteem of 'inferiors' exercised by any *one* of these élites, but it does not necessarily diminish the *overall* control of the profession over its members; the multiple élites may, indeed, share the same basic standards of 'professionalism' – as is true, for example, of the various specialities within the field of medicine.

[...]

The particular strength of professional socialization is rooted in the length and the institutional character of training. A vocation is, by definition, something one follows full-time, and changes of vocation are psychologically as well as financially difficult in fields protected by monopoly of practice and lengthy training. The heavy investment of time, energy, and money that most professions require insures, for one thing, the stability of a recruit within the field. Unless the benefits are too low, or the costs too high, the investment already incurred reinforces commitment – by inertia, if nothing else.[34] This *stability* – which is distinctive in highly mobile socities – effects a particulary strong identification of the person with the role, both subjectively and for others; popular novels, films, and TV serials emphasize this permanence – you cannot *really* unfrock a priest, unmake a doctor, or disbar a lawyer. Occupational stability immediately evokes *career*, of which it is both a condition and an effect.

While biography is looking backward on one's life, an after-the-fact search for order and meaning, career is looking forward, with a sense of order to come, which depends crucially on the stability of institutions. Thus, career closely binds the projected self to organizations or to the professional institutions which insure 'continuity in status in a labor market'.[35] The expectation of career is therefore a powerful factor of conformity with the existing social order and a source of basic conservatism. Careers, Wilensky remarks:

> give continuity to the personal experience of the most able and skilled segments of the population – men who would otherwise produce a level of rebellion or withdrawal which would threaten the maintenance of the system. By holding out the prospect of continuous, predictable rewards, careers foster a willingness to train and achieve, to adopt a long view and defer immediate gratifications for the later pay-off. In Mannheim's phrase, they lead to the gradual creation of a 'life plan'.[36]

This life-plan is a privilege, enjoyed only by a minority within the labor force. Orderly careers, it has been emphasized, may well be one of the most significant expressions of inequality between different individuals and different categories of workers.[37]

Career expectations are an essential component of profession, to such an extent that asking what is happening to professionals today is almost equivalent to asking what is happening to their modal patterns of career. Stability and orderly progression through a work-life were the goals of the professionalization movement. Today, they make professions into prestigious and desirable occupations. Subjectively, career is a pattern of organization of the self. It epitomizes, therefore, the professional's self-involvement with his work as well as the legitimacy he confers to the élites – professional or organizational – on whom his future depends, both materially and psychologically.

For most recognized professions, an orderly career begins with training in professional schools or universities. The authoritative and authoritarian framework of relations between teachers and students is a fundamental element of institutionalized professional socialization. The hierarchy of excellence and prestige by means of which a profession legitimizes its internal stratification is produced in the university; professional recruits internalize it, first, in that context. The student's inevitable subordination and acceptance of his teachers' supervision are immediately and tacitly justified in terms of the teachers' greater expertise. The interrelations between the context of training and the contexts of practice are personalized; the teaching élites of a profession are often élite practitioners in the field. In any case, their personal sponsorship guarantees the proper socialization of the students to the professional world outside the school. As Freidson and Rhea remark: 'Successful completion of a professional education is an objective measure of . . . technical and normative socialization, but its inadequacy seems to be implied by the characteristic tendency of professionals to rely on personal testimonials and recommendations'.[38]

These personalized warrants do more than simply insure the adequate socialization of the new professional, guaranteeing that his 'compliance and consent' will not be too difficult to obtain; they reinforce the control by an élite and the latter's legitimacy. Prestige filters down, from the 'great men' in a field to those who study or work under them, through ideological mechanisms; the formation of cults and the vicarious enjoyment of the great man's prestige by his underlings are characteristic of the training situation, but they also extend to the world of work. They insure the new professional's willing and even happy acceptance of the hierarchical order of his profession and of the élite-defined ideology that underlies it. Vicariousness gives him, indeed, a sense of belonging to a society of peers, in which differential prestige can be ideologically redistributed.

Finally, the ideology of equality within a stratified profession depends crucially on the content and on the social meaning of training and expertise. The content of professional education is, in part, a function of its length. One author remarks:

> Practitioners are typically *overtrained*. . . . Admission to any skilled occupation is so hedged about with rules that the entrant must learn far more than he will typically apply in the course of his practice – with a consequent overlap in the abstract knowledge base of adjacent occupations. . . . A physician still knows much more than an electrician, although both may have the same ratio of used knowledge to learnt knowledge. . . . The social pressures within the major professions as well as in the larger society demand that *all* the available knowledge be mustered for crises, or at least be on call.[39]

It is almost impossible to distinguish the real from the ideological effects of this overtraining. First of all, there is no effective guarantee that the individual practitioners one deals with will, in fact, mobilize such comprehensive competences 'in a crisis' for there is no guarantee that they have been keeping up with the advance of knowledge in their respective fields and that their training is not obsolete in all but a relatively narrow area of practice. Overtraining, however, aims at creating *complete* skills and at eliciting the layman's trust. Because of such overtraining, specialization is not seen by the public (or by the professional) as a narrowing down of competence, but as a deepening of knowledge, an *added* skill.

[...]

This share in monopolized knowledge brings them dividends of another kind: every profession, because of the monopoly of competence which it has or claims, 'considers itself the proper body to set the terms in which some aspect of society, life, or nature is to be thought of'.[40] Sharing in this general function of reality construction gives every professional a minimum of social authority. In this sense, 'all professionals are priests; they interpret mysteries which affect the lives of those who do not understand'.[41] Narrow specialization cannot achieve this mystical effect. For instance, the secret knowledge attached to certain roles within bureaucratic organizations seldom has general social significance; its specialized possessors do not contribute to defining and constructing for the public a usable segment of social reality. It is doubtful, therefore, that specialities whose functions are not really understood by any significant sector of the public, whose place on the 'general cognitive map' is vaguely traced, can sustain the full ideology of profession.[42]

The visible professions which have a clear monopoly of competence – and not only a monopoly of practice – have *authority* over a kind of knowledge that is important for every man's life. The gap in competence between professionals and laymen, institutionalized by the monopolies of training and certification, *ipso facto* sets *every* professional apart: he belongs to a privileged society of 'knowers', which the public tends to identify with its élite spokesmen. The 'mysteries' interpreted by the individual professional have been named and partially revealed to the public before he comes in. It is a rare individual who can challenge by himself the whole image of a field and the social construction of an aspect of reality in which professional élites are particularly active and influential.

We began by asking what elements bind professionals to their work and maintain a sense of 'community' and basic 'equality' in stratified professions. Individualism and a sense of privilege and importance *vis-à-vis* the laity and other occupations emerged as general dimensions of professional consciousness. On the one hand, vocation, career, training, expertise, and authority are individualized attributes of *privileged work*. On the other hand, the unconscious (or conscious) comparisons with other kinds of work, made by professionals themselves and by the larger public, ultimately set professions out as communities of 'superior' workers. These general elements of consciousness elicit 'consent and compliance' from educated workers and underplay the realities of professional stratification. The minimal internal equality of professions is only relative and relational. The question is whether the ideological effects of professional consciousness can resist the forces which objectively undermine the privileges of professional work.

[...]

The closure of the 'mastership' renders obsolete a traditional and still-cherished conception of the professional career: that 'independence' can be achieved after apprenticeship. Professional lives either tend to be increasingly organized by bureaucratic career patterns, or they 'progress' – in smaller, less bureaucratized professional firms – up to a point, beyond which almost nobody goes. In this latter situation, the arbitrariness and personalism of management are likely to be great; recognizing this, subordinate professional workers may organize to demand more bureaucratization, in the form of specified criteria of advancement and institution-alized and predictable promotions.[43] These attempts to stop the erosion of career hinge on 'universalistic' bureaucratic standards which are – or should be – binding for *both* management and professional employees. These standards are, nevertheless, an expression of alienated work, of the employees' lack of control over their whole work setting. As such, they make manifest the general subordination of work to a preestablished division of labor, to a synthesis achieved at the top. Writing about the 'malaise of technicians' in industry, an Italian political collective observes:

> One explanation of these difficulties, close to the technicians' heart, invokes the insufficient rationalization of the company – the persistence of archaic organizational forms, the inadequacy of channels of information, the manager's lack of training – in contrast with the superior organization of American firms. We argue that the technicians' malaise is rooted in the capitalist division of labor and that further rationalization will intensify rather than alleviate it. ... Even where personal arbitrariness plays a restricted role, careers are dependent on two basic criteria: on one hand, social facility, adaptability, aggressiveness, talent for public contact, [and] on the other, conformity to the model by which the system operates, ability to innovate without altering pre-established plans, loyalty and 'discretion' in relaying information to the top, and 'legitimate' ambition.[44]

Technicians in large organizations may even appear to constitute a 'new working class', precisely because of the specialization of their training and work, the threat of skill obsolescence, and the consequent greater subordination to management.[45] However, at the lower levels of the hierarchy, 'professional' work in all fields (except *perhaps* medicine, scientific research, and academic work) exhibits the same trends to specialization and fragmentation.

The tendencies to proletarianization of educated labor have, potentially, great political consequences. The phenomenon has preoccupied the theorists of the 'new working class', both in Europe and in the United States, especially since the events of May 1968 in France and 1968–70 in Italy.[46] Describing conditions of increasing specialization, blocked mobility, skill obsolescence, and erosion of the market value of educated labor, these studies emphasize a double set of contradictions: between ideological expectations and work conditions, on the one hand; and between education and other areas of social experience, including work, on the other.

In his classic study of industrial work, Robert Blauner noted:

Self-estranged workers are dissatisfied only when they have developed *needs* for control, initiative, and meaning in work. The average manual worker and many white-collar employees may be satisfied with fairly steady jobs which are largely instrumental and non-involving, because they have not the need for responsibility and self-expression in work. ... One factor which is most important in influencing a man's aspirations in the work process is education. The more education a person has received, the greater the need for control and creativity.[47]

Blauner's observations, however, no longer appear to accurately depict a new generation of workers.[48] The traditional legitimations of alienated labor are now in crisis, and they contradict the 'search for self', however individualistic and alienated its forms, that is abroad in the general culture.

The growing importance of 'educated labor', in both productive role and numbers, exacerbates the crisis and the contradictions: the amount of critical information available on society as a whole to an increasingly educated labor force contrasts with the narrow definition of functions and rank in most work situations. For educated labor within large organizations, this broader contrast takes the form of a contradiction between the powerlessness and apathy which are the lot of the average citizen and the discretionary power granted to the worker, who is expected to exercise technical skills and theoretical intelligence, if only in limited functions. Managerial and technobureaucratic functions, moreover, are in sharp contrast with the tendency to overspecialization in many areas of technical and professional education. It can be said that 'The technician, the employee, and the cadre have not been trained to be stupid, but to be intelligent: and this practical and theoretical intelligence cannot always be sufficiently controlled by the system, because the very kind of know-how that is demanded is already, in itself, contradictory'.[49]

The political potential of this 'new working class' is still undocumented by clear evidence, and is much too broad a subject to be considered here even speculatively; but we may suggest how the ideology of profession counteracts the structural contradictions of educated labor.[50]

[...]

We have seen earlier how management manipulates both the real and the symbolic dimensions of freedom at work and social prestige, in order to conceal the fact that 'professional ladders' *do not* lead to increasing power and control in decision-making. Because it shapes the expectations o. professionals, the ideology of profession contributes to the success of these strategies: it confuses, that is, discretion at the level of execution with real power and freedom of choice.

There is, first, the archetypical professional concern *with status*. In the newer professions, the creation, expression, and protection of special status tend to be the most central dimension of the professionalization project. *Relative* prestige and privilege, tacitly based on the invidious comparison with other occupations and other workers, influence, however unconsciously, a professional's assessment of a specific work situation.[51] Who he implicitly compares himself with is significant: it should be noted, in this respect, that the frequent *isolation* for professional departments and 'enclave' professional workers in large organization focuses comparisons on similar occupational categories. In theory, the very sense of ideological community fostered by professionalism should have the same effect, and keep comparisons from deflecting upward toward managerial ranks and their different kind of work and responsibilities.

The concern with status not only prevents *alliances* with other workers or with clients.[52] It also works as a preventive against the unity – and the unionization – of professional workers themselves. Unions are, in fact, an instrument of power of the working class, and as such are symbolic of a loss in general social status; for analogous reasons, even when there are unions, professionals are more reluctant than other workers to engage in militant tactics.[53] This ideological effect, in which concern with status can become a trap for subordinate professionals, is maximized by the second archetypical feature: professional *individualism* with all its facets.

Professional work conditions (and not only the general ideology) foster individualism. The professional's sense of power and authority flows not only from his actual command over special knowledge but also from his control over interpersonal situations. The first established professions – medicine, law, the ministry, and architecture – were typically concerned with the problems of individuals. Only indirectly did they define society as their client. Today, individualized service becomes an ideological remedy for the ills of a social situation, a screen for the social problems caused by the bureaucratic systems through which services are delivered – most notably in the medical and teaching professions.

The ideological insistence on individual aspects, the neglect of the whole, merges with specialization to confine the professional in an ideological conception of his role: the importance of narrow responsibilities is consciously and unconsciously emphasized, exaggerating the 'dignity' of the functions. The dominant ideology attributes to professionals and experts special prestige as well as 'moral and intellectual superiority': sharing in this ideology, professionals can easily mystify to themselves their actual power. Moreover, they are locked into conformity with the role society offers them to play – locked in by their vocational choice, by the particular mystique of each profession, and by their whole sense of social identity.

Finally, the technocratic *ideology* of science and objectivity excludes from the specialist's concern the social and political consequences of his acts. Nowhere is this truer than in the technical and scientific fields. Robert Merton notes that 'engineers, not unlike scientists, come to be indoctrinated with an ethical sense of limited responsibilities'.[54] As the technical auxiliaries of capitalist production, engineers, in particular, could never gain the power to define the social aims of technology, the overall purpose of their work. In this sense, they are a typical example of *powerless discretion*.

Scientists, engaged in the loftier and apparently more autonomous function of advancing knowledge for the whole of society, are similarly socialized into corporate irresponsibility, beyond the immediate and circumscribed area of their specific task. For the positivistic ideology on which most technical and scientific training tends to be based, 'science and ethics are rigidly separated domains with distinct methodologies and subject matter. As a result, the purposes of science are shaped by the dominant class, while ethics is understood as personal, vague, and increasingly without foundation'.[55] As 'the citizen-self threatens to become submerged in the occupational self', the narrow conception of autonomous and responsible function becomes a support for the technocratic ideology and its premises of general privatization and depoliticization: 'Paradoxically, the same ideology of the "expert", which gives the technician a certain autonomy within his or her own speciality, simultaneously prepares the technician to execute blindly the designs of others'.[56]

In sum, the expert's and the professional's outlook on their work lives tend to be shaped, today, by individualism and narrow specialism. Thus, the 'needs for control, initiative, and meaning in work' of which Blauner speaks tend to be defined, *by education itself*, in a way that is compatible with the requirements of production in advanced industrial capitalism. Flexibility, autonomy, and circumscribed responsibility are precisely the qualities expected from expert labor: as long as the protests of subordinate professional workers ask for more of these *individual* privileges, as long as that is the main purpose of their corporate associations, their potential disloyalty can easily be managed. Within the ideological constellation of contemporary professionalism, the ideology of expertise and of partial irresponsibility coexists with traditional components and with profession's own emphasis on individual career and individual solutions. With its persistent antibureaucratic appearances, the ideology of professionalism deflects the comprehensive and critical vision of society which is necessary to reassess the social functions of profession. In this sense, professionalism functions as a means for controlling large sectors of educated labor and for co-opting its élites.

[...]

Notes and References

1 On the concept of genealogy in Marxist analysis, see BALIBAR, E. (1970) 'Sur les concepts fondamentaux du matérialisme historique', in ALTHUSSER, L. *Lire le Capital*, Paris, Maspero, Vol. 2, pp. 182–92.
2 MARX, K. (1867) *Capital*, Vol. 1, p. 104 (my italics).
3 *Ibid.*, p. 36.
4 *Ibid.*, p. 88.
5 *Ibid.*, p. 109.
6 *Ibid.*, p. 45.
7 *Ibid.*, p. 39.
8 *Ibid.*, p. 170, Note 1.
9 *Ibid.*, p. 168.
10 POLANYI, K. (1957) *The Great Transformation*, Boston, Beacon Press, p. 72.
11 On the extension and use of credentials see, in particular, BERG, I. (1971) *Education and Jobs: The Great Training Robbery*, Boston, Beacon Press, Chaps. 2 and 3.
12 That this is not a self-evident proposition is illustrated by the example of the French system of Grandes Ecoles, founded by Napoleon: the students recruited by contest, are completely subsidized by the state (and often board in the school as well). They *owe their services to the state* at least for a period of time on completion of their studies. Private industries who wish to employ the members of this selected élite have to 'buy them back' – that is, to financially compensate the state for the expense of their education and the loss of their services.
13 I do not intend to enter the controversy that exists in Marxist theory about which kinds of labor are productive or unproductive (on this see GOUGH, I. (1972) 'Marx's theory of productive and unproductive labor', *New Left Review*, November–December, pp. 47–72). I believe that the issue becomes a matter of pure exegesis when, first, large proportions of heretofore 'unproductive' workers now sell

their labor to capitalist firms and when, second, the production and realization of surplus value increasingly depend on scientific and technical services, on the integration of distribution and supply with production, and also on a large range of governmental services. I will merely use the terms 'productive' and 'unproductive' as symbolic references to the different kinds of link that different kinds of professional labor form with the production of surplus value.

14 MARX, K. *Theories of Surplus Value*, Part 1, Moscow, Foreign Languages Editions (1969), Vol. 1, p. 157. Professional labor of this kind – if it was not exchanged on a market of services – could be considered akin to the labor of small peasants or craftsmen, which is 'neither productive or unproductive' according to Marx.

15 MARX, K. *op. cit.*, (1969), p. 404.

16 *Ibid.*, p. 152.

17 MARX, K. (1867) *op. cit.*

18 MARX, K. *op. cit.*, (1969), p. 457.

19 Ernest Mandel, quoted by GOUGH, I. (1972) *op. cit.*, p. 71.

20 See LARSON, M. (1977) *The Rise of Professionalism*, University of California Press, Chap. 11 for a discission of managerial encouragement of professionalization by employees.

21 Claus Offe writes, 'The services performed by the bureaucratic worker are based on a social relation in which value expansion through surplus value production does not take place ... and [they] are directly absorbed by social consumption. They have no market. This means that the conditions under which such labor power is socially put to use are not determined by the criterion of the production and realization of surplus value. Such labor is *concrete*, not 'abstract', it is not a commodity and produces no commodities. The social utilization of this kind of labor is determined by its *concrete results*; it is deployed with regard to its use value and to the use value of its performance and not, as in the case of abstract labor, with regard to its exchange value, where use value is not the primary factor, but only a necessary by-product'. And he adds, 'of course, such concrete labor can and does enhance the productivity (i.e. the surplus value yield) of other kinds of labor eventuating in exchange value'. OFFE, C. (1973) 'The abolition of market control and the problems of legitimacy', *Working Papers on the Capitalist State*, 1, pp. 109–10.

22 This tentative classification, quite unorthodox from the strict Marxist point of view, incorporates in rough form some dimensions outlined by GOUGH, I. (1972) *op. cit.*, pp. 60 and 67.

23 On the hopes for a political role of the engineer, see VEBLEN, T. *The Engineers and the Price System*, New York, Harcourt, Brace and World (1963 edn.); and LAYTON, E.T. Jr. (1971) *The Revolt of the Engineers*, Cleveland, Case Western University Press. On the inherent structural subordination of the engineer, see LARSON, M. (1977) *op. cit.*, Chap. 3.

24 LARSON, M. (1977) *op. cit.*, Chap. 5.

25 These comments are based on the classic works by HALEVY, E. (1966) *The Growth of Philosophic Radicalism*, Boston, Beacon Books; and MACPHERSON, C.B. (1962) *The Political Theory of Possessive Individualism*, New York, Oxford University Press. The quotation in the text is from MacPherson, p. 263.

26 In Hobbes' thought, for instance, 'the model of the self-moving, appetitive possessive individual and the model of society as a series of market relations between these individuals, were a sufficient source of political obligation. No traditional concepts of justice, natural law, or divine purpose were needed' – MACPHERSON, C.B. (1962) *op. cit.*, p. 265. Locke, however, refused to 'reduce all social relations to market relations and all morality to market morality'. His thought presents interesting analogies with the professions' combination of traditional and bourgeois legitimations for their own market project. See MacPherson, pp. 269ff.

27 *Ibid.*, p. 269.

28 SENNETT, R. and COBB, J. (1973) *The Hidden Injuries of Class*, New York, Vintage, p. 256.

29 HALEVY, E. (1966) *op. cit.*, p. 502.

30 John Stuart Mill deserves to be quoted for his clarity in formulating the articulations of liberal Uttilitarianism. In a discussion of voting, he wrote: 'When two persons who have a joint interest in any business differ in opinion, does justice require that both opinions should be held of exactly equal value? If with equal virtue, one is superior to the other in knowledge and intelligence, or if, with equal intelligence, one excels the other in virtue, the opinion ... of the higher moral or intellectual being is worth more than that of the inferior .... The only thing which can justify reckoning one person's opinion as equivalent to more than one is *individual mental superiority; and what is wanted is some approximate means of ascertaining that. If there existed such a thing as a really national education or a trustworthy system of general examination, education might be tested directly*. In the absence of these, the nature of a person's occupation is some test. An employer of labor is on the average more intelligent than an ordinary laborer, and a laborer in the skilled trades than the unskilled. A banker, merchant or manufacturer is likely to be more intelligent than a tradesman, because he has larger and more complicated interests

to manage .... Subject to some such condition [of successful performance], two or more votes might be allowed to every person who exercises any of these superior functions'. MILL, J.S. *Considerations on Representative Government*, Indianapolis, Bobbs Merrill, (1958), pp. 135–8 (my italics).

31 On ideological processes, see HERBERT, T. (1968) 'Remarques pour un théorie générale des idéologies', *Cahiers pour l'Analyse*, Summer, pp. 74–92.

32 FREIDSON, E. (1970) *The Profession of Medicine*, New York, Dodd and Mead, p. 171.

33 STINCHCOMBE, A. (1965) 'Social structure and organizations', in MARCH, J.G. (ed.) *Handbook of Organizations*, New York, Rand McNally, pp. 181–2.

34 Incidentally, the same notion of 'heavy investment' tends to weaken colleague control. Freidson's studies of medicine show that colleagues tend to encourage the culprit to 'resign from their company' – to bar him, that is, from the informal net works, rather than expel him from the profession. The latter is a last recourse, forced by publicity given to a gross offence. Otherwise the rationale tends to be 'to avoid ruining a man's life'. See FREIDSON, E. (1970) *op. cit.*, pp. 181–3, and FREIDSON, E. and RHEA, B. (1972) 'Processes of control in a company of equals', in FREIDSON, E. and LORBER, J. (Eds.) (1972) *Medical Men and their Work*, Chicago, Aldine-Atherton, pp. 185–99. The reactions of the organized profession to the case of a New Jersey surgeon who was clearly suspected of murdering a number of patients were neither rapid nor unambiguous, until the *New York Times* exposed the case of 'Dr. X'. The case came to a head in February and March of 1976.

35 STINCHCOMBE, A. (1959) 'Bureaucratic and craft administration of production', *Administrative Science Quarterly*, 4, p. 186.

36 WILEWSKY, H. (1960) 'Work, careers and social integration', *International Social Science Journal*, 12, p. 555.

37 See BERGER, P. (1964) 'Introduction', *The Human Shape of Work*, New York, Macmillan; FORM, W.H. and MILLER, D.C. (1949) 'Occupational career patterns as a sociological instrument', *American Journal of Sociology*, 54; TOURAINE, A. (1965) *Sociologie de l'Action*, Paris, Seuil; and WILENKSY, H. ( ) 'Measures and effects of social mobility', in SMELSER, N.J. and LIPSET, S.M. (Eds.) *Social Structure and Mobility*, pp. 98–140.

38 FREIDSON, E. and RHEA, B. (1972) *op. cit.*, p. 198.

39 GOODE, W. (1969) 'The theoretical limits of professionalization', in ETZIONI, A. (Ed.) (1969) *The Semi-Professions*, New York, Free Press, pp. 282–3.

40 HUGHES, E. (1971) *The Sociological Eye*, Chicago, Aldine-Atherton, p. 376.

41 SENNETT, R. and COBB, J. (1973) *op. cit.*, p. 227.

42 In this respect, see the interesting study of nuclear technologists by VOLLMER, H. and MILLS, D. (1966) 'Professionalization and technical change', in VOLLMER, H. and MILLS, D. (Eds.) (1966) *Professionalization*, Englewood Cliffs, N.J., Prentice-Hall, pp. 22–8.

43 Preliminary observations in a union of architectural employees suggest that this tendency is present at all levels, both leadership and rank-and-file.

44 'Technicians and the capitalist division of labor', *Socialist Revolution*, 2, (1972), pp. 79–81.

45 On the 'new working class' see GINTIS, H. (1970) 'The new working class and revolutionary youth', *Socialist Revolution*, 1, pp. 13–43; STODDER, J. (1973) 'Old and new working class', *Socialist Revolution*, 3, pp. 99–110; and SZYMANSKI, A. (1972) 'Trends in the American working class', *Socialist Revolution*, 2, pp. 101–22. More recently, see BRAVERMAN, H. (1975) *Labor and Monopoly Capital*, New York, Monthly Review Press.

46 On the European approach to the new working class, see GORZ, A. (1967) *Strategy for Labor*, Boston, Beacon Press; JERVIS, G. and COMBA, L. (1970) 'Contradictions du technicien et de la culture techniciste', *Temps Modernes*, April, pp. 1601–12; LOW-BEER, J. (1974) 'The new working class in Italy', Ph.D. thesis, Harvard University; MALLET, S. (1975) *Essays on the New Working Class*, St. Louis, Telos Press; and TOURAINE, A. (1971) *The May Movement*, New York, Random House.

47 BLAUNER, R. (1967) *Alienation and Freedom*, Chicago, University of Chicago Press, Phoenix Books, p. 29.

48 See, for instance, the report of the Special Task Force for the Secretary of Health, Education and Welfare (1973) *Work in America*, Cambridge, Mass., MIT Press.

49 JERVIS, G. and COMBA, L. (1970) *op. cit.*, (my translation).

50 Besides the recent work I have cited, Lipset and Schwartz draw on almost all the sociological work published before 1968. See LIPSET, S.M. and SCHWARTZ, M.A. (1966) 'The politics of professionals', in VOLLMER, H. and MILLS, D. (Eds.) *op. cit.*

51 Hence the often heard exaggeration among low-paid professionals (I heard it from an architect): 'the man who pushes the broom can earn more than the fellow who designed the building'. This observation should be read in conjunction with the intimate relation between personal worth, social esteem and money that is manifest everywhere in our society.

52 Engineering professional associations were convinced by management to abandon their former

sponsorship of collective bargaining. 'The societies now argue for commitment to a professionalism that excludes any kind of collective bargaining. *By stressing the differences between professionals and workers and by urging management to emphasize and respect these differences,* they have tried to make engineering unions unnecessary'. KUHN, T. 'Engineers', p. 93 (my italics). The 'professional' union of Italian pilots, independent of the large union confederations, repeatedly goes on strike against the state-owned airlines (forcing the services to stop a large percentage of flights) because they do not want to sign collective contracts with the other categories of workers, but want the right to renegotiate differentials in between general contracts. (See, for instance, the strikes of August 1975 and May 1976.) So much for the 'professional' defense of the public interest!

53 On strikes and professionals see, amongst others, DANIELS, A. and KAHN-HUT, R. (Eds.) (1970) *Academics on the Line,* San Francisco, Jossey-Bass; HAUG, M. and SUSSMAN, M. (Eds.) (1971) 'Professionalization and Unionism', in *Professions in Contemporary Society,* Special Issue of *American Behavioral Scientist,* 14, pp. 525–40; KUHN, T. *op. cit.*; PRANOY, K. (1965) *Professional Employees,* London, Faber and Faber; and WILDMAN, W. (1971) 'Teachers and collective negotiations', in BLUM, A. *et al.,* (Eds.) (1971) *White Collar Workers,* New York, Random House.

54 MERTON, R. 'The machine, the worker and the engineer', in NOSCOW and FORM (Eds.) *Man, Work,* p. 86. For a development on technocratic 'irresponsibility', see SARFATTI-LARSON, M. (1972–73) 'Notes on technocracy: some problems of theory, ideology and power', *Berkeley Journal of Sociology,* 17, 1–34.

55 'Technicians', p. 76, (see note 44).

56 *Ibid.,* p. 76. The quotation in the text is from MERTON, R. *op. cit.,* p. 87.

22   The Teachers and Professionalism: the Failure of an Occupational Strategy

Noel Parry and Jose Parry

[...]

Factors Inhibiting Professionalism among Teachers

The Teachers and the State

In England, the state first became involved in a direct way in education in 1833 when a small grant was paid by way of subsidy to the two principal charitable religious societies. These were providing elementary education for the working class and the decision of the Whigs to become involved was, in a sense, a negative one, because it was the increasing difficulty of raising enough charitable finance which led the societies to turn to the government. For its part the government took the view that it was better to subsidise than to see the societies go into a decline; this might lead in the long run to the government having to bear the whole cost of education for working people. The anglicans worked within the Tory party to oppose the measure. Failing this, it was they who insisted on the establishment of an inspectorate (1839), members of which were in fact principally recruited from the ranks of clergymen. After pressure had been exerted nonconformists were also appointed to inspect their own schools (1843). The involvement of the state was in the first instance only with elementary education and elementary teachers. The Minutes of 1846 established state certificates for teachers in this group, and also led to the expenditure of state money by means of both capital grant and recurrent expenditure on training colleges and teacher training. During the nineteenth century the state was scarcely involved in secondary education at all, except in its minimum role as 'ringmaster' as stipulated by liberal theory. There were Royal Commissions, debates in Parliament and legislation primarily concerned with the regulation of endowments, but no intervention on the lines which became established in elementary education.

Source: FLUDE, M. and AHIER, J. (Eds.) (1976) *Educability, Schools and Ideology*, Croom Helm.

The introduction of the inspectorate, and the Minutes of 1846, defined the 'state-control' relationship over the elementary teachers and the institutions in which they trained and worked. In the early days this was welcomed rather than resented by the teachers themselves. Improvements in training, remuneration and the provision of pension rights were all advantages likely to encourage a positive attitude, as was the light rein with which Kay-Shuttleworth's inspectors were encouraged to carry out their duties.[1]

The educational reaction after 1860, and particularly the alterations caused by the Revised Code which reduced remuneration, abolished pensions and disposed of capital grants to training colleges, was felt by the teachers as a savage blow. Hostility to the state was exacerbated by harsher methods of inspection. The reduction of the elementary teacher from a status informally commensurate with that of the civil servant to a lower position more firmly subordinate to the school managers heightened their sense of betrayal by the state. The effects of the code produced in turn a reaction among teachers which after a period of stunned acquiescence resulted in a swing toward unionism as the prime strategy for coping with the problem.[2]

The 1870 Education Act brought the state more firmly into the arena of elementary education and established the system of school boards which were the vehicle of administration until 1902. It is perhaps no accident that NUET was founded in the same year as the Education Act was passed (1870). It was by now apparent that school boards or no, the real power in elementary education was the state. Already it controlled the certification of teachers, and now increasingly, its hold of the purse strings was made manifest. It became clear that unionism *vis-à-vis* the state was the wave for the future. The NUET set up its headquarters in London in order to be able to negotiate with the government and act as a pressure group in Parliament. It was with central government that effective negotiations of real consequence could take place. [...] There is no doubt [...] that the state by virtue of its accumulated power in elementary education was an opponent of professionalism. The fact that the teachers were not organised on a professional basis prior to the entry of the state into the educational field, has meant not only that they were unable to obtain an initially favourable bargain compared with, for example, the doctors in 1911 and 1948, but also that they have had an uphill struggle to gain any purchase on the administrative structures which were laid down to control education. They have neither the formal status of civil servants nor the self-government of autonomous professionals.

England had been late in introducing government to education, but in the closing years of the nineteenth century, it became clear that shortly it would be closely involved also in secondary education. This sector in English education was relatively unorganised in the nineteenth century. The middle and upper classes were expected to provide appropriate secondary education for themselves through the mechanisms of the private market supported by a reorganised system of endowments. The 1902 Act brought the state directly into secondary education. [...]

The secondary sector of education comprised a diversity of schools including the public schools, endowed and grammar schools (both day and boarding) and the new County grammar schools which were created by local authorities as a result of the 1902 Act. In addition there were private (entrepreneurial) secondary schools of varying quality, some of which were not very satisfactory. [...]

In regard to teacher training, governments now had an interest in a good supply of secondary teachers. Until after the First World War, increasing opportunities were available for young men and women with degrees to take a professional diploma in the growing Departments of Education of universities. These were shared at least by some of the non-graduate trainee teachers from nearby colleges. Almost from their inception the lectures in Departments of Education were open to students from the colleges, and some of them went on to take degrees. Already by the turn of the century there was a large amount of degree work being undertaken in men's colleges, and a fair amount in women's. Much of this was attributable to the advent of the day-training college system which acted as a lever in breaking down the separate and closed residential system found in the teacher training colleges. After 1902 the new local education authorities began founding their own training colleges, free from earlier constraints, and with better staff salaries and accommodation. At the outset, like the universities, mixed colleges were founded catering for both men and women students and offering a better education. In these colleges, most students were taking a university degree course. In fact a number of the Departments of Education in universities originally started life as day-training colleges in this way. Only later did they become Departments of Education of the university. In 1918 a newly introduced set of Board of Education regulations encouraged the universities to specialise in four-year courses in which the diploma in education would be the final stage of professional training after a degree course. At the same time the training colleges were required, once again, to focus their attention upon two-year courses of study for non-graduates. In this way traditional divisions between elementary and secondary teachers were reaffirmed. In 1925 the Report of a Departmental Committee on the training of teachers warmly supported this move.[3] Colleges themselves were not to be upgraded; they were to focus on the development of professional skill in the student and not 'learning' or intellectual development as such. The separation between universities and training colleges was endorsed by the Committee's favourable view of the single-sex training institution.[4]

It was argued earlier that the state had come to have a vested interest in opposing the aspirations of teachers to professionalism. The divisions among teachers themselves enabled the application of the principle of 'divide and rule'. The activities of Morant at the Board of Education provide an excellent illustration of the manner in which this was done. Although the teachers themselves [...] were divided on the question of the form which a register of teachers should take, yet they were unanimous in wanting a register. By a clause in the Education (Administrative Provisions) Bill (1906) the Board of Education was relieved of the responsibility for continuing the teachers' register in any form. All the teachers' associations were dismayed. 'It seemed as though the Government and the Board had seized their opportunity to destroy all hope of teaching becoming a profession in a true sense'.[5] Morant took the opportunity to suggest that all that was necessary was the occasional publication of a list of schools recognised as fully efficient by his inspectors. He proposed that, in future, an increasing proportion of all new teachers should be trained. This administrative move succeeded in uniting both the National Union of Teachers and the Headmasters' Conference. Their representatives met and took action, through the House of Lords, to frame an amendment which had the effect of making it possible to set up a Registration Council representative of the teaching profession and a register consisting of one column only. An acrimonious struggle ensued between teachers' leaders and Morant, in which he used every tactic to delay and obstruct. Morant's delaying tactics were a portent of what was to be the continuing opposition by the state to professional self-government by the teachers.

Sexual Divisions in Teaching

Sexual divisions have proved to be a crucial factor inhibiting the development of professionalism among teachers and have also been a weakening element in the support for teacher unionism. The connection between the male sex and the anglican Ministry meant that there was an institutionalized predisposition to see teaching as a male role. [. . .]

Among secondary teachers the sexual division was of special importance in relation to professionalism. The male secondary teacher took his status, or aspired to take his status, from his university background, his general social background and the prestige of the school in which he taught, rather than from his training *per se*. Indeed 'training' was eschewed as smacking too much of the lower status elementary teacher. Among middle class women, who became employed as teachers in the new secondary schools for girls, these considerations acted as a stimulus towards the idea of training. The reasons for this were the mirror image of those which caused male secondary teachers to reject training. At first girls' schools were typically headed by a clergyman headmaster and often had male teachers on the staff. Men were usually to be found teaching religious knowledge and were often clergymen. Women teachers, who had not had the benefit of a university education and were excluded from the ministry, could only prove their competence *vis-à-vis* the male by claiming the benefits which were to flow from a certification of such competence after training. [. . .]

Among teachers' associations too, sexual divisions have played a very important part. In secondary education there are separate associations for Headmasters and Headmistresses respectively, as well as for Assistant Masters and Assistant Mistresses. In the elementary sector, the National Union of Teachers has always admitted teachers of both sexes as members, but in the early years of the twentieth century, a breakaway women's 'union' was created. The National Union of Women Teachers as it was called, respresented a feminist pressure group seeking objectives such as equal pay for women. On the other hand, as the balance of numbers within elementary teaching shifted in favour of women, many male teachers felt that the Union was being dominated by interests inimical to the advancement of the male. In consequence the National Association of Schoolmasters was founded as a splinter union during the First World War. Whereas the National Union of Women Teachers

dissolved itself in 1962 (with the achievement of equal pay), this event only served to invigorate the NAS which went on to press militantly for formal representation in the Burnham machinery. This it subsequently achieved.[6] The formal and institutionalized sexual division has weakened both the position of teachers' unions *vis-à-vis* the state and the struggle for teachers' professionalism.
[...]

Social Class Division

Class divisions are of great importance in enhancing the failure of teachers to create a unified and self-governing profession. From the outset elementary teachers were drawn from a lower class background than secondary teachers, and the question of the class basis of recruitment to the profession has thus been of continuing significance. In the early period, elementary teachers, as they were to be subsequently called, were recruited in the main from among men who had failed at other trades or occupations. Tropp reports that many of them had been semiskilled craftsmen, clerks, shopkeepers or 'superior' domestic servants. In other words, they had been in occupations for which a knowledge of reading, writing and simple arithmetic were required, or which offered the opportunity to acquire these skills. Teaching was often regarded as a 'respectable second best', although some became teachers from a sense of religious duty.[7]
[...]

Although Kay-Shuttleworth's proposal of 1839 for a National Training College was thwarted by sectarianism, his private efforts were thrown behind the development of a College of Education at Battersea. The Minutes of 1846 instituted the pupil-teacher system and served not only to improve the level of instruction given in elementary schools, but also to provide a supply of able candidates for the training colleges. In addition the government certificate, inaugurated by the Minutes, was underpinned by a direct financial grant from the government which augmented the salaries of certificated teachers.[8] From this time forward the remuneration of teachers in the elementary sector became dependent on the policies of governments, and their basic market situation could be 'manipulated' by decision of the state. The pupil-teacher system retained the character of apprenticeship and helped to preserve the notion that elementary teachers were part of the skilled working class rather than 'professionals'. [...]

Among middle class observers of the situation after 1846, there were those who feared that the elementary teaching 'profession' would come to be recruited solely from the lower orders. Moreover, they anticipated that such recruits would be motivated by personal ambition, and for this reason would concentrate more specifically on the secular subjects, which were examined for the certificate, rather than on the religious nature of the calling. The training colleges attempted to counter this by religious training designed both to inculcate a sense of missionary zeal, and also of personal humility. During the 1850s the HMI's collectively made every effort to prevent teaching becoming simply an avenue of social mobility for clever working class people. Rules of entry for the Queen's Scholarships were relaxed in the hope of encouraging applicants other than the five-year trained pupil-teachers.

Even before 1860 the proportion of female pupil-teachers was beginning to rise. In 1849 women made up 32 per cent of the total and ten years later, 46 per cent.[9] [...] Many girls entered teaching as a phase in life which they would leave behind on marriage. The relative advantages in income and position of certificated mistresses, compared with women in other occupations, was such that attempts were made 'to appropriate it for middle-class entrants'. Miss Burdett Coutts was among those who regarded recruitment of girls exclusively from working class backgrounds as not altogether 'socially advantageous'. She made efforts to get middle class young women to become elementary school mistresses and obtained the backing of influential people for her enterprise. Only the defective education of middle class girls at the time prevented the achievement of this objective. The fact was that they were extremely unlikely to be successful in the examination for Queen's Scholarships.[10]

In the fourth and fifth decades of the nineteenth century the elementary teacher had been offered a subsidised form of education which had provided an avenue of upward social mobility for such individuals into the middle class. The evidence from the period suggests that assimilation into the middle class was a widely held objective among teachers. For women teachers, there was a possibility of upward mobility through marriage, enhanced by education. For men, there was the chance that they, or their children, could obtain more solid middle class employment after a teacher training. Nevertheless, it had not been the intention of any government that elementary teachers should become upwardly mobile through state subsidisation. On the contrary, every effort was made to ensure that as a body, elementary teachers should remain in what was regarded as their proper place in society; that is, as teachers recruited from and serving the working class. The basis of the educational reaction of the 1860s was the middle class fear that this policy had broken down. At one level the debate which led to the establishment of the Newcastle Commission (1858) was related to both the religious question and to the matter of government expenditure, but each of these were manifestations of class prejudices and class antagonism. It was not just that as the Reverend C.H. Bromby said in 1862 there are those who 'in their hearts hate and fear the education of the lower classes' but, as another contemporary commentator, Wigram, thought, unless the middle classes made better educational provision for their children, the outcome would be 'an inversion of the orders of society'.[11] The teacher, with his certificate behind him, was thought by middle class people to be overeducated for his 'proper' social position. He was considered conceited, and overambitious. In copying the dress and manners of his social superiors he became discontented with his status and income. Often too, he gave up teaching to compete with middle class people in the white collar occupational world. The 'educational reaction' was more a social reaction against the aspirations of the elementary teaching occupation than it was a movement against the education of the working class. In fact, the elementary teachers symbolised something more important than the threat of revolutionary subversion; they represented an immediate threat to middle class people by former members of the working class who had acquired the very skills and manners on which middle class superiority was based. The powerful desire for assimilation into the middle class was the driving force behind both the teachers' aspirations and the reaction to them.

Thus the Revised Code of 1861 was an attempt, inspired by the mood of the middle classes, among whom were the secondary teachers, to clamp down on the aspirations of the elementary teacher. It signalled a definite blocking movement to the collective social mobility of the teachers, as well as an effort to check the upward social mobility of individuals. All direct payments to teachers and pupil-teachers were abolished; retirement pensions were swept away; building and furniture grants, book grants, grants for scientific apparatus and such like all disappeared. In their place a crude simulation of the market mechanism was introduced, which envisaged only one type of payment; this was to be made to the school managers upon evidence of the educational results of each child at an annual inspection: it was the system of payment by results. This was rightly understood by elementary teachers at the time as an attack upon themselves. They were firmly subordinated to the school managers and the attainment of self-governing professionalism was pushed further out of reach.

In turn, the Revised Code produced its own counter-reaction among teachers. At first, the teachers themselves, and the lecturers in the training colleges, were stunned by the new measures. The lack of a national organisation among teachers, at that time, made it difficult for them to effect an adequate collective riposte. Nevertheless, it was during this period that the idea of teachers' unionism began to crystallise. For a section of the elementary teachers, the rebuff to their middle class aspirations, eventuated in speculation about the possibility of an alliance with the working class movement. In any event, as a result of the Code, teaching became much less attractive and recruitment fell off. The morale of those who remained was low. Many, who were working as teachers or who were in training, took other employment as soon as they were able to do so. Although some teachers viewed positively the longer term prospect of serving their interests by an alliance with the working class movement, many took the alternative and supported the teachers' registration movement. The latter was used at this time by teachers' leaders as a means of arresting 'the disorganisation sure otherwise to result from the reaction arising from the late code agitation'.[12] The scholastic registration movement, although originated by middle class teachers in the private sector was seen by elementary teachers as a way of achieving a union between the different grades of the profession. Their objectives in giving support were to raise their own social position and to drive the unqualified teacher from the field. The middle class secondary teachers had no recognised certificate of efficiency and wished, for their part, to set up their own qualifying association within the structure of a self-governing profession. The elementary teachers feared that the success of such a movement, without their participation, would reduce the status of their own state-awarded certificate and thus reinforce the barrier to their own assimilation into the middle class.[13]

The foundation of the National Union of Elementary Teachers, in 1870, underlines the practical utility to the teachers of unionism. They needed an association which could engage in collective bargaining on their behalf. The union was necessary, both because the Revised Code controversy had raised the level of political consciousness of many teachers, thus transcending the sectarian differences which in other respects still divided them and also because the 1870 Act brought the state more firmly to the forefront as the power to be negotiated with in education. The union by no means gave up the teachers' aspirations for registration, or for professional self-government. It was just that the weakness of the teachers' position made such an objective only one among other more pressing considerations. The fact that the state controlled the certificate, and was able to 'manipulate' it, meant that the elementary teachers were in a market where the state was close to being a monopolist. In the 1870s and 1880s governments did not scruple to dilute the certificate and allow into practice increasing numbers of unqualified teachers, particularly women. In this way, the levels of remuneration for teachers, and thus ultimately their status, were controlled by the state. Aspirations for collective social mobility via self-governing professionalism were thus thwarted once again.[14]

[. . .]

Conclusions

[. . .]

Professionalism is an ideology of the middle class and has been practised as an occupational strategy; it is a vehicle for upward collective social mobility.[15] Teachers have either been concerned to defend their middle class status or assimilate themselves into that class (depending on which of the teaching occupations one starts with). Professionalism is *par excellence* an occupational strategy of groups who aspire to collective upward social mobility into the solid middle class. This is a major reason why it has long been attractive to teachers. On the other hand, divisions among teachers themselves based in class and religion, as well as in sexual divisions, have been important in preventing the emergence of a unified and self-governing profession. The opposition of established middle class groups to the assimilation of the elementary teacher was historically crucial. In the event, these forces were crystallized in the policies of governments, and in their record of educational legislation. The stark fact now is that the state, having become the most powerful force in education, has a vested interest in opposing the ideal of the teachers' registration movement; that is in blocking the establishment of a self-governing teaching profession. It is difficult to conceive of any way in which this basic situation is likely to change, and it remains the underlying reason why occupational movements of teachers have been organized on the model of unionism. Teachers' unions in Britain still aspire to professionalism but the overwhelming importance of them is, in itself an indicator of the failure of teachers to achieve the objective of professionalism. Meanwhile inflation, and the varieties of overt and covert incomes policies practised by the state in an attempt to combat it, have made manifest the extent of the distance between the ideal of professional self-government on the one hand, as opposed to the reality of state control on the other. In this situation incomes, and the number of teachers in training or employment, are determined by government, and in turn, by the latter's effort to manage the economy. Public sector employees, among whom teachers are prominent, are used against their will as a 'good example' to the private sector. All this seems far from teachers' self-interest and sometimes from that of education more generally. Here is the cause both of the outburst of militancy which has sometimes characterized union activity in recent years, but also and more importantly, the problem of lowered morale. This was noticed first in the inner city areas of London. Though only publicized in the media in the early 1970s, it had already been commented on by Kelsall in 1968.[16] Many teachers find themselves in a position where they are trying to live middle class lifestyles on incomes which make that aspiration impossible. This situation only serves to focus more sharply the issues of professionalism and unionism among teachers today.

Notes and References

1 RICH, R.W. (1933) *The Training of Teachers in England and Wales, during the Nineteenth Century*, Cambridge University Press.
2 TROPP, A. (1957) *The School Teachers*, Heinemann, pp. 10–11.
3 BOARD OF EDUCATION, (1925) 'Report of the Departmental Committee on the Training of Teachers for Public Elementary Schools', Cmd. 2409.
4 DOBSON, J.L. (1973) 'The Training Colleges and their Successors, 1920–1970', in COOK, T.G. (Ed.) *Education and the Professions*, Methuen.
5 BARON, G. (1954) 'The teachers' registration movement', *British Journal of Educational Studies*, May, pp. 133–44.
6 It has also subsequently been obliged to amalgate with the Union of Women Teachers (UWT) to comply with the Sex Discrimination Act.
7 TROPP, A. (1957) *op. cit.*, pp. 10–1.
8 RICH, R.W. (1933) *op. cit.*
9 TROPP, A. (1957) *op. cit.*
10 *Ibid.*, p. 23.
11 Striking quotations from contemporaries such as Bromby and Wigram are contained in TROPP, A. (1957) *op. cit.*, p. 59.
12 TROPP, A. (1957) *op. cit.*, p. 99.
13 *Ibid.*, p. 100.
14 *Ibid.*, Chaps. 8 and 9.
15 The concept of 'collective social mobility' is developed in PARRY, N.C.A. and PARRY, J. (1976) *The Rise of the Medical Profession: A Study of Collective Social Mobility*, Croom Helm.
16 KELSALL, R.K. and KELSALL, H.M. (1969) *The School Teacher in England and the United States: the Findings of Empirical Research*, Pergamon Press.

23   Women and Teaching in the Nineteenth Century

June Purvis

Introduction

In the nineteenth century, women entered and were concentrated in certain kinds of occupations. The 1851 Census, for example, reveals that in England and Wales, for adults aged 20 years of age and upwards, 1,421,354 males but only 454,421 females are recorded as 'Persons possessing or working the Land, and engaged in growing Grain, Fruits, Grasses, Animals, and other products' but 1,329,292 female and only 512,209 males are recorded as 'Persons engaged in entertaining, clothing, and performing personal offices for man'.[1] However, the extent of female waged labour is much wider than that recorded in such official statistics. Sally Alexander[2] has demonstrated that the work of married women in particular was often 'hidden': casual, home-based waged labour such as needlework, for example, was frequently unrecorded because it was both erratic and confined to the private sphere of the home.

One occupation that women did enter and become concentrated in was teaching, especially schoolteaching, which, because of its 'child care' function, was not far removed from a woman's domestic role. In this paper I shall look at the entry of women into schoolteaching not purely as a history in its own right but also as an important determinant of the forms and the quality of education provided for girls and women. A major theme will be that the position of women within the teaching profession in the nineteenth century can only be fully understood when ideological and material factors external to the occupation are taken into account. Here I shall focus upon the social class origins of female teachers and the class-specific images of femininity which I shall argue provide crucial variables in understanding the relationship between women and teaching.

Images of Femininity

Ann Oakley[3] emphasizes the important distinction between sex (based on biological

Source: First published in this volume.

differences) and gender (based on psychological and cultural differences). The terms male and female are usually applied to sexual differences and the terms masculinity and femininity to gender differences. Masculinity and femininity are thus historically specific social constructs that are determined by economic, social and cultural factors. In the nineteenth century, the bourgeois ideology of femininity, which was meant to apply to all women, was that of domesticity, and the ideal location for women was within the private sphere of the family as full time wives and mothers.[4] Men, on the other hand, were to be located within the public sphere of work where it was assumed that sufficient could be earned to support the economically dependent wife and children. The relationship between such definitions of femininity and masculinity and the development of capitalism cannot be adequately covered here. What I wish to stress, however, is that British society in the nineteenth century was not only a capitalist society but also a patriarchal society. Though patriarchy[5] as a power structure predates capitalism,[6] the dominance of men and subordination of women can be found within a variety of 'sites' and sets of social relations within capitalist work processes, but especially within the family. Consequently, masculinity, which was closely tied to the world of work, was the high status gender form while femininity, which was closely linked to the family and domesticity, was of secondary importance.

Within the dominant ideology of femininity as domesticity, we find class-specific images – that of the middle class 'lady' and that of the working class 'woman'. These images help us to understand the relationship between women and teaching since they will influence both the kinds of education that are given to women and also the entry of women into specific occupations. Let us examine these images further.

The dominant ideal image of the middle class 'lady' underwent a number of transformations during the course of the nineteenth century. In the first half of the century, the concept of femininity for middle class women involved the ideal of the *perfect wife and mother* who organized an efficient and emotionally stable home environment. This ideal is epitomized in the writings of middle class women such as Mrs. Sandford and Mrs. Ellis. Thus Mrs. Ellis in 'The Wives of England' suggests that when a husband return home from work, if his taste is for:

> neatness and order, for the absence of servants, and for perfect quiet, it would be absolute cruelty to allow such a man to find his house in confusion, and to have to call in servants to clear this thing and the other away after his return, as if he had never once been thought of, at least thought of with kindness and consideration, until he was actually seen. . . . At home it is but fitting that the master of the house should be considered as entitled to the choice of every personal indulgence, unless indisposition of suffering on the part of the wife render such indulgences her due.[7]

The 'perfect wife and mother' image involved almost saintly virtues of love, patience, self denial, suffering and resignation.[8] Ruskin in his lecture *Of Queens' Gardens* alikened women to 'lilies' who exercise queenly power over the separate sphere of the home[9] even though they must be wise 'not for self-development, but for self-renunciation'.[10] Other writers such as Mrs. Sandford emphasized that femininity involved dependence rather than independence, and inferiority rather than superiority:

> There is, indeed, something unfeminine in independence. It is contrary to nature, and therefore it offends. We do not like to see a woman affecting tremors, but still less do we like to see her acting the Amazon. A really sensible woman feels her dependence. She does what she can, but she is conscious of inferiority, and therefore grateful for support.[11]

The 'perfect wife and mother' image therefore involved some fundamental contradictions for the middle class woman: though femininity epitomized the Christian virtues of humility, self sacrifice and 'grace', women were still given an inferior and secondary status in a patriarchal society where men were in power and masculinity was the high status gender form. As Ruskin noted:

> The man is always to be the wiser; he is to be the thinker, the ruler, the superior in knowledge and discretion, as in power.[12]

During the second half of the nineteenth century, the middle class image of the 'perfect wife and mother' who was active within family life was challenged by another image of femininity, that of the *perfect lady*, the symbol of conspicuous consumption. As Hamilton[13] has noted, she was a person who could afford to do nothing. Vicinus suggests[14] that the 'perfect lady' ideal was most fully developed in the upper middle classes. Here a woman was not meant to work within the home since servants were available, her social and intellectual growth was confined to the family and friends, and her status was totally dependent upon the economic position of her father and husband. Thus the 'perfect lady' did not actively engage in child rearing but met her children at set times of the day, especially in the evenings before bed-time. Beatrice Potter (later Webb), for example, born in 1858 of upper middle class parents, was largely 'brought up by servants'[15]: a similar upbringing was experienced by Gertrude Pearson (later Lady Denham) born in 1884 of parents who later became the first Viscount and Viscountess of Cowdray.[16] Being a 'perfect lady' involved learning a ritual of social etiquette.[17] But above all else, the 'perfect lady' did not engage in waged labour, though she might participate in unpaid philanthropy. A letter to the editor of *The Englishwoman's Journal* in 1866 succinctly expresses this viewpoint:

> if a woman is obliged to work, at once, (although she may be Christian and well bred) she loses that peculiar position which the word 'lady' conventionally designates.[18]

Thus when Sophia Jex Blake, daughter of wealthy parents, was offered the paid post of mathematical tutor at Queen's College, London, her father was horrified: in a letter written in January 1859, he argued 'to be "paid" for the work would be to alter the thing "completely" and would lower you sadly in the eyes of almost everybody'.[19] Despite some pleadings, Sophia eventually bowed to convention and refused the offer.

Towards the end of the nineteenth century, another definition of middle class femininity began to emerge – the image of the *new woman*. The 'new woman' was to widen her sphere of action and participate in some of the various economic and social changes that accompanied industrialization. She could be found in paid employment, seeking education and fighting for legal and political rights.[20] Writers such as John Stuart Mill, Frances Power Cobbe and Josephine Butler[21] argued for the recognition of women as autonomous beings rather than as creatures defined only in relation to some man. Such a line of argument was one important aspect of the changing definition of femininity in the 'new woman' image. Typical examples of this new type of woman were those middle class pioneers, like Emily Davies, who fought to establish higher education colleges for women. In 1878 Miss Davies argued that parents should recognize the simple fact that

> their daughters, no less than their sons, need all that a complete and thorough education can do for them, and that where it would be a matter of course to send a boy to the University, it should be equally a matter of course to do as much for a girl.[22]

Yet the image of the 'new woman' who might enjoy equal opportunities in education and in employment was itself beset with contradictions since such behaviour, which attempted to break the link between femininity and domesticity, was defined as 'unfeminine' by the dominant, male, middle class culture. A number of writers equated higher education with masculinity. Maudsley[23] for example, in stating his case against higher education for women, argued that the aim of female education should be the development of womanhood, not manhood. Similarly, an article 'The British Mother Taking Alarm' in the right wing *The Saturday Review*, 19 September, 1871, asks the following question when discussing the issue of education for women:

> Is it altogether a fanciful notion that the masculine proclivities assuming such large proportions among women evidence a sort of moral senility? Just as ancient hens put on secondary male attributes and try to crow – but feebly – so old women grow more like old men than they were like young ones when both were in their prime. Is it really true, then, that the world is in its dotage, and that humanity as a race is tottering to its end? And is one sign of this to be found in the modern woman who thinks she can put the world of nature on a new footing, and who imagines that to be the bad imitation of a man is better than to be the perfect embodiment of true womanhood?[24]

The educational pioneers were probably conscious of such criticisms and aware of the contradictory nature of their demands. Thus Emily Davies[25] while arguing for the higher education of women was also careful to point out that an education which did not make good wives and mothers could not be justified. Anne Clough accepted the link of femininity with domesticity and justified higher education for women as a means of extending their intellectual interests and thus making them 'better' wives, mothers and companions.[26]

The gender definition of femininity for working class women was quite distinct from that of middle class women. The dominant image for working class women in the nineteenth century was of *the woman*. Since the middle class images of femininity were the most prestigious, 'the woman' image was subordinate. In every way, 'the woman' was regarded as inferior: she neither possessed the household management skills of the 'perfect wife and mother' nor the leisured life style and ritual of etiquette of the 'lady'. Thus the working class woman was seen as inefficient both as house-keeper and as wife and mother: she was frequently blamed for various social problems amongst the working class such as crime, drunkenness, poor educational effort, squalor, disease and a high infant mortality rate. Mrs. Ellis for example, when speaking of poor men's wives warns that crime might be traced to

> the early training of a low-principled mother. . . . The influence of low-principled mothers, and the general confusion and disorder as regards right and wrong which necessarily prevails in households governed by such women, are universally acknowledged to constitute the great counter-acting difficulty which stands in the way of educational effort, when directed to the working classes.[27]

Both single and married working class women were perceived by the middle classes as inadequate. It would appear that what tarnished the working class woman in particular was the experience of waged labour both before and after marriage. From a middle class perspective, her waged labour was a departure from the bourgeois ideal of domesticity and economic dependence. Thus middle class critics often confronted the reality of such economic activity not by redefining femininity but by classifying such women as 'unfeminine'. Lord Ashley, for example, in a speech in the House of Commons in 1844 notes that in the mills in the Manchester area where the men's labour was gradually being dispensed with, the women

> not only perform the labour, but occupy the places of men; they are forming various clubs and associations, and gradually acquiring all those privileges which are held to be the proper portion of the male sex. These female clubs are thus described: fifty or sixty females, married and single, form themselves into clubs, ostensibly for protection; but, in fact, they meet together, to drink, sing, and smoke; they use, it is stated, the lowest, most brutal, and most disgusting language imaginable ... on women are imposed the duty and burthen of supporting their husbands and families, a perversion as it were of nature, which has the inevitable effect of introduc-ing into families disorder, insubordination, and conflict.[28]

During the second half of the century, as the working classes became organized, the trade unions in particular campaigned for a family wage that would protect working class females from the brutalizing effects of waged labour: the ability to keep a wife at home became a sign of working class strength.[29] Yet even so, for the middle classes, a working class woman would never attain the middle class ideal of 'the lady': her social class background would always betray her.

The social class differences between women in the nineteenth century were reflected, then, in the different images of femininity and imposed by the bourgeoisie on their own women and on working class women. Such images had at least two important educational implications. First, they would influence the kinds of education considered appropriate for girls of different social classes and, second, they would influence the choice made in regard to the type of school that women might teach in. Thus, as we shall see, by the end of the nineteenth century, female teachers of working class background were concentrated in state elementary, mixed sex schools which catered for working class children while female teachers of middle class background were mostly found either as governesses or in private secondary, single sex schools which catered especially for middle class girls. What both groups of female teachers held in common was the fact that each was involved in low status education: the elementary education of working class children was considered inferior to that of middle class children while the education of middle class girls was considered inferior to that of middle class boys. For both groups of teachers, too, it was commonly assumed that teaching was an extension of femininity. Let us explore this issue further.

Teaching as a Feminine Activity

During the nineteenth century, reference was often made to the female capacity for teaching since teaching was regarded as a 'natural' part of femininity[30] (see Rev. Butler[31]). This view may be summed up in the following statement by Davenport Adams (1880):

> Women seem endowed with a natural capacity for teaching. Their quick sympathy, their patience, and their facility of expression are gifts which bring them readily into accord with their pupils.[32]

This natural capacity for teaching was of course based upon the link between femininity and domesticity, especially child care. In an article 'At Home and At School', it is argued:

> all mothers are teachers of evil if not of good. Women have an instinct for teaching given to them. The little girl in the nursery is quite ready to set herself up as guide and monitress to brothers two or three years older than herself; girls become mentors at a very early age.[33]

Thus within teaching, women were often associated with the care of young children. Nowhere is this more evident than among dame teachers who flourished especially in the first half of the century.

Though Leinster-Mackay[34] claims that the term 'dame school' has been used to denote schools providing education for all social classes, the term is usually applied to those small, self-financing ventures where for a few pence per week, a working class child might obtain the rudiments of education. Though the quality of such schools varied considerably, the general impression tends to support the complaints of the Manchester Statistical Society Report of 1834–35 about 'deplorable' conditions in dame schools:

The greater part of them are kept by females, but some by old men, whose only qualification for this employment seems to be their unfitness for every other. Many of these teachers are engaged at the same time in some other employment, such as shopkeeping, sewing, washing, etc., which renders any regular instruction among their scholars absolutely impossible. Indeed, neither parents nor teachers seem to consider this as the principal object in sending their children to these schools, but generally say that they go there in order to be taken care of, and to be out of the way at home.[35]

Thus Mary Smith,[36] the daughter of an Oxfordshire shoemaker, claims that she learnt very little at Dame Garner's school which she attended for two years from the age of four: the old dame just kept the children quiet and did small household tasks. At the age of seven, Mary was sent to another dame school, mainly to learn to knit and sew.[37] On the other hand, Thomas Cooper,[38] the self-taught, working class radical, recollects how 'Old Gatty', who ran a dame school, was an expert and laborious teacher of reading and spelling: in addition, her knitting – for she taught girls as well as boys – was the wonder of the town. The level of knowledge and extent of training necessary for dame teaching was often minimal: recruitment was open and no standards of entry were required. Dame teaching was usually seen as an easy means for a woman to earn a living in times of hardship, and such independent ventures into schooling were indigenous to working class culture before the development of mass schooling.[39] For working class women there were certain advantages to being a dame since it involved not just a means of income but also an opportunity to use certain skills in her job that were learnt and used in her domestic duties within the family.

Women also taught in some of the other forms of privately organized schooling offered to working class children – for example, charity schools, Sunday schools, day schools of the British and Foreign School Society (largely supported by religious dissenters) and of the National Society for Promoting the Education of the Poor in the Principles of the Established Church, ragged schools, factory and industrial schools. It has been estimated that in England and Wales in 1818, 452,000 children attended school on Sundays, 168,000 attended charity schools and 53,000 attended dame schools.[40] In some of these schools, female teachers taught a common curriculum to boys and girls but often they were expected also to teach sewing and knitting to girls alone: thus in the 1830s, at a factory school at Belper, Miss Phoebe Gregory taught factory children aged 9–13 reading and writing with additional sewing and knitting for girls.[41] Similarly, at the school of industry at Gower's Walk, Whitechapel, both sexes were taught the 3Rs but boys were taught the industrial occupation of printing while girls were taught needlework.[42] Female teachers in the factory, British and National schools were, however, inspected – unlike teachers in dame schools. Though, as we shall later see, middle class women might participate in some of these ventures on an unpaid, voluntary basis, it is the paid female elementary teachers (especially pupil teachers), recruited almost solidly amongst working class girls and teaching working class children, who are probably the typical women teachers of the nineteenth century. Amongst pupil teachers, the proportion of women rose from 32 per cent in 1847 to 46 per cent in 1859[43] and then to 78 per cent in the mid 1890s.[44]

The pupil teacher system was initiated in 1846 by Kay Shuttleworth. In this scheme a five year, state aided apprenticeship could be offered to a pupil who had completed elementary education to the age of 13. Certain educational entry requirements were demanded. Thus, amongst other things, each prospective candidate was expected to read with fluency, ease and expression; to write in a neat hand (with correct spelling and punctuation) a simple prose narrative which would be slowly read aloud; to write, from dictation; sums in the first four rules of arithmetic; to point out the parts of speech in a simple sentence; to possess an elementary knowledge of geography and to show an ability to teach a junior class to the satisfaction of the Inspector. But, in addition to such modest requirements, female pupil teachers were also expected to be able 'to sew neatly and to knit'.[45] In this way, female pupil teachers became a resource for teaching working class girls specific domestic skills. Anna Davin[46] has shown that the reading text books which would be used within the London School Board area espoused the domestic ideology for working class girls. By being able to teach domestic skills, female teachers could be used to maintain the sexual division of society and to promote the differential gender expectations that were a part of being masculine or feminine.

At the age of 18, a pupil teacher could sit the Queen's Scholarship and, if successful, enter one of the teacher training colleges organized under various voluntary schemes (university day training colleges were not established until the late nineteenth century). As expected, the Queen's Scholarship Questions reflected the differential expectations for male and female pupil teachers in terms of subjects to be taught. Thus in the Moffatt's Reprint of the July 1894 questions, both male and female candidates took the same examinations in dictation, penmanship, grammar, composition, school management, music, history, geography, French, Welsh, German and Latin, but only men took algebra, mensuration, Euclid and Greek and only women took domestic economy and needlework. The needlework paper shows how female pupil teachers were examined in the forms of 'useful' sewing considered suitable for working class girls rather then the 'ornamental' sewing common in the middle class household: thus the paper includes questions on the making of the lower or knee part of 'knickerbocker drawers' and on the making of a woman's gored petticoat.[47] The domestic economy paper shows that females were examined in health care issues such as the prevention in young children of earache, toothache and rheumatism: questions were also asked on how to cope with accidents in school such as a cut finger, an epileptic fit, nose bleeding and scalding.[48] It would appear then that female elementary teachers were expected to teach those skills which were linked to that form of femininity deemed appropriate for the working classes. A female elementary schoolteacher could never become a 'lady' teacher – she would always be a 'woman' teacher in both senses of the term.

Of course, not all pupil teachers passed the Queen's Scholarship and amongst those who did pass, not all could afford to attend training college. The shortage of college places aggravated the problem and it was women, in particular, who remained uncertificated. In 1875, only 9 per cent of the men and 13 per cent of the women were uncertificated but by 1914 this had risen to 12 per cent for the men and a staggering 41 per cent for the women.[49] During the last decades of the nineteenth century, the expansion of uncertificated female teachers took place especially amongst the category called 'supplementary teachers': the only qualifications necessary for such work were that the candidates should be over 18 years of age, vaccinated against smallpox and approved by an HMI as suitable for the general instruction of scholars, including the teaching of needlework.[50] Such teachers, later called 'Article 68s', could therefore be recruited without having passed any examinations at all.[51] The expansion of a state system of education, made possible by the 1870 Education Act, was therefore largely met by a supply of uncertificated, lowly paid women teachers. In 1861, the Newcastle Commission found that the average annual pay of a sample of certificated men was £94. 3s. 7d. and of certificated women £62. 13s. 10d.; whilst among the uncertificated the amounts were £62. 4s. 11d. and £34. 19s. 7d. respectively.[52] Such pay differentials, based on sex, extended well into the twentieth century. In the 1880s *A Practical Housekeeper* gave advice on how a village schoolmistress could live upon £70 a year: the money saving tips included the following recipes:

> 'Saturday' – Half neck (best end) of mutton, boiled, with parsley sauce. . . . Rice pudding (made with 'old' milk i.e., after cream has been skimmed from it. 'Monday' – Mutton broth (made on Saturday from part of the other half neck of mutton and the liquor in which Saturday's dinner was boiled; carefully skimmed and the fat put aside for future use). . . . 'Thursday' – 'Toad-in-a-hole' to use up any scraps of cold meat, and two eggs added.[53]

If elementary schoolteaching was a poorly paid and probably arduous occupation, what then was its appeal for the working class girl? First, the method of training, i.e. an apprenticeship whereby one was trained in the world of work, was indigenous to working class culture, especially amongst the skilled artisan occupational group. Indeed, one anonymous writer in the *Cornhill Magazine* 1873, claimed that the fathers of female pupil teachers were 'usually labourers, artizans, or small tradesmen'.[54] Second, teaching offered many advantages in comparison with other occupations open to working class girls – occupations such as domestic service, dressmaking, factory work. School-teaching demanded some degree, however basic, of scholastic ability and it had, therefore, a certain status. It also offered clean working conditions, the potential for intrinsic job satisfaction and the opportunity of limited social mobility since it was not manual labour. The price to pay was an ambivalence in terms of social status: the elementary schoolteacher was separated from the class from which she originated and was also unacceptable to those above her. This was the contradictory nature of the situation in which she found herself. Frequent references are therefore made to her social isolation.[55]

Tropp[56] suggests that many working class girls expected to abandon teaching once they married. This indicates, that for such girls, the marital state was meant ideally to exclude waged labour outside the home. Such an attitude, of course, may have been reinforced by the employment policies of employers. In the 1880s, Flora

Thompson remembers that after the failure of the schoolteacher Miss Matilda Annie Higgs, the previous teacher – now married as Mrs. Tenby – temporarily returned: she stayed only a few weeks either because 'she did not wish to teach again permanently or the educational authorities already had a rule against employing married-women teachers'.[57] Indeed, by the early twentieth century most local authorities had imposed a marriage bar which remained legal till the passing of the 1944 Education Act.[58] A host of factors probably contributed to such a discriminatory policy: e.g. the belief amongst employers that once married, a woman's prime responsibility should be child rearing and care of the home; the attitudes of the male dominated NUT and its fears that the flood of uncertificated female teachers would depress the status of the profession; the supply of teachers exceeding the demand.[59] The entry of women into teaching must be seen, therefore, in relation to the patterns and expectations of marriage. If married women were encouraged not to work and were usually forbidden entry into teaching, then the supply of women teachers would be mainly composed of single women. This, however, did not necessarily mean a short supply of entrants since, by the early twentieth century, the surplus of single women of marriageable age had reached a new peak.[60] The relationship between women's position within the family and their entry into teaching is therefore a complex one.

By the turn of the century, female elementary teachers had concentrated in the low status sectors of girls' and infants' departments and in the lower grades of boys' departments: the advanced work in the latter was almost always undertaken by men.[61] Female teachers, on the other hand, were responsible for the teaching of cookery, laundry work and needlework which had gradually become an integral part of the curriculum for girls.[62] This state of affairs reveals only too well the cyclical relationship between the forms and quality of girls' education and the level of skills and professional status of women teachers. Since female elementary teachers now formed three quarters of the teaching force,[63] any attempt to improve the quality of elementary teachers, either through raising the entrance requirements or improving the standard of training, had at least two effects. First, it would open up the possibility of more advanced education for such women teachers and, second, such changes would help to improve the quality of education for girls within the classroom.

Now let us discuss the entry of middle class women into teaching. Middle and upper class girls were mainly educated within the home, especially up to the 1870s – thus the governess was one of the most common categories of female teachers of middle class background. According to the 1851 Census, there were 20,058 governesses in England and Wales[64] though the total number may have been much larger. Sometimes a governess lived in with the family, sometimes she visited on a daily or even hourly basis. The subjects she taught might vary from a wide range to only a limited range of accomplishments. The rich father of Florence Nightingale, for example, taught his own daughters Greek, Latin, German, French, Italian, History and Philosophy but engaged a governess to teach music and drawing.[65] Governessing was of course a suitable job for a woman of gentle birth who had fallen upon hard times.[66] In particular, the clergyman's daughter had 'immense snob value' to those middle class parents who wished to give their daughters the polished manners of polite society.[67] In addition, she might have had previous teaching experience in teaching her brothers and sisters or in teaching in her father's Sunday schools. Despite Charlotte Yonge's claim[68] that the governess is 'a lady with a profession', the governess suffered from status incongruence, as Peterson has ably shown: she had a lady's status yet was also in paid employment.[69] In addition, she had failed in the marriage market: after all, the apogee of middle class feminity was finding a husband. The ambiguous nature of the governess's 'lady-like' position inevitably imposed severe strains upon her: for example, the insecurity of tenure, especially in old age, often meant destitution. Harriet Martineau[70] quotes a physician who said that the largest group of females in lunatic asylums were governesses.

Most governesses had no training for their job. Only a minority attended courses such as those offered at Queen's College for Women, London (founded in 1848) or at small training schools such as that at Bolham, near Tiverton.[71] The level of payment, like the level of training, was inadequate, probably about £20–45 a year: as Davidoff *et al*[72] have pointed out, even such a low level of pay would 'degrade' the femininity of a middle class lady. Though there was some improvement in the standard of training, level of pay and conditions of employment for governesses during the nineteenth century, in 1901 Mary Maxse could still claim that it was a career without a future.[73]

Of course unpaid teaching, of a philanthropic nature, was congruent with middle class definitions of femininity and with the 'lady' image. Virtues often associated with philanthropic work, such as compassion and tenderness, were considered to be peculiarly feminine virtues.[74] Through unpaid, part-time, philanthropic teaching, many middle and upper class women found an outlet for their suppressed energies without tarnishing their reputations. For example, in the Mechanics' Institutes, a major form of adult education in the nineteenth century, there was a strong tradition of middle class ladies teaching basic literacy and sewing to working class women: at Halifax Mechanics' Institute, which in 1859 had 74 female members amongst a total membership of 747, Mrs. Carpenter, the Misses Stansfield and Miss Birtwhistle all gave their teaching services free.[75] Middle class ladies also taught working class men for no pay. At Newham College in the 1880s female students gave lessons to groups of working men.[76] At this time too, Juliet and Winifred Seebohm, daughters of a Quaker banker, taught working class men in an adult Sunday school.[77]

Another category of female middle class teacher in the nineteenth century was the schoolmistress in a private day or boarding school. In 1867–68, the Taunton Commission exposed an overall deplorable standard of teaching in such schools: the education given was described as unthorough, slovenly, superficial, unorganized – with too much emphasis given to the teaching of accomplishments.[78] The general inferiority of educational standards in schools for middle class girls, in comparison with those for middle class boys, came as no surprise to education campaigners such as Mary Buss, Dorothea Beale, Emily Davies and Elizabeth Wolstenholme. The problem was of course a circular one since, as Isabella Tod[79] said some years later, women trained under such a system will seldom be able to inaugurate anything better when they become teachers. The problem was, amongst other things, partly a reflection of the cultural definitions of feminity and its practical implications in regard to educational opportunities between the sexes. Women could not be expected to provide as high a standard of education as that given by male teachers in boys' schools since women were given only very limited access to higher education. Even some of the colleges that had been established especially for women, such as Queen's College, London, offered education mainly of a secondary school standard and was a college in name only. Though women could attend lectures from 1828 at both King's College and University College, London, it was not until 1878 that London University admitted women as full members. Other universities showed even greater reluctance: thus it was not until 1920 and 1949 respectively that Oxford and Cambridge awarded degrees to women on the same terms as those for men.

The struggle for women to enter higher education was inevitably interwoven with the struggle to improve the educational standards of women teachers in middle class girls' private secondary schools. Many of the early female students (1870s) from the Oxford and Cambridge colleges became teachers in the newly developing girls' public schools and the girls, in their turn, helped to increase the pool of recruits for the colleges. Thus a new category of female teachers was created – an educated elite of public schoolmistress and head mistresses. As Pederson[80] illustrates, this new élite encouraged values of academic excellence and academic achievement through public examinations. The process of schooling for middle class girls became much more rationally organized than had been possible in the familial setting of the small private schools. In particular, the authority of the new teachers stemmed much less from their personal relationships with their pupils than from the position they held. A new kind of professional awareness and pride developed so that teaching was no longer seen as the refuge of needy ladies but as a desirable profession for women. A typical representative of this new category of teachers was Miss Buss, headmistress of the North London Collegiate. Sara Burstall,[81] who was a pupil there remembers that it was one of Miss Buss's principles that if girls and women wished to 'keep an honourable standing in the profession like men' then they must take the same examinations and keep to the same rules that applied to the opposite sex. Yet, as Delamont[82] has shown, such female teachers and their pupils were caught in a snare of double conformity: they had to meet the standards of the dominant male cultural/educational system as well as the expectations of ladylike behaviour. Education must not unsex girls or women and make them 'masculine'. Thus, even though Miss Buss introduced mathematics into the curriculum at the NLC (an experimental subject for girls at this particular time) Sara Burstall recollects that she still insisted on typically feminine attire on prize giving day:

> We were instructed to wear light summer dresses, the pretty Leghorn straw hats, trimmed with flowers and ribbon streamers, usual for girls in those days, and to carry real flowers. Those of us who had prizes were carefully taught to curtsy to the distinguished personage who made the presentations.[83]

In this way, the female teachers tried to impose upon their pupils at least an outward appearance of conformity to ladylike behaviour. The reality, however, within the wide range of middle class girls' schools may have been less conformist than Delamont suggests. Vera Brittain,[84] for example, suggests that the average teaching in such schools in the early twentieth century 'sterilized' all sexual charms and made the pupils into hockey-playing hoydens with awkward manners and an armoury of inhibitions.

This new élite of female teachers was interested in the training of teachers too. A number of them were associated with the Women's Education Union which in 1876 established a Teachers' Training and Registration Society. In 1878, the Maria Grey Training College was founded. Student teachers could also be trained in some of the schools. At Cheltenham Ladies College, for example, under the guidance of Miss Beale, the Secondary Training Department became a recognized division in 1885.[85] Towards the end of the century, many of the intending secondary teachers began to use the university training colleges too. By this time, professional associations had been formed: in 1874, Miss Buss had founded the Association of Headmistresses and in 1884, under the chairmanship of Mrs. Henry Fawcett, an Association of Assistant Mistresses had been established.[86] Overall, we might say that the public schoolmistresses were representative of the 'new woman': they engaged in paid employment and sought improvements in the working conditions and social standing of the teaching profession. Thus they helped to change the educational context with which women schoolteachers were usually identified. Even so, the rank and file of the profession were 'loth to do anything so vulgar as to press their claims to more adequate salaries'.[87]

In the closing decades of the nineteenth and the early twentieth century, more girls of lower middle and middle class backgrounds began to be recruited into elementary teaching. Teresa Billington, for example, a Lancashire suffragist, came from an impoverished middle class family: she earned only £26 annual salary in her first pupil teacher post, half as much as a mill worker might earn, yet she described herself as 'shabby, happy and absorbed'.[88] Even though such teachers – like their counterparts in the girls' secondary schools – were typical of the 'new woman', there was much debate about whether it was 'genteel' for middle class girls to enter elementary teaching. As early as 1857, Miss Burdett-Coutts had began an unsuccessful campaign to recruit middle class girls into elementary teaching and another campaign was launched by Lousia Hubbard in the 1870s. It was an essential part of Miss Hubbard's plea to insist that in no way would a lady cease to be a lady simply because she was in paid employment, though the punctual payment of her salary should be made 'with all the more thoughtful consideration' since a 'natural but false delicacy' may make it more difficult for her than for others to press her claims.[89] Many middle class supporters of Miss Hubbard's campaign believed that only middle class ladies could improve the quality of elementary education. The Rev. Brooke Lambert, for example, claimed in 1897, that a lady elementary teacher, in her dealings with the parents of children, would not be snubbed in the way that present teachers were since her manner and bearing would command respect.[90] Bishop Otter Training College, Chichester, which re-opened in 1873, was one of the few colleges that, in a small, family-like, Church of England setting, attempted to provide teacher training for the lady recruit. Such training was badly needed since the standard of education of most middle class girls was so low that many prospective teachers failed either the examinations by which they might become uncertified teachers or the acting teachers' certificate: the failure rate was especially high in the early days after the 1870 Education Act.[91] But it is doubtful whether middle class girls entered elementary teaching in any great number before 1914. Widdowson[92] concludes that they largely avoided such an occupation because of its equivocal status. In addition, of course, the manners, speech and lifestyle of many working class children might have acted as an effective deterent to close contact within the classroom. For the middle class girl who had to earn her living, the reality of such a culture shock could be avoided by entering some of the other expanding occupations such as clerical work and retail selling.

Conclusion

In conclusion, we may note three main points. First, the ideology of domesticity in the nineteenth century helped to facilitate the entry of women into teaching but class-specific images of femininity helped to determine what kinds of educational institutions women taught in. Second, as the state became increasingly involved in the provision of education, it upheld and supported a sexual division of labour within teaching whereby female employees, who were mainly of working class origins, were expected to teach certain domestic skills and engage in certain child caring activities. Third, the entry of middle class women in particular into paid employment as schoolteachers led to increased demands for improvements in the education of women, especially the right to enter the male preserve of higher education.

In this paper, I have tried to show that the nineteenth century link of femininity with domesticity posed a number of dilemmas and contradictions for female teachers, especially as the occupation became increasingly concerned about its professional status. Such dilemmas and contradictions are still relevant for female teachers today. However, much more research is needed before we can fully understand the relationship between women and teaching – not as an isolated, marginal analysis but as a question which, of necessity, must arise in any study of the development of mass schooling.

Acknowledgements

This paper is a part of a research project currently being undertaken in the Faculty of Educational Studies, The Open University. The research is funded by the SSRC and I would like to express my grateful thanks for this financial support. I would also like to thank Madeleine MacDonald for many helpful, constructive criticisms upon earlier drafts of this paper.

Notes and References

1 Census (1851) Summary Tables 'Occupations of the People', Table XXIV, p. ccxviii.
2 ALEXANDER, S. (1976) 'Women's work in nineteenth century London: A study of the years 1820–50', in MITCHELL, J. and OAKLEY, A. (Eds.) *The Rights and Wrongs of Women*, Harmondsworth, Penguin, p. 65.
3 OAKLEY, A. (1972) *Sex, Gender and Society*, Temple Smith, p. 158.
4 See, for example, the discussion offered in BANKS, J. (1954) *Prosperity and Parenthood: A Study of Family Planning Among the Victorian Middle Classes*, Routledge and Kegan Paul; BANKS, J. and BANKS, O. (1964) *Feminism and Family Planning in Victorian England*, Liverpool University Press; CROW, D. (1971) *The Victorian Woman*, George Allen and Unwin; DAVIDOFF, L. (1976) 'Landscape with figures: Home and community in English society', in MITCHELL, J. and OAKLEY, A. *op. cit.*; BRANCA, P. (1974) 'Image and reality: the myth of the idle Victorian woman', in HARTMAN, M. and BANNER, L. (Eds.) *Clio's Consciousness Raised*, Harper and Row; BRANCA, P. (1975) *Silent Sisterhood: Middle-Class Women in the Victorian Home*, Croom Helm.
5 The concept of patriarchy is problematic, as discussed in BEECHEY, V. (1979) 'On patriarchy', *Feminist Studies*, 3. However, she does suggest that at the 'most general level patriarchy has been used to refer to male domination and to the power relationships by which men dominate women', p. 66.
6 ROWBOTHAM, S. (1973) *Women's Consciousness, Man's World*, Pelican Books, p. 117; ALEXANDER, S. (1976) *op. cit.*, p. 77.
7 ELLIS, S. (1843) *The Wives of England, Their Relative Duties, Domestic Influences and Social Obligations*, Fisher, Son and Co., pp. 90–2.
8 DYHOUSE, C. (1978) 'The role of women: from self-sacrifice to self-awareness', in LERNER, L. (Ed.) *The Victorians*, Methuen, pp. 174–5.
9 RUSKIN, J. (1865) *Sesame and Lilies*. The page numbers here refer to the small edition published by George Allen in 1905, p. 113.
10 *Ibid.*, p. 138.
11 SANDFORD, Mrs. J. (1831) *Woman in Her Social and Domestic Character*, Longman, Rees, Orme, Brown and Green, p. 13.
12 RUSKIN, J. (1865) *op. cit.*, p. 130.
13 HAMILTON, M. (1936) *Newnham: An Informal Biography*, Faber and Faber.
14 VICINUS, M. (1972) 'Introduction', in VICINUS, M. (Ed.) *Suffer and Be Still: Women in the Victorian Age*, Indiana University Press, p. ix.
15 COLE, M. (1945) *Beatrice Webb*, Longmans, Green and Co., p. 14.
16 HUXLEY, G. (1961) *Lady Denham, G.B.E. 1844–1954*, Chatto and Windus, p. 18.
17 See, for example, DAVIDOFF, L. (1973) *The Best Circles: Society, Etiquette and the Season*, Croom Helm.
18 Vol. vii, (1866), p. 59.
19 Quoted in HOBMAN, D.L. (1957) *Go Spin, You Jade! Studies in the Emancipation of Women*, Watts, p. 82.
20 VICINUS, M. (1972) *op. cit.*, p. ix.
21 MILL, J.S. (1869) *The Subjection of Women*, Longmans; BUTLER, J. (1869) 'Introduction', and COBBE, F.P. (1869) 'The final cause of women', both in BUTLER, J. (Ed.) *Women's Work and Women's Culture*, Macmillan and Co.
22 DAVIES, E. (1910) 'Home and the higher education' (1878), reprinted with additions in DAVIES E. *Thoughts on Some Questions Relating to Women, 1860–1908*, Bowes and Bowes.
23 MAUDSLEY, H. (1874) 'Sex in mind and in education', *Fortnightly Review*, p. 481.
24 *Ibid.*, p. 335.
25 DAVIES, E. (1866) *The Higher Education of Women*, Alexander Strahan, p. 11.
26 MARKS, P. (1976) 'Femininity in the classroom: An account of changing attitudes', in MITCHELL, J. and OAKLEY, A. *op. cit.*, p. 185.
27 ELLIS, S. (1856) *The Education of Character: With Hints on Moral Training*, J. Murray, pp. 252–3.
28 *Hansard* (1844), 15 March, Col. 1096.
29 FOREMAN, A. (1977) *Femininity as Alienation: Women and the Family in Marxism and Psycho-analysis*, Pluto Press, p. 92.
30 See Bryce's evidence to the *Schools Inquiry Commission*, Vol. V, Part 11, 1867–68, p. 882.
31 BUTLER, Rev. G. (1869) 'Education considered as a profession for women', in BUTLER, J. (Ed.) *op. cit.*, p. 52.
32 DAVENPORT ADAMS, W.H. (1880) *Women's Work and Worth in Girlhood, Maidenhood and Wifehood*, John Hogg, p. 485.
33 'At home and at school', *All Year Round*, (1859), 8 October, p. 572.

34 LEINSTER-MACKAY, D.P. (1976) 'Dame schools: a need for review', *British Journal of Educational Studies*, February, p. 33.

35 Quoted in KAY SHUTTLEWORTH, J. (1862) *Four Periods of Public Education as Reviewed in 1832–1839–1846–1862*, Longman, Green, Longman and Roberts, p. 102.

36 SMITH, M. (1892) *The Autobiography of Mary Smith, Schoolmistress and Non-Conformist, A Fragment of Life*, Bemrose and Sons, pp. 16–7.

37 *Ibid.*, p. 24.

38 COOPER, T. (1873) *The Life of Thomas Cooper, Written by Himself*, p. 7, (the page number here refers to the reprint by Leicester University Press (1971)).

39 JOHNSON, R. (1976) 'Notes on the schooling of the English working class, 1780–1850', in DALE, R., ESLAND, G. and MACDONALD, M. (Eds.) *Schooling and Capitalism*, Routledge and Kegan Paul, p. 44.

40 SOLOWAY, R.A. (1969) *Prelates and People*, London, p. 351.

41 JOHNSON, M. (1970) *Derbyshire Village Schools in the Nineteenth Century*, David and Charles, p. 71.

42 HILL, F. (1836) *National Education: Its Present State and Prospects*, Vol. 1, Charles Knight, p. 20.

43 TROPP, A. (1957) *The School Teachers*, Heinemann, p. 22.

44 HORN, P. (1978) *Education in Rural England 1800–1914*, Gill and Macmillan, p. 66.

45 Minutes of the Committee of Council on Education (1846) 21 December.

46 DAVIN, A. (1979) 'Mind that you do as you are told': reading books for Board School girls, 1870–1902, *Feminist Review*, 3. pp. 92–8.

47 *Moffatt's Reprint of Queen's Scholarship Questions*, (1894) July, Moffatt and Paige, p. 30.

48 *Ibid.*, p. 26.

49 HOLCOMBE, L. (1973) *Victorian Ladies at Work: Middle-class Working Women in England and Wales 1850–1914*, David and Charles, p. 36.

50 HORN, P. (1978) *op. cit.*, p. 112.

51 WEBB, B. (1915) 'English Teachers and Their Professional Organization', *The New Statesman*, Special Supplement, 25 September, p. 3.

52 Quoted in HORN, P. (1978) *op. cit.*, p. 222.

53 A Practical Housekeeper *How a Schoolmistress May Live Upon Seventy Pounds a Year*, (n.d.), pp. 12–3. The date given by the British Library is 1887.

54 'Ladies as Elementary Schoolmistresses', *Cornhill Magazine*, (1873), p. 703.

55 See, for example, THOMPSON, F. (1954) *Lark Rise to Candleford*, Oxford University Press, p. 213; TROPP, A. (1957) *op. cit.*, pp. 39 and 60; HORN. P. (1978) *op. cit.*, p. 158.

56 TROPP, A. (1957) *op. cit.*, p. 23.

57 THOMPSON, F. (1954) *op. cit.*, p. 220.

58 HOLCOMBE, L. (1973) *op. cit.*, p. 46.

59 PARTINGTON, G. (1976) *Women Teachers in the Twentieth Century in England and Wales*, National Foundation for Educational Research, p. 7, claims that the supply of teachers exceeded the demand up to about 1909.

60 *Ibid.*, p. 9.

61 *Ibid.*, p. 2.

62 See, for example, YOXALL, A. (1912) *History of the Teaching of Domestic Subjects*, London; SILLITOE, H. (1933) *A History of the Teaching of Domestic Subjects*, Methuen; DYHOUSE, C. (1977) 'Good wives and little mothers: Social anxieties and the schoolgirl's curriculum 1890–1920', *Oxford Review of Education*, Vol. 3, No. 1 and (1978) 'Towards a "feminine" curriculum for English schoolgirls: The demands of ideology 1870–1963', *Women's Studies International Quarterly*, Vol. 1.

63 PARTINGTON, G. (1976) *op. cit.*, p. 2.

64 Census (1851) Summary Tables 'Occupations of the people', Table XXV, p. ccxxv.

65 WOODHAM-SMITH, C. (1950) *Florence Nightingale 1820–1910*, Constable, p. 11.

66 PERCIVAL, A. (1939) *The English Miss Today and Yesterday: Ideals, Methods and Personalities in the Education and Upbringing of Girls During the Last Hundred Years*, George Harrap, p. 99; DAVIDOFF, L. *et al.*, (1976) *op. cit.*, pp. 166–7.

67 HOWE, B. (1954) *A Galaxy of Governesses*, Derek Verschoyle, p. 112.

68 YONGE, C. (1876) *Womankind*, Mozley and Smith, pp. 34–5.

69 PETERSON, M.J. (1973) 'The Victorian governess: status incongruence in family and society', in VICINUS, M. (Ed.) *op. cit.*, p. 166; BRYANT, M. (1979) *The Unexpected Revolution: A Study in the History of the Education of Women and Girls in the Nineteenth Century*, National Foundation for Educational Research, pp. 31 and 35.

70 MARTINEAU, H. (1859) 'Female industry', *Edinburgh Review*, April, p. 307.

71 *Schools Inquiry Commission*, (1867–68), Vol. V, Part II, p. 625.

72 DAVIDOFF, L. *et al.*, (1976) *op cit.*, pp. 166–7.

73 MAXSE, M. (1901) 'On governesses', *The National Review*, May, p. 401.

74 PROCHASKA, F.J. (1974) 'Women in English philanthropy 1790–1830', *International Review of Social History*, p. 431.

75 *Report of the Yorkshire Union of Mechanics' Institutes*, (1859), Edward Baines and Sons, pp. 80–1.

76 GLENDINNING, V. (1969) *A Suppressed Cry: Life and Death of a Quaker Daughter*, Routledge and Kegan Paul, p. 52.

77 *Ibid.*, p. 38.

78 See, for example, the discussion offered in KAMM, J. (1975) *Hope Deferred: Girls' Education in English History*, Methuen, pp. 199–213; and in TURNER, B. (1974) *Equality for Some: The Story of Girls' Education*, Ward Lock Educational, pp. 103–7.

79 TOD, I. (1874) *On the Education of Girls of the Middle Classes*, William Ridgway, p. 7.

80 PEDERSON, J.S. (1975) 'Schoolmistresses and headmistresses: Elites and education in nineteenth century England', *The Journal of British Studies*, Autumn, p. 160.

81 BURSTALL, S. (1933) *Retrospect and Prospect: Sixty Years of Women's Education*, Longmans, Green and Co., p. 55.

82 DELAMONT, S. (1978) 'The contradictions in ladies' education', in DELAMONT, S. and DUFFIN, L. (Eds.) *The Nineteenth Century Woman: Her Cultural and Physical World*, Croom Helm, pp. 134–63.

83 BURSTALL, S. (1933) *op. cit.*, p. 58.

84 BRITTAIN, V. (1933) *Testament of Youth*, Gollancz, p. 33.

85 RAIKES, E. (1908) *Dorothea Beale of Cheltenham*, Archibald Constable, p. 249.

86 WEBB, B. (1915) *op. cit.*, p. 15.

87 *Ibid.*, p. 15.

88 LIDDINGTON, J. and NORRIS, J. (1978) *One Hand Tied Behind Us: The Rise of the Women's Suffrage Movement*, Virago, p. 104.

89 HUBBARD, L. (1873) 'Elementary teaching, a profession for ladies', in *Transactions of the National Association for the Promotion of Social Science*, p. 376.

90 LAMBERT, Rev. B. (1873) discussion in *Transactions of the National Association for the Promotion of Social Science*, p. 383.

91 HOLCOMBE, L. (1973) *op. cit.*, p. 36.

92 WIDDOWSON, F. (1976) 'Elementary teacher training and the middle-class girl', M.A. dissertation, Essex University, p. 75.

24 Accountability, Values and Schooling

Trevor Pateman

In this paper I argue that preferences among different possible forms of account-ability in education relate to and serve different orderings of socially-available values. I distinguish [four] such values and for simplicity treat each as if it was the only value governing the choice of accountability procedures. On this basis, I try to show what procedures will be preferred, why and with what consequences. Though my discussion is not, I hope, unreal, I do not discuss combinations of accountability procedures in relation to combinations of values (which is how we find things in the real world), for I wish to emphasize the distinctive nature of each value and of its possible translations into forms of accountability.

The [four] values I distinguish are these: schooling (which I use interchangeably with 'education' for the purposes of this paper) should, first, respond to parental preferences; second, use public resources efficiently; third, allow teachers pro-fessional freedom; [and] fourth, meet the requirements of society. [. . .]

As for *accountability*, this is a concept distinct from that of *responsibility*, as Mary Warnock has urged in a different context[1] where she distinguishes the accountability of an institution to another institution, with legal or quasi-legal authority over it, from the responsibility which an institution may owe or feel it owes to those it affects, but where those affected do not, directly, exercise authority over it. In the real world, the accountability which an institution owes fuses insensibly with the responsibilities which it feels, and this should be kept in mind in reading my paper, which concentrates on the accountability end of the spectrum.

Parental Choice

In the exercise and performance of all powers and duties conferred and imposed on them by this Act the Secretary of State and Local Education Authorities shall have regard to the general principle that, so far as is

Source: BECHER, A. and MACLURE, S. (Eds.) (1978) *Accountability in Education,* Slough, NFER, Chap. 3, pp. 61–94. This extract omits Pateman's final section dealing with a fifth value, children s'needs.

> compatible with the provision of efficient instruction and the avoidance
> of unreasonable public expenditure, pupils are to be educated in accordance
> with the wishes of their parents – *1944 Education Act, Section 76.*

In the present context, I take 'parental choice' to mean that parents should be able, collectively or individually, to determine the general character of the education which their children receive in maintained schools in relation to curriculum, method of teaching, discipline etc. On this interpretation of 'parental choice' there are no existing institutions in the public sector of education which provide for the direct translation of parental wishes into educational practice, subject even to the constraints specified in the 1944 Act as quoted above. Yet it is plainly possible to create mechanisms, such as voucher systems or the democratic election of school boards (an expression I use to avoid the cumbersome 'managers or governors'), which would give parents considerably more power than they have at present to translate whatever wishes they have into reality. Voucher systems and democratically elected school boards are possible mechanisms for making schools accountable to parents for whatever parents wished schools to render them account. We do not have the mechanisms because we reject parental choice as an overriding or even an important value, and this is simply a consequence of a history in which the claim of market mechanisms or democratic procedures to govern central areas of our existence has been rejected. Instead the state has successfully developed extensive activities which take place outside the marketplace, and the state has developed as a representative government: Parliament has conceded much to what nineteenth century liberals called the 'numerical principle', but it has not conceded it dominance. Our practice remains faithful to the aspirations of John Stuart Mill's *Representative Government*, not Rousseau's *Social Contract*. And where nineteenth century liberalism perfected the case for representative government, twentieth century social democracy has entrenched the case for extensive state activity, the 'mixed economy'. Both together made provision of education a central part of the state's activity. The private education ghetto reflects the relegation of market principles to a secondary role in education, and the purely token representation of elected parents on school boards, as also the auxiliary functions of parent-teacher associations (as fundraisers, etc.), indicates that recognition of the numerical principle is only a concession.

If parents were successfully to assert that schools should be accountable to them, through the obvious mechanisms I have indicated, they would have to throw overboard the inherited cultural-ideological baggage alluded to in the previous paragraph. That would involve them in arguments at least one of which seems particularly relevant to my discussion.

In our practice in relation to the government of education, there is still embodied a theory which may well seem culturally outdated, even offensive when put in the terms in which it was developed in the nineteenth century, and employed explicitly for much of the present century. That theory held that if education was to have – as it should – a progressive, civilizing function, as opposed to a non-progressive, merely socializing one, then power to determine its contents and forms must rest with those who had reached the higher eminences of the achieved level of culture, not those still engaged on the fatiguing climb, or happily encamped at the bottom. Since most parents are at the bottom, it follows that educational power cannot rest in their hands, unless it can be shown that they are best able to see the summits, know how to get their children there, and want to do so.

Now the general break-up of faith in progress and in the existence of non-relative values makes this position impossible any longer to rationalize, which leads those whose practice still commits them to the old theory either to silence or to purely verbal substitutions, such as the replacement of the nineteenth century's 'civilizing purposes' with our positivistic 'socializing functions', which will not, however, do the job required.

For those with no faith in 'progress' and 'absolute values' it is easy to justify market and democratic forms of educational accountability, since they no longer recognize the existence of summits which they have yet to climb. For those who retain the faith, it is difficult but not impossible to believe in parent power, as Rhodes Boyson has shown. He takes the view that parents, though not themselves representatives of the higher culture out of which further progress will come, are qualified and eager to recognize those who do stand high (though not *very* high) above them and able to detect the false prophets among the true.[2] In this way, he is able to combine a belief in market accountability with adherence to traditional values.

Boyson's way of reconciling belief in the traditional values with parental power will, of course, be unacceptable and unnecessary to those who take their stand with twentieth century relativism, and my general feeling is that the long term factor working to push up parental choice on any list of educational values is the breakdown of the old hegemonic value system, and its replacement with patterns of preference which are perceived as merely personal and subjective.[3]

But commitment to value relativism is not a sufficient condition of a belief in parental power, any more than it is a necessary condition. A relativist can dispute the assumption, which has tacitly been made, that parental wishes or choices are or would be original or non-derivative – that is, in some sense *genuine*. Just as Schumpeter argues that the political values held by citizens are outputs from the political system, not inputs to it,[4] so parental preferences could be argued to be creatures not creators of a system. To privilege parental preferences would then merely represent a confirmation of the power of those institutions or constellations of influence which had created those preferences in the first place, and a relativist could consistently give that as a reason for refusing to take parental preferences at face value. (The believer in progress is most likely to find in parental preferences a demand that their own educational experience be repeated on their children, a demand which – to use a favourite Victorian expression – would reduce society to a state of 'Chinese stationariness'.)

So both the believer in progress and the relativist can find arguments to bring for and against claims for according parental choice a high place among the values education is supposed to serve. There are other possible arguments, and two other negative ones deserve mention here. First, a sociologically-minded critic would point out that democratic values are rarely realized in class and status divided societies, even where the necessary legal mechanisms exist, and this because of variations in political participation rates. So if we had elected school boards, they might well be legally representative yet not at all socially or politically representative. And if we had direct democratic government of schools, through parents' meetings, they would not be representative either. In other words, formally democratic procedures can create or leave unrepresented minorities, and even majorities, just as much as existing systems for the appointment of school boards.[5] Second, a logically minded critic would use Arrow's general possibility theorem[6] to show how even a voucher mechanism could not consistently represent parental choice where more than two choices are available.

These are not decisive criticisms: they serve only to indicate some of the dimensions along which we might argue about the weight to be accorded to the value of parental choice, and hence of accountability to parents.

Efficient Use of Public Resources

Education, like any other public service, is answerable to the society which it serves and which pays for it – *Education in Schools, a consultative document, para.* 1.5[7]

To measure the efficiency of resource allocation requires a prior specification of performance or output objectives. This is as true for schooling as for soap powder. In an educational system where determination of objectives was effectively delegated to individual schools, the assessment of efficiency had to be correspondingly individualized. In British educational practice this is where, so it seems to me, the Inspectorate fitted in; for it was able to offer assessments of efficiency which took into account a school's own specification of its objectives. Theoretically, an unholy row might be going on about the aims of a school, but the national or local inspectorate could remain above it, confining itself to study of and advice about the means – end relationship. There are elements of this in the relation which the ILEA inspectorate had to William Tyndale Junior School.[8] In general, like exhibits in a horticultural show, schools were judged good or bad of their kind, but not all of them were expected to be apples.

This is an oversimplified account, and a number of modifications are required to approximate it to reality. Notably, there were fewer actual differences than the system theoretically permitted since there existed mechanisms, formal and informal, through which schools were made much more alike: appointments policies; managerial and parent pressure tending in a common direction; the occasional open bust-up; and, notably, public examinations.[9] Yet I want to argue that the oversimplified picture was useful to both teachers and inspectors, since it justified a practice with which both were reasonably satisfied. This can be seen if we look at a phenomenon which seems anomalous if it was indeed the case that inspectors were mainly concerned with the 'subjective and qualitative'[10] judgment of efficiency in relation to individualized systems of ends.

That phenomenon is, or was, the absence of explicit, written-down policies, objectives, targets or plans in most schools. If schools were autonomous and valued their autonomy as a means of creating difference, would they not have stressed this in written formulations? Is their lack of explicitness compatible with the thesis being argued? The answer to these questions can be made by employing distinctions drawn by Weber:[11] schools had goals, but they were expressed in *traditional* terms (ritual, routine, implicit understandings) rather than *rational-legal* ones (aims, objectives, rules, regulations). No doubt this was connected with the actual existence of an educational consensus, the breakdown of which Rhodes Boyson laments.[12] Now this traditional mode of operation increased the power of both teachers and inspectors. In the case of teachers, it made it difficult for them to be held to account by parents or managers with whom it was possible, if desired, to pursue a 'catch us if you can' game. In the case of inspectors, it required of them a hermeneutic understanding of the schools, the efficiency of which they were assessing. They could not do their job with a standard inventory, but had to engage in the kind of interpretation at which only insiders can be really adept. I suggest that this put them at a distance from their political masters, at both local and national level. That we still have Her Majesty's Inspectors, not DES Inspectors, may be symbolic of this. Education, like medicine and the law, had its mysteries to which teachers and inspectors were privy, and parents and politicians were not. Politicians were dependent on their inspectors to interpret to them these mysteries, the secret garden. There was no question of their barging in on something they could not fully understand, even when the value in question was such an eminently rational one as efficiency.

This is now changing: as *Education in Schools* puts it, 'Growing recognition of the need for schools to demonstrate their accountability to the society which they serve requires a coherent and soundly based means of assessment for the educational system as a whole, for schools, and for individual pupils' (para. 3.3). Now I suggest that this change, ironically enough, has been made possible by the 'legitimation crisis', to use Jürgen Habermas' expression,[13] in which some teachers' own acceptance of the traditional curriculum and values has crumbled, and in which the traditions have been challenged to justify and rationalize themselves. This has permitted the politicians to intervene legitimately and on an equal footing, something those same teachers never desired.[14] For the breakdown of a traditional consensus constitutes not only a sort of desacralization, but also re-equalizes rights to contribute to argument. There are no longer self-evident specialists. In other words, when the priests have doubts, then is the laity free to make its intervention again, of which history affords numerous examples. Congregationalism is analogous to demands for parent power, and where in the seventeenth century demands were heard for the cashiering of kings, now it is for the cashiering of teachers. In the present conjuncture politicians have emerged principally as flag carriers for the fourth value in my initial list, (i.e. 'meeting the requirements' of society) and so I shall have something to say about them when I discuss that.

In summary: efficiency as a value would have been less important if there had been no traditionally-expressed consensus, and the inspectorate has derived its importance from its ability to assess efficiency against unwritten standards. Efficiency was the only value for which politicians felt able to demand accountability. Inspectors have consequently enjoyed considerable independence, and schools have felt more accountable to them, perhaps, than to anyone else. In this way, schools have been held accountable to inspectors.

It is consistent with and indeed part of this analysis that the role of the national and local inspectorates has become increasingly advisory. For if it can be ruled out that schools are wilfully inefficient or hopelessly incompetent, then by definition they are committed to being efficient, and must rationally be willing to accept advice on improving their efficiency, advice which the inspectorate has been able to offer.[15]

The Professional Freedom of Teachers

The type of freedom claimed by teachers is professional freedom. Just as the doctor claims the freedom to treat the patient according to his own best judgement, formed in relation to available knowledge, technology and resources, so the teacher claims the freedom to teach the pupil. In both medicine and teaching, as in science, recognized hierarchies of knowledge and status define who is best qualified to decide in case of conflict over what constitutes the appropriate course of action.[16]

This notion of professional freedom is acceptable so long as the ends or different ends being pursued are not generally contested, and can co-exist, if diverse, without creating a pressing awareness of incompatibility. If there was no consensus on the meaning of *health* and *cure*, then doctors would not be able to make the claims to professional freedom which they do. The same applies to teachers. More strongly, once the ends are agreed it is rational to institutionalize professional freedom, for that is only to grant what is the due of expertise, and professionals are simply experts in the means required to achieve given ends.[17] In the consensual situation, the extent to which, for example, a school board can hold teachers or a school to account for its performance is strictly limited, since by definition its members are not expert and can at best only claim to be able to identify cases of gross incompetence, gross inefficiency and plain corruption – and even here they may well feel constrained to rely on the advice of the head teacher or an inspector.[18]

As for accountability, where the value of professional freedom thrives the notion and practice of intra-professional accountability will thrive too, though the fact that teaching has never achieved this to the degree that law and medicine have indicates that neither consensus nor professionalism have been so strongly developed in teaching as in these other occupations.

When the ends of education cease to be consensual, and differences can no longer peaceably co-exist, becoming territories to defend or attack, the claim to professional freedom logically collapses. For in such a situation there is no longer a neutral professional practice dealing in expertly-assessable means.

The contrast which is being made here will appear over-simplified, though just as teachers have an interest in exaggerating their professionalism, so in a crisis of values, politicians and parents have an interest in painting the consequences for professionalism more bleakly than is really warranted. In practice, means and ends are not so sharply distinguished as I have painted them: 'ends' are never simple matters of subjective preference, and 'means' are never neutral techniques. Even in a crisis situation, teachers can claim some special competence: they can claim to know something about what ends it is possible to pursue within the school system; they can point out that the miracles expected of them do not come cheap; and they can claim to understand something about the relation of secondary ends (e.g. teaching basic skills) to primary ends (e.g. meeting the child's needs). Most importantly, a good part of current disputes concerns not conflicting ends, but whether means alleged to be effective in reaching agreed ends are actually so, a dispute which could be eminently scientific.[19]

Nonetheless, the collapse of agreed values – the legitimation crisis again – has put teachers on the spot, and put 'professional freedom' in danger of being relegated to the fourth division of values. It is not surprising, therefore, to find teachers actively suggesting new forms of accountability which are effectively proposals for more effective and responsive forms of intra-professional accountability than have hitherto been used, though there are plainly limits beyond which they cannot go. Thus, at the time I write this, politicians are putting the question of getting rid of dud teachers on the agenda (*Education in Schools*, paras. 6.36–6.39) – something teachers could scarcely do themselves.

In this context, we can appreciate proposals like Margaret Maden's[20] for CNAA-style validation of school plans which would be drawn up internally by each school showing targets, curricula, teaching methods, resources, etc., and arguing out the relations conceived to exist among the elements of the plan. This is a particularly interesting idea, and the borrowing of an approach from higher education strikes me as significant. For it ties the disputed idea of teacher-control to the still consensual value of academic freedom. This is legitimate, since teachers are plainly involved to some degree in the same line of business as academics – the transmission of knowledge, over the production and dissemination of which it would be irrational to introduce formalized administrative and political controls, since that would require of politicians and administrators that they know better than those who are defined as those who know best.[21] But the proposal's weakness is that it takes no account of the important fact that schooling is universal and compulsory, whereas higher education is selective and voluntary. Is it really enough for one group of professionals to certificate another group of professionals to practice their skills on children who have little or no say in whether they wish those skills to be exercised on them, and whose parents have as little say, too? Furthermore, schooling is not only about the transmission of knowledge, but also about the civilizing, socializing, or controlling of a new generation. Could a CNAA-style panel successfully legitimize a claim to deal authoritatively with the non-intellectual aspects of schooling, such as discipline regulations?

In reality, such proposals as Margaret Maden's seem to have come too late. Traditional forms of intra-professional accountability have ceased to satisfy, and critics will not be satisfied with more rigorous versions of the old mechanisms. This is partly a dissatisfaction specific to teaching, but partly belongs to a more general movement of distrust of autonomous professional groups, including lawyers and doctors. Individuals do their own conveyancing and defend themselves in court cases; the Women's Movement has developed a critique of doctors and started alternative forms of medical practice. As these examples should make clear, these criticisms cannot always be associated with traditional right-wing and left-wing political positions: some of them hark back to traditional self-help doctrines; all of them dissent from the social democrat's confidence in the state. Of course, there are critics whose positions are typically right- or left-wing, especially in relation to schooling. Thus on the one hand, we have those who argue that teachers have abandoned their own previous good standards, to which the rest of us allegedly remain attached. On the other hand, it is argued that teachers retain a typical professional attachment to barbaric practices no longer acceptable to lay people, such as their retention of corporal punishment, uniform,[22] and curricula which stereotype children into traditional sex roles.

In conclusion, this section has relied on fairly intuitive notions of 'professional freedom'. I suggest that a useful research project would concern itself in analyzing and differentiating varieties of professional freedom, the sorts of arguments which can be advanced for each of them, and the kinds of accountability procedures which would put them out of existence.

Social Needs

Whether or not it is found that standards have remained constant, risen or fallen over some past period is less important than whether the standards which are being achieved today correspond as nearly as possible to society's needs – *DES Guidelines for the regional conferences of the Great Debate.*[23]

The speech (by the Prime Minister at Ruskin College, October 1976) was made against a background of strongly critical comment in the Press and elsewhere on education and educational standards. Children's standards of performance in their school work were said to have declined. The curriculum, it was argued, paid too little attention to the basic skills of reading, writing and arithmetic, and was overloaded with fringe subjects. Teachers lacked adequate professional skills, and did not know how to discipline children or instil in them concern for hard work or good manners. Underlying all this was the feeling that the educational system was out of touch with the fundamental need of Britain to survive economically in a highly competitive world through the efficiency of its industry and commerce – *Education in Schools*, para. 1.2.

The interpretation of 'social needs' is no more, and probably much less, consensual than the interpretation of the other educational values we have considered. For in practice its meaning is not established by argument, but by the authoritative definition of the state. The epigraph to this section from *Education in Schools* illustrates this splendidly: education has been criticized for all sorts of reasons, apparently from numerous different standpoints. The Green Paper disabuses us: all along, you know, you have *really* been feeling 'that the educational system was out of touch with the fundamental need of Britain to survive economically'. And this is not just a persuasive definition in the philosophical sense,[24] but an authoritative one, for it is a definition on which Government intends to act and has the ability to act.

In the nineteenth century the state defined society's needs primarily as a need for *citizens*. As everyone knows, universal compulsory education was introduced after the second great Reform Act of 1867. Its citizen-forming purpose was immortalized by Sir Robert Lowe: 'Educate your Masters'.[25] Today the definition has radically altered and society's needs are defined principally as a need for *workers*, a concern largely absent from nineteenth century political debate.

For the purpose of this paper there is no need to document the emphasis being placed on education as a preparation for working life; one has only to read *Education in Schools*. Parents plainly regard education as the principal determinant of job prospects; politicians have sought to make it so – here they again differ from their predecessors;[26] employers complain about the failure of schools to produce workers competent in the required skills. However, the volume of and stress placed on these positions should not lead us into assuming that each party is making a correct judgement.

For instance, while parents are more or less right, individually, in thinking that if their children achieve higher standards in core subjects then their job prospects will be improved, collectively this does not hold, for a fallacy of composition is involved in the transition from individual to universal case. If job opportunities are relatively fixed in number and distribution and determined by the semi-autonomous and slow development of the economic system (and leaving aside policy-created unemployment), then if all children achieve higher standards all that can happen is that either employers raise job qualifications all round (as in the USA)[27] or they resort to non-meritocratic selection criteria (jobs for the boys).

Again, individual employers may be right in protesting the lack of skill displayed by school leavers, but it can also be true that overall there is a secular trend towards a deskilling of work, job requirements becoming increasingly polarized between very high and very low skill jobs. Roy Edgley summarizes some of the evidence which points this way in a recent paper.[28] Even if it is not the case that work is being deskilled, a belief that it is may be involved in pupil perception of the world of work. For there do exist 'reluctant learners' who justify their opposition to school in terms of the pointlessness of learning what they are taught. Habermas categorizes such phenomena as belonging to a general 'motivation crisis',[29] pretty obviously connected to phases of economic crisis and which in Britain's case are chronic rather than acute, with the dole queue the certain destination of a proportion of school leavers. Youth unemployment may be small percentage-wise, but it has a ripple-effect impact on morale. It is all very well for *Education in Schools* to list as an aim of education 'to help children to appreciate how the nation earns and maintains its standard of living and properly to esteem the essential role of industry and commerce in this process' (para. 1.19, v), but this is not a lesson anyone can teach young people who think that they are destined not for industry and commerce but unemployment, or even for what were called, when I worked in the Youth Employment Service, 'dead-end jobs', to the elimination of which we looked forward. Some school leavers might have to put up with such jobs; we did not consider it our business to make them esteem them. But that was a dozen years ago.

Rhodes Boyson seems to me entirely wrong in denying the existence of a motivation crisis among pupils, other than one brought about by the schools themselves. He has to take this position since he also takes the view that parents have not changed, but only the schools. *Education in Schools* also makes light of the 'lack of motivation and unco-operative attitudes displayed by some pupils' (para. 2.16), but these seem to me of quite fundamental importance. Partly, we do not adequately understand them; partly, we are reluctant to face up to them, since we realize that their resolution (as opposed to their repression) may lead us outside the range of policies we are prepared to consider – a range which threatens to get more, not less, restricted.[30]

Unfortunately, I must leave such issues aside, and return to the current advancement of 'society's needs' as a value to be served by schooling, for this emphasis explains many of the most important new forms of accountability being canvassed, such as a government-defined core curriculum and government-administered national testing or monitoring in specified subjects at various ages.[31] Some of the connections are fairly obvious. A government can no more have an active manpower policy without predictive knowledge of and ability to influence the qualifications which school leavers will have, than it can have a rational teacher training policy without a registry of births. If the analogy serves to raise a grim smile, it may also introduce some remarks on the possible limitations of accountability procedures designed to permit the implementation of labour market policies. (Though these procedures are not designed for this purpose alone.)

My first and central question is this: Are we witnessing an overestimation of the possibilities of central planning? My second question is: Is an extension of political and administrative power, through the activation of existing legal rights (*Education in Schools*, para. 1.14, iii), being proposed in response not to a crisis of administrative rationality, but to a crisis in belief (legitimation) and motivation which cannot be solved by administrative means?

My answers to the two questions are interconnected. Habermas uses the expression 'rationality crisis' to refer to the systematic failure of an administrative system to produce the required quantity and quality of rational decisions.[32] He has in mind, for example, the apparent inability of governments to translate the theoretically simple Keynesian stabilizing strategies into effective economic management policies. Not only have grandiose National Plans had to be abandoned, but even more limited, expert-formulated wage and price policies have had to be ditched in favour of *ad hoc* coercion, political bargains, compromises and understandings.[33] Habermas' explanation is partly in terms of the inherent limitations of administrative rationality as such; partly in terms of the workings of uncontrolled forces outside the power of individual governments (such as the level of oil prices); and partly in terms of the political resistances which supposedly neutral, technocratic policies create, and which administrative procedures are unable to process.

This general argument of Habermas' seems to me relevant to the appraisal of the kinds of national educational planning-through-accountability-mechanisms which are being proposed. For these are also vulnerable both to the impact of autonomous economic and social developments which they cannot control (such as crisis-enforced educational cutbacks in which the Assessment of Performance Unit may be an early victim!) and to political resistances: the day that the Secretary of State puts on the agenda the question of getting rid of incompetent teachers, the General Secretary of the National Union of Teachers warns her that she is 'entering a minefield'.[34]

Political resistances will be that much stronger to the degree that the government is reacting not to failures, internally or externally recognized, of its own administrative system, but to a crisis of belief and motivation arising independently of actions by the administration. Now it seems to me that the government *is* reacting to such an external crisis, and is advancing the value 'social needs', to be pursued through core curricula and national monitoring, as a means of resolving that crisis. I suggest that this underestimates the actual autonomy and rationality of the belief and motivation crisis, and cannot possibly resolve it, though it may suppress it. Maladjustment, truancy, vandalism and radical educational innovations (which are often only reactive crisis-avoidance adaptations) will not go away because government enforces a core curriculum and national monitoring of standards in the interests of British industry, or for any other motive. If there really is a deep-seated crisis of motivation and belief, the effect of the political and administrative measures being proposed may only be to increase conflict at the classroom chalk face; and to deepen antagonisms between teachers, government and parents, and within the teaching profession itself. In the crudest terms, the list of aims which *Education in Schools* hopes that 'the majority of people would probably agree with' (para. 1.19) may just not be consensual enough for the most relevant groups – parents, teachers and pupils. To return to the analogy with British economic policy, governments are prone to launch policies on the assumption that they are broadly supported (and they may even have reason to suppose this from opinion polls and the like). But then trouble develops, the government calls on us to stand up and be counted – and we all remain sitting down. I am not saying that governments should avoid political battles; far from it. I am saying that governments seem to be naive about the extent of agreement which they can achieve or enforce by administrative means. Nor do government systems learn rapidly from mistakes, so that the tragedies of history have plenty of opportunity to return as farce.

The above discussion leaves aside the larger question of whether in principle administrative systems can meet the increased demands which are now likely to be placed upon them. Yet this is relevant too. I do not know enough about organization theory to enter into this; I only know of arguments to show that the bounds of possible administrative rationality are quite limited.[35] Fortunately, it is the task of other contributors to consider whether the road to hell is paved with good intentions, and I do not enter into the topic here.

[...]

Postscript

In a comment on my paper, Michael Eraut pointed out that schooling is expected to serve a value which cannot be assimilated to any in my list, a value which he calls 'generational control'. By this he means that schools are expected to ensure that children behave as children are expected to behave in relation to adults, in terms of manners, politeness, deference etc. Acceptance of this value by schools explains their insistence on such things as school uniform, and a great deal of popular criticism of schools is concerned with their failure to secure an acceptable level of generational control.

I agree that such a value exists, and I overlooked it because it seems to me illegitimate. However, it is socially legitimate and is therefore required in any explanation of what schools do. I take the view that schools are able to do much less towards meeting children's needs than otherwise they might be able to achieve, just because they also have to secure acceptable inter-generational control. This does not come across in my paper, which paints schooling in its most favourable aspects and is misleading insofar as it suggests that schooling can and does do a great deal for children; it does not, and one of the reasons for this is that it has to control the children assigned to it.

Too optimistic about schools, I was too negative about parents in section II of my paper. For from the way in which parents behave in an exclusionary system, we cannot infer how they would behave in a participatory system. (Consider how people can express anger that criminals 'get away with it' when interviewed by pollsters, but prove quite reluctant to convict when converted into jurors.) It was the genius of John Stuart Mill to realize that participation civilizes people – less tendentiously, that it broadens their outlook in forcing on them awareness of conflicting imperatives.

In a low growth economy, conflicting imperatives of special importance seem to me to exist between individual demands on the educational system and social requirements. For example, individuals may demand socially expensive higher education, though the economic system is unable to make use of their qualifications. Fairness to the rest of society may demand that opportunities for higher education be restricted, or else made available in diluted form as a consumer good to the whole population. Only in a participatory system is there any hope of reconciling such conflicts in a mutually acceptable way.

Acknowledgements

I had the benefit of discussion with Tony Becher, Judy Keiner, Heather Lyons before putting pen to paper. Tony Becher, Maurice Kogan and Ian Lister made written comments on the draft version of this essay. None of these people, who were so generous with their time, necessarily agrees with my arguments; none of them has read the final version.

Notes and References

1 In relation to broadcasting, see *Report of the Committee on the Future of Broadcasting*, (1977) Chairman Lord Annan, Cmnd. 6753, HMSO, Paras. 4, 11.

2 BOYSON, R. (1975) *The Crisis in Education*, London, Woburn Press. The question, how does a relatively uninstructed person distinguish false from true prophets? is an important preoccupation of both French and English political theory in the eighteenth and nineteenth centuries. For France, see DARNTON, R. (1968) *Mesmerism and the end of the Enlightenment in France*, Cambridge, Mass., Harvard University Press, especially the extract from a paper by Condorcet, pp. 189–92. For England, see Sir George Cornewall Lewis, (1849) *An Essay on the influence of Authority in Matters of Opinion*, London, John Parker. I discuss the question at length in my M.Phil. thesis, *How is Political Knowledge Possible?*, University of Sussex, 1978.

3 Central to Boyson's argument is the claim that parents have not changed, and from this follows the necessity of denying that children have changed. In his view, it is only schools that are different, see e.g. p. 13 of his book, *op. cit.*

4 SCHUMPETER, J. (1950) *Capitalism, Socialism and Democracy*, (3rd edition), London, George Allen and Unwin, pp. 250–83, reprinted in QUINTON, A. (Ed.) (1967) *Political Philosophy*, Oxford University Press.

5 In the case of William Tyndale School, the extent to which managers of a school can be socially unrepresentative can be gathered from AULD, R. (1976) *William Tyndale Junior and Infants Schools Public Inquiry*, London, ILEA. The evidence there, interpreted in the light of more general knowledge of developments in inner London, seems to confirm the analysis of HINDESS, B. (1971) *The Decline of Working Class Politics*, London, MacGibbon and Kee.

6 ARROW, K. (1963) *Social Choice and Individual Values*, (2nd edition), New Haven, Yale University Press. Arrow rediscovered and generalized an inherent limitation of voting (aggregation) procedures which had first been pointed out by CONDORCET (1785) in his little read *Essai sur l'application de l'analyse à la probabilité des décisions rendues à la pluralité des voix*, Paris, Imprimerie Royale, and periodically rediscovered since then. Roughly, if there are more than two choices, no voting mechanism can be devised which consistently represents voters' preferences; it will sometimes produce less preferred to more preferred results. This is sometimes called the 'paradox of voting'. See ARROW, K. (1963) *op. cit.*, esp. pp. 59–60.

7 DES/WELSH OFFICE (1977) *Education in Schools, a Consultative Document*, London, HMSO, Cmnd. 6869 (Hereinafter *Education in Schools*).

8 See AULD, R. (1976) *op. cit.*, and ELLIS, T., McWHIRTER, J., McCOLGAN, D. and HADDOW, B. (1976) *William Tyndale: the Teachers' Story*, London, Readers' and Writers' Publishing Co-operative.

9 See the account of the functioning of the 11+ in BOYSON, R. (1975) *op. cit.*, p. 57.

10 *Education in Schools*, (1977) *op. cit.*, Para. 3.6.

11 WEBER, M. (1964) *The Theory of Social and Economic Organisation*, Glencoe, Free Press.

12 BOYSON, R. (1975) *op. cit.*, p. 141.

13 HABERMAS, J. (1976) *Legitimation Crisis*, London, Heinemann.

14 Compare Boyson, (1975) *op. cit.*, 'The malaise in schools in Britain has followed from a breakdown in accepted curriculum and traditional values. There was little concern about either political control or parental choice so long as there was an 'understood' curriculum which was followed by every school. Schools may have differed in efficiency but their common values or curriculum were broadly acceptable. The present disillusionment of parents arises from their resentment that their children's education now depends on the lottery of the school to which they are directed. Standards decline because both measurement and comparisons are impossible when aims and curriculum become widely divergent. These problems can be solved only by making schools again accountable to some authority outside them. The necessary sanction is either a nationally enforced curriculum or parental choice or a combination of both', (p. 141).

15 On the role of the inspectorate, see the interesting letter from Val Arnold-Foster and Sarah Wood, of CASE, in *The Guardian*, 21 June 1977.

16 On the theory of this in relation to science, see ZIMAN, J.D. (1968) *Public Knowledge, an Essay Concerning the Social Dimension of Science*, Cambridge University Press.

17 This seemed obvious to early social scientists who embraced what we should now call social engineering approaches to policy formation and administration, since they were confident that scientific knowledge could be secured about both ends and means. Condorcet, Comte and Saint-Simon fit this bill, though Condorcet has more democratic spirit than the others: see BAKER, K.M. (1967) 'Scientism, Elitism and Liberalism: The Case of Condorcet', in *Studies on Voltaire and the Eighteenth Century*, Vol. LV, Geneva, pp. 129–65; and, more generally, BRAMSON, L. (1961) *The Political Context of Sociology*, Princeton

University Press. But see FAY, B. (1975) *Social Theory and Political Practice*, London, Allen and Unwin.

18 The Auld Report (1976) *op. cit.* is instructive in this connection. See, for example, Paras. 346–51, pp. 109–11.

19 Often it is scientific, which is not to say it is without shortcomings, such as biases in the research design. But all science is open to misuse, and this is what will happen to educational research in a crisis situation, especially where its shortcomings match social prejudices. See the reception of BENNETT, N. (1976) *Teaching Styles and Pupil Progress*, London, Open Books.

20 Reported in the *Times Educational Supplement*, (1977) 18 March.

21 Marx takes great pleasure using this argument in his 'Comments on the latest Prussian censorship instruction', in EASTON, L.D. and GUDDAT, K.H. (1967) *Writings of the Young Marx on Philosophy and Society*, New York, Doubleday, pp. 67–92.

22 To intrude a personal concern, I do think that the commitment given in *Education in Schools* to discriminate 'in favour of children who are under-privileged for whatever reason' (Para. 1.13) ought to be followed by legislation outlawing compulsory school uniform or by large increases in school clothing grants. For, whatever the intentions, schools which impose school uniform requirements discriminate *against* 'under-privileged' children, as the Child Poverty Action Group has argued.

23 Quoted in the *Times Educational Supplement*, (1977) 11 February, p. 3.

24 STEVENSON, C. (1938) 'Persuasive definitions' in *Mind*.

25 Quoted in GREGG, P. (1964) *A Social and Economic History of Britain 1760–1963*, London, Harrap, (4th edition), p. 247. Trevelyan observes, 'It was characteristic of the two nations that whereas the German people already enjoyed good schools but not self-government, the rulers of England only felt compelled to "educate their masters" when the working-men were in full possession of the franchise. It was felt that for so important a purpose as voting for Parliament, if for nothing else, it was good that a man should be able to read', TREVELYAN, R. (1937) *British History in the Nineteenth Century and After*, London, Longmans, Green and Co., new edition, p. 353.

26 See the further quotations from Sir Robert Lowe in GREGG, P. (1964) *op. cit.*, p. 508.

27 See BERG, I. (1973) *Education and Jobs, The Great Training Robbery*, Harmondsworth, Penguin.

28 EDGLEY, R. (1977) 'Education for industry', *Educational Research*, November.

29 HABERMAS, J. (1976) *op. cit.*, esp. Chap. 7.

30 In the period that I am writing this, ILEA has cut off its grant to White Lion Free School, which has had to be rescued by the National Association for Mental Health.

31 *Education in Schools* (Para. 3.6) refers to the work of the Assessment of Performance Unit and says that it is concentrating at the moment on the development of tests suitable for national monitoring in English language, mathematics and science. The emphasis is revealing. The original intention of the APU was to assess six areas of the curriculum: the verbal, mathematical, scientific, ethical, aesthetic, and physical. The last three are taking second place in the APU's work, not just because of the intrinsic difficulties in assessing them but also because of political decisions which have been taken. See the interesting article on the APU by LEONARD, M. (1977) 'Art of the impossible?', *Times Educational Supplement*, 17 June, p. 19.

32 HARBERMAS, J. (1976) *op. cit.*, esp. Chaps. 4 and 5.

33 Compare the numerous *post mortems* on British incomes policy.

34 As reported in *The Daily Telegraph*, (1977) 22 July, p. 6.

35 See, for example, ARROW, K. (1974) *The Limits of Organization*, New York, Norton.

25 Professional Control and the Engineering of Client Consent

William Bacon

Introduction

Having [...] examined some of the scripts of the major social actors taking part within one of the most radically democratized school-governing systems in the country to date, and one which clearly anticipates most of the main recommendations of, if not all the details contained within, the Taylor Report, we are now in a better position to return to the central focus of this study and ask ourselves two questions. Firstly, how far does this type of reform facilitate the development of a more democratic school system? Secondly, how far does it serve to make our schools more responsive to local needs and accountable to a general public interest?

[...] how far do these innovations work to extend the common good? [And] how far do they function to maintain existing centres of privilege and balances of power?

Education and the State

[...] It seems that the evidence we have examined [...] leads us tentatively towards the conclusion that there is often a surprisingly wide gap between our publicly expressed democratic sentiments and the realities involved in the citizen's daily interaction with the various social organizations of the welfare state. The reasons for this development are complex, but in part may be understood if we recognize that all modern industrial societies, whether they pay a nominal lip service to liberal-democratic or collectivist utopian ideologies, attempt to solve their problems by the adoption of centralized planning strategies and the creation of large public organizations which are charged with the pursuit of specific objectives in such fields as welfare, industrial development, recreation, the environment and, of course, education.

Source: An abridged version of BACON, W. (1978) *Public Accountability and the Schooling System*, London, Harper and Row, Chap. 8, pp. 179–207.

However, the evidence tends to suggest that in all industrial societies these relatively new and often large departments of state suffer from an inherent, if continuing, paradox. On the one hand they exist to provide a series of services designed to make life more comfortable or richer for the bulk of the population. At the same time their personnel are, in the course of their daily work, forced to make moral judgements about how people ought, and ought not, to lead their lives. Largely as a result of this situation, many of their clients come to feel a sense that they feel they are gradually losing control over some of the more important and intimate aspects of their lives – their ability to care for their own health; the freedom to educate their own children, plan their own leisure life-styles, and so on. This feelings of 'powerlessness' is not only a subjective articulation of a series of individualistic cultural values, it may also be substantiated empirically in the sense that modern industrial man's remaining spheres of autonomy are largely confined to his home, garden, and family life, and by contrast he enjoys relatively little influence over most of the major decisions taken by the officials of those state bureaucracies providing for his educational or social needs, or indeed, those who provide for his immediate employment or related life-support services.

This pervasive feeling of estrangement is perhaps intensified because of the refractory tendencies inherent in any large organization. Although these institutions are set up to attain a specific series of general and public goals or objectives, they also tend to develop their own private ethos and momentum. In the case of the state welfare institutions, it is not always easy to distinguish between these two areas of formal and informal activity. Indeed, from a critical vantage point some of these services seem to share many of the characteristics of 'rambling medieval fiefdoms', rather than rationally ordered public services. Thus, most of them recruit their key personnel in their late teens or early twenties, and these people then tend to spend the remainder of their working lives within the institution they have chosen to serve. Moreover, since all recruits tend to take part in a common series of training programmes and induction processes, then they also share a common series of loyalties, not only to the general official doctrines justifying their work, but also in the sense that they have a specific occupational interest in maintaining and, if possible, extending their estate's claims over the resources of society. In turn, their leaders play an active role, both at local and national levels, of decision making, and are naturally, if not always overtly, concerned to maintain the stability of the prevailing socio-economic system within which their status flourishes.

Largely as a result of this complex social situation the leaders of all welfare bureaucracies are forced to adopt a quasi-political role, in the sense that they don't operate within a social vacuum but must constantly pay heed to the consequences of their actions upon other competing groups and forces in society. Thus, whatever specific interest they serve, be it education, welfare, planning, or recreation, they must consistently address themselves to three key and universal issues. Firstly, the need to maintain their authority. Secondly, the need to maintain the stability and security of their organization. And thirdly, the need to justify their continued claims upon the wider sources of society.

[...]

Co-optation

One of the key tools in the armoury of the leaders of all large organizations is a social device sometimes known as co-optation. This concept has been extensively described and analysed by Phillip Selznick in his pioneering study *T.V.A. and the Grassroots: A Study in the Sociology of Formal Organisation*,[1] and refers to the process of ' . . . absorbing new elements into the leadership or policy determining structure of an organisation as a means of averting threats to it's stability or existence'.

This concept is a very helpful one, in the sense that it helps us to delineate more systematically some of the social processes which often take place in the kind of institutional innovations we have been examining [. . .]

Informal co-optation The concept of informal co-optation is used to refer to the kind of response which typically takes place when an organizational leadership decides to share effective power with a group which it had previously ignored, but which can no longer be avoided, since it has gained a position where it can make specific and concrete demands for a claim upon the organization's wider resources. This process usually typically occurs when a leadership finds that its authority, or ability to dominate, is in a state of imbalance with the true state of power within the community it serves. However, it is not always a readily identifiable state of affairs since this exercise is typically conducted in an informal manner and no explicit public statement describing and no recognition of this changing balance of power takes place.

Formal co-optation In contrast formal co-optation refers to the kind of social processes which often take place when the leadership of an organization formally seeks to develop new and publicly acknowledged relationships with previously disenfranchised, or excluded, groups of workers, clients, or dependents. It generally involves the establishment of a series of new, formally ordered and publicly recognized relationships. Thus, appointments are made to newly created official posts, constitutions are drawn up, and new and sometimes extremely elaborate organizational structures are developed. The whole of this social process tends to convey, both through the creation of new symbolic interactive devices – committees, community councils, and local assemblies and joint meetings – and through the development of a new ideology stressing the value of interaction, consultation, participation and dialogue, that the organizational leadership now intends to adopt a new and more democratic style of government.

In general Selznick suggests that the leaders of an organization tend to adopt formal co-optative strategies when they face either one or both of two classical, if recurrent, problems. In the first place, these tactics are often used when an organization lacks a sense of historical legitimacy. This may happen simply because its leaders no longer feel they possess an unquestioning belief in their own right to rule, or in the 'correctness' of their policies and actions. However, as is more usually the case, co-optation also tends to occur simply because the organization's right to rule is called into question by those it has traditionally dominated.

Co-optation and Social Control

The reasons for these responses are in theory quite simple, though in practice often complex and difficult to describe in detail. The leaders of any organizational system, be it an army, a prison, a hospital, or even a local educational authority, depend for the effective day-to-day maintenance of their rule upon the tacit consent and co-operation of those they govern. Although they may wish from time to time to employ coercive measures, these tactics are rarely employed on a widespread scale; rather they are at their most effective when they are employed in critical and symbolic situations such as punishment systems, and they are not effective as enduring weapons of mass control.

One of the most effective ways for a leadership to maintain its own confidence and the confidence of the mass of clients it rules is to formally co-opt into its public structure representatives from groups which in some way reflect the sentiments, or possess the confidence of, the relevant public or mass it governs. This is because these new elements lend not only a substantial degree of public respectibility to, but also help to re-establish the legitimacy of, the group which is in control. This policy has obviously been and is still widely used, particularly when a leadership is responding to a potentially 'threatening' or 'revolutionary' situation. Thus, for example, colonial administrators typical co-opt tribal leaders into the machinery of their imperial administration in order to gain the support and confidence of the mass of their dependent subjects. In West Germany industrial leaders have included representatives from trade unions on their managing boards for many years, and the evidence suggests that this has been a most effective means of gaining a wider support for their policies and also establishing the legitimacy of their rule at a time when in much of the remainder of Western Europe the legitimacy of the capitalist system is increasingly being called into question. In the same way this theory also offers us an effective means of making some sense of the complex social processes we have examined in Sheffield. Here again the leaders of many formerly disenfranchised and outsider groups – parents, auxiliary staff, pupils, and teachers – have now been incorporated into the formal administrative structure of nearly 300 local school systems. And, as we have seen, these administrative innovations have not only served to lend a substantial degree of democratic respectability to, but have also served to reinforce the authority of, these groups effectively controlling the city's school system.

However, formal co-optative tactics are not only a means for maintaining or even restoring the public's confidence in its rulers; they may also be used to solve quite different and essentially administrative difficulties. These typically tend to occur when the business of an organization grows so complex or extensive that its leaders' control is significantly weakened. This is because they find themselves swamped in a sea of administrative detail and have insufficient time or energy to continue to co-ordinate all sectors efficiently or to dominate their constituents effectively. This situation is most easily resolved if a substantial amount of everyday, detailed administrative decision making and minor policy execution is delegated to committees of clients, workers, or formerly disenfranchised groups. These essentially logistical objectives may again be achieved through the establishment of a series of new, formally ordered and publicly recognized procedures which incorporate the leaders of many subordinate groups into a series of self-governing structures set up within the general framework of, and under the overall control of, the wider organizational leadership.

The essential point about this latter type of participatory innovation is that it helps a leadership to substantially reinforce its dominant tactical position, and thus achieve three quite fundamental strategic objectives. Firstly, it helps to create a series of reliable and orderly mechanisms for communicating with a wider public or groups of clients. Secondly, it effectively devolves a great deal of burdensome minor administration, and thus gives a leadership more time to address itself to central policy objectives. Thirdly, it reinforces a widespread public impression that decision making has been substantially devolved and consequently the responsibilities for the successful achievement of policy objectives are no longer borne exclusively by one group, but are substantially shared with a variety of local committees and associations. However, these strategies are not usually intended to devolve substantial powers of decision making to subordinate participating groups; rather the latter are simply intended to be concerned with the details and responsibilities associated with the execution of a leader's policies. Once these basic premises are challenged and attempts are made to substantially question or influence a leadership's general policy, then characteristically one finds participatory policies are abandoned in favour of a more centralized, if less flexible, type of direct rule. [. . .]

In this case [of the Sheffield school boards] the establishment of many hundreds of local school-based executive committees serves to facilitate a substantial devolution of many minor administrative burdens and leaves a central administrative/political élite with more time and energy to address central policy objectives. However, these committees are [. . .] essentially concerned with the implementation of policy, and once they step outside this administrative and co-ordinative role then their actions are likely to be tightly restricted.

Co-optation and the schooling system

It seems then that any formal act of co-optation offers the leadership of any large organization, including a school system, a number of very definite tactical advantages if it finds that its authority or right to rule is being called into question. These benefits may be extremely important in a social period when the total public educative process is itself increasingly being seen as problematic both by those working within it, disaffected groups of clients, and people in the wider community. Moreover, co-optation also has the added attraction that it promises to ease the work load within an administrative system which is generally growing more elaborate and burdensome to finance and gives its leadership more time to think about central policy-related issues. This is because the type of 'people-oriented technology' implicitly associated with the co-optative processes tends to fulfil two analytically distinct if interrelated functions. In the first place, it may fulfil the important political function of restoring the wider public's sense of confidence in the policy of their ruler, and thus serves to legitimize their continued dominance in society. In the second place, it provides a ready solution to many key administrative problems, and provides a more reliable channel both for effective communication with, and maintenance of, control over a series of subordinate client groups. However, as we have seen, although formal co-optation largely allows a leadership to achieve these aims, it does not lead to a transfer of substantive power to either the workers, clients, or subjects involved within the school system. This situation largely explains why so many Sheffield governors appeared to be unsure of their duties and to have an ambivalent attitude to their new role; they were aware that they now occupied a conspicuous and status-giving office within their community, but at the same time they were acutely aware that they had little substantive power in the sense that their work was mainly symbolic and there was little tangible they could do either to mould their local school to their own wishes or alter the educational authorities' general policies. On those rare occasions when school boards threatened to challenge this opaque but nonetheless very real structure of power, then their formal constitution was quickly revised to divert this threat. Thus, although the original participatory scheme introduced in 1970 allowed the key office of chairman to be appointed by open election, the revised scheme introduced in 1975 substantially modified this procedure and specified that this office must be filled by a candidate chosen from a restricted list composed of local education authority nominees. Although the overt rationale for this change was never made very clear, one of the key factors at stake was the issue of power and ultimate control. The city's leaders were probably worried that if a school board's chairman was elected in a totally open contest, then in many areas of the city this key office might fall into the hands of people who were politically unacceptable to them or substantially critical of their policies. In the same way, when a key decision had to be made, such as whether to phase out a school or reduce the number of teachers in the city, then the city leaders also went ahead without consulting the relevant interests concerned. [. . .]

The Iron Law of Oligarchy

It seems then that although participatory schemes often create a widespread public impression that the local community is 'fully involved', and 'a great weight of concerned manpower is now working for the school', in fact from a critical perspective these reforms do little to alter the loci of power within the local school system, and most key decisions are not made by the people ostensibly being served by the organization, but by its full-time coterie of officials, advisors, and professional managers. The reasons for these refractory tendencies are complex, but some of the key factors have been elaborated by Michels in his classic study – *Political Parties, A Sociological Study of the Oligarchical Tendencies of Modern Democracy*.[2]

In the first place, effective power remains in the hands of the full-time official, be he the headmaster or school board clerk at the local level, or the administrator or adviser at the local authority level, simply because this group is in effective control of the school system's communication network. Thus, as we have seen, parents, teachers, or community representatives on governing bodies are often totally dependent upon their headteacher's co-operation if they wish to communicate effectively and rapidly with their constituents. This situation also means that the full-time officials are in a key position to decide which information to dispense or withhold from the public, and most important of all, which issues to raise and which to omit from the agenda of public boards of control. In this way, a subtle but none-theless censorial process takes place in the sense that, as we have seen, school boards tend to discuss those issues which trouble the city's caretaking élites and do not, of necessity, address those perhaps more critical issues – the private troubles of the clients, workers, or dependents of the local school system.

In the second place, the power of the full-time official is reinforced by his extensive, if not necessarily superior, knowledge of educational affairs. Their official role of necessity enables them to travel, visit different schools, read extensively, and conduct private research. In all of these ways they are able to build up such an elaborate and sophisticated rationale for their own actions that most lay people find it difficult to offer an effective critique of their policies. The root of the client's dilemma rests not in a fundamental intellectual inferiority, but in an unequal power relationship, for since the officials usually ultimately decide which educational issues are publicly addressed, which ignored, and which systematically devalued, then most of the public debate about educational policy is conducted from a dominant conceptual perspective, and thus even the most 'concerned' of diligent laymen finds it difficult to make an effective critique of or offer a substantial alternative to their policies.

Finally, the power of the officials is substantially reinforced by the general in-competence of the mass of the people they serve, and their own superior skills in writing, talking, and organizing. This is not to suggest that their clients are con-genitally inferior; rather it is merely to state the obvious, that, in their case, the competing demands of work, leisure and family life leave them with insufficient time or energy to acquire the detailed knowledge or communicative skills necessary to build up an effective counterbalance, or act as a significant check upon the role of the expert. Ironically, even in cases where people do make great efforts to acquire these skills – through reading, attending adult education classes, talking to teachers or children – they may still remain ineffective since they are, by the logic of their situation, denied access to the internal and private communicative network of their local educational system.

The Division of Educational Labour

It seems then that the social processes we have examined in the case of the Sheffield school board system may be seen as further examples which are generally consistent with the social law that the 'need to elaborate the division of labour', including educational labour, creates interests peculiar to itself. Thus, although [...] effective power within the school system originally lay within the hands of the local bourgeoisie, the need to create a sophisticated structure of education in the late nineteenth century necessitated the growth of a complex national organization and a concomittant cadre of full-time officials, ideologists, and professional managers. This diffuse, but nonetheless recognizable, status interest naturally possessed an intuitive set of characteristics which are commonly found within all organization structures, be they established to pursue military, religious, welfare, or in this case educational objectives, namely an instinct for self-preservation and the maintenance and, if possible, expansion of one's claim upon the wider society.

In the case of education, this task has become increasingly difficult in the context of wider economic and political developments during the late 1960s and early 1970s. In the first place a more general economic malaise has meant that society's resources are necessarily limited, and expenditure on education is constantly criticized since it is a labour-intensive and thus costly enterprise. Secondly, a more wide-ranging political crisis has developed in the sense that the postwar consensus between capital and labour has gradually broken down, and many politicians now view the school system as a mechanism which can be used to facilitate wider social changes, including the development of the first stages of a more meritocratic, if not egalitarian, society. Naturally, many other groups feel threatened by this process; they see state education as a machine which is not only transmitting 'socialism', but is also part of a wider process intended to undermine their class interests and traditional values. Largely as a result of this situation, the stage of public education is both more socially visible and more widely discussed than it has been since the late nineteenth century. Thus, what evidence there is does seem to suggest that the demand for local control of schools, and greater democratization and devolution of power to school boards, does tend to be a primarily middle-class and professionally orientated movement. One convincing explanation for this group's awakening concern with the issue of 'Who controls the local school system?' may be found if one relates it to the gradual introduction of comprehensive education, and the phasing out of traditional grammar schools and, more recently, direct grant schools. Largely as a result of these developments, one powerful and articulate section of upper middle-class society has largely lost control over its children's education. Many families have suddenly, for the first time in their lives, found that they have little choice but to educate their children within the state system. This very new situation has naturally facilitated the type of reaction which is best summed up in the words of one anxious parent when he told me, 'We were not sure what these places (that is, state schools) were about, so we said let's set to and jolly-well tell them'.

In view of all these developments, it seems reasonable to assume that the leaders of the educational interest, both nationally and locally, are currently working out strategies for coping with two analytically distinct, if at the same time interrelated, problems. Firstly, how can they maintain their claims upon the wider resources of society in a period when many other well-organized interests, including the military industry, the social services, and so on, are also competing with them for their own share of a relatively finite total budget? Secondly, how can they effectively engineer a widespread public acceptance of, and belief in, the legitimacy of their policies in an age when education is no longer widely thought of in terms of consensual models, which tend to assume it is a neutral and independent area of activity, but is increasingly being perceived, both by providers and clients, as a process which may profoundly effect both their child's life chances, and ultimately the culture of the society we live in?

The gradual espousal of various types of co-optative devices, including the retrieval of a Victorian anachronism – the school board system – from the lumber room of educational administration, the gradual development of an allied and complex system of school's consultative councils, community groups and academic boards, may all be seen as one quite natural and largely managerially sponsored response to this quite new and delicate situation.

Thus, as we have already seen, it is extremely naïve to assume that the pressure for greater parental, work, or communal involvement in the management or government of schools represents a genuinely spontaneous 'grassroots' activity in the sense that it might be compared in any meaningful way with a shop stewards' movement, a tenants' association, or a neighbourhood action group. Rather, it seems to be apparent when we analyse the aims, aspirations, and tactics of those groups currently pressing for school board reform, that most of the momentum has been generated by a diffuse, but nonetheless, in part, recognizable metropolitan intelligentsia, either employed directly or indirectly in élite roles within the nation's public educational industry. Similarly, and for reasons we have already identified, most of the mass support for, and responses to, these initiatives has been confined to the professional middle class.

Similarly, at the local level in Sheffield, most of the pressure leading to school board reform did not emanate from the community at large, but sprang from three fairly identifiable though closely related sources. Firstly, a district branch of the metropolitan intelligentsia which was primarily employed in, or indirectly involved with, the local educational industry, and which had formed local branches of such nationally organized pressure groups as the Campaign for State Education and the National Association of Governors and Managers. Secondly, a group of administrative officials who were dissatisfied with the city's extremely centralized system of organizing its educational service and who wished to see a greater degree of public participation and community involvement in the running of the city's schools. And finally, a group of local politicians, many of whom were employed in education or in other professional occupations and had grown increasingly influential in the city's ruling Labour Party.

All of these people, who may from one perspective be seen as members of Sheffield's new educational establishment, also tended to be generally critical of the city's long established paternalistic tradition of running its schools and were generally in favour of participatory democratic philsophies. They also, either overtly or implicitly, in their daily actions tended to question the conventional English tradition that public education was a politically neutral and value-free activity. In the main, they tended to support the view that the school system ought to be used as a tool to forge a more socially just and egalitarian society, while a few were proponents of a new radical orthodoxy and explicitly maintained that public education was an overtly political act which effectively maintained the continued oppression of the working classes.

Quite obviously an educational establishment which, either consciously, or implicitly, adopts this type of view is working within a potentially volatile political situation. It must not only address the central question of maintaining its claims upon the wider financial resources of society, but must also attempt to engineer a wide degree of client and worker consent for its policies, while at the same time working to effectively deflect, or neutralize, its critics or opponents. In other words, it may find it expedient to critically review the utility of maintaining the fairly centralized administrative and 'closed school system' traditionally associated with the traditional representational framework of local democracy, and think about the wisdom of employing new techniques to achieve its aims, including, of course, the rhetoric of participation and the machinery of co-optation. The old 'closed system' may well have been suited to a political climate in which there was a normative consensus about the aims of, and values to be transmitted within, a public educational system; however it appears to have less utility in a period when the national and local leaders of the educational interest are not only attempting to stimulate rapid social change but are also facing the challenge of an increasingly hostile environment.

Obfuscation and Impression Management

If one accepts the legitimacy of an alternative perspective which seeks to centrally question established conventions and ideologies, then one may perhaps see Sheffield's experiments in school board reform as an initial and still relatively crude response to changes which are taking place in the wider society. The city has become a 'test bed' for a series of ongoing experiments in the application of a new kind of 'people manipulating' technology which is effectively achieving two basic objectives. Firstly, the appropriate deflection or diffusion of groups who may be critical of, or actively hostile to, the policies being pursued by the educational establishment. Secondly, the engineering of an effective level of client consent for, and support of, the local educational system.

Most of the evidence seems to suggest that the new board system has been remarkably successful in achieving these aims. Although, as we have seen, these bodies have not facilitated any effective devolution of power to the community, at the same time their presence has helped to create, certainly amongst those groups most overtly interested in and vocal about education, the widespread impression that representatives of all concerned client and working groups are now intimately involved in the management of their own schools.

At the same time, the existence of the new boards also offers the local educational establishment a series of tactical advantages it lacked when it worked within a strictly and overtly centralized system of school administration. Today, if any of its policies generates bitter local criticism or violent public opposition, then it no longer occupies the kind of exposed and vulnerable situation where its leaders, be they politicians or administrators, must meet their enemies in a direct and damaging confrontation. Rather, in all but the most extreme cases of local discontent, these potentially troublesome and damaging conflicts are now likely to be deflected into a new '*decelerating* arena', the world of school board politics. These quasi-administrative bodies serve an invaluable obfuscatory function; this is because while in theory they can claim to represent local parental, worker, and other communal interests, in practice they tend, for reasons which should now be familiar to my readers, to identify themselves with and support the policies being advocated by the local educational establishment.

Consequently, if a contentious local issue such as a disputed catchment area, a school closure, or a discipline issue were to arise, then this is less likely to lead to the creation of local action group which will publicly seek to confront the town hall with a series of political demands. Under the new participatory system, two things may happen. Firstly, the issue may be deflected into the arena of school board politics, and in this way effectively deflected from a direct confrontation with the loci of power within the city. Secondly, the issue may still be serious enough to lead to the emergence of a local pressure group which seeks to publicly challenge the local authority. However, if this conflict does occur, then the tactical situation of the 'protestors' will now be a weak one, for the school boards in the area concerned are likely to support the local authority and call into question the action group's right both to speak for the local community and the legitimacy of the policies it seeks to advocate.

The new participatory structure also gives the leaders of the educational interest a number of strategic advantages in their fight to maintain what they see as their just share of public resources for the schools. This is because the new system effectively supplements the 'regular army' which is always fighting for the educational interest – the teachers' unions, the education committee, the education officers, and so on – with a new 'volunteer force' which can be rapidly mobilized in a time of crisis, which usually means the threat of financial cuts to the existing service. Thus, when Sheffield introduced it's new board system in 1970, it not only effectively provided each school with its own board of managers; at the same time it formally enrolled the services of many hundreds of people previously unconnected with education, and familiarized them with all the problems and difficulties schools were currently trying to cope with. In other words, it created 300 public bodies which were nominally representative of the communal interest, which had become actively involved in education, and which were naturally prepared to fight energetically for their own school's interests in particular and the interests of education in the city in general. This additional reservoir of support was of particular importance to a leadership operating within the kind of social context existing in Britain in the mid-1970s. It provided them with more troops to fight against those who seek to question the burgeoning cost of education in general, or the usefulness of schools in particular. Moreover, at the same time the new board system also extends the depth of their power base, and this in turn gives them a greater degree of flexibility and manoeuvre within the new system of corporate management which was introduced into local government after the major reorganization of 1970–71. This innovation threatened to effectively reduce the relative freedom and autonomy once enjoyed by senior officers and members of the education committee, in the sense that it sought to make them more accountable to people such as 'chief executives' and treasurer, and bodies such as finance or personnel committees not directly and intimately concerned about education or the day-to-day needs and interests of the schools.

[. . .]

Education and Democracy

It seems then that the evidence I have examined in the course of my field work leads us tentatively towards the following general conclusions. Firstly, the kinds of participatory school governing structures which have been pioneered by such innovatory authorities as Sheffield in the early 1970s, and whose main features have now been incorporated into the Taylor Committee's proposals, offer many easily recognizable advantages to those responsible within the present statutory framework for the effective day-to-day administration of the local schooling system. Secondly, despite the rhetoric which is typically used to legitimate these innovations, these new kinds of participatory structures do little to reallocate power in favour of either groups of clients, students or workers, or even people in the wider community. Indeed, the perhaps unintended paradox associated with this type of reform is that all of the latter groups may suffer from an increasing sense of estrangement simply because the effective loci of power within the school system has not only become overtly collectivized, but is also effectively obfuscated.

In making their own assessment of how far this type of quasi-democratic structure is necessarily concordant with the long-term public interest or wider societal values, my readers may find it useful to distinguish between two very different types of initiative. The first of these, which we may reasonably classify as 'substantive reforms', explicitly seeks to involve representatives of clients, workers, and also the wider community in the determination of an institution's public policy. The second of these, which are in essence simply 'administrative innovations', are radically different in the sense that they serve, while giving the public a semblance of democracy, to enmesh those people who participate in these schemes into an essentially executive process serving the wider interests of a power élite.

Although many people often assume that the latter process is consistent with wider democratic values, a more critical inspection of these systems will reveal, as we have already seen, that the loci of decision making is not substantially altered. Thus, at best in most school boards, what tends to happen is a social process which we may label 'discrete manipulative co-option'. This means that although a process of formal and elaborate consultation now takes place with all interested parties, teachers, parents, students, community groups, local political workers, and so on, at the same time the differential knowledge of, or structural position occupied by, certain key actors – the headteacher, the chairman, the officers of the local authority clerking the meeting – means that in the main the responsible officials of the organization decide not only what issues are to be raised but also have a heavy influence upon the subsequent discussions and any final decision which is taken. Of course, in a minority of schools little attempt is made to maintain even the fiction of 'full and open' consultation, and power is openly exercised by a small sub-committee again typically composed of the clerk, the chairman, and the headteacher.

The reasons this situation develops are complex; however, they are perhaps best understood in terms of the unintended consequences of a complex number of social actions and not, as is often suggested, in terms of a Machievellian plot or a conspiritorial theory. This being said, this rather pessimistic overview of the current position and work of democratized school governing bodies, and by implication future 'post-Taylor' developments, does, I believe, offer a more satis-factory interpretation of the work of these bodies than the conventional eulogies written on this subject. Moreover, this conclusion does, I think, do much to counter the conventional assumption that economic and educational developments will, of themselves, help to create naturally a new highly articulate and self-contained class of people who will be able to form a natural counter to the co-optative techniques, and incorporative strategies, typically employed by the officials of all large organizations. This thesis, which was I think best elaborated by Bukharin in his classic work, *Historical Materialism*,[3] is an attractive one in the sense that it clearly consistent with our social hopes and ambitions, if not the realities involved in particular programmes of democratic reform. However, as we have seen in the case of Sheffield, where so many governors were typically highly educated, socially concerned, and selfless professional people, there was little evidence to suggest that as yet this group was any more likely than any other to resist the inexorable pressure to become incorporated into an existing and continuing power structure. Indeed, from one point of view one might well argue that generally those less well-educated and less overtly socially conscious members of Sheffield's working class were simply showing, by their general indifference to the new board system, a more acute awareness of the reality and nature of the distribution of power in the city.

Authority and the School System

[. . .]
It seems to me that the type of technical malfunction which seems [. . .] likely to happen in reformed school board systems of the Sheffield and of the 'post-Taylor' era is not an open confrontation of the William Tyndale type, but a more subtle long-term process of factionalization. Thus, local people may gradually organize themselves into groups based upon ethnic, class, or local allegiances in order to mobilize the largely dormant powers presently exercised by school boards – general oversight of the curriculum, teacher appointment, direction of conduct, and so on. In turn this movement may be stimulated both by national developments such as the report of the Taylor Committee and the kind of radical analysis I have attempted in this study, in the sense that it may make people more conscious of, and thus prepared to challenge, the way in which school boards are presently used as in-struments of impression management and political obfuscation. However, for reasons I have already identified in past chapters, this movement when it finally develops is one which is very likely to be dominated by the professional middle

classes, and largely because of this a revitalized school board system might well in the long term facilitate the development of a series of 'runaway' situations in which one articulate and politically sophisticated section of the community could capture control of the local comprehensive or primary school and seek to run it in the interests of a sectional, not a general interest.

[...]

Obviously an author is treading on dangerous ground when he attempts to predict the future course of public events in the United Kingdom, for these developments are all obviously contingent on so many unpredictable and some still unrecognized factors. However, if as seems likely the major recommendations contained within the Taylor Committee's report are implemented nationally, then the kinds of situations I have simply schematized above may well develop and in their turn generate a counter-reaction leading perhaps to the reintroduction into the nation's educational system of tighter, more centralized systems of control, and the consequent downgrading of democratized school boards.

However, while this long-term development might well result from the inherent technical instability of co-optative systems of participation, it seems to me that they are equally likely to result from wider social developments. This is because, whatever framework of accountability, be it direct and local public participation or strict centralized state control, is eventually introduced into the nation's schooling system, the sociological reality is that these structures must be generally consistent with the philosophies and day-to-day practices which typically occur in other sections of the wider society. Because of this complex inter-relationship, it is always a useful exercise when one studies the overall structures of a school system, to relate its various subsidary elements and modes of control to the wider cultural context of the society within which it operates. Thus, in the same way that the Victorian school system [...] may be usefully analysed in terms of the radically different needs of three quite separate social orders, so is the current wave of interest in democratizing all aspects of social life, including the reform of school boards, usefully seen as part of a wider cultural movement which is at its strongest in the industrial sector of society. [...]

Notes and References

1 SELZNICK, P. (1949) *TVA and the Grass Roots*, University of California Press.
2 MICHELS, R. (1959) *Political Parties*, New York, Dover Publications.
3 BUKHARIN, N. (1925) *Historical Materialism, A System of Sociology*, New York, International Publishers.

List of Contributors

Paul Adams is assistant professor in the School of Social Work, University of Iowa.

Jean Anyon is assistant professor of education at Rutgers University, Newark, New Jersey.

William Bacon is lecturer in sociology in the Division of Continuing Education, University of Sheffield.

Veronica Beechey is lecturer in sociology at the University of Warwick.

Rhodes Boyson is Parliamentary Under-Secretary of State for Education and Science and Member of Parliament, Brent North.

John Clarke is lecturer in sociology at North East London Polytechnic.

Roger Dale is lecturer in sociology of education, The Open University.

Ross Fergusson is course co-ordinator in the Faculty of Educational Studies at The Open University.

John Fitz is research student in the Faculty of Educational Studies at the Open University.

Simon Frith is lecturer in sociology at the University of Warwick.

John Hargreaves is lecturer in sociology at Goldsmiths' College, University of London.

Heidi Hartmann is acting associate executive director of the assembly of Behavioural and Social Sciences, at the National Research Council, Washington, D.C.

Dick Hebdige is lecturer in sociology at Wolverhampton Polytechnic.

Richard Johnson is director of the Centre for Contemporary Cultural Studies at the University of Birmingham.

Hilary Land is reader in Social Administration at the University of Bristol.

Magali Larson	is associate professor at the University of Pennsylvania.
Madeleine MacDonald	is lecturer in sociology of education, The Open University.
Angela McRobbie	is editor of Screen Education.
George Mardle	is lecturer in education at the University of Keele.
Margaret May	is lecturer in sociology at the City of London Polytechnic.
Nicola Murray	works in a community law centre in South West London.
Jose Parry	is research fellow at Goldsmith's College, University of London.
Noel Parry	is head of the sociology department at the Polytechnic of North London.
Trevor Pateman	is lecturer in education at the University of Sussex.
June Purvis	is lecturer in sociology of education, The Open University.
Jenny Shaw	is lecturer in the School of Social Sciences, University of Sussex.
Paul Willis	is research fellow at the Centre for Contemporary Cultural Studies, University of Birmingham.
Anne Marie Wolpe	is senior lecturer in sociology at Middlesex Polytechnic.

Author Index

Abramowitz, J. 38
Adamson, O., Brown, C., Harrison, J. and
    Price, J. 139
Adderley, J. 279
Adorno. T. and Horkheimer, M. 76, 77, 85
Albonico, R. and Pfister-Binz, K. 68
Alexander, S. 121, 122, 139, 359, 373
Althusser, L. 47, 94, 95, 302, 344
Anyon, J. 176
Apple, M. 37
Arrow, K. 380, 389, 390
Arthur, C. 226
Ashley, Lord 363
Auld, R. 317, 389

Bailey, P. 68
Baker, K.M. 389
Baker, T.B.Ll. 281
Bales, R.F. 117
Balibar, E. 344
Ball, R. 39
Bane, M.J. 210
Banks, J. 373
Banks, J. and Banks, O. 373
Bannister, R. 61
Bardwick, J.M. and Schumann, S.I. 177
Barker, D.L. and Allen, S. 52, 139, 176
Baron, G. 357
Barrell, G.R. 261, 262, 265, 268
Barron, R.D. and Norris, G.M. 115, 123, 124,
    125, 126, 127, 128, 129, 140
Barthes, R. 87, 95
Barton, L. and Meighan, R. 317
Basini, A. 85
Basnett, D. 71
Baxter, I. and Eberts, M. 302
Beale, D. 369, 371
Beames, T. 276, 282
de Beauvoir, S. 160, 164, 175
Becher, A. and Maclure, S. 306, 317
Beechey, V. 140, 373
Bell, C.S. 209
Bell, D. 236, 238
Bennett, N. 390
Benston, M. 207
Berg, I. 390
Berg, L. 305, 317

Berger, P. 346
Bernstein, B. 39, 164, 165, 167, 175, 176
Bernstein, B. and Bourdieu, P. 175
Bernstein, B. and Davis, B. 157
Beveridge, W. 45, 249, 250, 254
Beynon, H. 53
Beynon, H. and Nichols, T. 53
Blackstone, W. 270, 282, 290, 302
Blake, S.J. 361
Bland, L. 52
Blauner, R. 341, 342, 344, 346
Blum, A. 39
Bogdanor, V. 309, 314, 317
Bonachea, R.E. and Valdes, N.P. 226, 227
Boulding, E. 255
Bourdieu, P. 141, 142, 157, 165, 166, 175, 176,
    268
Bourke, J. 302
Bourque, S. and Grossholz, J. 176
Boyer, R. and Morais, H. 37, 38
Boyson, R. 379, 381, 386, 389
Bragdon, H., McCutchen, S. and Cole, C. 35,
    36, 37, 38
Bramson, L. 389
Branca, P. 373
Branson, M. 35, 37
Braverman, H. 36, 39, 52, 127, 133, 137, 139,
    140, 346
Brett, M.R. 293
Brittain, V. 371, 375
Brittan, S. 238
Brody, D. 36, 37, 38
Brohm, J.M. 68
Bromby, Rev. C.H. 354
Brougham, H. 4, 6
Brown, B. 207, 211, 226
Brown, C. 202, 204, 209
Brown, R. 268
Brownmiller, S. 208
Buchanan, J. 276
Buchanan, W. 282
Bukharin, N. 403, 404
Burkett, E.C. 226
Burns, T. 68
Burraway, M. 209
Burstall, S. 370, 375
Busby, L.J. 177

Subject Index